Navaho Material Culture

Navaho Material Culture

Clyde Kluckhohn
W. W. Hill
Lucy Wales Kluckhohn

The Belknap Press of Harvard University Press
Cambridge, Massachusetts, 1971

Purpose and Development of this Monograph
By Clyde Kluckhohn

Professor Leslie Spier and others have often commented that Southwestern ethnologists have tended to neglect descriptions of material culture in favor of accounts of ceremonialism, social organization, and other topics. The present study had its inception as an attempt to meet this criticism as far as the Ramah Navaho were concerned. In 1944–45, Elizabeth Colson brought together the data available in the files of field notes (as well as a large amount of comparative material in the literature). Gaps were of course revealed, and these led to further fieldwork by Clyde Kluckhohn in 1946 and by George Mills in 1947. Other checking was done intermittently by Kluckhohn through the summer of 1958. Katherine Spencer, Robert Greengo, and Philip Smith have incorporated in the manuscript information on material culture obtained by other fieldworkers since 1945. However, except where otherwise specified, the ethnographic present for the Ramah Navaho materials is the 1935–1945 decade. The aim is to present—with certain exceptions— everything that was observable or obtainable from the memories of informants during that period. The exceptions involve three topics so complex that they have each received extensive monographic treatment from other authors: rug weaving, silversmithing, and sandpainting. (Adair [1944] includes some Ramah data on silversmithing; Ramah data on sandpainting are included in Wyman and Kluckhohn [1938] and Kluckhohn and Wyman [1940].) Other exceptions are two topics where Ramah data have already been published: pottery making and basketry (Tschopik, 1938, 1941). On ceremonial objects our policy is not fully consistent. We have included certain facts, but have not attempted comprehensive coverage or full citations of the literature in view of voluminous reporting by Father Berard Haile, Gladys Reichard, W. W. Hill, Kluckhohn and Wyman, and others.

Since the Ramah materials would be more valuable if seen in the context of information from other Navaho areas, I asked W. W. Hill if he would collaborate and work in unpublished data from his 1933–34 field trips. Later, Stanley Fishler made available his field notes from work in 1949–50 in the Western Navaho country. The descriptive portion of the text begins with the data from Ramah which are followed by Hill's data and Fishler's data, and concludes with a comparative section, which covers the ethnological, archaeological, and historical literature. In the last section we have also incorporated certain materials from the unpublished manuscripts of the late Louisa Wade Wetherill. These are not of professional quality, yet it seems worthwhile to spread them upon the record since they were obtained early in this century in a remote part of the Navaho country (the Oljeto-Kayenta region) by an observer who spoke Navaho and who had opportunity for daily and intimate contacts.

So many people have contributed to this study that authorship is difficult to assign fairly. Colson wrote a first draft which we have continued to use. Spencer, Greengo, and Smith completely rewrote (among them) Colson's original draft. The field notes of more than twenty workers have been utilized, and those of Harry Tschopik constitute a substantial proportion of the Ramah data. However, during the past twenty-five years of intermittent work on this monograph, W. W. Hill and I have continually made all decisions of inclusion and exclusion, and of weighing the evidence generally; we must assume the responsibility for these decisions.

While we hope that anthropologists, sociologists, psychologists, and historians will find something of value in the theoretical portions of this monograph, it is intended primarily as a source book or reference work for comparative studies of various sorts. It presents an accumulation of details, often minute, upon obsolete or obsolescent objects and cultural habits and attitudes related thereto.

Cambridge, Massachusetts
1958

After the death of Clyde Kluckhohn in 1960, the completion of the manuscript was undertaken by W. W. Hill and Lucy Wales Kluckhohn, formerly a research assistant to Dr. Kluckhohn. At that time, the manuscript consisted of descriptions of over two hundred and fifty traits, grouped into some twenty-five categories. Introduction and analysis were lacking, save for an excellent summary written by Elizabeth Colson for the first draft; parts of this are incorporated in the present manuscript. Kluckhohn's plans for the organization were unclear, and various research assistants had conflicting ideas. We have consequently made several over-all revisions, arranging and regrouping the traits in the present order; it was our decision to present the data that Louise Lamphere collected at Sheep Springs in 1965–66 in a separate section, following Hill's data. L. Kluckhohn undertook the task of condensing redundant material; the typescript was sent to Hill for revision or comments. Although we are deeply indebted to Colson, Greengo, and Smith for many of the ideas and occasionally phrases expressed in the analytical section, we must accept the responsibility for this section and for the work as a whole.

Grateful acknowledgment is made to the following people and institutions for their contributions to *Navaho Material Culture*. For fieldwork at Ramah: Clyde Kluckhohn (1935–1958); Harry Tschopik, Jr. (1937–38); Monro Edmonson, David P. McAllester; John M. Roberts (1946); George Mills (1947); and many others whose notes are in the Values Study Files now at the Laboratory of Anthropology, Santa Fe, New Mexico. For fieldwork in the Central, Eastern, and Western areas: W. W. Hill (1933–34) and Louise Lamphere (1965–66) at Sheep Springs, New Mexico. For fieldwork in the Western Navaho reservation: Stanley A. Fishler (1949–50).

For research and help with the manuscript: Elizabeth Colson, for processing early data, and for library research which resulted in the first draft of the manuscript; Katherine Spencer, Robert Greengo, and Philip Smith, for incorporating materials from Tschopik, Mills, Fishler, and others into the second draft; the late Frederick H. Douglas and the late Harry Tschopik, for their comments on the second draft; Olaf Prufer and James Sackett, for additional library research and data processing, 1958–1960.

This Monograph   For assistance on the third draft (written by Hill and L. Kluckhohn): Elizabeth Colson, for her introduction to the second draft; Philip Smith, for many stimulating queries and suggestions; and Ione Howson Burke, for her suggestions and data tabulations. David Aberle, Harry Basehart, Philip Bock, David De Harport, Richard Kluckhohn, Louise Lamphere, William Martin, who checked the botanical terminology, Stanley Newman, Terry Reynolds, Bruce Rigsby, Leland Wyman, and Robert W. Young read portions of the manuscript and furnished many helpful comments and ideas.

The line drawings were done by Symme Burstein and the map was drawn by Eliza McFadden. Beverly Chico, Elizabeth Warner, Helen Lorenz, and Marta Weigle typed the manuscript.

Hill expresses his thanks to the National Research Council for a fellowship which made possible his fieldwork in 1933–34. The work in the Ramah area was made possible by grants from the American Philosophical Society, the Ford Foundation, the Carnegie Corporation, the Social Science Research Council, and the Wenner-Gren Foundation for Anthropological Research.

L. Kluckhohn's work on the manuscript was made possible by a grant from the Ford Foundation to Clyde Kluckhohn, and by the efforts of Florence R. Kluckhohn and "The Committee" of J. O. Brew, Evon Z. Vogt, and Talcott Parsons to maintain the grant after the death of Clyde Kluckhohn, and by a patient and understanding husband. To all, many thanks.

W.W.H., Albuquerque, New Mexico
L.W.K., Canoga Park, California

January 1970

Contents

Chapter 2. Shelter, 143

Chapter 3. Clothing, 203

Contents

Chapter 4. Ritual, 317

Contents

Illustrations

Plates

Credits for text illustrations.

American Museum of Natural History, New York, 103.c. Arizona State Museum, Tucson, 54.b, 107.c–d, 107.h, 109.a–b, 256.a. Bureau of Indian Affairs, U.S. Department of the Interior, photo by Milton Snow, 54.a. Harvey Caplin, 107.g. David De Harport, 107.a–b. Stanley Fishler, 10.3–5, 19.5. Franciscan Fathers, *An Ethnologic Dictionary of the Navaho Language* (St. Michaels, Arizona, 1910), 5.2, 8.12, 20.2, 27.2, 37.1, 38.1, 54.1, 111.4, 113.1, 123.1, 130.4, 131.2, 132.1, 180.1, 184.13, 199.1, 214.2–3, 220.1, 222.1, 224.1, 225.1, 229.4, 230.1, 240.1, 248.2, 256.1. W. W. Hill, *The Agricultural and Hunting Methods of the Navaho Indians* (Yale University Press, 1938), 1.1–3, 4.2–3, 8.2–5, 8.7–9, 8.11, 37.a, 38.b. Laboratory of Anthropology, Santa Fe, 227.b, 245.a.

Louise Lamphere, 96.a–b. Maxwell Museum of Anthropology, University of New Mexico, photo by Richard Donachek, 240.a. Museum of New Mexico, Santa Fe, 2.a. Museum of Northern Arizona, Flagstaff, 90.a, 107.f, 209.a, 226.a, 256.b. Navajo Land Claim, photos by Lamar Newton, 50.a, 55.a, 211.a; by Clifford Gedekoh, 137.a. New Mexico Department of Development, 107.e. Peabody Museum of Archaeology and Ethnology, Harvard University, 13.a, 15.a, 19.a–b, 23.b, 41.a–b, 45.a, 65.a, 66.a, 67.a, 68.a, 82.c, 82.d, 103.a–b, 128.a, 141.a, 156.a, 164.a, 170.a, 177.b, 182.a, 184.a, 195.a, 208.a, 214.a, 215.a–b, 233.a, 253.a, 256.d, 262.a. R. H. Lowie Museum of Anthropology, University of California Berkeley, California, 37.b–c, 38.a and c, 111.a, 112.a; 217.a, 252.a, 254.a. Smithsonian Institution, Division of North American Anthropology, 127.a, 170.b, 178.a, 184.b–e, 189.a, 247.a; Office of Anthropology, 73.a, 164.b, 226.b–c, 235.a, 256.c; Soil Conservation Service, U.S. Department of Agriculture, photos by Milton Snow, 44.a, 72.a, 82.b, 85.a, 198.a; Harry Tschopik, Jr., 4.1, 5.1, 8.1, 18.1, 19.2, 23.1–2, 35.1, 35.a, 61.1, 77.1, 82.a, 96.1, 98.1, 98.a, 107.1–5, 116.1, 117.1, 119.1–2, 135.a, 141.b, 162.1, 170.1–4, 171.1, 174.1, 177.1, 177.a, 184.1–5, 187.1, 189.1–4, 191.1, 214.1, 248.1. Paul J. Woolf, 120.a, 227.a; Leland C. Wyman, 166.a, 175.a.

Navaho Material Culture

Note on Apparatus

The name of each trait is followed by the Navaho term for the trait and its source. A translation of the term is given if it differs from the trait name. The sources of Navaho terms are Ramah, Hill, and Lamphere (terms obtained in the course of fieldwork); Haile (Father Berard Haile's *Stem Vocabulary*, 1950, 1951); and the Franciscan Fathers (*An Ethnologic Dictionary of the Navaho Language,* 1910). Many literal translations have been provided by informant CC, from Sheep Springs, and these are so identified.

Except for the trait headings, all Navaho in the text has been anglicized. We have used the "h" in spelling Navaho as this was the accepted practice among anthropologists at the time most of the book was written. Although we recognize that "Navajo" is the contemporary spelling and the one preferred by the Navajo Tribe, we have retained the spelling "Navaho" because the task of changing at this time would be prohibitive.

Informants from the Ramah area are designated by numbers, for example, Inf. 1, in accordance with the practice used in other publications (such as Kluckhohn and Wyman, 1940). Other informants are designated by letters, usually initials of their names, and their areas are noted at the first mention in each trait.

Text illustrations are designated by trait number, followed by a letter, identifying a half tone, or by a number, identifying a line drawing.

Introduction

The Navaho are the most thoroughly studied of any tribe in the Southwestern United States. The range of investigation includes research by social scientists from almost every discipline. With the exception of Roberts' (1951) study, however, recent treatment of material culture is conspicuously absent. To a certain extent such studies have disappeared from anthropological vogue. But traits of material culture are an appropriate focus for study in a rapidly changing world: not only are they the first to change, but also, preserved as heirlooms, they frequently offer the only available link with the past. Inference from material remains is essential for archaeological interpretation. The descriptive material presented below, containing Clyde Kluckhohn's intended "accumulation of details, often minute, upon obsolete or obsolescent objects and cultural habits and attitudes related thereto," provides a basis for such interpretations. In addition, the data are useful for cross-cultural comparisons and studies of technological acculturation.

Over a period of thirty-six years (1933–1969) the present study has undergone a transition from a series of notes about a collection of Navaho objects to a monograph dealing with Navaho material culture. In this transition new orientations were evolved, several collaborators were added, and arbitrary decisions had to be made. With the publication of Osgood's *Ingalik Material Culture* (1940), the Navaho study gained momentum and pattern. Perhaps in anticipation of similarity between the two Athabaskan cultures, information on the Navaho items was organized according to material, construction, maker, user, owner, and the like; Osgood's format was adopted at least for the major part of the Ramah material. But, during the course of more than two decades of field and library research, it became evident that the data and their sources for *Navaho Material Culture* differed markedly from those of the Osgood study. The result was a reanalysis of the Navaho materials in search of a new ordering, or theoretical framework. How could an accumulation of cultural data best be presented to give a cogent picture of the Navaho material culture? What—beyond the obvious—is meant by Navaho material culture?

Ethnologists, archaeologists, museum directors, and collectors of all sorts have been dealing with traits of material culture for over a century without particular concern for the problem of definition. As far as Alfred Kroeber is concerned, the distinction, if one must be made between material and nonmaterial culture, is of little consequence, "except that it is sometimes of practical convenience to observe" (1948:296). Having elected this practical convenience, we shall attempt to define material culture. To call it the material manifestation of culture, or as Shapiro has done, "the product of culturally determined activity" (1956:176) is too sweeping. The definition should be sufficiently broad, to be sure, to include the rock that is used as a hammer and discarded and, at the same time, sufficiently narrow to exclude the geographical features, such as rivers and mountains, that are "used" in culturally patterned ways. Clellan Ford resolves this problem by describing material culture in terms of the *actions* "of manufacture and use, and the expressed theories about the production, use, and nature of material objects" (1937:226). These are subdivided into "unit actions"—kneading clay as opposed to making a piece of pottery—that should be examined in terms of purpose, materials, means, method, and result. Osgood prefers a definition phrased in terms of *ideas* "about objects external to the mind resulting from human behavior as well as ideas about human behavior required to manufacture these objects" (1940:26).

In our description of the individual traits of material culture we have incorporated the ideas of the authors mentioned above whenever appropriate. To these we have added other concepts that we developed in the course of our analysis of the data. Our descriptive criteria include actions and technical knowledge associated with the manufacture and use of the product, and ideas, both secular and religious, that promote or inhibit the manufacture and use of the product as well as place it in the Navaho cosmos.

Having arrived at a decision as to the various components included in trait description, we approached the problem of the organization of traits into related categories or complexes. The organizational patterns of classical and contemporary ethnographies that deal with material culture we found unsatisfactory; in the earlier ones data were neither collected nor organized systematically; and the same failure to organize data in comparable categories characterizes the work of more recent ethnographers (Buck, 1950; Osgood, 1940; Gifford, 1940; Murdock, 1938 and 1950). We decided to employ a basic framework of human needs, consisting of subsistence, shelter, and clothing. To this we added ritual and recreation, which cannot be separated from Navaho life. This framework is broad enough to lend itself to cross-cultural comparisons. Furthermore, it is congruent with much of Navaho thinking in relation to their culture.

Next we considered the possibility of arranging the data within this basic framework according to Navaho classifications frequently observed in particular spheres. As one of Wyman and Harris' (1941:9) informants stated, "Navahos are great categorists," a fact which was noted by Matthews (1866:767–777) as early as 1866. In the field of ethnobotany Wyman and Harris (1941:9) found plants consistently classified on the basis of "male" and "female," similar usage, or similar external features. Kluckhohn and Wyman (1940) and Kluckhohn (1960) were able to establish the presence of major ceremonial categories, systematically arranged, and subgroups within them. These were founded on other but consistently applied components. Similarly Hoijer (1951) was able to demonstrate a system of classificatory Navaho verb stems connoting (aside from verbal actions or states) the physical characteristics, number, or animate nature of the objects to which they apply. An excellent synthesis of the above and other categories in Navaho culture is given by Kluckhohn (1960). Although these (emic) classifications were not evident throughout the culture, our data in part support the finding of Matthews (1886:767–768) that Navaho "generalizations among allied species" are similar in certain respects to our own. We therefore utilized patterns of Navaho organization as far as possible in establishing categories of traits within the basic framework of subsistence, shelter, clothing, ritual, and recreation. One of these is the concept of a completed activity. The food category, for example, we first arbitrarily subdivided into headings of storage, preparation, and consumption, as Gifford (1940) had done. When questioned on this particular organization, an informant (DS, Thoreau, 1962) agreed that all items were pertinent to the category, but said they were not in the proper order. For instance, the informant classified stirring sticks, which we had included as an element in "consumption" (since they were used for tasting as well as stirring), with the metate and mano. The completion of a single activity—from grinding to the tasting of corn—was her criterion, and we have organized accordingly.

Another example of patterning occurs within the major heading of shelter. Houses and items associated with them are thought of as a unit. It might be said that "the hogan its insides" is the determining concept. In this instance the pattern is also reflected in the language. Many objects are described in terms of a possessive formed by adding some form of the prefix *bi,* meaning "its." Such a form is used to describe the area around a hogan: "a hogan its surroundings," *hogan binaa.*

Other Navaho classifications had more limited application. Hill examined the concept of "hard goods" and "soft goods," for example turquoise, "hard," as opposed to buckskin, "soft." He attempted to apply this to a variety of traits, but informants exhibited no consistency of categorization beyond grouping a limited number of traits used in a ceremonial capacity. This observation was also confirmed by Haile (1954:20–21).

Occasionally an item seems totally out of place in a given category. These are instances where the use of the item is limited to a single context; glue, though hardly a weapon, was used only for making a sinew-backed bow and thus is found in that category. Similarly the drill, though not an ornament, was used exclusively to perforate beads for necklaces and earrings, and has been classified as an ornament.

Several complexes of traits that are extensively treated elsewhere have been omitted or treated superficially here; these include weaving, basketry, sandpainting, housing, and silverworking, as well as traits known to be recent importations. Traits included as Navaho are considered Navaho not because they necessarily belonged to some hypothetical past culture, but because they have been incorporated into Navaho life through actual manufacture or are represented in myths and tales.

For clarity of presentation and for comparative purposes, we classified the descriptive field data on traits geographically. We divided the Navaho territory into four districts: Ramah, East, Central, and West. Informants living east of an imaginary line northwest from Ramah through the Chuska Mountains formed the Eastern group; those living between this line and the eastern boundary of the Hopi Reservation were considered Central; the remainder formed the Western group (see map, p. 4). Ramah, containing an isolated and relatively homogeneous Navaho group, was considered a separate entity. This area was settled shortly before 1875, and most of the present inhabitants are descended from two groups who moved to the area at that time or from families who immigrated to the area between 1875 and 1890 (see Kluckhohn, 1956; Spuhler and Kluckhohn, 1953). In part the areal division was an arbitrary one, because the ecology tends to be similar throughout the Navaho Reservation. However, the investigations of Kluckhohn and the Harvard group (1935–1958) were conducted at Ramah; most of Hill's (1933–34) in the East and Central areas; Lamphere's (1965–66) in the East (her work at Sheep Springs, near the foot of the Chuska Mountains, has been placed in the Eastern area rather than the Central because the Navaho there have more dealings with their eastern than their western neighbors); and Fishler's (1949–50) in the West. Thus, the areas represent locations where the fieldwork of different people was concentrated.

The field data for each trait are presented under the following headings:

The Navaho territory: informants living east of an imaginary line northwest from Ramah through the Chuska Mountains formed the Eastern group; those living between this line and the eastern boundary of the Hopi Reservation we considered Central; the remainder formed the Western group.

Ramah, Hill, Lamphere, and Fishler. (When data are lacking for any of these divisions, the heading is omitted.) Data from published sources, notably Gifford's fieldwork in the East and West and the Franciscan Fathers' in the Central area, are given in the Comparative sections at the end of each trait.

Chapter 6 contains a summary and analysis of the descriptive material in Chapters 1–5. There we examine the data on Navaho material culture in terms of areal distribution through time. We also include a summary of the use of natural resources, and of the manufacture and use of the traits. In the first case, we wished to determine the degree of homogeneity in Navaho culture as a whole and whether there was evidence of differential acculturation with any of the areas. Second, we examined the individual traits through time to discover whether they would produce significant insights on the causal factors resulting in cultural change, periods of accelerated innovation, and differential acculturation in Navaho history.

Chapter 1 Subsistence

The unifying theme in this chapter is the acquisition of food. Means of procurement are discussed in an order based partly on ethnological cliché (for example, hunting and gathering) and partly on the basis of chronology. Prior to their arrival in the Southwest, the Navaho presumably depended upon hunting and gathering for subsistence. Sometime after their appearance in their present habitat they acquired agriculture from their Pueblo neighbors. The pastoral aspects of their economy, including horses, cattle, and sheep, were derived from the Spanish in the sixteenth century.

The Navaho distinguish clearly between two types of hunting: ritual and nonritual. The hunting of certain animals, particularly deer, antelope, bear, and eagles, is highly ritualized. Other animals are hunted without special ritual observance; according to the Navaho, they are merely "killed." This distinction has been preserved and the hunting devices are described according to the presence or absence of ritual prescriptions.

Gathering, like hunting, involves exploitation of natural resources rather than the production of food. Unlike hunting, however, gathering tends to be a secular rather than a ritual pursuit unless the plants or other items are destined purely for ceremonial purposes. Salt is the only commodity gathered for which ritual is prescribed.

Though the agricultural processes were and are highly ritualized, the tools used in production, like those used in gathering, have no ritual association. The only exception is the digging stick, possibly because it is thought to symbolize snakes or lightning, which are potentially dangerous. In the first decades of the present century animal husbandry supplanted agriculture as the principal subsistence pursuit. Hunting and gathering were practiced only sporadically. Livestock are still important to the Navaho, particularly in terms of prestige. The Navaho admire a man who possesses a fine herd or flock. Extension by association is the basis for classification of the categories related to the livestock industry; for example, corrals, horse equipment, transportation and burdens.

The final category in this chapter is food itself, which has been divided into four subcategories. One item, the water bag, provides an appropriate transition between the category of transportation and burdens and the category of food, since it is used not only for transporting water, but also for storing it in the hogan. Storage devices are followed by items used in the preparation of food. Informants are responsible for the arrangement of these traits; they associated logically those used progressively in the preparation of food, especially corn foods—for example, mano, metate, grass brush, and stirring stick. Devices used in cooking are similarly arranged. General utensils, particularly those used as food containers or in serving food, are not consistently differentiated in Navaho parlance, perhaps as the result of historical factors. Sapir (1936:224–235) noted a number of Navaho and Apache reflexes of Proto-Athabaskan lexical items whose earlier referents seem out of context culturally and environmentally in the Southwest, but appropriate in the Northern Interior of Canada. The word *adee*, horn, is one of these. The Navaho use this term for horn but also frequently use it to designate bowls, dippers, ladles, cups, and dishes, as well as gourds. We have chosen to treat these utensils according to the materials from which they are manufactured.

Hunting
Ritual Hunting

1. Antelope Corral

ní·ʒį́   (Lamphere)

Ramah

Although the remains of antelope corrals have been observed in the Ramah area, only Inf. 115 contributed information about them: "The hunter sang, and the corral was raised to shoulder height." This paucity of data is understandable since the Corral Way is now obsolete.

1.a. Antelope corral (Kluckhohn)

Hill (East, Central, and West)

Hill has published a full description of the corral used in antelope hunting (1938:145–156). He doubts its use for deer. Since antelope were more numerous in the Western area, most data come from that region.

Corral Way, the appropriate ritual, involved more people than other ritual hunts and was more of a communal effort. The leader chose the site, and marked the outline of the corral with pollen. A juniper branch was placed at the southwest corner of the entrance, others in the west, north, and east sides. No one might enter the corral after it was outlined, and the walls were built from the outside.

Whenever possible, builders used juniper and pinyon boughs and logs, starting at the entrance and working back with the tips pointing to the rear. The corral was circular in form with an opening in the front and back. Walls were ten to twelve feet high to prevent the escape of the antelope. Before metal axes were available, all trees were burned down. One informant gave the diameter as about one hundred yards; another said the area enclosed

Antelope corrals (Hill)

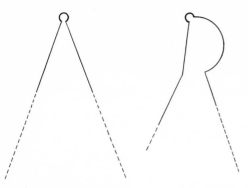

1.1. After RH, C, PP, GH   **1.2.** After MDW

1.3. After T

was one to two acres. The construction of one side generally took about two days and the average time required to complete the corral was five days.

When the corral was finished, a chute was built. The wings extended out from the corral from four hundred yards to a mile on each side of the entrance. Both might be straight (1.1) or one wing might be straight and the other a huge semicircle (1.2, 1.3). The right wing (facing away from the corral) was built first. One informant said wings were as high as the corral walls, but another said they were somewhat lower. The tips of the boughs used to build the chute pointed toward the corral. If wood was scarce, forked poles with stringers were erected and the chute walls made by hanging boughs, tips downward, on these stringers. If wood was plentiful, the wings could be built in two or three days.

Beyond the wings of the chute, piles of brush were erected at intervals for a distance of one to two miles, the intervals decreasing from about thirty yards at the extremities to about five yards near the entrance of the chute. From the end, the brush-pile "wall" appeared to be continuous. Occasionally uprooted yucca plants were turned upside down and a sagebrush was placed on top to give the appearance of a sitting person. An all-night Blessing Way was held when the construction was completed and during the Way no one was allowed to sleep.

Lamphere (East)

PM knew of a stone corral for trapping antelope. It was made of piles of rocks "funneling" into the corral. Antelope were chased into it. Neither EP nor her mother (MS), however, had heard of an antelope corral.

Fishler (West)

Before a hunt, a sing was held, and the corral was prepared. Old corrals were often repaired and abandoned ones occasionally rebuilt. Several informants expressed their fear of working with abandoned corrals because of ritual associations; they stated, "The power has now gone and no Navaho has the power to use these corrals today." Corrals were usually built at the end of small steep canyons.

Fishler's data on the construction of antelope corrals corroborate Hill's. The only shape he mentions is the symmetrical one (see 1.1). The men formed a semicircle and began shouting and moving toward the corral, driving the animals before them. When all were inside the corral, the opening was closed. Animals were killed as needed, unless the pound was poorly built, in which case all animals were killed to prevent their escape.

Comparative

Bourke has given a short description of corral use in 1881 which is useful as an eye-witness account:

> We passed close to an antelope "corral" of the Navajoes; these are made of two converging lines of stone and brush. The Navaho warriors, mounting their fleetest ponies, will scour the country for miles, driving before them the luckless game, which after a while reaches the narrowest point of the corral, and there falls a victim to the hunters in ambush. The Indians are careful not to kill all, but allow a few to escape; this forbearance is

partly based upon a desire to allow the game to reproduce, and is partly religious in character.

(Bourke, 1884:72.)

By 1910, the Franciscan Fathers stated that the hunting rites were not strictly observed, although some of the ancient customs were. The corral which they described was used for deer, antelope, and elk; the opening was to the east (Franciscan Fathers, 1910:475).

Gifford (1940:7, 85) reported the game corral for both Eastern and Western Navaho. He noted that the corral was so constructed that it was invisible to animals entering the wings; this advantage was achieved by building on two sides of a ridge or in a curved valley or canyon.

2. Antelope and Deer Disguise

be·dá (Haile)   "sitting with it"—stalking antlers

Hill (Central and West)

A detailed account of the use of the disguise and the Stalking Way has been published by Hill (1938:122–131). The costume was made of dressed "sacred buckskin" carefully prepared to retain the hair. A framework of twigs kept the head and nose extended, and juniper branches were used to represent the horns (real ones were too heavy and forbidden). The shirt was made of a series of loops of buckskin twisted in a chain stitch. A drawstring at the bottom prevented unraveling. Four "jewels" (beads of white and abalone shell, turquoise and red stone) were attached to this garment. From the waist down, the costume consisted of dressed buckskin pieced together to form long strips; these were wound clockwise, like puttees, one on each leg. Canes made from mountain mahogany or cliff rose wood wrapped with buckskin represented the front legs. Bow and arrows were carried in a quiver over the left shoulder.

Imitation was important in the actual stalking. The hunters "had to lie as an animal does" when sleeping, and to walk as an animal when stalking. Songs were sung as the hunter started toward the deer. Skinning, butchering, and the disposition of the accumulated bones were all carried out according to strict ritual requirements.

This disguise was used primarily for hunting deer. A second type was used largely for stalking antelope, and according to accounts was confined to the Western area. This ritual involved a large party of men, and included a camp tender (who might be a woman if she knew the songs).

Fishler (West)

The hunter wore a disguise consisting of the head and hide of an antelope (2.a). He moved slowly, creeping on all fours toward the game. He carried a bow and arrows, either on the antlers or in his hands (FG, TT, Coalmine; TH, Moenave).

Comparative

Gifford (1940:5, 81) stated that the antelope mask disguise was used by both the Eastern and Western Navaho. The deer mask was present in the Western, but absent in the Eastern district. He suggested that the antelope masks were

2.a. Navaho hunter stalking deer, from a painting by Quincy Tohoma

used in the open country and the deer masks in the mountains. The Franciscan Fathers (1910:475–476) recorded that the body was smeared with clay when deer or antelope masks were worn, and two small sticks were held in the hands to assist in walking in a stooped posture. Bow and quiver, or gun, were "slung under the belly."

3. Pitfall

čákeh kèhgò (Ramah)   "deer fell in there" (CC)

Ramah

Deer and antelope were the only animals hunted by means of a pitfall. A number of people cooperated in selecting a likely site. "Then if there was a man there who knew the ritual, they went ahead and made it" (Inf. 7). A fence (*andii*) was constructed on either side of a game trail in a narrow canyon, or on a mountain pass. It was open in the center. Here a pit was dug, about six feet deep (Inf. 7) and about three by four feet across (Inf. 8). Hurdles, straight poles set in two forked sticks (*nadahasta*), were erected in such a way as to force the animal to jump over them into the pit. It contained four sharpened sticks and was concealed by crossbars covered with dirt and leaves. Animals were killed by falling upon the stakes, which were not poisoned.

According to Inf. 7, deer were not driven nor was any bait placed on the pitfall, but Inf. 12 said that a group of hunters drove the deer down the trail, forcing them to jump the hurdle. The pitfall was used only during the winter months, and it was abandoned after a hunt (Inf. 7). It is not known if it was reused. Inf. 12 added that Pit Way was rarely used since it was dangerous if the hunter made a mistake in ritual.

The principal informants (Infs. 7, 8, 12) did not claim to have used a pitfall. One man who died in 1929 (Inf. 257) was said to have known Pit Way. He is the only Ramah inhabitant who may have taken part in the ritual construction and use of the pitfall. Abandoned pits and fences may still be seen in the vicinity of Ramah, but this method of hunting is no longer used.

Hill (Central and West)

Hill has published a detailed description of the pitfall hunting of deer (1938:131–132). According to C (Chinle), deer were the only animals hunted intentionally by this method; but it was considered fortunate if other animals fell into the pit. Informants differed as to the construction of the pit. PP (Fort Defiance) said that the pit was empty, that the deer's antlers would keep the front legs off the floor of the pit and prevent escape. According to C, a forked pole placed at either end of the pit caught the deer as it fell and held it suspended; it was impaled on a single stake. This was denied by MDW (Jeddito) and K (Black Mountain); they said several stakes were used (as at Ramah). Hunters either flushed the game and "coaxed" the animals toward the trap, or the hunt was left to chance and the pit visited each morning. Ceremonies accompanied not only the construction of the traps but the morning visits.

Fishler (West)

IJun (Kaibito) said that pits were used for deer, antelope, and sheep. TN (Kaibito) denied their use for mountain sheep. Informants did not mention the use of sharpened stakes, but said that the hunter killed the animals he found in the pit. According to TT (Coalmine), antelope were captured in camouflaged pits; deer were taken in pits with a log and brush hurdle. TH (Moenave) confirmed the second type of pit. None of the informants had ever used pitfalls, but they had heard of or seen them.

Comparative

Pitfalls are mentioned only in the recent literature. Corrals were apparently observed before pitfalls, but this may be because they were more obvious (see Bourke, 1884:72; 1936:80). The Franciscan Fathers (1910:475, 477) were the first to describe the pitfall, which seems to resemble that described by Ramah informants. They also included a variant which consisted of a series of pits constructed in a zigzag row.

According to Gifford (1940:6, 82), both the Western and Eastern Navaho used the stick-covered pitfall for deer. The Western Navaho pitfall had impaling stakes, the Eastern the straddling bar. Both pits were between six and nine feet deep, built on trails. The Eastern Navaho placed them in "gates," or openings on the trail, the Western did not. The Western Navaho placed them behind a hurdle, "sometimes." Neither group built pitfalls in series.

4. Eagle Pit   ʼaca ʼaxi·ńí·łʒí (Ramah, Haile)   eagle pit (method); "eagle we are grabbing" (CC)

ʼo·d (Haile)   eagle pit trap (structure)

Ramah

Small hills "a long way from home" were selected as sites for eagle pits; the proximity of an eagle aerie was unimportant. Hunting was done in midsummer, about July. Only those men who knew Eagle Way could hunt eagles. "Not any man can do this, he has to know songs, prayers, and the way to paint his body." Eagles and hawks were hunted in this manner.

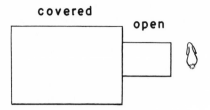

4.1. Eagle pit, after Tschopik

Eagle pits (Hill)

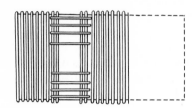

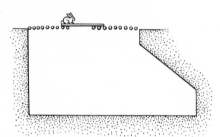

4.2. After GH

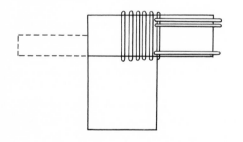

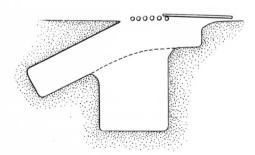

4.3. After MH

A pit, with the doorway to the east, was dug large enough to accommodate a seated man. Sticks were placed over most of the pit to conceal it, and these were covered with earth. A live rabbit was tethered by one leg to a stake at the entrance to the pit (see 4.1). The hunter then hid in the pit and sang the proper ritual songs, calling the eagle by its sacred name. When an eagle flew down to seize the bait, the hunter reached through the hole and caught it by the feet. The eagle was then tethered to a second stake to decoy others.

According to Inf. 7, the hunter who first made a pit had exclusive rights to its use. He later said that a hunter did not reuse the pit, since in the prayers after killing an eagle the hunter said "a lot of good things so he can't kill anything there anymore." It is possible that the hunter either returned periodically and regarded the pit as his own, or abandoned it.

According to Inf. 7, no one in Ramah knew this method of hunting eagles. He said that the ritual had become obsolete before his time. This statement was confirmed by Infs. 12 and 21. An old man who died some years ago (Inf. 257?) was supposed to have used this method to secure eagles (Inf. 8); Inf. 1, however, had never heard of the method being used at Ramah.

Another means of obtaining eagle feathers for ceremonial purposes was to remove the young from the nest and raise them in captivity until they were fully feathered; Kluckhohn saw this done near El Morro.

Eagles are now shot with rifles or caught in metal traps, but the feathers of these birds may not be used ritually. The pit ritual may be extant at Crownpoint and Keams Canyon (Infs. 7, 8). It is possible that the Ramah Navaho have always relied on other areas to supply them with eagle feathers, gall, dried meat, and claws for ritual use. Various persons in the Ramah area possess eagle feathers, but the origin of the feathers is unknown.

Hill (Central and West)

Hill's description is published (1938:161–166). According to Hill, ritual hunting of eagles took place in late November and continued until January. A hunting party might be limited to two men, or consist of as many as ten. The duration of the hunts was twelve days. Hill's informants described two types of pits, larger and more complex than those described by Inf. 7. In one of these (see 4.2) the excavation was extended to one side to accommodate the captured eagles. The opening was covered with closely set poles, then bark and earth; an aperture was left in the middle for the hunter to enter, and through which to pull the captured eagles. The other pit (see 4.3) was similarly covered, although the aperture might be at one end. The excavation included an extended supplementary pit, in which the hunter could lie down.

Fishler (West)

TN (Kaibito) mentioned two methods of catching eagles; in both the nest was robbed of the young. In the first, a burlap bag was lowered to the nest by a rope. The claws of the young birds became entangled in the bag and they were pulled to the top. In an alternative method, a rope was tied to a log above the nest and a man was lowered. The young birds were taken, and any down feathers in the nest were gathered. Young birds which were not fully feathered were kept and fed rabbits and mice until they matured. GB (Tuba city) confirmed the second method, and said that eagles were also shot with bow and arrows from ambush near the nest.

Comparative

The pit for eagle catching may be implied in Matthews' statement (1897:232) that "the Navahoes, like the wild tribes of the north, catch full-grown eagles in traps, and pluck them while alive." If so, this is probably the earliest reference to this trap.

According to the Franciscan Fathers (1910:476–477), eagle pits were usually dug in some spot much frequented by eagles. In other respects the pit is as described elsewhere. They specified the use of a rabbit dummy, controlled by a stick.

The account by Sapir and Hoijer parallels those found elsewhere, except that their informant said that eagle pits were not made in the Navaho country. Those who planned to catch eagles traveled to the edge of the Navaho territory to do so (Sapir and Hoijer, 1942:317–319).

Gifford's Western Navaho informant denied the use of the pit for taking eagles. His Eastern informant, however, said that such pits were used, and that the hunter was accompanied by a "shaman" who made "medicine" to prevent his getting boils or carbuncles (Gifford, 1940:7, 84). All other accounts, however, indicate that the hunter himself had the necessary knowledge for hunting eagles and did not need an assistant. (See Hill, 1943:31–36; Newcomb, 1940b:50–78.)

Data confirming the present existence of the pit hunting of eagles are lacking. One statement from the Eastern area suggests that pit hunting is no longer practiced: "Formerly the live feathers were obtained from eagles trapped according to the methods described by Matthews" (Kluckhohn and Wyman, 1940:36).

Nonritual Hunting

5. Bird Snare   cídi·łcoí be·γʷóλe·hé (Ramah, Haile)   "canary loop" ("canary a loop catch it") (CC); snare for yellow birds (Haile)

5.1. Bird snare, after Tschopik

Ramah

Bird snares were used to catch birds for ritual purposes. Several variations were described. In the first, a frame was made of four sticks wrapped with flowering weeds. To this two transverse sticks were attached, one above the other. From the upper one were hung as many horsehair nooses as possible (see 5.1). The frames were hung in the branches of trees, or among sunflowers where birds congregated. "There was not enough room for the birds to perch on the upper stick, and they hung themselves when they moved to the lower one" (Inf. 7). The informant had seen this snare, but had not used it. He originally said that it was used for bluebirds as well as smaller birds, but later retracted, saying bluebirds were too heavy and would break the loops.

A second type was constructed as follows. Four sticks were pushed into the ground, with about sixteen inches left above the surface. Two transverse sticks were added; horsehair loops, about one inch in diameter, were placed on them at three-inch intervals. The horsehair was twisted, to stiffen the loops and project them upward. These snares were used for small birds (type unspecified) and were set near ponds or springs. Birds entangled their feet in the nooses when they flew down to the water (Inf. 15). A variation of this type consisted of a series of individual loops staked to the ground with wooden pins (Inf. 8). This type is still used by some Zuni (Inf. 8). A stick with many small loops attached to it was also used.

Snaring was done mostly by children, who sold the feathers to singers (Inf. 7). But according to Inf. 8, men were the only trappers, not women or children. Birds were snared at any time, and feathers stored until needed. Feathers of bluebirds and yellow birds are still used for ritual purposes, but the birds are shot with guns or slingshots. Only eagle feathers must be taken from live birds.

Hill (East, Central, and West)

Hill's informants (MC, Sawmill; C, Chinle; IS, Lukachukai; MH, Head Springs; MLH, Crownpoint) confirmed the sunflower stalk trap described by the Franciscan Fathers (1910:323), stating that it was generally used for the bluebird and yellow warbler (see also Fishler section).

PP (Fort Defiance) described a variation similar to the second Ramah type. Holes were bored through a sunflower stalk near its top and a crosspiece inserted. On this were placed nooses of horsehair with the ends secured to the transverse piece. Nooses were arranged in the following manner. Horsehair was doubled and the ends tied to the stick. The loop thus formed was twisted and a bale sling hitch formed in the end (see Trait 155, Knots). The loop of this formed the noose. Several nooses were tied about an inch apart on the stick. The twisting of the horsehair strands gave a springlike action to the noose. These traps were placed in the fields.

Snares used for snowbirds (eaten in times of famine) were horsehair nooses tied to a stick and covered with horse manure. When the birds scratched in it they were caught. This type of snare was also described by JJ (Crownpoint), PP, and IS. According to IS, blackbirds and bluebirds were also caught in this manner. Snares were baited with meal or bread crumbs.

Fishler (West)

A snare was used for catching doves, bluebirds, or other small birds. Horsehair loops were tied to a stake (TN, Kaibito), or to the top of a large sunflower (TH, Moenave). These snares were placed where birds were known to flock, or set when birds were seen in any particular location. Corn meal was sprinkled on the ground for bait. Hunters frightened the birds and attempted to drive them toward the snare. The doves caught their feet in the loops as they walked around. Three or four birds were caught at a time; the snares were employed during the winter.

GB (Tuba City) described a similar type used for bluebirds. A large sunflower stalk was hollowed out from seven to eight inches below the flower. A length of horsehair was then pulled up through the hole in the center of the stalk, and through one in the side, seven to eight inches below the top. A loop was formed at one end; the other was tied to a stick. Two or three small willow twigs were placed parallel on top of the flower. Birds landing on the sunflower slipped on the twigs and were snared by the loop.

Fishler's informants stated that males made these snares.

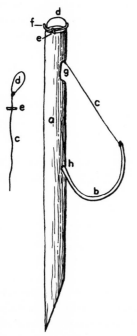

5.2. Sunflower stalk bird snare, after the Franciscan Fathers. Sunflower stalk (*a*), is cut at points *g* and *h;* a greasewood twig (*b*) is inserted at the lower cut (*h*); horsehair (*c*) is twisted and looped (*d*), pulled through the top of the stalk (*a*), and attached to the twig (*b*). A split reed (*f*) and a small stick (*e*) keep the trap set until a bird lands.

Comparative

The Franciscan Fathers (1910:323) described the sunflower stalk snare used by Fishler's informants (see 5.2). They specified that all parts in contact with the snare were to be polished and smooth. The bird's foot was pulled into the hollow stalk when the trap was sprung.

According to Gifford (1940:6, 83), the Western Navaho used the sunflower stalk snare, the Eastern did not. One snare used by the Western Navaho was drawn shut by the release of a bent stick (as above), that used by the Eastern Navaho was drawn shut by a stick weight. The type of snare described at Ramah, the "sinking perch," was described by Gifford's Zuni informant. Neither Navaho informant was questioned, unfortunately. The Eastern Navaho also used a horsehair snare attached to a vertical stick which projected up in the center of the noose; the weight of the bird drew the noose shut.

6. Blind   ʾił (Lamphere)   "evergreen branch"; "pinyon tree branch" (CC)

Ramah

Additional boughs were leaned against a small tree to form a more effective screen. The quarry included the bluejay, whitebreasted nuthatch, chickadee, and several unidentified species. The hunter crouched behind the blind, and shot at birds with a bow and arrow. The arrows had crossed sticks near the tip (see 19.3). When branches of the blind broke, they were replaced. If it was frequently used, the blind did not last long.

"Just kids did this" (Inf. 8). Blinds were used to kill birds to prevent them from eating drying corn or meat (Inf. 7). Inf. 8 said that he had made such a blind when he was a child, but he indicated that blinds are no longer used. Instead birds are killed with a rifle, shotgun, or slingshot.

Hill (East, Central, and West)

Hunters sometimes built blinds at waterholes. These blinds were used to hunt deer or antelope, rather than small birds (Hill, 1938:97).

Lamphere (East)

PM said that the blind was made of juniper or pinyon, or whatever kinds of branches were available.

Comparative

Gifford's data confirm Hill's. The Western Navaho sometimes hid behind rock piles to hunt various animals; the Eastern did not. Gifford's statement that both used blinds for hunting deer probably refers to the pitfall fence (Gifford, 1940:7, 84).

7. Rodent Snare   naʾalλoˑ ši beˑʾóλehé (Haile)   "four-legged animals loop" (CC)

Ramah

Nooses were set around prairie dog holes, and the free end of the string was tied to a stake driven into the ground near the hole. These snares were not regarded as efficient for catching prairie dogs because the animal usually bit through the cord and escaped. Inf. 39 did not state when this snare was introduced, whether he saw it, or when (and if) it became obsolete. Prairie dogs are now secured by drowning, or by steel traps; traps have been observed in at least five or six establishments.

Hill (East, Central, and West)

Hill's data confirmed the Ramah material. Horsehair nooses, twisted for tension, were attached to a stake or rock and set at the entrance to the hole. When the noose was set, the entrance was hidden with grass (Hill, 1938:172).

8. Deadfall

·àlǯiǯ (Ramah)   "crushing"

Ramah

A stone was set on edge by resting it against a straight pole which in turn rested in the fork of a stick set in the ground (see 8.1). Corn bait was suspended by a string from the end of the straight pole. When the animal reached for the corn, the pole was disturbed and the stone dropped. Deadfall traps were set near the garden (Inf. 7), for catching both jack and cottontail rabbits, as well as rats and mice. Anyone in the family could set them. Traps were set in the daytime; animals were caught at night.

Both Infs. 7 and 12, the only informants, denied any other types of deadfall traps. The former stated that he had never made a deadfall and that they are no longer used at Ramah. Neither informant indicated whether he had seen such a trap made. Rodent traps are mentioned fairly frequently in the field notes, but these may be commercial metal ones.

Hill (East, Central, and West)

Hill also questioned Inf. 7 from Ramah—his informant MM—about deadfall traps. Hill's description includes a trigger mechanism: a stick fit into notches in the upright forked stick and the horizontal lever. Bait was suspended by a string from the upper end of the trigger (see 8.2).

Other informants described a variety of different deadfalls, used not only for rabbits and other small animals, but for coyotes, wildcats, and foxes. Some of these are illustrated (see 8.3, 8.4, 8.5, 8.7, 8.8, 8.9, 8.10, 8.11). The trigger on one described by N (see 8.3) was dislodged when the animal attacked bait placed at its midpoint; the upright slab fell into the indented rock. On another (see 8.4) a stone slab was set in a trough between two low rock walls;

Deadfalls

8.1. After Tschopik

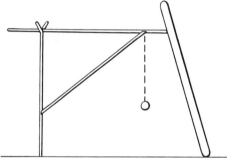

8.2. Hill, after MM (Inf. 7, Ramah)

Deadfalls (Hill)

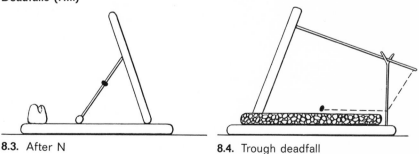

8.3. After N

8.4. Trough deadfall

Deadfalls (Hill), cont.

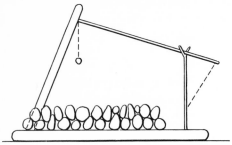

8.5. Trough deadfall with suspended bait

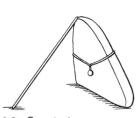

8.6. Coyote trap

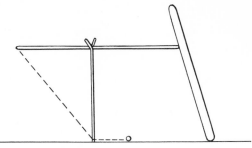

8.7. After YLH, C

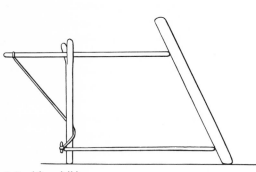

8.8. After MH

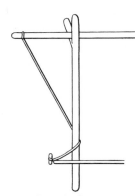

8.9. Detail of 8.8

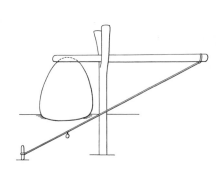

8.10. After C

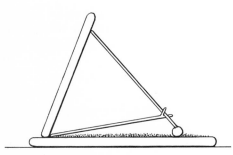

8.11. After PP

bait was set on a small stick across the walls, tied by a string to the trigger stick. In a similar trap (see 8.5) rock walls were also used, built slightly higher than in 8.4, and bait was suspended. Details concerning the construction and operation of most of these traps are in Hill (1938:168–173).

The simplest coyote trap was a stone, propped up by a stick smeared with blood or tallow. Several of these traps were often set on a trail (Hill, 1938:169). Or, for the small rodents, bait was hung from a string tied around the stone (C, Chinle; see 8.6).

A lever was often used, with a string attached to it at one end and to bait at the other. In one such trap a slip knot at the base of the upright forked stick maintained the necessary tension (see 8.7). In a triggered version, the string was wrapped one or more times around the base of the upright, then tied to a small piece of wood. Corn kernels were attached to a stick balanced between the trigger chip and the stone (MH, Head Springs; see 8.8, 8.9). Or, according to C, the string attached to the lever was staked out, across the deadfall. Bait was suspended on this string, directly below the stone (see 8.10).

In several instances a base rock was used, to prevent an animal from digging free if he survived the impact of the upper stone. The stick which supported the stone often rested on a small rock, and was thus easily dislodged (see 8.3, 8.11). Hill's informants also described other traps, similar in principle to those described above.

Fishler (West)

Men used a flat stone propped up with a stick; corn was scattered under the trap for bait. GB (Tuba City) said that deadfalls were used especially for squirrels; BN (Kaibito) specified squirrels and chipmunks; TH (Moenave), bluebirds, sparrows, snowbirds, and quail; and TN (Kaibito), rabbits.

Comparative

Bourke found a deadfall in use among the Fort Defiance Navaho in 1881. This trap was described as a heavy stone resting on a slender stick to which the bait was attached. He said, however, that these deadfalls were used only for killing field rats (Bourke, 1936:231–232). The trap mentioned by the Franciscan Fathers thirty years later was used specifically for rabbits and mountain rats (Franciscan Fathers, 1910:322; see 8.12). This type was described by Hill's informant MH.

Gifford (1940:5, 82) stated that both the Eastern and Western Navaho used the baited trigger type of deadfall with a stone weight, that described by the Franciscan Fathers (1910:322). They also used an unbaited trigger-bar trap, placed along the trail, for rodents or rabbits. The Eastern Navaho used the deadfall for rodents, rabbits, wildcats, and coyotes.

The statement by the Franciscan Fathers in 1910 that deadfalls were used "in former days" but are "at present . . . rarely used" confirms the Ramah suggestion that they are now nearly obsolete. Since they are easy to make, they may still be used by poorer families. They have apparently been displaced by traps purchased at the trading post.

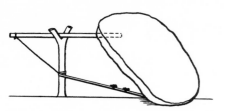

8.12. Deadfall, after the Franciscan Fathers

9. Reflector

ʼe·š diłła·· (Lamphere) "to make it shine?"; "is that shining light?" (CC) or "is that shiny?" (CC)

Ramah

A reflector of polished rock was used in hunting prairie dogs. To make the animals emerge, sheep were driven over their burrows. The hunter then reflected the sun in their eyes, and shot them with bow and arrow (Inf. 7).

Hill (East, Central, and West)

A piece of mica three or four inches square, placed in a split stick, was set near the entrance of a prairie dog burrow to reflect sunlight as far down the hole as possible. When the animal emerged, he was blinded and was easily shot with a barbed arrow (Hill, 1938:171–172).

Lamphere (East)

PM said that after the advent of traders, the Navaho used the lids of baking powder cans to reflect light into the prairie dogs' burrows. Now, she said, they put water in the holes to drive the animals out. The holes are watched (one person for each five holes), and when the prairie dogs emerge, they are hit with a stick and killed.

Fishler (West)

A stick one and a half to two feet long was split at one end, sometimes sharpened to a point at the other. A piece of glass or mirror, or tin can, was inserted in the split. When the device was correctly placed, sunlight was reflected into the prairie dog burrow.

Comparative
The Franciscan Fathers (1910:476) mentioned the method described by Hill's and Fishler's informants; they also confirmed the use of water to drown the animals. Gifford's Western informant described a device made from crystal (?) or mica. "Animal comes out to see what it is and is shot" (Gifford, 1940:83).

10. Throwing Club

cįha·ł (Ramah)   "weapon" (CC) (specific to throwing club)

tsin hathl ntelí (Hill)   "the wide flattened throwing stick"

Ramah
A limb of dry oak, or a green juniper branch, one and a half to three inches in diameter, was cut with an axe to the proper length, one and a half to two feet. The clubs were slightly curved, or straight; they were not grooved, nor were the edges sharp. Men made them, in a special, but unspecified, place.

Both cottontail and jack rabbits were hunted with clubs, in communal rabbit hunts held either in winter or summer. If there had been a heavy snowfall, hunters went on foot, but in summer they hunted on horseback. At a prearranged time and at an appointed place, they gathered with their fastest horses. Some carried two clubs; others had bows and arrows. Either they scattered and ran the rabbits down, or they formed a long line which gradually closed in a circle. When near the quarry, they clubbed or shot the rabbits. Either men or women participated in the hunt (Infs. 3, 7); but Inf. 8 insisted that only grown men used clubs. He had done so, as had Inf. 256, before 1942.

According to Inf. 8, it was "just a little over thirty-nine years ago," or about 1915, when the Navaho stopped using these clubs. By 1940, clubs were employed only for sport, as indicated by Inf. 256. Other descriptions of rabbit hunts all mention the use of firearms instead, save for one ambiguous statement by Inf. 90. It appears that the functional role of the throwing club ended at Ramah about the second decade of this century.

Throwing clubs (Hill)

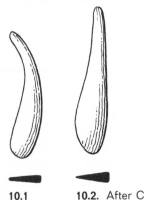

10.1   **10.2.** After C

Hill (Central)
Several types of throwing clubs were distinguished. The first—that described by Ramah informants—was quickly and often carelessly made, and was considered a makeshift weapon. It was straight, with a diameter about the size of a fifty-cent piece. The second type was carefully constructed. It was curved, with the grip left round but the body flattened and the blade tapered from the outside to the inside edge. Shaping was done by rubbing the wood with a coarse-grained stone (see 10.1). All informants agreed on both these types.

A third type (see 10.2) was described by C (Chinle), called "the wide flattened throwing stick" (*tsin hal nteeli*). Also made by rubbing, it was not curved, and had a greater taper than the second type. In a fourth type, described by PP (Fort Defiance), the stick was left round. It was heated, and when hot bent to lunate shape. A cord was tied to each end to set it until it cooled in the desired shape. C denied that the flat "boomerang" Pueblo type of rabbit stick was used by the Navaho.

Hill's informants also stated that hunters practiced throwing at targets until they became expert, and that some could kill at forty or fifty yards. Both men and women with clubs were said to have taken part in communal hunts directed by a leader (Hill, 1938:170–171).

Fishler (West)

A heavy length of seasoned wood was peeled, and worked to one of several shapes. TT (Coalmine) described a short, round, uncurved stick (see 10.3) used at short distances (cf. Ramah and Hill sections). Hill's second type was also described, although IJun (Kaibito) stated that this type of club was of equal width along its length (see 10.4). TT described an oak club curved with a flat inside and a round outside. At one end was a handle, round and larger than the opposite end (see 10.5).

Informants stated that men used clubs for killing rabbits, but other small animals were also killed or stunned. Clubs were grasped by the narrow end and thrown with a horizontal or an overhand swing. GB (Tuba City) said that boys nowadays did not know how to throw the club. TN (Kaibito) stated that at one time men were very accurate with these clubs at long distances. He also said that while hunting prairie dogs "you could whistle and the prairie dog would come back to see what was making the noise. Then you could hit him with a club," which was "any available stick." He had seen this done, but had not done it himself. TN said that rabbits were clubbed from horseback, but that the purpose was to improve the individual's horsemanship rather than to secure game.

Comparative

The Franciscan Fathers described an oak "boomerang" whittled to the shape of a battenstick, then heated, and bent over the knee to create a slight curve. The object in throwing it at rabbits was to break the animals' legs. Rabbits were also clubbed (Franciscan Fathers, 1910:324, 476).

Both of Gifford's informants denied the curved throwing club, and confirmed the straight variety for hunting rabbits and other game. Only the Western informant used a club while surrounding game. The Eastern informant claimed that hunters shot the animals instead of clubbing them (Gifford, 1940:7, 33). An informant in the Blanco-Largo Canyon area denied the use of the rabbit stick (Farmer, 1938:6).

Throwing clubs (Fishler)

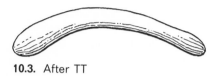

10.3. After TT

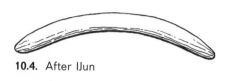

10.4. After IJun

10.5. After TT

11. Rodent Stick

be·há·aldiʒ (Ramah) "(pole) pulling out by the fur" (CC)

Ramah

A straight pole was trimmed of branches, but the bark was not removed. Diameter and length of the stick varied with the size of the animal to be caught. The tip was worked to a rounded point, then spit upon or smeared with gum to increase its adhesiveness. This end was thrust into a rodent's burrow, and twisted into the hair of the animal, which was then pulled out.

Men, women, and children made these devices just before hunting. "Kids use it all the time" (Inf. 256). "One could hunt in the winter in this way" (Inf. 8). They were used for catching cottontail and jack rabbits, chipmunks, ground squirrels, rats, and porcupines. "Prairie dogs live too far underground" (Inf. 7). Hill doubts the use of this stick for the last four animals, on the grounds of insufficient—or inappropriate—fur. Rodent sticks were either thrown away or kept around the hogan. If one could be found, it would be used again.

Both Inf. 8 and Inf. 256 have used the rodent stick. A more common method of hunting rodents, however, was to pour water into the burrows to drown the animals (Infs. 7, 39); or to build a fire at the edge of the hole and smoke them out.

Hill (Central)
Data from IS (Lukachukai) and MC (Sawmill) confirmed that from Ramah. According to Hill's published material, the cottontail is the only animal caught in this manner. The point of the stick was abraded, to catch more readily in the fur (Hill, 1938:171).

Fishler (West)
When rabbits were driven into their burrows, a long, blunt-ended stick, thrust into the hole, was twisted in the belly fur of the rabbit and the animal was pulled out. If it caught in the animal's back, the fur came loose and the quarry escaped. TT (Coalmine) and TH (Moenave) had hunted in this manner; BN, TN, IJmo (all of Kaibito) had seen this method practiced.

Comparative
Bourke's description (1936:231), probably from the Fort Defiance area, indicates that a forked stick, twisted until it caught in the animal's fur, was used to pull rabbits from their burrows. Both of Gifford's informants confirmed this means of catching rodents. Both informants mentioned the stick moistened with saliva, and both denied the use of a split stick. A rough stick was used by the Eastern Navaho; the Western informant was not questioned. All of the Southwestern tribes investigated by Gifford used some such device for catching small animals (Gifford, 1940:6).

12. Rabbit Net

Hill (East, Central, and West)
Hill's informants denied the use of nets in rabbit hunts (Hill, 1938:171).

Lamphere (East)
PM had never heard of using nets. She said that rabbits were chased from horseback until they tired, and then were killed with rocks.

Fishler (West)
TN (Kaibito) stated that in the old days, communal hunts were held for cottontail and jack rabbits, but not for snowshoe rabbits. The animals were driven inward and caught by nets. TN did not think that fire or torches or noise were used to drive the rabbits. TT (Coalmine) said that a net was never used to catch rabbits.

Comparative

Gifford's informants denied the use of the rabbit net (Gifford, 1940:6). The Franciscan Fathers (1910) did not mention the use of nets; they stated that rabbits were rounded up, then clubbed to death (1910:476).

Weapons

13. Sinew-backed Bow

ˈałtį·diłxił (Ramah, Haile)   dark bow; "arrow, black" (CC)

ˈałtį̂·ˈ yiŝ̌é·ˈ (Ramah, Haile)   pitch-covered bow; "arrow carving (whittling)" (CC)

Ramah

According to Inf. 7, the best material for bows was a plant known as *tselkani*,* which grew on a mountain some hundred miles south of the Ramah area. Bow songs were associated with this material. Oak was also frequently used, and Inf. 2 said that juniper made good bows; Inf. 16 spoke of sumac bows, but Inf. 7 denied the use of either sumac or willow.

A straight piece of wood was cut, usually about four feet long, but sometimes shorter. "Each man picks his own size" (Inf. 7). Men made bows, but whether every man made his own is not known. Bark was removed with a hatchet; the stave was then shaped with a knife or hatchet. It was approximately two and a half to three inches wide at the center, or grip. It was tapered slightly and thinned on the inside toward each end. The back of the bow was rounded, and the inside surface flat. When the shaping was completed, sheep fat was rubbed on the wood and the stave was placed near the fire to dry and to allow the grease to penetrate; the stave was worked with the hands to give it resiliency. The bow was curved by bending it in a crotch of a tree.

13.a. Sinew-backed bow

* The species to which this term refers has not been identified botanically, and sources differ on its nature. It has been variously translated as "yellow mahogany" (Kluckhohn and Wyman, 1940:32) or "mahogany," possibly a species of *Cercocarpus*, the genus which includes mountain mahogany (Wyman, 1964, personal communication). The Franciscan Fathers (1910:318) referred to it as a "very hard wood used for war bows," and Haile later (1951:198) identified it as mock orange. F. H. Douglas suggested that it might be Osage orange. Elmore (1944:93) translated it as "wood that is hard and sweet," a translation which fits the stems "stone," (*tse*) and "sweet," (*likan*) (Haile, 1951:283, 289). Pending botanical identification, the term "mahogany," following Wyman's designation, is probably most appropriate.

The back was then reinforced with three or four layers of sinew which were glued to the surface. The ends of the bow were wrapped with sinew and covered with glue for about two inches from each tip. Finally a grip of braided buckskin and a handle were attached to the center of the bow. The grip consisted of three buckskin thongs plaited over and under, parallel to the long axis of the bow; these encompassed the bow, but were not glued to it. Or, according to Inf. 16, the grip was made from soft scrapings from the inside of a buckskin glued on the center of the bow. Both Inf. 7 and Inf. 16 agreed that the center was not wrapped with sinew.

Care had to be taken of the bow, especially of the bowstring, made of sinew or buckskin, which would stretch if it became damp. When not in use the bow was loosely strung. It was stored in a buckskin case attached to the quiver (Trait 23); this case was hung from the roof of the hogan (Inf. 34). Bows were kept and reused, but there was no estimate of their durability. When the bow was carried, the butt end was always toward the ground.

The sinew-backed bow was more highly prized than any other type and was accorded particular care (Inf. 7). Inf. 8 said these bows were formerly used only for war and that only warriors could make them. Other types of bows were used for hunting (Inf. 8) and for archery contests.

For shooting, the bow was held in the left hand, diagonally and sloping to the left. The thumb was parallel to its long axis and the fingers gripped around the front. The string was drawn to the shoulder with the second and third fingers of the right hand. Boys were taught to shoot both right and left handed (Inf. 1).

Women and girls were not supposed to use bows, but Inf. 177 stated that Inf. 4 made a little bow and arrow and they "used it to shoot at the lizards. Sometimes we hit them and sometimes we didn't." Boys began to play with bows and arrows when they were about eight years old, and were urged by their parents to increase their skill by playing games which involved archery.

Older informants regarded the bow as a part of the old Navaho culture. When asked to explain its presence they gave it a mythical origin. Many adults were familiar with archery games and most of the males had played them. Some, including the younger men, had made bows in recent years; Inf. 256 said that he made an oak bow with a leather bowstring. Observers noted that several informants owned bows (Infs. 20, 101, 106, 138, 258); Inf. 39 had two which he used for shooting rabbits and prairie dogs around his dwelling but not for large game. Miniature bows are still part of the ritual equipment of chanters, especially those who perform Evil Way chants (Kluckhohn and Wyman, 1940:32). A small boy was seen making a miniature bow from a piece of heavy wire.

The gun has now largely replaced the bow for hunting game and for killing birds and rodents in the fields. There has been a change in the hunting pattern, however, for both men and women use guns, although women do so infrequently. According to Inf. 1 the toy bow has been replaced by the slingshot.

Hill (Central and West)

The sinew-backed bow appears to have been the most frequently used and the preferred type. There was little difference among the several varieties either in the shape or the length, which depended on the strength of the man. The carrying power was about a hundred yards. Bows appear to have been rarely effective at half that distance, and, to judge from samples of present-day archery, dangerous only under a hundred feet.

Informants confirmed the use of oak, sumac, juniper ("but this is soft"), and *tselkani* (not native to Navaho country), and said that occasionally black greasewood and wild rose were used (PP, Fort Defiance; AM, Lukachukai; SG, Keams Canyon). While nearly all men were able to make bows, some were recognized for their proficiency and were often hired to make them for others. Payment might consist of a pair of antelope skin pants, a pair of leggings, or a blanket (MH, Head Springs). No ceremony attended the making of a bow; anyone could make one who had had an Enemy Way performed over him (PP).

Opinions differed about the selection of straight-grained wood. According to SG, a limb three to five inches thick and ten feet long was cut and the best section chosen. AM said that the limb should be about one inch in diameter and five hand spans and five finger lengths long. According to PP, any convenient length was chosen. Bark was removed with a flake of stone and the stave set aside to season for a week to ten days. The bow was shaped as at Ramah.

After the stave was roughly shaped it was straightened over the knee or with the aid of a forked stick. If a curvature was desired, the center of the stave was heated and this section placed against a tree trunk or limb. The ends of the stave were then tied to other limbs, and the bow was left to set for three or four days. Removal of some of the wood between the ends and the grip accentuated the curve (PP).

Notches for the bowstring were cut in the sides near the ends. The growing end of the wood always formed the lower end of the bow (AM), the outside of the tree the back of the bow (PP). The bow was then rubbed with mutton tallow and heated over the fire, as at Ramah. "This kept the bow from cracking" (AM). It was then placed in the sun to dry, for two to seven days.

Glue and sinew were prepared for backing (see Trait 14, Glue). The sinew used came from the back or legs of deer, and in later times horses (AM, PP). Sinew from the back was preferred. A bundle a foot and a half long and four finger widths in diameter was necessary (SG). According to SG, the sinew was soaked in water until it began to soften and was then chewed. "If the sinew is not chewed it will not stick." This process was repeated until the sinew became pliable. AM said the dry sinews were placed on a block of wood and pounded with a stone. Then they were placed in water to soak, taken out from time to time, and scraped until pliable.

Informants differed on the method of application. SG stated that the glue was put on the back of the bow and allowed to harden. When the sinew was ready the bow was held over a fire until the glue "came almost to a boil." Sinew was then placed on the back of the bow starting from the bowstring notches and overlapping at the grip. This sinew was allowed to dry; then more glue was applied and more sinew added in any convenient way until the back of the bow at each end was covered. The sinew was passed from back to front over the ends of the bow. AM stated that the back of the bow was tallowed, then hot glue was applied, and finally sinew. The first application of the sinew covered about four finger widths both front and back over each end of the bow. The first layer was allowed to dry before the second was applied.

All informants agreed that three or four complete applications of sinew were necessary. After each, the sinew was allowed to harden; then more glue was applied. While the work progressed, the back of the bow was rubbed with a stick or stone, or (according to SG) with a square of horsehide which was first placed on the fire for a moment and then soaked in boiling water, in order to smooth the sinew and press it into the glue. When the last application had dried, the sinew overlapping the ends of the bow was covered by more sinew wrapped for about three inches around the ends of the bow. Wrapping began just below the bowstring notch. The grip and other points of stress were reinforced in the same manner and with an additional buckskin wrapping. The ends of the sinew were thinned out and they adhered without tying. The ends of the buckskin wrapping were tucked under the wraps.

The Navaho distinguished two kinds of sinew-backed bows: the "black bow" and the *tselkani.* Their methods of manufacture were the same except for the final step. The "black bow" was finished by rubbing burned pinyon boughs and tallow into the wood, giving it a dark color. The *tselkani* bow was rubbed with tallow and scorched cedar boughs, which gave it a yellow color. The distinction was a ritual one. The "black bow" was the male, the *tselkani* the female, and they were mentioned respectively in the sections of the war and hunting rituals where the two sexes played a part (AM, AS, Lukachukai; C, Chinle; MH, Head Springs; SG; PP).

As soon as the bow was finished, a bowstring was made and the bow loosely strung. It was then set aside to dry thoroughly. From time to time the string was tightened to keep the bow taut in the desired shape and to stretch the bowstring. In shooting, the bow was held either diagonally across the body or in a vertical plane with the body. The secondary arrow release was practiced: the nock of the arrow was held between the thumb and first joint of the index finger of the right hand with the middle and third fingers laid beside the string. The arrow was held to the left of the bow.

The bow was used extensively until Fort Sumner times (AM). There were still many bows and arrows on the reservation in 1933–1934, and although they were not used as weapons, archery contests were witnessed at Lukachukai.

Fishler (West)

TN (Kaibito) said that oak was used, and juniper, but the latter broke easily when dry. He denied pinyon bows. GB (Tuba City) said that juniper and pinyon bows broke easily, but others lasted for a long time. FG (Coalmine) stated that an oak bow with a yucca bowstring and a greasewood arrow were used in certain ceremonies.

Bark was removed and the wood was seasoned and shaped, then smoothed with sandstone. Horse sinew was boiled with horsehide (formerly deerskin) until it was viscous, then smeared over the bow to strengthen it. Glue was not mentioned. After the sinew had dried, a deerskin (or cowhide, TN) grip was wrapped around the center. Pitch was warmed and then smeared and smoothed over the deerskin; this process was denied by TN. The ends of the bow were notched for the bowstring.

Men made and used the bow to hunt mountain sheep (TH, Moenave; IJun, Kaibito; TN), prairie dog, antelope, and deer (TH), rabbit (IJmo, TN, BN, Kaibito; GB), and buffalo (TT, Coalmine). It was also used in warfare and in ceremonials. The bow was held in the left hand as at Ramah; the arrow rested on the left hand and was held between the second and third fingers of the right hand as the bowstring was pulled.

That there were specialists in making bows was confirmed by TN. He said that formerly one might pay a good-sized dressed deerskin for a bow and arrows.

Comparative

The first reference to the Navaho bow is by Benavides, in the seventeenth century, but the type was not described (Ayer, 1916:45). According to Matthews (1897:142), the self bow was the original type used by the Navaho; they later "learned to put animal fiber on the backs of the bows."

Other observations in the nineteenth century, however, indicate the sinew-backed bow. Pattie, in 1827, observed that Navaho bows were similar to those of the Mescalero Apache, which he described as of elastic wood backed with buffalo or elk sinew (Pattie, 1905:164–165). Letherman's description (1856:293) is of a bow "made of some kind of wood which is said not to grow in the Navaho country, and covered on the back with a kind of fibrous tissue." Some twenty-seven years later Bourke described bows made of white juniper backed with sinew, strung with a deer, cow, or horse sinew bowstring (Bourke, 1936:231). Both bows pictured by Mason, presumably collected in the 1880's, are sinew-backed. They have grips wrapped with buckskin thongs, ends wrapped with sinew, and bowstrings of two-ply sinew. Both are slightly less than four feet long. One is of mesquite, the other of an unidentified hard wood (Mason, 1894:pl. LXI and opposite page, pl. LXXIX and opposite page).

The bow described by the Franciscan Fathers (1910:318) is the self bow (see Trait 15). Gifford's informants confirmed the use of both the sinew-backed bow and the self bow. The Eastern Navaho made the sinew-backed bow from oak, mulberry, or juniper. The sinew was from the leg tendons of the deer, and was soaked and glued to the bow. The ends of the bow were recurved. The Western Navaho bow was of oak reinforced with back sinews of deer or other animals, rather than leg tendons; these were glued to the bow. The ends were not recurved. In both areas, bowstrings were of two-ply sinew (Gifford, 1940:29–30). Farmer (1938:6) was told by a Blanco-Largo Canyon informant that only sinew-backed bows were used. These were of oak or chokecherry, never of juniper.

Pope experimented with a Navaho specimen to obtain ballistic data. The bow which he described was made of mesquite, and showed good workmanship and signs of use. It was "stiff and quick in action, with no jarring in the hand." The string gave a "good musical hum," and the bow, when pulled to 26 inches, weighed 45 pounds and shot 150 yards (Pope, 1923:337; pl. 47, fig. 7).

According to Shufeldt (1887:784), the bow was held with the upper end obliquely to the right. Gifford's informants specified an oblique position (Gifford, 1940:30), but the Franciscan Fathers said that the bow was held vertically (Franciscan Fathers, 1910:319).

Little is known about bow makers. Left Handed's first bow was made by his mother, and it was only after he had worn out several of her productions that his father made him a bow of oak (Dyk, 1938:74). According to Gifford (1940:30), each man made his own.

I. Barbas Huero or Light Beard (prior to 1877). Note bow (Tr. 13–15), arrows and arrow release (Tr. 19), quiver (Tr. 23), and hair tie (Tr. 181).

By 1827, the bow was being replaced by the gun. Pattie met a Navaho war party with guns (Pattie, 1905:165). As late as 1850, however, Simpson stated that Navaho encountered in Canyon de Chelly and en route were generally armed with bows, arrows, and lances; rifles were few (Simpson, 1850:108). Hopi traditions include an account of their last fight with the Navaho, who were armed with bows and arrows, shields, war clubs and a few guns; this account probably refers to an event in the early or middle nineteenth century (Voth, 1905:262). At about this time Letherman (1856: 293) reported that the Navaho had guns but were not yet sufficiently accustomed to them to be deadly shots. The Powell expedition in 1871 met Navaho armed with bows, rather than guns (Dellenbaugh, n.d.:170. Cf. also Dyk, 1938:182, in which the narrator says that guns were very scarce in the

1880's. His family possessed only the bow and arrow.). Bows appear to have been the predominant weapon until about 1890, for three years later Stephen (1893:362) observed that guns had largely replaced the bow and arrow, and by 1910 bows were used only for shooting small animals and in archery contests (Franciscan Fathers, 1910:319, 325).

Today, the bow and arrow may still be seen in the Navaho Mountain district, "the only place where the bow and arrow are seen regularly each spring and summer" (Dunn, 1939:n.p.; Kluckhohn, 1942:4). Here they are apparently used in games and rituals, rather than for hunting. Adair, however, observed the bow and arrow in the Chilchinbitho area in 1938, and the trader there said "quite a few men in this area still hunt with the bow" (Adair, personal communication).

Miniature bows are used in the ritual of Evil Way, as part of the ceremonial bundle. These are about nine inches long and are "made of 'yellow mahogany' . . . or fendlera and strung with wolf or mountain lion sinew" (Kluckhohn and Wyman, 1940:32).

14. Glue   čah bé·ʒ (Ramah)   "hoof boiling" (CC)

Ramah
The hooves of sheep and goats were boiled in a pot for a day and a night. A little pinyon gum was added and the glue was ready for use (Inf. 7). According to Inf. 16, glue was made from the thick skin of a deer head. This was partially burned, then boiled until sticky. Its consistency was determined by testing with a stick. Inf. 12 said glue was made from pinyon gum and some other material. Glue was prepared only when it was to be used immediately. While still warm it was applied to the back of the bow, which was also heated. Sinew was then put on.

All information was obtained from men, and it is reasonable to assume that they usually made glue According to Inf. 8, it is no longer made, but was used "a long time ago, where there was war."

Hill (East, Central, and West)
Hooves, horns, and hide of deer and domesticated animals were specified; each informant seemed to have his own preference. SG (Keams Canyon) said that glue was made from hooves alone. These were boiled until reduced to a liquid state. AM (Lukachukai) specified all three materials; he said horns and hide were boiled together in a pot for five to seven days. According to PP (Fort Defiance), TLLSS (Crownpoint), and MH (Head Springs), only the hide was used. MH said that it was boiled for three days. PP stated that it was soaked in warm water until it soured, then was dehaired and pounded or cut into pieces. This preparation made it necessary to boil the hide for only one day. One of Hill's informants made glue from boiled deer horns and the edges of fresh deer hides (Hill, 1938:145).

Fishler (West)
Sinew from both wild and domesticated sheep was boiled in water and used for glue (TN, Kaibito).

Comparative

Both of Gifford's informants confirmed glue made from horsehide, but denied glue made from horn or pitch. The Eastern informant said that at an earlier period glue was made from deer hide, later from horsehide or cowhide. Hides were boiled (Gifford, 1940:30, 199). There is no indication that glue was used for any other purpose than to affix sinew to the bow.

15. Self Bow

čahba·· (Ramah) bow; "thing that makes one ready for war" (Haile)

·ałt̜·· (Ramah, Haile) "arrow" (CC)

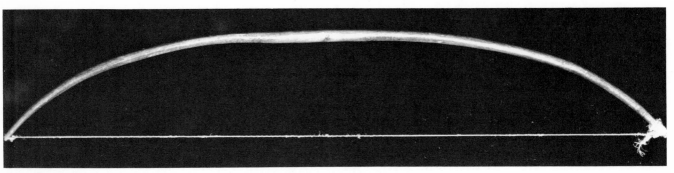

15.a. Self bow

Ramah

The self bow was shaped in the same manner as the sinew-backed bow. After the wood was heated and rubbed with tallow, the center portion was bent slightly toward the inside. The grip was pared to fit the hand, and the ends were notched but not grooved. Bows were not decorated, nor were ownership marks placed on them. According to Inf. 7, the self bow may have been used only for hunting.

Other data presented with the sinew-backed bow (Trait 13) are also pertinent here.

Hill (Central)

Self bows were used by those who could not afford, or obtain, sinew for backing (SC, Crystal). The self bow was reinforced with a wrapping of mountain sheep, deer, horse, cow, or goat sinew at the grip, for about four inches at the ends, and occasionally for short distances in the intervening spaces.

Fishler (West)

The description given by TN (Kaibito) appears to be that of a self bow. An oak bow, round on the outside and flat on the inside, was smoothed with sandstone. A strip of wet deerskin or cowhide was put around the grip and allowed to dry. No pitch was used.

Comparative

The bow described by the Franciscan Fathers is the self bow. They confirmed the use of oak, *tselkani,* juniper, sumac, and, recently, black greasewood.

Shaping was accomplished by heating the bow over a fire, placing the foot on the center of the stave and bringing the ends inward. Both ends were then pressed against the knee, to recurve them slightly. Points of stress including the center were bound with sinew, and the whole covered with pitch (Franciscan Fathers, 1910:318). Mountain sheep (bighorn) sinew was specified; this was denied by Ramah informants, as was the recurving and the binding of the center of the bow.

Gifford's Eastern informant made self bows of mulberry, oak, and other wood. Bows were nearly straight, and the tips were either notched or wrapped with sinew. The Western Navaho bow was made of oak. The nearly straight form of the Eastern Navaho bow was denied, but other description was lacking. Tips were wrapped with sinew (Gifford, 1940:29–30).

16. Trussed Bow

Hill (East, Central, and West)
The trussed bow was made in the same manner as the self bow, except that additional notches were cut at each end. Two, three, or four strings were twisted as were bowstrings. These were placed on the back of the bow and run over the ends in the notches, down the front a short distance, and fixed there in two separate places at each end, by wrapping sinew around the bow. Additional wraps were made at the grip and midway between the grip and each end; there were seven ties in all. The trussed bow was said to have more elasticity than the sinew-backed bow (SC, Crystal; C, Chinle; T, Chaco Canyon). PP (Fort Defiance) and SG (Keams Canyon) denied the use of the trussed bow.

Comparative
See Trait 13.

17. Elkhorn Bow

Ramah
Horn-backed bows were denied. Other data were lacking.

Hill (East, Central, and West)
Elkhorn bows were known by several informants (IS, Lukachukai; WH, Wheatfields; OTKM, Manuelito; C, Chinle). They were denied by inform-ants from other regions (SG, Keams Canyon; PP, Fort Defiance; T, Chaco Canyon). MH (Head Springs) knew them only from the Utes.

Horns were boiled and while soft bent and worked to bow shape with a stone chip or knife. Horns were occasionally split to make two bows. The bow was then backed with sinew. These bows were used in hunting and warfare.

Lamphere (East)
PM said that no elkhorns were used in making bows.

Comparative
See Trait 13.

18. Bowstring

ʼałtį x̌óˑł (Lamphere) "bow, string" (CC)

Ramah

Bowstring material varied, although sinew was common and regarded as best. Sinew was taken from the hind leg of a deer or horse (Infs. 7, 16); others (Infs. 12, 39) said that it came from the back of a deer or horse rather than the leg. The bowstring was made twice the length of the bow, doubled on itself and tightly twisted, and then stretched between two sticks and left to dry. Vegetable fiber bowstrings were denied by Inf. 7.

A noose (see 155.11) was formed at one end of the bowstring and secured to the lower end of the bow; the other end of the bowstring was looped loosely about the top when the bow was not in use. To string the bow, the lower end was placed on the ground and the upper end held firmly in the left hand. The bowstring was untied at the top, and the bow was bent with the left knee. With his right hand, the archer wrapped the string once about the upper end, pulled the end through the loop, and knotted it twice (see 18.1).

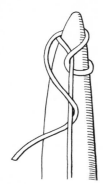

18.1. Bowstring fastening, after Tschopik

Hill (Central and West)

Sinew was preferred for bowstrings, but buckskin was occasionally used (PP, Fort Defiance). Sinew from the back of animals was best. Two arm span lengths were required. After the sinew was softened by soaking, it was doubled and twisted into a string by rolling it forward on the thigh. (Wool is rolled in the opposite direction, that is, toward the body.) "It is just handier; there is no particular reason for doing it this way" (C, Chinle). The string was tied to the lower end of the bow. A noose (see 155.11) was used at the upper end, or a crossing knot (AM, Lukachukai; see 155.12b). Thus it was possible to unstring the bow when it was not in use (C; AM; PP; SG, Keams Canyon).

Lamphere (East)

MS said that sinew from the hind leg of the deer was used, both for the bowstring and for wrapping the bow.

Fishler (West)

Horse or deer sinew was soaked in water. When pliable, it was split and joined, if extra length was needed. It was rolled between the hands, and tied between two posts to stretch. After it had dried, one end was tied to the bottom of the bow, the other to a piece of deerskin. The bottom of the bow was placed on the ground, and the bow bent against the knee. The bowstring was wrapped around the top of the bow, tightened, and the end tucked under. Finally water was put on the sinew and it was left to dry.

Comparative

The bowstring was made of twisted bighorn or deer (goat, cow, or other) sinew, secured at one end, and looped about the other (Franciscan Fathers, 1910:318). Both Gifford's informants confirmed the use of two-ply sinew bowstrings, made of sinew from the back and leg of deer. The Western informant was not questioned about the use of sinew from the back versus that from the leg. Both denied vegetable fiber bowstrings, and multi-ply bowstrings (Gifford, 1940:30).

19. Arrow   ka·' (Ramah, Haile)

·ałtį· bika·' (Lamphere)   "bow, its arrow" (CC)

Ramah

19.a. Arrows

The stems of flowering ash (*Fraxinus cuspidata*) were preferred (Inf. 7), but other woods were also used, including mountain mahogany (*Cercocarpus montanus*), Fendlerbush (*Fendlera rupicola*), Apache plume (*Fallugia paradoxa*), wild currant (*Ribes inebrians*), flowering currant (*Ribes sp.*), and Gambels oak (*Quercus gambelii*). Bone and horn arrows were denied (Infs. 7, 16).

Sticks were cut to lengths varying from one and a half to three feet. Bark was removed with a knife, and they were allowed to dry for a day or two. The shafts were straightened with an arrow wrench (see Trait 20) or with the hands and teeth, then cut flat at both ends. Work on the shafts could be done either in the hogan or outside.

The shaft was painted before fletching. Nine informants said that some paint must be used on the shaft, or the user would go blind. According to Inf. 1, however, paint might be omitted without ill effect, and Inf. 259 declared that he had never used paint.

The paint was called "the eye" (*binaa*) (Inf. 7). The shaft was painted in bands, and various colors were specified. These included four bands of any color, one black and two red, one red and one black, two alternating red and black, or an unstated number of red, black, and blue bands. Infs. 12, 56, and 256 said two marks were made on each side of the arrow where it was notched to receive the point. The old men called these "the arrow's eyes." It was believed that if they were omitted the range of the arrow would be shortened and its accuracy impaired. The marks were black (Inf. 12), or red and black (the red a "store dye," and the black charcoal), covered with a protective coat of melted pitch.

Red paint was also made from pinyon gum and the red dust (galls) from oak bark: Vestal (1952:22) specifically identified red leaf galls of the Gambel oak, mixed with red clay or gum, or pinyon gum and red clay. Juniper gum was also used as a base when oak galls were used (Elmore, 1944:18). Black paint was made by mixing pinyon gum and charcoal. The mixture was warmed and then rubbed on the shaft. Recently, however, commercial dyes have been used.

Lines were also incised the length of the shaft. These represented lightning, the zigzag line for Male Lightning (*atsinitlish*), the straight line for Female Lightning (*hatsoolghal*). There should be four lines, stated Inf. 12, but he and his father, as well as Inf. 256, used only one straight and one wavy line. Other variations included one wavy and two straight lines (Inf. 16), or one straight and two wavy lines (Inf. 7). Thirteen informants affirmed, and none denied, that both wavy and straight lines were used on the same arrow. The lines were thought to increase the speed of the arrow, and to act as protection against lightning.

Deer, rabbit, or prairie dog blood was smeared on the shafts (Infs. 7, 16, 259). There were no property marks (Infs. 7, 16), but since each man made his own, each was able to recognize his own.

Fletching formerly had to be done at a distance from the hogan. The reason for the prohibition given by twelve informants was that fragments from the feathers might get in the food or be swallowed and endanger women and children. Some said that fletching might be done inside, however, if the feathers had previously been prepared; one informant said that only eagle feathers were dangerous. Opinion was divided on the prohibition of watching an arrow fletcher at work. Four informants said that no one was allowed to watch, four that only strangers were prohibited, and eight stated that anyone might watch. Women and children were allowed according to Inf. 81, but prohibited by Infs. 16 and 56.

Eagle feathers were preferred for fletching; next were those of the red-tailed hawk, the "yellow-tailed eagle" (Infs. 7, 39). Other feathers used included those of the turkey, two varieties of hawk, and crow and owl. Tail feathers and the secondaries were used. Arrows fletched with eagle feathers were called *atsee bestaan,* those with yellow-tailed eagle feathers *astee kisdiichoi,* and those with turkey feathers, *kaa.*

Feathers were split longitudinally and three sections were used on each arrow. Sinew, dampened by chewing, was used to tie the feathers to the shaft, distal end first. They were laid straight, not spiraled. No gum was used for fastening. When secured, the feathers were trimmed and the nock cut. Both Inf. 7 and Inf. 16 said the arrow was slightly larger at the butt end. The feathers were trimmed to slant slightly toward the front of the arrow (Infs. 12, 16), or they were cut straight except for one plume at the front (Inf. 7; see 19.3). The nock was described as a square U in shape (Infs. 7, 12).

Arrow points were made from chert or other stone, and informants said that points were usually gathered around ruins rather than manufactured. In some cases the end of the shaft was merely sharpened; and although Inf. 7 denied that it was ever fire-hardened, this practice was confirmed by Infs. 8 and 81. Specialized points were made for small game, such as prairie dogs (see 19.2). Iron points have been used recently: Inf. 256 cut arrow points from a barrel hoop with shears. Points were bound to the arrow shafts with sinew.

The following five types of points were recognized by Inf. 7.

1. Blunt point. Arrows with blunt points were made for hunting birds and for practice. This point was denied by Inf. 16.

2. Sharpened wooden point. This had no special name.

3. Chert point. The shaft was split for about one and a half inches, and the point inserted. The base of the point was ground flush with the shaft; it was then wrapped tightly with sinew and left to dry for half a day. Gum was not used to secure it to the shaft. This point was no longer made after iron was introduced.

4. *Ka askaal.* This type was made for hunting warblers and bluebirds whose feathers were used by chanters. Four pieces of hardwood, or greasewood (Inf. 16), about one and a half inches long, were sharpened at both ends and tied with sinew to the arrow shaft about two inches behind the tip. These cross-pieces were said to make it easier for the hunter to hit the bird (see 19.1 and 19.b).

5. *Ka azhah.* This point was made for hunting prairie dogs (see 19.2). The shaft was cut obliquely, and a point, slightly bent in the center, was hafted to the arrow. The projecting back section functioned as a harpoon barb. Hardwood was formerly used; this has been replaced by iron or a nail.

19.1. Arrowhead for hunting warblers and bluebirds, after Hill

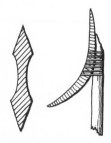

19.2. Prairie dog arrowhead, after Tschopik

19.b. Detail of bird point

The completed arrow was approximately two feet (Inf. 12) or twenty inches (Infs. 7, 39) long. It was measured in terms of a span twice the length between the thumb and middle finger plus the length between the thumb and index finger.

According to Inf. 7, a composite arrow (*bikii*) was made only when hardwood was scarce, although the old people regarded it as the better arrow. The foreshaft was about nine or ten inches long, made of hardwood. It was cut and thrust into the shaft, which was somewhat longer and made of reed (*Phragmites sp.?*) or rabbit bush (*Chrysothamnus depressus*). The joint was covered with pinyon gum and secured with a wrapping of deer sinew.

The foreshafts of hunting and war arrows were painted with poison (*kasda*) made from yucca juice and the black paint used on the shaft. "This made the wound swell" (Inf. 7). Vestal noted several formulas for arrow poison. In one the juice of the narrow-leafed yucca was mixed with charcoal from a lightning-struck pinyon or juniper; this mixture was used to blacken about six inches of the tip of the arrow. In another, juice from a yucca leaf was mixed with the ashes from porcupine quills. A third specified the use of poison ivy (*Rhus radicans*), mixed with charcoal from a lightning-struck tree and deer blood (Vestal, 1952:21, 35). Other informants said that the juice of any sharp plant might be used without blackening material, and that yucca was the poisoning substance (Infs. 20, 101, 180). Infs. 8, 63, 99, and 192 had heard of *kasda*, but had never used it; four others (Infs. 11, 16, 106, 111) denied hearing of it. Inf. 16, however, knew of an arrow poison made from weeds, charcoal, and fresh deer blood. The use of rattlesnake venom was denied by Inf. 3, who refused to discuss the use of deer blood. Inf. 12 said a "little stick" was left in the wound, and this caused blood poisoning.

Each man usually made his own arrows, but if a man made superior ones, others might obtain them from him. Thirteen of the informants had made arrows. Fathers or grandfathers made them for small boys who were learning archery, but Inf. 256 observed children making their own arrows in 1938. According to twelve informants, women were not allowed to make arrows or to handle them. This was a recent development, said Inf. 1, who also stated that formerly elderly women could handle them; Inf. 7 stated that women could use arrows but never own them. "Boys started to play with arrows at about four or five years; by the age of twelve they had better arrows, and when they were about fifteen they had real arrows and were able to make a quiver" (Inf. 7).

When not in use, arrows were kept in the quiver, which hung with the bow from the roof of the hogan. According to Inf. 256, old arrows were stored in a safe place. Arrows were used in hunting, archery games, chantways, and formerly for warfare. Arrow shafts were also used as drills in composite firedrills. In shooting, the archer did not sight before releasing the shaft, but "just figured in his head."

The arrow was said to have a mythical origin, and to have been given to the ancestors of the Navaho sometime far in the past. Other than the substitution of metal points for stone ones, and the use of commercial dyes to color the shaft, there has been little change in the arrow. Iron points have been in use as long as informants can remember, though they are familiar with stone ones recovered from ruins. Inf. 8 thought that stone points were the only kind used in war and that they are no longer used "because we are not at war now."

At one time every man and boy probably owned arrows; there are now few (seven in 1945) who do. A large number of men have the requisite knowledge and skill to make arrows, but the generation represented by Inf. 256 may be the last to do so. He learned the art from his father when he was about thirteen, and has made arrows as recently as the summer of 1940. He said that all of his friends knew how to make them, each having learned from his father. There is no evidence, however, that children today are taught to make arrows, or are practicing archery.

Hill (East, Central, and West)

Informants confirmed the use of mountain mahogany, Fendlerbush, and wild currant, and stated that black greasewood and juneberry, and occasionally goldenrod and cane, were used (SG, Keams Canyon; AM, Lukachukai; PP, Fort Defiance). Specialists were sometimes hired to make arrows (MH, Head Springs). The tools employed were the wrench, smoother, and engraver. Straight-grained wood was always chosen. Limbs of the approximate diameter and some inches longer than the finished shaft were cut and set aside for a few days to dry. Bark was then removed with a knife and the limbs cut to a length slightly longer than the distance from the point of the elbow to the tips of the fingers. According to PP, shafts were cut to size after they had been straightened and smoothed with the arrow wrench (see Trait 20). Long curves were straightened with the hands. The shafts were then bundled up and put aside for three or more days to season (SG, AM, PP). Shafts were run back and forth through the arrow smoother to polish them. Then the nock was cut, always in the growing end of the wood (SG, AM, PP).

The butt end of the shaft was painted with black and red pitch (after heating, according to PP). Red paint made from pinyon pitch and oak fungus was confirmed by AM, that from red ocher by PP. The base of the black paint was charcoal. Three stripes were painted, each a finger width wide. They were put on in the order red-black-red or black-red-black. All the shafts were painted at the same time. "This was just for looks." According to the myth, these marks represented parhelion, "the stubby rainbow" (AM).

Next, one straight and two zigzag lines were made in the shaft with the engraver. These lines ran from either the upper or the lower point of the fletching to the point of the arrow. The operator placed the shaft on his thigh and set the groove against the projecting point. The wavy lines were made by rotating the shaft as it was forced along (SG, AM, PP). These marks were said to represent the straight and zigzag lightning which the culture hero Monster Slayer used when he killed the monsters.

> He was like a god. He was going to give lightning to the Navaho for arrows. However, the Navaho were afraid that the lightning would kill them and that they would kill each other with it. Instead they put two wavy lines and one straight line on their arrows to represent the lightning. The straight lightning was called "the friend" because it always followed the zigzag. These marks make the arrow go fast and follow a straight line.
>
> (SG, Keams Canyon)

No ownership marks were placed on arrows but it was said that every man was able to identify his own by his workmanship (SG; AM; C, Chinle; Hill, 1938:97).

When the arrow had been marked, the notch for the point was cut (AM). Others (SG, PP), however, stated that this was not done until the fletching was finished. The shaft was rubbed with sheep's blood from the point where the fletching was to be attached to the point of the arrow. "This was done to harden the shaft." The portion to be covered by the fletching was rubbed with red ocher. "This made the arrow pretty, kept it from breaking, and made the man who used it brave" (SG).

The tail feathers of eagles were preferred for fletching. Wing feathers were also used and in this case feathers on each arrow were taken from the same wing so that they matched (SG, AM, PP). Feathers less in demand were those of the turkey, western red-tailed hawk, red-shafted flicker, owl, crow, and dove (SG, AM, PP). Those of the owl, crow, flicker, and dove were used on arrows destined for children or for sport (PP). According to AM, hawk feathers other than those of the western red-tailed hawk might not be used for fletching. "If you used feathers of other hawks you would be afflicted with boils." PP, however, denied this, saying that the feathers of the cooper and marsh hawk were allowed. "The feathers of the buzzard could not be used, because that bird ate dead flesh" (AM).

The outside of the quill of the selected feather was scraped both front and back. Then the large end of the quill was placed between the feet and split from the top down with the hands. Pith was removed and the quill was scraped until pliable. Feathers were removed for about an inch from each end to allow for wrapping on the shaft. According to SG, a tuft of feathers was sometimes left at the base of the quill. This was bent to cover the bare portion of the shaft (see 19.3). "Not everyone did this; it was simply an ornament." After this, the feathers were buried in moist earth. During this time the sinew to be used in affixing the feathers was shredded and soaked in water (AM, PP).

When the feathers were removed from the earth they were straightened by stretching. Then the fletcher wrapped three or four turns of the sinew around the butt of the shaft about an inch from the nock. The wrapping progressed toward the nock. Holding the loose end of the sinew in his mouth, he placed the first feather on the shaft and took one turn, then the second feather and another turn, the third feather and another turn. After this the

19.3. Fletching (Hill), after SG

shaft and quills were wrapped as far as the nock. The sinew was not tied but was reduced to a fine thread, wound back on the wrapping, and stuck there. The arrow was set aside until the upper binding of the fletching dried. When six arrows had been prepared, the first was sufficiently dry to secure the rest of the feathers. If more than ten arrows were made, two men worked (PP). The feathers were pulled tight and straight on the shaft, and wrapped as before except that the wrapping progressed toward the point. The arrows were set aside, and when dry, projecting feathers were cut even with the nock. Those on the side were cut to the width of a finger. They were placed on a flat piece of wood and cut with a sharp knife (AM, SG, PP).

The average length of an arrow was two hand spans and two or three finger widths. The fletching varied in length from four inches when flicker feathers were used to a hand's breadth when the feathers of larger birds were used (AM). PP said the span was measured from the thumb to the tip of the middle finger.

Arrow points were of wood, bone, stone, or iron. In former times, the end of the shaft was merely sharpened (PP; AM; Hill, 1938:96–97). These arrows were called "with no point." According to PP, plain wooden arrows were occasionally decorated by a type of negative painting. Sinew was wound spirally, with intervals between each turn, from the point of the arrow to the fletching. The whole shaft was then painted with a solution of yucca juice and allowed to dry. When dry, the sinew was removed, leaving a spiral design. Black and white diamonds resulted if two pieces of sinew were wrapped around the shaft from opposite directions.

Bone points were made by working a piece of bone to the desired shape on a piece of rough stone (SC, Crystal). Three types of stone points were distinguished on the basis of shape. A point with a single shoulder barb was known as *zazhah*. This generic term for barbed points might be applied to points with two barbs, but these were usually called "arrow point barbs something is there," or arrow point with barbs. Unshouldered points were called "arrow points without barbs." The Navaho never made stone points (AM; PP; OTKM, Manuelito); it was forbidden (Hill, 1938:96). According to mythology, the Horned Toad People and the Giant made these points and scattered them around for the Earth People to use. The Earth People deposited prayersticks which the Holy People picked up, leaving arrowheads in exchange (OTKM, AM). With the introduction of iron, points of this material were fashioned after the old patterns.

Several specialized forms were also in use. Several informants (T, Chaco Canyon; AM; PP) described the arrow with crosspieces which was used for killing warblers, bluebirds, and woodpeckers (see 19.b). The centers of the crosspieces rested against the shaft, and they were lashed transversely to it. If the point missed, one of the crosspieces would usually strike the bird and stun it sufficiently for capture.

Another type was made for hunting prairie dogs. The shaft was about a foot longer than usual. It was unfeathered, but a piece of sinew was wound just above the nock. A barbed point was hafted, and if stone was used, one shoulder was broken off. This long shaft and barbed point made it possible to pull the prairie dog from its burrow when shot (SG, AM, PP; see 19.2).

Composite arrows for hunting small game were of cane, *Phragmites communis, lokaa tsoh* (obtained from the Apache country), or "a jointed grass" (PP). The

19.4. Arrowhead for hunting rats and mice, after Hill

cane was gathered, seasoned, and cut to size. If the reed was crooked, the worker heated a stone, spat on it, and placed the crooked portion of the reed on the saliva, bending it straight (AM). The shaft was then smoothed and feathered as above (not feathered, stated PP). The nock was always cut just below a node in the cane. The foreshaft was made of black greasewood or a hardwood and was fitted to the pith channel of the cane. The joint was wrapped for about an inch with sinew. Lightning marks were placed on the foreshaft, not the shaft (C; AM; SG; PP; MLH, Round Rock).

Still another type of arrow was used for killing rats and mice. About two and a half inches of the tip of a corncob was forced on to the tip of a wooden pointed arrow (see 19.4). The animals hit with this blunt point were stunned and then dispatched (AM, PP).

Arrows were commonly treated with one of several preparations believed to make them poisonous. As at Ramah, yucca juice and charcoal from a lightning-struck tree (or soot from the roof of a hogan) were mixed (RH, Crystal); or yucca juice and blood from the heart of a deer (T). According to C, black paint was mixed with rattlesnake blood, or the stingers of ants, bees, or other insects. "A man or animal who was scratched with one of these poison points would get an infection and immediately die." Another type of poison was produced in the following manner: a rattlesnake was caught and killed on a rock; a yucca leaf was heated over the fire and the juice squeezed on the blood of the snake; finally charcoal made from the leaf pitch of the "wide cactus" was added (TLFOS, Shiprock and Fort Defiance). Arrows were painted with these mixtures from the point to about six inches down the shaft.

Aside from the symbolic marks and paintings which were believed to add to the efficacy of the arrow, very little ritual was connected with the manufacture of bows or arrows. If either were made in preparation for a war raid, however, the leader of the party sang over them to "bless them." There were instances reported of warriors who, immediately before a charge, addressed their weapons as persons and told them to conduct themselves in a brave manner (RH, C).

Lamphere (East)
PM said that an arrow was called "bow, its arrow."

Fishler (West)
Oak, willow, greasewood, or any light wood was used (TN, Kaibito). The arrow was seasoned, then shaped in a wrench as above, or by heating the shaft in a fire and using a grooved stone smoother.

FG (Coalmine) stated that arrows were incised with designs thought to increase the speed of the arrow. These were derived from the Twin War Gods, and only those with "the story and the power" could make them. "The First Twin's designs were crooked, while the Second Twin's were straight, and each used four designs on each arrow." Those who knew the myth could use two crooked and two straight lines, but a man who lacked "the power and the song" could use only three. A notch was cut, and the arrow was fletched, as above. Eagle, owl, or turkey feathers were used, three in number (GB, Tuba City; TN).

There were several types of points. The first two were used "in the old

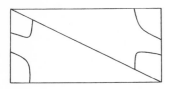

19.5. Pattern for iron arrowheads, after Fishler

days." The shaft was sharpened to a point with a knife, and fire-hardened in the ashes. It was said that these points did not shatter like stone points. Chert (and other varieties of stone) was chipped to produce points, but the process was not known to informants. TN said that points found in Pueblo ruins and in other areas were used, as was obsidian. According to him, the Lightning made and shot the small, black obsidian points. TH (Moenave) confirmed this statement.

Iron points were made from barrel hoops cut in strips approximately three inches long, and half that wide. Each rectangle was then cut diagonally, from corner to corner. This process produced two blanks, the ends of which were cut, leaving a narrow stem (see 19.5). The point was serrated with a file.

The barbed arrow used for hunting prairie dogs was also described. TT described one of oak. The shaft was shaped, and a barb was carved below the point. It was then placed in the coals, or smeared with cactus juice to harden it. GB and the other informants indicated that the barbed arrow was made like a regular arrow, except that it was from three to three and a half feet long; one type was unfletched. It had an iron point with one barb.

Arrow poison was made from yucca ashes, raw yucca, spiders (any kind with poison), snake venom, and poisonous weeds mixed together in water. Only a few men knew how to make this poison (TN). FG said that there was an antidote for the arrow poison used in warfare, but would not say what it was. "I want to die of old age with it." Neither informant had seen poison made, but both had heard of it.

Anyone could make bows and arrows, but better craftsmen made and sold them. GB said that the Navaho had lost their strength. "In the old days an arrow went through a deer at one hundred yards, but now the Navaho cannot even shoot an arrow through a prairie dog at this distance."

Comparative
The earliest reference to Navaho weapons is that of Benavides in 1630, who stated that the arrows were tipped with white flint (Ayer, 1916:49). By the time detailed descriptions were published, stone points had been superseded by iron ones (Letherman, 1856:293). This substitution occurred sometime between the mid-seventeenth and the mid-nineteenth centuries.

Arrows in the Harvard Peabody Museum collections differed slightly from those described at Ramah. In general, nocks were slightly expanded; notches were cut in a rounded V or U; although feathers were laid straight and secured with sinew, the trailing ends usually protruded over the notches; tangs of iron points were ground to the diameter of the shaft, although several were wider, and a few had serrations to engage the sinew binding.

Putnam in 1879 described one of the earliest collections of Navaho arrows, from near Fort Defiance (deposited in the Smithsonian Institution). All thirteen arrows had iron points. Five with wooden shafts about two feet long he compared to those of the Santa Clara; the others were the composite arrow, about three feet long. "The feathers on the reed shaft are not as long as those on the wooden" (Putnam, 1879:390).

Various authors have confirmed the use of hardwoods such as wild currant, Fendlerbush, black greasewood, willow, and oak (Franciscan Fathers, 1910:316; Mason, 1894:pls. 40, 43; Gifford, 1940:30). Left Handed's father made him oak arrows, although Dunn stated that oak was not used for arrows since one who used it would die young (Dyk, 1938:74; Dunn, 1939:n.p.).

Painting of the shaft was confirmed, although red and blue were the colors used, rather than the red and black common at Ramah (Franciscan Fathers, 1910:319; Mason, 1894:pl. 43). Gifford's Eastern informant denied arrow shaft painting; his Western informant was not questioned (Gifford, 1940:30).

Incised lightning marks were commonly mentioned. Two straight and two zigzag lines along the length of the shaft were noted by the Franciscan Fathers (1910:319), and the arrow illustrated by Mason (1894:pl. 43) has one wavy and two straight lines. Three rills "for the escape of blood" were noted by Bourke (1936:238). Other observers stated that lightning designs were marked on the shaft but did not specify the number or the type (Haile, 1938:32; Dunn, 1939:n.p.; Gifford, 1940:30). (Gifford's Eastern informant said that these designs represented lightning and the rainbow).

Dyk indicated that the custom of smearing fresh blood on the arrow before shooting it was practiced in the northern Navaho area (Dyk, 1938:322). Coolidge (1930:135) recorded a mythological reference to clan marks on arrows, and an informant in the Blanco-Largo Canyon area told Farmer that each person placed ownership marks on his arrows (Farmer, 1938:6). This statement contradicts data collected by Hill and those from Ramah.

Eagle feathers were most commonly mentioned for fletching. They were preferred, according to Haile (1938:31), because their barbs were usually of equal width. Crow feathers were also cited fairly frequently (Franciscan Fathers, 1910:318; Sapir and Hoijer, 1942:427; Dyk, 1938:74; Gifford, 1940:31). Hawk and turkey feathers were also known. Although both were denied by Gifford's Western informant, others indicated a more general usage for turkey feathers (Franciscan Fathers, 1910:318; Gifford, 1940:31; Dunn, 1939:n.p.). Owl feathers were mentioned only in connection with children's toy arrows (Haile, 1938:31; Dyk, 1938:74). The feathers were split and three halves were fastened to the shaft with sinew (Franciscan Fathers, 1910:318; Haile, 1938:31; Bourke, 1936:238), or with sinew and glue (Mason, 1894:pl. 43, and opposite page; Gifford, 1940:30, 31). According to Gifford, three is standard in the Southwest.

Blunt arrowheads were used for practice (Franciscan Fathers, 1910:319; Gifford, 1940:30). Arrows were often pointed simply by sharpening the wooden shaft, and no source mentioned fire-hardened points. Bone and stone points were denied by Gifford's Eastern informant. Gifford's Western inform-ant said that they were found, not made, and that throughout his lifetime iron arrowheads had been used. Points were inserted into a split end of the shaft and bound with sinew (Bourke, 1936:237; Dellenbaugh, 1926:147; Franciscan Fathers, 1910:318–319; Gifford, 1940:30–31; Letherman, 1856:293; Mason, 1894:pls. 43, 60; Sapir and Hoijer, 1942:427. See also Hill, 1938:96–97). Mason (1894:pl. 60) is the only one to confirm the bone points mentioned by Hill.

The special bird arrow existed in several areas. Arrows with one and two crosspieces were reported, but this trait was denied by Ramah informants who said that four crosspieces were used. According to Gifford, this arrow was used only by the Eastern Navaho (Gifford, 1940:30, 120; see also Hill, 1938:175).

Arrows, with barbed heads, for shooting prairie dogs, had a wider distribution. Observers stated that these were not fletched, a feature not reported by Ramah informants. Gifford confirmed the long barbed or hooked arrow for both the Western and Eastern Navaho, and stated that the Western Navaho had a special arrow with two crosspieces, which "caught in the burrow" (Gifford, 1940:83).

Several authors referred to the composite arrow. Quoting the origin legend, Matthews (1902:240) noted that reed arrows tipped with wood were formerly common, although wooden ones were also made. Pattie saw Navaho reed arrows with hardwood foreshafts and flint points in 1827; these, he stated, were similar to those of the Mescalero Apache (Pattie, 1905:164). According to Gifford, only the Eastern Navaho had the composite arrow (Gifford, 1940:30; see also Putnam, 1879:390, above).

The use of arrow poison is fairly well attested. Bourke was told by Chee Dodge in 1881 that long ago arrow points were dipped in the juice of a plant like the sunflower, but the practice had disappeared (Bourke, 1936:231). Voth described a poison attributed to the Navaho by the Hopi; it was made from the putrid matter from a decaying rattlesnake and the previously extracted venom (Voth, 1905:note 1). The black pinyon gum-like substance smeared on the tips of the specimens in the Peabody Museum collections is probably a poison.

Data on arrow makers were less complete than those on technology. Dyk indicated that women might make arrows at least for children, but Newcomb stated that women never made arrows (Dyk, 1938:74; Newcomb, 1940a:39). Dyk and Dunn asserted that arrow making was a specialized occupation, and that a man usually bought his arrows from a recognized specialist (Dyk, 1938:321; Dunn, 1939:n.p.).

The only account of the Navaho arrow release is quite detailed (Shufeldt, 1887:784–786). Shufeldt was given a demonstration of technique. This method was essentially the secondary release, except that the middle finger overlapped the ring finger; normally both fingers were on the string. In the demonstration, two spare arrows were held against the bow, but Shufeldt was told that spare arrows were usually kept in a quiver in front of the archer. He observed that on all occasions where distance was required, the secondary release was used, but where the range was short, the primary release was employed.

Archaeological evidence of arrows for the Navaho is equivocal. Arrowheads are commonly found at Navaho sites, but other data are lacking. Keur could find no evidence that the Navaho made points, and said that the assortment suggested random acquisition from those discarded by the Pueblos. Points collected were made from obsidian, chert, chalcedony, and petrified wood. No bone points were reported (Keur, 1941:56, 1944:79; Farmer, 1942:72).

In the nineteenth century, the bow and arrow were gradually replaced by the gun. Arrows still form a part of the ceremonial bundles, especially in the Shooting Way rites. Wyman (1936a:637) described those used by a singer in the Pinedale area in 1935. Kluckhohn also observed arrows among the chant equipment for the Shooting Way rituals, presumably in the Ramah area. These were similar to those described by Wyman, and were decorated with more feathers and turquoise. Haile also gave a detailed description of the making and symbolism of five different arrows used in the Shooting Way

(Haile, 1947c:15–21, 191; see also Haile, 1946:18–27; Matthews, 1902:24–25, 240; Reichard, 1950). It is abundantly clear that arrows are still intimately involved in the rich ceremonial complex of the Navaho.

20. Arrow Wrench

bé·éką́ʒí (Ramah, Haile)   "with it to sharpen" (CC)

Ramah

A section was cut from mountain sheep horn, and two holes were bored through the sides with a hot iron; one hole was smaller than the other.

Four informants confirmed the use of mountain sheep horn, and Inf. 8 remembered an old man who had such a wrench. He said it must have been quite old, for it was smooth and "all worn out." Old ram horns pierced with a hot iron were used by Inf. 256 and others. Inf. 34 said his grandfather used a bone wrench and Inf. 7 who had made wrenches of both horn and bone, said that the bone used was from the lower front leg of a deer. Bone arrow wrenches, however, were denied by Infs. 2 and 16. Inf. 39 used a round, flat rock with a hole in it; Inf. 8 used a piece of wagon wheel rim.

The straightening of arrow shafts was done by men while the wood was still slightly green. If it was too green, it might be dried by the fire. The shaft was rotated through the hole in the straightener.

Stone and ram horn wrenches still exist in the Ramah community (Infs. 39, 256), but none of any other material is known. Many of the older men have undoubtedly used arrow wrenches, for no tool is known which has replaced it.

20.1. Bone arrow wrench, after Hill

Hill (East, Central, and West)

Arrow wrenches were made from the horns of female mountain sheep (MLH, Crownpoint; SG, Keams Canyon; Hill, 1938:168), the horns of domestic goats (PP, Fort Defiance; SG), or from any animal bone of convenient size (AM, Lukachukai; SG). Usually the bone from the foreleg of the animal was split and the sides smoothed by rubbing on a stone. One to three perforations were made (see 20.1). At one time these were bored, but in recent times they have been made with a hot iron.

The worker ran the shaft back and forth through the hole. Occasionally a short piece of wood was tied transversely to one end of the arrow shaft to afford a better grip (AM). The man sighted along the shaft; the crooked portions were straightened by bending in the wrench.

It was generally believed that paralysis would follow if any part of a mountain sheep other than the flesh was used other than ceremonially. The use of its horns in the arrow wrench was one of few exceptions.

Fishler (West)

Fishler's informants confirmed the data above. The end of the shaft was inserted in the hole and twisted and revolved until it was forced completely through (GB, Tuba City; TT, Coalmine).

Comparative

Both stone and horn arrow straighteners were mentioned in the literature, although many sources seem to have confused the straightener with the

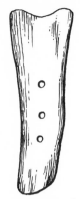

20.2. Bone arrow wrench, after the Franciscan Fathers

smoother. According to the Franciscan Fathers (1910:318), arrow shafts were "smoothly polished and straightened," either by pressing them between the teeth, or by running them through narrowly grooved stones or a punctured mountain sheep horn (see 20.2). Gifford's informants both confirmed straighteners made of female mountain sheep horn, and both denied those of stone and pottery. The Eastern Navaho used a perforated wooden wrench, and straightened arrows on a warm ungrooved stone. The Western informant denied the wooden implement. He said that holes in the horn were drilled with an iron tool; the Eastern informant said that they were bored with "flint" points (Gifford, 1940:31, 121).

Archaeology has produced little on the subject. No arrow wrenches were found in the Gobernador area and Big Bead Mesa in sites dating from the mid-seventeenth century to the beginning of the nineteenth century, unless some of the stone smoothers were actually straighteners. Keur apparently found no mountain sheep bones in sites she excavated (Keur, 1941:50, 63; 1944:80).

Farmer suggested that one stone with a longitudinal groove in one slightly rounded side was a straightener, rather than a smoother. Although shaft polishers were reported in some numbers, other data from mid-eighteenth century sites in the Blanco and Largo Canyon areas were lacking. There were few bone artifacts and no evidence that the Navaho living at these sites used mountain sheep (Farmer, 1942:72, 74). Malcolm found a grooved straightener associated with a burial dated by textiles as early nineteenth century. He did not designate the material (Malcolm, 1939:19).

21. Sandstone Shaft Smoother

be··edzí·hí (Ramah)   smoother; "with it smoothing (i.e., sandpaper)" (CC)

Ramah
Two pieces of sandstone, each about three inches long, two inches wide, and one inch thick, were obtained and a groove made in each (Inf. 7; see 21.1). An unmodified piece of sandstone might be used instead, or a rough stone grooved with a piece of metal or harder stone (Inf. 8). Inf. 8 had never seen the smoother described by Inf. 7, but had used the other types.

The two pieces were placed together with the grooves in the same axis. The arrow shaft was pushed back and forth in the grooves. This type of smoother was used with all arrow shaft materials. Smoothers were kept indefinitely and owned by the men who made them.

21.1. Sandstone shaft smoother, after Hill

Hill (Central and West)
Data were obtained from Keams Canyon, Lukachukai, and Fort Defiance; they confirmed those from Ramah.

Fishler (West)
TN (Kaibito) described a pair of grooved stones; another informant said that two flat, unprepared pieces of sandstone were used. When the shaft had been straightened with the sheep horn wrench, it was placed between the two stones and pulled back and forth until the crooked and uneven parts were removed (GB, Tuba City; TN).

Comparative

Unlike the arrow wrench, this trait is well attested archaeologically. Keur reported a number of polishers from both the Big Bead and Gobernador sites. In the latter site, all were of the elongated single-groove type (Keur, 1944:80). At Big Bead Mesa, most of the smoothers were of this type, but at least one was found with more than one groove. All were of sandstone with the exception of one which was of limestone (Keur, 1941:60). In the Blanco and Largo Canyon area, Farmer (1942:72) reported elongated shaft smoothers, usually of reddish sandstone. Both Gifford's informants used two-piece grooved stone polishers (Gifford, 1940:31).

Two of the types outlined by Woodbury in an interpretation of grooved stones in the Southwest are pertinent here (Woodbury, 1954:101–111. He has continued the analysis by Toulouse, 1939:80–89). Woodbury's "Simple Grooved Abraders" coincide with the variant forms mentioned by Ramah informants. There is little or no intentional shaping, and the grooves vary greatly in number, size, and shape. (The abraders are known to be at least as early as Basketmaker III times in northeastern Arizona.) The second type, "Elongated Shaft Smoothers," consists of a pair (probably) of oval or rectangular pieces with a groove in approximately the center of the flat surface parallel to the long axis. They were common in the Plains area, where they dated from the Signal Butte I Period, but were typical only of the southern Pueblo region in the Southwest and are common only after the Pueblo II times (Woodbury, 1954:104, 111).

22. Engraver

Ramah

For incising lightning marks on arrow shafts, a small piece of wood was notched with a knife and a knife blade inserted from the opposite side so that the point protruded part way into the notch (Infs. 7, 8; see 22.1). Or, a piece of wood the length of the thumb was grooved and a nail was inserted in the groove (Inf. 180). Other informants did not describe the incising tool. The arrow was drawn through the groove or notch. It was drawn straight or twisted depending on the type of line desired. A new engraver was made whenever necessary.

It is not known how widespread this tool was in the Ramah area. Apparently it is no longer made or used.

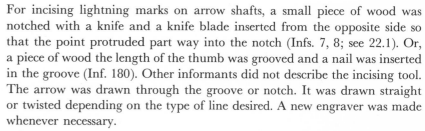

22.1. Engraver, after Hill

Hill (Central and West)

Information obtained from Keams Canyon, Lukachukai, and Fort Defiance confirmed that from Ramah.

Comparative

Gifford's Western informant confirmed, but the Eastern denied, rills on the arrow shaft. (Both confirmed lightning marks.) According to Gifford, the Llanero Apache made the rill by drawing the shaft over a sharp point, formerly of rock, now of metal. The Walpi drew the arrow over a sharp fragment of chert set between two pieces of wood. Gifford did not state which method was used by the Navaho (Gifford, 1940:30, 120).

23. Quiver

ka·γé·ł (Ramah, Haile)

ka·ʼazis (Ramah, Haile)   arrow bag; "arrow cover" (CC)

ʼałtí·ʼbiʒis (Ramah)   bow, its case; "bow cover" (CC)

Ramah

Quivers for carrying a bow and arrows were made anywhere around the home and at any time. They consisted of two pouches, sewn or lashed together, the arrow pouch or quiver proper ("arrow bag"), and the bow case ("bow, its case").

Quivers of mountain lion skin with the fur on were preferred, but other materials were used. Some were of dressed goatskin, with the hair, legs, and tail removed; buckskin and antelope hide were also used. Antelope hide was not dressed because it would be too soft. The hair was removed, the flesh scraped away, and the cases cut and sewn. The arrow case—but never the bow case—was sometimes made of wildcat skin, with the fur out; the legs and tail were removed. If the bow case was of mountain lion skin and the quiver of wildcat skin, the two were not sewn together. Quivers were not made from the hides of bear, fox, coyote, or fawn. Mountain lion skin lined with dressed antelope hide might be used for the quiver (Inf. 16).

The material for the two cases was cut from the same skin if a mountain lion hide was used (see 23.1). The quiver was cut and sewn on only one side; the other side was formed by the fold. A round piece of dressed buckskin was sewn into the bottom. To keep the quiver extended, a stick or unworked arrow shaft was attached on the outside of the side seam and laced in place with buckskin. The quiver was about two feet high and open at the top. The bow case when cut from a small skin (23.1) was sewn on both sides and the bottom, with either mountain lion skin or buckskin thongs. A large skin was so cut that each case could be made with a single seam (see 23.2). The hair side of the skin formed the outside. The legs of the animal were left attached to either the bow case or the quiver; as long as they hung down, it did not matter where they were placed.

The two cases were then attached with buckskin thongs at two points along the arrow shaft or stick. The bow case was several inches longer than the quiver, and the mouths of the two were not flush (see 23.6). A shoulder strap was then sewn to either end of the stick. Quivers do not seem to have been ornamented. The flap which closed the top of the bow case was fringed, however, as was the bottom.

Men usually made quivers; Inf. 8 specified grown men. Inf. 7 said, however, a boy had "real arrows" and could make a quiver by the age of fifteen. He said there were some specialists.

When not in use, the quiver was hung in the hogan to keep it dry. According to Inf. 8, it "lasted long time," but he was not explicit; he said that the quiver was buried with the dead and was not inherited. The bow and arrows were carried in their separate cases. The quiver hung on the left side; the strap passed over the right shoulder. Arrows were drawn under the left arm. Except when traveling, one never carried the quiver on the back.

Infs. 7, 8, and 16 provided most of the data. Another (Inf. 34) said that he could remember his grandfather's quiver full of arrows hanging in the

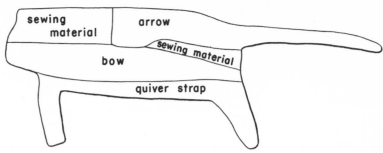

23.1. Mountain lion skin

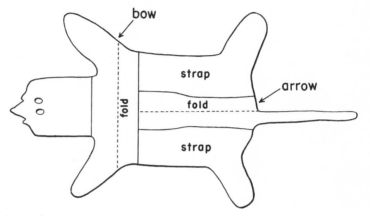

23.2. Large skin

hogan, but that no one had such things any more. Inf. 7 had seen people using the quiver; Inf. 8 said that the only one he had seen was carried by an old man who was a "chief." He carried it to indicate his status. This occurrence was "quite a while back." Various men at Ramah still have bows and arrows, but data on their containers are lacking. Apparently the quiver disappeared from use around the turn of the century. Kluckhohn, however, disagreed, saying that the quiver was used in the 1930's.

Hill (Central and West)

Informants confirmed the preference for mountain lion skin. According to C (Chinle), otter skin quivers were occasionally made. "This required three skins." Less valued were those made from deer or goat hide. The poorer Navaho were satisfied with quivers made from the skins of badger and wildcat; these were pieced and lacked most of the ornamental features. Informants agreed that a combined quiver and bow case was desirable. If materials were lacking, however, the bow was carried in the hand and the arrows in a quiver slung over the shoulder (C; PP, Fort Defiance).

Quivers averaged from two to three hand spans long for blunt arrows and several inches or so longer for pointed arrows. The nocks of the arrows projected above the edge of the quiver. Bow cases were from three and a half to four feet long; the bow was used to measure for length. About six inches of the bow projected from the case.

According to C, to insure that the parts corresponded in size, the dressed mountain lion skin was folded along the back and various sections marked for cutting. The hide was then laid flat and cut along the pattern (see 23.3). The circular piece of the bottom of the quiver was cut from any convenient area.

PP followed a slightly different procedure. He said the hide was not marked before cutting. The worker placed a foot on one section of the hide, held the remainder off the ground with one hand, and cut the various sections. "In this way you did not damage the fur as you would if you laid the skin on a board and cut it." The pattern differed from that used by C. Carrying straps were cut not from the edge of the hide, but from a section between that used for the quiver and those sections used for the bow case. The remainder of the hide was used for fringes and the quiver bottom (see 23.4).

Seams were sewn with sinew (from the tail of a mountain lion according to PP) in a simple running stitch. For the quiver, the fur was usually placed on the outside, especially when mountain lion skin was used (C). On the bow case, it was always on the inside, according to PP. He stated that as soon as the bow case was completed it was painted on the outside (flesh side) with a yellow dye made from dock, sorrel, or golden rod.

Quiver patterns (Hill)

23.a Quiver, from Jeddito (Hill)

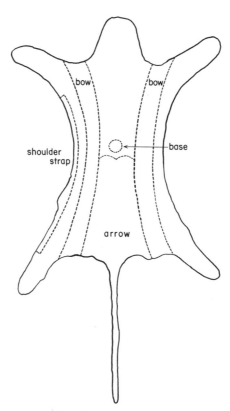

23.3. After C

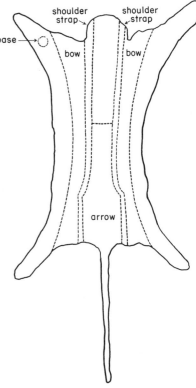

23.4. After PP

Quivers (Hill)

23.5. Pieced quiver, observed by Hill at Jeddito; *a* and *c* show piecing; *b*, stitch used

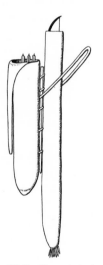

23.6. Completed quiver

The hair was on the inside on a deerskin quiver examined at Jeddito; because the original hide was small, the quiver was pieced out by an additional section (see 23.5). As at Ramah, a slender pole was cut and notched at either end. It was always currant or Fendlerbush (PP). "This had to be gathered secretly and sacredly. It must be free from a bush against which a deer had rubbed its horns." After the quiver and bow case were lashed to the median pole, the carrying strap was tentatively attached and the quiver tested for balance. It was supposed to hang at the back with the opening over the left shoulder at about a forty-five-degree angle from the vertical. Except for decoration the quiver was complete (see 23.6).

For ornament, the tail was allowed to hang free from the quiver; the ends of the carrying strap were fringed and fringe was attached to the bottom of quiver and case. According to PP, additional decoration of buckskin, bayeta, and feathers was added if the owner possessed the materials. A strip of white dressed buckskin about two and a half inches wide and the length of the median pole was fringed on one side. The unfringed side was placed on and just over the median pole from the right. A similar strip of red-dyed buckskin was put on top of the first from the left. This was occasionally double width and folded; if so, both edges were fringed. Next a folded strip of bayeta was added. This was fringed on one side, and wide enough so that only the buckskin fringes appeared beyond its margins. These strips were secured by a white buckskin lace which ran from bottom to top and was crossed like a shoelace to add to the aesthetic effect.

Added to the base of the tail on the quiver was a rosette of turkey breast feathers; from its center were suspended two eagle tail feathers with eagle plumes attached to their ends. To make the rosette, the end of each quill was cut off, the sides scraped, and the pliable section bent over a foundation string and tied. The eagle plume was tied with a square knot to the end of the tail-feather quill. The two tail feathers were then affixed to the center of the rosette with a string.

There is evidence that ritual was once associated with the manufacture of quivers. According to PP, individuals who had participated in warfare were eligible to make quivers, shields, and lances, which might be made at home with no ceremony. Those who had not participated in warfare might assist the worker at certain stages, but no "ordinary" man should cut or sew the circular section for the quiver bottom. It was believed that illness would result, and such a breach could be cured only by the Enemy Way. The most highly considered and efficacious quivers, however, were those which were made during the course of an Enemy Way. Therefore, individuals normally waited to make quivers until this ceremony was held. "There are eight different songs while the quiver is being made. These songs should not be sung unless there is a ceremony" (PP).

Fishler (West)

Wildcat skins were used for quivers but in spite of the beauty of the pelt they were not more highly valued than other skins (TN, Kaibito; TT, FG, Coalmine), such as mink and mountain lion. According to legend, the Navaho learned to make quivers from the Twins. The First Twin had a mountain lion skin quiver and the Second Twin a mink one.

Comparative

Benavides in 1630 stated that the Navaho used the quiver (Ayer, 1916:49), but neither he nor Simpson, the next to mention it (Simpson, 1850:101), described the article. Many of the early photographs in the Harvard Peabody Museum photograph collection confirm the existence of quivers like those described by various informants (see also Hill, 1936b:pl. 1). A sketch by Möllhausen in 1853 or 1854 shows a mounted Navaho warrior with such a quiver. It is worn on the right side, and appears to be slung from the waist rather than the shoulder (Whipple, *et al.,* 1855:pl. 22). About 1858 Möllhausen depicted a Navaho man with a quiver slung from his left shoulder over his right hip (Ives, 1861:pl. 7). It appears to be similar to those in the Harvard Peabody Museum collections.

Specimens in the Harvard collection are good examples of the late nineteenth-century Navaho type. One quiver was collected in 1892 from Navaho in southern Colorado (see 23.b); the other, from unspecified Navaho, was received by the Museum in 1924. Both quivers are made of mountain lion skin, the arrow cases with the hair side out, the attached bow cases with the hair side in. Both quivers were made from a partially cased skin with the head toward the bottom, which was closed by an inset piece. In both specimens the split tail portion of the skin formed an appendage equal in length to the case. In the Colorado specimen, both the arrow case and the tail piece measure nearly thirty-one inches; both dimensions on the other case are twenty-seven inches. Both arrow cases are wider at the top than at the bottom: the Colorado specimen narrows from approximately eight inches to almost two inches, the other from seven inches to more than three inches. Both bow cases are approximately thirty-nine inches long, and slightly more than an inch wide at the bottom. The Colorado specimen is nearly three inches wide at the top; the other is about two inches wide at the top. Each bow case was fringed around the top, each arrow case around the bottom. The Colorado specimen was sewn with a buckskin thong, the other with fiber. Both were laced to sticks with buckskin thongs. Incorporated into the stitching of the stick on the Colorado specimen were a strip of red cotton cloth, a piece of black corduroy, and a green ribbon. One straight and two wavy lines were incised at the top of the stick, and a string of small white beads was also wound around the top. On the other case, the stick was decorated with "American" red wool flannel cloth, and a varicolored string of beads.

These quivers were similar to one described by Mason in 1894 (pl. 79). The bow case is forty-four inches and the arrow case twenty-eight inches. He noted that the wooden support was an integral part of the arrow case, and that the bow case was an afterthought. This observation pertains to the Peabody Museum specimens as well, but the relationship between the rod and the two cases is more functional than sequential.

Other late nineteenth-century observers noted Navaho quivers of "panther" or "cougar" skin (Bourke, 1936:90; Dellenbaugh, 1926:147). According to an origin legend recorded by Matthews (1897:140, 239), in early legendary times the Navaho did not have large skin quivers, but used something like a "modern shawl-strap" for carrying arrows. One of the Peabody Museum specimens (see 23.b) was supported by a mountain lion skin strap attached at two points on the lower half of the stick; the ends were slashed into nine or ten long fringes. The other quiver was supported by an old piece of dressed

23.b. Mountain lion skin quiver from southern Colorado

skin reinforced with blue denim; this was tied to the stick near the point where the bow and arrow cases were joined.

Most sources confirmed the use of mountain lion skin (Franciscan Fathers, 1910:321; Sapir and Hoijer, 1942:429; Gifford, 1940:32, 121). Goatskin, wildcat skin, and beaver skin were mentioned (Franciscan Fathers, 1910:321; both informants, Gifford, 1940:32, 121; Eastern informant, Gifford, 1940:32, 121). Gifford's Western informant said that in battle the quiver was carried at the side, under the arm, but the Eastern informant said it was carried on the back; he also confirmed separate pockets for bow and arrows, which the Western informant denied. According to the Franciscan Fathers (1910:321), the quiver was carried on the back in war, attached at the waist in peace. Shufeldt was told by a Navaho warrior that the Navaho used to carry a buckskin quiver "full in front of them, from which [arrows] could be removed with great rapidity while firing" (Shufeldt, 1887:786). His observation that most archers at that time preferred to carry the bow and a few arrows in the hand was confirmed by the Franciscan Fathers in 1910.

There is no information on the present distribution of the quiver. In 1932, F. H. Douglas saw a Navaho at Zia Pueblo carrying a cougar skin quiver but it was uncertain whether it was intended for actual use or display.

There is little information in the literature about the makers of quivers. Newcomb (1940a:39) stated that the work was forbidden to women, although women were permitted to work on them at least in some areas and at some periods, and specialists were not always required. Left Handed, who told how he made a mountain lion skin quiver in the 1870's or 1880's, said that his mother told him not to sew across the nose of the skin because only a woman could do that. The quiver was decorated with ribbons and beads (Dyk, 1938:321). Left Handed's pride in this decoration revealed the value of the bow, arrows, and quiver as articles of display rather than as purely functional objects.

24. Wrist Guard   keˑʼtoh (Ramah, Haile)

Ramah

A man who had bows and arrows made his own wrist guard, which was worn on the left wrist to protect it from the snap of the bowstring.

A strip of rawhide about four inches long was cut and thongs were attached. These were laced on the underside of the arm. The guard that Inf. 8 had "a few years ago" had no design on it, but Inf. 7 said that he had never seen one without a groove around each end. Both informants were familiar with the more ornate guards decorated with silver. According to Inf. 16, the wrist guard was of buckskin, and rawhide was an innovation.

Inf. 8 said that he had made one "a long time ago" and that wrist guards did not wear out. Storage was no problem since they were worn on the wrist at all times.

The old functional wrist guards have been replaced in Ramah Navaho culture by richly ornamented wristlets of rawhide and silver. These are a recent innovation, according to Inf. 7, and are made by silversmiths, not necessarily in the Ramah community. Not every man owns one.

Hill (Central)

According to PP (Fort Defiance), the earliest type of wrist guard was made of cottonwood. A section of the root was reduced to a thin rectangular piece carved to fit the wrist. Four holes were bored to carry thongs which secured it to the arm.

Wrist guards were made from the hides of badgers, buffalos, cows, and horses. There were several patterns (see 24.1–24.4). The hide was folded before cutting to insure a symmetrical form. Four holes were bored for the securing thongs. According to AM (Lukachukai), when the serrated type (24.2) was used, the guard was turned and the serrations pushed forward over the protruding bone of the wrist back of the thumb, in order to present a flat surface for the bowstring to strike. When not in use, the serrations lay on the back of the wrist.

According to PP, silver ornaments began to be used on wrist guards after the return of the Navaho from Fort Sumner. He stated that turquoise and silver did not come into use until about 1890. Silver mounts were equipped with copper eyelets on the underside. The hide guard was perforated, the eyelets pushed through the openings, and a tongue of skin placed in the eyelet to prevent it from slipping out (see 24.5).

Wrist guards (Hill)

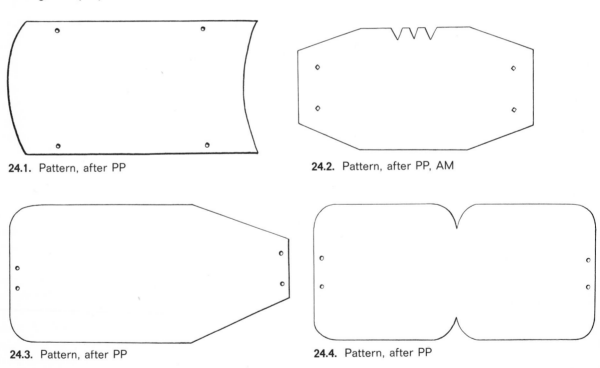

24.1. Pattern, after PP

24.2. Pattern, after PP, AM

24.3. Pattern, after PP

24.4. Pattern, after PP

24.5. Detail of wrist guard fastening, after PP

Fishler (West)

A piece of deerskin or cowhide three and a half to four inches long and wide enough to wrap around the arm was obtained. Two holes were made at each end. Not all Navaho made or used wrist guards (GB, Tuba City). Other data confirmed those from Ramah and Hill.

Comparative

A wrist guard of plain leather was found on a burial site regarded as Navaho in Chaco Canyon (Malcolm, 1939:19). It presumably dates from the early part of the nineteenth century.

By the 1880's bow guards were no longer purely utilitarian; although some plain ones existed, many were ornamented with silver (Bourke, 1936:231; Shufeldt, 1887:786). By 1910 the Franciscan Fathers described them as largely ornamental and usually decorated with a heavy silver plate set with turquoise (Franciscan Fathers, 1910:312).

According to Woodward (1938:40–41), this change from the simple leather wrist guard began in imitation of the Utes, who used broad brass wristlets, and, later, plates of copper and brass cut and fastened to leather. Adair has traced the change in designs of the silver decorations. He found that leather guards are still used in the northwestern part of the Navaho area, where the bow is still used to some extent. Other Navaho wear their wrist guards largely for ornament (Adair, 1944:34–35).

25. Sling   be·ˑediⁿλ̣́ (Ramah, Haile)   "with it a throwing loop" (CC)

Ramah

A hole was cut at each end of a diamond-shaped piece of buckskin and thongs were attached. Pebbles of any type might be used for ammunition, but round ones of a certain size were preferred and saved for that purpose.

Slings were made by anyone who knew how, and at any time or place. They were kept in the pocket or hung on the hogan wall. The maker was the owner and could dispose of his sling as he wished. If used frequently, slings wore out quickly. When a man died, his sling was given to another man, thrown away, or burned.

Slings could be used at any time of the year, for hunting rabbits and frightening birds from the fields, but they were not used for large game. Boys used them as toys. Warriors used to rely on slings when their arrows were expended.

Apparently slings are no longer used by the Ramah Navaho, although in 1946 Roberts was told by Inf. 90 that Inf. 234 knew how to use one. Two adults (Infs. 8, 256) had used them as boys, and Inf. 8 said that his father made him one for rabbit hunting. Others (Infs. 1, 7, 16) knew of the sling, and may have used one. The sling is no longer an adult's weapon, and it has been replaced as a boy's toy by the rubber-band and forked-stick slingshot, which boys began to make "a few years ago" (Inf. 8).

Hill (Central)

Slings were used for frightening birds and animals from the corn fields; for killing rabbits, prairie dogs, and birds (WH, Wheatfields); as toys; and for turning sheep during herding (PP, Fort Defiance).

Data on form and construction confirmed those from Ramah. According to WH, if the sling's over-all length was greater than three feet, it was difficult to shoot efficiently. When the sling was used, the index or middle finger (WH), or the middle finger (PP), was passed through the loop or split in one thong; the other thong was held between the thumb and index finger. According to PP, the sling was whirled once above the head before the pebble was released.

Lamphere (East)
PM confirmed the word for sling known at Ramah.

Fishler (West)
Deerskin thongs about one foot long were tied to each end of a wide piece of deerskin. TN (Kaibito) said these slings were quite accurate and were used to kill or stun small animals such as squirrels, rabbits, and prairie dogs. BN (Kaibito) claimed that the sling was not large enough or strong enough to kill large animals. IJun (Kaibito) said that slings were toys and were not effective for hunting.

Comparative
Slingshots were used in 1881 by the Fort Defiance Navaho. Bourke said that they were used by children, but did not describe them (Bourke, 1936:225). The Franciscan Fathers (1910:325) described the sling used for killing birds and throwing stones at the sheep during herding. By 1910, however, the Navaho had obtained the rubber-band and forked-stick slingshot. They also described a toy gun made by the boys, which used stones, nails, small arrows, or bullets for ammunition. It was made from a grooved stick, shaped like a small bow attached to the muzzle. A string fastened at either end of the bow was passed over a notch in a wooden trigger that served to release the string and propel the shot forward. It was used to kill birds. Such a crossbow has not been described for the Ramah area.

Both Gifford's informants confirmed the sling for killing birds to protect crops. According to the Western Navaho, slings were used for killing foxes and rabbits, and as boys' toys. These uses were denied by the Eastern informant, who said that slings were used in war; the Western informant denied such use (Gifford, 1940:33, 123).

26. Firearms   be·eldǫ (Haile)   "with which to cause noisy explosion"; "gun" (CC)

Ramah
Data on firearms were not collected, although it is known that they were used. Inf. 7 owned a Winchester rifle which he purchased new, probably in the 1880's. Both men and women were (and are) allowed to use firearms.

Hill (Central and West)
Muzzle loaders obtained from the Mexicans were used, according to SG (Keams Canyon). Hill also observed a few modern rifles in use in the Crystal, Keams Canyon, and Lukachukai areas.

Comparative

Firearms were observed by several of the nineteenth-century travelers, such as Pattie (1905:165) and Letherman (1856:293). By the turn of the century, firearms seem to have replaced the bow and arrow in most parts of the Navaho area, although the transition was gradual and uneven. A vocabulary for the gun and its parts was recorded by the Franciscan Fathers by 1910. Although the rifle and revolver were common, the shotgun was not (Franciscan Fathers, 1910:325–326). According to Haile (1950:64) the term for the gun meant "with which to cause noisy explosion."

27. Powder Horn

biˑnáȝihiˑ ˑadeˑˑ (Lamphere) "put something in that horn" (CC)

beˑeldǫ́ baˑhihiˑ (Lamphere) "its for the gun"

Powder horns

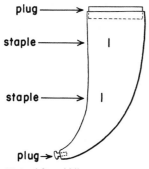

plug →
staple →
staple →
plug →

27.1. After Hill

27.2. After the Franciscan Fathers

Ramah
Adair was told by Inf. 7 that powder was carried in horns of the domestic cow. They were hung at the right side by a strap over the left shoulder. Powder was poured out into silver measures worn on the strap of the leather pouches that every man wore by his side. Powder could thus be easily measured and poured into the gun (Adair, 1944:7–8, pl. 2B).

Hill (Central and West)
Cattle horns were allowed to dry and the core removed (SG, Keams Canyon), or else the horns were covered with mud and placed in the hot ashes after which a slight tap easily dislodged the core (RH, Crystal).

The tip of the horn was cut off (SG), or a hole was burned in the tip with a wire (RH). A leather (SG), rawhide, or wooden plug (RH), was inserted in the opening. A pinyon plug was placed in the open end of the horn. Wire staples were inserted in the side of the horn (see 27.1), and these were used to fasten it to the bottom of the shoulder pouch (SG). According to RH powder horns were also suspended from the shoulder on a strap.

Lamphere (East)
PM contributed the words for powder horn.

Comparative
According to the Franciscan Fathers, the powder horn was made of the horn of a goat or cow, and the opening was covered with goatskin (see 27.2). By 1910 these horns were no longer in use (Franciscan Fathers, 1910:325).

Only older Navaho informants knew of the powder horn, which apparently disappeared from use when cartridges became available in the latter part of the nineteenth century.

28. Ammunition

beˑeldǫ bᵃkaˑ (Haile) "gun bullet" (CC)

Ramah
No data were collected, but Inf. 7 was known to possess cartridges for his rifle.

Hill (West)

Wire was rolled into balls and used for bullets. These were fired from the muzzle-loading guns which the Navaho obtained from the Mexicans (SG, Keams Canyon).

Comparative

Rifle cartridges were used when they became available. By 1910 they were included in the vocabulary collected by the Franciscan Fathers (1910:326). According to Haile (1951:44), the term for ammunition applies to cartridges.

Gathering

29. Cactus Picker

xoš be·γʷóbehé (Haile)   "cactus with it you pick"

Ramah

A stick of young green juniper about one foot long and about one and a half inches in diameter was split about halfway down its length. Grass was sometimes inserted in the split to provide elasticity, but the split was not tied. Bark was removed. When Inf. 8 made a cactus picker, he selected a branch with a fork in it and pulled it apart to split the piece. He used a sharp stone to cut it to the proper length when no knife was available.

Anyone could make this implement, at any location. It was used for twisting off the fruit of the prickly pear, *Opuntia phaeacantha* (Wyman and Harris, 1941:27).

The tool was grasped near the distal or split end, and the stem of the fruit was pinched between the two sections of the split and twisted off. Further splitting of the stick was prevented by the position of the hand; and, when the fruit was ripe, it was easily detached. Picking cactus was easy, and anyone could do it. The stick was thrown away after the fruit was picked.

Not all informants who mentioned the use of cactus fruit included information on the cactus picker. According to Inf. 8, who gave the most explicit data, cactus fruit is no longer gathered; and Inf. 7 knew of no such implement recently used at Ramah.

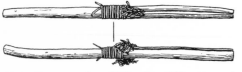

29.1. Cactus picker (Hill), after GH; side and top views

Hill (Central and West)

Oak as well as juniper was used. Grass, juniper bark, or, according to LW (Lukachukai), a piece of wood was inserted at the base of the split to keep the prongs apart. GH (White Cone) stated that the cactus picker was tied to prevent further splitting (see 29.1); tying was denied by LM (Canyon del Muerto).

This implement was used for picking cactus fruit, especially that of the prickly pear (MS, Sawmill; C, Chinle; SG, Keams Canyon; GH, LM, LW). It appears to have been used until very recent times. One was constructed by GH at White Cone.

Comparative

The Franciscan Fathers (1910:211) were the first to describe the cactus picker, although the device was probably in use in the nineteenth century. According to them, the Navaho gathered the prickly pear fruit with cactus pickers or a forked stick. It is impossible to tell from their illustration whether the cactus picker was a split or a forked stick. Elmore (1944:64) believed a forked stick was used. Gifford's Eastern informant confirmed the split stick, his Western informant confirmed the forked stick; each denied the other (Gifford, 1940:11).

30. Cactus Brush

Hill (Central)

When cactus was gathered, the spines were removed by brushing the leaves or fruit with a plant called "cactus cleaner" (LM, Canyon del Muerto) or "cactus brush" (C, Chinle). According to MS (Sawmill), this operation was performed with a juniper branch.

Lamphere (East)

PM said that the small spines (*hosh bichii*) on the cactus, not the larger ones, were knocked off with any kind of stick. She did not know about a plant.

Comparative

Gifford credited the Eastern Navaho with brushing the spines off the fruit, but he gave no further data. His Western informant said that spines were singed off (Gifford, 1940:11). Thorns were also removed by rubbing the fruit in the sand with the foot (Franciscan Fathers, 1910:211; Bryan and Young, 1940:8, 26).

31. Seed Beater

cintel (Ramah)   "wood" (CC)

Ramah

A paddle-shaped piece of wood about one foot long, and "as wide as your palm," was used for separating seeds from stems. Anyone could make seed beaters (Inf. 7), but women probably used them more often than men. Usually, however, the seeds were detached by a blow of the hand, or with any convenient stick. A basket or some other container was placed under the plant to catch the seeds as they fell. Inf. 129's mother had done this. Another method was to gather the plants or stems with seeds intact and to free the seeds by scorching them over a fire.

The seed beater was confirmed by Infs. 7, 14, and 32; but Inf. 32 said that it might be used for any type of seed, and Inf. 14 specified *Mentzelia pumila* var. *multiflora*. Infs. 15 and 50 told of using sticks; Inf. 192 denied the use of a seed beater or sticks for gathering seeds. Vestal (1952:72) listed nineteen species of plants which yielded seeds used for food by the Ramah Navaho, but he did not specify the method of gathering all of them.

It is not known whether the seed beater exists at present in the Ramah area. Seeds are still gathered occasionally, mainly by the older women, and the seed beater may be used.

Hill (East and Central)

Both informants, PP (Fort Defiance) and D (Crownpoint), denied the use of seed beaters, meaning in this case the classic woven seed beater of the Intermontane and California areas. The idea of using this tool or a substitute was considered entirely foreign.

Comparative

Gifford's informants for both Eastern and Western Navaho denied the use of a seed beater (Gifford, 1940:11). Morris, however, found seeds of a gray-white weed in Navaho caches in Canyon del Muerto, and stated that an old Navaho man had told him that twice since their return from Fort Sumner the people had been reduced to eating this seed. It was gathered by sliding a basketry tray under the plant and "knocking the seeds into it with a beater of spread twigs" (Morris, 1939:118, pl. 99b). The weed is called *tlo tai,* which resembles the word translated by Wyman and Harris (1941:33) as seed grass, *Chenopodium leptophyllum* (see also Vestal, 1952:25).

32. Pinyon Beater   ne·šǐ·· naniłxa·ł (Lamphere, Haile)   "you beat it with a club" (Lamphere); "pinyon, beating it" (CC)

Ramah

Any straight oak pole was used to knock down pinyon nuts. Formerly, it was a special pole, but Inf. 7 did not "haul it around." Sticks were thrown at trees, or branches were struck with the poles to dislodge the nuts (Infs. 7, 8, 50). Pinyon beaters were discarded after each season because good pinyon crops occurred at intervals of three or four years. The stick was not absolutely necessary, for when the cones were ripe the nuts fell to the ground.

The time for gathering pinyon nuts was carefully calculated, however, since a substantial snowfall put an end to the pinyon season, not only by covering the crop but also by making travel difficult. Thus, as Inf. 8 said, "In the old days people might be in a hurry to gather the nuts and beat them off the trees while they were still green." These factors are still important in the gathering of pinyons but apparently the long pole beater is no longer used by the Ramah Navaho.

Some informants observed a taboo against beating trees, and Inf. 8 mentioned one against climbing, although he did not know the sanction for this belief. Some claimed the reason was the fear of bears. It is apparent from the data that not everyone observed the taboo against beating trees, but no one is known to have climbed them.

Hill (East and Central)

According to LW (Lukachukai), K (Mariano Lake), and TLLSS (Crownpoint), long poles were used to dislodge pinyon cones. This was denied by MS (Sawmill), who said that the cones (or limbs carrying cones) were stripped from the tree by hand, or the nuts were gathered from the ground.

Lamphere (East)

PM said that the stick used for pinyon beating could be called "you beat it [pinyon nut] with a club."

Fishler (West)

TN (Kaibito), TH (Moenave), and GB (Tuba City) said that people waited until the cones had been opened by frost before traveling to the pinyon groves. After the nuts had fallen to the ground, they were picked up by men, women, and children. Some informants placed blankets under the trees and struck the branches with a large stick. The older Navaho, however, believed that if the tree were struck, the spirit of the bear would cause them to become ill. GB had never heard of a bear spirit associated with the tree. All of the informants had gathered pinyons.

Comparative

The only published reference to the pinyon beater among the Navaho has been by Gifford (1940:11, 91). His Western informant said that poles were sometimes used, but his Eastern informant said they were never used, for fear "bears would attack them." They gathered only those nuts which had fallen naturally. Adair saw and photographed a Navaho family near Marsh Pass, Arizona, using a pinyon beater. When the branches were too high to strike with the poles, the poles were thrown at the higher branches to dislodge the nuts. He said specifically that they did not climb the trees (Adair, personal communication).

33. Pinyon Screen

ne·ščí·· be·biγá̜h de·he> (Lamphere)   "pinyons with it, shaking them"

ne·ščí·· be·binkan ʎe·he> (CC)   "pinyon, with it two persons are shaking" (CC)

Ramah

Wire screening was attached with narrow strips of wood to a wooden frame. This device was used to screen pinyons after they were gathered, or to clean beans or other seeds.

One of Inf. 12's daughters constructed a pinyon screen which was used by the whole family in sorting beans for a neighboring white family, and for gathering pinyons (Inf. 12). Everything under a tree (nuts, needles, and all) was swept up and dumped on the screen. The needles passed through the mesh, leaving the nuts behind. This method was said to be much more efficient than picking pinyons one at a time. In this manner 100 to 150 pounds can be gathered in a day. A similar screen was seen at Inf. 45's place, and more recently Inf. 166 was seen to use one. Each of the three households studied by Roberts (1951:28–29) owned a pinyon screen similar to the one described above, and Inf. 29 described a "big square screen" used in gathering pinyons in the 1920's (Leighton and Leighton, 1949:173).

Lamphere (East)

PM and EP stated that the pinyon screen was called "pinyons with it, shaking them."

Comparative

The only reference to the pinyon screen among non-Ramah Navaho is that of Sapir and Hoijer (1942:409). They were told that the nuts were winnowed first in a flat, broad dish, and then in "that which is like a box." "They hold it between them, put the pinyon nuts with the rubbish in it, and then they screen them with it."

34. Gathering Bag

ci·zis (Ramah, Haile)

Ramah

A large circular piece was cut from a fresh undressed goat or sheep hide. The skin was not necessarily dehaired. Two pieces of wood were crossed and tied together to serve as a framework and keep the skin extended. The skin was placed hair side out over the framework and then pulled up. The edge of the skin was sewn with deer or sheep sinew, in "any old way" (Inf. 8), to an oaken ring which served as the rim. On each side of the rim was a loop of unspecified material. A spun wool cord connected the two loops to form a handle. Some bags were as large as three feet deep and two feet in diameter. These bags were used for gathering yucca fruit and wild seeds (Infs. 7, 8) and for storing dried meat (Inf. 7).

Both men and women made gathering bags, at any place and at any time (Inf. 8). Inf. 7 made conflicting statements: first he said they were made only during the yucca fruit season, then dismantled and stored; then he said they were used to hold dried meat, as well as for gathering yucca fruit and wild seeds. According to Inf. 8, they were used to store clothes in between gathering seasons. He said his mother had used one, and there was one in each hogan. They were said to last about a year (Inf. 8), and when used for storage, they were kept "in a safe place." Inf. 32 confirmed the data given by Inf. 7.

The only person known to have used a gathering bag is Inf. 8's mother, who died about 1921. Inf. 8 said that these containers were no longer used after about 1916, and that yucca fruit is now gathered in a carton or any sort of a container. Gathering bags do not appear to be extant in the Ramah area.

Hill (East and Central)

Information was obtained from Wheatfields, Lukachukai, Red Rock, Mariano Lake, Canyon del Muerto, and Fort Defiance. It confirmed that from Ramah.

Comparative

The first reference to gathering bags occurs in the account of the Franciscan Fathers (1910:299). Their description confirmed that from Ramah, and they stated that the implement was "sometimes made on the field for conveying the fruit." Both of Gifford's Navaho informants denied the gathering basket, but so did all but one (a Lipan) of the twenty Southwestern groups he investigated (Gifford, 1940:42).

35. Carrying Basket

ci·zis (Ramah, Haile)

Ramah

Data are abstracted from Tschopik (1940:458–459). Informants agreed that no ritual was necessary for the manufacture of carrying baskets (Infs. 21,

32, 169, 192). These were used exclusively in collecting yucca fruit and edible wild seeds (Infs. 7, 32, 169, 192; see 35.1). This type of basket is no longer used in the Ramah area.

Hill (East, Central, and West)

Carrying baskets were made of willow (usually, according to PP, Fort Defiance; K, Mariano Lake), sumac (PP; LM, Canyon del Muerto; MH, Head Springs; LW, Lukachukai; RH, Crystal), sumac and yucca (WH, Wheatfields), or oak twigs (PP).

Informants differed in descriptions of the weave. PP stated that two oak twigs were bent to U-shape and crossed to form the foundation. A hoop of oak was then tied to the upright twigs. LM stated that two twigs were crossed at right angles, and the first weft element introduced. Additional warp elements were inserted as needed and bent to give the necessary conical shape (see 35.2). A stick or loom batten was used to pound down the weave (LM), which was a simple wicker (LM, MH, PP). Informants agreed that weaving was done clockwise, and that the side of the basket nearest the weaver was worked. This process was the opposite of that employed in the manufacture of the basket tray (LM, LW, PP; see Trait 98, Hill section).

Loops of buckskin (PP, LM) or horsehair (PP) for affixing the tumpline were tied along the main warps, at the balance of the basket. Sometimes a goatskin bottom was laced to these baskets (LM).

SG (Keams Canyon) described a different weave, twined with a two-rod foundation. This consisted of two pairs of four elements each. These were twined together for about an inch in the center (see 35.3). The two sets of four warps were crossed and the regular twining process began. An additional warp passed diagonally under both pairs of foundation warp; this was included in the weave about three inches from the base. New warp and weft elements were added as needed (see 35.4), giving the appearance of a three-rod foundation.

In finishing the basket, warp elements were bent over the top weft or a hoop at the top and the ends pushed into the basket (MH, LM, WH, PP). A split piece of wood (MH) or a buckskin wrapping (WH, LM) was laced in to hold the rim in place.

Baskets were colored either red or white, depending on whether or not the bark was removed (LM, LW). RH stated that the sumac was dyed. He never saw a carrying basket with the buckskin fringed: "The Apaches do that, not the Navaho."

35.a. Beginning to make a carrying basket, Ramah

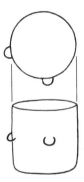

35.1. Carrying basket, after Tschopik; top and side views

Carrying basket weaves (Hill)

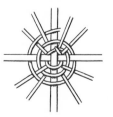

35.2. Starting a basket, after LM

35.3. Twining elements at start of basket, after SG

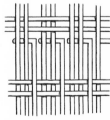

35.4. Two-rod foundation with new wefts, after SG

35.5. Shape of carrying basket, after Hill

Carrying baskets were made by women (PP), or by men and women (LM). They were used to carry corn, and were woven so closely that shelled corn could be transported (LM). The basket was either placed on the ground and filled with corn or carried on the back and the ears tossed into it over the shoulders (PP). When in use the bottom tip of the basket (see 35.5) reached to about the belt line. The upper rim extended above the shoulders (C, Chinle). C said that the Navaho never carried things on their heads.

These baskets had been in use as long as LM could remember, and according to SC (Crystal) they were in general use while the yucca was still plentiful on the reservation.

Fishler (West)
Large baskets were made from brush or yucca to transport seeds (FrJFa, Tuba City).

Comparative
According to the Franciscan Fathers (1910:298–299), a basket made of willow twigs was used for gathering yucca fruit. The rim of the basket was unfinished. A cord was fastened to two of the staves (upright warps) and the basket was carried by tumpline, or occasionally on horseback or by burro (one on either side). The same framework was sometimes covered with goatskin or sheepskin instead of wickerwork. By 1910 the carrying basket was rarely seen.

Both of Gifford's Navaho informants confirmed the use of a carrying basket or a skin sack for carrying gathered foods. The Western informants said that any basket, or piece of hide, might be used (Gifford, 1940:11, 92).

36. Salt tˣáłx̌á xata·h (Ramah, Haile)   "spring bottom clay" (CC)

ʼášįh (Haile)

Ramah
Men ordinarily gather salt from a deposit at Zuni Salt Lake, sixty miles southwest of Ramah. Salt is dried and brought home in sacks. It is ground on the regular metate before use.

It was said that a man had to know the proper songs and rituals before he could enter the volcanic cone where the salt was located. According to Inf. 7, the old men knew many songs for collecting salt. He said that when two enemies met at Salt Lake they would not kill each other, but he was unfamiliar with the idea that only warriors who had killed enemies could visit the volcano.

Inf. 34 said, "Kids are not supposed to go nor women either," and Inf. 16 noted that women do not go to Salt Lake. Her sister-in-law assured Inf. 82 that it was not dangerous for women to go, and she herself had made one trip to the lake. No matter who gathers the salt, women do help with its preparation and probably do most of the grinding.

Expeditions are usually undertaken in the summer or late fall, and generally take six or seven days. According to Inf. 34, expeditions are made every one or two years, depending on the supply of salt.

Salt is used for seasoning food, as a medicine, and for ceremonial purposes, in which case ordinary "store" salt can not be substituted. Because salt for ritual purposes is not easily obtained, it serves as an exchange medium. Navaho may make long expeditions trading this easily transportable commodity for other goods.

Even the most acculturated among the Ramah Navaho, Inf. 82, prefers the lake salt to "store" salt, saying the latter is too "bitter." Salt is still gathered from the Zuni Salt Lake and many expeditions have been noted. For example, Inf. 3 sent his grandson for salt because he was too old to make the trip; Inf. 83 asked Inf. 128 to bring her a load of salt from the lake; Inf. 2 was seen leaving for a journey in 1937; and Inf. 104 visited the lake in 1940. Additional information from Roberts, Kluckhohn, and Vogt indicates that trips were made in 1946, 1949, and 1950.

Hill (East and Central)

Hill has published an extended account, including comparative material from other Southwestern groups and a good bibliography (Hill, 1940b:1–25). Data were obtained from Coalmine, Round Rock, Fort Defiance, Red Lake, Chinle, Black Mountain and Nazlini, Crystal, and Chaco Canyon. Ramah data coincided with Hill's account.

Fishler (West)

GB (Tuba City) stated that there were two locations where the Navaho went for salt. One was Zuni Salt Lake, the other was the Grand Canyon, near the junction of the Colorado and Little Colorado Rivers, where the Hopi obtained their salt. TN (Kaibito) confirmed both. Few Navaho went to the Grand Canyon because of the distance from the floor to the top of the canyon. Trips were formerly made on foot, later on horseback.

On arrival at the salt deposits, a prayer was said thanking Salt Woman for the gift of salt. Presents of turquoise, oyster shell, small white shells, obsidian, and corn pollen were given to her, and were deposited in a special place for protection. The man then went down to gather the salt. If he were a good man without evil thoughts he would get clean pure salt; if his thoughts were evil, he would get dirty salt. TN denied a ritual similar to that practiced by the Hopi when gathering salt. He does know the location of the stone at the Grand Canyon with which the Hopi simulate copulation (Simmons, 1942:235–236; Titiev, 1937:247). His brother broke off a piece of this stone as a souvenir. Simulated copulation with Salt Woman was also done by the Hopi with the water at Zuni Lake (Simmons, 1942:254).

FG's (Coalmine) description of the Hopi "hole" near the junction of the Colorado Rivers is similar to that above. "Salt Woman now dwells in Zuni Lake. When you have gathered your salt and leave the lake along the trail, if you look back or juggle the load or try to adjust the pack, it becomes heavier and heavier."

TN's brother and father have made many trips to Zuni Lake and Grand Canyon; the other informants have either gone or had close relatives who have gone for salt.

Comparative

The gathering of salt from saline lakes, especially the Zuni Salt Lake, is confirmed by the Franciscan Fathers (1910:410). Gifford was told that the

Western Navaho obtained their salt from the deposit at the confluence of the Little Colorado and Colorado Rivers. The Eastern Navaho sometimes used alkali deposits, but usually obtained salt from Zuni Salt Lake. The Western informant said that salt was gathered informally, and denied a ritual journey. Salt was stored in a rock shelter, in a pot with a flat stone lid (Gifford, 1940:15, 96–97).

Agriculture

37. Digging Stick

giš (Ramah, Haile) "cane" (CC)

Ramah

A stick of hard wood, such as *Quercus gambelii* (Vestal, 1952:22) was brought to the hogan to be shaped. Bark was peeled from the dry stick. The end might simply be sharpened with a knife or stone, in which case the whole tool was about two feet long. Or, as one informant stated, one end might be shovel-shaped, the other pointed. If so, the tool was about as long as a modern shovel handle. The point was neither fire-hardened nor horn-tipped. The stick was thrown away as soon as the point became dull, usually in about three or four days (Inf. 8).

A special stick made from greasewood (*doghozhi*) was fashioned for digging the root *Phellopterus bulbosus* [*Cymopterus bulbosus*] (Inf. 14; Wyman and Harris, 1941:22). The stick was about one and one half feet long and pointed at one end. It was used because greasewood grew in the same locale as the root and was very tough. This tool was apparently discarded after the roots in an area had been gathered.

Digging sticks were used not only for gathering roots, but for planting. For corn, the stick was driven into the ground about eight inches, twisted, and pulled out; then seed was dropped in (see Leighton and Leighton, 1949:79). Wild potatoes were gathered in the fall, about the end of October. They grew to a depth of about six inches, and were dug with a motion like paddling a canoe.

Men usually made digging sticks and dug the holes, but according to Inf. 9 only women dropped the seed. Women also dug wild roots.

That information on digging sticks was obtained from a young group of informants indicates its recent use in the Ramah area. The implement was seen in use by many (Infs. 8, 9, 34, 45), several of whom had apparently used it as children when they helped with the planting.

Metal implements, including even the cultivator and tractor, have displaced the digging stick in agricultural work. Roots are not often dug, but when such work has been observed a spade has been used. No known digging stick is in existence in the Ramah area. Smaller versions of the digging stick, however, form part of the bundles of the Singers of Life Way and Shooting Chants (Wyman, 1936a:637; Kluckhohn and Wyman, 1940:31–32, 159–160).

37.a MH using a digging stick

Digging sticks

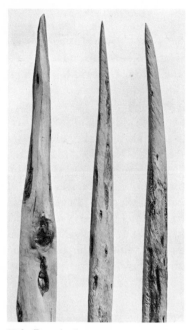

37.b Detail of points

37.c Detail of broad ends

Hill (East, Central, West)

Digging sticks were made of juniper (PP, Fort Defiance; C, Chinle; MLH, Crownpoint), greasewood (MH, Head Springs; C, MLH), and oak (C). (See also Hill, 1938:32.)

Two types of digging sticks were reported. The older type was approximately two and one half to three feet long. The diameter varied according to the size of the limb from which it was made. The sticks had beveled blades which varied in breadth. For working in heavy soil, a sharply pointed blade was used; for sandy soil, a broad blade. Before the introduction of iron and steel tools, the digging stick was shaped by rubbing with a coarse sandstone. A smaller stone with a finer texture was then used to smooth and sharpen the stick.

In planting, the operator knelt on one knee, scraped away the dry surface soil, and loosened the moist earth beneath. The point of the stick was then forced straight downward and the resulting hole filled with moist soil. Seeds were planted just above this hole, and the loosened soil gave easy access to the roots. Digging sticks of this type were also used to gather the roots of wild plants, among others the tubers of the wild onion and mariposa lily (GH, White Cone; SG, Keams Canyon; T, Chaco Canyon; PP, MH, MLH, C).

The second type of digging stick was longer, greater in diameter, and had a broader blade than the preceding one. It also had a projecting fork near the base for a footrest. It was manufactured as the other. It was operated from a standing position in the manner of a shovel. The point was driven into the ground, and twisted with the foot to loosen the soil. According to the majority of informants, this type of digging stick is of Pueblo provenience and was introduced in some areas as late as ninety years ago. Most attributed the introduction to Jemez Pueblo (PP, C, MH). GH referred to this footrest digging stick as the Zuni type. MLH denied its use in his area. Digging stick weights were never used (PP).

Both types were used by men, although women planted the seed (Hill, 1938:32).

Digging sticks appear to have survived until very recent times, and informants at Head Springs and Crownpoint had no difficulty in reproducing specimens (see 37.b, 37.c).

Fishler (West)

A long greasewood stick was flattened and pointed at one end. This was used for planting corn (to a depth of thirteen to fourteen inches), beans and melons (to a depth of three to four inches). FG (Coalmine) said the Navaho formerly planted their corn in a "circle," a ceremonial circuit in a clockwise direction. "The corn was still in straight rows, even though it was in a circle. A good crop resulted from planting this way." Both informants (GB, Tuba City; FG) had used digging sticks.

Comparative

The use of wooden implements in agriculture was reported in the Rabal documents, 1706–1743 (Hill, 1940a:397), but the types were not specified. This is perhaps the earliest reference to the digging stick.

37.1. Digging stick, after the Franciscan Fathers

A single archaeological find apparently indicates the antiquity of the straight digging stick: in the Gobernador region Keur found two manzanita sticks, averaging forty inches long, with flattened lower ends tapering to rather blunt points. The upper eight or ten inches had been smoothed and the bark removed (Keur, 1944:79). These were identified as digging sticks by Inf. 12 from Ramah.

Two types are illustrated by the Franciscan Fathers. One, of greasewood, confirms the similar type from Ramah. The other, with a footrest (see 37.1), confirms Hill's second type. Men dug the holes; women planted the seed and closed the holes with their feet (Franciscan Fathers, 1910:265).

Both Gifford's informants confirmed the hardwood sticks for digging bulbs and roots. The Eastern Navaho made them of greasewood or wild cherry, whittling them with a knife and then rubbing them on sandstone. They sometimes drove them into the ground with a cobble (Gifford, 1940:11, 91). Both informants confirmed the straight stick for planting, and both denied the footrest (Gifford, 1940:17, 101).

As modern tools became available, digging sticks disappeared from other areas as well as from Ramah. For example, around 1892 Old Mexican dug holes with a hoe because he found it quicker than the digging stick (Dyk, 1947:51). In 1910 the Franciscan Fathers reported the use of mattocks rather than digging sticks, and the adoption of the plow (Franciscan Fathers, 1910:266). In 1939, however, Kluckhohn observed that the digging stick was still commonly used in some parts of the Navaho reservation remote from centers of white influence (Kluckhohn, 1942:4).

38. Hoe

łe·ž be·xalka·dí (Ramah, Haile)   "with which dirt is scooped"

behégod (Lamphere, Haile, Franciscan Fathers)   modern hoe

ałtʼsáji behégudi (Franciscan Fathers)   "either side hoe"

agástsin behégud (Franciscan Fathers)   "shoulderblade hoe"

nabehégudi (Franciscan Fathers)   "the side hoe"

Ramah

The entire hoe was made of one piece of wood, usually oak or very dry pinyon. The blade was flat and pointed. The hoe was approximately as long as a modern shovel, but was sometimes shorter. It was made with a stone axe and required about a month to fashion. A hoe made from the sharpened scapula of a cow was also used to break the ground for planting.

One Ramah informant used the first term above, "with which dirt is scooped," to designate both types of hoe. The scapula hoe was described by Inf. 9, who said it had been used by Infs. 44 and 134 and some of their women (see Leighton and Leighton, 1949:79). Wooden hoes were described by Inf. 7, and Inf. 34 remembered them during his youth.

Tools purchased from the trading post have replaced both types of hoe, which were probably used by Navaho who lacked money for new tools. "There is some store all right, but they too far to go and they ain't got no money to buy any kind farm tools" (Inf. 9). According to Inf. 7, the Navaho first started to farm around Ramah after their return from Fort Sumner, when they were issued farm equipment.

Hill (East, Central, and West)

According to informants, the oldest type of hoe was made from the scapula of deer (WP, Canoncito; RH, Crystal); of deer, sheep, and goats (LH, Aneth; PP, Fort Defiance; C, Chinle; GH, White Cone; SG, Keams Canyon); of horses (PP, GH); and of elk (GH, RH). At first these hoes were not hafted (C, PP, RH). According to WP, thin slabs of stone were also used instead of an unhafted scapula. Later, the blades were hafted in juniper, two and one half to three feet long (PP). The haft was either split, the blade inserted, and wrapped with yucca (C, GH), or a right-angle joint was cut, the blade placed flat and bound with buckskin (SG; see 38.a). Handle and blade were always in the same plane. The operator, squatting, shoved the blade ahead of him to remove weeds (Hill, 1938:36, pl. 2; see 38.b). The cutting edge was sharpened from time to time on a stone. LH denied the use of the scapula hoe.

A second type of hoe was made of a single piece of juniper (PP), oak (MLH, TLLSS, Crownpoint), or greasewood (TLLSS). It was about two and a half to three feet long, spade-shaped, in a single plane (see 38.c). The blade was beveled on each surface to produce the cutting edge. Shaping and sharpening were done on a coarse-grained slab of rock. This hoe was operated in the same manner as the scapula hoe (PP, TLLSS, MLH, SG; IS, Lukachukai). Occasionally the sides of the blade were also beveled (MLH, SG), to enable the operator to remove weeds with a side-swinging as well as a shoving motion. This hoe appears to conform roughly to the type reported by the Franciscan Fathers (1910:266) which, according to PP, was not used by the Navaho but by the Zuni and Hopi.

38.a. Scapula hoe made by SG

38.b. SG using a scapula hoe

38.c Wooden hoe made by MLH

LM (Canyon del Muerto) denied anything but iron hoes. He said that the first hoe he ever saw was obtained in trade from the Mexicans around 1860. It would appear, however, that both scapula and wooden hoes were in fairly common use until recently. Informants had no difficulty in reproducing specimens (see 38.a, made by SG, Keams Canyon, Arizona; and 38.c, made by MLH at Crownpoint, New Mexico), and discarded wooden hoes are still extant (see also Hill, 1938:35-36).

Lamphere (East)

PM confirmed the term used for the modern hoe.

Comparative

Hill has interpreted the reference found in the Rabal documents to wooden tools used in working the soil to mean the digging stick and the hoe (Hill,

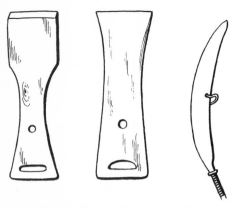

38.1. Hoes, after the Franciscan Fathers

Subsistence

1940a:397). This interpretation seems confirmed by Keur's finds at sites dated in the eighteenth century, where one large cist was discovered that held twelve heavy pinyon and juniper sticks, all with curved, projecting basal ends. They were found associated with the "pure" Navaho hogan group in Pueblito Canyon, in the Gobernador area. Many sticks showed evidence of flattening and fire-hardening, a trait denied for the Ramah area. Keur suggests that they may have served as "hand-ploughs" (Keur, 1944:79).

Several types of hoes (see 38.1) were described by the Franciscan Fathers (1910:266). A straight hoe with a beveled edge was made from wood ("either side hoe"), or from deer or elk scapula ("shoulderblade hoe"). A different type ("the side hoe") consisted of a curved blade to which a wooden handle was secured with an elk hide thong.

By 1910, implements purchased at the trading posts had replaced all four types. According to the Franciscan Fathers, the term used at Ramah ("with which dirt is scooped") described the modern shovel.

Gifford's Eastern informant, but not the Western, confirmed a spatula weeder of "weaving sword type," which cut with a side motion. Both groups used a hoe made from the scapula of a horse or other animal set in a wooden handle; this type was used like a shovel (Gifford, 1940:17, 102).

Two kinds of hoe are mentioned in Matthews' version of the Origin Legend. Deer scapula hoes were noted, as were hoes of thin split cottonwood boards, which were shoved ahead of the worker to clear the weeds (Matthews, 1897:70).

39. Shovel

łe·ž be·xalka·dí (Lamphere, Haile, Franciscan Fathers)   "with which dirt is scooped"

Hill (East and Central)
Replicas of metal shovels were made from wood; WP (Canoncito) specified cottonwood. These were used for piling dirt on hogan roofs (IS, Lukachukai) and for making furrows in the fields (WP).

Lamphere (East)
Both PM and EP confirmed the word for shovel.

Comparative
Data pertaining to the hoe undoubtedly pertain to the shovel as well. Haile gives several forms of the term used for the implement, depending upon its use, "all of which shows that the shovel is a borrowed, not a native tool" (Haile, 1951:263).

Informants did not differentiate terminologically between shovel and hoe. Either the wooden or scapula hoe described in Trait 38 was also used as a shovel. The Ramah term for this implement ("with which dirt is scooped") was translated by the Franciscan Fathers and by Haile as "shovel," and it referred to the modern tool (Franciscan Fathers, 1910:267; Haile, 1950:327, 1951:262–263).

40. Rake   be náxʷi·ʒidí (Hill, Haile)   "the thing you gather trash with," "trash"

Ramah

Although information from the Ramah area is scanty, it is known that "metal lawn brooms" were used around Fence Lake to sweep up pinyons. In 1948 Rapoport observed "a new rake, thin but wide toothed, for raking pinyons. It was bought from the Lambson store." Manson noted a year later that a "good man with a broom could best them [various types of tools] all."

Hill (East and West)

The rake was called "the thing you gather trash with," or "trash." The forked branch of a tree was obtained. The main portion of the limb formed the handle, and the branches beyond the fork were cut to equal length to produce the tines. Rakes had two, three, or four tines (SG, Keams Canyon), three or four (MH, Head Springs), three (T, Chaco Canyon), or two (GH, White Cone). According to MH, tines were about a foot long. He stated that a brace located midway on the tines was occasionally lashed to the fork with yucca. T stated that a limb with only two branches was always selected. A separate piece was then tied to the handle bottom and crosspiece to form the third tine.

These implements served the purpose of both rake and fork. They were used to clear weeds from the fields and to pile them for burning. Hill has noted (1938:36) that "the absence of these implements from the entire Central area suggests their late diffusion from the pueblos."

Comparative

Comparative data are scanty. The rake mentioned by the Franciscan Fathers (1910:268) is a modern tool. The term cited by Haile confirms that noted by Hill (Haile, 1951:238). Gifford (1940) has mentioned no such tool, and there seems to be no reference to it in the myths.

41. Flail   be· élxàʎí (Hill)   "something to beat with"

čéčil bici·n (Lamphere)   oak stick; "oak stem" (CC)

Ramah

An oak flail, about as long as an axe handle, was used for threshing corn (Infs. 7, 8, 34) or any kind of seeds (Inf. 14). The branches were trimmed from the oak pole for easier handling. Either a woman or a man might make a flail. The material to be threshed was placed on a blanket and beaten until the seeds separated. Threshing was usually done by adults, since the work quickly tired children.

Flails were kept from one season to the next. They were usually stored in the hogan, where they would be available, but in no special place. The flail was still used by Inf. 8 in 1954.

Hill (East, Central, and West)

The flail was called "something to beat with." Flails for harvesting corn were fashioned from juniper (SG, Keams Canyon) or oak (PP, Fort Defiance). They were about four feet long, shaped somewhat like a baseball bat, with the distal end slightly upcurved (PP; GH, White Cone). Corn was placed in an oblong pit, and beaten by men; then the women gathered and winnowed the detached kernels (Hill, 1938:41). Formerly, kernels were removed from the cob with a pointed stick, one row at a time, or the ears were struck against each other until the rows of kernels were removed. This method is still used in some localities.

Flails were also used for threshing various types of wild seeds, principally grasses, such as lambs quarters (*Chenopodium album,* identified by Vestal, 1952:24–25, and Elmore, 1944:43–44, also called white pigweed), pigweed (*Chenopodium cornutum* [*Chenopodium graveolens*], or *Chenopodium fremontii,* identified by Elmore, 1944:44), and green amaranth, or rough pigweed (*Amaranthus retroflexus,* identified by Elmore, 1944:46). The flails were used if available, but more often any convenient stick was employed. The plants were pulled, piled up, and beaten, the operator removing the larger twigs as the work progressed (D, Crownpoint; C, Chinle; MS, Sawmill; MDW, Jeddito; LW, Lukachukai; PP, SG).

Lamphere (East)

According to PM, the following method was employed in threshing corn. First a piece of canvas was spread on the ground; on this was placed a goatskin flesh side up, then the husked ears of corn. Finally another goatskin, flesh side down, was placed on the corn. This pile was then beaten with the flails until the kernels were detached.

Comparative

Both of Gifford's informants reported the shelling of corn by hand, and the Eastern informant added that an "awl" was used to loosen the kernels, or the corn was beaten with a stick. The frijole was also threshed on the ground, according to the Eastern informant; but the method was not specified. In both areas the work was done by women (Gifford, 1940:18).

There are two flails in the Harvard Peabody Museum collection. One, made from a dark, relatively hard wood, is some twenty-two inches long and slightly curved. In cross section it is triangular, two inches on a side. A leather thong is inserted through a hole in the rounded handle end. This flail was designated as a club, "Macena Para Natar" (collected by Grace Nicholson in 1912; see 41.a). Another specimen, used for threshing beans, is somewhat paddle-shaped (collected by Kidder and Guernsey in 1914 in the Kayenta region of Arizona; see 41.b).

Flails

41.a. Club, 1912   **41.b.** From Kayenta

42. Drying Platform and Frame

Ramah

A wooden platform some eight to twelve feet square and "high enough so you can load corn on" was constructed near the living area, where it could be protected from birds. Poles were placed across a framework, and "wheat" (probably straw) was strewn on it to keep the corn from falling through (see 42.1, 42.a). The framework was apparently supported by uprights at each corner. The height provided for the free circulation of air.

These platforms were made by men, and were used from one season to

42.1. Drying platform

42.a. Drying platform

the next; repairs were made when necessary. Women spread the corn to dry in the fall, after harvest.

Corn was also dried on a frame made of poles or ropes suspended between trees in the dwelling area. The corn was hung in bundles of ears tied together by the husks. Later, according to Inf. 7, the ears were laid on weeds spread on the ground. Inf. 9 said greasewood brush cut and spread on the ground as a bed for the ears of corn was used instead of the platform. Inf. 7 said that meat might be dried on a tripod.

Information was derived from Infs. 8, 9, and 7. Of the three, Inf. 8 is still using a platform, the only one definitely stated to be in the Ramah area. Information from Inf. 9 was derived from Inf. 134 (see Leighton and Leighton, 1949:79), and Inf. 7 gave only enough information to indicate a vague familiarity with the device. He admitted that the platforms were used, but not widely.

Hill (East, Central, and West)
According to Hill's informants, no special platform was built for drying corn; it was spread out on the roof of the sunshade or ramada. Informants also confirmed the drying of corn on the ground, bare rock, or brush (Hill, 1938:41).

Corn was also hung from a stringer to dry. Two forked sticks were erected and connected by a stringer. Husks were removed from the ears except at the base; then the husks of two ears were tied together and placed over the stringer (MH, Head Springs; SC, Crystal; PP, Fort Defiance). MH stated that the husks might be entirely removed and the ears tied together with cord and then placed over the stringer to dry. According to PP this was the correct way to dry seed corn, since it took less time.

Lamphere (East)
PM had never heard of a drying platform. She said that corn was dried on tumbleweeds or on the tops of houses. One might say of the second method that "the corn is lying in the sun at [against, or outside] my grandmother's house."

Fishler (West)
Fishler's informants described platforms similar to those at Ramah. Heights varied, but some were as high as five or more feet. These were used for drying not only unshelled corn, but beans and other vegetables, fruit, and meat. Peaches and apricots were cut open and dried. They were turned several times a day so they would dry thoroughly. TT (Coalmine) stated that buffalo meat was cut into long thin strips and placed on the platform. If it rained, produce and meat were brought into the hogan. When hunting, men built these platforms to dehydrate meat.

Comparative
Gifford's Western informant, but not the Eastern, confirmed drying corn on the roof of the shade. Both dried it in braids, which were hung up. Apparently neither group had platforms (Gifford, 1940:18, 102). Both groups sliced and dried meat; but the Plains type of drying frame was denied by the Eastern informant and the Western informant was not questioned (Gifford, 1940:16).

43. Dam   dádesẋin (Haile)   "mud wall" (CC)

Ramah

Simple dams for storing water for irrigation during the dry season, or for watering stock, were sometimes made of earth. Inf. 45 remembered helping to build such a dam as a boy. The site chosen was a small arroyo that had running water. Since they had no tools, the builders picked up lumps of earth and piled these one on the other. "It wasn't a very good dam that we made, but we stopped some water and we used the water a little of it, and then the dam was washed away."

A larger dam was made by Inf. 12, with the help of four other men. The main wall was constructed of earth, and behind this brush was piled. A rock spillway was constructed at one side of the dam to carry off excess water.

Men or boys built dams, in the summertime. The dam was apparently owned by those who made it. Those who helped Inf. 12 with his dam agreed that they would share the water. Therefore they asked to feed themselves; if Inf. 12 had fed them, his action might be considered payment for their work.

Dams are built at present. In 1941 Inf. 9 built a small dam, and Landgraf observed five check dams near Inf. 45's place. These were not very substantial, and all had been partially washed out by the last heavy rain.

Hill (East, Central, and West)

Land was prepared for planting in one of several ways. Formerly, seed was planted in land inundated by floods or runoff. Later, dikes were sometimes built across arroyos to deflect the water and hold it on the fields, thus insuring a thorough soaking. This type of irrigation was widespread and probably became prevalent during the mid-nineteenth century. The Navaho believe that it was copied from the Pueblos, and TLHO (area unknown) specified Jemez (Hill, 1938:24; see also Bryan, 1929:444–456).

TLLSS (Crownpoint) described dikes that were built across arroyos, as at Ramah. The earth was transported in buckskins, and as it was laid brush was added to prevent erosion. When completed, the top of the dam conveyed the water to diversion dikes in the fields. The construction of dams was a communal effort. TLLSS had known only one such dam prior to Fort Sumner. WP (Canoncito) associated diversion dikes with the introduction of the iron hoe after Fort Sumner.

Comparative

The Navaho began impounding water at an early date. The deponents of the Rabal documents (1706–1743) described water holes dammed with sand dikes (Hill, 1940a:402, 404). No remains of dams have been reported in connection with archaeological material, however, probably because construction was such that they were soon washed away.

Information from the nineteenth-century travelers is scanty. Simpson stated that he saw no evidence of irrigation in 1849 (Simpson, 1852:53, from Hill, 1938:25). Letherman in 1855 said that some of the localities did irrigate, and Bandelier in 1880 confirmed this, although he did not acknowledge his source (Letherman, 1856:288; Bandelier, 1890–1892:176). In August 1881 Bourke (1884:73) was shown a dam in eastern Arizona, near Hopi country, built by the Navaho for watering their sheep. "A little cleft in the rocks" was dammed by branches of trees, stones, and mud.

The Franciscan Fathers (1910:49, 264) also reported dams for impounding water for stock and for irrigation. Small banks were thrown up around fields near available water, such as the Little Colorado and San Juan Rivers, Tseili, Whiskey, Chinle, and other creeks and arroyos. Permanent dams and reservoirs were not very common. Gregory (1916:104) also reported the fairly extensive use of dams. Diversion dikes were built, a few inches to a foot or more high. Check dams in arroyos were built fifty to two hundred feet apart, and two to five feet high.

According to Gifford (1940:16–17), the Eastern Navaho had the dam; but the Western Navaho lacked it and relied on natural flooding for irrigation.

A vivid account of the technology and requirements of post–Fort Sumner Navaho farming is given by Old Mexican in his autobiography, which includes a number of references to the part played by dams and irrigation ditches. His description of building a temporary dam to prevent overflooding a field coincides with that of Hill's informants, except that the dam was constructed of brush and poles, on top of which he plastered mud. A big dam was subsequently built below the temporary one (Dyk, 1947:69).

According to the Navaho origin legend, the descendants of First Man and First Woman built a dam to irrigate their farm (Matthews, 1897:70).

44. Ditch

tˣo xa·gʸe·d *or* tˣôigʸe·d (Lamphere, Franciscan Fathers)

"digging out water" (CC)

Hill (East, Central, and West)
In addition to flood water irrigation and the use of dams, irrigation ditches were used. According to informants they were introduced after the return from Fort Sumner (Hill, 1938:24–25).

Lamphere (East)
Both PM and EP confirmed the word for ditch given by the Franciscan Fathers (1910:264).

Fishler (West)
GB and his father, while at Fort Defiance, built a ditch two to three miles long from the government reservoir. When they finished, all used it, even though they had not helped in the construction.

Comparative
This trait is merely listed by the Franciscan Fathers. It is called a "ditch" (Franciscan Fathers, 1910:264). The term is confirmed by Haile (1951:89).

Guernsey in 1914 observed near Mitchell's Butte (near Monument Valley, Arizona) "trenches built at intervals across the orchard (peach) to hold back any water that might fall from the cliffs" (Guernsey, 1914:21). Ditches to divert excess water from the fields were confirmed by both of Gifford's informants (Gifford, 1940:16–17).

Old Mexican described the digging of his own ditch. He refused assistance or food from other men whom he had helped, because "they might ask me

44.a. Digging the diversion channel for a dam

for a piece of the land after I have finished the ditch." To test the gradient, he used a spirit level borrowed from a white trader, but this usually was done by letting some water run through the ditch. Some years later (1902) he dug a ditch in twenty days, "straight, even when trees were in the way." One of his ditches—possibly this one—was two miles long (Dyk, 1947:35, 68, 70).

According to the Navaho origin legend, an irrigation ditch was built in connection with the dam (Matthews, 1897:70; see also Trait 43).

45. Well

tˣó báxá·o·λin (Haile)   "walled up for water"

tˣóha·λi (Lamphere)   "water coming up"; "taking water out" (CC)

tˣóha·snil (Lamphere)   "water standing there"; "water already out" (CC)

Ramah

Wells were made by digging down about eight feet to the water level and walling the sides of the hole with a crude dry masonry. The mouth, which was left uncovered, was about four feet in diameter, and slightly raised above the surface of the ground because of the earth thrown out in excavating.

A hoist was sometimes built for lifting water. Two posts were set on either side of the mouth of the well, and a beam was placed across these. A bucket was suspended by a rope and pulley from the center of the beam.

This type of well was seen in 1937 by Tschopik, near Inf. 2's hogans. Wells were also dug in the fields. A well of the same dimensions as those given above was built for Inf. 6 (see Leighton and Leighton, 1949:58–59). According to Inf. 9, four men (Infs. 6, 9, 27, 45) worked for two days before they reached the water table. It was six days before the well was completed.

45.a. Well; note pitched basket bottles (Tr. 82), bow (Tr. 15), and arrows (Tr. 19)

Although a number of men often worked together in the construction of a well, the owner was apparently the person upon whose land it was located. Those who helped dig the well, and possibly other neighbors as well, had the right to use it. The owner might expect them to help keep the well clean.

It is not known when the Ramah Navaho began to build wells, or from whom they borrowed the idea; but well building is presumably a modern trait, as is the pulley. Vogt was told by Inf. 7 that the Navaho were the first to dig a well at Nutria, and that they used to farm the land around Ramah before they were sent to Fort Sumner. "We moved around from place to place searching for wells and grazing land" (Vogt, unpublished data). The Indian Service has constructed a number of wells with windmills for pumping water. Most families have no immediate access to a well, and haul their drinking water from government tanks or springs which may be some miles away. In some few cases they have access to the wells or tanks of white neighbors. In several instances springs have been cleaned to insure a better supply (Infs. 7, 86, 84, 153). Inf. 16 depends upon cisterns in the rocks near his fields; whether these are artificial or natural, however, is not known. In winter, the Navaho gather snow and melt it over a fire.

Hill (Central)
Pits were excavated in the floors of washes. Such storage devices were supplied either by running water after rains or by subsoil seepage (LM, Canyon del Muerto; LW, Lukachukai). These were in use in Canyon del Muerto in 1933.

Lamphere (East)
EP said that the word for well meant "water coming up." PM said a well meant "water standing there."

Comparative

According to the Franciscan Fathers (1910:49), cisterns and wells were not made. Their informants confirmed Hill's storage pits and the melting of snow in the winter. To insure purity, the hogan was built at some distance from the water supply. No word was recorded for a well until later. Haile (1951:317) has recorded the term translated above as "walled up for water," indicating a specific well below Hopi down the valley from Polacca, also others (Haile, 1950:109). Both of Gifford's informants stated that snow was melted for drinking and cooking water, but the well was not mentioned (Gifford, 1940:14).

Animal Husbandry

46. Water Trough cin bi·ˑ xaˑoˑcéˑl (Ramah, Haile)   log trough; "wood it's hollowed out" (CC)

Ramah

Troughs for watering stock or for storing drinking water were made from logs. These were about two and one half feet long and six to eight inches wide and deep. They were made only by men. They are now common in the Ramah area, and were reported near the hogans of Infs. 16, 53, 109, 139, and 4027. In 1941 the Leightons saw a stone trough similar to the wooden ones in the Two Wells area. This had been made by Inf. 36's grandfather.

Although they probably date from before the beginning of the twentieth century, water troughs are a recent and borrowed trait. Their exact derivation is not known.

Comparative

The name for the log trough given by the Franciscan Fathers (1910:269) and by Haile (1951:185) confirms that from Ramah. Although other references are lacking, it is improbable that water troughs occur only in the Ramah area.

47. Corral ·ił názti· (Haile)   fence; "circle of boughs"

Ramah

Brush, barbed wire, or railing corrals were common features of almost every establishment and many of the Ramah people now enclose their fields with one or a combination of these materials. According to Inf. 45, a half mile of brush fencing could be made in a day. These fences are still common in remote regions of the reservation such as Navaho Mountain (see Kluckhohn and Leighton, 1946:30), and Roberts has illustrated a brush circle for goats and sheep (Roberts, 1951:fig. 2, HC-2). He has also noted that "horse corrals

II. Sheep corral (Tr. 47) in Monument Valley. Goats and sheep are herded together.

77

were invariably associated with the more permanent habitations." An enclosure for the storage of feed was often built in connection with the corrals. In addition, two pig pens and six barns, one of which was built under the same roof as the family dwelling, were also noted for the Ramah area (Roberts, 1951:41).

Hill (East, Central, and West)

Sheep and goat corrals (see Plates II and III) were prevailingly circular in form and there was general agreement among informants that the earlier forms were made of brush; TLLSS (Crownpoint) said brush corrals were built before Fort Sumner. He said that the animals were corralled every night, and that sometimes timbers were placed on the brush to fall and wake the owners if an attempt were made to steal the sheep or goats. According to GH (White Cone), the sheep dogs always slept in the corral with the animals (see Trait 52, Chicken and Turkey Pens).

In a frequent variation of the circular corral, the face of a cliff was utilized for one section. This obviated the necessity of collecting much material for construction and afforded protection from wind and rain.

At lambing time, ewes who rejected their lambs were placed with them in small corrals (PP, Fort Defiance; SG, Keams Canyon). The same was true for goats. Corrals were also built if necessary when a Blessing Way was held over the sheep, and this special corral was blessed (PP).

Informants agreed that corrals formed of upright pickets or posts were a comparatively recent innovation (RH, Crystal; OTKM, Manuelito; SG). Presumably they were coincident with the introduction of the axe.

Comparative

Circular corrals of upright posts set side by side near the hogan were confirmed by the Franciscan Fathers (1910:335). Stables for horses or cattle were not built. Their term for the "permanent corral" (*anazti*) resembles that given by Haile to indicate the brush corral. According to Haile, the term for corral is hogan, with a prefix to indicate whose home it is.

Both of Gifford's informants confirmed the "circular enclosure of boughs (corral)" but his Western informant stated that it was for a hunters' encampment (Gifford, 1940:23, 110).

Coolidge (1930:61–62) also noted the use of brush corrals, particularly during April and May, the lambing season. These were built as near water as possible, and were surrounded by smaller brush pens for ewes and lambs abandoned by their mothers.

48. Snow Drag   cin ná·lʒo·di (Lamphere)   "branch, wood, dragging" (CC)

Ramah

To clear the ground of snow for the sheep, two pinyon trunks were tied together and made fast to a singletree. They were dragged around by a team of horses. Inf. 90 used a drag during a heavy snow in 1942. He is the only one known to have used this device, and it is possible that it is his invention.

Lamphere (East)

PM said that the snow drag was made from any kind of wood. Limbs were cut and the branches removed. A framework consisting of three logs placed across another pair was then constructed. This framework was dragged across the ground to remove the snow. A similar device was used to smooth the field after plowing.

Comparative

According to the Franciscan Fathers (1910:257), pinyon and juniper branches were cut off for the sheep to graze on when the snow was deep. There are no other references.

49. Ram Apron   ɫe·sco·z (Lamphere)   "loincloth" (CC)

Hill (Central and West)

Buckskin thongs or cords were attached to the corners of rectangular sections of cloth, preferably canvas. These aprons were tied beneath the bellies of rams to prevent them breeding except during the desired season (MH, Head Springs; PP, Fort Defiance).

Lamphere (East)

PM said that the word for ram apron was the same as that for breechcloth.

Comparative

There is no information on this trait. According to the Franciscan Fathers, there was much room for improvement in Navaho methods of sheep raising, although by 1910 the Navaho were beginning to herd their animals separately (Franciscan Fathers, 1910:257–258). Reichard (1936:10, 11) denied the separate herding but Roberts (1951:32) stated that males were herded separately.

50. Sheep Shears   bé·š ·axédiɫi· be· tˣádígʸéši· (Haile)   "metal, with it you do shearing" (CC)

Ramah

Shearing was done with ordinary sheep shears. Power shears were known, but infrequently used (Roberts, 1951:32).

Hill (East, Central, and West)

According to RH (Crystal), a smith pounded a piece of iron into butcher-knife shape. The shearer kept a whetstone handy during the shearing, which was done by pulling the wool tight and sawing it off. TLLSS (Crownpoint) also said that shearing was done with a knife. Other informants (PP, Fort Defiance; SG, Keams Canyon; OTKM, Manuelito; IS, Lukachukai) agreed that sections of tin cans were often used to saw off wool (see 50.a).

50.a. Shearing knife made from a tin can

Comparative

Welsh (1885:25) found the method of shearing sheep among the Navaho "crude, wasteful, and barbarous in the extreme." It was done with a case knife, a piece of tin, or any instrument that could be whetted on a piece of sandstone. Wool was hacked off rather than clipped, with the result that the sheep was sheared unevenly.

According to the Franciscan Fathers (1910:257–258), shearing was done with commercial shears in the fall and after the spring storms. Coolidge (1930:62) noted that "a rich owner may hire as many as thirty or forty shearers, each one bringing his own shears."

51. Kennel

łį· ho·γe·d (Lamphere) "dog, storage; dog garage" (CC); dog run

łį·čą·i biγan (Lamphere) "dog, its house" (CC)

Hill (Central and West)
An oblong pit was excavated with an incline at one end running from the ground level to the bottom of the pit. With the exception of the incline the excavation was roofed with poles covered with earth. Juniper bark bedding was placed in the bottom of the pit and it was ready for occupancy (AS, Lukachukai). GH (White Cone) said that such a pit was not roofed over. PP (Fort Defiance) said that herders and children often built small brush houses for their dogs.

A doghouse of stone and earth, a variation of that above, was in use at Coalmine in 1934. Presumably such structures were innovations since they were lacking in most of the areas.

Lamphere (East)
PM gave the first word for kennel (above), which she called "dog run." EP said that it was called "dog house."

Comparative
Both Gifford's informants confirmed the keeping of dogs as pets (Gifford, 1940:20), as did the Franciscan Fathers (1910:142–143), but no mention was made of kennels.

52. Chicken and Turkey Pens

nahóxai biγan (Lamphere) chicken house

tˣąži· biγan (Lamphere) turkey house

Ramah
A number of Ramah informants (Infs. 12, 21, 32) said that wild turkeys were formerly caught and kept in pens "in the type now used for chickens." These were presumably of the type observed at Inf. 34's place by the Leightons. Seven families were known to have chicken houses between 1937 and 1949, but the chicken house does not seem to have been a prevalent structure.

Lamphere (East)
PM and EP said that these structures would be called either chicken houses or turkey houses.

Comparative

According to the Franciscan Fathers (1910:162), the "Navaho do not raise chickens, nor do they, as a rule, eat eggs." Turkeys and the use of turkey feathers were frequently mentioned, but nothing was said of pens or cages. Gifford's Eastern informant said that wild turkeys were caught when young and successfully raised in cages, which were probably domed willow cages (Gifford, 1940:20–21, 106–107). Chickens were seen running free around Thoreau (L. Kluckhohn, 1960, 1962).

53. Eagle Cage

Ramah

Kluckhohn observed that young eagles were raised in captivity to obtain feathers for ceremonial purposes. The type of cage was not stated (see Trait 4, Eagle Pit).

Hill (East, Central, and West)

Cages for captive eagles were usually made of poles. These were cribwork structures with a diameter of about four feet and a height of five; they converged slightly toward the top. The roof consisted of horizontal poles. Perches were placed inside the cage to prevent the eagles from soiling their feathers on the ground (TLLSS, Crownpoint; OTKM, Manuelito). C (Chinle) stated that the cage consisted of a circular rock wall roofed with poles. A perch was made by inserting a pole between the rocks; the eagle was tethered to the perch.

According to MH (Head Springs) and OTKM, a simple platform of poles was erected in a tree and the eagle tied to it. SG (Keams Canyon) stated that eagles were merely tethered to a log.

K (Black Mountain) said that feathers were plucked and the eagles freed when they were full grown. He said that only Coyote Pass clan members were allowed to raise eaglets (Hill, 1938:165).

Comparative

Informants of the Franciscan Fathers stated that eagles were not kept, but were released after the necessary feathers had been plucked (Franciscan Fathers, 1910:157, 477). This practice was confirmed by both of Gifford's informants, who agreed that eagles were not caged. The Eastern informant said that eagles were tied to a log in the nest until they were old enough to be plucked and released. He confirmed the domed willow cage, but did not specify the occupant (Gifford, 1940:20, 106).

Horse Equipment

54. Bridle and Bit

·azá·ti·í (Haile) "horse mouth rein" (CC)

Ramah

Although both men and women used bridles, Inf. 7 said that men usually made them. He did not know whether women could make bridles. Inf. 128

has a silver bridle which belonged to his grandfather (Inf. 265) and was made by Inf. 148. A silver bridle was part of the bride price paid by Inf. 9 for his first wife. At present, the majority of bridles are purchased through the trading stores, rather than made by hand.

Hill (Central and West)

Prior to the introduction of iron bits, horses were guided with rope bridles. A loop was made in the rope (a woolen rope, according to RH, Crystal) and was placed over the lower jaw of the animal, the knot on the underside. The ends of the rope served as reins (RH; PP, Fort Defiance; SG, Keams Canyon). PP denied the use of the hackamore.

The Spanish bit was still extant but rarely used in 1933 and 1934. PP had one such bit with a silver-mounted headstall. IS (Lukachukai) stated that he had seen bits made from horseshoes and other scrap iron. Bits used by women had a connecting bar across the bottom to which spangles were attached. These were lacking in men's bits.

Fishler (West)

TN (Kaibito) had heard of the use of the rope bridle in the early days, but he had never seen one.

Comparative

Palmer (1869:95) commented that the Navaho bridle, "which consists of a rein attached to the lower jaw, is very hard on the animal." A rope looped over the nose of the horse also served as a bridle without a bit (Franciscan Fathers, 1910:150, 281). According to Sapir and Hoijer (1942:423), in 1929 a young man near Crystal said the bridle was made of slender pieces of goatskin tied together and braided into a cylindrical form. Bits were made from metal acquired from the Mexicans. Adair (1944:42–43) also confirmed the frequent use of braided buckskin bridles.

Most of the other references in the literature pertain to the silver-mounted bridle. The Navaho were known to have them as early as 1824, as evidenced by an article in the *Missouri Intelligencer* of that year, which described leather bridles "embellished with silver ornaments" (*Missouri Intelligencer,* April 3, 1824, p. 3; reference from Woodward, 1938:50). By 1885 the Navaho were making bridles and metal bits; according to Davis (1857:412), there were several native blacksmiths in the Navaho territory. In 1864 a correspondent of a weekly newspaper stated that the Navaho "warriors" could make bridles; and in 1865 Herrero, regarded by Woodward as the first Navaho silversmith, said that he worked in iron and made bridle bits (Woodward, 1938:16–17, 53). A picture published by Whipple and Ives (1854:31) shows a fringed bit. Letherman (1856:292) described a bit with a ring attached to it through which the lower jaw of the horse was partly thrust; the bridle was decorated with small pieces of steel attached to the bit. He added that the Navaho were excellent judges of the purity of the silver used. Bourke, in 1881, noted that the silver-mounted bridle had "no throat latch" (Bourke, 1936:238).

The Franciscan Fathers (1910:150, 281) confirmed the type of bit noted by Letherman, and added that it was made by native smiths from old horseshoes and iron scraps (see 54.1). By 1910 bits and headstalls were usually purchased at the stores.

54.a. Silver-mounted bridle

54.b. Bridle and bit

A good description of the Navaho bridle is included in Adair's study of Navaho silversmithing (1944). His informant reported that Atsidi Sani was the first Navaho to work silver and iron, and that he had learned how from a Mexican. He wanted to learn so that the Navaho would buy their bridles from him, rather than from the Mexicans. Adair's informant, from the vicinity of Ganado, stated that he had formerly made silver-mounted bridles, and that at that time every Navaho who could afford one had such a bridle. But now, he said, they were rarely seen (Adair, 1944:4, 8).

Headstalls were ornamented with silver secured by copper loops, and seven to thirteen closely fitting pieces of silver encased the straps. A concha was placed on each side. An ornament like the crescent necklace pendants was suspended from a small metal loop on the central silver piece on the head-strap. The crescent was called *najahe*. A fringe of metal loops was often attached to the bit (Adair, 1944:41; see also Mera, 1944b).

The early bridle designs were very plain, according to Adair (1944:42–43). A specimen in the Laboratory of Anthropology, Santa Fe, he suggested, might date as far back as 1875. Later bridles were marked with dies; still later they were sometimes set with turquoise. Silver-mounted bridles are infrequently seen at present, except on the pawn racks of the trading posts, where they are held as collateral.

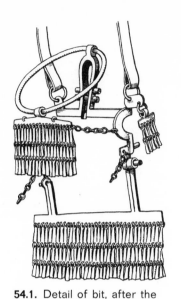

54.1. Detail of bit, after the Franciscan Fathers

55. Saddle

ʼaxasilahi (Ramah, Hill) "lying side by side"

łį·· biɣé·l (Hill) "horse load"

Ramah

The old type of saddle was "just something laid over the horse, so there was no saddle horn to it, no back piece to it. All they had was stirrup and cinch. They could fold up a blanket or whatever they had and sit on top of that" (Inf. 12).

The "Indian saddle" described by Inf. 9 consisted of a wooden tree covered with rawhide. He had one made for his wife by a man who knew how to make this particular type. He paid one saddle horse and supplied the leather. In 1939 Inf. 256 purchased a saddle from Inf. 34, who said it was "an old Indian saddle" that he had acquired from Inf. 16, who had had it for "years and years." According to Inf. 12, when the materials were prepared, it took about a week to make a saddle. He learned to make saddles from his father and could still make them.

A pregnant woman was not allowed to work on a saddle, according to Inf. 3, nor was her husband, according to Inf. 48, because saddles were cut and notched. If they did, the baby would be born with a hair lip.

At present, most of the Ramah Navaho use saddles obtained from the trading post.

Hill (Central and West)

The saddle was called "lying side by side" or "horse load." The simplest and, according to RH (Crystal) and PP (Fort Defiance), oldest type of saddle consisted of two cylinders, about eighteen inches long and four inches in diameter (PP), fastened together by strips of hide. Cylinders were made of

Pommels, after Hill

55.1. For woman's saddle

55.2. For man's saddle

55.3. For man's saddle

55.4. For man's saddle; slits (*y*) show cuts for quarter straps

55.5. Cantle, after Hill; slits (*x*) show cuts for quarter straps

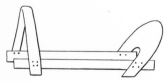

55.6. Assembled saddletree, after Hill

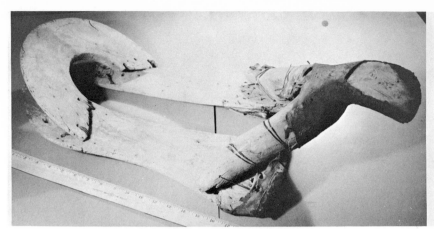

55.a. Wooden saddletree covered with leather (wire added to hold fragments together)

dressed horsehide (PP), cowhide (RH), and stuffed with cliff rose bark (PP), juniper bark (RH), deer or antelope hair. They were moistened before packing, the hair or bark pounded tightly into the container with a stick, and the opening stitched together. The constriction of the hide in drying insured that the filler would be even more tightly packed.

The cylinders were placed about six inches apart and three strips of horsehide (two strips from the ventral section of a cowhide, RH) were secured to them by thongs. The widest and longest strip was in the center, and a cinch strap was attached to one end, the cinch to the other. Saddles with two cinch straps were unusual at this early period (PP). RH stated that the cinch was of wool, the cinch ring of oak bent in circular form and covered with buckskin. He added that stirrup straps were attached to the cylinders, and stirrups made from bent sections of oak were tied to the straps.

According to RH, "Every time a Navaho saw a Spanish or Mexican horse they would remember the equipment and copy it. That is the kind of saddle that was later made." Modern saddles for men and women were distinguished by the pommels. Those for women were equipped with a broad flat horn on which the cradle might be rested (see 55.1). The pommel of the men's saddle was oval and lacked the horn; otherwise construction was identical.

The saddletree consisted of four parts, made from pinyon or cottonwood (PP), or pinyon (SG, Keams Canyon). According to SG, a forked branch was selected for the pommel of a woman's saddle, but the base was carved to make the horn. According to PP, forked branches were prone to split and when possible the pommel of a woman's saddle was fashioned from a single block of wood. For the man's pommel a branch with a curve conforming as nearly as possible to the desired shape was selected. Some variation in shape was allowed for men (see 55.2, 55.3, 55.4). The limbs were cut and scraped to shape. The diameter in the pommel area was about an inch and a half, the legs about three inches wide.

The cantle was shaped from a second curved limb (see 55.5). The legs were about three inches across, and the width varied. Two lengths of pinyon (or cottonwood, PP) three inches wide formed the sides of the saddletree. Four to six holes were burned through the ends of each piece with a hot wire.

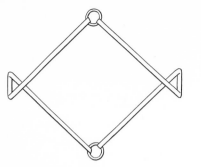

55.7. Quarter straps, top view as if attached

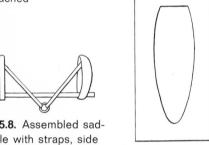

55.8. Assembled saddle with straps, side view

55.9. Skirt, after Hill

55.10. Stirrup pattern; kerf lines marked *x*

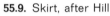

55.11. Assembling stirrup; kerf lines marked *x*; joints, where dowels are inserted, marked *y*

The ends of the pommel and cantle were tapered to insure a snug fit for the side boards, and grooves were cut between holes so that the lashings would be flush with the outside surface. Lashings were either single or double and were tied on the inside (SG). According to PP, either lashings or wooden dowels might be used.

When the saddletree was assembled (see 55.6), it was covered with wet rawhide. The hide was cut and pieced to insure a snug fit; it covered all parts of the wood. As it dried the seams were pounded to remove unevennesses. Pairs of three-inch slits were cut on the inside of the pommel (see *y* on 55.4) and cantle (see *x* on 55.5), and sticks were placed in these to prevent their closing as the hide dried. Quarter straps about three inches wide were run through the openings, crossed, and joined by rings (see 55.7, 55.8). PP said the quarter straps might also be nailed to the tree. Cinch straps were attached to the quarter strap rings, and passed through the cinch rings when the horse was saddled (PP, SG).

A skirt was fitted to the underside of the saddletree. It covered the area which came in contact with the horse and prevented the animal being galled by the frame. A rectangular piece of hide (later leather) from which the center section was removed (see 55.9) was secured by buckskin or saddle strings. A second strip of hide or leather ran under the center of the saddletree, one end of which was brought over the outside of the cantle and nailed or screwed to the inside near the top. On a man's saddle, the other end was passed under the pommel, brought up and over and secured at the inside top. On a woman's saddle, the strip was slit near the end and secured by the horn.

With the addition of stirrups these saddles were considered usable, and many Navaho merely threw a dressed skin or blanket on the seat for additional comfort and rode them. If material were available, however, several additions were made. A second skirt similar to the first was placed to cover the sides in front of the pommel and back of the cantle. Those sections extending beyond the pommel and the cantle were further covered with transverse strips, the rear one often equipped with pockets. Finally, a leather covering was placed over the whole tree, secured on the sides by saddle strings and along the cantle and pommel by brass studs. Occasionally the covering was stamped to heighten the aesthetic value of the saddle (PP).

Stirrup straps, either double or single, were secured to the side boards of the saddletree. The stirrups were made of oak and pinyon. A piece of green pinyon three feet long and six to eight inches in diameter was split and shaped (see 55.10) and kerfs were cut (lines marked *x* on 55.10). The board was heated and the sides bent up along the kerf lines; the inside angle was slightly less than ninety degrees. A fork of a tree was used instead of a vise. Next a piece of oak, left in the round, was kerfed and bent in the same manner; this was gauged to fit over the top of the stirrup shoe. It rode in the loop of the stirrup strap. The top was attached to the shoe by pairs of dowels (three cottonwood dowels, according to SG) inserted at the joint (see points marked *y* on 55.11). Finally the stirrups were covered with wet rawhide, seamed on the inside, and allowed to dry (PP, SG). Tapaderos were not used by the Navaho (PP).

These saddles were current among the Navaho in 1933 and 1934. Western stock saddles were also used, but these were purchased, not made locally. The Navaho were weaving both double and single saddle blankets and using them in 1933 and 1934.

Comparative

An illustration published in 1854 indicates that the Navaho were using saddles, although the details are not clear (Whipple and Ives, 1854:vol. IV, pl. 23). Davis (1857:412) stated that the tribe at that time made its own saddles, bridles, bits, and stirrups. Newcomb (1940a:39) stated that all work on saddles was done by men.

Both types mentioned by Hill's informants were confirmed in the literature. According to Palmer (1869:95), the first type consisted of two rolls stuffed with straw, covered with deer or antelope skin; rawhide was used for the girth and stirrups. Wool was used for stuffing according to Bourke in 1881, and from the saddle hung "two leather straps terminating in flat, wooden, Turkish stirrups" (Bourke, 1936:236). Worcester (1945:139) confirmed the use of animal hair, and stirrups of wool or rope. According to Wissler (1915:31), these stirrups and saddles were of the Shoshonean type.

Letherman (1856:292) observed Navaho saddles of the Mexican type, and noted that the stirrup was short, and placed farther to the front than on a Mexican saddle. Palmer (1869:95) also confirmed the Navaho imitation of the Mexican saddle, and said that hard ash was the material used. The description of the manufacture of a Navaho saddle published by the Franciscan Fathers (1910:148–149) agreed with that by Hill. The Franciscan Fathers noted that by 1910 the old box stirrups had been replaced by iron ones; girths were usually purchased, but some were woven of yarn and plaited with horsehair. Saddle blankets were, "of course, of native fabric." A weave of diamond-shaped figures was most often used for this purpose. The blanket was called "that which is put up on something" (*akidah iinilii*) (see also Haile, 1950:22, and 1951:252). By 1910 American saddles were much in demand, and were replacing the older style.

Hill's description was also confirmed by Sapir and Hoijer's informant. Stirrups were called "the foot is in it" (*biideeseez*) and the girth was made of woven wool. The saddle was finished when a sheep's hide was sewn under it (Sapir and Hoijer, 1942:421–423).

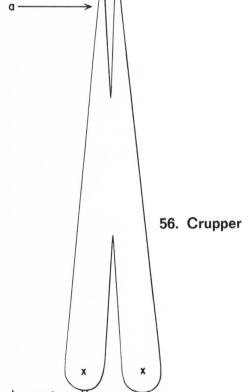

56. Crupper

bitsâ ᵓâtíꞏgi (Franciscan Fathers)   crupper (includes crupper and belt attached to rear of saddle)

Hill (Central and West)

Cruppers were called "suspended." Leather was cut to the appropriate pattern (see 56.1) and the crupper, a roll of soft leather (*b* on 56.1), was sewn to it. The area at the back (*x, x* on 56.1) was usually decorated by designs stamped in the leather, or by the addition of brass studs.

A crupper was used to prevent the saddle from slipping forward. It was placed under the saddle and above the saddle blanket. The ends (*a* on 56.1) were tied to the pommel. The crupper proper passed under the tail of the horse. Cruppers were considered a part of the women's horse equipment, but were occasionally used by men (PP, Fort Defiance; SG, Keams Canyon).

56.1. Crupper pattern, after Hill; ends (*a*) were tied to the pommel and the leather roll (*b*) was passed under the tail of the horse; *x* marks areas of design

Comparative

According to the Franciscan Fathers (1910:148), the crupper, "which in the early days was connected to the rear of the saddle by a wide belt of rawhide, has almost entirely disappeared." It does not appear to be noted elsewhere in the literature.

57. Quirt

be·ec^xis (Haile, Lamphere) "whip for horses" (CC)

Ramah
Quirts were made of cowhide, horsehair, and wood. Until his death in 1942, Inf. 16 made cowhide quirts, and Inf. 12 said he knew how to braid them. Whether any others knew how is unknown. Quirts are now used in the Ramah area, but whether they are made or purchased is not known.

Hill (Central and West)
Quirts were considered an essential part of the riding equipment. The oldest form of quirt was fashioned from a single strip of rawhide, bent double and knotted just below the bend. The knot formed the grip, the two loose ends the lash (SG, Keams Canyon).

According to SG, four-ply braided quirts were a later innovation. The lash varied in type. A single or double strip was inserted at the base of the stock, or all or half of the plaiting elements were knotted at the base, the free ends forming the lash. Most quirts of this type were equipped with a wrist thong.

PP (Fort Defiance) described several variants of braided leather quirts. One was round in diameter, braided in four ply around a leather filler. Others were made in twelve ply and square four ply. Lashes were inserted or formed from plaiting elements.

Lamphere (East)
PM confirmed the word for quirt, which could be made of buckskin or cowhide.

Fishler (West)
When quirts were made, "live" eagle feathers were sometimes included in the plaiting in order that the horse would win races. A few Navaho still own these (FG, Coalmine).

Comparative
Although by 1910 quirts and ropes could be obtained at the trading posts, many Navaho were skilled in plaiting them. According to the Franciscan Fathers (1910:314), a bone or hardwood awl was the only implement used in braiding. Rawhide was plaited around a stick, which was removed after the quirt was dry, and a wrist thong was put through the loop. By 1910, "black or tanned leather strips" were being used, as many as sixteen for large quirts. These were plaited around a center of twisted rawhide, which was often wound with cord. The ends were concealed, and the grip ended in a plaited knot and a wrist thong. "A very attractive quirt of alternating white, red, and black horsehair" was occasionally made for sale. Sapir and Hoijer (1942:423) confirmed whips braided of cowhide.

58. Chaps

ʾakaˑł ƛaˑžiˑeˑ (Lamphere)   "pants set in a circle"

ʾakaˑł ƛaˑkaˑł (Lamphere)   "skirt set in a circle"

xadiˑłžiʾí (Haile)   "slipped on"

Ramah
Chaps are worn in the Ramah area, and Inf. 4415 was seen wearing them in 1949; further information is lacking.

Hill (Central)
Leather chaps are of recent introduction, and are purchased at neighboring white communities. They are not manufactured by the Navaho (PP, Fort Defiance).

Lamphere (East)
PM called chaps by the terms above, meaning either "pants set in a circle," or "skirt set in a circle."

Comparative
This trait was not mentioned by the Franciscan Fathers (1910), but Haile (1950:164; 1951:47) listed a term for chaps. The Navaho term is also applied to the woman's dress, coveralls, one-piece underwear, and a Franciscan's habit. The term refers to that which is "slipped on" the body.

59. Pack Saddle

ɫíˑˑ biɣéˑl ʾałná ʾiˑˑáhígíˑ (Haile)   "saddle crossed for carrying" (CC)

Ramah
There is no information on this trait. Dog packing was denied by Inf. 7, as was the travois.

Hill (Central)
Pack saddles (see 59.1) were not made by the Navaho but were obtained in trade from the Mexicans (PP, Fort Defiance). Their use seems to have been limited. Occasionally burros were packed, and accompanied the herds of sheep to the mountain pastures. The informant had never heard of dog packing or the use of the travois.

Comparative
According to the Franciscan Fathers (1910:149), the pack saddle was not much used since "light transportation, such as of wool, flour, or eatables," was done with the ordinary saddle.

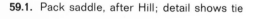

59.1. Pack saddle, after Hill; detail shows tie

60. Skin Saddlebag

ʾabaniˑazis (Ramah)   "deerskin bag" (CC)

Ramah
A bag, about three feet long by a foot and a half wide, was constructed from a rectangular piece of buckskin. The neck was tied with a thong. Either men or women made such a bag.

For transporting goods on horseback these bags were tied to the saddle strings in front and behind. They were also used for carrying burdens on the back. It is quite possible that Inf. 7, the sole informant, had never seen these in use, for they were replaced by blanket bags. None are known in the Ramah area today.

Hill (East and West)

The dressed skin of a deer or elk was trimmed along the sides and laid on the ground. The head and tail sections were folded so as to meet in the center of the hide. Seams closed the sides, and were sewn across part of the head and tail sections. The seams began at the edge, but did not meet in the center, and formed a constricted opening for both compartments of the saddlebag (GH, White Cone; see 60.1). Dressed sheepskins were trimmed, folded longitudinally, and sewn across each end. The open edge was sewn part way toward the center as above (TLLSS, Crownpoint).

Saddlebags were used for transport; they were thrown over the back of the horse (GH, TLLSS).

Comparative

Letherman (1856:288) noted that the only mode of transportation of goods used by the Navaho was buckskin bags on horses. Gifford's Eastern informant affirmed a type of bag similar to that described by Hill. He said it was made of buckskin, not rawhide, and that before the Navaho had horses, the bags were carried over the shoulder. The Western informant knew nothing of such containers (Gifford, 1940:42, 134).

Saddlebags and cantinas were usually added to modern saddles by 1910, and "buckskin saddlebags, studded with white beads (which are purchased from the Utes)" were a part of ritual paraphernalia (Franciscan Fathers, 1910:149, 372).

When such bags were first used by the Navaho is not known, but considerable antiquity may be inferred from data from Inf. 7 at Ramah and Gifford's Eastern informant. Whether they are still used, or whether they have been replaced by saddlebags and gunnysacks purchased from traders, is not known.

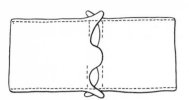

60.1. Skin saddlebag, after Hill

61. Woven Saddlebag

na·kai· bičidí (Ramah)   "Mexican's car"

Ramah

A large blanket was woven on the regular loom. When completed it was about the size of the Pendleton blanket. It was spread out and the material to be packed placed at the ends. The blanket was then folded over the contents and the ends bunched and tied (see 61.1).

For packing goods on horseback, it was thrown over the seat of the saddle, never in front or behind. Anyone could use this device, and Inf. 8 said that any blanket could be used. Inf. 7 said that no regular saddlebags were utilized and that blankets were a substitute for double saddlebags. According to Inf. 8, permanence was difficult to determine, since a heavy load might tear the blanket. At the death of the owner these blankets were either buried with the dead or burned.

Since woven blankets of Navaho make are seldom used in the Ramah area,

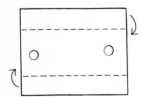

61.1. Woven saddlebag, after Tschopik; arrows indicate direction of fold

except as saddle blankets, it is improbable that saddlebags are specially woven. Blankets (not necessarily Navaho woven) are still used for saddle packing if a sack is not available (Inf. 8).

Comparative

By 1881 blankets were being used for packing on horseback, and Bourke observed that the Navaho were "keen at a bargain and as each unpacked his ponies and ripped open the blankets full of wool he had brought to market, he acted as if he knew its value and meant to get it" (Bourke, 1936:83).

According to the Franciscan Fathers (1910:247), the Ramah term for the woven saddlebag was translated as "Mexican rug or pelt," and referred to a specific pattern of black, white, and blue strips made for the Mexican trade. Skin saddlebags were the only ones specified.

When Son of Old Man Hat and his father took peaches from the Oraibi orchards they used impromptu containers made by sewing their double saddle blankets into sacks. "We gathered some soap-weed stalks and tore them into strips and began sewing up our saddle blankets" (Dyk, 1938:336).

62. Hobble

ł̧·· behéx̱ó·l (Ramah, Haile)   "horse cinch, or horse hobble" (CC)

Ramah

Rawhide was buried in the damp ground until it was pliable, then removed and beaten with a rock to soften it. The hair was removed, and the hide greased with mutton tallow. After this it was again placed in damp ground. When the hide was next removed, a long strip was cut; a hole was made near one end and the other end slashed into several strands. It was cut narrower in the center section. The strip was then doubled over one arm with the hole and strands opposite one another. The center portion was twisted, and the arm removed; a loop was left at one end. It was then allowed to dry. The strands were tied in a round knot which was inserted in the opposing hole to form the second loop (see 62.1, 62.2). A wooden peg was sometimes used to shape the first loop. This was inserted while the hide was wet and remained in place when it dried (Inf. 8).

62.1. Drying the hobble

62.2. Twisted hobble

The hobble was attached to the forelegs of the horse, just above the hoof. Each leg was fettered by one of the loops.

Either men or women could make a hobble, although men usually did so. Ownership was not specified. A hobble made from thick hide would last about a year. It was carried on the saddle or hung on a nail in the hogan; Inf. 8 put "a little grease or something on it so it won't get too hard."

When data were collected there were one or two such hobbles in the Ramah area. One was owned by Inf. 7, who said that this type had once been used, but currently anything was used (meaning, probably, a piece of hemp). Until his death in 1942 Inf. 16 made hobbles and quirts of rawhide. He and Inf. 8 are the only ones who are actually known to have made rawhide hobbles. In 1939 Inf. 256 saw "an old fur hobble," which belonged to Inf. 34; he did not know who made it.

62.3. Threaded hobble, after Hill

Hill (Central and West)

Hill's informants (SG, Keams Canyon; PP, Fort Defiance) confirmed the Ramah type of hobble, with variations in manufacture. A strip of rawhide approximately two inches wide was thoroughly soaked, and placed around a stick of three or more inches in diameter. Next the ends were twisted together for about eight inches, and the free sections beyond the twist tied around another block of wood the size of the first. It was left to dry. An eye was then cut in one of the free ends. The other was split in four sections and braided. The braid formed a knot which was inserted in the eye and secured the hobble. According to PP, the ends projected beyond the knot to assist in pulling it through the eye.

Another type (PP) was made by taking two strips of rawhide and cutting slits in them at intervals. The strips were threaded together alternately through the holes, and allowed to dry. In this type, eyes and braided knots were made at both ends (see 62.3).

According to SG, short lengths of twisted wool an inch in diameter or of four-ply braided wool, rawhide, or buckskin were used for hobbles. These were doubled, placed around one of the horse's forelegs, and twisted several times; the ends were passed around the other leg and tied in a square knot on the outside.

Comparative

The hobble described at Ramah and by Hill's informants was confirmed by the Franciscan Fathers (1910:313–314). These devices were two to three inches wide, and two and a half feet long. This type of hobble was said to be convenient and durable. The term for hobble given by Ramah informants was confirmed by Haile (1951:153).

In the collections of the Harvard Peabody Museum is a hobble collected in the Kayenta area in 1914 by A. V. Kidder and S. J. Guernsey. It is fifteen inches over-all, and the loops are about twelve inches apart. It was made from two pieces of rawhide, stitched together at one end with a rawhide thong. A small piece of rawhide was sewn in the eye to prevent the slit from tearing. In all other respects, it appears to confirm the description above.

63. Hitching Post

Fishler (West)

Holes were dug in the four cardinal directions, approximately fifty feet from the hogan. In the bottom of each was placed turquoise, white shell, obsidian and oyster (olivella?) shell; medicine was put in the hogan to insure the increase and good quality of the horse herd. A song was sung as this was done. Posts with the figures of the sun and moon carved on each were placed in the holes and the holes filled in with dirt.

These posts were used for tying horses for ceremonial purposes, and only those who knew the Blessing Way could erect them. Horses were tethered to the post which coincided with the direction from which the rider had come on his return to camp. It was also believed that the posts would prevent horses from straying if they broke their hobbles.

Whether such posts were constructed is not known. It is possible that the description is derived from mythology, although the informant (FG, Coalmine) claimed that such posts were used by the early Navaho.

64. Yucca Rope

cáʼásziˑ ʼaháˑdadisɣaˑn (Ramah) "yucca, tie it together to make it long" (CC)

cáʼásziˑ X̌óˑł (Lamphere) yucca string; "yucca string" (CC)

Ramah

Wide yucca leaves were picked and cut into thin strips. These were tied together to form a long strand, which was doubled and twisted between the fingers of the right hand. Twisting was done away from the worker. Rope was also sometimes braided of fiber obtained from pounded yucca roots. It was made by women, and used for drying meat or for hanging clothes. It was strung between two trees.

Yucca rope is still used. It is a temporary contrivance, since it must be used while still green. Most of the data was obtained from Inf. 7, although Inf. 16 mentioned yucca string. Roberts noted a horse being led by an improvised yucca-leaf cord (Roberts, 1951:37), and Kluckhohn saw Inf. 97 making a fiber rope.

Hill (Central)

Yucca was the only plant from which rope was made. The leaves were pounded to loosen the fibers, which were dried thoroughly in the sun. They were then twisted into rope. Size varied, but some ropes were "as large in diameter as a silver dollar." This size was used by individuals to reach food stores located in the cliffs. Smaller sizes were used in connection with livestock. According to the reports, yucca ropes disappeared from use soon after sheep became numerous, and were replaced by woolen ones (C, Chinle; SC, Crystal).

Variations were reported. According to PP (Fort Defiance), yucca leaves were beaten to loosen the fibers. These were allowed to dry, and used to make three- and four-ply braided ropes. The finished rope was extended between two posts and the leaf of a prickly pear cactus was heated and run back and forth over it; the glutinous material from the interior of the leaf smoothed the yucca fibers and "strengthened the rope." Then it was pulled several times through the crotch of a tree or a rope wrench to remove stiffness and to make it pliable. "When correctly braided and prepared they are as strong as a dressed skin rope."

According to LM (Canyon del Muerto), green yucca fiber was used for temporary rope and twine. The leaves were beaten to loosen the fibers and a braided three-ply rope or twine produced. The size depended upon the intended use. Such ropes were used for packing wood and tethering horses. If the owner desired to reuse them, he buried them in moist earth or sand, which prevented the fibers from drying out and becoming brittle.

Lamphere (East)

PM said that the first term was not used for real rope, but strands of yucca used to tie the warp to the loom, before the Navaho had wire. She said the yucca was covered with earth to keep it moist. Then when a woman needed some, she would split a piece off and tie the loom with it. When it dried, it would break, and would have to be replaced by another. She gave the second term, a literal translation of "yucca rope."

Comparative

Gifford's Eastern informant said that wide-leafed yucca leaves were tied together in an emergency and used for packing. Plant fibers were also braided into rope for lashings and other cord. He said that these ropes were sometimes made pliable by pounding, sometimes wilted over a fire. Usually they were split. Both informants confirmed twisted yucca cord, and both denied braiding yucca for lassos (Gifford, 1940:47, 140).

The term for yucca rope given by the Ramah informants was not listed as such by Haile. He gave translations for yucca *tsa aszii* and rope (*tlool*) as given by Lamphere's informant. In addition, his term for any "hard rope" (*noodatlool*) seems to combine terms for both yucca and rope: *nooda* (compare *noodah*, "it falls along") refers to a species of yucca which occurs in Yucca Mountain of the southern Apache country, and *tlool* refers to rope (Haile, 1950:159; 1951:250, 326).

65. Rawhide Rope

beꞏgašiꞏ bikágí ƛ́óꞏł (Lamphere)   "cowskin rope"; "cowhide string" (CC)

Ramah

Ropes made from cowhide or horsehide were manufactured and used by men. Inf. 7 said they were used any time, but buckskin ropes were used for "dress up" occasions.

Hill (Central and West)

Ropes were made from cowhides and horsehides, which the worker cut spirally, beginning at the outside edge, to produce continuous lines. These were braided and made pliable by running them through the crotch of a tree or a rope wrench. Spun or twisted ropes were not made of this material (PP, Fort Defiance).

Ropes of this type were primarily for use in connection with animal husbandry. According to SG (Keams Canyon), this trait is of comparatively recent introduction.

Lamphere (East)

PM said such a rope was called "cowskin rope."

Comparative

Lassos of plaited rawhide were of recent introduction, according to the Franciscan Fathers (1910:314), although other materials had previously been used. Both of Gifford's informants denied the use of braided lassos (Gifford, 1940:47–48, 140).

There is an eight-strand rawhide lasso with a noose at one end and a knotted fringe at the other in the collection of the Peabody Museum, Harvard University. This lasso, collected in 1912, is thirty feet in length and rectangular in cross section (see 65.a).

65.a. Rawhide lasso

66. Buckskin Rope ·abanⱤóꞏł (Ramah, Haile, Lamphere)   "deerskin string" (CC)

Ramah

Dressed deerskin, goatskin, or antelope skin was cut into thin strips. Goatskin was used most often because it was most readily available. Two or three large buckskins or three doeskins, goatskins, or antelope skins were usually required to produce a rope. Cutting began in the center of the skin and continued spirally. Ten to thirteen strips were cut and then stretched so that all were the same length. The edges were evened with a knife, and the strips then braided. In braiding, one end of the strands was tied to a tree, and each strand was rolled into a ball. As braiding progressed the worker moved away from the tree and unrolled the material as needed.

Ropes were round in cross section or rectangular with rounded edges, depending on the number of strands. Apparently the round form required three or four strands, the other type ten to thirteen. Inf. 7 specified an odd number of strands, although he later described ropes with from four to twelve. Inf. 12 had made ten- or eleven-strand ropes, and Inf. 16 said that any number of strands might be used.

When the rope was destined for use as a lasso, one end was tied or knotted to form a fringe, and a noose was made at the other. Sometimes a piece of rawhide was sewn around the noose to permit the rope to slip easily. For an ordinary rope both ends were tied off.

Braided buckskin was probably used for bridles as well as for lassos and ropes. Either men or women made ropes. According to Inf. 7, women made ropes and men made bridles, but both he and Inf. 12 had made braided ropes. Apparently there was some specialization in rope making. Whoever made a rope owned it and could sell it or give it away.

Ropes were used by anyone in the family, "when you want to dress up" (Inf. 7). They were stored in the hogan to protect them from moisture.

Braided buckskin ropes have been used until recently in the Ramah area. According to Infs. 7 and 8, none was extant in 1947 except on the reservation. Inf. 12, who gave much of the information above, at one time made ropes for sale to Navaho in the vicinity of Two Wells; and a Two Wells man who has lived a short time in the Ramah area has made bridles. Inf. 7 said that Inf. 274 had made and sold buckskin ropes in Ramah. Although buckskin rope has been replaced by manila, it has a functional advantage, since old white stockmen agree that buckskin rope is much less likely to "burn" an animal than hemp rope. The same is true of buckskin hobbles. The antiquity of this trait is unknown.

Hill (East and Central)

Buckskin, later goat hide, and according to TLLSS (Crownpoint) occasionally horsehide, was used in producing dressed skin rope, which averaged between thirty-five and forty feet in length. Hides intended for this purpose were more carefully prepared and softer than those for ordinary use. The legs and neck were removed from the hide. Then, beginning at the outside edge, the worker cut the hide spirally to form a continuous strip. Five, seven, nine, or eleven strands were braided to produce the rope; seven or nine strands were preferred. PP (Fort Defiance) said that these materials did not lend themselves to twisting or spinning.

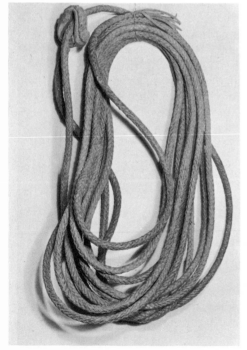

66.a. Plaited buckskin lasso

These ropes were in current use in connection with animal husbandry, but they also represented a form of wealth and were prominently displayed at all social and ceremonial gatherings. According to TLFOS (Shiprock and Fort Defiance), they were also used to lower individuals to eagles' aeries.

Lamphere (East)
Both EP and PM confirmed the term for buckskin rope.

Comparative
Robinson, who was in the Navaho country in 1846, noted that the Navaho used lassos, but he did not state how they were made (Robinson, 1932:44). Bourke, in 1880, noted that the Fort Defiance Navaho made ropes of twisted goatskin and buckskin, and that those of goatskin were most highly prized (Bourke, 1936:232). The Franciscan Fathers (1910:314) reported that three- to eleven-ply braided lassos were commonly made from goatskin because of the scarcity of buckskin, and that ordinary hemp rope was usually preferred since it was less expensive. Both Gifford's informants confirmed braided buckskin ropes, and both denied the use of such ropes as lassos. The Western informant braided ropes of three, five, seven, nine, and eleven strands for use on horses. The Eastern informant spoke of three-, four-, and six-ply ropes, and said that eight and twelve strands were in use but that this was a modern innovation (Gifford, 1940:47–48, 140).

A buckskin (possibly rawhide) lasso in the Peabody Museum, Harvard University, is forty feet long and appears to be four-strand square plaiting (see 66.a).

67.a. Wool rope

67. Wool Rope

ʼaɣaˑˑ *ʌ̓óˑɬ* (Lamphere)

ʼaɣaˑsis (Lamphere, Haile) wool belt, twine

Ramah
Wool or mohair was prepared as for weaving, then braided. Women did this "in the old days" (Inf. 7).

Hill (Central)
Wool strands were spun and several twisted together to produce rope. This was done with the aid of a rope twister (see Trait 69) (PP, Fort Defiance; SC, Crystal). PP said that wool ropes were not strong enough to make good lassos.

Lamphere (East)
PM said that wool was spun, then braided, then braided again. This process produced a large rope which was used in tying up and tightening the loom.

Comparative
There is in the Harvard Peabody Museum an eight-ply Navaho wool rope (see 67.a) collected by G. H. Pepper in 1897 from northwestern New Mexico. It is plaited flat, of white, brown, or black wool. Over-all length is approximately twenty-nine feet and four inches.

Palmer (1869:5–6) noted that "a strong rope made of coarse woolen yarn" was used by the Navaho at Fort Sumner to tie bundles of wood. The Franciscan Fathers (1910:314) stated that lassos were braided of wool. According to Haile (1951:324), the second word for wool rope was translated "wool twine," made from twisted or spun wool.

68. Horsehair Rope

łį·· bice·· ʼXó·ł (Ramah, Haile)   "horsehair string" (CC)

Ramah

Hair from the tail of a horse was made into ropes, some as long as sixty feet. Two people, usually men, cooperated in making a rope. One pulled horsehair in the desired thickness from a pile behind him, and the other twisted it with a rope twister. Then two posts were set in the ground and the strand wrapped around them in three double thicknesses. With the removal of one post, the rope began to twist on itself. One man twisted it further with his hands, a section at a time. If the posts were not used, the strands were twisted by hand, doubled, and allowed to twist on themselves. This process was repeated as often as necessary to achieve the required thickness. Finally the rope was moistened, tied between two trees, and left to dry. These ropes were used "for everyday work" with horses. Ornamental ropes were made by mixing white and black horsehair.

According to Inf. 7, no horsehair ropes are extant in the Ramah area. He learned rope making from his father, who in turn had learned from the Mescalero Apache. The technique may be derived from the Plains area where buffalo or human hair ropes were made (these were denied by Ramah informants), or it may be an adaptation of Navaho cordage techniques of great antiquity.

Hill (East, Central, and West)

Horsehair rope was produced in two ways. The hair from the mane and tail was twisted with the aid of a rope twister, or it was braided. According to SG (Keams Canyon), spun strands of small diameter were sometimes later braided or spun into a rope with a spindle. Horsehair rope was braided in three, four, five, or nine strands. Its primary use was in connection with animal husbandry (PP, Fort Defiance; SC and RH, Crystal; TLFOS, Shiprock and Fort Defiance). PP said that bridle reins were often made from braided horsehair.

Comparative

Bourke noted that horsehair ropes were extant, but rare, in the 1880's (Bourke, 1936:32). Horsehair was one of the materials cited by the Franciscan Fathers (1910:148–149) for rope lassos. Both the Western and Eastern Navaho confirmed twisted and braided horsehair rope, but the Eastern informant regarded it as modern. Both denied human hair ropes. The Eastern informant denied buffalo hair ropes; the Western Navaho was not questioned (Gifford, 1940:47–48).

A horsehair rope in the Harvard Peabody Museum was collected by

68.a. Horsehair rope

R. S. Taylor and attributed to the Navaho. It is fifty-three feet long, twisted of six individually twisted strands (see 68.a). A note in the catalogue stated that the rope was placed around a sleeping person to keep off rattlesnakes. The author of a clipping inserted with the note discounted the myth, however, because he had seen rattlers climb over the horsehair rope.

69. Rope Twister

daha·zdi·tˣa·z ʎ́ó·ł ła ʒi·la (Lamphere)   "twisted, some rope to make"; "one end is tied, twist string" (CC)

Ramah

A piece of wood about nine inches long was perforated at both ends with a hot iron. A stick was inserted through one hole, then fastened loosely. This served as a handle for the L-shaped tool. Rope was passed through the hole at the other end, or attached to the wood at this point (see 69.1).

For twisting horsehair into rope, two persons were usually required. One whirled the implement in a clockwise direction, the other released the fiber in the desired thickness. Either men or women could do this.

According to Inf. 7, the Ramah Navaho derived the rope twister from the Apache (probably Mescalero Apache).

Hill (East, Central, and West)

This device consisted of two pieces of hardwood, a stationary handle and a movable arm. A shallow groove was cut about half an inch from the tip of the handle, and the arm was perforated at one end. This perforation was barely large enough to admit the handle. The protruding tip of the handle was wrapped with yarn to prevent slipping when in use. The distal end of the arm carried a notch to which fibers could be tied (see 69.1).

Rope twisting was normally done by two individuals, as at Ramah (TLLSS, Crownpoint; TLFOS, Shiprock and Fort Defiance; SC, Crystal; SG, Keams Canyon). According to SG, it could be done by a single individual. The fibers were placed in a pile. Several were twisted with the fingers and attached to the end of the twister which was then whirled. "Other fibers will catch on as you whirl the twister."

Rope twisters were used in the production of horsehair, wool, and (according to SC) yucca rope. Informants also stated that the rope twister used on wool and hair from horses' manes was smaller and lighter than that used for yucca and hair from horses' tails.

Lamphere (East)

PM said rope was twisted by looping it around a fence post, inserting a stick and twisting it around. She gave the name for the rope twister.

Comparative

Gifford is apparently the only person to have published on this tool. The rope twister was used by the Western Navaho for twisting buckskin and horsehair, but the Eastern informant considered it a modern innovation (Gifford, 1940:47, 140).

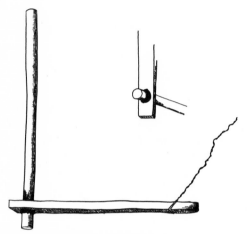

69.1. Rope twister, after Hill

70. Rope Wrench

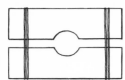

70.1. Rope wrench (Hill), after PP

Hill (Central)

Semicircular notches were cut in two pieces of wood. These were matched to form a circle and the two sections were tied together (see 70.1). One individual held the wrench while another pulled yucca or rawhide ropes through the opening to increase pliability (PP, Fort Defiance).

71. Branding Iron

be·ʾadi·λí·d (Lamphere)   "with it branding is done"; "with it burning with metal" (CC)

Ramah

The branding iron was used in Ramah, but, because it is known to be of recent introduction, no data were collected.

Hill (East, Central, and West)

Branding is a trait recently acquired by the Navaho. TLLSS (Crownpoint) believed that it was introduced sometime after 1870 by government employees. PP (Fort Defiance) and MH (Head Springs) could give no date but agreed that the practice was not old.

Branding was usually limited to horses. Brands were crudely applied with any convenient piece of iron or wire. According to MH, several applications of the metal were necessary before the brand was completed. The Navaho do not appear to have manufactured branding irons of the type used in the modern cattle industry.

Lamphere (East)

PM gave the word for branding iron. She said, however, that sheep were not branded but that ownership marks in the shape of a brand were painted on them with "homemade" paint consisting of a mixture of pine pitch and ashes.

Comparative

According to the Franciscan Fathers (1910:258), branding was done "after American fashion, with branding irons obtained at the agencies, or otherwise purchased from blacksmiths."

72.a. Wagon

Transportation and Burdens

72. Wagon

cina·ba̧·s (Haile)

Ramah

The wagon was the principal vehicle in the three households studied by Roberts. It was used to haul wool sacks, people, household gear, and water (Roberts, 1951:54).

III. Many-legged hogan (Tr. 107) and corral (Tr. 47) near Lupton, Arizona. Note also wagon (Tr. 72). A loom is set up outside at which the women are working.

Hill (Central)

According to PP (Fort Defiance), the first time the Navaho saw wagons was just before they went to Fort Sumner, when the troops came to Fort Defiance. Before that the Navaho had always packed.

Comparative

The mid-nineteenth-century introduction of the wagon was confirmed by the Franciscan Fathers (1910:151). Wagons were issued by the government, although many Navaho preferred to purchase their own. The farm wagon was used for freighting, hauling wood, and often for traveling.

73. Tumpline

ʼawéˑčáˑl n̆aˑlʒidíˑ (Lamphere)   tumpline, used when carrying cradles

Ramah

A strap of rawhide was used for carrying burdens. It was three inches wide at the middle and about one inch at the ends (Inf. 18). Length was measured from one knee, back up over the neck and down to the other knee.

The strap was placed over the forehead or across the chest. A narrow strap was padded with a blanket. There was no forehead protection on the strap. When worn over the chest, it was sometimes held in place by the thumbs. Both men and women used the tumpline.

The material to be transported (such as corn, meat, or wood) was wrapped in a dressed buckskin, or tied together, and the bundle was fastened to the ends of the strap. Bailey (1950:80) stated that the cradle was also carried on the mother's back with the tumpline. Roberts (1951:54) stated and Inf. 90 confirmed that carrying the cradle was the only use for the tumpline.

The principal informant (Inf. 7) specified that tumplines were used "in the old days." Inf. 76 had heard of them, but only in connection with tribes other than the Navaho. Inf. 18, however, had made and used a tumpline, and in 1938 Inf. 47 was seen using a canvas strap as a tumpline. It was placed across the chest, but not held with the thumbs. This method of transport is very rare or nonexistent in Ramah today.

The use of braided or woven tumplines and carrying nets was denied (Inf. 7). Burdens were not carried on the head.

Hill (East and Central)

Tumplines were made from a wide range of materials and in a variety of methods. For temporary needs a number of yucca leaves were tied together (C, Chinle; K, Mariano Lake; LM, Canyon del Muerto). More permanent forms were made from wool (C; K; PP, Fort Defiance; MM, Lukachukai) or cotton and buckskin (C). MM stated that she had never seen a buckskin tumpline. Those of wool were woven (MM, C), plaited (MM, PP, K), or twisted (PP, K). Those of cotton were woven (C).

According to informants, the tumpline was the most common device used to facilitate the transport of weighty materials or objects. It was employed by both sexes and by children. The length of the line varied depending upon the size of the load and the strength of the packer. The strap might be alternated from chest to forehead; according to C, head and chest tumplines were never used simultaneously. They were used principally to transport wood (LM, C) and carry cradles (PP), secondarily to move meat, field products, and water (C, PP).

Meat from a hunt was packed on a frame used with the tumpline. Two poles were placed about a foot to eighteen inches apart, and three crosspieces were tied with yucca leaves to make the frame. Meat was placed on the frame, covered with hide, and tied in place. When the frame was carried, its top often extended above the head of the packer (C; Hill, 1938:111).

Lamphere (East)

PM confirmed the use of tumplines for carrying cradles; the term she gave applies only to this use. EP did not know about this trait.

Comparative

None of the observers who visited the Navaho area before the twentieth century indicated that tumplines were an early device among the Navaho.

In a photograph (see 73.a) published by James (1902:pl. 26a), two Navaho women were shown carrying basketry water bottles with tumplines. One bottle was suspended by a cord running over the top of the wearer's head; the other was supported by a band (either cloth or skin) slung over the chest and upper right arm.

A "carrying cord" was confirmed by the Franciscan Fathers (1910:510, 472). It passed over the forehead or chest, and was used to carry a blanket bundle or wicker bottle. The cradle was also carried in this manner; the cord passed over the forehead and shoulders. Gifford's informants confirmed the pack strap, which was worn both across the forehead and across the chest. The Western informant said that an extra thickness of buckskin was used to prevent the strap from chafing the forehead. Both groups said that the hide pack strap was used, and both used the blanket sling. Both denied woven pack straps, but the Eastern informant said that sometimes Spanish bayonet yucca leaf tumplines were used. The Western informant said that burdens were carried on the head by both men and women; the Eastern informant denied this trait (as did Ramah informants) (Gifford, 1940:41–42).

73.a. Navaho women carrying basketry water bottles (Tr. 82) with tumplines; note also their hair ties (Tr. 181)

74. Carrying Pole   cinbeꞏʼoꞏgeꞏł (Ramah)   "wood with it carrying" (CC)

Ramah

A juniper pole (Inf. 18) about five feet long and one inch in diameter was balanced over one shoulder, with loads tied at each end. It was not used over both shoulders as a yoke. Inf. 18 said only men made this device, but either sex used it, sometimes, for carrying meat.

Inf. 18 had transported meat with the carrying pole as recently as 1945; Inf. 7 knew of it but did not say whether he had ever used it. Inf. 76 had heard about it from her father, who said it had been used before his time. Inf. 261 said that the Zuni and the Navaho used the same type of pole, and that the Zuni got it from the Navaho. According to Roberts (1951:54), carrying poles were never used.

Comparative

There is little information in the literature on this trait. Both of Gifford's informants denied the use of the carrying pole (Gifford, 1940:133). Since it was confirmed by Gifford's Zuni informant, it may be an acquisition from the Zuni that is restricted to some members of the neighboring Ramah group.

75. Litter bita·h ne·sgai be·elλé·· be·elcos (Lamphere) "his body aches, blanket, carries"; "sick, blanket, carrying it" (CC)

Hill (Central)

Litters were constructed from juniper. Two straight poles were selected and the branches removed. The poles were laid parallel, from two and one half to three feet apart. Green juniper boughs were tied across the poles at frequent intervals to complete the litter. Although the construction seems not to have been very substantial, it was adequate for the temporary use for which the litter was intended.

Litters were used for transporting persons who were ill. "If a man were sick and became restless you might move him to another place. Naturally, you would always move him south, since the dead go to the north." The sick person lay on a blanket placed on the litter. A chanter always accompanied the group and sang as the journey progressed. Trips as long as three miles were reported. It was believed to be bad luck for a person to pass in front of a litter. Likewise, if an animal crossed in front of the party it was thought to portend evil for the sick person.

It was mandatory that the litter be dismantled at the end of the trip. "If you left it intact it would be just asking for another patient." The boughs were placed some distance from the hogan, "where children would not find them," with their growing tips toward the east. No wood from a litter could be used for firewood, nor could lightning-struck wood be used in the construction of litters (PP, Fort Defiance).

Lamphere (East)

PM did not know of the juniper litter. She said that a blanket was used to carry the sick. Her term referred to this method.

Comparative

"A carrying frame, constructed for temporary use in the early days," was vaguely remembered by informants of the Franciscan Fathers (1910:510). This frame was not described.

According to Gifford's informants, a ladder-like litter was used by both groups for transporting disabled persons (who were also carried on the back with a blanket or rope sling). The Eastern informant said that a litter with yucca leaf crossties was used, but a buckskin stretcher was denied. (Gifford, 1940:41).

76. Buckskin "Trunk" ·abani·azis (Lamphere) "deerskin bag" (CC)

Hill (Central)
Buckskins were used for storing and transporting personal effects. Clothing was placed in the center of the buckskin and the legs of the hide tied together (SC, Crystal). According to PP (Fort Defiance), when the legs were tied the neck was pushed under the knot and another buckskin tied over the bundle in the opposite direction. Buckskins were also used to transport wild seeds (LW, Lukachukai), and green hides were used to transport meat from the hunt (RH, Crystal).

Lamphere (East)
PM said that this trait was called "buckskin, a purse or holder."

Comparative
According to Gifford's Eastern informant, meat from a hunt was carried home in bundles tied with yucca leaves. The Western informant sometimes carried meat home from a hunt, usually in a hide (Gifford, 1940:9, 89). Other data were lacking.

77. Sled na·lžo·dí (Ramah, Haile) "slide" (CC)

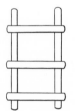

77.1. Rough sled, after Tschopik; side and top views

Ramah
A wooden sled was built for hauling wood over the snow. It was about four feet long (see 77.1).

Tschopik observed a sled at Inf. 34's place in 1938, and was told by Inf. 270, his interpreter from Two Wells, that it was used for hauling wood. Murray saw one used by Inf. 256 and his family in 1941 for hauling water. According to Inf. 16, however, sleds were never used by the Navaho, even for amusement.

Comparative
The Franciscan Fathers (1910:270) listed the word for sled in the roster of modern tools. No other data were presented. Two terms were cited by Haile (1951:267), both of which were similar to the Ramah term.

78. Raft na·škǫ·ł (Ramah, Haile) "floating" (CC); "floating here and there"

Ramah
A wooden pole about one foot in diameter and about four feet long (Inf. 16) was cut but not shaped. According to Inf. 2, "any piece of wood would do." The raft was a temporary device (Inf. 16), used for crossing rivers (Infs. 16, 7). It was placed crosswise under the armpits. The individual paddled with his arms and kicked his feet. Inf. 16 had seen this device in use on a "big" river near Albuquerque.

A raft made by cutting a cottonwood tree in half and attaching two crosspieces with cordage was described by Inf. 3. Inf. 7 said that rafts were from one and a half to two feet wide and square at both ends. The user lay full length on the wooden support and kicked his legs to propel the craft. He had never seen a raft and said that no one had ever used one in the Ramah area.

Inf. 2 had heard of the raft, and Inf. 1 knew the name but nothing more. It is possible that Inf. 3, who lived on the San Juan River before the Fort Sumner period, had seen or even used the raft he described. None of Roberts' informants had ever used any sort of water transportation (Roberts, 1951:54). At the present time there are no boats or rafts in use among the Ramah Navaho, although there is a lake in the area.

Hill (East and Central)

Rafts were used for transporting goods across rivers. They were made from logs approximately twelve to fourteen feet long (TLFOS, Shiprock), or driftwood (TOMC, Red Rock), tied together with yucca. According to TLFOS four logs were used; TOMC said the size depended on the size of the load.

Goods were placed in the center of the raft—on a cribwork to prevent them from getting wet (TLFOS). Men grasped the sides of the raft and pushed it as they swam. TLFOS had used such a raft.

One- and two-log rafts for human transport were described by SC (Crystal). The individual sat astride the raft and poled it across the river. PP (Fort Defiance) had never heard of rafts or boats among the Navaho.

Comparative

One of the more substantial accounts of water transportation in Navaho mythology is that by Washington Matthews (1897:161–162), in the legend of Natinesthani, who hollowed a boat out of a cottonwood log. None of the accounts in the legends, however, are applicable to the current or historic scene. (For other accounts of the floating log story, see Goddard, 1933:161; Sapir and Hoijer, 1942:25; Matthews, 1902:172–175; Hill, 1938:100.)

The Franciscan Fathers stated that flat boats were used to ferry streams at high water. These were drawn upstream and allowed to drift with the current, while steered diagonally across it. Canoeing was not in vogue. "The Navaho in general are inexperienced swimmers and usually steer clear of water" (Franciscan Fathers, 1910:49). Gifford (1940:24) reported that only the Eastern Navaho had any method for crossing streams other than swimming. They used a single log or pole to aid the swimmer. The Western informant denied this method and both groups denied any more elaborate craft (such as one made by lashing two logs together). According to Gifford (1940:111), the Western Navaho learned to swim while in exile at Fort Sumner, although there was no swimming in the Western Navaho region.

Old Mexican related how he "got a pole and swam across the river" with a goat carcass on his back (Dyk, 1947:69). Underhill stated that on the return from the Fort Sumner captivity, "the men made rafts and boys swam, as the soldiers had taught them," to cross the flooding Rio Grande (Underhill, 1956:146).

The term for raft given by Haile (1951:237) confirms that from Ramah (see also Haile, 1950:143).

79. Bridge   na·ńžo·ž (Haile)   "log bridge" (CC)

na·ná·ái (Haile)   "across extension"

Hill (Central)
Log bridges were constructed over crevices in the rocks. These were reportedly made whenever the necessity arose but were most plentiful in the area of Canyon del Muerto and Canyon de Chelly. One in del Muerto was three logs wide. Depressions were cut in the rock and the ends of the logs fitted into them. The logs were notched on top to prevent slipping (C, Chinle).

Comparative
The only bridge reported by the Franciscan Fathers (1910:264) was used in connection with irrigation. The term confirmed that given for log bridge by Haile. Haile's informants gave a slightly different term (the second above) for an unidentified, bridged river mentioned in Shooting Way and Flint Way legends; this term also refers to any modern single-span highway bridge over a canyon or arroyo (Haile, 1950:140; 1951:34). Gifford's informants denied the use of a log bridge across a stream (Gifford, 1940:24).

Food
Storage

80. Water Bag   tˣo ·abi·d (Ramah, Haile)

Ramah
An undressed goatskin or the hide of a small deer was used, but elk skin was not (Inf. 7). The worker cased the hide, beginning at the heel of the hind leg, cutting up the back of the leg, across the perineum, and down the other leg. The bones were broken, and the hooves left attached to the skin. The rest of the skin was pulled off toward the head. The neck opening was sewn and tied to make it secure; the legs were also tied. A string was tied around the leg-perineal opening, which was used as the mouth of the water bag. The stomach of a sheep or goat was also made into a water bag. It was removed and cleaned, and the apertures were then tied with buckskin thongs or string. These bags were made by women (Inf. 36).

For storing water around the hogan, the bag was suspended by the hind legs from a tree. Liquid was dipped out with a small dipper. The bag was also used for transporting water for irrigating plants, usually when a horse was available, since when full the bag was heavy. It hung from the saddle horn, and was filled from a small container. It was also used as a container for an alcoholic drink made from corn (Inf. 8).

Women and children were the ordinary users, especially during the summer months when the plants needed watering. No one in particular owned the water bag; Inf. 267 said it belonged to the household.

The best descriptions of this type of water bag were given by Infs. 7 and 36; Inf. 36 stated that there were a number in use when she was a girl and that they were still being made at that time. An older informant (Inf. 12) had never seen this item, and knew nothing of its manufacture. It is possible that the bag survived later in the Two Wells area, where Inf. 36 lived as a girl, than at Ramah.

Inf. 8 had seen one in the Ramah area near El Morro, called "twopit." He thought the bag was procured from the Apache, and that its obsolescence began when buckets and pails became available at the trading posts about 1900.

At present, bottles are used for carrying small amounts of water. Large quantities are transported and stored in barrels loaded on wagons or trucks. The barrels are purchased by the Navaho or obtained as containers of purchased goods.

Hill (Central and West)

The use of cased sheepskins and goatskins for the storage and transportation of water was confirmed by GH (White Cone) and WH (Wheatfields). The apertures were tied and the hide allowed to dry. GH confirmed the use of the stomachs and large intestines of goats and sheep.

Comparative

How long the Navaho have used skin water bags is uncertain. The Franciscan Fathers (1910:298) stated that one was formerly made by stretching a piece of buckskin over a hoop to form the bottom. The ends were then brought upward and attached to a second and very small hoop. Later, the paunch of a cow or sheep was used instead of the buckskin.

The Ramah type was seen by Guernsey in 1914 near Mitchell's Butte (Monument Valley, Arizona). "While there we saw Indians filling goatskin water bottles which were packed down to cornfields on the back of a burro, where a little water is poured in every corn hill. The goatskins are complete and have a life-like, but bloated, look when filled" (Guernsey, 1914:21).

Both of Gifford's informants confirmed the use of the skin bag for carrying water. The Western informant said that goatskin or sheepskin was used, but not deerskin; the Eastern informant mentioned the use of fawn skin. He said that paunch bags were used, but only in emergency, as on a hunt, and that they rotted after two days. The Western informant denied their use (Gifford, 1940:41, 133).

The convenience of cased sheepskins and goatskins for water bags was noted by Haile (1951:314).

81. Gourd Canteen

tˣóšʒeˑh (Lamphere)   water bottle; "water with pitch"; "barrel" (CC)

Hill (Central)

The largest gourds available were selected for making canteens. The end of the neck was removed and small pebbles dropped into the aperture. These were shaken about to dislodge the seeds and pith. When the interior had been cleared, it was rinsed with a solution of juniper leaves to remove the taste of the gourd.

A sagebrush bark stopper was made. Strips of bark were folded back and forth on themselves until the plug attained the desired diameter. This bundle was then wrapped and tied with a strip of bark (C, Chinle) or yucca (PP, Fort Defiance). Allowance was made for expansion to prevent the plug when saturated from cracking the neck of the canteen.

Canteens were covered with hide or cloth to protect them from breakage. A handle or shoulder strap was sewn to the covering and the container was either carried in the hand or suspended from the shoulder (PP, C).

Lamphere (East)
PM described large gourds that were used to hold water. She said the seeds were taken out and a stone was used to smooth the inside. This device was called by the same term as that used for the pitched basket bottle.

Comparative
Both of Gifford's informants confirmed the use of gourds for canteens (Gifford, 1940:20, 41).

82. Pitched Basket Bottle

tˣóšʒeˑh (Ramah, Haile) "water with pitch"; "barrel" (CC)

Ramah
Obsolete by 1940, the pitched water bottle was used regularly for transporting water (Infs. 15, 32, 192) until the middle of the nineteenth century. Infs. 15, 32, and 192 probably made them, and their mothers certainly did, for Inf. 32 stated that "in the old days, a lot more women made baskets." She agreed with Inf. 192 that there were no ritual restrictions involved. According to Inf. 15, however, when making water bottles "you have to be careful like when you make medicine baskets. This is because they use the same plants" (Tschopik, 1940:459). Metal buckets purchased at the trading posts are now used for carrying water.

82.a. Inf. 32 putting pitch on a bottle

Hill (East and Central)
Sumac twigs were gathered about the first of October (K, Mariano Lake), after the first frost (LW, Lukachukai). They were split with the teeth into three wedge-shaped pieces; from these the triangular core of the twig was removed and discarded. The remaining pieces were put in the sun for two or three days to dry. Bark was removed by pulling the splints through a cloth; it was saved and used later for dye. Splints to be stored were dried, bent into a coil, and tied. Those to be used immediately were soaked, and pulled through a rectangular notch for sizing (see Trait 83).

Two sumac rods (C, Chinle) were used for the foundation. These were scraped at the ends to facilitate bending in as small a circle as possible. Stitching began at the point of overlap, and was done under and over toward the worker. A deer bone awl was used. New rods were tapered to make a smooth joint, and were added clockwise. The basket was turned counterclockwise. A short splint was broken off inside the basket, and the new one introduced from the outside in order to place the overlap under the coil. Care was taken to place the last coil in line with the first one; the stitching

82.b. Materials used to make a pitched basket bottle, left to right. Bottom row: metate and mano used to pulverize the paint, graniteware plate used to mix the paint, stones used in applying pitch to the interior. Center row: awl, butcher knife, and sieve for straining the melted pitch. Top row: completed bottle, vessel used to melt the pinyon pitch (note stirring stick and mop).

82.c. Coiled basket covered with pitch

82.d. Pitched basket bottle

element was run back two stitches, then through to the inside where it was broken off.

A handle of three-ply braided horsehair was woven into the basket at the appropriate point. The ends of the horsehair were tied together and doubled. One loop thus formed was placed over a foundation rod and secured by the coiling. The other loop was usually introduced four coils above the first; on a larger basket, the cord was thicker and the distance between the loops greater.

The finished basket was coated with pitch inside and out. Pinyon pitch was heated to the boiling point and poured into the bottle, which was then rotated until the pitch filled all the interstices. After the inside hardened, a small hair brush was used to paint the outside of the basket with boiling pitch (K). C said that three rocks were heated and placed in the water jug with the pinyon pitch to coat the inside. According to K, heated rocks were used to repair any leaks incurred after use. Water jugs were sometimes covered with buckskin. A very large basket would hold from three to five gallons of water (K). Shredded sagebrush bark or cornhusks were used to plug the opening (K).

Pitched basket bottles were also used by the bride and groom at the wedding ceremony and in the Night Way dances.

Fishler (West)

TN (Kaibito) said that women made water baskets, and specified yucca for the material. Details of manufacture confirmed those above.

Both basket bottles and pottery bottles were formerly used for transporting water. GB (Tuba City) said that the bottle was carried tumpline fashion on long deerskin straps tied to the sides of the basket, or two basket bottles were tied on either side of a saddle.

Comparative
According to Matthews (1897:18–19), the Navaho "buy most of their baskets and wicker water jars from other tribes" and would "lose the art of basketry altogether" if it were not for ritual requirements. Curtis (1908:77) stated that even basket bottles used in ceremonies were purchased from neighboring tribes, "especially the Havasupai and Paiute, who weave them primarily for purposes of trade." The Franciscan Fathers (1910:297) also described the wicker bottle, and stated that willow or other pliable twigs were used as well as sumac. Their informants confirmed the use of a heated pebble to smooth the inside surface and to remove any hardened lumps. The exterior surface was daubed with red clay to obtain the reddish hue. According to the Franciscan Fathers, the usual capacity was from one to two gallons, although some bottles were larger. Even in 1910, these were being displaced by the pail and bucket. Both of Gifford's informants confirmed the use of the pitched basket bottle (Gifford, 1940:41).

83. Sizer

Hill (East and Central)
A notch was filed in a piece of silver, the case of a pocket knife (K, Mariano Lake), a scrap of iron, or some unidentified material (LW, Lukachukai). The depth and width of the notch corresponded to the size desired for the coiling element used in making baskets. These elements were pulled through the notch to insure uniformity in size.

Lamphere (East)
PM did not know about any specific tool for sizing. She said that when sumac was used, it was just evened out with a rock or a flint (chert) arrow.

Comparative
Although it is probable that women who wished uniform pieces of sumac for their baskets used a sizer of some sort, there is little information in the literature. According to the Franciscan Fathers (1910:293), each part of the split sumac was "scraped clean of its bark with a knife or piece of tin," but this was apparently a preparation for dyeing, and not for sizing. Gifford recorded no information on this trait (Gifford, 1940).

84. Storage Cave céní·ˑnoˑˑ (Ramah) "rock hiding there" (CC)

Ramah
Small natural holes in the face of a cliff were swept and food placed inside them. A flat rock was used to close the aperture, which was sealed by an adobe plaster. Reeds were inserted through the mud in three or four places to allow air to circulate (Inf. 7). Sometimes, according to Inf. 45, the opening of the cave was walled up with mud and rock, but this description may merely indicate a more elaborate masonry.

The caves were used in the summer for the storage of meat (Inf. 7) and in winter for the storage of corn (Inf. 45). Yucca fruit (Inf. 7) was also stored in this manner, and Inf. 14 said that dried meat or dried wild potatoes mixed with partially dried fat were placed in a partially tanned buckskin and the bundle stored.

Presumably the cave was owned by either an outfit or an individual family. Storage places were hidden (Inf. 14) and only the family knew their location. "In that time the people did not touch anything that did not belong to them. Even [when] they had the corn stored there for one whole winter nobody would ever touch it" (Inf. 45).

There was nothing to indicate that any present member of the Ramah community had ever helped construct such a storage cave. When he was a small boy, Inf. 45 had seen one made and corn stored in it. Except where noted data obtained from Infs. 7, 14, and 280 confirmed that from Inf. 45. Storage caves had also been found at Inscription Rock in the Ramah district (Inf. 280). They are apparently no longer used.

Hill (Central)

Hill's informants (PP, Fort Defiance; LW, Lukachukai; LM, Canyon del Muerto) confirmed the use of natural cavities for storage. Small cavities were treated as at Ramah. Stone walls were built across the openings of large caves, and "flat stones were then laid on edge in front of the walls and rubbed with moss to give the appearance of a solid cliff face" (Hill, 1938:43).

Comparative

The earliest reference in the literature to storage pits seems to be that by Matthews (1897:240). Walled up natural caves and rock shelters were in use at the time of his writing. They escaped the notice of the Franciscan Fathers, perhaps because they were no longer in use in the early twentieth century or because they did not occur in the area most familiar to the Franciscan Fathers. There was no mention of this trait either in the *Ethnologic Dictionary* or in the *Vocabulary* (Franciscan Fathers, 1910, 1912).

Apparently the Navaho have long used such natural cavities whenever they were conveniently available. In several areas they were found in association with Navaho sites, some of which date back to the early eighteenth century. At Big Bead Mesa, Keur not only found storage places in small cavities in the hogans where a natural sandstone ledge formed part of the wall, but also located a few specially constructed independent caches. A front wall of masonry bounded the cache near "complex A." Two wind-eroded cavities had been used in two large caches in association with the "D complex," which had one wall of piled up boulders across the front of both. About five hundred corncobs were discovered in the northern of the two caves. The wall in front of another nearby cache was of coursed, thin, red sandstone slabs, with a "neat rectangular opening or window in the middle." Two other, similar, caches in this area were also described by Keur (1941:33, 34–35). In the Gobernador area she also found a cist of this general type which had been used both as a burial cist and for the storage of corn. It occurred in association with a hogan, and was unusually large (eight and a half feet in maximum length). "A semicircular wall had been erected on an adobe base under a large overhanging boulder. It was made of well-matched stones, evenly laid and interspersed with adobe and roughly finished on the outside with a heavy coat of adobe" (Keur, 1944:77). The masonry in this structure is more elaborate than that occurring in the Ramah area. Evidence from other parts of the Navaho area also indicates that the storage cists were somewhat more elaborate than the Ramah type.

Malcolm found enclosed rock shelters on ledges in the Chaco Canyon area. These were about the size of the average hogan, and were usually formed by an overhanging rock with a wall of stones and mud beneath it. At another site, cists were found in the sides of rock tables and ledges. Some had been "walled up to a more or less airtight condition to serve as storage places for corn and other staples." About a dozen ears of dried corn were found in one sealed cache. "Some of the cists had been blocked at one end to improve their utility." Others showed traces of use as burial vaults, first by the Pueblos, and later by the Navaho (Malcolm, 1939:11, 15–16). Farmer (1942:70) stated that he found in the Blanco-Largo region enclosures of the same type as those encountered by Malcolm and Keur.

Gifford reported that both Western and Eastern Navaho stored food in clay pots which were then cached in rock shelters. The pots were covered with lids, for which the Western Navaho used another pot. Food placed in skin bags was stored on the ground in dry caves, according to the Western informant (Gifford, 1940:16, 99).

85. Storage Pit

nǫkeh (Ramah, Haile)   "underground place"

no·keh bahahoged (Ramah)   "store things pit"; "hole dug under the ground" (CC)

Ramah

One or more pits were dug in the ground near the hogan (Infs. 192, 32), but never in the hogan floor (Inf. 50). They were hidden as well as possible (Inf. 192), and sometimes located in out-of-the-way places away from the hogan. "Just one family would know where its own corn was stored" (Infs. 50, 280, 45).

The pits were trapezoidal in cross section; the bottom diameter was greater than the top and the sides were smoothed (Inf. 192). Depth varied from two and a half to three feet (Infs. 50, 280), to four feet (Infs. 45, 15), or five feet (Inf. 192), or the height of a man (Inf. 14), or six or more feet (Inf. 32). The diameter was about two feet (Infs. 50, 280) or three feet (Inf. 192).

The bottom and sides were lined with juniper bark (Infs. 192, 32, 45, 15). Inf. 280 said it was used for the bottom layer; Infs. 192 and 32 said it was placed over a layer of pinyon. According to Inf. 50, only the bottom of the pit was lined; Inf. 14 said that the pit was not lined.

The pits were used for storing corn or wild seeds such as pinyon (Inf. 192), squash or sunflower (Inf. 280), or wild potatoes (Inf. 14). Infs. 50 and 14 agreed that corn was not placed in the same pit with other seeds. Each type of wild seed was stored in a separate pit (Infs. 50, 192). Seeds were stored as gathered, not cleaned or placed in bags, but merely poured into the pit. According to Inf. 14, however, seeds were stored in buckskin sacks or blanket bags; she said that one pit might hold two or three kinds of seeds. Potatoes were dried, then placed loose in the pit for storage. When the pit was filled, it was sealed with juniper bark (Inf. 50), closed with a large flat rock, and covered with dirt (Infs. 192, 14, 280, 45, 15). If necessary, poles were placed across the top of a large pit, and smaller sticks were placed across them. These were then covered with juniper bark and earth (Infs. 14, 32). Inf. 50 said poles were never used. The surface over and around the pit was camouflaged with dirt and leaves (Inf. 50).

Information was obtained from a large number of informants, all of whom were older members of the community. All but Inf. 45 were women. Although the whole family helped in the construction of storage pits, "mother had most to do with it" (Inf. 280). Inf. 45 remembered seeing such a pit made by his family in his youth and helping to store the corn in it.

Apparently these pits are no longer made nor are old ones used. Corn is stored in hogans built for that purpose or in any unused hogan belonging to the family. Some families have built vegetable and root cellars. The one once used by Inf. 12's family had a screen door in addition to the "solid" door, to provide circulation of air and prevent molding.

Hill (East, Central and West)

Hill's informants described storage pits that varied in shape from those described by Ramah informants, but in most other respects seem to have been the same (see Hill, 1938:42–43). A globular pit, somewhat constricted at the neck, was said to be the oldest; it was the most common. Depth was about five to six feet. It was constructed as at Ramah. According to WP (Canoncito), a fire was built in the pit to harden it and to insure the removal of any moisture. The globular pit was given a mythical origin in the legend of the Plume Way chant (SC, Crystal).

In parts of Canyons del Muerto and de Chelly, a circular pit was dug, and a circular wall of stone and adobe added for extra storage room. This type was closed by poles placed across the opening, on which a cloth was laid and covered with earth (LM, Canyon del Muerto).

A large rectangular pit was also built, about five feet deep, three feet wide, and six feet long. This too was lined with juniper bark, but an air space was left above the stored produce. Poles were placed across the pit; space was left for an entrance, which was covered by smaller sticks. Juniper bark and earth covered the cache, as at Ramah. A few pits had a hatchway in the center for the removal of produce. Occasionally it was necessary to thaw the ground with a fire before the pit could be opened (MH, Head Springs). When supplies were removed, the earth, bark, and poles were carefully replaced.

In a variant of the rectangular storage pit, two supports were set up at the ends of the pit and a stringer placed between them. Poles were then leaned on the stringer from the ends and sides, and the whole covered with bark and dirt. The entrance was made in either of the two sides (TLLSS, Crownpoint; PP, Fort Defiance; see Hill, 1938:43).

Storage pits were located near the summer hogan or in the field. Although each family usually had from one to four such pits, occasionally two families shared them. If so, produce was separated by juniper bark. Hill's informants confirmed the careful concealment of the pits, and said that a landmark was noted to aid in locating the cache.

Corn was usually stored in the globular pits, either shelled or on the ear,

85.a. Storage pit

either loose or in goatskin or, preferably, elk hide containers. It would keep for two years if properly dried and if the ground remained dry. Squash, watermelons, and muskmelons were stored in one or another of the pits described above. The mature fruit was carefully wrapped in bark or corn-husks, and was said to last for several months. The dried fruit was also stored. Beans were separated from corn by bark partitions or placed in individual sacks; they were said to last indefinitely. Dried peaches were stored in buckskin or goat hide sacks, and kept separately in pits lined with rock (PP; see Hill, 1938:43–45, 49).

Fishler (West)

Storage pits were dug near the hogan, but occasionally in the fields where crops were grown, or in areas where pinyon nuts were gathered. According to informants, storage pits were dug about six to seven feet deep, and four to five feet in diameter. GB (Tuba City) said that a fire was built in the pit. When it had cooled, one to two inches of dirt were removed from the sides; the resulting surface was hard. Each pit was covered with closely placed logs, juniper, weeds, or brush, and one and a half to two feet of earth, first dry earth and then wet, which was then tramped down. This surface was convex for drainage. According to TN and IJmo (Kaibito), no fire was necessary. IJmo stated that excavations lined with rocks were sometimes constructed near pinyon trees to store the nuts; GB and TN, however, denied the use of stone- or mud-lined pits.

After the corn was dried, kernels or ears were placed in the pit, either loose or in bags; according to TN, corn could also be put in the hogan. Beans, apricots, and peaches were dried before storage, but pumpkins, squash, and melons were placed in the pit without drying.

GB said that when dried food was taken from the cache, it was placed in water for a few minutes and then rubbed to clean it. Food stored in pits never spoiled.

Comparative

There is little information on storage pits in the archaeological literature, perhaps because of the difficulty of discovering the carefully hidden caches. The known antiquity, however, goes back into the early eighteenth century, as confirmed by the deponents of the Rabal documents (Hill, 1940a:397, 402).

Bourke observed storage pits near Keams Canyon in 1884; they were lined with juniper bark, roofed with juniper poles, and covered with earth (Bourke, 1884:78). In the Black Mountain area in the 1880's, the family of Son of Old Man Hat had stored squash and pumpkin in separate pits (Dyk, 1938:110, 221). Around 1903, Old Mexican "got a box from the store, and we put all our grub into it and dug a hole and stored it and covered it with dirt" (Dyk, 1938:62; see also Dyk, 1947:64, 140–141).

The globular pit was also confirmed by the Franciscan Fathers (1910:267), who noted its use for storing supplies beyond the daily requirements. Digging was formerly done with the planting stick.

"Cisterns like holes with openings at the top stoned up like a well" were seen by Guernsey in 1914 near Kayenta Creek in Arizona. These were used for corn storage, and confirm one of Hill's types.

Gifford's informants differed, although both used storage pits. The Eastern informant confirmed the use of the bottle-shaped pit and a skin sack for storage. Dried muskmelon was sometimes preserved this way. The Western informant denied the globular pit, but confirmed pits lined with juniper bark, which the Eastern informant denied (Gifford, 1940:16, 99).

In Navaho mythology, the storage pit has been noted as part of the Game Story (Goddard, 1933:161). It was used to preserve corn.

86. Storage Bag

yige·l azis (Ramah)   Type I: carrying bag

ʾazisnacǫ́·dí (Ramah)   Type II: storage bag, "rubber bag" (CC)

ʾałcá·ʾazisí (Ramah)   Type III: storage bag; "eagle bag" (CC)

Ramah

Informants described three varieties of rectangular storage bags. The first, Type I, was made from dehaired rawhide, obtained from the hides of horses, cows, sheep, goats, buffalo, or deer, but not from coyote or mountain lion (wildcat?) hide (Inf. 7). Two pieces were sewn together on three sides. A flap folded over the pocket. The maximum dimension of this bag was about two feet. It was closed with thongs, as were all three types; draw strings were denied. According to Inf. 7, this type was used for storing dried meat, but not for gathering seeds or for transport.

The second type, Type II, was made from a single piece of dehaired buckskin; it was folded and sewn on two sides. This container was about three and a half feet long and two feet wide. In addition to dried meat, corn, corn meal, and clothing were stored in this type of bag. In some cases, dried meat was apparently wrapped in a partly dressed buckskin for storage.

Types I and II were undecorated, and both men and women could make them (Inf. 7). The third type, Type III, was fringed and was used for storing ritual equipment (see Trait 217, Medicine Bag).

Storage bags were kept in the hogan, suspended from poles placed in cracks in the walls. The undecorated buckskin bag (Inf. 280), and possibly the rawhide bag, were also used for storing dried meat in caves (see Trait 84, Storage Cave).

To what extent the first two types of storage bag were and are made or used by Ramah inhabitants is unknown. The primary material for the rawhide sacks probably changed from buffalo and deer hide to the hide of domestic animals as the latter became more readily available. Whether any are now used or preserved as heirlooms is unknown. At present, some jerky is still made, but it is stored in gunnysacks or in roof crevices within the hogan (if there are no cats) and consumed soon after it is made. Clothing is stored in suitcases or trunks purchased at the trading posts or hung on hangers. The third type, however, is used at present, and has been in continuous use as long as Inf. 7 can remember.

Hill (East, Central, and West)

Several varieties of skin storage bags were constructed. One type was made from elk skin traded from the Ute (C, Chinle; GH, White Cone), buckskin, or goatskin (GH). "Elk skin is more flexible and lighter in weight than buckskin, but not as tough. These elk hide sacks lasted for years" (C; see Hill, 1938:45). Two hides were normally used; these were trimmed and sewn together. The finished bag was trapezoidal in shape, wider at the bottom than at the top. Note that an error exists in the description of this bag as given previously in Hill (1938:43). Bags of this type were approximately two feet deep and four to five feet wide at their broadest part. They were employed primarily for storing farm products (C, GH).

A second type of bag resembled a barley sack in shape. Two elk hides were trimmed, and the resulting rectangles sewn together. It was also used for storing farm products (C).

A third type was made from a single hide, of elk (C, GH), deer, antelope (GH), sheep, or goat (TLLSS, Crownpoint). GH said that mountain sheep skin was used, but this is doubtful since the animal was normally used only in a ceremonial capacity. The hide was folded lengthwise, the edges trimmed and then sewn along the bottom and side. This bag was used not only for storage but also for transportation. The top was closed with a drawstring or tied with a buckskin thong. According to GH, a portion of the neck skin might be left to form a flap at the top of the bag.

AM (Lukachukai) stated that sacks of buckskin, later of elk hide, and more recently barley sacks, were used to transport pinyon nuts. Jerked meat was commonly put in buckskin sacks and placed in stone storehouses in the cliffs (Hill, 1938:145).

Fishler (West)

Deerskins or antelope skins (TN, Kaibito), buffalo hides, or mountain sheep skins were used to make storage bags. The hair was left on the hide. TN stated that skins of small animals were never used to make sacks. According to FG (Coalmine), a cased skin was used.

These bags were used, as above, for the storage of food and ceremonial objects. TT (Coalmine) specified that sheepskin bags were used to transport dried buffalo meat. "Pemmican" (TN) and pinyon nuts were also stored in skin bags (TN; GB, Tuba City). "Using skins kept food much better" (TN). FG said that formerly small bags were used for tobacco.

Comparative

There is little information on storage bags in the literature. None of the early reporters on the Navaho mentioned them, although they were probably used in the storage pits and caves noted by the earlier writers.

Gifford's Western informant said that food was stored in deer hide sacks in dry caves. Later, sacks were made from the hides of horses, sheep, and goats. The Eastern informant spoke of storing meat and dried muskmelon in skin bags (Gifford, 1940:16, 99).

According to Newcomb (1940a:43), seeds were never stored in skin bags, because "in the early days sacks were made from the skins of animals and were so nearly air-tight that the contents were liable to mold."

In a description of traditional foods, Mrs. Wetherill stated that buckskin bags were used for storage for bread and dried meat (Wetherill, n.d.:2 pp.).

Preparation

87. Mortar   biki·idcidi (Ramah)   "pounding meat (corn) on a sheepskin" (CC)

,áčǫbike··ecidí (Ramah, Haile)   "pemmican anvil"

Ramah

A pit about six inches in diameter was pecked in the center of a stone about the size of a metate (about eighteen inches long and four inches thick). A small hard pebble (*tse ewozi*) was used. The pit was further deepened with the same rock (*tselgai*) used in finishing the grooved axe and hammer. Neither sand nor water was used in the grinding process, since the pit was meant to be somewhat rough in texture. "You don't have to get it smooth" (Inf. 7). A woman, if she knew how, could make a mortar, but usually men made them (Inf. 8). There was no specified time or place.

Mortars were used mainly by women just before meal time for pounding dried meat "so that it won't spill off." If women were busy elsewhere, a man might perform the task. Inf. 50 declared that dried deer meat had to be pounded before eating, but dried goat or mutton did not. Unpounded meat was often eaten (Inf. 8).

Bedrock and bowl-shaped mortars were denied by Infs. 7, 14, and 2, and Inf. 192 denied mortars of any type. Most of the information was given by Inf. 8, who had seen and used a mortar, but had never made one. He said that an axe and a hammer are now used for pounding meat. The unimportance of hunting in Ramah at present may account for conflicting statements and the disappearance of the mortar.

Fishler (West)

FG (Coalmine) was told about a wooden mortar for grinding seeds "in the old days before corn was grown," but he had never seen one.

Comparative
There is almost no information in the literature, either archaeological, mythical, or ethnographic, that deals with the mortar. Various authors, including the Franciscan Fathers, Matthews, and Gifford, have described the preparation of jerked meat, which was softened by pounding with a stone; but not even by implication was it suggested that pounding was done in a mortar. Mortars and pestles of any sort were denied by both of Gifford's informants, but both informants confirmed the making of pemmican: dried meat was pulverized by pounding with a cobble on a rock. According to the Eastern informant, pounding was not done on the metate for fear of breaking it (Gifford, 1940:16, 25, 98). No mortars are reported for any archaeological site regarded as Navaho.

88. Metate

cé da·šžé·· (Ramah, Lamphere, Haile)   "stone for grinding"; "flat bottom rock" (CC)

bika ·aka·ha· (Lamphere)   "on it grinding is done"

Ramah
A piece of hard lava—abundant around Ramah—was selected, approximately the size of the finished metate. One surface was pecked with a hammerstone, then ground with another until the desired size and shape was achieved. The shape varied from oval to rectangular with rounded corners. Dimensions also varied. The length, width, and thickness of three metates which were measured were (in centimeters): 24.0 by 7.6 by 2.5; 45.7 by 30.5 by 5.0–7.6; 41.0 by 25.0 by 2.5–5.5. (See 82.b and Plate IV.)

Corn and other grains, salt, clay, bark for dyes, and sandpainting minerals were all ground on the metate. Occasionally, several metates might be reserved for different purposes, although Inf. 192 said that the back of the regular metate was used for grinding material other than food.

Either a man or a woman could make metates, although they were usually owned by women. Inf. 15 made the one she uses today. Inf. 7 was forced to use his whetstone to grind bark because his wife thought this process would dull the metate used by the household: "The women folks won't let me use it."

Grinding was done either inside or outside the hogan. The metate was placed on a sheepskin or goatskin, hair side down. A stone was placed under the hide at the thinner end of the metate nearest the worker, so that the stone sloped away from the operator. Women or girls usually did the grinding, but a man might occasionally use the metate, and sometimes boys ground corn.

Metates lasted a long time. The one owned by Inf. 15 was made many years ago, and she had worn out two manos but the metate is still serviceable. Storage was not specified, but Inf. 8 kept his on the floor near the wall behind some old sacks. An informant from Thoreau kept hers "out of the way, because it is not used much any more."

Sanction for the metate occurs in mythology and it is regarded today as a part of the early Navaho culture. Although most families still possess at least one, many no longer use metates. Lava metates were seen at the hogans

Subsistence of several informants (Infs. 8, 15, 61), and Roberts (1951:22) noted that each of his households had at least one metate and one household had two. Bailey (1940:275) reported that most families that she worked with around the Ramah, Smith Lake, Pinedale, and Chaco Canyon areas still possessed the metate and mano. Hand gristmills were introduced by the traders about 1900; and as commercial flour, salt, dyes, and other products became available, the metate was less frequently used.

The metate is not entirely obsolete, however, since it is utilized in the preparations for the puberty and marriage ceremonies and for sandpaintings. Informants know how to make metates, and some of the older ones have done so.

IV. Grinding corn on the metate (Tr. 88). Note also the loom with partially woven blanket (Tr. 127). Goatskins (cf. Tr. 126) are used to catch the corn as it is ground with the mano (Tr. 89) on the metate (Tr. 88). The woman is wearing a cotton skirt (Tr. 166), velveteen blouse (Tr. 167), hair tie (Tr. 181), turquoise and shell necklace (Tr. 197), earring (Tr. 198), and bracelets (Tr. 200).

Hill (East, Central, and West)

Metates were manufactured from lava and other rocks of similar hardness. The Nazlini area was a noted source for the appropriate material (MS, Sawmill). The rock was tested by pounding. If it did not chip or crack when pounded and gave a ringing sound, it was considered suitable (C, Chinle). As at Ramah, an attempt was made to select a stone with the approximate dimensions of the finished product. This was transported, usually on horseback, to the home of the maker.

The standard metate for general household use was about two feet long and fifteen inches wide. Its width was gauged by the size of the mano, which should be about an inch and a half shorter.

Shaping a metate was a tedious process, done intermittently during leisure periods. It was accomplished by chipping and abrading with petrified wood or a hammerstone, or both. The implements of petrified wood were of three sizes, each with at least one sharp edge. The largest was used to outline the metate. The stone was struck at an acute angle; the blow was struck away from the operator and toward the outside of the metate. According to MS, it was customary for the worker to say a prayer at the time work began. "You say this outline is the spider's web." Once the utensil had been roughly shaped, a medium-sized piece of petrified wood was used to smooth the edges and grinding surface. A mano was run over the face from time to time, to enable the operator to detect any ridges or unevennesses that existed. Water was poured on these high spots and they were chipped and abraded until the face was level. Finally the smallest piece of petrified wood was used to pit the surface irregularly to give it a cutting or working edge (MS; PP, Fort Defiance; IS, Lukachukai; C; TW, Keams Canyon).

According to MS, a short ceremony was necessary before the new metate could be used. A handful of white corn was ground on it and the meal placed in a container. The operator took pinches of this and "marked" (blessed) the four principal support posts of the hogan. The remainder of the meal was sprinkled clockwise around the hogan. This procedure was followed by a prayer to the metate.

As at Ramah, the metate was placed on a goatskin. Corn was poured on the metate from a basket and the mano worked back and forth until the meal was of the desired texture. A metate brush (see Trait 90) was used to clear the surface of any meal that had not already fallen onto the hide. This whole process was repeated until sufficient meal had been ground (LW, Lukachukai). According to TW and MS, new cutting surfaces were chipped in the metate each time it was used. Grinding on the bottom side of the metate or reversing the ends of the mano while it was in use was believed to bring bad luck (MS).

Some informants (MS, IS, PP) reported that a smaller and lighter metate and mano set was used when the family traveled; this set was approximately eight to twelve inches in size. Its use was denied by TW. According to IS, when green corn was ground, several metates were customarily placed side by side, after the manner of the Pueblos. Slabs of rock were placed around three sides, since the ground material was too liquid to be held on the goatskin.

Metates and manos were customarily given by mothers to their daughters at the time of their marriages (MH, Head Springs).

There is some evidence that at an earlier period grinding songs existed among the Navaho. According to K (Mariano Lake), the singing was done by young men. When several girls were grinding boys sang, beating an inverted basket to keep time. Some of these songs were believed to bring rain. Others had only entertainment value. One in particular referred to the fact that girls would often "talk back and sass" their mothers when asked to grind corn:

What are you going to do with the corn you are grinding?
What are you going to do with the corn you are grinding?
Why don't you chew it instead of grinding it?
Why don't you grind it instead of talking back?

According to PP, songs of this type occurred most frequently during preparations for the girl's adolescent rite. The men sang, keeping time on a rolled-up sheepskin. "These songs were for fun and to speed the work." From time to time the girls would throw meal on the men, and the men would throw meal back at them. All would be covered with meal when the grinding was completed. GH (White Cone) denied that grinding songs were in common use. He stated that they were part of Blessing Way, but were not for secular use.

Lamphere (East)

PM confirmed the term for metate, and said it might also be called "on it grinding is done."

Fishler (West)

Fishler's informants (GB, Tuba City; TN, IJmo, Kaibito) confirmed data obtained at Ramah and by Hill. Often, according to his informants, metates and manos were also secured from ruins. The metates were used for cracking pinyon nuts and for grinding juniper berries and corncobs, as well as for grinding corn. When cracked, the nuts were placed in a flat basket and winnowed to remove the shells. IJmo said that her grandmother told her of making a flour with corncobs long ago. The corn was shucked, and the cobs were cooked in the ashes. They were then ground on the metate, and mixed with ground corn. Juniper flour was also used; the berry was shelled, soaked in water, and ground. Other informants said that juniper flour was mixed with a "blue clay" and eaten when other food was in short supply.

Comparative

The metate appears to have been a standard item for all Navaho groups, although opinions differ as to the amount of work expended in shaping it and the value attached to the shaped stone. Palmer, the first writer to report the metate, stated that it was invariably flat and that any concavity was the result of wear. When the Navaho moved, they took their metates with them (Palmer, 1869:49). According to the Franciscan Fathers (1910:63), the metate was used for grinding corn, coffee, or wheat. By 1910, however, it was already beginning to be replaced by flour and coffee mills obtained from commercial sources. The term confirms that at Ramah (Franciscan Fathers, 1912:127).

Both of Gifford's informants confirmed the movable rectangular metate set at an angle for grinding corn and seeds. Both denied metates of vesicular lava or bedrock. The Eastern informant denied sandstone metates. He also denied that metates were used for grinding anything but food. He said that four stone slabs were set on edge around the metate, but not actually against it; hardened clay on the floor inside the slabs kept the food clean, and buckskin at the lower edge of the metate received the food. According to the Western informant, yucca detergent was also crushed on the metate (Gifford, 1940:24, 111–112).

Metates have been found at sites, presumably Navaho, dating from the seventeenth century. Keur found one on the vesicular volcanic rock at Big Bead Mesa that save for its length (53.34 cm.) seemed comparable to the Ramah type, as did two of the three metates found in the Gobernador region (Keur, 1941:59; 1944:79, pl. VIIIa). At sites in the Largo and Blanco Canyons, Farmer found two types of metate, both of sandstone. One type was slab-shaped; specimens fell within the range of sizes found at Ramah and by Keur. The other type had a trough open at one end and seemed to be more common at campsites (Farmer, 1942:71).

The Navaho seem to have preferred what Woodbury has called the flat metate. This is most common in the north and central areas of the Southwest, and is typical of Pueblo III sites, although occasional specimens have been found in earlier Pueblo sites (for example, Alkali Ridge, Site 12; Marsh Pass, Arizona, Site RB551; see Woodbury, 1954:54–59). Reiter pointed out that plain surface metates were found where igneous rock was available, and other types where igneous rock was not available (Woodbury, 1939:68).

It has been suggested that the metates found in old Navaho sites were not Navaho made, but taken from nearby Pueblo ruins. Given the Navaho penchant for making full use of their environment, this is possible. Undoubtedly diffusion of both artifact and pattern took place; the flat metate was late in the Pueblo culture sequence, and it was the predominant type in the areas of Pueblo-Navaho contact (Woodbury, 1954:58–59).

There are numerous allusions to metates in Navaho mythology, and they are represented in some of the sandpaintings. Different color combinations for metates and manos were reported by Reichard (1950:15, 157, 586), including pairings of black and blue, black and white, and blue and white (see also citations of corn grinding in Spencer, 1947:25).

89. Mano

cé da·šʒíń (Ramah, Haile, Lamphere)   "upper millstone"

kosče·be·ká (Ramah)   small mano

nabé··ʼélka (Ramah)   "grinding stone"

Ramah

The mano was used with the metate for grinding (see 82.b and Plate IV). Details of manufacture correspond to those for the metate. According to Inf. 8, pecking was done with petrified wood, but a hammer is now used. In grinding, the mano was rubbed over the metate with short backward and forward strokes, the movement being from the shoulders rather than the elbows.

A small mano (about three inches by four inches) known as *kostse beeka* was used for grinding seeds, not corn, as was the "grinding stone" (Infs. 50, 14). According to Inf. 50, who had a small mano, one was used when it was feared the greater weight of the regular mano would crush the seeds. This type of mano was rocked back and forth over the seeds. An unshaped sandstone cobble might be used for rough work such as grinding bark for dye (Inf. 7) or clay (Inf. 15); it was feared that such grinding might injure the regular mano.

Another use of the mano was as a weight to facilitate removal of the placenta after childbirth. This use was confirmed by all but two of Bailey's informants (Bailey, 1950:68).

Hill (East, Central, and West)

All of Hill's informants had seen the mano and metate in use, and both were being used to a limited extent in 1934 and 1935. Manos were manufactured at the same time as the metate, from the same materials, with the same implements, and in the same manner. The standard mano was about twelve inches long (about an inch and a half shorter than the width of the metate), with a cutting face about four inches wide. This face was usually pitted to enhance its grinding efficiency (MS, Sawmill; TW, Keams Canyon; LW, Lukachukai; C, Chinle; PP, Fort Defiance). According to MS, two manos were always made for each metate—one of the standard size, the second with a cutting face only two inches wide. As at Ramah, the motion of the mano was always back and forth, never rotary (K, Mariano Lake; LW; PP).

Specialized forms were used in grinding seeds. According to K, these were about four inches square and two inches thick. C and MS said a rounded boulder-like mano was used for grinding mustard seed (MS) or the seed of the bladderpod (C).

Lamphere (East)

PM confirmed the first term for mano.

Fishler (West)

According to Fishler's informants, the mano was pecked until it was round on top and flat on the bottom; it was about ten inches long and three inches wide. Both men and women made these (TN, Kaibito). FG (Coalmine) stated that when a woman had difficulty dispelling the placenta after childbirth, pollen was placed on the mano and it was rolled over the stomach. Prayers and songs were sung by a chanter to induce the placenta to leave the woman.

Comparative

The mano, like the metate, is reported from many parts of the Navaho area. Palmer collected one, probably before 1870 (Palmer, 1869:49). According to the Franciscan Fathers (1910:63), a fairly rounded stone of a convenient size was used and discarded when the job was completed. Sometimes, however, petrified wood was used to resharpen the surface, and the mano was not discarded. Gifford's informants used a mano of stone other than vesicular lava; it was fifteen inches long and shaped like a flattened ellipse. It was used with both hands. The mano used by the Western Navaho was long, thin, "elliptical in cross section, of close-grained granitic stone" (Gifford, 1940:25, 122).

Apparently both types are known archaeologically. Small rounded or rectangular manos, evidently for use with one hand, and longer ones (up to eight and nine inches long) were found by Keur (Keur, 1941:58–59; 1944:79). Farmer also found both oval and rectangular manos, usually of sandstone. The oval type had two usable surfaces and could be worked with one hand; the rectangular type was long and narrow, "probably two-handed" (Farmer, 1942:72).

Hurt (1942:95) distinguished three types of rectangular sandstone manos from Canyon de Chelly. One type was relatively thin, with rounded corners and a beveled top; another was very thick, with rounded corners and a convex top; another was flat on the top as well as the bottom. Hurt suggested that the majority of his specimens might have been found by the Navaho in the nearby Pueblo ruin. He indicated that the lava specimen, however, might be a "Navaho" type.

90. Grass Brush

bé·éžó·· (Ramah, Haile) "broom"; "brush" (CC)

cé be· ná·lžó· (Lamphere) "metate brush"; "rock brush" (CC)

Ramah

Ripe stems of grasses such as Three-awn, Wiregrass, Muhly, Timothy (Vestal, 1952:15–17), or wheat (Inf. 261) were collected. The stems of some, such as Muhly (but not Timothy), were stripped of leaves; Inf. 261 said that wheat heads were not removed. The stems were gathered into bunches, from one to three feet long and from three quarters of an inch to three inches in diameter. The bundle was cut square at one end, and tied with a piece of cloth or string about two inches from that end. Leather was used to bind the metate brush observed by Mills in 1947.

Men, women, and children could make these brushes, although women usually did, and Inf. 8 said that women owned them. They were made in the hogan, in the fall or winter after the grass was ripe.

The long end was used to clean material from the metate after grinding, three times a day (according to Inf. 18). It was also used for sweeping the hogan floor (see Trait 120, Broom) and as a strainer. In the latter case the loose ends were spread and the liquid poured through. In 1946 Roberts noted that sometimes a bundle of stiff grass was used to stir the ashes when making corn bread and also to strain the "blue water" (blue corn meal in water). The short end was also used as a hairbrush (see Trait 181, Hair Tie).

Because stems were broken through use, the grass brush often had to be retied. Inf. 8 spoke of a brush made eight years previously; he thought it would last another two years, but admitted that it was not used much. Inf. 18 said that a brush used three times a day would have to be retied after three days, and that it would last only nine months. Inf. 8 said his brush was thrown on some box shelves along with mush sticks; Inf. 18 said his was kept on the dirt floor near some old sheepskins.

Bailey found these brushes still in general use in the late 1930's in several Navaho areas, including Ramah–Two Wells, Smith Lake–Pinedale, and Chaco (Bailey, 1940:274; 1942:212). Roberts (1951:22, 24, 48) noted three grass hairbrushes in one of his households and one in another.

Hill (East, Central, and West)

Descriptions of material, construction, and use of the metate brush or hairbrush coincided with those obtained from Ramah (C, Chinle; IS, Lukachukai; PP, Fort Defiance; K, Mariano Lake; GH, White Cone). Brushes of this type were in use in 1933 and 1934.

Informants also confirmed the use of the brush as a strainer to remove undesirable materials from liquids (C, IS, K). K made specific mention of this in connection with dyeing. In recent times a piece of cloth has been used as a strainer (IS). PP denied the use of strainers.

Lamphere (East)

PM said that the second term (above) designated the grass brush used for cleaning the metate. The term means "rock, with it sweeping, or brushing."

Fishler (West)

FG (Coalmine) said that brushes were made from grasses which were tied together; they were used to clean metates.

Comparative

There is no known occurrence of the grass brush in archaeological sites regarded as Navaho.

The Franciscan Fathers (1910:190) confirmed the use of the grass brush as described above. Several varieties of grasses were used. Elmore identified some of the grasses as species of Muhly (as did Vestal); he also stated that a twig of Rocky Mountain juniper was inserted into the brushes "supposedly for protection against evil influence" (Elmore, 1944:25–26).

Gifford's informants used the grass brush for sweeping meal and as a hairbrush. It was also used as a strainer when "ashy water" was added to maize meal (Gifford, 1940:25, 112–113).

A grass brush in the Harvard Peabody Museum is about twenty inches long and an inch and a half in diameter at the point where it is tied with a piece of cloth. It was collected in 1913 by C. C. Willoughby and R. G. Fuller at Chinle, Arizona.

Mythical references to the grass brush may indicate that it is a long-established Navaho trait; Matthews (1902:197) mentioned it in his account of the Night Chant.

90.a. Grass brush. This is also used as a hair brush (see Tr. 181).

91. Mush Stirring Sticks

ʾádísci·n (Ramah, Haile)   "mush sticks" (CC)

Ramah

A number of sticks, preferably of greasewood, were stripped of bark and smoothed, then tied together with buckskin, string, or cloth. Inf. 12 said that any number of sticks was used, "as long as they filled the hand." According to Inf. 47, sticks were always used in groups of four. Bailey's informant said that four was the preferred number (Bailey, 1940:272). Inf. 8's stirrer contained five sticks; it was about two feet long, tied six inches from one end. This type of implement was the only one used for stirring corn mush (Inf. 7).

These sticks were made at any time usually by women. Inf. 8 thought that men might also make stirrers, but his was made by a woman, Inf. 178, from material gathered on a trip to Atarque. Children did not make stirrers. The maker was the owner (Inf. 8).

Whoever did the cooking could use this device. It was held butt down with both hands for thick mush, with one hand for thin mush. According to Bailey (1940:274), it was used for corn dishes only, and was often reused. It was held in the right hand like a pencil, and after use, leaned against the edge of the pan on the ground.

Inf. 8 said that prayers were offered after stirring corn meal (apparently before the stirrer was taken out of the mush). The sticks were removed and cleaned, then held in the right hand with the butt ends up at about a forty-five-degree angle; they were moved slowly in a circle while a prayer was said. In winter Inf. 8 prayed that the sun would warm the land; in summer, prayers were for rain. He was the only informant to mention prayers in connection with this trait, and he had not seen (or heard) anyone else saying prayers recently.

Mush stirrers are still used in the Ramah area, although how extensively is impossible to judge. Inf. 12's family made stirrers for ceremonial use and retained them for daily use after the ceremony. The set owned by Inf. 8 was two years old, and he expected it to last for another ten years if not used too often. According to Inf. 8, people generally ceased using the mush stirrers when meal became available in the stores.

Hill (East, Central, and West)

Greasewood or black greasewood for stirrers was always gathered in the spring. It was placed in the coals to remove the spines and loosen the bark. When the bark was removed, the sticks were cut the same length (PP, Fort Defiance), about two feet long, each a quarter of an inch in diameter (TW, Keams Canyon). Several of these lengths were tied loosely in a bundle with cotton or woolen cord, a buckskin thong (WH, Wheatfield; MH, Head Springs; K, Mariano Lake), or yucca fiber (C, Chinle). According to MS (Sawmill), if wood other than greasewood was used a famine would result. As at Ramah, the number of sticks specified varied: two to three (BW, Keams Canyon), four to six (TW), seven to nine (C), or occasionally as many as fifteen or twenty (PP).

According to AS (Lukachukai), stirring of corn meal mush always had to be done in a sunwise (clockwise) direction; this was denied by TW. No songs were sung while stirring (K).

This implement was highly valued since prayers were addressed to it when it was made (MS, MH) and each time it was used (MS, C, AS, MH, TW). When the cooking was completed the woman held up the stirrer and said,

May I live until I have white hair;

May it rain;

May the good fortune which has occurred in the past continue.   (TW)
or

May it be cool; may it be warm;

May I acquire property;

May my neighbors and I have good health;

May my neighbors feel friendly toward me.   (AS).

Women used the same stirring stick over a period of many years and the implement habitually was passed down from mother to daughter. "The reason for this was because it was prayed to" (MH).

Lamphere (East)
PM said that stirring sticks were made from black greasewood. She confirmed the term.

Fishler (West)
FG (Coalmine) had used stirring rods of black greasewood in ceremonies.

Comparative
According to the Franciscan Fathers (1910:218), from one to eleven greasewood sticks were used for stirring mush, the number depending on convenience. Both of Gifford's informants confirmed this implement, and denied the use of more than ten sticks. According to the Western informant, three, five, or seven sticks might be used; the Eastern informant said that stirrers might contain from one to seven sticks (Gifford, 1940:25–26, 113).

The stirrer also figured in daily ritual according to most observers. The Franciscan Fathers, for example, stated that grace was spoken by the head of the family while holding the sticks upward (as at Ramah), a ritual considered indispensable "at a time when the Navaho relied completely upon the yield of corn and herbs." Although the diet had changed by 1910 to include staples bought at the trading posts, the custom of saying grace had not entirely subsided (Franciscan Fathers, 1910:220).

92. Stirring Paddle

Ramah
According to Inf. 7, stirring paddles or loop stick stirrers were never used.

Hill (East, Central, and West)
Paddle-shaped stirrers with square blades (TW, Keams Canyon) were made from juniper. TW said that they were not extensively used, and were made only when black greasewood for stirring sticks was unavailable. K (Mariano Lake) stated that they were used only when making thick corn meal mush.

MS (Sawmill) had never heard of the stirring paddle. According to her, if such an instrument were used, the mush would become lumpy. PP (Fort Defiance) denied knowledge of both this trait and the looped stirrer.

Lamphere (East)
PM had never heard of a stirring paddle. She said a juniper stirring stick was sometimes used in a ceremony.

Comparative
Both of Gifford's informants denied the use of a stirring paddle (Gifford, 1940:25). Other information on this trait is lacking.

Cooking

93. Griddle   céte·s (Ramah, Hill, Haile)   "stone slab"; "rock cooker" (CC)

biki·te·sí (Ramah, Haile)   "metal slab"; "metal cooker" (CC)

bice·ʼxólóní (Ramah, Haile)   modern griddle; "frying pan (purchased)" (CC)

Ramah
A flat rock was placed over the fire and used as a griddle on which to bake bread. At present, a metal griddle is used (Inf. 82). It is supported over the fire by stones, or empty evaporated milk cans (Bailey, 1940:275); and as the fire burns down, the coals are raked back under the sheet with a stick. Metal griddles about twenty inches square were observed by Bailey in Ramah, Chaco Canyon, and the Pinedale–Smith Lake areas. "This and the coffee pot are the household's most frequently used articles." In 1949, Manson observed Inf. 10 grilling mutton on a small wire grill over a bed of coals.

Hill (Central and West)
Hill's informants confirmed the term for "stone slab," above. Griddle stones were about half an inch thick and varied in size to an upper limit of a foot in width and three feet in length (C, Chinle). A soft stone was selected since it withstood the heat and was less apt to crack; this was abraded and pecked to the desired shape by harder stones. The surface was then rubbed with a rough rock to remove unevenness and produce a smooth face (C; PP, Fort Defiance; TW, Keams Canyon; MS, Sawmill).

Then peach kernels, pumpkin and squash seeds, and pinyon needles were chewed and spit upon the stone. This mixture was rubbed with a smooth hard boulder to produce a polish on the face of the griddle. When this polishing was completed, pinyon pitch was spread on the surface; a fire was built, and as the pitch melted, it was rubbed back and forth with branches of pinyon. After the final polishing, the griddle was ready for use. "Your first bread will taste pitchy but the pitch will finally burn or wear away" (C).

Several variants in curing and polishing the stone were encountered. PP stated that pounded pinyon needles were soaked in water and rubbed on the stone to give the initial polish. For the final polish the spinal fluid of sheep was used. "It will become smooth as glass." TW applied pitch, then pinyon needles, and allowed these to burn off. "This makes the rock slick and prevents the bread from sticking." MS first rubbed powdered squash seeds on the griddle. "This makes it possible for the stone to withstand heating and smooths the surface." Next the stone was placed over hot coals and when thoroughly heated an inch-thick layer of pinyon needles was placed on it. These were cooked until they turned brown or yellow, then removed. Finally, pinyon pitch was rubbed on the surface and it was allowed to cool gradually. All treatments were believed to season and to give polish to the griddle.

Griddles were manufactured by the women. "Grandmothers usually seasoned them; the other women of the family assisted in sizing and smoothing." Normally these utensils descended from mother to daughter; occasionally they were lent to neighbors (MS).

Griddles were used for making piki or wafer bread. The griddle rested upon several boulders that raised it three or four inches above a bed of hot coals (PP, MS). When the supports were removed and taken from the fire, the impression left in the ashes was eradicated and a short prayer was said (MS). According to MS a different griddle was made for cooking corn bread; it was oval in shape and an inch and a half thick.

Fishler (West)

A flat stone fourteen or more inches long and nine inches or more wide was shaped by pecking with a hard rock. It was heated over the fire (as at Ramah), then rubbed with pinyon branches. The pinyon pitch turned the surface black, hard, and smooth. GB (Tuba City) described a stone "pan" used for roasting pinyon nuts. A flat stone (as above) formed the bottom, two rocks the same size formed the sides, and a smaller one the end of the "pan." Pinyons were placed in this, and stirred with a stick while cooking to prevent burning.

The griddle was usually made in the hogan or outside in the brush shelter. It was used for cooking fried bread or other foods, or for roasting pinyons. GB denied its use for frying meat. He said that marrow was used to grease the stone and to keep the fried bread from sticking. Piki was made from finely ground corn meal, with ashes for leavening. TN (Kaibito) believed the stone was used only for cooking bread.

Comparative

Most observers of the Navaho have confirmed the use of the griddle. The baking of a thin, broad, flexible corn cake on a large, flat, polished stone slab was described by Matthews (1902:47). A flat round stone was still used in 1910, although by that time frying pans and skillets were used by many Navaho (Franciscan Fathers, 1910:63, 219). According to Sapir and Hoijer's informant at Crystal in 1929, corn bread was baked on a griddle; his description confirmed that above (Sapir and Hoijer, 1942:403). Steggerda and Eckhardt (1941:218–219) described various types of bread baked on the hot stone griddle.

According to both of Gifford's informants, maize bread was baked "on hot stones, in coals, or on pottery pan"; ashes were added to the batter. The Western informant denied the baking of paper bread, which the Eastern informant had confirmed. He said that goat's milk was used with red maize flour to make red piki; "without goat's milk red maize makes white paper bread [piki]" (Gifford, 1940:19, 104). It was probably baked on a griddle.

94. Skewer (Spit)   atsa bildizi (Hill)   skewer; "meat cooking" (CC)

Ramah

The ribs of the wildcat were placed on the end of a pointed stick held over the fire (Inf. 7). This was presumably a common method of broiling meat, although it is not known whether the method is still used. Meat was also roasted in the coals, or cooked in a pan.

Hill (East, Central, and West)

A convenient length of juniper less than an inch in diameter was pointed at one end (SG, Keams Canyon). Meat was forced over the point and held over the fire to broil (SG; TOMC, Red Rock). According to C (Chinle), meat was placed in the cleft of a forked stick. The butt was placed in the earth and the stick inclined at an angle to let the meat hang above the fire.

MS (Sawmill) described an oak skewer, three feet long and half an inch in diameter. Two or three layers of stomach fat were wrapped about this pole, covering all but four inches at one end and ten at the other. Over the fat was wrapped the diaphragm. Two stones were placed in the coals and the free ends of the spit rested on these and above the fire. The pole was rotated from time to time as the broiling progressed. The use of skewers was denied by PP (Fort Defiance).

Fishler (West)

GB (Tuba City) and TN (Kaibito) said that a piece of meat was put on a pointed stick and broiled over the coals. Both informants had broiled meat this way.

Comparative

Davis (1857:410) was apparently the first to report the skewer among the Navaho. He saw a woman broiling the side of a sheep on a stick held over the coals. This method of roasting over the coals was confirmed by the Franciscan Fathers (1910:212), who mentioned it briefly. Gifford (1940:15) recorded the use of a spit in broiling for the Eastern Navaho; the Western informant was not questioned on this trait. Both groups had used another common method of cooking, roasting meat on the coals.

95. Pot Supports

cé biʒáˑd (Lamphere)   "rock leg" (CC)

Ramah

Three large pieces of sandstone were used to support containers which were placed over a fire. These were observed by Tschopik in use at Inf. 7's establishment in 1938.

Hill (Central)

MS (Sawmill) confirmed the use of conveniently sized stones placed in the ashes to support oval-bottomed pots. C (Chinle) and PP (Fort Defiance) contended that if the base of the pot were worked into the ashes it would stand without support. Griddles, and in some cases spits and ears of corn (MS), were rested on stones (PP, MS). All informants agreed that the depressions left by the stones and the pots were erased and a short prayer said.

Lamphere (East)

PM and EP agreed that if one used a stone griddle on the open fire, the rocks set underneath it would be called "rock, its leg."

Comparative

Stones were used to support the griddle according to Sapir and Hoijer (1942:405). Three stones were used to support pots according to Gifford's Eastern informant. The Western informant used no supports, but instead worked the bottom of the pot into the ground (Gifford, 1940:15, 98). Stones or empty evaporated milk cans are now used as supports, according to Bailey; she saw these at Chaco Canyon, Smith Lake and Pinedale, and at Ramah. She also described a method of steadying a hot vessel while its contents were being stirred. A strip of metal about eighteen inches long and two inches wide was grasped in the middle with the left hand while one end rested on the ground and the other on the rim of the vessel. The contents of the pot were stirred with the right hand (Bailey, 1940:274–275).

96. Roasting Pit

Xe·ná·álbiš ·á·á·n (Ramah)   "cooking fire in a hole" (CC)

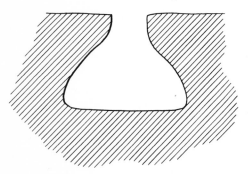

96.1. Roasting pit, after Tschopik

Ramah

According to one of Bailey's informants, the roasting pit was about five feet four inches deep, about eighteen to twenty inches in diameter, and like the storage pit (see Trait 85), larger at the bottom than the top (see 96.1). Tschopik observed a similar pit at Inf. 19's place in 1938. It was five and a half feet deep, with a bottom diameter of four feet and a top diameter of three feet. A pit seen at Inf. 45's place in 1938 was five feet deep, three feet long, and two and a half feet wide.

Smaller pits were also observed. A sample corn cake was baked for Bailey in a pit six by eighteen inches; the baking took only a few hours (Bailey, 1940:281). The Leightons in 1940 observed the roasting of a porcupine at Inf. 12's place; the pit used was twenty-four by eighteen by twelve inches.

Several methods of cooking in this type of pit were observed. Usually a fire was built in the pit and allowed to burn all day (Bailey), for twenty-four hours (Tschopik at Inf. 19's or Inf. 12's), or for two days (Roberts, at Inf. 34's). According to Bailey's informant and Inf. 47, the coals were then raked out, corn was put in, covered with cornhusks and then dirt. Tschopik observed unhusked corn thrown directly on the coals. The mouth of the pit was filled with corn stalks, parallel sticks, and dirt. According to Inf. 45, the order was poles, cornhusks, then dirt. In each case, the corn was left to cook overnight.

Corn cake, used in the girl's adolescence ceremony, was baked in a pit at Inf. 12's home in Two Wells. After the fire had burned in the pit for a day, the bottom and sides were covered with cornhusks. Batter was poured in and covered with a layer of husks; then the pit was filled with dirt and a fire built on top. The cake baked from about sunset to almost dawn. Roberts observed at Inf. 34's place that the ashes were removed and covered with dirt. Then the hole was lined with cornhusks "criss-cross first and go round and round the hole" (Inf. 12).

Meat was also cooked in pits. The cooking of a horse's head was witnessed at Inf. 12's place. The head was placed on the coals in a large pit; then more coals were added, then earth, and it was left to roast overnight.

When a porcupine was cooked in a small pit at Inf. 12's place, hot stones were used instead of coals. According to Inf. 50's mother, flat, hot stones were also used for cooking yucca shoots (*ndeesgai*) from *Yucca glauca* (identification by Wyman and Harris, 1941:21). The stones were placed in the pit and the shoots laid directly on them. More heated flat rocks were laid on the shoots, and finally dirt was added. The buds of the yucca were also roasted in this manner.

Both men and women might make the pit and roast corn. Several women were observed helping Inf. 19; they were paid for their labor with roasted corn. Inf. 34 said that both he and his wife had helped prepare a pit, and Inf. 180 helped Inf. 8 dig his pit.

According to Inf. 47, the roasting pit was used "when the frost is on the ground." Field notes from most observers usually indicated September and in one case October, or when the corn was ripe. It was probably used earlier in the year for other plants. The porcupine noted by the Leightons was roasted in March. Inf. 12 said corn cake might be baked at any time but usually was made only once a year at some large ceremonial. The roasting pit was repaired when necessary, and reused frequently.

According to Infs. 45, 47, and 50, the Navaho have always used the roasting pit. It survives in the Ramah community, and pits have been observed at the homes of several informants (Infs. 7, 8, 9, 19, 45, 58, 274). Although its present incidence is not definitely determined, probably most Ramah families use the pit at some time during the fall. For large ceremonials, some have the earth oven (see Trait 97). For daily cooking, the makeshift stoves or the camp fire are used.

Hill (East, Central, and West)
According to C (Chinle), when corn was hit by frost it was picked immediately and roasted. Fire was kept burning in a pit all day. At sundown the ashes and coals were removed; the corn was thrown into the pit, covered with cornhusks and dirt, and left to cook. The next morning, it was eaten freshly roasted (*leeshibeezh*) or dried in the sun and shelled (*nashjizhi*). MH (Head Springs) said that a second crop of corn was planted when the first was half grown to insure a supply of these two products (Hill, 1938:41).

As at Ramah, hot flat stones were used when a porcupine was cooked. They were covered with a layer of wet mud, the porcupine, another layer of mud, and more hot stones. The animal was cooked for about an hour (Hill, 1938:173–174).

Lamphere (East)
Lamphere attended a *kinaalda* at Sheep Springs in July 1966, and supplied the following data. The pit was dug, and a fire built in it that burned for two days. Near sunset, the fire was removed and the bottom of the hole swept clear of ashes. Then the first cornhusk cover was put in the hole. The cover was made from husks that had been softened in water, and clipped on the pointed end; two of these were crossed and sewn together by the *kinaalda* girl to form the center of the large sheet. More husks were sewn to the first two by the women who were helping with the ceremony until a large circular cornhusk cover was formed (see 96.a). A similar cover was sewn for the top and set aside.

Batter was then prepared in a large tub. Corn, ground traditionally on the metate but recently commercially, was mixed first with cold water to form a grainy mixture, then with hot water to form a thin soup, which was

96.a. Lining the roasting pit with a sheet of cornhusks

thickened by adding more and more corn. This batter was stirred with the traditional stirring sticks until the mixture was about the consistency of soft cement and free of lumps. The batter was carried to the side of the hole by a male relative of the kinaalda girl. He then poured it so as to overflow a container placed in the pit (see 96.b) in order to prevent tearing the cornhusk cover and to allow the batter to spread gently around. Women placed additional husks around the edge of the hole as the batter rose. Next the kinaalda girl blessed the cake by sprinkling white corn meal over the batter in a ritual manner; then the second cornhusk cover was put in place. Lamphere added that at this ceremony a layer of wax paper was then spread over the husks. Next came a layer of dirt, then ashes, and finally small long sticks which were set afire.

The cake cooked all night and was uncovered and cut in the morning. Usually the cutting was done by a male relative of the kinaalda girl. Pieces of cake were taken from the outside of the pit first; four pieces were left in the middle. A bit from each of these was given to the four people who sang special Blessing Way songs during the previous night. Other pieces were given to women and men who helped with the singing or with the work.

Comparative

The earliest reference to the roasting pit seems to be that of Matthews (1887:430; 1902:47). According to his description, batter for corn cakes was prepared in one hole lined with fresh sheepskin. It was cooked in another pit, after the fire, which had been burning for many hours—"until the surrounding earth was well heated"—was removed. As at Ramah, cornhusks surrounded the cake. This practice was confirmed by many other observers (Franciscan Fathers, 1910:207; Sapir and Hoijer, 1942:405; Wyman and Bailey, 1943:6–7).

In addition to the method above, the Franciscan Fathers (1910:207–209) confirmed the roasting of unhusked ears in the coals. The name for this method was that given by Hill's informants (*leeshibeezh*). Dyk's informant also confirmed the roasting of green corn as described by Hill (Dyk, 1947:25).

The roasting pit was well known to both of Gifford's informants. Both cooked meat and a variety of corn breads and cakes. The Western informant said that the pit was used for cooking deer, antelope, and elk. The Eastern informant used hot stones and mud to cook prairie dogs, in the same way that Hill's informants cooked porcupines. The Eastern informant, however, cooked porcupines with layers of stones and earth on top of the ground. He also said that several families often used a single pit. The Western informant said that they did "sometimes." The Eastern informant said that maize batter, saliva sweetened, was "cooked on maize foliage in preheated stoneless pit." It was "poured over gourd cup in center to run in different directions. Several families combined. Head woman made maize-meal cross, prayed for future crops." Then the hole was covered with cornhusks, mud, and hot coals (Gifford, 1940:15, 19, 98, 103).

Newcomb (1940a:49) stated that ground squirrels and prairie dogs were roasted "wrapped in green-corn leaves" in a pit, usually placed under the campfire. Legs and heads of sheep and goats were also baked in such pits.

Frisbie (1967:78–81) discussed regional variations in the Central and Eastern areas in the preparation and use of the roasting pit for baking the kinaalda cake. She said that at Pinedale the husks for the first cover were

96.b. Pouring the corn cake batter

sewn in a circle, and at Crownpoint a double cross of husks was pinned together. Husks were then pinned to the circle or double cross to make the mat for the bottom of the pit. The cake was covered with loose husks. At Chinle, the double cross was sewn together, then separate husks were placed around in a circle; no circle was sewn together either at Chinle or at Lukachukai.

There is little or no archaeological evidence for roasting pits, possibly because of the difficulty of discovering them, since they were often dug near the fields rather than the hogans. Very tentative evidence was found by Keur in the Big Bead Mesa sites where cobs were found with kernels which "appear to have been removed in an immature or 'roasting ear' stage" (Keur, 1941:45).

Mrs. Wetherill recorded a traditional mythological account of the use of the roasting pit for corn meal cakes similar to those called *leehiilzhozh* described by Bailey (1940:281). She also described the roasting of "spreading bread," which was cooked in a shallow pit from which the fire had been removed. The pit was cleaned with a grass brush, and the batter poured in. It was made as smooth as possible, to keep the hot sand which was next spread on it from penetrating. Live coals were placed on the whole, and it was left to bake (Wetherill, 1947:39; 1946:5–6).

97. Earth Oven

bá·h biɣan (Lamphere)   "bread's house" (CC)

97.a. Woman baking in an earth oven

Ramah
A few of the Ramah informants, such as Inf. 259, have the Pueblo type of mud and stone beehive oven. It is used for large ceremonials.

Hill (Central)
According to C (Chinle), adobe ovens of the Spanish-Pueblo type were introduced after Fort Sumner and were first used for baking green corn. Recently they have been used for baking bread.

Lamphere (East)
Lamphere observed PM in the construction of an earth oven. She first gathered some flat, thin stones and covered a circular area with them. Wet sand was then plastered on top of the rocks until a smooth platform was made about one-half inch above the ground level. PM said that this platform should be very smooth so as not to leave impressions in the bottom of the loaves of bread. Next she placed large rocks in a circle, leaving an opening for the door. (The door should usually face the east, but PM was not careful about it.) Next, PM poured water on the ground near the oven and used the wet earth (called by the term for clay) to plaster the rocks. She planned to add rocks and earth (adobe) plaster until the beehive shape was achieved. A large, flat stone was placed at the top, and another was to be put in the doorway.

Fishler (West)
TN (Kaibito) said that animals were cooked by putting them in an oven. The Navaho learned this method from the Puebloan people. TN had cooked this way.

Comparative

According to the Franciscan Fathers (1910:218), the roasting pit was originally the only oven possessed by the Navaho, but "in modern times ovens, similar to those in use among the Pueblos, have been introduced for baking purposes." Both of Gifford's informants denied cooking "dough-filled husks in domed (Spanish) ovens" (Gifford, 1940:19).

Utensils

98. Basket Dish

ċa·· (Haile)   basket

Ramah

This description is abstracted from Tschopik (1938, 1940). Baskets were made from sumac (*Rhus tribolata*), yucca (preferably *bacatta*, but also *glauca*), willow, and cottonwood. Other grasses which occur in the Ramah area were not used, usually for fear that the baskets would be rejected for ceremonial use (Infs. 15, 41, 43, 192). The sumac was split into three parts (as it was for the basket bottle), but informants believed it dangerous to use the teeth for splitting (Infs. 15, 32, 41, 43).

Many ritual restrictions attended the manufacture of a basket. The butt ends of the rods always radiated from the center of the tray, "the way the plant grows" (Infs. 39, 41, 192). The butt of one rod always was placed against the tip of the next (Infs. 15, 32, 41, 43, 192). An opening or "trail" was always left in the design; the last coil was supposed to end at this point (see 98.1). In ceremonials this opening faced the east. The technique known as "false braid," a herringbone braid, was used to finish the rim. Care was taken to prevent any blood from coming into contact with the basket; otherwise a singer could not use it (Infs. 41, 32).

At the close of the Fort Sumner captivity, the basket was the principal container for food, particularly corn breads and mush of wild seeds (Infs. 32, also Infs. 7, 15, 192). Baskets were also used as receptacles for winnowed seeds (Infs. 32, 169, 192), for parching seeds (Infs. 15, 32, 169, 192), and for carrying seed corn to the field for planting (Infs. 15, 192).

There was apparently no differentiation in the manufacture of baskets for use in ceremonials or for food. Distinctions, however, were made among finished baskets. Blood was not allowed to touch a finished ceremonial basket, but bloody food was often placed in food baskets; ceremonial baskets were not allowed to come in contact with fire, but hot coals were placed in baskets to parch seeds. By the 1930's ceremonial baskets were no longer buried with the dead, but they have been found in nineteenth-century graves (A. V. Kidder to H. Tschopik). It was Tschopik's belief that most of the ceremonial restrictions were recent developments.

At present, the basket dish is used in ceremonials, but rarely for food. Baskets that have been mended—thus no longer fit for ceremonial use (Infs. 14, 32, 41, 43)—may be used for food, but plates and dishes from the trading post are more common.

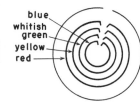

blue
whitish
green
yellow
red

98.1. Designs for basket dishes, after Tschopik; note opening near top of each

98 / Basket Dish

Hill (Central)

Sumac was gathered and prepared as for the pitched basket bottle. LW (Lukachukai) said that there was no taboo against holding the twig in the teeth. Next it was pulled through a notched implement for sizing. Two—not three—of the slender twigs were chosen for the foundation; LW said that the Paiute used three rods. Twigs and yucca were kept wet to maintain pliability while the work was in progress. The rods were whittled until they were pliable, then placed together tip and butt reversed, and bent in a circle. A strip of yucca was put on top and between the two rods; it was secured and hidden by the coiling process. The yucca was twisted like wool. Loose ends were pulled through as far as possible and pinched off; new elements were not overlapped. Work was done from right to left, and sewing was always done on the edge of the basket away from the weaver. The center of the basket was used as a guide for the weaving of the ceremonial opening (*atiin*, the trail), which LW said should be in a straight line from the inner edge of the rods (see 98.2). If the trail was omitted, she believed the weaver would go blind. She said that the Ute and Paiute, who now make these baskets

Patterns of basket dishes, observed by Hill at Lukachukai

 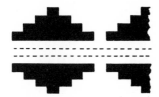  

98.2. Diagram showing "trail" **98.3.** Continuous pattern **98.4.** Five patterns per basket **98.5.** Four patterns per basket

98.a. Putting rim on basket; note metal awl (Tr. 150) and earring (Tr. 198)

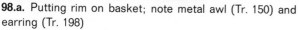

98.b. Baskets in the trading post at Lukachukai, 1933

135

for the Navaho, generally overlook this. As at Ramah, there was no special weave or restrictions in making a basket for ceremonial purposes.

Comparative

Many observers of the Navaho have published material on the significance of Navaho baskets, and their design. (See, for example, James, 1902, and Mason, 1904.) A basket described by Matthews (1897:211, note 5) was thirteen inches in diameter and three and three-eighths inches deep. It conformed to the requirements described by Ramah and Hill's informants.

The Franciscan Fathers (1910:291–300) have also published a description of basketry among the Navaho, including several of the taboos involved. Baskets and the materials and persons involved in their manufacture were considered dangerous. Paiute baskets were often indistinguishable from Navaho ones, except possibly for the finishing, and were readily accepted.

Gifford's Eastern informant confirmed the "coiled basket food dish" and said it was also used for winnowing seeds, and for parching pinyon nuts. Twilled, twined, or wicker baskets were denied. The Western informant was not questioned (Gifford, 1940:44, 136).

99. Stone Bowls   cé biotcil (Hill)   "stone, rock bowl" (CC)

Hill (Central and West)

A stone with one flat side was selected. The opposite side was pecked and abraded with a hard stone to form the depression of the bowl. No attempt was made to smooth the interior. When the bowl was completed, the blood of a wild animal was rubbed over the interior and allowed to dry. "This leaves a smooth surface" (SG, Keams Canyon).

Both SG and PP (Fort Defiance) reported that stone bowls were used as food containers and SG said they were also used for seed storage. DM (Ganado) had heard of this utensil but had never seen one. TW (Keams Canyon) said that stone bowls were unknown among the Navaho.

Comparative

This trait was not mentioned by the Franciscan Fathers (1910). Gifford's Western informant said that a stone cup was used; the Eastern informant denied this (Gifford, 1940:26).

100. Wooden Utensils   cin ·ade·· (Ramah)   "wood cup" (CC)

Ramah

To make a wooden cup, cottonwood, golden aspen (Vestal, 1952:22), or juniper burls were trimmed with an axe, then shaped with a knife. When completed, the cup was about the size of a coffee cup, with rounded sides and a flat bottom. The "handle like a frying pan" was flat and extended from the burl parallel to the rim. It was from two and a half to three inches long.

Inf. 18 said that he made cups in Mexico when he was nineteen years old. A burl eighteen by eight by five inches was whittled out with a knife, in one or two days. According to Inf. 7, such cups were not decorated in any manner.

Cups were probably made by men, since the only informants were men. They were used for drinking water or other liquids (Inf. 18). They were also used for stirring food (Bailey, 1940:274) and for dipping. According to Inf. 18, they lasted about six years, and were washed after use as are cups today. When a man died his cups were chopped in half.

According to Inf. 7, pan-shaped dishes were also carved from wood. These had no handles. They were used to hold food, although pottery and basketry dishes were more common.

Although Inf. 18 has made wooden cups, it is uncertain whether this trait was derived from his Navaho heritage or learned in Mexico. Inf. 7 spoke of the cups as articles which were formerly used; he denied the use of wooden ladles for stirring. No wooden utensils are known to survive in the Ramah community and it is not known whether the technique involved in their manufacture survives. At present, utensils are obtained from the trading posts.

Hill (East, Central, and West)

All informants stated that wooden ladles (or bowls or cups—the Navaho word is the same) were made from cottonwood burls. According to MS (Sawmill), they were also made from juniper and oak; according to C (Chinle) and TOMC (Red Rock), from aspen. The burl was detached from the tree by striking the trunk a sharp blow with a stone axe at a point at the top of the burl, which caused the wood to split around the edge of the burl. A cut was then made several inches beneath the burl, and the burl was removed. This lower section was used for the handle (GH, White Cone).

The burl was allowed to season and dry. When it was thoroughly dry, hot coals were placed on the section where the bowl or cup was to be formed (according to GH, opposite the outermost part of the burl). The worker blew on the coals and caused the wood to smoulder and burn. When the coals had cooled, the charcoal was scraped away with a flake of stone. The process was repeated until the bowl had attained the desired form and depth (GH; C; PP, Fort Defiance). According to TOMC, the burl was buried and the edges covered with earth during the burning process to facilitate the work and to decrease the chance of spoiling the cup or bowl during manufacture. The handle and outside were shaped with a rough stone (GH, MS, TOMC). SG (Keams Canyon) said that a cottonwood burl was whittled into bowl form with a knife.

Wooden ladles were the same size as gourd ladles (BW, Keams Canyon); six inches in bowl diameter (C); six inches in diameter and four inches deep (TOMC). According to GH, a large wooden ladle would have a bowl diameter of eight inches. These were manufactured by the old men (BW, C, TOMC, GH). They were used as dippers and as utensils from which to eat and drink (GH). They were considered more difficult to make than pottery vessels, a fact which may explain their comparative rarity.

Fishler (West)

TN (Kaibito) said that wooden spoons were never made or used by the Navaho.

Comparative

Bourke apparently found wooden utensils still in use in the Fort Defiance area in 1881, for he noted that "their spoons and dippers are made of cottonwood 'knots' and also of gourds" (Bourke, 1936:232). He is the only person who appears to have seen the actual objects. By 1910, "burnt out pine warts" and other such utensils had "long since been displaced by china and tinware," according to the Franciscan Fathers (1910:219).

Gifford differentiated several wooden utensils, of which only wooden bowls were known by both informants. The Western informant confirmed the use of a cottonwood spoon or ladle for mush, a cup made from a burnt-out pine wart, a wood platter for meat (which was sometimes only a bark slab), and a wooden bowl made from an oak bole (a shaman used this). These were denied by the Eastern informant. According to him, the wooden bowl was made from a mountain tree, probably quaking aspen (Gifford, 1940:26, 113–114).

101. Gourd Ladle or Spoon ·ade·· (Ramah, Haile) "cup" (CC)

Ramah

Ladles or spoons were made from gourds, *Lagenaria siceraria* (Molina) Standl. (Vestal, 1952:47). According to Inf. 7, gourds were never grown but were obtained from Laguna and Zuni; Inf. 192 agreed, and said that they might also be obtained from the Hopi. In 1946, Inf. 34 told Roberts that "some Indians around here have gourd spoons, or I can get one from Zuni or Laguna."

These were used for dipping liquids; otherwise people ate with their fingers. Inf. 9 said a gourd ladle was used in the wedding rite when he married Inf. 7's daughter.

Whether or not gourd utensils are still used in the Ramah area is not known. According to Bailey (1940:274), they are no longer in favor.

Hill (East, Central, and West)

Gourds, a long- and a short-necked variety (PP, Fort Defiance), were selected and thoroughly dried in the sun. Then a series of holes was punched around the circumference with a needle (MH, Head Springs), awl (K, Mariano Lake), or sharp piece of chert (TM, Round Rock). The cuts followed the inside and outside curve of the stem, never the side. The spaces between the closely punched holes were cut with a knife. All cutting implements had to be sharp to prevent the gourd from splitting (K, MH).

Before the gourd could be used, a solution of juniper ash and boiling water was placed in the bowl and allowed to remain for some time. This turned the gourd yellow and hardened it (MH), and removed the bitter taste (MH, TM). Gourds were never decorated (TM).

Lamphere (East)

PM confirmed the use of gourds as spoons.

Fishler (West)

A dried gourd was perforated as described above. To split it, it was "put behind the back," with the fingers placed along the holes; a quick pull separated the halves. The larger gourds were used for dishes, the smaller ones for dippers or spoons.

Both men and women made them. GB (Tuba City) had not made any himself, but had seen his mother do so before 1914. Because he believed that the seeds of domesticated plants were derived from the Cliff Dwellers, he attributed gourds to that source.

Comparative

As noted in Trait 100, Bourke observed the use of gourds and wooden utensils in the Fort Defiance area in 1881 (Bourke, 1936:232). According to the Franciscan Fathers (1910:286, 288, 447–448), the gourd ladle was used not only for dipping water but also in pottery making: the bottom of the gourd was used to smooth the wet clay. Its use in the wedding ceremony was also mentioned. Both of Gifford's informants said that gourds were cultivated and that they were used for canteens, dishes, and spoons. Smoothing pottery with a section of gourd was also noted (Gifford, 1940:20, 50).

102. Horn Spoons

Ramah

Spoons of any type of horn or bone were denied by Inf. 7. He specifically denied the use of deer skull, or mountain sheep horn. "Mountain sheep like lightning—we are afraid to eat out of their horns."

Hill (East, Central, and West)

The core of a cattle horn was removed and the shell boiled until pliable. When it was soft, one half to three quarters of the inside lower section was removed. The remaining portion of the base was bent back and upward and the sides pulled out to form the flaring bowl of the container (RH, Crystal; WH, Wheatfields; SG, Keams Canyon). When the horn had cooled, the edges were smoothed with a rough rock (WH).

RH stated that he had heard that spoons were also made from elk horn. They were never made of mountain sheep horn (Hill, 1938:168). K (Mariano Lake) denied that the Navaho made horn spoons, attributing their manufacture to the Zuni. These utensils were both spoons and ladles (RH, WH).

Lamphere (East)

PM said that horn spoons were not used.

Comparative

The paucity of references to horn spoons among the Navaho may confirm the attitude expressed above by Inf. 7. This trait was not reported by the Franciscan Fathers (1910). Although Gifford's Eastern informant did confirm a ladle of mountain sheep horn with a wooden bottom, he specified its use by shamans as a grease container. He also described a ladle with no handle made of deer's chin skin; it was for drinking soup (Gifford, 1940:26, 113).

Haile (1951:275) has noted the similarity between the Navaho words for spoon (adé) and horn (dé), and stated that "originally [adé] may have been part of a deer or other game horn [dé], but now a gourd spoon or ladle is meant."

103. Pottery
ʾadeˑˑ žiní (Ramah)   pottery spoon; black spoon

xašʌiš ʾadeˑˑ (Ramah, Haile)   earth gourd; mud spoon; "mud cup" (CC)

Ramah
Data were obtained from Tschopik (1941). Tschopik's informants (Infs. 5, 192) described two types of ladles, both of which were made in one piece. The first type ("black spoon") was not painted and was coated with pinyon gum after firing. It was used for serving food, but not for drinking (Infs. 7, 32, 192). The second type ("earth gourd") was shaped like a gourd ladle and served as a cup for drinking soup, water, or boiled milk (Infs. 7, 192). The handle was perforated for suspension (Inf. 192). Dippers were "baked with gum," according to Inf. 192; but Inf. 32 said that they were slipped red or yellow, but not painted with designs.

Hill (East, Central, and West)
According to Hill's informants, ladles and dippers used in the Central and Eastern Navaho areas were molded in one piece, as above. In the West, however, a lump of clay was flattened on a board or rock. Next, the worker lifted the edges of the clay to form the side walls of the bowl and squeezed one end together for the handle. The ladle would be about two finger widths deep. Two coils of clay were then added, one around the bowl to give it depth, the other to strengthen the top of the handle (Hill, 1937:20).

Fishler (West)
GB's mother (Tuba City) made pottery from red or gray clay mixed with sherds found in nearby ruins. Shapes were formed by coiling; the coils were moistened with water and smoothed with a corncob, or a broken piece of gourd, and finally with a smooth stone. Designs were painted with plant dyes, but no slip was used. The vessel was then fired; it was surrounded by layers of sheep manure on which hot ashes were placed. TN (Kaibito) stated that blue clay was used and that vessels were not coiled but shaped around a

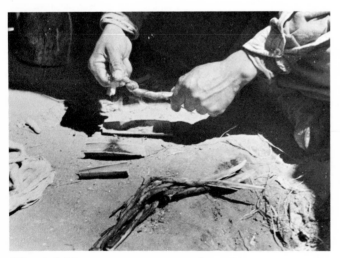

103.a. Inf. 24 squeezing yucca juice for paint

103.b. Inf. 32 applying slip to bowl; Inf. 24 mixing paint

103.c. Navaho pottery: bowl, cooking pot, cup, cooking pot, bowl

form, such as a basket. Pottery making was women's work, but TN and FG (Coalmine) said that berdaches also made pottery.

Comparative
Navaho pottery has been extensively treated in the literature; see, for example, works by Tschopik (1938, 1941), Hill (1937), James (1937), Gifford (1928), and others.

Pottery making was considered women's work. Clay was obtained locally where possible, and tempered with crushed sherds. The vessel was usually coiled. Except for cooking vessels, pottery was decorated, according to the Franciscan Fathers (1910:286). Ladles and spoons were shaped like the gourd ladle, and like it, used for dipping liquids. The Franciscan Fathers stated that because commercial wares were available at the trading posts, comparatively little earthenware was being used, even in 1910. Gifford has also collected data on Navaho pottery making, but the ladle was not specified (Gifford, 1940:50, 141). According to Keur (1941:62), "a crudely formed ladle of unfired clay" was recovered from a hogan site.

104. Cornhusk Spoon

Hill (East)
A cornhusk was tied at the small end and the open or oval end was used in the same manner as a spoon (K, Mariano Lake).

Lamphere (East)
PM said that only gourds, not cornhusks, were used as spoons.

Comparative
A spoon made from a cornhusk may have been an uncommon trait among the Navaho, or one used only when other implements were not available. The use of a husk of dead mescal butt as a container—perhaps a comparable trait—was denied by both of Gifford's Navaho informants (Gifford, 1940:26).

105. Liquid Swab and Sucking Stick

beichisi (Hill)   liquid swab; "that which you suck"

Ramah

A foot was cut from a rabbit and apparently used without further preparation. It, or a stick, was dipped into the liquid and then sucked. According to Kluckhohn (1945:268), Inf. 7 used a stick dipped in boiled goat milk.

Hill (East and Central)

The term for this is "that which you suck." The inner bark of juniper or bundles of cornhusks were tied four finger widths from one end. The other end was shredded for a distance of an inch and a half. The shredding was done with the fingers or by chewing.

These swabs were used in eating any type of liquid food, usually mush, milk, and soup. The brush was dipped into the container and the food sucked from it (PP, Fort Defiance; IS, Lukachukai; K, Mariano Lake).

Lamphere (East)

PM had never heard of such a swab made from a rabbit's foot. She said that a stick was sometimes used to poke at dumplings and to pick them out of a stew.

Comparative

Gifford reported that both Eastern and Western Navaho used a swab for imbibing liquids. The Eastern informant used a juniper bark swab for deer soup, but not for goat milk; the Western informant used a deer's tail (Gifford, 1940:25, 113).

106. Toothpicks

xaɣʷóˑkis naˑacihi (Haile)   "tooth in between going through"

Ramah

Toothpicks are made from fresh juniper twigs. Kluckhohn observed these in use in 1940 among the Ramah Navaho. It is not known, however, how prevalently they are used, or whether they are a trait of any antiquity.

Chapter 2 Shelter

Traits in this section pertain to protection from the environment. Houses and, by extension, the various items which make a house more comfortable, such as heating and furnishings, have been included. It might be said that "the hogan, its insides" is the determining organizational concept. Such extension is consistent with Navaho patterns of thought. Descriptions of Navaho house types have been reduced to a minimum because of the vast amount of published material. Data are presented only when they have historical, acculturative, or distributional significance.

As noted above, an integral part of the hogan is the fire, used for heat, illumination, and of course cooking. Cooking was done both inside and outside the hogan, but the devices for making fire formed part of the household equipment. Many of these are now obsolescent and some (such as the firedrill and wooden poker) are reserved almost exclusively for ritual use.

Cooking utensils (described in Chapter 1) form an appropriate transition to the section on household furnishings, and might well have been included here. Clothing might also have been included but, for reasons cited in the following chapter, is described in a separate section. Both are part of "the hogan, its insides." Several of the artifacts found within the hogan, such as the axe, hammer, and knives, form a group of multipurpose tools. These have been treated as a category, a grouping preserved from the original manuscript. Brooms and other miscellaneous household equipment form the next category.

In the bedding section, descriptions of weaving patterns and techniques are minimal, again because of the wealth of published material. The reader interested in the Navaho blanket should consult some of the many sources which pertain specifically to that subject.

Cradles are doubly appropriate to this chapter. The Navaho love children, and it is common to see many children at any establishment. Infants are swaddled and placed on the cradleboard, where they spend most of their time until they are able to sit up or walk. The cradleboard affords protection from various household hazards, and enables the child to view the world from a secure position.

Housing

107. House Types

xo·γan (Ramah, Haile)   hogan

Ramah

According to Inf. 1, before Fort Sumner the Navaho constructed shelters by piling stones against the walls of cliffs and roofing these with poles. Stone hogans existed in the Alamo area (Inf. 1), but Kluckhohn neither saw remains nor heard of any in the Ramah area; both Inf. 1 and Inf. 15 stated that the Ramah Navaho had never built this type of hogan. Inf. 34 had gathered rocks to construct such a hogan but as of 1946 the project had not progressed beyond that point (Roberts, 1951:42). Inf. 265 (died 1923) lived in a stone *house,* the ruins of which still stand in Inf. 7's canyon near Ramah.

Shelter   The conical forked-pole hogan (see Plate V, 107.a–107.d) was the traditional type, according to Infs. 3 and 32. They claimed that the "four-legged" hogan was a recent development and that the hexagonal cribwork type was post–Fort Sumner. Inf. 45 said that when he was a boy there were only brush hogans in the Ramah area. They were for winter use; in summer, people camped under a tree.

In the early days dead wood, particularly pine, was used since the Navaho had no axes with which to fell live trees (Inf. 7). It took about three days to build a hogan, although all the neighbors assisted.

Inf. 12 said that in the Ramah area, pine was the preferred material because of its straight grain, next best was pinyon, and last juniper. Spruce was not used because of its ceremonial associations. The reverse order was given by Inf. 17: juniper was best, but too crooked, and pinyon was better than yellow pine, which rotted rapidly.

107.a. Interlocking forked poles for traditional hogan

107.b. Detail of interlocking poles in 107.a

107.c. Traditional forked-pole conical hogan before mud is applied

107.d. Traditional forked-pole conical hogan after mud has been applied

V. Navaho silversmith outside the hogan. Note that the hogan (Tr. 107) is of the traditional forked-pole conical type. The silversmith, at the left, is wearing a headband (Tr. 183), silver necklace (Tr. 197), woolen blanket (Tr. 127), cotton trousers (Tr. 175), and moccasins (Tr. 189). The boy is holding the bellows. The man at the right is using the drill (Tr. 199).

107.e. Polysided hogan with cribwork roof. Note also the man's headband (Tr. 183), necklace (Tr. 197), two belts (Tr. 180), pouch for personal equipment (Tr. 195), and moccasins (Tr. 189).

In warm weather hogans were often left unplastered on the sides, to allow air to circulate more freely. At least one instance of a "house-hogan" with windows was noted (Inf. 42).

In January 1940, the Leightons photographed the building of a hogan in Two Wells for Inf. 12 by his son and son-in-law (Leighton, 1941a; a story in pictures). This hexagonal cribwork hogan was built in six days, although actual construction started on the third. Most of the work was done by the two young men; Inf. 12's two daughters assisted, but only with the caulking of the holes with mud and the final plastering. Small children helped keep the fires burning and heat water for making mud, but otherwise did no work.

Some logs for the hogan walls came from a dismantled house of Inf. 12's; others were cut from a nearby stand of juniper. Trees were notched with a double-bitted axe, then cut with a two-man crosscut saw which was oiled from time to time. The lumber was hauled to the hogan site in a wagon by Inf. 12's son-in-law and daughter.

While the logs were being cut, Inf. 12's son-in-law cleared sagebrush from the house site, an area about ten or twelve feet in diameter, then broke the ground with a grub hoe. He excavated about two inches, at which depth the ground was too frozen to dig further.

At the site the two men trimmed and squared the logs; the larger ones were trimmed and split so that one side was flat. Before they began construction of the walls, they laid out the roof structure in a hexagonal pattern: five logs were arranged on the ground; the sixth side of the hexagon was left open. Crosspieces were placed on these, apparently to discover whether there was a sufficient quantity of timber available for the roof.

The walls were constructed of notched logs laid horizontally without a framework of vertical posts. The two men put a log in place, marked the location for the notch with the axe or a nail; then turned the log over in place, cut the notch with a saw and axe, trimmed it if necessary, and rolled it back into place. Some logs fitted snugly, but there were large gaps between others. A door opening was left toward the east at one of the angles in the walls. The completed walls were shoulder high and consisted of five tiers of logs. The doorway was trimmed with the crosscut saw to widen it and to produce a more finished appearance. A door frame was made and fitted. In this case the first frame was too large and had to be dismantled and remade.

The first roof timbers were placed directly on wall logs. Roof logs were measured with a length of rope and cut by the son. While he was doing this, the son-in-law began filling the wall interstices with any readily available wood. The following day both men caulked the roof with wooden chips. The son then continued work on the walls, fitting logs into the large spaces and splitting pieces of suitable size from a large log when gaps were smaller. He used an axe but no wedges. The son-in-law continued with the roof, covering it with another layer of chips; these chips were smaller and were thrown on with a shovel.

Next a fire was built in the hogan. The two men then alternated in breaking the ground and grubbing out the earth for the floor. The son-in-law mixed some of the earth with water heated over the fire to make a mud plaster, which Inf. 12's daughter threw into the cracks from about a foot away and smoothed with her hand. When the gaps were greater than an inch, a chip of wood was often used as well as the plaster. Later another daughter also helped to smooth. Plastering began to the north (right) of the door, and continued around the room. The inside plastering took about an hour.

Meanwhile the son was throwing dirt on the roof. This came chiefly from the thawed ground around a stump which had been fired the previous day. When he had a supply of earth on the roof, he climbed up and leveled it. The son-in-law helped pack down the earth with a spade after he finished plastering the inside. Then the son banked the hogan with earth to cover the gap between the bottom log and the ground. The son-in-law caulked the outside with mud, which he brought from the inside on a spade. (See 35.a for an example of a caulked wall.)

On the sixth day, the hogan was finished and consecrated with corn meal by Inf. 12's son. There was still work to be done, such as making the door and adding log eaves so the dirt roof would slightly overhang the walls; this work was completed later, as was the construction of a plank floor. Ownership of the hogan was not determined. Inf. 12 said it would belong to his son when finished, but Inf. 12's son-in-law and daughter occupied it.

This kind of structure may be regarded as a common type in the Ramah area. The lack of an internal post framework is typical and has been observed elsewhere (at Inf. 112's, for example). In front of one such hogan an earth platform faced with logs served as a porch.

The ownership of hogans by sixty-eight families in the Ramah area was confirmed during the period between 1936 and 1946. Of these, three families used forked-pole hogans of the old type, four the pentagonal type, four the hexagonal type, and one an octagonal hogan. On the others no data were obtained. Five individuals or families had no hogan. During the same period forty-six families owned wooden houses and four owned stone houses. Of the wooden ones, nineteen were described as log cabin in type, four as paling, and one as frame. In addition, two families were said to be living in a "Spanish-American style" house. Only three brush hogans were observed in the ten-year period between 1936 and 1946, although two were seen as late as 1944. For twenty-four families no house was observed during this period. The common practice was to own both a hogan and a log cabin simultaneously, or an establishment often consisted of several of each. Whether the ratio of houses to hogans has changed radically in recent years could not be ascertained from the data; it is doubtful, however, since both were present in 1936 and 1937, and both have since been built.

Landgraf, in his study of land use in the Ramah area (1954), noted that most dwellings were the hexagonal or octagonal hogan, and that "small, rectangular, one-roomed log cabins, with gabled earth-covered roofs and packed earthen floors" were associated in these clusters. No hogans had windows in 1941, when his data were collected. He also noted that when hogans were to be used for ceremonial purposes, plank doors were removed and replaced by blankets; chimneys, sometimes made by stringing up bottomless buckets, were also removed (Landgraf, 1954:47).

Roberts collected data in 1946, and published (1951:18, 40–41) a detailed description of Inf. 34's hogan. He also compared its structure, furnishings, and associated buildings with the other two households he studied.

In 1949 an innovation was observed by Vogt and Roberts in a hogan built by Infs. 256 and 84. The structure had the traditional log sides, but the roof was made from lumber cut at the sawmill. Boards were nailed in concentric rings on rafters which radiated from a central smokehole frame down to the eaves. The roof was sloping; it was covered with green tar paper. This mixture of white and Navaho architecture was copied by Inf. 256 from a house he saw near Lupton, Arizona. It was so well received, even by Inf. 7, an old man, that a similar structure was being planned. A similar roof was seen on a structure near Thoreau occupied by Inf. 84's father.

Vogt noted that in 1949 hogans still lacked windows in the Ramah area, but windowed hogans in the Thoreau area seemed more numerous than in 1947. In the same year (1949) Roberts discussed with an informant the cost of building a hogan and agreed that it would be at least $200.00 depending on the price and availability of lumber. In 1952, Mills noted a degree of professionalism in hogan building; Inf. 24 was building a hogan for someone else, and was "a well-known hogan builder in the area."

Hogans were and are used chiefly during the winter months. Kluckhohn observed that in the Ramah area families seldom stay in the same hogan for more than a year or so at a time, although some have done so; Inf. 17 lived in one place for at least eighteen years. Nearly every family moves to a new location at lambing time, and again for shearing, in May and June. During this time the family camps (see Trait 109, Shade).

Since there is little detailed information on house types now being built by the Navaho, Tschopik's description of a "Spanish-American style" house is presented (see 107.1–107.5); Inf. 12 occupied this house in 1937. The derivation of this type of structure is uncertain. Many of the Ramah men have worked as herders for the Spanish-Americans of the area. Another such

Spanish-American style house, after Tschopik

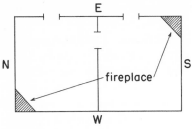

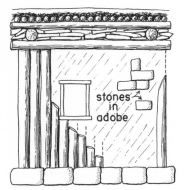

107.1. Floor plan, showing location of doors and fireplaces

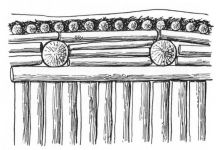

107.2. South side; showing construction

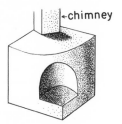

107.5. Fireplace, inside

structure, with three rooms, belonged to Inf. 134, who had spent much of his life as a herder.

The house occupied by Inf. 12 was eleven yards by six yards and had two rooms of equal size connected by a door (see 107.1). An exterior door in each room faced east. The walls were of upright pinyon logs plastered with adobe (see 107.2). Other logs were placed horizontally across the top of the walls, two on the ends (north and south) and three in the front and back (east and west). The logs were caulked with adobe and small pieces of sandstone. At the south end of the house the corner posts rested on large stones (see 107.3), and others were placed against the base of the wall to prevent erosion, since the ground sloped in that direction.

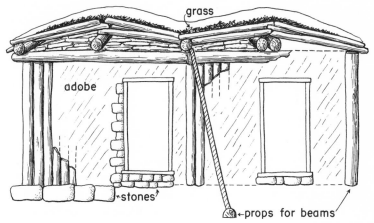

107.3. East side, showing construction

The roof (see 107.4) rested on five large beams, two of which seemed to be of yellow pine, the rest of pinyon. These extended from east to west. Split pinyon logs lay between and across the beams (north to south); the sections met end to end at the beams and did not overlap. At the north and south sides of the building, the logs overhung for about two feet and formed a ragged and uneven eave. A layer of short lengths of unevenly cut wood was then added; these pieces extended beyond the walls for about two feet, forming additional eaves (east and west). A thin layer of grass and brush was covered with a layer of adobe five to six inches thick to complete the roof. When finished, the roof had a slight double pitch, raised by the beam in the center of each room. Because of the adobe covering, however, it was practically flat.

The doors were set in wooden plank box frames and were once painted red; one door hung on iron hinges, the other was missing. There was a window in the south wall, but none on the north; the one built on the west was subsequently filled in with stones and adobe.

Inside the house an upright post in the center of the south room supported the central roof beam. The walls were plastered with adobe. The floors were of hard-packed clay, and that of the north room was a step lower than the one in the south. In a corner of each room (southeast and northwest) was an adobe fireplace with a square chimney (see 107.5). The square chimney on the roof was of adobe and stone.

149

Two houses belonging to Inf. 45 were observed by the Leightons in 1941. These were set close together with their roofs touching. One was square and made of horizontal logs caulked with adobe, the ridgepole producing a roof pitch; the roof was earth-covered. The other was of vertical logs, caulked and covered with adobe. One house had a red painted window frame, and both had doors facing south with white painted frames. The Leightons were told by Inf. 12 that in a house a door might be on the east, north, or south, but never on the west because the snow drifted from that direction.

Most families in the Ramah area build their own homes at present; in one case, a Spanish-American neighbor came with a team and assisted in hauling logs and in raising the posts into position. Techniques involved in house building, however, may have been learned through apprenticeships, for a number of the Ramah men have worked for their Anglo neighbors. A group of middle-aged men were employed for several years by a local trader two decades or more ago, and among other things, they built various structures. In at least one case, however, Anglos have built a cabin for a Navaho (Inf. 102).

Hill (East, Central, and West)

Informants from a dozen areas reported positively on the occurrence of the traditional forked-pole type of hogan (see 107.a–107.d) in their locality (TLLSS, Crownpoint; K, Mariano Lake; LH, Aneth; TOMC, Red Rock; PP, Fort Defiance; SC, Crystal; LM, Canyon del Muerto; WH, Wheatfields; C, Chinle; IS, Lukachukai; MH, Head Springs; SG, Keams Canyon). None stated that it was a recent development and nearly all volunteered that it was the oldest and most prevalent form of dwelling among the Navaho. According to C, when timber was scarce, hogans of this type were constructed over a pit four to five feet deep. TOMC stated that before axes became common builders were forced to use lumber that could be picked up or cut with a stone axe. This, plus difficulty of transport, resulted in a smaller domicile than was current after Fort Sumner. He said that before this period a hogan with a diameter of six feet was considered large.

Types of the "many-legged" or four-pole hogan were confirmed by informants from six localities (Crownpoint, Fort Defiance, Crystal, Canyon del Muerto, Chinle, Lukachukai). Informants disagreed about the antiquity of this kind of hogan, apparently because of different opinions about the place where convergence of the poles began: two structures were indicated.

One began converging immediately from the foundations. The entire structure was of cribwork, and rounded or beehive in shape (see 107.f). According to TOMC, this house type was small in size until the introduction of iron tools. Evidence supported the antiquity of this type, and C, WH, and TOMC stated that it was known prior to Fort Sumner. Recently a variation—walls of vertical posts—has become popular. It is perhaps this variation which resulted in controversy. (See also the Comparative section, work by Haile, 1952.)

The second type of "many-legged" hogan had vertical walls and a converging cribwork roof (see 107.g). Forked poles were erected in each of the four corners, and stringers were placed in these to form a rectangle. The walls of vertical paling rested against these. The roof produced a slightly gabled effect. Two rafters were added, oriented in an east-west direction. These rested

107.f. Conical cribwork hogan, beehive in shape. Walls of this type converge from the foundations.

107.g. Partly constructed many-legged hogan, Monument Valley. This hogan will have vertical walls and a converging cribwork roof.

on the north-south stringers, about a third of the distance toward the center from each wall. Poles were then laid, one end resting on the rafter, the other on the adjacent stringer. After this, the distance between the two rafters was bridged by poles. Finally, the interstices were closed with bark and the roof covered with earth (SC, PP, C, LM). This "four-legged" type of dwelling was said to exist before Fort Sumner, but did not become popular until after that period (IS, C, LM). PP, MM (Lukachukai), and TLLSS said that it was recent. (See also Plate III.)

The cribwork hogan as described at Ramah was reported from many localities. Structures varied from pentagonal to nonagonal and were produced by overlapping the ends of horizontally laid logs (TLLSS, K, TOMC, SC, AS, MM, WH, C, PP).

There was ample evidence of the permanent occupation of the lean-to type of house. Several variants existed. The foundation of the double lean-to consisted of two forked poles and a ridgepole. Poles were leaned against the ridgepole from both sides and at one end. TOMC and PP said that the limb of a growing tree was often utilized instead of forked poles and the ridgepole. They added that this form was quite prevalent during the unsettled period prior to Fort Sumner and before axes became common. According to PP, such houses were still being used in 1933 in the more isolated areas of the reservation; they were reported from Fort Defiance, Crystal, and Red Rock, and the remains of one were still standing in Lukachukai in 1933. SC considered this kind of dwelling a late development.

Another variant was constructed with only one forked pole. In this case one end of the ridgepole rested in the fork and the other on the ground. The ground plan tended to be oval rather than rectilinear (PP).

Several variants of the lean-to were specifically adapted to areas where timber was scarce (IS). Pit houses with lean-to roofs were reported from several areas (Chinle, Canyon del Muerto, Lukachukai, Mariano Lake). Pit excavations were four to five feet (C), five feet (LM), four to seven feet (IS) deep. Two forked poles were set in the corners of one side of the pit and connected with a stringer. The lean-to poles rested on this and the back of the pit. Occasionally poles were placed in the front as well (LM). According to C, this was an old form of dwelling; according to K, it was a late form. Excavations were also made in the side of a bank to form a room. These were covered with flat or cribwork roofs (IS, PP, SC).

Cave dwelling was validated by PP, K, and C. A rock wall about five feet high was erected in front of a cave or, more often, a cliff overhang. A cribwork (PP) or lean-to (C) roof rested on the wall and the side of the cliff. C stated that caves were occasionally occupied as temporary habitations; MH said that no Navaho would live in a cave for fear of illness.

Circular rock-walled hogans with cribwork roofs (see 107.h) occurred in several areas (Fort Defiance, Crystal, Chinle, Canyon del Muerto, Mariano Lake, Lukachukai). Hill photographed a structure of this type in the Alamo area in 1934. All informants agreed that this type of house was recent and occurred in regions where deforestation was advanced. PP placed the date of its introduction around 1910, K said it was after United States occupation. AS stated that stone hogans were quite common on the east side of the Chuska Mountains.

107.h. Stone hogan with circular rock walls and a cribwork roof

VI. Ramada shade (Tr. 109) and circular stone hogan (Tr. 107). Note also the ladder (Tr. 110) to the roof of the shade where corn is often stored for drying (cf. Tr. 42). In summer the family will live in the ramada shade.

Fishler (West)

TN (Kaibito) and TT (Coalmine) described the conical, earth-covered hogan, similar to that described by Hill (page 150).

Comparative

There is no doubt that the earth-covered, conical forked-pole dwelling was the dominant type in use by the Navaho during early contact and late pre-contact times. That this was not the only type of housing is abundantly indicated by the remains of several varieties of stone structures presumably used as dwellings by seventeenth-century Navaho (Keur, 1941, 1944; Farmer, 1938, 1942, 1947; Malcolm, 1939). The deponents of the Rabal manuscripts, in the early eighteenth century, stated that the Navaho in the Largo-Gobernador area lived on mesa tops in stone houses, or houses of stone, mud, and timber (Hill, 1940a:392–415). When Benavides referred to their "sort of lodgings under the ground" (Ayer, 1916:45, 138), he was probably alluding to the conical earth-covered hogan, though he gave no further descriptions.

In his investigations in Canyon de Chelly of Navaho architecture presumably dating from the eighteenth and early nineteenth centuries, De Harport noted that only two of the nineteen abandoned hogans built in Puebloan sites are of the forked-stick type. The others, designated as the "stone ring" type, had circular stone masonry walls. All entrances were on the east. These, he stated, were constructed out in the open; they were built after the return from Fort Sumner, when such a location was safe from raids. The smaller size of the old hogans—contrasted with modern ones—was striking. He noted that approximately four out of five dated before Fort Sumner; the hogans were ten feet or less in diameter (De Harport, personal communication). De Harport concluded that there was no reliable evidence for the so-called "pit hogans" which according to Page (1937a:47–48) and Farmer (1938:9) were supposed to be unique to the Canyon de Chelly during the Fort Sumner period (De Harport, n.d.).

Travelers in the mid-nineteenth century saw and described various house types. Descriptions were not always sufficiently clear to distinguish the different types. Several observers indicated the traditional conical forked-pole type. The hogan described by Backus (1853:70) was seldom over five feet high, built of pinyon or juniper sticks, covered with flat stones and earth. It had a triangular opening in front. The fire was made in front of the lodge. Backus stated that the Navaho were nomadic and often sheltered themselves in caves or fissures of the rocks.

This account of the use of flat stones over the conical pole framework is apparently unique. Letherman (1856:289) confirmed the temporary nature of Navaho houses and the use of caves, which he termed "the only foundation for the assertion that they build stone houses"; but he stated that the framework was covered with branches and dirt. The hogans were from six to sixteen feet in diameter, and in many a man could not stand erect. The door was "a hole covered with an old blanket or sheepskin" (see also Cremony, 1868:306).

The hogan described by Ostermann (1917:22) was not unlike the beehive type described by Hill's informants; the logs converged from the base, and it was rounded in shape. This type was described as the "Logs-stacked-up-House" by the Coolidges (1930:81, 79V), and as the "round hogan" by Corbett (1940:105, 103V).

According to Simpson (1850:93, 103), the typical hogan was about eight feet high and about eighteen feet in diameter at the base; it was built of poles set tipi style and covered with bark or brush and mud.

Later nineteenth-century descriptions of Navaho houses were more detailed, the product of observers who were more ethnographically oriented (see, for instance, Shufeldt, 1893; Matthews, 1887:418, 1897:13–17). In 1898 Mindeleff published his classic description of then extant Navaho architecture together with mythological background (Mindeleff, 1898:475–517).

The conical hogan was the most prevalent type until the early part of the twentieth century. According to the Franciscan Fathers (1910:330) it was "generally preferred as typical and better suited for ordinary purposes." They described in detail the construction of this type of hogan. By 1946 it was less popular than the hexagonal or polygonal type (Kluckhohn and Leighton, 1946:44); and although Underhill (1953:270–271) noted that the conical hogan was still in use on the reservation, she described it in the past tense. In the Fruitland area, there was only one conical hogan, and this was no longer occupied (Tremblay, *et al.,* 1954:195).

The polysided cribwork hogan was probably a post–Fort Sumner innovation, but when and where the first one was built is difficult to determine. The earliest reference to this type of structure is that of Matthews (1897:14), who was in the Southwest between 1880 and 1894 and published a picture of a hogan "made of logs in a polygonal form" (1897:fig. 11). The walls were vertical, of seven horizontally laid logs. The logs apparently were trimmed but unpeeled, not well matched, and neither notched nor thinned to fit at the ends. Two vertical poles extending up beyond the roof formed the door frame, and supported blankets instead of a door. The roof was earth-covered, but appeared too flat to be of cribwork construction. A very similar hogan was described by Page (1937a:pl. VIII), except that several walls slanted in toward the top.

The first description of the polygonal hogan in its most common form was that of the Franciscan Fathers (1910:333–334). These hogans were "occasionally built in mountainous and other districts" where timber was available. They were built as described at Ramah. A crosspiece supported by piles driven into the ground on each side of the entrance held the logs in position and framed the door. This type was the most spacious of Navaho houses, since no uprights were necessary.

The Coolidges (1930:83–84, 79VII) noted that the hexagonal hogan made of closely fitted and joined logs was rapidly supplanting the older forms wherever timber was plentiful. Page (1937a:48, pl. V) observed that only a general plan was followed in construction, and that a builder used the most accessible materials for a square, rectangular, or polygonal hogan, whichever was desired. The polygonal hogan he described differed in several respects from that described by the Leightons (see also Haile, 1937:3).

Both of Gifford's Navaho informants knew of the polygonal hogan, and he was told that the smokehole was increased in size in hot weather, reduced in cold (Gifford, 1940:107).

The prevalent type of Navaho house about 1945 was the polygonal hogan made either with logs or in some areas with rock slabs laid in adobe mortar. This type is sometimes circular. Until recently the roof, regardless of wall materials, has been predominantly of cribwork (Pepper, 1902:7; Haile, 1937:3; Corbett, 1940:104). With the increasing availability of sawed lumber, a plank and tar paper roof has become popular, as at Ramah and Thoreau. In the Western part of the reservation, however, the conical hogan was commonly found (Leland C. Wyman, personal communication).

A study of Navaho housing in the Fruitland district in 1954 indicated modern trends. Four types of hogans were distinguished: (1) conical, no longer occupied, although used for ceremonial purposes; (2) a rough stone structure, usually round in shape and the most common; (3) a structure of logs laid horizontally, with either six or eight sides, or a round structure with upright logs; (4) a stone type constructed with skillful masonry, with either six or eight sides. Most of the hogans were round and roofed with planks and tar paper; in most cases the smokehole was replaced by a chimney. Stone and log hogans (types 2, 3, 4) numbered 13 in a sample of 72, ranking third in frequency after frame and stone houses. House types were divided by categories: Conservative (hogans, pole and daub, log cabins) numbered 25; Acculturated (adobe, stone, frame and brick) were in the majority—there were 41 (Tremblay *et al.*, 1954:195, 206, 211). It would appear that the Fruitland Navaho are less conservative than the Ramah Navaho, since hogans and log cabins predominate in the Ramah area.

Navaho mythology has yielded references to the ancestral Navaho dwelling type. Parsons (1923:374) recorded a folk tale which described hogans without doors. Entrance and exit were through the smokehole by means of a ladder. According to the Franciscan Fathers (1910:327), the dwelling was "a mere dug-out, with a rude covering of a grass and yucca mat secured with yucca cords." A ladder was used. This type was also described by Haile (1942:39–56), who stated that "these prototype hogans mention either a four or five-pole type of hogan." He also discussed rather fully the significance of the hogan in Navaho ceremonial life.

It is in the mythology associated with the Blessing Way that the hogan is particularly important. The intent of the ceremonial is to insure good things in any phase of the life cycle. Father Berard Haile (1952) discussed the hogan. "In the beginning," the creators who planned the hogan serenaded the white bead, turquoise, abalone, and jet, the pole materials of which the first hogan was made. Later, three forked poles were found to be the most convenient framework for building. The south pole was interlocked with the north pole, and both were held in the fork of the west pole. A straight pole was leaned in on the east, and another was placed slightly to the north of it; these two, so placed as to leave room for a smokehole and entrance structure, were known together as the east pole. Stone slabs were "set for it," below the uprights of the entrance. These were for the benefit of the people; the stone, outlasting wood, was meant to symbolize the continuity of the hogan and its songs. Many door slabs have been found, often with the remains of poles still interlocked. It is strange that SC (Crystal) and C (Chinle), both chanters of the Blessing Way, did not mention door slabs to Hill. These ritual requirements made the hogan distinctive, and were believed to unify its inhabitants into a tribe of "hogan dwellers," distinct from the neighboring Pueblo and tipi dwellers.

The Blessing Way myth described different types of hogan. Significant differences related only to two types: the conical and the round-roofed. For Blessing Way, the smaller, conical forked-pole hogan was preferred. For chantways, the round-roofed type was preferred because it provided more space for spectators, large sandpaintings, and the like. The round-roofed hogan could be either the "many-legged," the polygonal cribwork, the bee-hive, the stone-walled, or other type of cribwork hogan; the lower structure mattered little, as long as the roof converged to a smokehole.

108. Woven Doorway Mats

cá·ászi· yisX̌ó (Lamphere)   "woven yucca"; "yucca woven" (CC)

Hill (East, Central, and West)
Mats were placed in the doorway of the hogan to prevent drafts. Doorway mats were woven in both twine and checker techniques. Twined mats with yucca twining elements and "slim grass" (PP, Fort Defiance; K, Mariano Lake) or juniper bark (SG, Keams Canyon) bundles were reported. Checker-work mats of cliff rose bark were described by MH (Head Springs), of juniper bark and yucca by MC (Sawmill) and SG.

The mats were made rigid by bundles of juniper bark sewn around the edges (MC), by sticks tied to the edge (K), or by sticks cut the size of the doorway and inserted at intervals in the mat along both edges (SG).

Lamphere (East)
PM said these mats were called "woven yucca."

Comparative
Haile (1942:44) commented briefly on the trait. According to him, the grass mat has been replaced by "blanket curtains, or even by makeshift doors made of scraps of lumber." By 1910, the "curtain made of an old blanket" was all that the Franciscan Fathers (1910:332) noted for a door in the conical hogan.

109. Shade

ča··oh (Haile)   brush shelter

Ramah
No detailed description of the shelters used by the Ramah Navaho is attempted because all types of construction have been dealt with at length by numerous observers. The data presented are based on information supplied by informants or on observation.

Kluckhohn observed both brush windbreaks and shades in the Ramah area. The windbreaks were either waist or stature high; the shades seemed to be high windbreaks with covered tops. Occasionally living pinyon trees were used, at which time the pitch was covered with mud to prevent it from dropping on the occupants or their belongings.

According to Inf. 14, the old style of shade was earth-covered, and in 1938 her family still had such a shade. She implied that it was not prevalent at that time.

A shade of the ramada type (see, for example, Plate VII) was observed at Inf. 107's in 1937. This structure was seventeen yards long, six yards wide, and eight feet high, and, according to Tschopik, extremely well built. It was used as the kitchen during a Squaw Dance held by Inf. 107's family.

It was constructed of upright pinyon posts, which supported the principal

VII. Ramada shade (Tr. 109). Note also the wagon (Tr. 72) in the background, the cooking fire (Tr. 95), the modern ladder (Tr. 110), the women's blouses (Tr. 167) and skirts (Tr. 166), belts (Tr. 180), and bracelets (Tr. 200).

roof beams. Poles were placed across the beams and covered with juniper boughs. The walls of the shade were constructed of irregularly crossed poles of the same size. Smaller poles were leaned against this frame, then juniper boughs, butt down. Three doors were built in the east side. Two stout pinyon logs were leaned against the frame to form each doorway. Inside, the structure was divided in half by a canvas partition. One section was used for cooking, the other apparently for storage and sleeping. The roof of the ramada was often used for drying corn because the circulation of air was good (see Trait 42, Drying Platform and Frame).

Smaller shades were seen at other establishments. In 1941, Inf. 256 built a shade in two days for the women of the family, for weaving. It had a frame of five posts, covered with crosspieces. Oak branches were then placed over the top and along the sides.

The shades in the Ramah area generally were associated with a group of hogans or cabins, and were the principal summer residence of the family. Only twenty-two shades were recorded, and two windbreaks. At least eight families used tents for summer shelters, and a few others have made makeshift tents from tarpaulins. Vogt noted several brush shelters near Crownpoint in 1947. Some of these were made of Russian thistle, others were of rabbit brush (Vogt, field notes, 1947).

Hill (East, Central, and West)

Shades of the ramada type (see Plates VI and VII) were commonly used, and were noted by informants in several regions (SG, Keams Canyon; C, Chinle; LM, Canyon del Muerto; IS, Lukachukai; SC, Crystal; TOMC, Red Rock).

A large variety of other temporary shelter types was encountered. The Navaho frequently used brush circles or windbreaks (see 109.a) when hunting, traveling, and at sheep camps. According to PP (Fort Defiance), it was

109.a. Brush circle shade or windbreak, Kayenta

formerly the custom for the family head to occupy a hogan and the younger married children to live in brush circles in the near vicinity. WH (Wheatfields) stated that these shelters were extensively used for dwellings in the unsettled period prior to Fort Sumner.

Temporary lean-to structures (see 109.b) were employed in the fields and on journeys. These were less substantially made than the permanent type (see Trait 107, Hill's description of the lean-to), but were constructed in the same manner. Brush often replaced much of the paling (AS, Lukachukai; SG, PP, C, SC).

A more ambitious rectilinear temporary structure was described by SG. It consisted of four forked poles connected by stringers. The front elevation was seven to nine feet, the rear three feet. Vertical poles were leaned from the sides; a wall of horizontally laid poles formed the back. The front was open. The roof was of poles and mud.

A temporary brush hogan was seen in the Steamboat Canyon region in 1934. In one instance, a polygonal hogan was apparently extended and walled with boards to make a summer shelter (see Plate VIII).

Fishler (West)

Several types of temporary shelters were utilized. A windbreak was constructed of pinyon branches with juniper bark piled on top. If blankets were lacking, juniper bark was also used as a covering. A fire was built and the person slept near it. TN (Kaibito) described a hogan-shaped windbreak used by hunting, trading, and war parties.

A hogan-like structure was sometimes built of juniper logs or brush. Juniper bark was put in the cracks and if time allowed dirt was piled over the structure. TT (Coalmine) said that a shelter similar to this was used when large numbers of people were hunting.

Sometimes the hunter or traveler dug a hole about three feet wide, three feet deep, and seven to eight feet long. Brush was placed in this and burned. The ashes were removed and the person lay inside the excavation, which would hold the heat for a long time. Heated rocks were put under the feet, and some men put a layer of dirt over their feet and the rocks. Using his saddle as a pillow, the sleeper then covered himself with a blanket.

Often, through accident, men became isolated and were without protection from the weather. While working for the government, GB (Tuba City) was accompanied by the supervisor of the reservation and another official. When their car broke down and no hogans were nearby, they warmed themselves with heated rocks placed under their feet.

Comparative

Matthews (1897:14–15) reported the building of brush shelters, usually contiguous to the hogan. These he called "corrals" and differentiated them from summer houses, which were merely lean-to structures. Both were used by the family.

Mindeleff (1898:494–497) described several types of shelters used in the summer. They ranged from lean-to structures and brush circles which may only have been useful in locating the family's belongings and as protection against the drifting sand, to the winter hogan, also comfortable in summer. He also described an earth-covered "half hogan, or house with the front part

109.b. Lean-to brush shelter, possibly used for a Squaw Dance, Kayenta

VIII. Polysided hogan extended and boarded by logs to make a summer shelter, near Lukachukai, Arizona. Note the top of the loom (see Tr. 127) inside the house on the left. The men are wearing headbands (Tr. 183), cotton shirts (Tr. 172), cloth trousers (Tr. 175), concho belts (Tr. 180), necklaces (Tr. 197), and moccasins (Tr. 189). The women are wearing velveteen blouses (Tr. 167), cotton skirts (Tr. 166), shawls (Tr. 169), necklaces (Tr. 197), woolen belts (Tr. 165), concho belts (Tr. 180), hair ties (Tr. 181), silver buttons (Tr. 202), and moccasins (Tr. 189).

omitted," which may have been the type mentioned by Inf. 14 at Ramah. It was semicircular and faced not necessarily east, but away from the prevailing wind.

According to the Franciscan Fathers (1910:334–335), the shade was constructed of four forked posts (or two, or even one), set into the ground and connected with crosspieces. The number of available posts seemed to determine whether the structure would be a ramada or a lean-to. The framework was covered with brush. The use of rapidly constructed shelters of brush and small timbers and of brush windbreaks by travelers was also confirmed.

Both of Gifford's Navaho informants confirmed the use of a shade made by inserting sticks horizontally in the branches of a tree. They also confirmed the use of a square, flat-roofed shade, which was free-standing and sometimes had side walls. A man could stand erect in it. The Western informant said the top of this shade, which was earth-covered, was used as a storage place; the Eastern informant said that it was sometimes used for storage. Both informants also confirmed the use of a "circular enclosure of boughs (corral)" for hunting parties and said that unroofed windbreaks were sometimes used as camps. The Western informant stated that the lean-to was a modern structure. A brush hogan "with little or no earth covering" was used in hot weather (Gifford, 1940:23, 109, 107).

Gifford referred the reader to Page (1937a:48–49), who stated that the common type of shelter was the ramada, built as described above; a "forked-stick tripod overlaid with brush," not earth-covered, was also common. According to Page, those who could afford to do so lived in a tent in the summer.

110. Ladder xaˑsˑái (Haile) "extends upward"

Hill (East and Central)

Ladders were of two types: one was a simple notched log (WH, Wheatfields); the second was made from aspen (PP, Fort Defiance) or any convenient wood (WH). In the latter type two poles were selected and notched at intervals. Rungs were set in the notches and tied in place with yucca leaves (PP, WH; TLLSS, Crownpoint). After the introduction of iron, holes were bored in the poles with a hot iron and the rungs inserted (WH).

Ladders were used to reach the tops of ramadas when an individual wished to examine the drying corn (WH, TLLSS; see Plate VII). They were also used to reach cave storehouses and were used extensively in and about Canyon del Muerto and Canyon de Chelly (PP).

Comparative

A ladder with rungs was illustrated by the Franciscan Fathers (1910:327). They stated that it was used to enter Navaho dwellings in the old pre-hogan days. The only other ladder mentioned by the Franciscan Fathers (1910:352) was that used in the emergence myth. Gifford's informants denied the use of ladders of either type (Gifford, 1940:22).

Fire Making

111. Firedrill γʷoˑlk̯ą (Ramah, Haile) firedrill

ceγadindeˑ ł (Ramah) tip

biki·dét̯ą (Ramah) shaft

be·ˀo·lk̯ą (Ramah) hearth

ˀaǯi·h (Ramah) tinder; bark

ni·xikáhí (Ramah) firedrill plant

Ramah

This implement was used for kindling fire; it consisted of a hearth and a drill. The hearth was a block of cottonwood four to twelve inches long and two inches wide, containing no fixed number of pits (from one to four have been observed), with notches cut at one edge to allow sparks to fall out on the tinder. Inf. 3 specified the roots of a big cottonwood for the hearth, but Inf. 7 said that it was made from an unidentified plant called *niihikahi*. The tinder was juniper bark rubbed between the palms until soft (Inf. 7).

The drill was normally a single piece of sagebrush or cottonwood five to seven inches long. A composite drill was also known and used by several informants. The tip, approximately three inches long, was made of *niihikahi*, lightning-struck white oak, or cottonwood. The tip and the shaft were either tapered or notched at one end to make a smooth joint, then secured with either buckskin or sinew. Shaft length varied, but the composite piece was about one and a half feet long (see also Kluckhohn and Wyman, 1940:4). No hafted drills, bow drills, or cane shafts were used (Infs. 7, 16).

Either men or women made the firedrill and hearth, according to Infs. 7 and 21; Inf. 8 specified only men and boys, and said that boys sometimes made firedrills for toys. They were made either inside or outside the hogan, at any time. A household contained only one at any given time, and when it broke another was easily made.

The firedrill was owned by the old man of the family, even if manufactured by someone else. It was used at any place and at any time fire was needed. Usually the fire in the home was kept alive from day to day, but Inf. 8 said it went out about once a month.

To kindle fire, one man rotated the drill between his hands in one of the notches of the hearth, which was held—slightly tilted—between his feet or by another man. Tinder piled beside the hearth caught the spark. Neither charcoal nor dirt was used to increase friction (Inf. 16); but warm ashes, or a type of sand called *kodiditlish* might be used (Inf. 7).

In the hogan, fire-making equipment was stored between the beams of the roof where it would not get wet. When traveling, the Navaho often manufactured a drill on the spur of the moment or used an arrow shaft instead. Thus it was only necessary to carry the hearth and tinder. These, and sometimes the drill, were wrapped in a small piece of buckskin and carried in

Shelter a skin pouch made especially for this purpose. Sometimes the implements were carried in the quiver with the arrows (Inf. 7), but this was denied by Inf. 16.

Infs. 7 and 16 stated that the simple firedrill was the older form, the composite drill the more recent, although both implied that the two types had been known for many years and were used interchangeably. Both forms were rooted in mythology according to Inf. 7, who stated that "the simple form was made of sagebrush which had spoken to the people when they were still beneath the earth and told them to use it for fire. Later they found the *niihikahi,* growing on the mountains, and began to use this in the composite drill."

The firedrill still exists in the Ramah area, but only as a ceremonial article. It is used for making fire during some of the rituals, and is part of the equipment of singers (Infs. 1, 21). For daily use matches obtained from the traders have replaced it.

Hill (Central)

Hearths were made of cottonwood root, sagebrush, and the stalks of *Yucca baccata, Yucca glauca,* and an unidentified yucca or cactus which grew in the territory of the Western Apache. Depressions and notches were cut as at Ramah (see 111.a and 111.1). Tinder consisted of either finely shredded juniper or sagebrush bark.

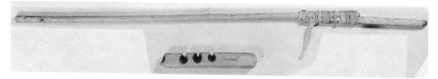

111.a. Firedrill and hearth

The composite drill was described. Drill points were made of the same material as the hearth (C, Chinle) or of any hardwood (PP, Fort Defiance). The drill handle was constructed of any available wood. The point, about five inches long and a half an inch in diameter, was attached to the handle by a right-angled joint (C; see 111.2), or a diagonal joint (PP; see 111.3). Any available cordage or buckskin was used to wrap the joint.

The drill was operated with as much constant and downward pressure as possible. Sand was placed in the depression of the hearth to increase friction.

According to C, each family formerly possessed a drill for household use. Men had extra drill sets which they carried on hunting trips, or firedrills were manufactured in the field when necessary.

At present firedrills are used only ceremonially (see Plate IX). PP stated that they must be made of ritually gathered materials: lightning-struck sagebrush, yucca, and juniper bark for the drill point, hearth, and tinder, respectively. A pollen offering was made to the plants before removing the desired materials. Even the sand was obtained from a rock which had been struck by lightning; pollen was placed upon the rock, and a piece of chert or chalcedony was used to dislodge fragments. Before making fire, the operator dropped the sand (or charcoal from a lightning-struck tree, or both) on the hearth, first from the east, then from the south, west, and north.

Firedrill construction (Hill)

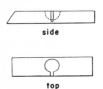

111.1. Hearth, side and top views

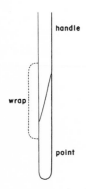

111.2. Right-angled joint for handle, after C

111.3. Diagonal joint for handle, after PP

IX. Making fire with a firedrill (Tr. 111). This is for the "sweat and emetic" ceremony of the Five Night rite of the Female Shooting Evil Way, to be performed over the girl in the background.

If, on trips, a ceremonial drill was the only one available, it might be used. First, however, the owner made a pollen offering to the drill, explaining the necessity for fire and apologizing to the drill for using it in a secular capacity.

All informants denied the use of a simple drill by the Navaho. Bow or pump drills were never used in making fire. Fire fans were unknown. The Navaho blew on the coals to produce a flame.

Fishler (West)

Fishler's informants described the composite drill. The hardwood (not oak) point was tied to a greasewood shaft with a deerskin thong. The cottonwood or dried yucca (TN, Kaibito) hearth was pitted to receive the point of the drill. Tinder was of juniper bark, rolled until soft. These drills were made and owned by men.

Juniper bark was placed around a hole in the hearth. The drill was inserted and rotated between the hands to exert a downward pressure. Rotation was continued until the cottonwood became hot and the juniper began to smolder. The drill was then removed and the bark blown on until it ignited.

Comparative

Descriptions of both the composite and simple form of the firedrill occur frequently in the literature on the Navaho. Though similar in general, they vary in specific details. Nearly all observers commented on the rudeness of Navaho fire-making equipment.

Materials for the point of the composite drill included sagebrush (*Artemisia tridentata*), yucca, lightning-struck juniper or white oak, juniper, cottonwood, willow or any hardwood. Hearth materials included pine, cottonwood, cottonwood root, weed stalk, yucca, sagebrush, lightning-struck juniper or cottonwood, beeweed stalk, and white oak. Sand was the only material mentioned for use in increasing friction. Tinder was made of shredded sagebrush or juniper bark, punk, dried grass, or horse manure (Palmer, 1869:84; Bourke, 1936:232; Matthews, 1897:169, 246; Mindeleff, 1898:501; Hough, 1901:585–586; Matthews, 1902:27; Franciscan Fathers, 1910:65–67; Hough, 1928:14–15; Gifford, 1940:28—both informants confirmed the use of the simple firedrill; Kluckhohn and Wyman, 1940:40; Haile, 1946:13). The friction material mentioned by Inf. 7 at Ramah could not be identified. The Franciscan Fathers (1912:110) described a yellow clay used as an incense; its name was similar to that given by Inf. 7.

According to the Franciscan Fathers (1910:65–66, 415), the hearth was about one inch wide and thick, and about eight inches long, with small holes (usually four in number) cut into it (see 111.4). Hough (1928:5) stated that the drill was rarely shorter than twelve inches long.

The displacement of the firedrill by other types of fire-making equipment of European introduction is also reflected in published accounts on the Navaho. Bourke indicated that the firedrill was in fairly common use in the 1880's (Bourke, 1936:232), and Mindeleff (1898:501) stated that the production of fire by friction was such a simple matter that the Indians often did it in play. At about the same time, however, Matthews (1897:246) declared that the firedrill was used commonly only in rites. It was used about 1883, but in an emergency when matches were wet (Dyk, 1938:169). By 1910, the firedrill had become purely a ritual implement (Franciscan Fathers, 1910:

111.4. Firedrill, after the Franciscan Fathers

65–66; Kluckhohn and Wyman, 1940:40). It is evident that the simple firedrill survived in the Ramah area, but in most of the other areas it disappeared; the composite form remained for ceremonial use.

112. Strike-a-Light

bé·š x̣é·ł (Haile)   "metal striking" (CC)

Ramah

A piece of U-shaped steel was held in the right hand with one arm of the U extended across the knuckles. A chert arrow point was held in the left hand between the index finger and the thumb, and was struck with the steel. Tinder made from a red dust found in oaks (*chechil bizhi*) or juniper bark might be used. The chert and steel were carried in a skin pouch with the tinder, which was wrapped in a small piece of buckskin.

According to Infs. 7 and 16, the use of chert and steel was adopted from the whites, and both agreed that pyrites were not used. Inf. 16 said the strike-a-light was adopted from the Mexicans and was in use before Fort Sumner.

With the introduction of matches, this technique of fire making disappeared. It is possible that no living Ramah Navaho (mid-1940's) used the technique or saw it used, since Inf. 16 said that he had heard of it but not seen it, and he died in 1942. It is not known when this device ceased to be used in the Ramah area.

Hill (Central)

Use of the strike-a-light for fire making was confirmed by three informants (RH, Crystal; PP, Fort Defiance; C, Chinle). According to C, the apparatus was carried in a mountain lion skin bag hung over the shoulder. In making fire, a small fragment of spongy material from a rotten oak was placed on the edge of a piece of chert or chalcedony. The stone was then struck with the steel, the operator being careful not to dislodge the tinder. The spark that ignited the tinder was blown upon and a fire was built from it. "This was quicker than the drill."

It is not known when this technique was discontinued. A cloth bag containing a fire-making kit of this kind was purchased at Fort Defiance in July 1933 (see 112.a). It was, however, not in general use at that time.

Fishler (West)

Gall from an oak tree (as at Ramah and confirmed by Hill's informants) was shaped into a ball for tinder. Shredded juniper bark was also used. The tinder was held in the left hand. A piece of chert was placed on the tinder, and the steel was struck downward against the chert until a spark fell into the tinder. When the tinder began to smolder, the striker blew on it until it ignited.

Comparative

It is probable that the use of the strike-a-light was confined to a period of about forty years from about 1860 to 1900. Both Matthews and Mindeleff, working within that period, reported that the flint and steel were being used (Matthews, 1897:246; Mindeleff, 1898:501). Dyk (1938:36–37) described the

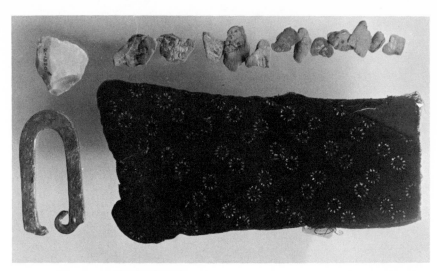

112.a. Strike-a-light fire-making kit

first appearance of matches in the household of Old Man Hat, probably in the late 1870's. At that time the strike-a-light was also in use. Matches were obtained only after the establishment of the trading post in Keams Canyon. By 1910, according to the Franciscan Fathers (1910:66), the strike-a-light had been entirely displaced by matches.

Both of Gifford's informants believed that the chert and steel was a modern introduction, derived from the Mexicans. The Western informant stated that this method succeeded an earlier one employing two stones. The Eastern informant denied this method of making fire (Gifford, 1940:28, 117).

113. Slow Match and Torch

xono·γé·ł (Ramah, Haile)   "firebrand"

Ramah

To make a slow match or torch (the same device was used for both), strips of dry juniper bark were made into an uncoiled bundle approximately one yard long and three to four inches in diameter. Bark on the outside of the bundle was left untouched while the inside was shredded soft. The bundle was tied with strips of *Yucca baccata*.

The Navaho used slow matches, containing a spark smoldering inside, to preserve fire while traveling in rain or snow; they burned best on calm days. They were held in the hand, and three or four were usually carried in case some were extinguished. Apparently live coals were never used for transporting fire. These devices were also carried blazing as torches and were so used in the Fire Dance.

There were no ritual proscriptions associated with the torch and anyone who needed one could make it if the materials were available. The torch was thrown away after use.

This device is no longer used in the Ramah area, and according to Inf. 8 became obsolete about 1908. Inf. 16 had only "heard about" it and Inf. 7 called it a custom of the "old days." Possibly no member of the Ramah community had ever seen one in use except at a Fire Dance; and these dances normally were held outside the Ramah area.

Hill (Central and West)

As at Ramah, a tightly bound bundle of shredded juniper bark was tied with yucca (SG, Keams Canyon; RMW and IS, Lukachukai; PP, Fort Defiance). Sizes varied; some were as large as four inches in diameter and three feet long (IS).

These bark cylinders were utilized in a variety of ways. As slow matches, they were used for conveying fire from place to place (IS, PP). "They burn slowly; one will last all day" (IS). They were used as torches for lighting (IS, PP; GH, White Cone). "If you want it to flare up you hold it against the wind" (PP). According to IS, the flares used in the Fire Dance were of this type. PP stated that they were not used to illuminate hogans, but GH reported that at night lighted torches were brushed along the cracks and crevices in the hogan to kill flies. They were also used to facilitate the gathering of mountain rice. The gatherer put a lighted torch to the heads, the fire consumed the husk, and the grains fell into a receptacle, or on a cloth placed at the base of the plant (GH, RMW).

Fishler (West)

Juniper bark was wrapped as tightly as possible and tied with yucca or another piece of bark. FG (Coalmine) said these devices were used for matches "a long time ago." One might last a month if used carefully.

Comparative

The slow match or torch was probably the "fire-brand" to which Eaton (1854:217) referred as carried in the hand by travelers during the winter. Son of Old Man Hat told of using juniper bark torches tied with yucca during lambing time, in Western Navaho country in the late 1870's or 1880's (Dyk, 1938:67).

Both of Gifford's informants confirmed the use of the slow match and torch made of juniper bark. The Western Navaho also used cottonwood bark for this purpose (Gifford, 1940:28, 117).

Torches constructed of juniper bark bundles are attested in Navaho myths and in accounts of the Fire Dance (Matthews, 1887:441; Reagan, 1934:437; Wheelwright, 1942:88; Haile, 1946:41–43). The Franciscan Fathers (1910:375) illustrated a torch (see 113.1) used in a war dance.

113.1. Torch, after the Franciscan Fathers

114. Wooden Poker

xonešgiš (Ramah, Haile)   "fire cane" (CC)

Ramah

Juniper (Inf. 8) or green pinyon wood was used. Wood which had not been cut with an axe or knife was specified by Inf. 1. Pokers were from two (Inf. 1) or two and a half (Inf. 8) to three (Infs. 18, 44) feet long; Inf. 18's was somewhat over an inch thick. Inf. 8 said that the handle was smoothed with a knife; a poker at Inf. 44's hogan was roughly sharpened at one end.

Either men or women could make pokers. Those belonging to Inf. 8 and

Inf. 18 were made outside, near the hogan. No one in particular in a family owned the poker. If the head of a family died, the poker could not be used again; it was left "right where it is," and a new one was made.

When a poker burned to about a foot in length, it was discarded (Infs. 8, 18). Inf. 18 said his poker was reduced in length from three feet to two feet in twenty-four days. According to Inf. 15, the poker was a fairly permanent item: "When you move, take the fire poker with you." Inf. 8 said that two pokers were made and used at the same time.

It is unlikely that the poker has changed in form or construction over the years. Its prevalence at Ramah is not known, although pokers were observed (as above, and at the household of Inf. 106; see also 120.a). The use of various sorts of iron stoves has very likely restricted the poker's use, since Inf. 8 said that he knew of no one who used a wooden poker with an iron stove. He used a metal poker that looked like a flattened ladle or spoon; it was about a foot and a half long.

There were several requirements for gathering material for pokers for ritual use. In Holy Way chants, lightning-struck trees were prescribed. Materials varied somewhat according to the chant or ritual, but all were taken from carefully selected trees and cut in ceremonial order from the four sides. Informants stated that the initial cut was to be with a stone knife; then the limb could be broken or cut off with a metal tool. This is perhaps the requirement of which Inf. 1 was speaking.

Pokers intended soley for ritual use were consecrated with an odorous grass which was chewed and spit upon them. Each poker was treated according to the ceremonial order. When the pokers were not being used, they were placed to the west of the fire, tips pointing north (Kluckhohn and Wyman, 1940:84–85; see also below).

Hill (Central and West)
Pokers were made from juniper (IS, Lukachukai; TW, Keams Canyon), pinyon, or greasewood (IS). They were of any convenient length or width (TW), usually about three feet long and one inch in diameter (IS). One end was tapered. They were used for poking the fire, raking out coals, or removing pots from the fire.

Supernatural potency was also attributed to pokers. IS said that a headache would be cured if the person pressed a poker to his head while singing. A poker placed under the bedding was said to cure nightmares. The poker was also placed over the cradle of a child left alone in the hogan as a safeguard against accident.

Fishler (West)
Pokers made of small lengths of wood were used. Some were shaped, but often any convenient stick was used (FG, Coalmine).

Comparative
Most of the references to the wooden poker in the literature pertain to its ritual use, properties, and prescriptions. Newcomb (1940a:68) noted that the poker had "as definite a place in the furnishing of the hogan as the loom and the metate," and that even more superstition was connected with it than with the other traits. Newcomb specified mountain oak or ash for the material.

Sticks were about three feet long and seldom straight, and some were chosen because of four slight angles which suggested the body of a snake. To avoid bad luck, the growing end of the poker was used to stir the fire; and when not in use, this end was carefully pointed toward the fire. Anyone who reversed the ends of the poker would be called ignorant or simple-minded, and was often told that "even a child would know better." A poker was never passed to another person so that the end pointed at either one, for fear that the person at which it pointed would later suffer severe burns.

An informant told Reichard that the poker was "one of the first things the Navaho ever had." It was never to be destroyed. This informant also stated that the poker should always be kept with the point toward the fire. If a man moved, he was to place the poker where it would not be disturbed (pointing at the fire, of course) to insure his safe return (Reichard, 1934:131).

According to the Franciscan Fathers (1910:415), four pokers were used in a ritual context to "represent bull- or copperhead snakes, who lay with their heads to the fire at the cardinal points." For this reason, pokers were taken from branches pointing east, south, west, and north, and were placed butt to the fire in these respective positions. This was done on four successive days during the witch chant, after which the pokers were placed in the branches of a tree with their tips pointing northward.

Further discussion of the ritual use of the poker may be found in Reichard's work. According to Navaho mythology, Changing Woman used her poker to drive Big Monster from her home (Reichard, 1950:392, 516, 547, 581).

Haile (1951:226) noted that the poker was used "in ceremonies of the fire." Otherwise any convenient stick was used; in either case the word for poker confirmed that used at Ramah.

Kidder and Guernsey found two pokers in a *chindi* (*chiidii*) hogan (where someone died), near Say Odd Ne Chee, Arizona, in 1914. These are now in the Peabody Museum, Harvard University.

115. Firewood   čiž (Ramah, Haile)

Ramah

Pinyon, juniper, and chamiso were all used for firewood. Informants expressed various preferences for pinyon and juniper; but chamiso, which produced a vile odor and did not hold the heat, was used only when the others were unavailable. In the households observed by Roberts, pinyon was the wood used for heat; juniper was preferred for cooking since it did not blacken the pans, and gave a clear rather than pitchy smoke. Vestal stated that some preferred pinyon because it produced fewer sparks. Other woods used included Western yellow pine, oak, and big sagebrush (Roberts, 1951:30; Bailey, 1940:273–274; Vestal, 1952:12, 13, 73). Vogt was told that the Navaho in the vicinity of Crownpoint burned coal instead of wood. The informant preferred the Ramah area, "where there is lots of good wood."

All members of Inf. 90's household gathered firewood on occasion, and all except a one-year-old child were able to use an axe both in obtaining wood and in splitting it in stove lengths (Roberts, 1951:30).

A Navaho fire was usually small and compact, never so big that a woman could not get close to it when necessary. It was started with chips and twigs and larger sticks were added as necessary (Bailey, 1940:273–274). An empty oil drum was sometimes made into a stove (Vestal, 1952:12, 13, 73).

Hill (Central and West)

As at Ramah, pinyon and juniper were the principal woods used in cooking and heating; juniper was preferred for cooking because it produced less smoke. Conversely, when warmth was desired, pinyon was chosen because it was less likely to produce sparks (IS, Lukachukai; PP, Fort Defiance).

Both sexes gathered wood. Men were responsible for the heavier labor involved. Formerly ample supplies of wood were readily available, and only recently has it become necessary to haul fuel from a distance and to accumulate a surplus for winter use (IS).

Several restrictions were observed when gathering fuel. Wood used in the production of ceremonial equipment or for ritual purposes was prohibited. Included in this category was wood from lightning-struck trees, a grave, a tree clawed by a bear or on which a deer had rubbed its antlers, a hogan in which death had occurred (GH, White Cone; SC, Crystal) or the woodpile outside at the time of death, an eagle-catching pit, the brush circle used by hunters or in the Enemy Way, the corral in the Mountain Way (SC), or twigs from a bird's nest (GH). SC, GH, and PP agreed that wood from a sweathouse was not to be used; GH added that wood for domestic purposes and for sweat baths should be gathered separately. "If you should run short of wood at home you could use some gathered for a sweathouse fire. However, you must explain to the sweathouse why you needed it. This is because the first people who used the sweathouse offered prayers" (PP).

Wood for fires used in ceremonials was limited to juniper and pinyon, gathered particularly for the occasion; branches the diameter of a finger were selected. A new fire was required for each ceremony, and when it was concluded the coals were extinguished with water and removed from the hogan. During the ceremony no one could step over the fire until the patient had first done so and then only after he had circled the fire four times (PP).

Comparative

Firewood is so prosaic a trait that it has often been overlooked by observers of other features of Navaho culture. The Franciscan Fathers (1910:56) confirmed Hill's data, stating that cedar was used for cooking "in the open fireplace of the hogan," and that pinyon and pine were used for heating and illumination. Cottonwood was used only when other woods were unavailable. The Franciscan Fathers stated that coal was not mined and not in demand for domestic purposes, although there was much on the reservation.

By the 1950's the oil drum stove or small flat coal stoves were commonly used, both for heating and cooking. Fires in these stoves kept the hogan very hot. Pinyon, gathered by the entire family, was the principal fuel. It was the woman's duty to make the fire, and keep it going by adding fuel occasionally (Franciscan Fathers, 1952:11–12).

Gifford's Navaho informants affirmed the use of dead wood for fire, broken with or over a stone. Preferences for particular kinds of wood were not mentioned (Gifford, 1940:28, 117).

Multipurpose Tools

116. Axe

nił (Ramah, Haile)   axe head, stone axe

cénił (Ramah, Haile)   hafted axe

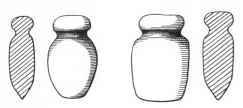

116.1. Stone axe heads, after Tschopik

Ramah

An unspecified type of hard stone, procured from ruins, was shaped by pecking with a small hard pebble (*tse ewozi*), which was also used to form a groove around the stone. The rough axe was then ground with a flat, hard stone (*tselgai*). Two shapes were made; both had full grooves and sharp edges. They were the size of the palm of the hand or slightly smaller.

The handle was made from straight, green oak (*Quercus gambelii*) (Vestal, 1952:22), one and a half to two inches in diameter and one and a half feet long. The part of it used to encircle the axe head was reduced to the diameter of a thumb with a large arrowhead. The wood was placed in hot ashes until "real hot," after which the thinned portion was bent around the axe head (see 116.2). Bark was then removed and the haft tied with buckskin thongs (or deer sinew or intestine, according to an Anglo trader). It was further secured by sewing a piece of wet rawhide around and over the binding with rawhide cord. The handle was greased with fat to prevent splitting; if it cracked, it was bound with buckskin.

Anyone could make an axe, according to Inf. 7; but Inf. 8 said that only men, old or young, could do so. The axe was owned by the whole family, and used when required. It lasted "quite a long time" (Inf. 7). The cutting edge was renewed by sharpening with a hard stone.

Inf. 7 said this type of axe was used for chopping down trees, although large trees were not felled; and Inf. 16 denied that trees were ever cut down. The worker sat at the base of the tree and hacked at all sides until it toppled. Bark was then removed with the axe, which was held with both hands on the haft. When Inf. 8 was a small boy, his grandfather told him about a stone axe used to cut wood for a deer pound.

The use of an axe in ceremonies or as a weapon was denied by Inf. 7. He said that axes formerly were difficult to obtain and were highly valued. They made a suitable gift from the groom to the bride's family.

No stone axes are preserved in Ramah today; both men and women now use the metal axe for cutting firewood and house timbers. Infs. 7 and 16 both denied that either adzes or wedges were known until after the introduction of the metal axe by whites.

Hill (East, Central, and West)

Information on the manufacture of axe heads obtained from several informants (RH, Crystal; K, Mariano Lake; GH, White Cone; SG, Keams Canyon) coincided with Ramah material. Informants from Keams Canyon (SG, BW) and Fort Defiance (PP) indicated that axe heads from ruins were frequently used; PP and DM (Ganado) stated that all were derived from this source.

Specimens were acquired from various locations in the Central Navaho area. In no case was it possible to ascertain whether they were of Navaho or prehistoric manufacture. Two specimens possessed a full median groove over the whole midriff of the axe, and a broken one appeared to. One of the two also had a three-quarter groove located between the full groove and the proximal end of the axe. According to RH, side- or half-grooved axe heads were also made.

Considerable variation was reported in hafting methods. The Ramah method occurred at Keams Canyon (see 116.2). At Keams Canyon and Lukachukai the head was placed at the center of a piece of oak and the wood bent around it and tied at the base and at intervals along the end to form the handle (see 116.3). The wood was sometimes wrapped twice around the axe head (LW, Lukachukai; see 116.4); this hafting may have been used on heads with both full and three-quarter grooves. At Crystal, an oak limb was split down the center, and one of the halves bent double. This bend formed the butt of the handle. The two ends passed over the groove of the axe from opposite directions and were tied at the base (see 116.5). At Mariano Lake, an oak limb was split at one end, the head inserted in the split, and secured with ties above and below (see 116.6). Yucca was sometimes substituted for rawhide or buckskin ties in the Crystal area.

Axes were used for cutting wood and felling trees (LW, RH, PP); for removing burls (GH, BW); for warfare (PP); and occasionally for pounding jerky (LW). There was no indication that any of the informants had produced or used stone axes. RH stated that his account was based on tradition. SG, however, indicated that axes were highly valued and somewhat rare. "If a man wished to get married he would give one of these axes to the woman or her father to get into the good graces of the family."

Fishler (West)
Smooth stones were pecked to an edge at one end; the other end was rounded if not already so. This type of axe was grooved, as in the other areas. TN (Kaibito) said that axes found in the area were used when possible; otherwise one was made when needed. The cutting edge was reworked and sharpened when necessary. Men did this work.

The haft was a green limb, fitted into the grooves of the axe and tied with deerskin thongs (TN). FG (Coalmine) described a similar axe with a more flexible handle. He gave Fishler a small axe which was being used as a doorstop. It was about three inches long, five inches wide, and an inch and a half thick. It was shaped to a round point and had two rudimentary grooves or notches on the upper and lower sides. GB's (Tuba City) grandfather owned such an axe.

TN said that the axe was used only to cut down trees, not for warfare. GB was not sure that the axe was used in warfare. TH (Moenave) stated that the Navaho believed that all stone axes were derived from those used by the giants on earth a long time ago. "After this, the Navaho used the axe."

Comparative
There is no record of anyone having observed a Navaho using a stone axe. According to Bourke (1936:231), it was no longer in use by 1881, and the Navaho at Fort Wingate in the late 1880's had only the discarded metal axes of the troopers (Shufeldt, 1893:279).

Axe hafts (Hill)

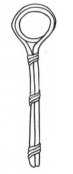
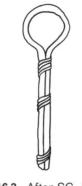

116.2. After SG, also Ramah method

116.3. After SG, LW

116.4. After LW

116.5. After RH

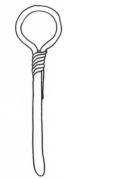

116.6. After K

Both of Gifford's informants affirmed the use of the grooved stone axe as a tool, but both denied the use of prehistoric axes. His Eastern informant said that trees were felled with fire and by girdling, processes denied by the Western informant (Gifford, 1940:27, 116). Both the Franciscan Fathers (1910:322) and Sapir and Hoijer (1942:429) referred to the stone axe used in warfare (see Trait 244, War Club).

Stone axes have been found in some but not all Navaho archaeological sites. A grooved axe of granite was reported from Big Bead Mesa, and Keur found hogan poles evidently cut by stone tools. Another grooved stone axe was found on a Navaho site in the Gobernador region (Keur, 1941:60, 1944:80). No such tools were found in Navaho sites in Canyon de Chelly, Upper Blanco and Largo Canyons, or in Chaco Canyon (Farmer, 1942; Malcolm, 1939). Hurt (1942:90) noted axe marks on hogan poles but did not specify whether stone or metal axes were indicated. Woodbury published a general discussion of stone axes in the Southwest including the distribution of grooved types, preferred by the Navaho; but the three-quarter grooved axe was also known (Woodbury, 1954:25–42; 1939:68–72).

There are a number of references to the stone axe in Navaho mythology; in most myths the axe killed anyone who grasped it other than the owner. Reichard collected a number of these tales (Reichard, 1950:440, 447, 454, 522, 538, 605). In the Beauty Way myth, when Frog Man and Box Turtle Man raided the Pueblos, the people tried to murder them with stone axes (of Pueblo manufacture, of course) (Wyman, 1957:22, 46). The only description of hafting in Navaho mythology indicated that a flexible oak twig was bent around the grooved head and secured with yucca fiber. Using this implement, two young men required a full day to cut four hogan poles (Matthews, 1887:388). In another myth, a tree was felled and hollowed by fire to make a canoe; but no stone woodworking tools were mentioned (Sapir and Hoijer, 1942:25).

117. Hammer

be·ʾecidí (Ramah, Haile)   "with it hitting" (CC)

117.1. Stone hammer, after Tschopik

Ramah

A grooved hammer was pecked out and hafted in the same manner as the grooved stone axe (see Trait 116). The stone hammer head was approximately two and a half to three inches wide and nine to ten inches long; both ends were flat (see 117.1). Unworked cobblestones were used for temporary hammers. The person who made the hammer owned it.

Hammers were used to peck out the pit in the stone mortar. They were also used to pound dried meat. According to Inf. 14, a pounder of petrified wood (*tsebeenatsil*) was held like a pestle for this purpose; the Navaho had no regular pestles.

Data on the hammer were obtained from Inf. 7, on the pestle from Inf. 14. Whether they ever saw or used these devices is not known. It seems certain, however, that they are no longer used in the Ramah area. The hammer purchased from the trading store is now a common tool; but it is not used for pounding meat or making mortars, both of which are no longer done.

Hill (East and Central)

Unworked stones of convenient size were selected and used as hammers. They were used in dressing sheepskins (PP, Fort Defiance; AM, Lukachukai; TLLSS, Crownpoint) and for softening jerky (MS, Sawmill; LW, Lukachukai).

Comparative

There is little information on the existence of a hammer (other than a natural cobble) from parts of the Navaho area other than Ramah. The Franciscan Fathers (1910:269) confirmed the term used at Ramah, but it clearly referred to the modern hammer. Gifford's Western Navaho reported a grooved stone hammer used for pounding bone and dry meat. This was denied by the Eastern informant, who said that grooved stone hammers were found, but not used (Gifford, 1940:27–28, 116). "The hammer end of the stone" was used for breaking bark into small pieces, according to Pepper (1903:8); whether this was the hafted hammer, a mano later used in grinding, or a cobble was not stated.

Hammers are common in archaeological sites (see Woodbury's general discussion of hammers in the Southwest, 1954:43–47). They were usually made of chalcedony and chert, quartzite, basalt, sandstone, or petrified woods. Most showed little or no workmanship, but all were battered from use. Only two examples of a grooved stone hammer ("maul") are known, one in the Big Bead area, the other in the Gobernador (Keur, 1941:60–61, 1944:80; Farmer, 1942:72).

118. Knife   bé·ž (Ramah, Haile)   Type I: knife, or metal

bé·ž ńnez (Ramah)   Type II: knife, long

bé·ž nahasdaníí (Ramah)   Type III: knife

Ramah

A knife was made by striking a flake from a chert or chalcedony pebble. For Type I, one end was wrapped with buckskin or string to provide a handle. This type of knife was used with an awl in making skin clothing, instead of an awl in making baskets, for skinning animals, and as a woodworking tool. Type II, which was about a foot long and single-edged, had a handle made of two pieces of wood wrapped in sinew and covered with wet rawhide. This knife was carried in a sack because of its length. It was sometimes used as a weapon, "when you ran out of everything else." Type III was a similar but shorter knife; it was carried in a rawhide sheath at the belt. Knives could be sharpened on rock and might last for some time.

According to Inf. 7, stone knives were never made by the Navaho since stone arrow or spear points were easily obtainable from ruins. These were required to make the first cut when knives were to be used for ritual purposes. The rest of the cutting could be done with a metal knife. Bone or wooden knives were never used (Inf. 7).

According to Inf. 7, the single informant for this trait, metal knives were obtained from the Mexicans; but he said that at one time some Navaho operated a blacksmith shop. Except for ritual purposes, metal knives are used at present, and most are imported. Adair (1944:64), however, reported that worn files were sharpened on grindstones to make short-bladed knives. With the introduction of scissors and other specialized tools, the knife has become limited to ordinary purposes; it is no longer used for sheep shearing.

Hill (Central and West)

The use of stone flakes for cutting was confirmed at Keams Canyon, Lukachukai, and Chinle. LW (Lukachukai) said that any sharp stone might be used in this capacity. SG (Keams Canyon) stated that chips were struck specifically for that purpose from a larger rock. Both informants denied that the chips were retouched or that hafts were added.

According to C (Chinle), metal knives were introduced from Spanish sources prior to Fort Sumner. They were not numerous, however, and the use of stone for cutting continued for some time after the return from the incarceration. The metal knives varied in size up to six inches and were equipped with wooden hafts. Shortly after the return from Fort Sumner, Navaho smiths began producing metal knives, according to RH (Crystal). The iron was pounded and roughly shaped to resemble the modern butcher knife. These were equipped with wooden hafts.

Knives were also made from tin cans (PP. Fort Defiance). The top and bottom were removed, and the can cut across the side. The tin was flattened. One section was rolled up to form the handle; the remaining edge was used as the blade.

In whittling and in most cutting operations, the blade edge was always held toward the operator; this was confirmed by observations in the field and by informants (see Newcomb, below). As at Ramah, knives were extensively used for shearing sheep before the introduction of modern implements for that purpose.

Fishler (West)

TN (Kaibito) stated that men made knives; a hard stone was chipped to a long pointed shape. These knives were formerly used for scraping and cutting, for preparing food and for defense; at present, they are used for ceremonial purposes.

TT (Coalmine) said that a flint knife or arrow was used in hunting to tell whether or not a porcupine was fat. The animal was turned on its back and held by its feet while the hunter made a scratch where the skin showed underneath the tail. If the scratch bled, it was not fat; if it did not bleed, it was.

Neither of the informants (TT, TN) had seen knives made, but both were told about them by older people.

Comparative

Stone flake knives were known in parts of the Navaho area other than Ramah although, as at Ramah, there were no eyewitness accounts of their manufacture and use. Stephen (1889:131) stated that stone knives were not used for practical purposes. He reported, however, that they were used in religious capacity and that those used in rituals involving surgery had to be of obsidian, although he had also seen Navaho using fragments of dark-colored glass.

According to the Franciscan Fathers (1910:62, 411), stone knives were used for cutting, whittling, and scraping; they were shaped like arrow points, and were still used for ceremonial purposes.

Newcomb (1940a:40) confirmed Hill's observations concerning the prescribed manner for using a knife. She noted that the point was never to be held toward the heart, or the operator would suffer from sharp pains in his heart.

Both of Gifford's Navaho informants confirmed the use of an unretouched flake, which the Eastern informant said was for skinning, but not for woodworking (the latter affirmed by the Western informant). The Western informant said that a chipped knife (possibly double-edged and set in a wooden handle) was used for butchering and possibly for carving wood. The Eastern informant denied that it was used for wood carving. Bone and wood knives were denied by both (Gifford, 1940:26, 114). There was a mythological reference to knives of "deer ribs nicely fixed up" (Sapir and Hoijer, 1942:81). Other archaeological or ethnological evidence for wood or bone knives was lacking.

Matthews (1897:233) stated that stone knives were used prehistorically, and they were found at several Navaho sites. Only three were found at Big Bead Mesa (Keur, 1941:56), and only three in the upper Blanco and Largo Canyons (Farmer, 1942:73); but sixty-seven were reported from the Gobernador sites (Keur, 1944:80). The cutting tool inventory of the prehistoric Navaho was undoubtedly augmented by the use of projectile points and scrapers, and this may in part account for the paucity of flake blades (see Woodbury, 1954:120–142).

It is evident that the Navaho acquired metal knives early in the period of contact with European culture. Once introduced, metal knives were quickly adopted. Gifford complained that they "so early and thoroughly replaced stone, bone, cane and wooden knives" that he found it difficult to gather information about these types (Gifford, 1940:114). According to Dyk (1938:53), immediately before and after Fort Sumner the Navaho not only imported knives, but made many from scrap metal. The stone knife continued to exist throughout the area only as a ceremonial object (see also Bailey, 1950:74; Haile, 1938:31–32; Kluckhohn and Wyman, 1940:34–35, 84, 90; Leighton and Leighton, 1949:71; Matthews, 1897:130–132; Wyman, 1936a:638–639, 642–643).

119. Knife Sheath   bé·ž bežis   "knife bag" (CC)

Ramah

Two sections of rawhide, sometimes thick buckskin, were cut the shape of a small knife (Type III, Trait 118) and sewn together. The edges of such a sheath were sometimes fringed. It was worn in the belt (Inf. 7). (See 119.1.)

Another type of sheath was made and used for holding a pen knife; Inf. 39 claimed to have invented it. It was about three inches long and was cut from a single piece of buckskin, which was folded and sewn on the bottom and side with a slender buckskin thong. Strips were left attached; these were

Knife sheaths

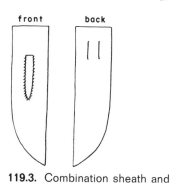

119.1. After Tschopik

119.2. Tschopik, after Inf. 39

front   back

119.3. Combination sheath and awl case (Hill), after C

twisted and tied together to form a loop through which the belt passed (see 119.2). When finished, the bag was turned inside out, so the sewing was on the inside. Whether anyone else used this type of sheath is not known.

Awl sheaths were denied (Infs. 7, 192).

Hill (Central)
Sheaths were formerly made from buckskin and more recently from leather. C (Chinle) described a combination sheath and awl case. Two sections of material were cut slightly larger than the blade of the knife; a third, slightly larger than the awl. The back of the sheath was slit in two places to allow for the passage of the belt. It was sewn to the front half, as was the awl case (see 119.3).

Sheaths were worn on the left side by right-handed men. They were formerly undecorated, but bead work has been added recently (C).

Comparative
The use of knife sheaths seems to have escaped all observers of the Navaho save Palmer (1869:48), who showed a photograph of the "Knife Sheath of Men." The sheath was apparently made from a single folded piece of leather or rawhide. The fold was not decorated, but small white shells or beads were sewn to the other edge. Palmer did not describe the knife sheath, its manner of construction, or use.

Gifford's Eastern informant confirmed the use of a buckskin "awl scabbard," but this article was not described. The Western informant was not questioned (Gifford, 1940:27, 115).

Miscellaneous Equipment

120. Broom   bé·éžó·· (Ramah, Haile)   "brush" (CC)

hašče·dá̹· (Ramah)   desert thorn; "god food" (CC)

Ramah
The leafy stems of the big sagebrush were wired together to make a broom, or desert thorn branches were used (Vestal, 1952:48, 42, 15–17). The grass brush used for cleaning the metate (see 90.a and Trait 90) was also a broom.

These brooms were used to sweep the hogan. The grass brush broom was "generally grasped with the little finger down toward the longer end and held nearly perpendicularly while sweeping." These were still being used in the late 1930's in three Navaho communities, Ramah–Two Wells, Smith Lake–Pinedale, and Chaco (Bailey, 1942:212).

Hill (Central)
Pinyon and juniper branches or bunches of goldenrod were utilized for sweeping the hogan (WH, Wheatfields).

120.a. Inf. 97 sweeping inside the hogan with a grass broom; note the poker (Tr. 114) by the coffeepot.

Comparative

The Franciscan Fathers (1910:190) confirmed the data obtained at Ramah, stating that the grass brush was also used as a broom (and as a hairbrush). It is not clear whether or not Gifford's Navaho informants, both of whom knew the grass brush, used it for sweeping (Gifford, 1940:25, 113).

121. Fly Swatter

céʼédǫ́ʼiˑ beˑ bitaˑʼiltˣasi (Lamphere)   "fly with it hitting" (CC)

Hill (West)

A wooden frame like the one used for a loop drumstick (Trait 234), but larger, was made. Two yucca leaf warp elements were tied to this. The remaining area was then filled out with yucca leaf wefts, the ends of which were tied to the frame. The checker weaving technique was employed.

Some sweet substance was used for bait, and when the flies gathered, they were killed. GH (White Cone) said that such fly swatters had been in use among the Navaho prior to Fort Sumner.

Lamphere (East)

PM said that her word for fly swatter referred to the ones that are bought in the store. She had not heard of the type described by GH. She said that people used to cut rubber from old tires and shoot it at flies, "like shooting rubber bands."

122. Clothes Hangers

ʾaheˑɬ baˑsitani (Lamphere)   "clothes hanging" (CC)

ʾaheˑɬ baˑdahastˣa (Lamphere)   "clothes pole" (CC)

Ramah
Inf. 19 put clothes on metal or wooden hangers; these hung from a pole placed across the corner of the room in his slab house. This practice was observed in 1949.

Hill (Central and West)
Many hogans were equipped with facilities for hanging clothing and personal effects. Commonly, these consisted of wooden poles placed horizontally and secured in the roof structure or side walls at the rear of the hogan (GH, White Cone; SC, Crystal). In other cases pegs were cut and driven between the logs of the wall or roof; occasionally limbs were left projecting on the logs used in the construction of the hogan. These were utilized for hanging (PP, Fort Defiance).

Lamphere (East)
PM said that clothes were hung on poles suspended from rope.

Comparative
The Franciscan Fathers (1910:341) stated that the Navaho wardrobe usually consisted of what the individual was wearing, "with additional coat and pants, jacket and skirt, for festive occasions"; such would hardly require storage facilities.

Bedding

123. Sleeping Mat

ƛohyaˑtˣeˑɬ (Ramah, Haile)   "yucca sleeping bag" (CC); "grass under wide"

Ramah
Bundles of grass, about an inch and a half in diameter, were twined together with strips of *Yucca baccata* (Vestal, 1952:14–15). Two strips were used at once, and these were twisted between every two grass bundles (double or plain twining). According to Inf. 32, crude checkerwork mats were also made. The finished mats were rectangular in shape, about the size of a man (Inf. 7). Mats were not decorated in any way.

Vestal's informants said that both rectangular and round mats were made from the Broadleaf cattail (*Typhus latifolia*). Only one informant confirmed this. Another (Inf. 15), who knew how to make cattail mats, said that they were used only as lightning mats (see Trait 215).

Inf. 7 said that either men or women could make mats, but he did not say whether he had seen them made. Infs. 7 and 32 agreed that formerly everybody slept on grass mats, although Inf. 32 admitted that she had never used them and Inf. 15 knew only of their ritual use. Apparently they have not been used in Ramah for a long time, and most informants have never seen them.

Hill (East, Central, and West)

Bast materials appear to have been extensively used in an earlier period in the production of sleeping mats that functioned in the capacity of both mattresses and bedding. LM (Canyon del Muerto) said that his grandfather used mats of this type. PP (Fort Defiance) and SC (Crystal) had heard of them but had never seen them.

With few exceptions these mats were twined with a bundle foundation. Yucca was usually used as the twining element, but materials for the foundation varied. Juniper bark was reported by several informants (TLLSS, Crownpoint; GH, White Cone; IS, Lukachukai; LM, SC); "slim grass" was popular (N, Coalmine; K, Mariano Lake; LM; PP); and PP and MB (Divide) agreed that cliff rose bark was used. SG (Keams Canyon) said that willow bark was not used. A blanket four to five feet long and three feet wide was described by MB. it had a cliff rose bark foundation twined the length of the blanket with wool.

No loom was used in the production of these mats. Bark or grass was gathered and placed in bundles side by side. Green yucca was obtained and the fibers stripped from the leaves. Fibers were tied end to end to form a long cord, but not spun or twisted. Enough fibers were included to give it the diameter of heavy wrapping cord. The yucca twining element was tied around the last warp, to secure it (K, GH). Twining elements were spaced about an inch apart.

GH described a variant of these mats. Bundles of juniper bark were wrapped with yucca and then with spirally cut strips of wildcat or rabbit fur. These were then twined, as above (see also Trait 124, Rabbit Skin Blanket, and Trait 125, Dressed Skin Blankets and Robes).

Checker weave mats were reported, made of juniper bark (RH, Crystal; SG), cliff rose bark (RH; LW, Ganado), and yucca (IS, TLLSS). The ends of the weft element were turned back over the first and last warp and tied on themselves. LW (Ganado) stated that blankets of cliff rose bark and rabbit skin weft were also made.

Shredded juniper bark appears to have been extensively used instead of a mattress (TLLSS, RH, SG; T, Chaco Canyon). SG said that a depression the size of the person was dug and filled with bark.

Comparative

According to the Franciscan Fathers (1910:467), by 1910 the grass mat had long since been superseded by buffalo robes and buckskin and sheepskin bedding. The yucca mat which they illustrated was round, woven sunwise, and used in connection with the grass blanket (see 123.1). Blankets braided of slender grass, and of slender grass and yucca, were reported by informants of Sapir and Hoijer (1942:403); both types were superseded by wool blankets.

Gifford's Eastern informant stated that the earliest mattress was merely a grass pile, superseded by hides "when Mexicans brought firearms." Mats of both juniper bark and grass were known; those of yucca were denied. Blankets were woven of any soft bark, or grass, according to the Eastern informant. He specified untwisted Cowania (*Cowania stansburiana*) or Apache

123.1. Yucca sleeping mat, after the Franciscan Fathers

plume (*Fallugia paradoxa*) bark, with a yucca weft. Sometimes shredded fibers were used for covering. The Western informant confirmed only the use of yucca for sleeping; it was shredded, or woven into a mat or blanket. He did not know the weave (Gifford, 1940:40, 132–133).

Matthews collected several references to the grass mat in Navaho mythology. Mats of hay were used for mattresses and to cover the doorway (see Trait 215, Lightning Mats), and fine juniper bark was used for blankets (Matthews, 1887:388). In one myth, blankets of juniper bark, yucca fiber, and skins sewn together were noted (Matthews, 1897:141).

124. Rabbit Skin Blanket

gáh čidí (Ramah, Haile)   "rabbit robe" (CC)

Ramah

Many rabbit skins were needed to make a blanket, one hundred according to Infs. 3 and 32. Sixty-two were used in a blanket made by Inf. 36, including skins of four jack rabbits. The blanket was about half the size of a Pendleton blanket. Either or both cottontail or jack rabbit skins could be used. According to Inf. 36, rat skins might be used to finish a blanket if sufficient rabbit skins were lacking. The use of rat, coyote, or squirrel skins was denied by Inf. 7.

Skins were stripped from the rabbit, dried, and used without further treatment (Infs. 32, 36) or rubbed with ashes and dried in the wind (Inf. 3). Inf. 7 said they were first buried in the ground, then rubbed between the hands until pliable. Each skin was cut down the middle, and strips were cut along the straight edge (Inf. 7). Skins were not cut spirally (Inf. 7). According to Inf. 32, strips were approximately the width of the large finger and were torn from the hide. They were then either folded (Infs. 7, 36) or twisted (Inf. 32) so that the fur was exposed.

Woolen yarn twisted by spindle into a two-ply cord formed the warp. Inf. 32 said that she had heard of yucca warp, but she had never used it. The use of buckskin warp was denied (Inf. 7).

The warps were strung on a regular loom: either a vertical two-bar loom supported on a four-bar vertical frame, or a loom set horizontally (Inf. 32). The two loom cords were strung along the ground beam to catch every other warp thread; they twisted on themselves in between. This selvedge was then tied irregularly to a smaller pole. A similar selvedge was made at the top.

The rabbit skin strips (weft) were placed in the center of the warp against the top supports, and were woven in and out between the twisted and untwisted warp threads; each strip was held by at least one twist. The strips were not tied or twisted together, but a new strip was inserted before the previous one ended, to make an overlap at the joint. Heddles were used, but no battens. When the blanket was finished, the warp threads were cut at the top, knotted, and the knots inserted back under the rabbit fur.

In 1937, Inf. 36 made two small (29 in. by 27 in. by 18 in.) blankets for Kluckhohn. These are now in the Peabody Museum at Harvard University. The weft strips were rabbit skin, about eight inches long and an inch wide when folded. The warp was two-ply yarn. Inf. 36 said there were twenty-five double warp threads in one of these blankets. Because of the grouping, this blanket gives the impression that the threads are paired. The two heddle

124.a. Rabbit skin blanket on the loom

sticks used by Inf. 36 were made from stems of the squaw currant (*Ribes inebrians;* Wyman and Harris, 1941:29), and were used only for this blanket. The weave was plain, and the warp strands showed clearly against the fur of the weft. When a rough place occurred, it was tied with deer sinew.

Either men or women might make rabbit skin blankets (Inf. 7). On the only occasion when the process was observed, a woman did the weaving. The materials were obtained by two men. Skins were sometimes sewn together to make blankets (Inf. 32).

These blankets were not used as mattresses. As soon as the sleeper arose, the blanket was rolled up or folded, since it was easily torn. According to Inf. 36, in the period immediately before Fort Sumner these blankets were used for carrying small babies. Softened juniper bark was used as a pad inside the blanket.

Data was provided by four informants, one of whom (Inf. 3) may have used this type of blanket. He and Inf. 7 gave a detailed description in 1937 and implied that they had seen them being made. In 1947, however, Inf. 7 said that although he had seen rabbit skin blankets, the Navaho regarded them as too fragile, and only the Zuni used them. As noted, Inf. 36 wove two blankets for Kluckhohn, and Inf. 32 had seen others being woven. Inf. 8 had merely heard of this type of covering. Although the technique survives, the blankets have disappeared. None is preserved as an heirloom. Woolen blankets purchased at the trading posts are now used.

Hill (East, Central, and West)

Rabbit skin blankets were woven on the loom (PP, Fort Defiance; SW, Nazlini; SG, Keams Canyon; GH, White Cone) and by hand (TLLSS, Crownpoint; TOMC, Red Rock; SC, Crystal; LW, Ganado). According to PP, when a man collected enough skins of either cottontail or jack rabbit, he soaked them, trimmed them, and, beginning at the outer edge of the hides, cut them spirally into single strips one-quarter to one-half inch wide. The strips were stretched between two stakes and allowed to dry. They were then bunched together, sprinkled with water, and rubbed between the hands. "This made them pliable and gave them a sort of dressing." According to GH, no dressing process was applied; the hides were merely cut spirally and two strips twisted together. SG said that hides were not dressed and were cut in straight strips, not spirally.

The ordinary upright loom was used for weaving. The warp material was wool (GH, SW, PP) or buckskin (SG). The size of the blanket depended on the number of skins a man had (SG).

Hand-woven blankets were produced in both twined and checker technique. According to TLLSS, rabbit skins for twined blankets were cut in straight strips that were tied end to end to form a long string. They were twisted spirally to place the fur on the outside. TOMC said that whole pelts were twisted spirally and tied together. The spiral strips were placed on the ground; the top and bottom ends were tied to lengths of twisted rabbit skin (TLLSS). The yucca (TOMC, SC) or buckskin (TLLSS) twining elements were introduced. The operator or operators—as many as five men might work at a time—started at the left and worked to the right. Wefts were introduced at intervals of about two inches. When two or three were completed, a weft was introduced across the center of the blanket to hold the warps in place. The loose ends of the wefts were tied around the last warp and two hoofs from the foreleg of a deer were attached. Two hind hoofs were tied at the point where weft elements were introduced. The sleeper always oriented his head toward the front hoofs (TLLSS). Rabbit skin blankets of this type were about two feet wide (TOMC) or two and a half feet wide (TLLSS).

Hides for checker-woven blankets were cut in strips about two fingers wide and placed in damp earth until they became pliable. They were then twisted spirally to place the fur on the outside and tied with sinew to make a long strip. Strips were then woven in checker weave (TLLSS). LW stated that for a checker weave blanket, rabbit skins were cut spirally and used for the weft; cliff rose bark was the warp.

Fishler (West)

According to TN (Kaibito), his great grandmother, who died in 1910, told him that small pieces of dressed rabbit skin were inserted between the warp and weft of a woolen blanket. BN (Kaibito) denied this; he said that in the old days, rabbit skins were sewn together with a needle and sinew to make blankets. GB (Tuba City) and TH (Moenave) agreed that blankets could be either woven or sewn.

Informants disagreed about the use of rabbit skin blankets. TN's great grandmother told him that they were used only as bedding, because if used for cloaks or bags they would wear out rapidly. GB claimed that they were never used as blankets, but only as cloaks.

Comparative

So far as is known, no observer of the Navaho has reported a rabbit skin blanket in use or being made by a Navaho, except for the two described above, which were made by request. The Franciscan Fathers (1910:457) illustrated a yucca blanket, a type which was "occasionally braided with rabbit fur," perhaps as described by Fishler. Handles of braided yucca were placed on the sides and end to enable the wearer to draw it close. Their term for the rabbit fur robe confirmed that used in Ramah.

James (1914:16) stated that the Navaho were familiar with the crude rabbit skin blanket loom still used by the Mohaves, Pimas, and Apache. He implied no evidence for its existence among the Navaho then or in the past.

Gifford's Western informant denied the rabbit skin blanket. The Eastern informant, however, said that these blankets, woven for bedding only, had a yucca fiber warp and a twisted rabbit skin weft. They were woven in checker weave around four pegs set in the ground to form the corners. Weaving was done by men (Gifford, 1940:40, 48, 140).

Although rabbit skin and other fur blankets were one of the most important Basketmaker textiles (Guernsey and Kidder, 1921:74–75) and were widely distributed in aboriginal America (from the Arctic to Yucatan, Wissler, 1938:57), they presumably became obsolete among the Navaho after the introduction of European textiles or sheep. By the late nineteenth century, certainly, they were rare. Around 1880 Dyk's informant saw a rabbit skin blanket on a visit to the Hopi. His father recognized it, but the informant had never seen one (Dyk, 1938:52).

125. Dressed Skin Blankets and Robes

ʼčidí (Ramah)   dressed buffalo robes

Ramah
Dressed buckskin and other pelts were used for bedding. Dressed buffalo robes were also known. Skins were sewn together.

Hill (East, Central, and West)
Blankets and robes were made from hides (see Plate X). These were sewn or woven. The sewn type was more prevalent than the woven. These appear to have been used both for bedding and for clothing.

Skins of several animals were used. Buffalo hides derived through trade with the Utes were reported (PP, Fort Defiance; C, Chinle; TLLSS, Crownpoint), as were mountain lion and elk skin robes (C) or dehaired deer hides (C; GH, White Cone).

Wildcat skin was by far the most popular material for sewn blankets and robes (PP, TLLSS, GH; LW, Ganado; N, Coalmine; SG, Keams Canyon). SG said that he had never seen or heard of robes of this type made of any other materials. TLLSS, however, said that they were made of fox and woodrat hides; C of otter ("it took four skins to make a robe"); T (Chaco Canyon) of rabbit; and PP of buckskin.

Dressed hides were trimmed along the sides and the heads and legs removed. The pelts were then sewn together with sinew (or yucca fiber, T). Hides were placed transversely, head to tail (TLLSS). How long this trait remained in use is not known; a wildcat skin robe was shown in a photograph taken some time prior to 1894.

Woven blankets were occasionally made from the dressed skins of wildcat (MC, Sawmill; GH, SG) or mountain lion (SG). These were woven on the upright loom. SG said that mountain lion or wildcat hides were cut into strips and introduced as the weft; the warp consisted of spirally cut strings of buckskin. According to MC and GH, woolen warp was used and the wildcat skins were cut spirally for the weft.

Lamphere (East)
PM denied the use of skins other than those of sheep and goats for bedding.

Fishler (West)
TT (Coalmine) stated that buffalo hides were used for bedding; when he was a boy, many Navaho still owned such hides. TN (Kaibito) and TH (Moenave) had only heard of them.

Comparative
Buffalo robes, buckskin, and sheep pelts were all used for bedding, according to the Franciscan Fathers (1910:341, 467). They were rolled up in the morning, but occasionally spread out for airing. The Navaho disposed of old pelts at the stores.

Gifford's Eastern informant said that wildcat skins, mountain lion skins, and dehaired buckskins were used for bedding, but not coyote, fox, antelope, or bear. He did not know whether badger skins were used, and said that the use of the buffalo robe was modern. The Western informant was not questioned (Gifford, 1940:40).

X. An aged tribesman (the grandfather of RH, Crystal) prior to 1894. Note the dressed bobcat skin robe (Tr. 125), woolen blankets (Tr. 127), mountain lion skin hat (Tr. 186), and the straw hat. The man is wearing a cotton shirt (Tr. 172), buckskin leggings (Tr. 177) with silver buttons (Tr. 202), woven garters (Tr. 179), a cloth headband (Tr. 183), and moccasins (Tr. 189).

Blankets of skins sewn together were included in Matthews' mythological inventory of original Navaho clothing (Matthews, 1897:141). In Reichard's transcription (1944:137) of the Hail Chant, Rat Woman laid a squirrel skin over Rainboy, but a blanket of woven or sewn skins was not indicated.

126. Sheepskin Bedding

dibéčidí (Ramah)   "sheep robe" (CC)

Ramah
Three or four dressed sheep pelts, preferably large ones, were trimmed straight along the edges and sewn together. If three were used, the pelts were laid parallel; if four, two were laid side by side and one of the other two was placed at each end.

Women did the sewing, at any time or place. These pelts lasted about a year (Inf. 7) or two years (Inf. 8). During the day they were hung on wires or sticks across the corner of the hogan, or hung outside.

Inf. 7 said that sheep pelts were used as bedding as long as he could remember. Today, almost every family uses sheep pelts for bedding. Roberts counted six, ten, and six in the three households he studied. He noted, however, that the sheep and goat pelts used for bedding and floor covering were untanned; the fresh pelt was merely staked out in the sun to dry. This work could be done by anyone, but it usually was done by the owner of the animal. Roberts had seen a young boy, an old man, and two adult women staking pelts at one time or another (Roberts, 1951:19, 37–38). It is probable that sheepskin bedding has replaced that made from the skins of wild animals.

Hill (East, Central, and West)
Several informants (C, Chinle; PP, Fort Defiance; MS, Sawmill; K, Mariano Lake; TLLSS, Crownpoint) reported the use of sheepskins and goatskins for bedding. According to WH (Wheatfields), anything convenient might be used as a pillow. GH (White Cone) said that if nothing better was available, a block of wood was used.

Lamphere (East)
PM confirmed the use of sheepskins and goatskins for bedding, and said that only these were used.

Fishler (West)
TH (Moenave) and TN (Kaibito) said that the skins of sheep were used for rugs and bedding.

Comparative
Sheep pelts are so frequently mentioned in the literature as Navaho bedding that it may be assumed that they are universal throughout the area. They were common by 1910, used almost to the exclusion of buckskin and buffalo robes (Franciscan Fathers, 1910:467). Gifford's Western informant confirmed the use of sheepskin bedding; the Eastern informant (who confirmed the other types) was apparently not questioned on this trait (Gifford, 1940:40, 132).

127. Woolen Blanket

beˑelʌádí (Haile) blanket; "shawl, or Pendleton blanket" (CC)

beˑelʌéˑˑ (Haile) "blanket" (CC)

Ramah

Woolen blankets were (and are) woven on an upright loom. The details of construction and techniques of weaving have been thoroughly and competently covered by others. There are no important variations from the Ramah area.

Ramah is not an area noted for the excellence of its weaving. The traders have described weaving as a "lost art" and have not found it financially lucrative. In 1937 traders paid ninety cents per pound for blankets and sold their stock for that or less. Most of the weaving was destined for the trading post, although quite often a blanket or rug was woven for some other Navaho in the region. A few families used blankets of their own manufacture; Inf. 12 said that such blankets were woven more carefully. Of the materials sold to the traders, most were double saddle blankets, many were chairback size pieces; perhaps one sixth were rugs.

Whether complicated weaves were used is unknown; a few informants knew diamond weaves, and one said that she could weave double-faced cloth. Dyes were usually commercial, although vegetable dyes were used by at least one family. A daughter learned of them at a government boarding school and instructed her mother and sisters in their use. In one household studied by Roberts, vegetable dyes were known but had not been used recently. Two households, however, owned sacks of white clay for washing wool yarn (Roberts, 1951:37, 99, fig. 12, HB-3). In 1937, half of the rugs in one trading post had complicated designs; most of the rest were simple striped patterns enclosed by short vertical bars of contrasting colors.

In the ten-year period between 1936 and 1946, eighty-four women in the Ramah area were known to weave. Girls usually learned from their mothers (fifteen of eighteen) when they were between the ages of ten and fifteen. No men were known to weave, although several said that they had learned as children. Two (Infs. 55, 264) stopped "because people teased us about it," after Inf. 55 had finished a very small blanket.

Adequate figures on output of the Ramah weavers were obtained only for 1938. Data were obtained from sixty-three women, twenty-five of whom wove less than six rugs during the year. Six women produced none, but three of them said they were too old to weave. Thirteen women wove between six and eleven rugs; nine between eleven and fifteen; seven between sixteen and twenty; one between twenty-one and thirty; and two more than thirty. The last two were helped by younger women in weaving and, presumably, in the preparation of materials.

Most of the weaving was done in the winter, although some women also wove during the summer. Many made excuses, saying that they had been sick, or that the trader had taken all the wool, or that they had to buy wool because they had no sheep. One trader did not receive a rug for several weeks in the summer of 1941.

In the households studied by Roberts, women and girls wove rugs and saddle blankets, but no belts or garters. They carded, spun, and wove inter-

127.a. Unusual poncho-like woolen blanket

mittently, fitting these activities into the domestic routine. Two of the women knew a variety of designs and several weaves. One wove two rugs during the period of study (March 4 to August 4, 1946), another wove one, and a girl who was learning to weave made a small rug (Roberts, 1951:37, 39, fig. 4, HA-2, HB-2; fig. 12, HB-1, HB-2).

Comparative

The Franciscan Fathers (1910:341, 467) confirmed the use of woolen blankets for bedding; they were generally used to cover the individual. Both of Gifford's informants agreed that woven wool or cotton blankets could be used, although the Eastern informant said that the trait was modern (Gifford, 1940:40).

For details on Navaho weaving see one of the many excellent sources, for example, Amsden, 1934; Franciscan Fathers, 1910:221–255; Hollister, 1903; Jeançon and Douglas, 1930; Matthews, 1884; Pepper, 1923; Reichard, 1936.

Cradles

128. Split-back Cradle ·awé·čá·l (Haile) "baby board" (CC)

Ramah

Western yellow pine (*Pinus ponderosa*) was preferred, and Inf. 9 said that it was taken from a tree not likely to be felled, in a place rarely visited. Inf. 76 said the flattest side of the tree was chosen; Inf. 3 said that wood was taken from the east side of the tree and that all parts of the cradle (except the canopy) must be made from one piece.

Transverse notches were cut in the tree and the wood between was removed (Inf. 76). The wood had to be so oriented that the direction from top to roots in the tree was the same as that from head to foot in the cradle (Roberts, 1951:70–71).

The two pieces of the cradle back were shaped as follows (according to Bailey's notes). A triangular section was cut from the top and bottom of each board, at the inner edge (where they were laced together). At the top, the cutting line was drawn from a point midway across the top to another a third of the distance down the inner edge. From this point, a line was drawn to another about a quarter of the distance across the bottom of the board. This narrow wedge was whittled, not sawed. Cut surfaces were smoothed with a knife, and sharp corners were slightly rounded. When the two boards were placed together, the upper diagonals formed a broad V-shape. A crosspiece was made to fit against the backs of the two boards at the point of the V (see 128.1). Its rough edges were beveled with a knife; the other side was unworked.

Inf. 81 and his wife (Inf. 82) made a cradle for Bailey, who obtained two pine boards ($\frac{1}{4}$ in. to $\frac{1}{2}$ in. thick) from the trading post. A model (Inf. 82's cradle) was placed next to the boards to determine the approximate length, after which it was measured in finger widths. Other measurements were made by sight. The new cradle was lighter than the model, and longer. Inf. 82 tested it in her arms for length, which was "just right," and remarked that the lighter weight was preferable. Cutting the board to size and cutting the first diagonal were done with a cross-cut saw, on a wooden bench; the board was held stationary by the knee. The diagonals were placed to avoid knots and a place which split during the first sawing. The first board was used as a pattern for the second, and the cut marked with a pencil. The second side was cut with more care and did not split. On both boards the long diagonal was sketched in with a pencil using a straight board as a square; it was then whittled. The jackknife was held in both hands, one at either end of the blade, and pulled toward the worker; Inf. 81 braced one end of the board against his abdomen and the other against a chair while cutting. He handled the knife very dexterously.

Holes were then bored with a heated wire at points previously marked. A stone was rubbed over the boards to smooth them. A mixture of ground red ocher and tallow, or other grease, slightly heated and rubbed on the boards, gave the cradle a reddish tint. According to Inf. 82, the reddening was done because "the evil spirits never paint their cradles red and therefore the Navaho must do so to distinguish between theirs and the *chiindi's.*"

Buckskin thongs about six inches long were cut, and the boards laced together in the center. The ties were on the underside of the cradle. Inf. 82 said buckskin lacings were formerly wider; now they are "like shoestrings." Some lacings are also made of canvas or other cloth rather than of buckskin.

The footboard and canopy frame were then attached. According to Inf. 29, the cradle was so constructed that the footboard could be extended as the child grew. No hole was left at the bottom for drainage of the child's wastes (Infs. 54, 3). Inf. 3 said that urine drained through the joint between the two boards.

A buckskin canopy was placed over the top of the cradle. A cloth was rolled and attached to the cradle to serve as a headrest; wood was not used for this purpose.

A bit of squirrel hide, such as the tail, was sometimes placed on the cradle to protect the baby (Inf. 50). The cradle was occasionally decorated with buckskin tassels (Inf. 48) or silver buckles. The latter were placed at the top two corners, attached by strips of buckskin threaded through holes burned in the frame, and tied on the underside. Inf. 12 said that sometimes beads or shells or a bell were placed on the cradle for ornament. Inf. 48 had never heard of placing turquoise on a boy's cradle or white shell on a girl's cradle.

The cradle was lined with cliff rose bark (Vestal, 1952:30), shredded to a fine straw. The bark was placed on the cradle, with a sheepskin, fur side up, over it. The bark absorbed water, and was removed, dried in the sun, and used again. The child was laced into the cradle with cords or thongs, which were tied in a double square knot across his stomach.

Either men or women made cradles (Infs. 12, 9, 48). Informants said that anyone who knew how (Infs. 35, 3, 9) and was available, or knew the accompanying prayers (Inf. 3), or anyone in the family (Inf. 9) could make cradles. A man might be paid a colt or sheep for making a cradle (Inf. 3). A man or woman who had been sick for a long time should not make a cradle. Often both sexes helped. According to Inf. 12, a man cut the tree for the boards, then helped hold them while the woman shaped them,

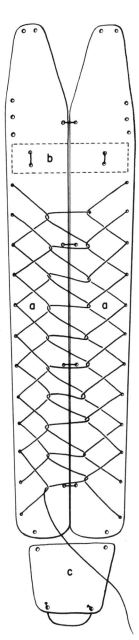

128.1. Split-back cradle (Hill), after K (Mariano Lake), showing backboards (*a*), crosspiece (*b*), and footboard (*c*)

punched the holes, and fixed the thongs. When making the cradle for Bailey, Inf. 81 did this work, and his wife (Inf. 82) helped judge the measurements, bored the holes, and rubbed the cradle with red ocher. Inf. 82 said that either the father or grandfather usually made the cradle while the mother made the buckskin wrappings and cover and fixed the cloth headrest. One father (Inf. 27) made the cradle for his daughter, born in 1940. Inf. 55 thought that his mother had made his cradle, and Inf. 15 made a cradle for one of Inf. 9's babies. It was destroyed at the child's death, and Inf. 9 and his wife made another for their subsequent child.

Work on the cradle started two or three days (Inf. 12) or a week (Inf. 82) after the baby was born; Inf. 82 said that if it began earlier the child would die. Inf. 27 began the cradle for his daughter three weeks after her birth; it was completed in three days. Cradles were made in the hogan.

According to Inf. 29, the child was placed in the cradle shortly after the umbilical cord fell off. The cradle was used until the child tried to crawl out of it, until he sat up or began to walk. Inf. 46 said that after a child was four months old he spent much of the time off the board, and this time increased until the cradle was finally abandoned.

The same cradle was used for successive children, and when not in use was hung on the wall without special covering, unless a baby died. In this case, it was dismantled and placed by the child's grave, or, according to Inf. 3, in a juniper or pinyon tree or a cave. Inf. 55 said that his cradle was used by his brothers; then he thought it was given away. Inf. 82 said that a cradle might be used for four successive generations. When a child outgrew a cradle, it was dismantled and stored (Inf. 3). The cradle was washed and painted with red ocher before being used by another infant.

The cradle is regarded by the Ramah Navaho as a trait of their early culture. It still survives, and it is probable that the majority of Navaho babies born in the Ramah area are placed in the cradle. The art of making cradles is still known in the area. The only change of which informants are aware is the occasional substitution of the blanket for the buckskin canopy. The use of hot metal for boring holes is also an innovation.

Hill (East and Central)

Cradles were made in five pieces: two backboards ("the whole cradle," or "baby cradle"), a footboard ("the sole of the foot"), a back brace ("its bottom"), and a bow-shaped canopy support. All but the last were made of pine. "Only this wood was wide enough" (SC, Crystal). A slab of pine was split from the tree and the four sections shaped with an axe and knife. These parts were perforated with a hot iron; through the holes passed buckskin ties for assembling the cradle and securing the child (SC; PP, Fort Defiance).

Four or five matching holes (depending on the size of the cradle) were burned through the inside edge of each backboard; buckskin ties passed through these holes held the sections together (see *a* on 128.1). Another pair of holes was made in the upper part of each backboard, for ties from a pair in the brace (see *b* on 128.1). Above these, on the outer edge of the backboards, were two or three holes to which the canopy support was lashed. Thongs through two holes at the top edge secured the canopy. Buckskin loops were tied through perforations made in the lower edges of the backboards; the lacing that held the baby in the cradle was run through these loops. These holes were spaced the distance between the thumb and the tip of the middle finger on the extended hand. Indentations were usually cut in the backboards for drainage (SC).

The footboards (see *c* on 128.1) had four holes. Two matched holes on the backboards were used to attach this piece to the cradle; the other two carried a buckskin loop to which the lacing was tied (SC, PP). Such a cradle (see 128.1) was obtained from K (Mariano Lake).

When the framework of the cradle was complete, tallow was rubbed into the various parts. Each piece was then held over the fire to allow the fat to permeate the wood. The worker repeated the process using tallow and red ocher (SC).

A pad of shredded cliff rose bark was placed on the backboards of the completed cradle. In recent times, a cloth has been laid over the bark or a cloth pad used instead. Usually a roll of bark was tied to the cradle under the neck and a small pad under the base of the skull (SC; C, Chinle). "This last would make the skull round" (SC).

Cradle lashings consisted of buckskin thongs, two inches wide. One pair was run through the loops on the outside of each backboard. Each thong was run through alternate loops and enough slack was allowed to form secondary loops (see 128.2). A fifth thong, tied to the top loop, was run through the remaining loops, from side to side, and tied to the thong on the footboard (SC, C).

Both sexes used the same type of cradle. There were no marks on it which identified the occupant as male or female (SC, PP, C).

When the child was born he was wrapped in a sheepskin and placed with his head toward the fire. "This will make the head round." After a while the child, still wrapped in the hide, might be tied to any board. When he was from seven to ten days old he was placed in the cradle. "The child remained in the cradle for about a year, until it was weaned or got uncomfortable and did not want the cradle any more" (SC).

If a child died the cradle was broken up or hidden. Children were never buried in cradles, although occasionally the cradle might be placed on the grave. If no deaths occurred the cradle was used for each successive child. Cradles were commonly inherited by daughters from their mothers (SC).

"Those who know the legend of the origin of the cradle think of the different parts as symbolic, but common, ordinary people do not know this" (SC).

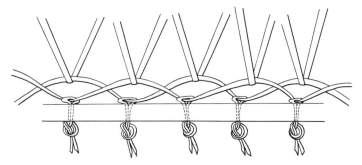

128.2. Securing the lashing on a split-back cradle (Hill), after K

Lamphere (East)
PM said the footboard was called "foot sits there."

Comparative

Apparently the earliest reference to a Navaho cradle is by Robinson (1932:51), who in 1846 saw a willow cradle carried on the back of a Navaho woman. Simpson (1850:88) observed a cradleboard with a canopy frame of willow bark. It is not clear whether their descriptions referred to the split-back cradle or the solid-back cradle. Bourke, in 1881, stated that the Navaho cradles were made "precisely like those of the Zunis," of flat juniper slabs, lined with "soft, tissue-like bark." He saw one being made by an old woman (Bourke, 1936:224, 237).

Mason (1889:193–194) described a cradleboard collected in the 1870's or 1880's by Dr. R. W. Shufeldt, U.S. Army. The upper end, he said, was "in shape like a boot-jack," an apt description. It was manufactured as described above. The pillow consisted of "soft furs and rags rolled up in soft buckskin and fastened to the board." Shufeldt noted that Navaho mothers always placed a pad in the cradle to protect the back of the child's head; at the same time, the head was not strapped but allowed all possible freedom (see also Mason, 1896:530–531, figs. 222, 223).

The Franciscan Fathers (1910:469–471) gave a complete description of the construction of the cradle, stating that most of the details applied to the construction of both the split-back cradle and the solid-back or "whole" cradle. Cottonwood, pine, willow, weeping willow, and pinyon were common materials, although wood from a coffee case or dry goods box had recently been used. Wood from a tree struck by lightning, broken by winds, or against which a bear had rubbed, was thought injurious and was prohibited. Thongs were of buckskin, or tanned goatskin if available, or of wool. Details of construction confirmed these described above. A fringed buckskin (now leather) tassel, knotted and passed through a hole at the top of the boards, was the only ornament. Turquoise (for a boy) or white shell (for a girl) was set near the tassel. By 1910, however, silver buttons had displaced the setting.

A description, translated from Navaho text, was published by Sapir and Hoijer (1942:279–281). Bark was pulled from an appropriate tree and shredded. The tree was marked with pollen on the east side, then cut; another cut was made, and an axe forced in as a wedge until a piece of the appropriate thickness dropped out. Pollen was again applied to the wood to be used for the cradleboard. Holes were burned through the wood, and the pieces lashed together with dressed skin. Then "the cradle-board, all of it, is made red with red clay." Shredded bark was then placed in the cradle, and the baby laid into it. "His bed being his home, he always lies in it."

According to Newcomb (1940a:28), the cradle was not made until the child was three or four weeks old for fear that he would die. The father made the cradle, using pine, ash, and cliff rose. Pine for the backboards was cut from a young tree growing in a secluded or almost inaccessible spot. It was believed that if during the life of the child the tree were cut down, struck by lightning, or broken during a storm, the child would die a violent death. Ash was used for the canopy arch; cliff rose bark was shredded for padding. Newcomb stated that the cradle was seldom reused; even when it was outgrown, it was considered the child's property and often served as a toy.

The Coolidges (1930:54–55) confirmed the prescriptions required for gathering pine; oak was cut for the canopy. Each piece was sprinkled with corn pollen. The cradle was painted inside and out with a mixture of sheep tallow and red paint; the bark lining was also rubbed with this mixture. When the baby was placed on a blanket in the cradle, he was laced in; lacing started at the bottom and crossed upward. The baby was supposed to lie upward, as the tree grew. The Coolidges stated that this was a temporary cradle, used while the father was preparing the permanent cradle.

Both of Gifford's informants confirmed a "board cradle," but the Eastern Navaho said it was modern. The baby was laced into the cradle with buckskin loops attached to the cradle frame, but the loops themselves did not pass through holes bored in the frame. Both informants affirmed a footrest; the Eastern informant said it was made of yucca fiber and was adjustable. Both confirmed a canopy covered with a skin drape or sometimes cloth (Eastern informant). Bedding was of shredded cliff rose (Eastern informant) or juniper (Western informant) bark. The Western infant was swaddled in buckskin, the Eastern in either a blanket of woven rabbit skin or of sewn woodrat skin, or in cloth. A buckskin pack strap was attached to the cradle, which was carried on the back either over the head or over the shoulder and chest. According to the Eastern informant, the cradle was sometimes carried against the hip (Gifford, 1940:45–47, 137–139).

Leighton and Kluckhohn collected data from Chaco Canyon (1938) and Navaho Mountain (1942) in addition to that from Ramah, and presented a detailed description of the materials, decoration, construction, and use of the cradleboard. Also included was material on customs and folk rites for the use of the cradle gathered by Louisa Wade Wetherill at Oljetoh or Kayenta, probably before 1920 (Leighton and Kluckhohn, 1947:18–26, 29, 30). The Wetherill manuscript (n.d.:2 pp.) contained a few notes not cited by Leighton and Kluckhohn: Lacings were reused until they were worn out, then placed in the top of a pine or pinyon tree with a special prayer. If a child died in the cradle, the board was broken up and buried with the child; in this case the strings could not be reused.

There is a split-back cradle in the Harvard Peabody Museum (see 128.a). Except for an oak hoop, all pieces were made of sawed pine (about $\frac{3}{8}$ in. thick), finished with a knife. The backboards (each $4\frac{1}{2}$ in. wide, about 31 in. and 32 in. long) tapered at the upper ends ($5\frac{1}{2}$ in. from the top). There were five pairs of holes in the inner edges for lashing the boards together and an additional pair in each board for securing the back brace (7 in. by 8 in.), the upper edge of which was seven inches from the top. Twelve holes lined the outside edges of the boards. The upper three were for lashing the canopy frame, the rest for lacing. All appeared burned. The footboard was trapezoidal ($5\frac{3}{8}$ in. high, $4\frac{1}{2}$ in. and 7 in. wide). Two holes in the wide (7 in.) edge corresponded to one in the center of each backboard; thongs through these secured the three pieces. A loop through two holes in the outer edge of the footboard secured it to the rest of the cradle lashing. Through the center one of three holes in the upper end of each backboard was passed a thong for suspension, secured by a handmade silver button. The cradle was suspended either from the top or from a stout buckskin tumpline (55 in. long) tied to the second hole from the top on the outside edge of each

128.a. Split-back cradle with buckskin wrapping

backboard. The cover and lacings were of buckskin, secured by knots in the lacings on the underside of the backboards. The only ornament was a small hemispherical silver button attached by a short thong to the upper part of the buckskin bedding cover.

Prototypes of modern cradleboards were mentioned in Navaho myths. Among specified parts were the backboards, footrests, canopies, and lacings, as well as fringed covers, pillows, and carrying straps (see Reichard, 1950:543).

129. Solid-back Cradle ꞌawéꞏčáꞏl ꞌałaꞏígí (Ramah) "baby board one" (CC)

Ramah

Only wood from a large pine was used. The cradle was shaped like the split-back cradle, but the back was made of one piece and was rounded in cross section, not flat. Either a man or a woman made this type of cradle, but the mother owned it. The solid-back cradle was used for the first month or two, "because baby is weak and tender" (Inf. 48).

Both types of cradles are now used, sometimes in the same family at the same time. If so, the older child is put in the split-back cradle. According to Inf. 48, the solid-back cradle is an old Navaho type but Inf. 3 denied its existence in the face of contemporary examples.

Hill (Central)

The "whole" cradle appears to have been a variant of the split-back type. Its occurrence was rare because of the difficulty of acquiring timber of sufficient width and because in earlier periods inadequate tools made it easier to fashion the backboards in two pieces. "If a wide enough board could be found, the back was made in one piece" (C, Chinle). "Only this wood [pine] was wide enough" (SC, Crystal).

Comparative

Many observers did not differentiate between the split-back and the solid-back cradle. The cradle described by Palmer (1869:94), however, appears to be the latter: "It consists of a flat board to support the vertebral column of the infant and soft wadding to give ease to the position." It was ornamented with a leather fringe, and had a canopy for protection. A leather strap was attached for carrying.

The Franciscan Fathers (1910:469) presented a detailed description of the "whole" cradle. It was used when the baby was about three months old, for a month; after that the split-back cradle was used. It was shaped like the split-back cradle, but a small hole was provided in the lower part of the back to allow for drainage. In this type of cradle, the Franciscan Fathers stated, the lacing and carrying cords were frequently not used, although holes were provided for lacing loops. In other respects, the two types were similar.

Both Gifford's informants denied the use of more than one cradle before the baby walked. Both confirmed the "wooden board cradle" although the Eastern informant said it was modern. It is not known whether this is the split- or solid-back type (Gifford, 1940:45, 46, 138).

130. Laced Rod Cradle

'awé·čá·l yisⱭonigi (Haile) "baby board woven" (CC)

Hill (Central)

According to informants (SC, Crystal; C, Chinle), a rod cradle was constructed prior to the introduction of iron tools. The pattern was similar to that of the split- or solid-back cradles. Rods were of willow, hardwood (*tsintliz*) (SC), sumac, or oak (C). They were held in place by yucca strips or buckskin thongs. The thong or strip was wrapped once around each rod and the ends tied to the outside rods (see 130.1). Ties were introduced at intervals of about eight inches.

Laced rod cradle, after Hill

130.1. Method of lacing   **130.2.** Top of cradle   **130.3.** Footboard

The V top of the cradle was achieved by shortening the rods in that area (see 130.2). A drainage hole was produced by placing two short rods in the center section of the cradle. The footboard was of rods, made in the same manner as the cradle. Lacings were of buckskin. The canopy support was of oak, willow, or hardwood (SC).

Comparative

The Franciscan Fathers (1910:468–469) described a cradle made of peeled twigs laced together in four places by strings (see 130.4); this was used for about two months, was then replaced by the "whole" cradle, and finally by the split-back cradle.

The laced cradle was also confirmed by the Coolidges (1930:54), but they stated that the "whole" cradle, rather than the split-back type, was the final form. Leighton and Kluckhohn (1947:18–20) also mentioned the four types of cradle cited by the Franciscan Fathers.

130.4. Laced cradle, after the Franciscan Fathers

131. Cradle Canopy

'awé·· bini·kidí (Ramah, Haile) "baby face over" (CC)

Ramah

A canopy was made for the cradles described above. The frame was of oak or juniper, usually an inch to an inch and a half wide, although one four inches wide was observed. Instead of a single flat curved piece, the canopy support was sometimes made of two curved pieces or two or more twigs bound together. The frame was rubbed with red ocher, as was the rest of the cradle. It was laced with buckskin to the backboards.

A buckskin was placed over the top of the cradle. The front was stretched over the arc, the rest draped over the back with the tail of the skin hanging down between the two prongs of the cradle; the rear legs were tied together under the cradle by a thong laced through holes punched in each leg. The tail on the buckskin was supposed to protect the baby and to insure good luck (Inf. 82).

A blanket is now used instead of the buckskin. Inf. 82 preferred a blanket because it was easier to keep clean and less warm than buckskin. On Inf. 83's cradle, a blanket covered the top.

A similar canopy was made to protect the head of a newborn baby; it was not used with the regular cradle. A framework of pliable oak or juniper sticks was covered with buckskin, dressed goatskin or antelope skin, or a blanket. The newborn child was wrapped in a sheep pelt and placed on the west side of the hogan, with the canopy over its head. This canopy was used for the first month of the child's life.

Although Infs. 81 and 82 stated that the canopy was not ordinarily made until several days after the child was born, Kluckhohn observed Inf. 242 the day after he was born and found his head covered by the canopy.

Anyone in the family, either man or woman, might make a canopy (Infs. 9, 28). According to Inf. 76, a skin canopy was owned by the man of the family, a blanket one by the woman.

When not in use canopies were stored in buckskin sacks hung on the hogan wall. An antelope skin canopy made by Inf. 76 when she was a young woman lasted about ten years.

Inf. 48 spoke of the canopy as an old Navaho device. She had not seen the type illustrated by the Franciscan Fathers (see 131.2). This type of covering is still in use in the Ramah area, although observers have seen children with no canopy protection.

Hill (Central)

The canopy support was made of oak (SC, Crystal) preferably or juniper if oak was unavailable (PP, Fort Defiance). When possible, it was constructed in one piece. A slab was worked to a quarter of an inch or less in thickness and three to four inches in width. This was bent in the shape of an arc. It was bent cold if pliable; if not, it was steamed and bent.

Two or three holes were burned in each end. Two pieces of hardwood, slightly larger in diameter than a pencil, were cut to fit the width of the support. These were placed at the ends of the arc. The lashings which secured the support to the cradle passed around these hardwood pieces, through the holes in the support and backboard, and were tied tightly beneath the cradle (see 131.1).

If wood of sufficient width was unavailable, the support consisted of two or three narrow arcs. These were wrapped to form a single unit and attached to the cradle (SC, PP).

The canopy was formerly of buckskin, and is now frequently of goatskin. It was fastened to the support at the center and at each end; three pairs of holes were punched in the hide for this purpose. The back of the canopy was tied to the top of the backboards. Squirrel skins, squirrel tails, or pieces of chert were often tied to the support to amuse the child and attract his attention (SC).

Lamphere (East)

PM confirmed the term for cradle canopy.

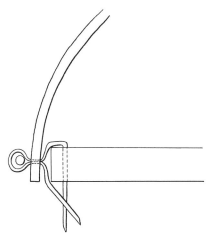

131.1. Lashing the cradle canopy (Hill), after K

Comparative

The canopy for the "whole" cradle was later used on the split-back cradle, according to the Franciscan Fathers (1910:467–470). It was made of bows of "thin and smoothened scrub oak, cedar [juniper], or other convenient wood, four of which" were laced together with four buckskin thongs to form a single arc. In 1910, some used a single wide or two fairly wide bows. The arc was tied to two holes in the backboards, loosely enough to allow it to move back and forth when the child was inspected. The frame was covered with a cloth or well tanned goatskin, secured to the sides of the backboard near the base of the bow.

A canopy cover without cradle was also described. As at Ramah, the newborn child was placed between the fireplace and the west side of the hogan, and covered with a canopy to protect him from sparks from the fire. The frame (see 131.2) consisted of three bows, a horizontal one as a base (*a*), a vertical one (*b*) attached with cords to the ends of the first, and a third as a brace. The third arc (*c*) was secured with cords at the center of the base and upright. A cord (*d*) was stretched from end to end of the bow at the base; the baby's weight on this cord kept the canopy in place. A blanket or cloth (a tanned goatskin in wealthier families) was placed over the frame.

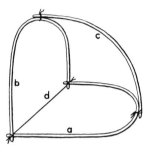

131.2. Frame for cradle canopy, after the Franciscan Fathers; showing base bow (*a*), vertical bow (*b*), brace (*c*), and cord (*d*) to secure the frame

According to Newcomb (1940a:28), mountain ash was used for the canopy frame; it was gathered with the same care as wood for the rest of the cradle. The Coolidges (1930:54) referred to this protective device, as did Leighton and Kluckhohn (1947:18–19), the latter specifying willow withes as the framework material.

Both of Gifford's informants confirmed the use of a canopy with the cradle. The Eastern informant described an arc of parallel oak withes, fastened with sinew twining; it was sometimes adjustable. The Western informant said an arc flattened on one side was used. Both agreed that a skin was draped over the frame. Buckskin was preferred, according to the Eastern informant, or a checker-weave fabric of Spanish bayonet fiber (Gifford, 1940:46, 138).

The canopy of the cradle in the Harvard Peabody Museum consisted of two splints ($1\frac{1}{4}$ in. by $33\frac{1}{4}$ in.) lashed together with wide buckskin strips (see 128.a). A hole at either end was provided for tying the splints to the backboards. Incorporated into the lashing on each side was a round stick ($\frac{1}{4}$ in. by 6 in.).

132. Cradle Swing

ʾawéˑndoba (Ramah)

Ramah

Inf. 48 said that she had heard of a swing similar to that illustrated by the Franciscan Fathers (see below). A "baby swing" and "baby walker" were observed in Inf. 99's hogan in 1941. Whether others occurred in the Ramah area is not known.

Comparative

The cradle swing described by the Franciscan Fathers (1910:472–473) consisted of a flat board with two holes in each corner. Two long cords, secured by short cords through the holes at each corner, passed under the board; they were tied over the center of the swing at the top (see 132.1). Another

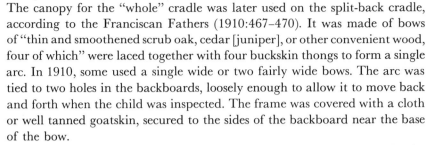

132.1. Cradle swing, after the Franciscan Fathers

cord was attached to the knot, and the swing, with the cradle on it, was suspended from a beam in the hogan, or from a tree outside. It was out of reach of other children and red ants. Occasionally the mother would give it a swing. The swing was apparently in use in 1910.

The only other reference to the cradle swing was by Gifford (1940:138). Both his informants confirmed it, but only that used by the Western Navaho was described. It was composed of buckskin supported on two parallel ropes. The cradle with the baby in it was placed on this swing.

The present distribution of the cradle swing is unknown.

Chapter 3 Clothing

This chapter is a continuation of the theme of the preceding one, since clothing serves to protect the individual and, as noted in Chapter 2, is an occasional part of "the hogan, its insides." Clothing merits separate treatment, however, because traits in the two chapters differ in terms of technological complexity. Most of the traits pertaining to shelter were manufactured directly from raw materials, but a number of preliminary processes were necessary before an article of clothing could be produced. Traits associated with these processes are grouped in categories, as were those pertaining to the preparation of food. Categories are discussed in the approximate order in which an individual would encounter the included traits if he were manufacturing an article of clothing. Skins must be dressed before they are sewn or otherwise fashioned into garments. Note here that although woven garments (for example, shirt, belts, garters) are discussed, looms and loom equipment (batten, carding implements, and so forth) have been amply covered elsewhere and are therefore omitted from this study (see Bibliography and Trait 127). Skins and skeins of wool are dyed before they are made into garments. Dyes are also used for non-clothing materials such as baskets; but this use has been fully discussed in other works and is therefore omitted from this book.

Where possible, types of clothing are described in order of historical sequence. Women's clothing is first discussed. The bast apron "worn in the old days" is followed by aprons or skirts of skin and cotton, by blouses or shirts of skin and cotton or wool; the two-piece costume is followed by the whole, or dress. Next is the section on men's clothing. (A few garments listed under men's clothing, such as the buckskin belt, are also worn by women, but are primarily male garments.) Finally, apparel worn by both sexes, including headgear, shoes, and winter clothing, is described.

Clothing involves more than protection from the environment. For this reason it is appropriate to include in the section materials on ornamentation and hygiene. Necklaces, earrings, bracelets, rings, and other pieces of jewelry are familiar accessories among the Navaho and are worn for adornment as well as for prestige. Additional ornamentation sometimes includes the use of paint on the face and body, and tattooing. Ornamentation is followed by a description of materials used for personal hygiene.

Skin Dressing

133. Rawhide biʰh biskạˑ (Ramah) "deer dry skin" (CC)

ʼakáˑɬ (Ramah, Haile)

Ramah
Hides from ritually hunted, nonritually hunted, and domestic animals were used for making rawhide. The method of skinning depended on the ritual, or lack of it; and for a ritually hunted animal, it varied according to the ritual used by the hunter. Small animals and fawns were sometimes cased,

but specific techniques were not known. Game animals were skinned where they fell and the hide brought home for processing.

When skinning a deer (a ritually hunted animal), the worker laid the body on the ground or on a bed of boughs. He made an incision on the ventral side from nose to tail tip, leaving a small strip of skin around the nose. He then made incisions on the inside of each leg, leaving a little strip of hide around the top of each hoof. The ears were left attached to the skin. In some instances, the knife was used; in others, the hand was pushed under the skin and worked along to loosen the hide.

For a domestic animal, the account by John Adair of butchering and skinning a sheep documented a recurrent behavior pattern of the Ramah Navaho. In this account, killing and butchering were done by a woman. She tied the animal's legs securely and, taking a hunting knife, parted the wool over the jugular vein. Standing behind the sheep, she pulled its head back with her left hand (held under its jaw), braced her left foot against the back of its head, and cut a slit across the bottom of the neck over the jugular vein. Blood was caught in a pan held under the neck. She gave a quick backward pull on the head, which appeared to break the animal's neck.

Next the animal was skinned. A cut was made from the sternum to the slit in the throat, another around the bottom joint of the left foreleg (the closest to her). After cutting from this joint down the inside of the leg to the shoulder, she held the loose edge of the skin and pulled upward while pressing down on the flesh with the knuckles of her right hand. She removed the skin from the leg, around the sternum and the neck. Then, with the knife, she removed the hoof at the joint. She slit the belly, from the sternum to between the hind legs. She skinned the left hind leg, removed the hoof, as above, and pulled the skin back from the belly and side toward the backbone. Then she moved to the other side of the animal and repeated the process, leaving the skin attached to the back.

Her son started a fire to the east of the shade, where Adair supposed they were going to roast the mutton. She strung a cord between the tibia and fibula of the left hind leg; and the two carried the carcass to a nearby tree and hung it from a limb. Then they pulled off the rest of the skin.

The front limbs were cut off and placed on an old sheep pelt. The body wall was slit and the entrails removed and placed on the pelt. She separated the mesentery from the viscera and gave it to her son to hold. The right hind quarter was detached, and she cut the ribs (first on the left side) back to the backbone and broke them off. She untied the leg and cut it from the spine. Then she went about stripping out the tripe. All of this took thirty minutes.

There is no available information on the method used in skinning a larger animal, such as a cow or horse, although the hides of both were commonly used in making rawhide.

Rawhide was prepared from either fresh or dried hides, any time from a few days to a month after skinning. The hide was fleshed, dried, and rubbed with fat, then buried in damp earth for about a day. When taken out, it was placed over a rock and beaten with another rock to soften it.

The hide was then folded and dehaired with a scraper, sometimes against a beaming post (see Trait 135), which enabled one man to work effectively.

Sometimes two men cooperated when the hide was large. It was dried and spread on the ground, and while one man held the hide the other scraped. Roberts noted two methods of stretching deer hide: one by pulling it over a pointed juniper post (see 135.a), the other by stretching it with the hands and feet from a sitting position (Roberts, 1951:fig. 3, HA-2, HB-2). Hides were never suspended on a tripod for scraping.

Dehairing had to be done at some distance from the dwelling area (between an eighth and a quarter of a mile away, according to Inf. 8. Inf. 7 added that the bones had to be "put away" because anyone who played with them might get sick. Both Inf. 7 and Inf. 8 specified that preparation of rawhide was done at a distance from the hogan, but it was not clear whether they meant to include in the stipulation processes other than scraping or the working of hides of domestic animals.

When the hair was removed, the pelt was greased again with fat and tallow. The worker forced tallow into the hide by beating the skin, which was placed near the fire. Finally the skin was buried in wet ground for about two days, after which it was considered dressed. The whole process took about three days, but it involved only intermittent work by the individual.

Men generally made rawhide, but women could help, even with the skins of ritually killed animals. Women could also help skin these animals, if they knew the proper ritual. A number of people generally assisted in the skinning of domestic animals; it was likely to be a family effort.

Hides of game animals were usually claimed by a hunter other than the one who made the kill. When an animal was shot by one of a group of three men, the other two raced for it. The first to arrive received the hide; the man who made the kill took the meat. When two men hunted, the partner of the one making the kill received the hide, but he had to butcher the animal, or at least help (Inf. 8). Inf. 8 stated that a man hunting alone kept both meat and hide, but Inf. 7 said even in this case someone else would be given the hide.

Rawhide was used by either men or women for making robes, moccasin soles, binding materials for tools, and bags of different types. It was also a preliminary stage in dressing hide for clothing.

These processes are common today in the Ramah area, and presumably everyone past early childhood knows how to skin a sheep. Men who hunt know the methods of skinning game. Rawhide making may be less well known, but it is probable that most adult men are aware of the process even if they have not practiced it.

Rawhide making was considered old in Navaho culture. The processes have not changed except for the substitution of metal scrapers and knives for bone tools, and domesticated animals for wild. These substitutions took place before any of the Ramah informants were born. The greatest change has been in the narrowing of uses for the finished product. Since most articles of daily use are now purchased from the trading post, rawhide is little in demand. It is now used for moccasin soles, or for combination "storeshoe" and rawhide soles, worn by some Ramah Navaho in the lower economic bracket. Moccasins are worn by most people only on ritual occasions, although some older individuals (Inf. 7, for example) still wear moccasins more often than shoes.

Hill (East and Central)

Informants confirmed the variations in the disposition of a deer hide observed at Ramah. Skinning, done by the man who claimed the hide with the assistance of others, was done according to ritual. The animal was placed on spruce or pinyon boughs, but never on juniper. Unlike sheep, deer were never suspended for skinning. Cuts were made as at Ramah, and care was taken not to cut the lip, or the anal or genital aperture, lest the hunter cut off his luck. According to C (Chinle), the hoofs were left on the hide; but OTKM (Manuelito) said that a cut was made around the leg just above the hoof, as at Ramah. The hind legs of a fawn were skinned first; then the animal was cased without further cutting (Hill, 1938:110, 115, 119, 126). Informants stated that buffalo hides were removed in two pieces by making an incision along the back and belly.

Data on further preparation of the skin for rawhide were collected in connection with the making of saddles. TLLSS (Crownpoint) said that a horsehide was buried in wet earth for three or four days. It was then placed flat on the ground and the hair removed by scraping. The hide was washed thoroughly and while still wet was fitted, stretched, sewn on the saddletree, and allowed to dry in that position.

Comparative

Skinning methods were generally similar throughout the Navaho area. The differences, when they occurred, were ritual ones employed in skinning certain wild animals, such as the deer, antelope, bear, and eagles (Shufeldt, 1889:59–60, pl. 23; Matthews, 1887:391; Matthews, 1897:214).

The Franciscan Fathers (1910:302) stated that deer, antelope, elk, and bighorn, among other animals, were once used for making rawhide and buckskin. By 1910, however, "as the early Navaho despised and shunned labor, and preferred to barter with the neighboring Utes for well tanned hides," they were using hides from this source. The hides of domestic animals were merely hung up or pinned down and covered with dirt to dry. Goatskins or calfskins were treated either in this manner or made into buckskin.

The disposition of deer hide, according to Gifford's informants, varied according to the number of hunters; and there were definite rules for division. Both informants stated that the companion received the hide. The animal was butchered on the spot and skinned either on cleared ground (Eastern informant) or on branches (Western informant). Care was taken in skinning around the eyes, lest illness ensue (Gifford, 1940:9, 88–89).

A description of skinning sheep was published by Sapir and Hoijer (1942: 411). It confirmed the Ramah account. Mythological allusion to skinning methods was made by Goddard (1933:162–163).

134. Buckskin   ʾabaní (Ramah, Haile)   "deerskin" (CC)

Ramah

Buckskin was made from the hides of many animals, although deer was preferred and, according to Inf. 39, was the only possible type for a chant. The skins of most animals, such as mountain sheep, mountain goat, deer, elk, and antelope, were dehaired before the dressing process began, although

Inf. 39 said that formerly antelope hides were not dressed. These hides were dressed in the same manner as was the domestic goat (Infs. 12, 39). Skins of several animals were dressed with the hair on, including gray fox, wildcat, coyote, bear, badger, skunk, cottontail, jack rabbit, and mountain lion.

The hide was thoroughly washed in clean cold water; at the same time it was pulled and twisted to soften it. Then it was wrung out (see Trait 140), and was left to drip.

Meanwhile, the skull of the animal was split and the brain and all small bone splinters removed. The brain was crumbled into small pieces with the hands, then boiled in water for about ten minutes; it was allowed to cool until lukewarm.

The hide was spread out hair side up on some protective material (now canvas) and moistened with warm water. The mixture of water and boiled brains was poured over it and rubbed in with the fingers until it was absorbed. Next the wet hide was hung over a line for a day. When thoroughly dry and stiff, it was rinsed in clean warm water and then allowed to soak for two days. During this interval it was periodically removed from the container and twisted and stretched. Finally it was wrung out with a wringing stick and left to dry for thirty minutes.

Next the skin dresser, sitting cross-legged, worked the hide between his hands, twisting and stretching it. The skin was usually held over the right knee and manipulated with the left hand, or it was secured by a foot and both hands were used. At this point the surfaces were again scraped with a knife to remove remaining particles of hair or flesh. Stretching and twisting continued, usually for an hour and a half, until the hide was thoroughly dry. Except for final smoothing with a rough sandstone cobble, the dressing process was complete.

A slightly different process was used for dressing mountain lion hides. The skin was dried for an hour or so after removal, unless too much flesh remained on the hide. In that event, it was soaked, pegged out on the ground, and fleshed with an arrow point. The skin was rubbed with a piece of liver that had been placed on hot coals for a few minutes. The liver was worked into the skin with the hands, and the skin softened by working it between the hands. When the liver was absorbed, the hide was left to dry, then buried overnight in wet earth. In the morning, it was removed and reworked, dried again in the sun, and reburied. This process was repeated two times (three for a large hide) and the dressing was then complete. Salt was also rubbed into mountain lion hides, but Inf. 39 said that using salt was a recent innovation and was likely to spoil the hide.

Rabbit, squirrel, and skunk skins were easy to dress. Skins were scraped, then moistened and worked until pliable.

Inf. 16 said that the spinal fluid as well as the brain was used, but not the liver. He also denied the use of fat, marrow, or ashes. The use of smoke was neither mentioned nor observed at Ramah.

Skin dressing was usually done by men, but occasionally by women. A hide was prepared for one observer by Inf. 43. Inf. 9 said that only a pregnant woman need worry about working leather.

Ownership depended on a variety of circumstances (see Trait 133, Rawhide). The person who did the dressing was not necessarily the owner. Skins were stored in a bag or hung over something until used.

There was no particular time for skin dressing. Formerly, when game was plentiful, groups of men brought back quantities of jerked meat and hides, and "they worked on tanning that all through the winter" (Inf. 104).

Scraping and wringing of hides were always done outside, but the other steps could be done in the hogan. According to Inf. 8, it was taboo for anyone but the worker to be in the hogan while a hide was being dressed; he then said that a man could enter (if the worker was male) as long as he did not walk in front of the skin dresser.

Buckskin is still made in the Ramah area, but no great amount is prepared. The source of buckskin is still primarily the skins of wild animals, and it is probable that the process of skin dressing has remained unchanged for a considerable period of time. Buckskin is now reserved for ritual use or for making moccasin uppers. Most items for which buckskin was once used are now imported, and even buckskin for rituals is purchased at trading stores in Ramah or Gallup (See also Kluckhohn and Wyman, 1940:23, 24, 116, 144, 160, 171, fig. 2; Roberts, 1951:37–39, fig. 3).

Hill (East, Central, and West)

A remarkable uniformity of practice was reported (SG, Keams Canyon; MLH, Crownpoint; K, Mariano Lake; C, Chinle; AM, Lukachukai; PP, Fort Defiance). Hides of animals killed in the autumn were considered best for making buckskin. According to K, as soon as a hunter returned, he was to go to his hogan, ask for luck, and sprinkle pollen on the deer hide and venison before either could be used. Skins were occasionally left to dry, but the green hide was preferred for dressing (SG, MLH). Skin dressing was predominantly a man's occupation, but women were allowed to prepare the pelts of sheep and goats or other domestic animals. There was a definite prohibition against women dressing the hides of mountain sheep. "There is more respect shown to these hides than to those of other game" (C, K).

The removal of hair from hides was usually done in the field, since deer hair was considered potentially dangerous. In fact, if time allowed, the entire process of skin dressing was done in the field. PP said the Navaho never dressed deer hides with the hair on—"the Zuni do that." But in actual practice some Navaho did leave the hair on.

The skin was thoroughly soaked in water for two or three days. The head of the hide was then placed over the upper end of the beaming pole, which was leaned against a tree, wall, or cliff face. The hide was scraped with a beaming tool, first with the grain of the hair, except on the neck and head. The pelt was then reversed (AM) and the neck and head hair removed against the grain. Hair was left on the lower portion of the legs.

The dehaired hide was placed in warm water to soak overnight. In the morning it was washed and rinsed, "just as you would wash clothes." At this time any noticeable fat, meat, or dirt was removed with the fingernails (PP). The water was changed and the hide twisted at intervals with a wringing stick, as at Ramah. The process was repeated three to five times or until the rinse water remained clear.

The clean hide was placed on a blanket or some other covering and saturated with a solution of brains (preferably deer) and warm water. AM said that brains were rubbed into both sides of the pelt; all others said only the outside. The pelt was then hung outside for the night (PP) or for two or three days (K) and allowed to dry. If necessary, the whole operation was repeated.

In warm weather, the final stage of skin dressing was accomplished outside. Otherwise it was done in the hogan. A fire was lighted, since it was believed that unless subjected to warmth the skin would dress poorly. First the dry skin was soaked and wrung several times. It was then stretched and twisted. The operator returned to the workplace, put an edge of the hide between or under his feet, and worked the hide to break down the fibers and make it pliable. According to K, the pelt was rubbed with shredded juniper bark to make it dress easily, and according to MLH any hard spots were rubbed with a rough rock. This final operation consumed from four to eight hours. "You can tell when the hide is finished because it feels warm. If the spots in the skin feel cold, you have more work to do" (AM).

The legs were dressed last. These were the most difficult since the skin was thickest at these points. This portion of the pelt was buried in moist earth for some time, then worked with the hands. If necessary, the legs were pounded with a stone to accelerate the softening (PP). All informants denied that buckskin was smoked as part of the skin dressing process.

Certain religious observances were a normal adjunct to the manufacture of buckskin. Most men allowed no one near them or in the hogan while they were working. It was believed that if they were watched or if someone walked between the worker and the fire, the skin would dry and dress unevenly (PP, AM, K, MLH, SG, C). SG said that if a menstruating woman entered the hogan while work was in progress, a red spot would appear on the hide and it would be ruined. MLH reported that some men contracted lung trouble while dressing skins. "This is because they do something wrong."

A variation of the skin dressing process was used for sheep and goat hides (C, PP, K; TLLSS, Crownpoint; MS, Sawmill), most of which were used for sleeping and sitting. These were usually dressed with the wool on; they were not so carefully done as was buckskin. Women as often as men prepared the pelts. The Navaho made a further distinction with regard to dressing hides of wild and domestic animals: hides of wild animals were never staked to the ground for stretching. "The Havasupai do that. We do it with sheepskins and goatskins. If you stake the hide of a wild animal to the ground it would be the same as boiling mutton and venison together and would bring bad luck" (PP).

The skin was washed, then staked for stretching. The hide was placed, wool side down, in a shaded area where it would not dry too rapidly. It was left for a day, during which time any remaining fat or meat was scraped off with a knife. When it was dry, a thin or "weak" solution of brains and water was applied until the skin was thoroughly saturated; then it was left to dry for about two days. According to MS, the hide was first placed in the hot sun for another half hour.

Dry pelts were then buried in damp earth or sand and worked in the same manner as buckskin. Hard spots were rubbed with rough sandstone to soften them. If the skin became dry while work was in progress, the hide was reburied until it softened. Dressing was done in a secluded spot, where sun and wind would not dry the skin too quickly. This type of skin dressing was considered definitely inferior to the work done on buckskin (C, K, TLLSS, MS, PP).

Some variations in this operation were recorded. MS said that the pelt was placed in a pile of damp earth for about an hour. Then a small mound of earth was erected and the skin placed on it, wool side up, and washed with warm water. The skin was then allowed to dry for a day before being worked with the hands. According to TLLSS, before being buried in the earth the hide was sprinkled with water, folded wool side in, and pounded with a rock.

Fishler (West)

Fishler's informants described the preparation of unwounded or "sacred" buckskin. Whenever there was a need for such skins, a hunt was held, often in the fall, but also in winter when the tracks could be followed easily.

A deer, or sometimes an antelope, was caught after being run until exhausted or by using an ambush or pit (IJun, Kaibito). Several hunters—good runners—tracked the animal; when one tired another took his place, until the animal fell from exhaustion. Pollen was then placed in the animal's nostrils and mouth, and the animal was smothered by holding the hands over these apertures. A deer killed by a wildcat or mountain lion (IJmo, Kaibito; FG, Coalmine) or wolf (FG) or by accident (IJmo) could also be used. Hides with too many holes or of animals killed by a gun, arrow, or spear could not be used ceremonially.

A pollen line was drawn from the hind legs along the belly to the forelegs, and to the neck and mouth. A prayer accompanied this operation. An incision was made along the pollen line or across the hind legs to the belly and the skin was cased. The hide was dressed in the usual manner (see Trait 139, Rubbing Stone).

TH (Moenave) said that deerskin was used primarily for clothing and that men used to make moccasins, shirts, and trousers. According to TN (Kaibito), women made the clothing. IJun stated that the Navaho traded with the Utes for buckskin shirts, trousers, and turquoise. They also traded with tribes to the west, exchanging buckskin for necklaces and shells.

Though not all the informants had run down animals, they had seen, or had in their possession, the skins of such animals. Fishler obtained two deer, a male and a female: one had died of exhaustion in the snow and the other had been killed by animals. These were given to GB (Tuba City), who said that the skins were acceptable for ceremonial use. It is possible that the ritual utilization of such hides is fairly recent and has arisen because of the current scarcity of deer.

Comparative

It is known that the Navaho possessed buckskin as early as 1630 (Ayer, 1916:49), and deponents of the Rabal documents mentioned trade in buckskin in the eighteenth century (Hill, 1940a:397–407).

Shufeldt (1889:59–66) published a description of the manufacture of buckskin, including six plates illustrating the dressing process. Although the account referred to the Fort Wingate Navaho in 1887, the process described was essentially like that now practiced at Ramah. Shufeldt stated that women never made buckskin, but boys learned the art at an early age. In the next decade or so, however, buckskins were also procured elsewhere. Matthews (1897:18) stated that the Navaho did not consider themselves expert dressers of deerskin, and purchased the best of their buckskins from other tribes. In Dyk's accounts, deer or buffalo hides were frequently mentioned as gifts or for trading, but the process of dressing was ignored (Dyk, 1938, 1947). In contrast, Hollister (1903:49) stated that the Navaho were "expert in tanning buckskin and making it into moccasins, leggings, and other garments."

The Franciscan Fathers (1910:302) confirmed the descriptions above of the dressing process (see Trait 133), but stated that the finishing was done in the hogan and that the smokehole and doorway were covered with blankets to exclude the air. Hides of goats, cows, sheep, and horses were also dressed. Gifford's data corroborated the accounts above. His Eastern informant believed that the hide would harden if someone approached the dresser (Gifford, 1940:28–29, 117–118).

An excellent summary of the literature on the ceremonial use of buckskin was presented by Reichard (1950:530–531).

135. Beaming Post

bíki·iɫzí (Ramah) "on it for scraping" (CC)

bináži ·azehé (Ramah) scraping frame; "around for scraping" (CC)

Ramah

The beaming post provided a firm base for scraping a hide. A post without branches, about six feet long and six inches in diameter, was stripped of bark on one side. One end was beveled to fit a notch in a tree about four feet above the ground. The other end was placed in a hole in the ground to prevent it from slipping.

Inf. 8 said pinyon was required; but Inf. 9 had a juniper post, pointed at the top, about seven inches in diameter at a point five inches above the ground. Another post was stripped of bark and rounded on all sides, and a third was stripped to about fourteen to sixteen inches above the butt. For removing bark, Inf. 39 used an axe. In one case, the notch for supporting the upper end of the post was made by stripping bark from the tree at the appropriate point.

The pelt to be scraped was thrown over the post, flesh side up, with the head end secured between the top of the post and the tree. After the flesh was removed, the pelt was reversed and dehaired. When one area was finished, the hide was moved to bring another surface immediately above the log where it could be scraped.

135.a. Scraping the hide on a beaming post

Work, usually by men but occasionally by women, was done away from the dwelling area (see Traits 133 and 134). The use of the beaming post enabled one man to scrape a hide; otherwise one had to hold the hide while another worked.

The beaming post is still used in the Ramah area. Infs. 12, 39, and 256 employed it. Presumably it has been known throughout the informants' lives, for it was not mentioned as a trait of recent introduction or invention.

Hill (East and Central)

Information coincided throughout with the Ramah material, with one exception. According to K (Mariano Lake), the post was constructed with a fork at the bottom to prevent its turning while the operator worked the hide. These posts were used in preparing skins of deer, elk, antelope, and calves (K; PP, Fort Defiance; AM, Lukachukai; TLLSS, Crownpoint).

Comparative

The post used at Ramah described above, is similar to that seen by Shufeldt in use at Fort Wingate, New Mexico, in 1887. The post he described (1889:60, 61) was of pine, cut and peeled on one side. A deep notch was cut in the large end to brace it against the limb of a small tree; the other end rested firmly on the ground about two feet from the base of the tree. The hide was caught and scraped as at Ramah. On this occasion, however, the post was used only for the removal of the hair. Fleshing had been done on the ground.

According to the Franciscan Fathers (1910:302, 303), the beaming post was used for removing both flesh and hair. The term for "scraping frame" was similar to that used at Ramah.

All of the tribes with which Gifford worked confirmed the use of the beaming post, especially for deer hides. He mentioned its use only for removing hair. The Western Navaho, but not the Eastern, used the post to work the skin soft (Gifford, 1940:29, 118).

136. Bone Beaming Tool

be· dahadi·tˣasí (Ramah, Haile)

ł̨į·· bicą̀ be·elʒéhí (Ramah, Haile)   horse rib beaming tool; "horse rib scraper" (CC)

Ramah

Deer bones were kept "put away" (Inf. 7) around the hogan and sharpened on rough rocks just before a hunt. Cow or horse ribs were cleaned of flesh and used without further preparation. Men and older boys made these tools at home, either inside the hogan or in the doorway.

Scraping was done at some distance from the hogan, about half a mile (Inf. 8), but in no particular direction. It was believed that one who urinated on the hair removed from a hide would become ill. Inf. 18 said only men scraped hides; Inf. 7 said men usually did the scraping but that women could do so if they knew how. Since the hide was supposed to be worked as soon as it was skinned, scraping was done at any time of the day or year.

The operator straddled the pole on which the skin was hung. He repeatedly drew the beaming tool down and toward himself until the hair was removed. The hide was then shifted and another area scraped. When the scraper was worn out, it was thrown away.

Inf. 8 had formerly used deer bone scrapers, but said that they are no longer used; Inf. 39 described the use of cow or horse ribs, but did not indicate whether he had used them. Field notes indicated that these tools may also have been used as "fleshing implements."

Hill (East and Central)

The shorter ribs of the horse (PP, Fort Defiance) and deer (K, Mariano Lake), bones from the forelegs of the deer (K; AM, Lukachukai; C, Chinle; MLH, Crownpoint), and the radio-ulnae of sheep (C) were employed as beaming tools. According to MLH, it was customary to sharpen and intensify one of the angles of the deer bone to heighten the cutting efficiency of the tool.

The utilization of beamers corresponded to that at Ramah. The tool was used in the same manner as a spoke-shave, pulled toward the worker, and usually with the grain of the hair. According to C, a quick jerky motion was most effective. Work on deer hide was usually done at a distance from the home. "If you should lie on deer hair you would have bad luck" (PP). "You must not allow the hair to blow about if you are near your home. You collect it and place it beneath a rock or under a pinyon or cedar tree" (K).

Comparative

Evidence from other areas indicated that the rib or ulna tool was formerly in use. Near Fort Wingate, New Mexico, in 1887, Shufeldt witnessed scrapers made from the ulna and radius of the deer that provided the hide. The sharp posterior edge of the ulna was further improved by scraping it with a knife. It was grasped at each end—the carpal bones were left to provide a better handle—and drawn toward the worker (Shufeldt, 1889:61, fig. 2, pl. XXIV). Matthews (1897:214) stated that both ulnae of a deer from which sacred buckskin was taken were used as scrapers, and no other scrapers could be used on that particular buckskin.

Gifford (1940:28, 118) reported that both the Eastern and Western Navaho dehaired hides with a cannon bone tool or with a rib drawn edgewise. The latter was of horse bone according to the Eastern informant. The term given by the Franciscan Fathers (1912:168) was similar to that at Ramah; the second term was so called "because a horse rib was used in scraping the hair from hides."

There is little or no archaeological evidence on the Navaho beaming tools. An implement similar to that described by Shufeldt, however, was found in abundance at Pecos. This consisted of the metatarsal bone together with the ankle bones which served as a handle (Kidder, 1932:233). Bone scrapers were either absent in Navaho sites or were not recognized as such. Bone tools of any kind are rare in Navaho sites (Keur, 1941:63; 1944:80). Farmer (1938:93) stated that bone was plentiful at his sites, but worked bone almost nonexistent.

137. Metal Beaming Tool

bé··iłʒí (Ramah)   Type I: "scraper, scraping" (CC)

bé··eɣołi (Ramah)   Type IIa: "scraper" (CC)

bé·šháha·stání (Ramah)   Type IIb: "metal . . ." (CC)

Ramah

An iron blade was secured in slits in the inner sides of a V-shaped piece of pinyon about sixteen inches long. The final form was that of a broad A. These tools were made by men. Infs. 39 and 12 owned and used this type (I).

Variations were noted. In one type, one end of a solid piece of iron was wrapped with buckskin as a handle. This was called by either of the last two terms (above); it was made, owned, and used by Inf. 7, and known by Inf. 16. Roberts (1951:38, HB) observed a two-handled implement made of metal set in a curved bone.

Like the bone beaming tool, this implement was used to remove flesh and hair from hides. It was held in both hands and drawn toward the worker. Work was done away from the hogan.

There is no information on the general distribution of this implement in the Ramah area, but it is possible that each worker varied the general form to suit his particular inclination.

Fishler (West)
A V-shaped branch of a tree from twelve to fourteen inches long was obtained. A sharpened piece of steel one half to three quarters of an inch wide and eight to ten inches long was embedded in the wood inside the mouth of the V, with the sharp edge facing inward and slightly downward. These tools were made as needed.

The hide was placed hair side up over a post or rock. The scraper was held with the V inverted, blade toward the worker. It was pulled toward the worker, never pushed.

Comparative
According to the literature, scrapers of the type used by Inf. 39 at Ramah were distributed beyond the Ramah area. No references to the type used by Inf. 7 were found. According to informants for Sapir and Hoijer, a piece of metal sharpened on one edge and inserted in the curved center of a bow-shaped piece of wood (see 137.a) was used to scrape hides (Sapir and Hoijer, 1942:419).

Both of Gifford's informants denied the use of a scraper with a curved wooden handle and a stone blade. The metal-bladed scraper was not mentioned (Gifford, 1940:28, 118).

By 1912, iron scrapers were known, but when they first were used is not known (Franciscan Fathers, 1912:168). According to the Franciscan Fathers (1910:302–303), a "scraping stick," much like a loom batten, was used for removing hair and remnants of flesh. It was called by a term similar to the first of the three above (Type I). This is apparently the only reference to a wooden scraper.

137.a. Beaming tool found near McElmo Creek, Colorado

138. Stone Scraper

bésistogi (Ramah, Haile)   "small stone, arrowhead" (CC)

Ramah
A chert or chalcedony projectile point, about three and a half to four inches long, was held in a piece of buckskin. It was used for fleshing hides for rawhide and buckskin, and was important in a number of ceremonials (see, for example, Kluckhohn and Wyman, 1940:34).

Inf. 39 referred to this tool as one used before the introduction of iron tools. Probably any chip of stone, not necessarily a shaped projectile point, served this and other purposes. It has now been replaced by the knife or scraping implements described above.

Hill (Central and West)
Flakes of stone, especially chert, were used as scrapers. These were not manufactured (MS, Sawmill; GH, White Cone), and no attempt was made to retouch them (SG, Keams Canyon). SG added that they were never hafted. Implements of this type were also employed in the manufacture of wooden ladles (MS, GH; see Trait 100).

Fishler (West)

GB (Tuba City) stated that pieces of sharpened stone were used to scrape hides.

Comparative

Various investigators referred to the use of the chert chip for scraping and working hides, but nowhere was it indicated that the stone fleshing tool was a specialized implement. According to Gifford's informants, the Western Navaho used a rough stone for scraping flesh and fat from the hide; the Eastern informant denied this trait (Gifford, 1940:28). According to the Franciscan Fathers (1912:28), the name given by Ramah informants for the stone scraper was that for a chipped chert or arrowhead.

139. Rubbing Stone

cebéiɣoɬí (Ramah) "stone it rubs" (CC)

Ramah

The Navaho used unworked cobbles to smooth rough places when dressing buckskins, to remove miscellaneous hairs along the rough edges of the hide, and to beat rawhide. "You just picked these rocks up any place, but never carried them around with you," Inf. 39 was observed using such a cobble while working on buckskin.

Hill (East, Central, and West)

Sandstone cobbles, selected at random, were often used in skin dressing. In the production of buckskin, the areas of the neck and legs were pounded with such a rock to break down the tissues and make the hide pliable (AM, Lukachukai). Hard spots in the body of the hide were rubbed to soften them (C, Chinle). In preparing sheep pelts, either the green hide, wool side folded in (TLLSS, Crownpoint), or the partially dried skin, spread out (MS, Sawmill), was pounded with this implement. Cobbles were also used to remove any wool that remained on sheepskins after scraping or clipping (TLLSS). Pieces of sandstone of varying size were also used to sharpen implements (RH, Crystal; MDW, Jeddito).

Fishler (West)

A rounded piece of stone was used to pound a hide to remove the hair which remained after scraping. When almost all of the hair was removed, the hide was buried in moist sand. Later it was taken out and pounded. Grease and brains were smeared on the pelt and it was again covered with sand. Finally it was removed and pounded once more to make it pliable. This process was observed by Fishler.

Comparative

There is little published information from other areas on the use of smoothers, probably because they are unobtrusive and were overlooked by observers. According to Gifford, the Western but not the Eastern Navaho rubbed the hides with a stone to soften them (Gifford, 1940:29).

Smoothers have been reported by Keur (1941:61), who found specimens of sandstone, vesicular volcanic rock, basalt, and quartz, at Big Bead Mesa.

One form consisted of a stone with one smoothed surface; another with two smoothed surfaces was ovoid in shape; and a third was a small rectangular block. These, she stated, were rubbing stones. Polishers were water-worn pebbles of quartz, chert, and jasper (see also Farmer, 1938, sec. III).

140. Wringing Stick

be· dahadi·t^xasí (Ramah, Haile)   "with it, twisting" (CC)

Ramah

A straight pole of cottonwood or juniper (always juniper according to Inf. 8) three to four and a half feet long and about two inches in diameter was obtained. The bark was removed and the ends rounded.

The hide was thrown over a branch from which the bark was removed, and the legs folded in until a loop was formed around the branch. The pole was inserted in the loop and twisted with the hands until the hide formed a hard knot. The stick was then locked behind the branch.

Men made this implement, and ordinarily used it. The hide was twisted during the dressing. Work was done outside, usually close to the hogan. The wringing stick was stored where it could be found and used again.

Hill (East, Central, and West)

Descriptions of this trait corresponded with those obtained at Ramah. The only discrepancies were that any kind of available wood was used and that the length of the stick was normally less than four and a half feet (MLH, Crownpoint; K, Mariano Lake; PP, Fort Defiance; AM, Lukachukai; C, Chinle; SG, Keams Canyon).

Comparative

The use of the stick for wringing hides was mentioned by all who described the dressing process in any detail. The wringing stick was widely used throughout the Navaho area. Reports of its use covered a span of fifty years (see Traits 133 and 134). The term for wringing stick published by the Franciscan Fathers confirmed that used at Ramah (Franciscan Fathers, 1910:303; 1912:50, 209). Both of Gifford's informants confirmed this process (Gifford, 1940:29, 118).

Dyes

141. Red Dye

cé·ésda·zi· bito·h (Ramah, Haile)   "mountain mahogany its juice" (CC)

Ramah

Roots of the mountain mahogany (*Cercocarpus montanus*) were dug, and the bark was removed by pounding them on a flat stone with a sharp rock (see 141.a). The bark was dried in the sun for a day or two, then crushed with a hammerstone (identifications from Vestal, 1952:30, 53, 21; Wyman and Harris, 1941:22, 26; Elmore, 1944:39).

The crushed bark was boiled overnight in a bucket, then left to cool, after which the pieces were removed. If basketry material was to be colored, it was put in the solution and placed "to the fire" where it remained overnight. In the morning the material was colorfast and ready for use.

For coloring buckskin, however, a mordant was usually required, and recipes and preparations varied. According to some informants, the buckskin was first spread hair side up and the bark solution poured on and rubbed in with the hand (Infs. 44, 46, 3). Then the mordant was prepared. Ground alder trunk bark (*Alnus tenuifolia; Alnus incana* [*sic*], *kish*) was mixed with juniper ashes (*Juniperus pachyphloea* [*Juniperus deppeana*], *gad;* Infs. 44, 7), or mountain mahogany (Infs. 3, 46), or used alone (Inf. 32). The mordant was rubbed into the hair side of the wet buckskin. The skin was then folded and left for fifteen minutes (Inf. 32), half a day (Inf. 44), or a day and a night (Inf. 3). It was spread in the sun to dry, and finally worked between the hands until the "powder" came off or it was soft. According to Vestal (1952:30), mountain mahogany bark was boiled for about thirty minutes, and the skin was soaked in the decoction for only thirty minutes before the color was rubbed in.

A slightly different preparation was described by Inf. 7. A mixture in the approximate proportions of three-fourths mountain mahogany to one-fourth juniper and oak (*Quercus, sp., chechil*) was placed in a pottery vessel (now a large kettle) and boiled in clean water for about two hours. Mountain mahogany and alder bark were then ground to a fine consistency on the metate; this mixture was sifted into a panful of the dye until the color changed from a dull reddish purple to the proper shade of reddish brown. An additional supply of alder bark was ground and put aside, and juniper limbs "not too young" were burned and the ashes collected.

Before any solution was applied, ashes were rubbed and kneaded into the hair side of the skin; superfluous ones were shaken off. "This makes it stay red." Red dye from the pot was dipped out and splashed over the surface of the skin, then rubbed in, first on the hair side, and second—with less

141.a. Pounding the roots of sumac to loosen the bark

141.b. Inf. 7's daughter dyeing buckskin red

care—on the flesh side. Then the solution from the pan was spread over the hair side of the skin. Finally the skin was dusted with dry alder bark. "This makes it real red [reddish brown, according to Vestal, 1952:30]. When the rain hits it, it won't hurt." After drying the skin was ready to use.

Intentional variations in color were produced. Ashes of dried yucca leaves were added to make a light red, (Inf. 12), a lighter brown or tan (Vestal, 1952:30). Juniper leaf ashes produced an unspecified red (Inf. 2) or a dark red (Vestal). Other reds were obtained from dyes of other plants. The lichen (*Parmelia conspersa, niihadlaad*) was used with other plants, and when mixed with the roots of plant coffee (*Thelesperma megapotamicum, chil gohweeh*) was used to dye wool a brownish red. The ashes of the leaves and twigs of fourwing saltbush (*Atriplex canescens, doghozhi*) were used for dyeing buckskin (Vestal, 1952:53, 21). All of the ingredients listed were found locally, except for the alder bark, which was obtained by trade or from trips to the Zuni Mountains.

Either men or women prepared dye for buckskin, but women made dyes for basketry materials.

Red dye is probably rarely made now. There are no data on the frequency of its use or the number of people able to prepare it. The Leightons were told that no one in Inf. 12's family knew all the necessary steps, and a fifteen- or sixteen-year-old daughter had never seen dye made. Despite this, red dye is probably more common than any other at this time, for buckskin is usually colored red.

Hill (East and Central)

According to K (Mariano Lake), mountain mahogany roots, juniper leaves, lichens, and alder bark were gathered. The process she described was similar to that described by Inf. 7 at Ramah. The mountain mahogany roots and lichens were boiled together until the liquid became red or brownish, when it was strained through a metate brush or hairbrush and put aside to cool and settle. While the liquid was boiling, juniper leaves were placed in a pan and cooked until reduced to a powder. While cooking, they were vigorously stirred with a metate brush. Water was added to the powder and this mixture was poured into the first solution.

Alder bark was ground to a powder and sprinkled on the hide, which had been spread on a flat surface. The dye solution was applied to the outside. Then the hide was folded and placed in the corner of the hogan for the night; in the morning it was unfolded and placed in the sun. Before it was dry it was worked, then buried in the earth for half a day. Finally it was removed, worked again, and allowed to dry. The various workings insured pliability of the buckskin.

PP (Fort Defiance) differed. He said that alder, always secured in the spring when it was tender, was boiled for a day. Pinyon pitch and "sulphur rock," reduced to powder by cooking, were added to the boiling water. When the solution had cooled it was applied to the buckskin. According to him, only leggings and moccasin uppers were dyed red.

AM (Lukachukai) stated that the inner bark of juniper, spruce, and pine were boiled with the dry bark from mountain mahogany root. Dry alder bark was ground and added. Finally juniper ash was added as a mordant. This mixture was applied to the buckskin after it had been sprinkled with powdered alder bark.

According to K, basketry material was dyed red with the same type of solution as that used for buckskin.

Comparative

The preparation described by Inf. 7 at Ramah was apparently common among the Navaho, although others were known. It was confirmed by several observers (Pepper, 1903:6–10; Amsden, 1949:81–82; Sapir and Hoijer, 1942:419–421). According to the Franciscan Fathers (1910:304, 293, 292), juniper and mountain mahogany roots were crushed and boiled; a mixture of alder bark and juniper ashes was added, and the solution allowed to boil again. While warm it was applied to the hide. The dye was used for buckskin, wool, and basketry materials.

Other red dyes were known. Amsden (1949:82–83) recorded two on the strength of statements from Pepper and Keam: one made by boiling the root bark of the aromatic sumac, the other by boiling the husk of the sunflower seed. The latter was apparently confined to the Keams Canyon area. Reichard (1936:42) reported five different methods of producing red dye for wool, one of which was a variant of Inf. 7's red dye for moccasins. Elmore (1944:108) mentioned seventeen different plants used for producing red dyes, and another for pinkish hues.

Both of Gifford's informants knew of red dyes made from boiled alder bark (used for coloring leather), from oak galls or the roots of an unspecified shrub root (used by the Western informant for face painting), and from a red mineral (ocher?). The Western Navaho said that the alder bark dye was applied to moccasins with a corncob (Gifford, 1940:29, 34, 118, 126).

The most intensive treatment of Navaho dyes is that of Bryan and Young at the Fort Wingate Vocational High School. Mrs. Nonabah G. Bryan, an educated Navaho woman who spent most of her life on the reservation, worked on the native dyes in collaboration with Miss Young. The basic recipes were those of her ancestors, but some were experimental. Bryan and Young (1940:75) listed only four plant species from which pink to red dyes were made. Only the use of fermented prickly pear cactus fruit (*Opuntia polyacantha*) was apparently unknown in Ramah (Vestal, 1952), and Mrs. Bryan stated that it was a recent innovation. She presented a more traditional recipe, using the thick, brick-colored rainwater (*tolchii*) from the red mesas in New Mexico and Arizona. Four gallons were to be collected from puddles immediately after a heavy rain. A half pound of wet yarn was added, and the mixture was stirred and boiled for four hours. Clear water was added as needed to maintain sufficient liquid in the pot. Finally the wool was rinsed. "The redder the clay used, the deeper will be the color of the yarn."

142. Yellow Dye   be·ʼi·łcohí (Ramah, Lamphere, Haile)   "with yellow" (CC)

Ramah

The buds and flowers of rabbit brush (*Chrysothamnus nauseosus,* var. *bigelovii, kiiltsoi tsoh;* Vestal, 1952:49) were broken from the bush (Infs. 8, 12). Other plants were also used, including snakeweed (*Gutierrezia sarothrae;* Inf. 39; Vestal, 1952:51; Elmore, 1944:86); *kii* (*Tetradymia canescens,* var. *inermis*) used with other plants (Inf. 45; Vestal, 1952:53; Wyman and Harris, 1941:24, who render it *chiindi chil*); and, according to Vestal, the young leaves and twigs of chamiso or fourwing saltbush (*Atriplex canescens;* Vestal, 1952:24). Two off-yellow hues, a yellow-brown and an orange-yellow, were also used. The former was made from the root of dock, also known as canaigre or wild rhubarb (*Rumex hymenosepalus, chaatini;* Vestal, 1952:24), the latter from the boiled roots of plant coffee (*Thelesperma megapotamicum, chil gohweeh;* Vestal, 1952:53; Wyman and Harris, 1941:24).

The buds and flowers (or roots) were boiled in water for two hours (Inf. 7), overnight (Inf. 15), or from early morning until noon (Inf. 32). The dye was ready for use when cool. According to Inf. 7, however, the decoction was mixed with rock alum; and Inf. 32 said that the ashes of rock lichen (*Parmelia conspersa;* Vestal, 1952:10) were added to the mixture, which was then boiled again for half an hour. Inf. 97 agreed that lichen was used to make yellow dye.

Yellow dye was used for wool, buckskin, and basket materials (Infs. 7, 15, 32), although Inf. 192 denied the last. Basketry material was placed in the dye and warmed overnight, but not allowed to boil. No mordant was necessary (Inf. 15); it is probable that the rock alum was only added for dyeing buckskins or wool. The decoction was splashed over the skin and rubbed into the surface with the hands. Unused dye was poured out on the ground (Inf. 15).

Either men or women made dye, but children were not supposed to watch. Only women dyed basketry material, but either men or women used dyes for other materials.

According to Inf. 15, dyes could not be made in cloudy weather. "Won't dye out for you . . . When the sun is clear, that's when we are supposed to dye . . . When you are working on dye you must not go away and leave your work . . . you will get sick in the head."

Inf. 15 prepared yellow dye in 1937 for coloring basketry material. Dyes are infrequently made today, although the knowledge persists, and there are several who are able to prepare the yellow. Except that lard pails or other metal containers rather than pottery vessels are used, the method of production seems to have remained unchanged.

Hill (East and Central)

Goldenrod petals (PP, Fort Defiance; C, Chinle; LW, Lukachukai) were gathered in the late summer or fall, "when they had the best color." These were placed in a sack to preserve the pollen and were stored until needed. To make dye, the petals were put into a pot and boiled until the water "showed a good color." The worker then removed the plant material with a loom batten or some convenient stick. "Salt rock" (rock alum) was placed on the open fire. When it turned white, it was dropped into the solution where it dissolved. This solution was used in dyeing wool. The material was placed in the container and boiled; it was constantly stirred to insure an even distribution of color. When the desired density of color had been achieved, the wool was lifted out, drained over the pot, and put out to dry. Unspun wool was dried on the ground, spun wool hung up to dry (LW).

According to K (Mariano Lake), to make yellow dye for buckskin, sorrel or dock (C) and rock alum were added to the goldenrod when it was boiled. Later "melted alum rock" was added to this solution and these four elements were boiled for four to six hours, then allowed to cool. The buckskin was spread and the dye rubbed on the outside with the hands. When completely covered, it was folded and placed in the corner of the hogan for the night. The following morning it was placed in the sun. Before it was completely dry, it was stretched and worked with the hands, then buried in damp earth for half a day to prevent it from hardening.

Recently, according to C, the bark and leaves of the walnut have been utilized to produce yellow dyes.

Lamphere (East)

PM confirmed the term for yellow dye.

Comparative

There were many yellow dyes used in the Navaho area, and a great variety of plants was used in their manufacture. Elmore (1944:108) listed twenty species from which yellow, yellow-brown, and orange dyes were made. Twenty of thirty-three dye plants listed by Bryan and Young (1940:5) produced one to four shades of yellow, gold, or mustard dye. The last was obtained by mixing the decoction in an aluminum vessel. Three additional species yielded shades of orange.

Other observers knew of fewer dyes. Pepper (1903:4–6, 11) was told of two different types, one of which was used at Ramah. Washington Matthews found the Navaho in 1881 making three different yellow dyes for wool (Matthews, 1887:377; 1893:613–616; 1904:6). Amsden (1949:83–87) mentioned three, as did the Franciscan Fathers (1910:230–232), who cited both Matthews and Pepper. Reichard (1936:38–40), however, knew of five. All of the observers were told of the dye made from the leaves and buds of the rabbit brush; yellow dyes derived from other plants were apparently less frequently prepared.

Gifford's Eastern informant stated that yellow dye was obtained by boiling the leaves of an unidentified plant with salt or other alkali; it was not used for dyeing wool. He knew of a yellow pigment or mineral, which the Western informant did not. Buckskin was colored yellow, but not smoked, according to the Eastern informant. He did not specify the dye (Gifford, 1940:29, 34, 118, 126).

143. Black Dye   beˑˑiˑlzíˑhį̇ˑˑ (Ramah)   "with black" (CC)

Ramah

A yellow mineral (*tseko*) was imported from west of Gallup or obtained from a deposit about a mile and a half from Inf. 192's hogan. It was finely ground on the metate, then placed in a frying pan over the fire until all moisture evaporated. This process took about half a day. Just before it began to burn, the mineral was removed from the fire and mixed with pinyon pitch; according to Inf. 32, two parts of the mineral were mixed with one part of pitch. The combination was returned to the fire and stirred constantly until the materials were well mixed. A piece of iron was used as a stirrer (Inf. 15) because wood was apt to catch fire. When the mixture turned black, it was removed, then ground on a metate (Inf. 15). Next water was added and the solution boiled for about half an hour (Inf. 15). Infs. 7, 32, and 280 said the mixture was not ground but was added directly to boiling water. When the solution cooled, the material to be dyed was added.

Infs. 7 and 280 stated that sumac bark (*Rhus canadensis*) was boiled in the solution before using it as a dye. Inf. 192 said that sumac leaves were boiled in water "all night," then the leaves were removed, and a roasted ocher-pitch lump was added: "Then it turns real black."

Vestal (1952:21, 24) noted that another black dye was made from the juice of *Yucca glauca* mixed with a yellow soil from the vicinity of Fort Wingate, and that redscale (*Atriplex rosea*) was formerly used.

Either men or women made black dye and used it for coloring buckskin, wool, or basketry material. The latter two were immersed in the warm solution; basketry material was left overnight (Inf. 15) or for half an hour (Inf. 32).

For dyeing buckskin, Inf. 7 said that the hide was first dyed red, and then the black mixture was poured over it and worked into the skin. If it were not first dyed red, "it would come out kind of blue."

Though black dye is presumably rarely made at present, knowledge of its composition and manufacture still exists. Variation among recipes is slight, especially in comparison to the red dyes.

Hill (East, Central, and West)

All informants (K, Mariano Lake; LW, Lukachukai; PP, Fort Defiance; SG, Keams Canyon) agreed that the essential ingredient in black dye was sumac. Bark, leaves, and stems were gathered early in the fall and stored until required. When needed, these materials were tied in a bundle and placed in a pot to boil overnight (LW) or for a shorter period (K). While they were boiling "sulphur rock" was "burned" and ground to a powder, which was mixed with pinyon pitch, placed in a pottery dish, and cooked until reduced to a dry black ash. The sumac bundle was removed from the pot and replaced by the black powder. This concoction was brought to a boil and then set aside to cool (K).

The buckskin to be dyed was spread on a flat surface. It had previously been colored a light red. A handful of wool was dipped into the black dye and rubbed over the outside of the skin. When completely covered, the hide was set aside for about two hours to allow the dye to soak in and set. After this interval the worker abraded the skin with a fingernail in several sections to discover whether or not the coloring had permeated to the desired depth and, if so, the skin was placed in the sun. While still moist it was stretched and worked to prevent stiffening (K). Black dyed buckskin was used for shirts and trousers.

K and LW agreed that this preparation was used in dyeing wool. The wool was placed in the boiling dye and stirred to insure that all parts were equally saturated.

Basketry material was treated differently. According to K, the elements were rubbed with alder bark, then placed in the dye, boiled for half a day, and allowed to soak in the dye two or three hours more while it was cooling. According to SG, sumac leaves were boiled for half a day. Meanwhile "rock coal" was ground and reduced to a powder by cooking. It was then mixed with yellow ocher and pinyon pitch and the cooking process repeated. Finally it was placed in the sumac solution and the dye was complete.

Comparative

Black dye prepared from sumac twigs and leaves, native ocher, and pinyon pitch was standard in the Navaho area for dyeing basketry materials and wool (Matthews, 1884:376; Pepper, 1903:10–11; Reichard, 1936:46; Amsden, 1949:74, 75, 76, 79–81). O'Connell (1939:272) identified the mineral ocher as carnotite, an ore of radium, uranium, and vanadium, usually occurring as a powder in the sandstones and conglomerates of the Colorado Plateau. Hough (1902:471) reported that the Navaho (and Hopi) had a black paint made from a clay "rich in oxides of manganese and iron with some organic matter," and Matthews believed this occurred in a natural state. In addition to sumac and pinyon, Elmore (1944:108, 68) mentioned only tea berry (*Gaultheria humifusa*) for making black dye. The last was also mentioned by Jeançon and Douglas (1930:2).

Ramah data for making black dye were confirmed by the Franciscan Fathers (1910:230, 293, 303). According to them, the method of preparation was similar and sumac, ocher, and pinyon pitch were used.

Gifford's Eastern informant stated that a black dye made from a boiled plant was applied to dressed skin. The informant denied the use of a mineral or of walnut-skin juice; the Western informant was not questioned. Both agreed that charcoal, sometimes obtained by charring greasewood gum, was used for making black dye (Gifford, 1940:34, 126).

144. Blue Dye

ci·ƛ̓ó·ł (Ramah)   blue dye; "hair string" (CC)

be·edi·lƛ̓í·š (Ramah, Lamphere)   indigo; "with blue" (CC)

Ramah

Blue clay (indigo), obtained from Spanish-Americans, was soaked in warm water in a large pottery vessel sheltered from the sun and rain until it became soft like mud. Children and adults were told to urinate in the pot. The material to be dyed was placed in the pot and left there for four days, then removed and dried, then soaked for another four days. When dried it was ready for use (Inf. 32).

According to Inf. 7, urine was collected in a pot and placed in the sun for four or five days. The indigo and material to be dyed were added; the pot was covered with rags. After an indeterminate time, when the material had turned dark blue or green, it was removed, hung up to drain, then washed in clean water and dried. In Inf. 192's recipe, a bucket was placed for children's urine; since "it took a long time to fill it," the urine stood for a few days. Then a handful of indigo was tied in a rag and dropped into the urine. It was stirred with the hand, not a stick. The material was soaked overnight. In the morning it was light blue in color. For a darker blue, it was returned to the dye until the desired color was obtained. This procedure sometimes took four days. Wool (Inf. 192) or wool and basket materials (Inf. 32) were dyed blue.

There is no indication that blue dye is now prepared in the Ramah area. It was probably never popular, since individuals who were familiar with other dyes have never heard of it, for example, Inf. 15. Infs. 7, 32, and 192 described the dye, and Inf. 41 said that in baskets she had used a blue dye purchased in Gallup.

Hill (Central)

LW (Lukachukai) said that the Navaho first obtained indigo for dyeing wool from the Pueblos; later, directly from the Spanish and Mexicans. The urine of children was used as a mordant. It was saved and stored in a Pueblo pot.

Greasewood roots and *hactan* were boiled until the water became light red in color. When this mixture had cooled, the indigo was placed in a cloth and submerged in the liquid. The cloth was squeezed and worked with the hands until all the coloring matter had dissolved.

In the meantime a pit was dug and a fire built in it. When the wood had burned down, a cooking pot was set in the coals and the urine and dye solution poured in. Wool was added and stirred until thoroughly saturated. Then a flat rock was placed over the top of the receptacle and it was covered with earth. The wool soaked for two nights and was then placed on the rocks to dry. "The odor soon leaves."

It was not unusual for this procedure to continue over a period of weeks or even a month. The pit was kept warm and the fire replenished from time to time. More urine was added each time a new quantity of wool was introduced. "You can even dye for your neighbors."

Lamphere (East)

PM confirmed the second term for blue dye.

Comparative

Indigo was the only material which the Navaho were actually seen using to produce a blue dye. The method was known before the middle of the nineteenth century, for Letherman mentioned it (1856:281). It was also observed by Matthews (1884:376) and by Pepper (1903:4) and others in the twentieth century.

According to the Franciscan Fathers (1910:232–233), before indigo was introduced the Navaho made a blue dye from a blue clay boiled with sumac leaves (see also Matthews, 1884:376; Pepper, 1903:37). Reichard (1936:44–45) discussed the additional possibility that the Navaho formerly used a molybdenum compound, as well as a blue solution found in the black sandstones near Ouray, Utah.

Amsden (1949:90) was told that indigo ceased to be traded to the Navaho about 1905 because the demand had fallen, and modern blue dyes were easily obtainable (Haile, 1951:166). In the 1930's Reichard (1936:43, 44) noted that wool was still dyed blue, "but the pressure of white prudery" made the process a secret. She added that for vegetable dyes any blue flower was used for coloring matter. "Since alfalfa, an introduced plant, is a favorite with them, this method may not be ancient." Elmore (1944:108) mentioned three plants used in making blue dye, but all may be of recent use.

Gifford's Eastern informant said that a blue pigment was obtained from small plant leaves or a mineral; both were used by a chanter, the latter for sandpainting. Both were denied by the Western informant (Gifford, 1940:34, 126).

145. White Dye

λe·š (Lamphere, Haile)   "ground white rock"; "white clay" (CC)

Ramah

White clay was obtained from nearby deposits, such as those south of the TWA emergency landing field at Ramah (Inf. 90) or near a coal mine near Pescado (Inf. 277). It was mixed with water to form a solution for whitening wool yarn or soiled buckskin caps.

Women apparently dug the clay and made the dye. They owned the clay and stored the excess in sacks until needed.

This trait is still extant at Ramah. Two of Robert's households had sacks of white clay. One woman (Inf. 276) was photographed digging the clay, and she used it for whitening yarn. Another (Inf. 278) possessed white clay, but did not wash yarn in it (Roberts, 1951:39, fig. 12, upper right). Inf. 84's household knows of this process and of a deposit of clay near Laguna.

Lamphere (East)

PM said that the word for white dye meant "ground white rock," a special kind, which was ground and rubbed into the wool.

Comparative

There is apparently no mention of white dye in the early literature on the Navaho. The Franciscan Fathers (1910:461, 463, 388) confirmed the use of white clay for a number of purposes. They specifically mentioned its use on a type of buckskin hat called "whitish cap," on the Talking God mask, and for a white line around the base of all masks. There was no reference to whitening wool with white clay. Both of Gifford's Navaho informants affirmed knowledge of white mineral clay but gave no uses for it (Gifford, 1940:34).

Bryan and Young (1940:16) presented a recipe for white wool dye which may be traditional. It called for half a cup of white clay, or two tablespoons ground, toasted gypsum (selenite variety), two cups of water, and one pound of yarn (natural cream color). The clay or gypsum was dissolved in the water and the yarn rinsed in it. "This will make a white rather than a cream yarn."

White clay was used for body painting and for ceremonial purposes (see Trait 203, Face and Body Paint, and Chapter 4).

146. Green Dye

táλid nahalinigi be·diλiži (Lamphere, Franciscan Fathers)   "with green" (CC);   "algae, the one like it, it is dyed"

Hill (East and Central)

Green yarn was produced by combining dyes. LW (Lukachukai) said that a woman first dyed the yarn indigo. Then she added more "salt rock" to

Clothing   a container of yellow dye and dipped the blue yarn. The mixing of the two colors produced a dull green. According to K (Mariano Lake), yellow-dyed buckskin occasionally had a greenish tinge.

Lamphere (East)
PM said that the term for green dye meant "algae the-one-like-it it is dyed."

Comparative
Although green dyes were probably known in the nineteenth century, the first references to them are from the twentieth century. Most observers agreed that green was produced by a mixture of indigo and yellow dye (for example, Franciscan Fathers, 1910:233). According to Reichard, the yellow used for a true and fast green was obtained from the tannin-producing canaigre plant (see Trait 142). She added that greens produced from native plants were apt to be more yellow than green (Reichard, 1936:43–45). Amsden (1949:88) also noted the yellowish color and confirmed the mixture of yellow and indigo. In addition, he stated that indigo alone would produce a green color if the material was left in the dyebath for only a short time. He considered green "perhaps the rarest of the old colors—a great deal rarer than the highly-prized bayeta red." It was used sparingly, in the background, on a large blanket.

Elmore (1944:108) listed eight different species of plants from which shades of green were produced, and Bryan and Young (1940:64, 70, 71) gave an additional three.

Although Gifford's Eastern informant mentioned a blue pigment obtained from small plant leaves or a mineral, Gifford did not distinguish between blue and green. Both dyes were denied by the Western informant (Gifford, 1940:34, 126).

147. Dye Stirring Sticks

xonešgiš (Lamphere)   stirring sticks; "fire cane" (CC)

ʼádísciˑn (Lamphere, Ramah)   stirring sticks; "mush stick" (CC)

Ramah
Slender sticks were employed to stir the dye used for basketry material. Sumac was the material specified by Inf. 15, but Inf. 8 said any dry stick might be used, especially one without bark. It is evident from various Ramah notes on basketry that a stick was used for stirring, but the species of wood was not stated.

These sticks were gathered only by women (Inf. 8), at any time or place, and used only by those who made baskets.

Hill (East and Central)
According to LW (Lukachukai), a loom batten or any convenient stick was used to stir dyes. K (Mariano Lake) said that a metate brush was used (see Trait 90, Grass Brush).

Lamphere (East)
PM confirmed the terms for dye stirring sticks.

Comparative

No information on dye stirring sticks was encountered in literature on Navaho basketry. Elmore's reference to the use of sumac for stirring basketry dye was based on Tschopik's observations at Ramah (Tschopik, 1938:259). The Franciscan Fathers (1910:234) noted the use of slender sticks "for dipping in and taking wool out of the dye pot." Women used two of these. They were called by the same term as that for mush stirrers (see Trait 91).

Sewing Equipment

148. Sewing Bag   λozdiłgai· ·azis (Ramah, Haile)   "squirrel bag" (CC)

Ramah

The cased skin of a squirrel, fur side out, was used to store sewing equipment such as sinew, buckskin, awls, and other implements. The bag was carried by the tail, which was left on the skin.

According to Inf. 8, women made these bags, at no special time or place, and only women used them; but one seen in Ramah was used by a man (Inf. 16). Inf. 8 said the full squirrel skin bag was placed in another bag and hung on the wall when not in use. He thought it might last two years.

Tschopik was shown the bag owned by Inf. 16. There is no information on its use by other members of the Ramah community, and whether this is an early form of bag is not known.

Comparative

Informants may have confused the sewing bag and the knife sheath (see Trait 119). Gifford's Eastern informant referred to buckskin awl scabbards, but other data were lacking (Gifford, 1940:115).

149. Bone Awl   c̓a·gai (Ramah, Haile)   white awl (also metal awl); "white needle, awl" (CC)

c̓in cah (Ramah, Haile)   "wood needle" (CC)

Ramah

Fresh metacarpals (Infs. 16, 192), metatarsals (Infs. 7, 32), or occasionally tibiae (Inf. 192) of deer were split with a knife. One end of each splinter was ground to a point on a rock. The opposite end was neither hafted nor wrapped. Awls might be made by anyone, anywhere, at any time (Inf. 7).

They were used for making baskets (Infs. 15, 16, 32, 192) and for punching holes in skins for sewing, but not for making moccasins (Inf. 7). One basket maker (Inf. 41), questioned in 1940, had never used such awls although she could remember seeing them in use. When the awl was not in use its point was wrapped in buckskin (Inf. 7). According to Inf. 16, it was carried with other sewing equipment in a squirrel skin sack.

No bone awls are known to survive in the Ramah area. Metal awls are now used. Bone needles, as such, were not known.

Hill (East, Central, and West)

Awls were fabricated from deer ulnae (PP, Fort Defiance; C, Chinle; MH, Head Springs), radii (MH), and metacarpals (SC, Crystal). C stated that the bones of any animal might be used, but those of deer were preferred. According to PP and C, the ulnae were split and several awls were produced from a single bone. All informants agreed that awls were shaped and pointed by rubbing on a rough-textured stone. C said that a stone of finer texture was used for a final polish. He also stated that the proximal end of the awl was commonly wrapped with buckskin to give the worker added purchase. Sizes appear to have been variable.

These tools were used in making baskets (PP, SG; K, Mariano Lake) and as perforators in sewing (PP, C). Awls were sometimes carried in a specially designed compartment in the knife sheath (C; see Trait 119).

Fishler (West)

A piece was detached from the ulna or radius of a deer or other large animal (TH, Moenave). TN (Kaibito) stated that bone from wild sheep was used, as were the fibulae and tibiae of other animals. The bone was smoothed by rubbing on a rough rock or sandstone, and one end was ground to a point. A hole was made at the opposite end.

These awls were used with sinew thread for making clothing and bags. Both TT and TH had either manufactured needles or seen them made.

Comparative

There is substantial ethnographic evidence for the use of the bone awl among the Navaho for making baskets and sewing skins. The implement was common at the end of the nineteenth century, and deer bone was the preferred material (Stephen, 1889:131, 134, figs. 5, 6). A deer bone awl was used in preparing sacred buckskin, and fibulae were specified in the sewing of masks for chants (Matthews, 1897:214; Sapir and Hoijer, 1942:77). Just prior to 1910 awls were still used in basketry (including wickerwork water bottles), as well as for sewing moccasins; but perforators of other materials were becoming more common for the latter purpose (Franciscan Fathers, 1910:293, 305).

Both of Gifford's Navaho informants affirmed the use of deer leg bone awls for coiled basketry and skin sewing, but not for boring wood. The Western Navaho also used an antler awl for making winter overshoes. The Eastern informant denied the use of an antler awl; he said that a long bone awl was used for baskets, a short one for moccasins. The handle was wrapped in buckskin; this was denied by the Western informant (Gifford, 1940:27, 115).

Keur found three deer bone awls at Big Bead Mesa. One was a nicely worked metacarpal, but the other two were merely smoothed and sharpened tips of a metatarsal and metapodial. At the Gobernador sites nine sharply pointed and well polished awls were discovered, made from the proximal end of metapodial bones of the mule deer (Keur, 1941:63; 1944:80). Farmer (1938:93) found "a few awl tips, one awl, a part of a flaker" on Navaho sites; the awls were split bones, sharpened for use.

The awl is mentioned in myths, and at one time there was an Awl Chant. According to the Franciscan Fathers (1910:363), A. M. Stephen recorded an account of the use of the awl in the manufacture of the first moccasin. Although the Franciscan Fathers suggested that this myth might be the origin of the Awl Chant, Wyman and Kluckhohn (1938:30) associated the Awl Chant with basketry. Sources agreed that the chant is probably extinct.

150. Metal Awl   ċaˑgai (Ramah, Haile)   white awl

béˑs cah (Ramah, Haile)

Ramah
A filed iron point, about an inch long, was inserted in the small end of a short (four and a half inches) wooden handle. Two incised lines encircled the handle near the butt and another near the point (see 98.a).

Inf. 41 used a metal awl to split coils for the insertion of sewing material when making coiled baskets. A similar implement, with a ring in the handle, was used for making holes in leather; it was observed by Murray in 1943. Inf. 7 used an ice pick for making moccasins.

A basket maker's awl was made for a woman by her husband; but if a woman knew how, she made it. Most women, however, used awls obtained at the trading posts. Only Inf. 41, from one of the poorer Ramah families, was observed using the homemade variety. Because it was made by her husband, Inf. 8, a man with Chiricahua Apache affinities, it may not represent a type manufactured by the Navaho before trading posts became easily accessible.

Hill (East and Central)
According to TOMC (Red Rock), iron since its introduction has been used to make awls. These were hafted with antler. WH (Wheatfields) was observed in 1938 using an iron awl hafted with wood for moccasin sewing.

Comparative
Implements similar to the awl made by Inf. 8 were widespread in the early part of the twentieth century. As early as 1889, Stephen (1889:131, 134, figs. 5, 6) reported a similar tool, an implement called by the same term ("*pec-tsa*") as the second one used at Ramah. He said it was a "very rough specimen of their metal awls," many of which were made "with great nicety" from long knife blades rubbed until they were slender and very sharp.

For making moccasins a needle was either driven into a wooden handle or secured between two pieces of wood with sinew or cord. Also used was a pocket knife with two blades, the smaller of which was ground to awl shape. Since, according to the Franciscan Fathers (1910:305, 293), moccasins were usually made by men, this tool was largely used by men. The bone awl was retained for basket making because the iron one was said to be impractical.

151. Yucca Thread

Ramah

Strips of yucca were used for sewing "lightning mats" (Inf. 15; see Trait 215).

Hill (West)

Yucca leaves were split in half or into smaller elements. These sections were used in lieu of thread for temporarily mending sacks or for making temporary containers out of a blanket (MH, Head Springs).

Comparative

The Franciscan Fathers (1910:308, 457, 327) stated that yucca leaves were boiled and pounded with a stone to extract the pith, then twisted and braided with mountain grass for making blankets, bedding mats, leggings, and shoes. They were also twisted into cords for securing yucca and grass mats over the doorways of early Navaho houses.

Gifford's Eastern informant stated that yucca leaves are sometimes pounded or wilted over a fire to make them pliable; both stated that they were twisted into a two-ply cord. This was presumably used for sewing, as well as for packing a load (Gifford, 1940:47, 140).

152. Sinew Thread

bičeˑˑaˑcid (Ramah)

Ramah

According to Inf. 7, sinew from the tail of the pack rat was formerly used to make thread. This was called *leetsoh* (pack rat) *bichee atsid.* Later deer sinew from the side of the spine began to be used. Sinew fibers were moistened and twisted on the right thigh with the right hand. They were rolled away from the worker. No stick was used in twisting the material, and no fixed number of fibers was required. Either men or women might make sinew thread.

Sinew was used for sewing moccasins and for bowstrings. In sewing, the end was twisted between the right thumb and index finger to bring it to a point, and was moistened in the mouth.

Data were obtained from Inf. 7 and confirmed by Inf. 16. Sinew is still used in making moccasins, but when it began to be used is not known.

Hill (East, Central, and West)

On a hunt, deer sinews were given to anyone who needed them. When an animal was killed, the sinew was detached from the meat and stretched by pulling it through the closed fist of one hand. This process was believed to strengthen it and to prevent it from curling when dry. Sinew for sewing was taken from the back; the leg tendons were used for sinew-backed bows and for wrapping arrow points and fletching (Hill, 1938:145).

Before use, the sinew was moistened in the mouth and twisted on the thigh. Twisting was always done forward and away from the worker, as at Ramah. When dry, the sinew was ready for use (PP, Fort Defiance).

Fishler (West)

Sinew from wild and, later, domesticated sheep was split and used for thread (TN, Kaibito). TT (Coalmine) said sinew was used to sew the skin bags. Both informants had seen sinew thread used for this purpose.

Comparative

According to Matthews (1897:240), the material commonly referred to as sinew was a yellow fibrous tissue taken from the dorsal region, not sinew in the anatomical or histological sense. The Franciscan Fathers (1910:305, 309) stated that loin sinew of sheep, goat, or deer was used in sewing moccasins, but deer sinew was rapidly disappearing from use. The fibers were detached from a supply kept on hand, moistened, and rolled into a stout thread.

Gifford's informants agreed that sinew was used for sewing. The Eastern Navaho said that a one-ply thread was rolled on the thigh, made by men, and used for bowstrings or for sewing skins. The Western informant said that a two-ply cord was used (Gifford, 1940:47, 139).

153. Thongs

ʼabaní·yisła·s (Ramah)   "deerskin, woven" (CC)

Ramah

Scraps of buckskin were cut into strips, which were pointed at one end and trimmed with a knife until they were narrow enough for use. A strip was held against a board by the thumb of the right hand, and the edges trimmed with a short sawing motion. Then the strip was held between another piece of scrap buckskin and the knife, and pulled to scrape it thin.

Thongs were made as necessary, usually by men. They were used for sewing buckskin clothing. Women who did this prepared their own thongs. Each thong was knotted at one end. The pointed end was twisted and inserted through an awl hole from the same direction as the awl, pulled through, and inserted in the next hole.

Thongs were prepared by Inf. 7 when making a buckskin shirt. He said that he had learned as a boy by watching his mother and father.

Hill (East, Central, and West)

Buckskin was used for thongs. Mountain sheep skin was never used, for fear the offender would become a cripple (Hill, 1938:145, 168).

Fishler (West)

GB (Tuba City) stated that thin strips of rabbit skin were twisted between the finger to make thongs.

Comparative

According to the Franciscan Fathers (1910:533), thongs of buckskin, goatskin, or mountain sheep skin were used for sewing and attaching objects. Haile (1951:298) stated that thongs might be cut from rawhide, sheepskins and goatskins, or from buckskin. Gifford (1940:47) indicated that buckskin was used for sewing by the Eastern Navaho, but the Western informant was not questioned.

154. Buckskin Cord

Ramah

To make cord a buckskin thong was twisted on the thigh with a motion away from the worker, then doubled and twisted toward the worker. Either men or women made cord. When cord was used for a bowstring, it was dampened (see Trait 18).

It is not known whether buckskin is still made into cord.

Comparative

According to Gifford (1940:139), the Eastern Navaho rolled cord of buckskin, sinew, or yucca fiber on the thigh.

155. Knots

Ramah

Although no specific information on knots was collected at Ramah, they were known to be present. The unraveling knot was mentioned in rituals and several types of knots were used in weaving and assembling the loom.

Hill (East, Central, and West)

The square knot (no. 1204, p. 220;* see 155.1) was apparently preferred and was the most commonly used for general purposes (PP, Fort Defiance, "tight knot"; C, Chinle; IS, Lukachukai; TLLSS, Crownpoint). "The Navaho teach their children only this kind of knot. They tell them not to use any other kind of knot" (C). According to IS, "The square knot is the knot of the Navaho."

The granny knot (no. 1206, p. 220; see 155.2) or "crooked knot" (IS, PP) was currently known as the "knot of the dead," and was avoided except in connection with preparation and dressing of the corpse prior to burial. "This knot should never be found on a living person" (IS). According to C, "the only place this knot could be used was on a corpse. If a person tied it by mistake it was all right, but if he tied it on purpose sickness would follow. There are really two knots, one for the living [the square knot] and one for the dead [the granny knot]." According to PP, "when a person is living he should never use this knot. The Navaho are afraid of it. It is only used on the dead. You tie the moccasin thongs and bead and earring strings of the corpse with this kind of knot."

The half or single bowknot (no. 1211, p. 220; see 155.3) was used for the same purposes as the square knot, but was easier to undo (C). The bowknot (no. 1212, p. 220; see 155.4), or "loose knot" (PP, IS), was another general utility knot, "easier to untie than the square knot."

The half hitch (no. 50, p. 15; see 155.5), or "knot slipping over and tying," was used in the making of juniper bark torches (PP). The clove hitch (no. 53, p. 15; see 155.6) was called "rope over knot" (PP). The bale sling hitch (no. 59, p. 15; see 155.7) was used in making the loop of bird snares (IS; see Trait 5), and at the beginning of the lashing that held the upper crosspiece of the loom on the upright (LW, Lukachukai; see *a* on 155.15).

The slippery hitch (no. 51, p. 15; see 155.8) was used to finish the lashing holding the upper crosspiece of the loom on the upright (see *b* on 155.15), to tie the warp threads to the yard beam (LW), and at the beginning of

---

*Nomenclature is taken from Ashley, 1944; page numbers and knot numbers refer to this book. Figs. 155.1–155.15, from *The Ashley Book of Knots* by Clifford W. Ashley, copyright 1944 by Clifford W. Ashley, are reproduced by permission of Doubleday and Co., Inc., and Faber and Faber, Ltd.

Knots, after Ashley

155.1. Square knot   **155.2.** Granny knot   **155.3.** Half bowknot   **155.4.** Bowknot

155.5. Half hitch   **155.6.** Clove hitch   **155.7.** Bale sling hitch   **155.8.** Slippery hitch   **155.9.** Single hitch

  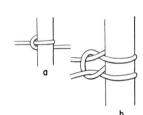 

155.10. Loop knot   **155.11.** Noose   **155.12.** Crossing knot, showing first turn (*a*) and finished knot (*b*)   **155.13.** Chain stitch

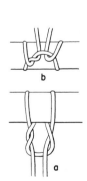 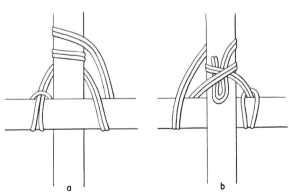

155.14. Cat's paw, loosely tied (*a*), pulled up (*b*)   **155.15.** Lashing the upper crosspiece on the loom, beginning with the bale sling hitch (*a*), finishing with the slippery hitch (*b*)

the lashing on the drumstick used in the Squaw Dance (GH, White Cone). This knot was also used at the beginning of the lashing on the male and female bluebirds used in the Corral Way (RH, Crystal; Hill, 1938:151). The single hitch (no. 49, p. 15; see 155.9) was used at the beginning and at the end of the lashing on a drumstick (SC, Crystal).

The loop knot (no. 1009, p. 186; see 155.10), when tied in the end of a rope to make a lasso, was called "lasso slip knot" (PP). This knot was also used in making the corner tassels on a blanket. It was tied and the loop cut, the cut ends forming the tassels (LW).

The noose (no. 43, p. 14; see 155.11) was used at the beginning of the knitted stalking costume (AM, Lukachukai).

The crossing knot (no. 206, p. 40; see 155.12) was used in attaching the bowstring to the upper end of the bow. For this purpose, two crossing knots were tied, the second placed over the first (AM).

The chain stitch (no. 2100, p. 341; see 155.13) or "ceremonial knot" (IS) was tied around a stick and unraveled over the patient in some chants (see, for example, Kluckhohn and Wyman, 1940:78, fig. 7).

Comparative

Although there were numerous allusions to knots in accounts of Navaho ceremonial practices, there were practically none in descriptions of Navaho secular life. The Franciscan Fathers (1910:315) noted several knots in connection with plaiting and said that the chain stitch was used in making quadrangular quirts.

The "holy stitch" mentioned by Matthews (1902:309, n. 8b) appeared to be a bale sling hitch. That which he called the "Navaho knot" appeared to be a modification of the cat's paw (no. 1891, p. 315; see 155.14), with two turns on the left bight and one on the right bight (Matthews, 1902:309, n. 8a).

According to Reichard (1950:182, 567), knots symbolized the concept of reversal, in which "square knots, normal to the living, are tied as grannies for the dead." Knots also symbolized the circle of frustration. Cutting the knots demonstrated "the freeing of the patient and control of the evils that tied him in." A closely related form of symbolism, unraveling, is to be found frequently in Navaho curing ceremonies (see, for example, Kluckhohn and Wyman, 1940:77–80, 117–118; Haile, 1938:70–71).

156. Knitting Needles

yisX̣é be·X̣ohí (Ramah)   wooden knitting needles; "sox with it knitting" (CC)

be··eX̣o·hí (Ramah)   wire knitting needles; "weaving tool" (CC)

Ramah

Wooden needles were made from a hardwood such as Fendlerbush. These were about five inches long. Metal needles were made of wire procured from the Zuni, or umbrella ribs broken to the desired length with the fingers. These were from six to eight inches long, and the number used was two, three, and five. One needle was used as the mobile element, while the other or others were used to hold the stitches.

156.a. Knitting socks (about 1890)

Both men and women used needles for knitting woolen yarn into mittens and leggings. The knitter made his or her own needles. They lasted a long time, and when not in use were kept in a sack hung on the wall (Inf. 8).

No one who had made knitting needles was questioned, although it is probable that some of the older people had done so. Inf. 32 had knit with wire needles, but said that she had abandoned knitting shortly after the return from Fort Sumner. Infs. 7 and 8 had seen needles of wire but not of wood.

This trait is now obsolete because mittens and leggings are now easily available from local stores.

Comparative

Indirect evidence indicated that the Navaho possessed knitting needles during the early days of American contact; several observers mentioned knitted leggings or stockings (Davis, 1857:411–412; see 178.a). Palmer (1869:47) believed that the trait was one borrowed from the Spaniards.

In 1881, Bourke saw a man knitting and was told that a considerable percentage of the Navaho were able to do so (Bourke, 1936:81). Most observers agreed with Thompson's statement that "more men than women knit stockings (I think)" (Thompson, 1871:32; Palmer, 1869:47; Bourke, 1936:81; Franciscan Fathers, 1910:256), but Hollister (1903:48) said that women did the knitting.

Matthews (1897:21) commented that wire needles obtained from the whites were used, usually four in number. Hollister (1903:48) confirmed the use of four. According to Pepper, however, five needles were used (Pepper, as quoted in Amsden, 1949:108). There was no reference to the use of three needles, as at Ramah.

The Franciscan Fathers (1910:255) stated that before steel and iron were available, needles were made of wood, either of Fendlerbush or black greasewood, since both could be given a smooth polish. By 1910 steel needles were common. They were purchased from the trading posts. Other metal needles were manufactured from pieces of wire or umbrella ribs. The ends of the latter were ground smooth on a stone, and in time the paint wore off from use.

Gifford's Western informant said that both men and women knit using wooden needles and that four were used. The Eastern informant said that knitting with wooden needles was a modern trait, but—perhaps in confusion—said that neither men nor women knit (Gifford, 1940:48, 140).

Apparel
Women's Garments

157. Bast Apron

Hill (East, Central, and West)

Bast aprons, worn back and front, were woven from cliff rose bark (LW, Ganado), cliff rose bark and yucca (PP, Fort Defiance), rabbit skin and yucca (SC, Crystal), "slim grass" and yucca (TLLSS, Crownpoint; C, Chinle). They were produced in checker weave (TLLSS, LW). According to LW, at the edge the warp or the weft (sometimes both) was bent back over the last element and tied on itself. The completed edge was further reinforced by sewing. Aprons reached almost to the knee and were held in place by a thong about the waist (C).

LW claimed to have seen these garments, and PP reported that his grandmother had seen them in use; SC said that the older people had described this type of dress to him. C had never seen an apron but had been told that they were made by unfortunate women who had no one to hunt for them. Only one informant (K, Mariano Lake) denied the existence of bast aprons.

Comparative

The earliest Navaho costume, according to the Franciscan Fathers (1910:457), "was very meager and constructed of yucca and grass fiber." Yucca leaves were boiled, pounded with a stone, then twisted and braided with mountain grass to make a blanket wrap, which was drawn around the body.

Gifford's Eastern informant described a woman's apron made of shredded juniper bark; it was knee length and tied to or over a cord at the waist. A tubular skirt was also made. This informant also described a woven dress of finely spun Spanish bayonet yucca fiber; it was made in two rectangular pieces which were sewn together down the sides. All of these garments were made when buckskin was scarce. The Western informant denied the apron and skirt and was not questioned about the dress (Gifford, 1940:38–39, 130–131).

Louisa Wade Wetherill collected some mythological materials dealing with traditional Navaho clothing. According to her, juniper bark clothing was worn, apparently by both men and women. The costume consisted of a short juniper bark skirt secured at the waist with a yucca fiber string. They also wore a knee-length tunic of juniper bark: two bark strips were tied with yucca cord at the shoulders and under the arms. A woven mat of grass (cf. Franciscan Fathers, 1910:457) was worn over the shoulder to protect them from the cold. They plastered their bodies with mud for the same purpose (Wetherill, n.d.:2 pp.).

158. Skin Apron

Hill (Central and West)

The two-piece skin apron consisted of rectangular sections of buckskin. Approximately one inch of the upper portion of the skins was folded over and sewn, to form a hem. A thong running through the hem openings fixed the aprons at the waist; the tie was on the side. Aprons extended to within three inches of the knee (GH, White Cone; SG, Keams Canyon). "When a woman sat down she pushed the front apron between her legs" (SG).

Two informants from the Central part of the reservation (MB, Divide; PP, Fort Defiance) had never heard of a buckskin apron being worn by the Navaho.

Lamphere (East)

EP's mother and PM had never heard of women wearing skins.

Comparative

Gifford's Eastern informant said that the two-piece apron which he described was made of buckskin if available (Gifford, 1940:130).

ʾλa·kał (Haile)   "skirt" (CC)

159. Skin Skirt

Hill (West)

One informant (MH, Head Springs) described a skirt constructed of two pieces of buckskin, with the skirt seams at the sides. Such garments were worn with a buckskin shirt.

Lamphere (East)

EP's mother and PM had never heard of women wearing skin skirts.

Comparative

Both of Gifford's informants said that a one-piece buckskin skirt was worn by women; the Eastern informant also confirmed a one-piece unfringed skirt (Gifford, 1940:39, 131). The Franciscan Fathers (1910:460) mentioned a waistcloth worn by women as part of the Navaho costume. The term was that which Haile (1951:266) translated as "skirt."

Mrs. Wetherill stated that traditionally the women wore skirts of buckskin or buffalo calfskin. The head and tail were left on the hide and were joined at the right hip. According to her, all hides but fox hides were dehaired before dressing (Wetherill, n.d.:2 pp.).

160. Skin Shirt

Hill (Central and West)

Buckskin shirts seem to have been occasionally worn by women. According to SG (Keams Canyon), they were of the same type worn by the men (see Trait 170); according to MH (Head Springs), they were sleeveless. C (Chinle) stated that poor women sometimes pieced together scraps of buckskin and produced a shirt "like a brassiere."

Lamphere (East)

EP's mother and PM had never heard of women wearing skin shirts.

Comparative

Both of Gifford's informants said that a fringed poncho-like short tunic of buckskin was worn with a buckskin skirt. The Eastern informant said that sometimes it was unfringed (Gifford, 1940:38). The Franciscan Fathers (1910:457) illustrated a fringed buckskin shirt, but did not state whether it was also worn by women.

According to Mrs. Wetherill, the Navaho women wore shirts of rabbit skin, swift, or blue fox. The skins of four swifts were sewn together over the shoulder and under the arm, with two in front and two in back. The shirt was secured at the waist with a squirrel skin belt. She stated that later shirts were made of elk skin and deerskin, with long sleeves and tight cuffs, and were fringed at the waist and around the armholes (Wetherill, n.d.:2 pp.).

161. Skin Dress

Hill (East, Central, and West)

Two variants of the buckskin dress appear to have existed. The first type (161.1) was made from two hides. These were roughly trimmed along the bottoms, sides, and shoulders to allow as much flare as possible toward the bottom of the skirt. The two halves were sewn together with sinew at the shoulders, and down the sides, from approximately eight inches below the normal sleeve opening to within eight inches of the bottom. The upper opening facilitated nursing (GH, White Cone; C, Chinle); the lower allowed freedom of movement. If additional length was required, a third buckskin was cut down the back and the two sections sewn to the bottom of the skirt. The heads of the skins were always placed at the upper end of the dress. These were trimmed to triangular shape and allowed to hang down in front and behind (GH). Dresses of this type were sleeveless and were worn with a buckskin belt tied about the waist (C).

The second type (161.2) of dress differed in cut from the first. The tops of the skins were squared, and the neck opening was formed by a medial cut of eight to ten inches in the front of the dress. The edges of this cut were folded back to form "lapels." Rudimentary sleeves were formed by removing sections from the sides. These features produced a fitted effect. Otherwise, construction was the same as the first example (C).

Differences of opinion existed concerning ornamentation. According to TLLSS (Crownpoint), the bottoms of the skirts were fringed. This was denied by WH (Wheatfields) and GH. According to TLLSS, fringed yokes were sometimes added to dresses. GH stated that buckskin dresses were never dyed and MH (Head Springs) and PP that no clothing of any kind was ever painted.

Skin dresses, after Hill; dotted lines indicate seams

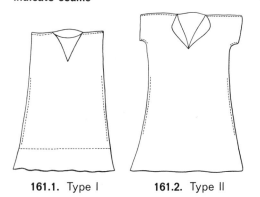

161.1. Type I   161.2. Type II

Buckskin dresses appear to have become obsolete about the period of Fort Sumner. Several informants (WH; GH; MB, Divide) stated that they were the prevalent type worn when the Navaho were taken to Fort Sumner, and others (SC, Crystal; SG) said that they disappeared soon after the return. MM (Lukachukai) did not remember ever having seen women wear these dresses.

Lamphere (East)
EP's mother and PM had never heard of women wearing skin dresses.

Comparative
Gifford's Navaho informants confirmed a short-sleeved buckskin tunic (dress?) which the Western informant said was open part way in front; both informants denied a long poncho-like tunic (Gifford, 1940:38).

Amsden (1949:96–98) also stated that the Navaho probably wore a deerskin dress made in two pieces that was the prototype of the woven two-piece dress, and added that a similar buckskin dress was found among the Apache (see also Mera, 1944a). Bourke confirmed the prototype and stated that the skin dresses of the Shoshone and Bannock women were similar to the Navaho woven dresses, the cut being "almost identical" (Bourke, 1936:82).

Mrs. Wetherill described a one-piece buckskin dress which came to about the knees, with fringe on the bottom and short sleeves (Wetherill, n.d.:2 pp.).

162. Woolen Dress, Type A

be·λé··é·· (Ramah) "blanket clothing" (CC)

Ramah
A rectangular blanket was woven, usually in black and white horizontal stripes. Some were plain white, but none was all black. The blanket was folded over and sewn down most of one side and across one end; an opening was left for the head (see 162.1). The dress was worn over the left shoulder and under the right. It was caught at the waist by a belt of twisted wool and reached to the middle of the lower leg.

These dresses were made by women, at any place, "just as weaving is done now" (Inf. 8). They were worn by women and girls after about the age of fifteen (Inf. 8). If well woven, they might last a year (Inf. 8). Each was stored "in a sack where it will be safe" (Inf. 8).

Most of the data were obtained from Inf. 192, who implied that such a dress was worn before the Fort Sumner exile. Although Inf. 7 denied knowledge of it, as did Inf. 48, Inf. 8 had seen Inf. 7's mother wearing such a dress. No dresses of this type are preserved in the Ramah area.

Comparative
Although observers stated that Navaho women wore dresses of the Pueblo type, descriptions were often insufficient for definite documentation of this particular style. The Rabal documents (1706–1743), for example, reported that Navaho women were dressed in a black woolen dress of Pueblo type (Hill, 1940a:398, 412, 413). The dress was not described by the Franciscan Fathers (1910:245–246), and descriptions by Amsden indicated its absence among the Navaho. In a burial dating from about the beginning of the

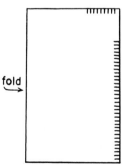

162.1. Woolen dress, Type A, after Tschopik

fold→

nineteenth century, however, there was a "shoulder mantle or dress of Pueblo (woman's) type, black with indigo blue border in diamond twill." Grave goods identified this man as a Navaho (Amsden, 1949:pl. 63, see pp. 96–97).

James (1914:41) did confirm the existence of this type among the Navaho. He said that it was a late development, worn by only a few women. He had several examples in his collection. Both of Gifford's informants denied this type of dress (Gifford, 1940:38).

163. Rope Belt

ʾaɣaˑsis (Ramah, Haile) "wool belt" (CC)

Ramah

A belt was made in the form of a twisted wool rope; it was worn with the woman's dress, Type A. Inf. 256 said this belt was also worn by men.

According to Inf. 192, the rope belt was worn before the Fort Sumner period. She implied that it was replaced by the woven belt. There are no data from other informants, and it is unlikely that the trait has survived. Silver-studded belts are now worn, if any.

Comparative

Only the Franciscan Fathers (1910:249) mentioned this belt, and they gave only its name, "wool girdle rope," saying it was woven like the sash.

164. Woolen Dress, Type B

biˑl (Ramah, Lamphere, Haile) "woven wool" (CC)

164.a. Woman wearing woolen dress, Type B

Ramah

Two blankets were woven about the size of a double saddle blanket, but not so wide. They were usually black, but some had stripes of yellow, red, or other colors. They were sewn together across the shoulders and down the sides; openings were left for the neck and arms. The dress was sleeveless.

Women wove these dresses and wore them with a woven belt. According to Inf. 7, girls wore these as soon as they could walk; but Inf. 8 specified the age of fifteen or so. They lasted a year (Inf. 8) or about three to four years (Inf. 7). They were stored in a sack.

Most data were obtained from Inf. 32, some from Inf. 48. The latter said that the dress was worn both before and after the Fort Sumner captivity. Infs. 7 and 8 both remembered seeing it during their youth, but the dress has since disappeared and none has been preserved as an heirloom. It has been replaced by the skirt and blouse.

The two types of woolen dress were regarded by the Ramah Navaho as the earliest type of women's costume. No descriptions of bast or skin clothing (see Traits 157–161) were obtained.

Hill (East, Central, and West)

Wool dresses consisted of two identical rectangular sections of woven material. These were sewn together as at Ramah; stitching along the sides went from a little above the waist to slightly below the knee. An awl was used for perforations and a running stitch was employed. Sewing materials were either blue or red yarn (LW, MM, Lukachukai; C, Chinle). Dresses extended to within eight inches of the ankles (LW, Lukachukai) or just below the knee (LW, Ganado). This type of dress was sleeveless (LW, Lukachukai; WH, Wheatfields; LW, Ganado; TLLSS, Crownpoint). Many of these dresses were plain blue or black in color (MM); others had horizontal stripes of red and indigo introduced at the top and bottom (LW, Lukachukai; TLLSS).

Nothing was worn underneath the dress (MM) and both WH and LW (Lukachukai) commented that these dresses were rough and scratched. According to LW, after Fort Sumner cotton linings were sometimes placed in the dresses to make them more comfortable.

According to tradition (C), woolen dresses were derived from the Pueblos. They were apparently common just before and at Fort Sumner (LM, Canyon del Muerto; N, Coalmine). According to WH, they were worn at this period but were not too numerous. SC (Crystal), GH (White Cone), and TLLSS reported both woven wool and buckskin dresses during the Fort Sumner period. MM remembered wearing this type of dress as a child. According to SG (Keams Canyon) and LW (Lukachukai), they continued to be worn for some time after the return from Fort Sumner, and AS (Lukachukai) remembered seeing one worn as late as 1908.

Lamphere (East)
EP's mother and PM confirmed the term for this dress.

Comparative
Woven dresses of this or a similar type have been in vogue since at least the middle of the eighteenth century and are documented by the Rabal manuscript (Hill, 1940a:398, 412, 413). Specimens were preserved from the early nineteenth century. One dress, taken from Massacre Cave, had a black center, with bayeta red stripes and indigo blue end panel figures. The dress dated from 1805 (or 1819, D. De Harport, personal communication; Amsden, 1949:pl. 49). In an article in the *Missouri Intelligencer,* April 3, 1824, Navaho women were described as wearing "a loose black robe, ornamented around the bottom with a red border, which is sometimes figured" (quoted in Woodward, 1938:51). Simpson, in 1849, encountered women dressed in blankets confined at the waist by a girdle (Simpson, 1850:88).

Amsden (1949:96–97) described the typical pattern for the woolen dress. As at Ramah, it was woven in two pieces, each about thirty inches by forty inches, sewn together down the sides and at the shoulders. Gaps in the side seam at top and bottom provided freedom of movement. "In color and pattern a rigid conservatism prevailed" (see also Sapir and Hoijer, 1942:413; Mera, 1944a). This dress—black, with a red and blue border—was the one most frequently cited by nineteenth-century observers, such as Palmer (1869), Bourke (1936:82), Matthews (1884:388), Thompson (1871), Stephen (1893:356), and James (1914:39–41, 118). James (1914:118) noted other color variations, including black, gray, red, and deep blue; red, black, and gray; deep maroon, red, bright green, and deep blue. He said that these ranged in age in the order given, the oldest listed first.

The Franciscan Fathers (1910:245–246) stated that the dress was originally woven in black and blue: the black a native dye, the blue an indigo. The body of the blanket was black, with four lines of blue at the top and bottom. "The whole was bordered and tasseled in blue." With the introduction of bayeta, red was substituted for the blue bands, but the blue border and tassels were retained. "Gradually various designs of red and blue were woven with the black at each side of the center belt." Amsden (1949:97) said that he had never seen this type of dress. James had seen several of this type, but they were scarce. He obtained one from Manuelito's widow, who regarded it as the last of its kind (James, 1914:118, and 112 showing Manuelito's widow dressed in this garment). It is possible that the black and blue garment was a local variation.

Both of Gifford's informants stated that women wore a "short-sleeved tunic," which according to the Eastern informant was woven of red yarn from Mexican blankets, but earlier was made of buckskin. Whether the *bil* was meant, however, was not made clear (Gifford, 1940:38, 39, 130–131).

By the late nineteenth century, the *bil* was by far the most common dress for women. It continued to be worn after the men had accepted garments supplied by the whites. It was common in the vicinity of Fort Wingate in 1877 (Shufeldt, 1893:280), common in the Fort Defiance area in the 1880's (Bourke, 1936:224), and typical in the Keams Canyon area in the 1890's, although "the young women now generally wear a calico dress under this rough tunic" (Stephen, 1893:356).

When the styles changed, the change was rapid. Amsden (1949:97) was told by a trader that the tribe was "going calico" in 1895, and there were so many native dresses in pawn at his trading store that he sold them for almost nothing. By 1900 this dress was rare. It was not mentioned in Hollister's description (1903:61–62) of the woman's costume, and by 1910 it was a thing of the past, according to the Franciscan Fathers (1910:245–246). A few old women, however, still clung to this dress; Amsden (1949:97) saw a woman wearing one in 1913.

In 1914, James (1914:39) stated that such dresses are "no longer woven, no longer worn, and are absolutely unobtainable anywhere, at any price, save from the collectors and dealers." Later, some of the younger women began again to make the woman's dress, not for wear but for sale to the traders (Reichard, 1936:121).

Mrs. Wetherill stated that the woman's costume, after the advent of the Spaniards and the introduction of sheep, was the squaw dress. It was at one time worn by all the women, and is now used in some ceremonies. The dress she described was black, red, and blue, although unmarried women sometimes wore a white dress, with designs in red and black (Wetherill, n.d.:2 pp.).

164.b. Woman wearing woolen dress, Type B

165. Woolen Belt sisłičí··ígí (Ramah) belt; "red belt, that one" (CC)

Ramah

Belts from two to four feet long were woven on belt looms. The belts were red with two longitudinal stripes and diamond designs in white (Inf. 192), or red with designs in red and white and a blue stripe at each edge (Inf. 7). At each end were long fringes in red and green (Inf. 192). Conch shells were sometimes tied to the fringe at one end; Inf. 192 has such a belt, an heirloom.

These belts were made by women, but only certain women (Inf. 256). The belt (see Plate VIII and 164.b) was worn with the *bil* (Trait 164) as a girdle

(Inf. 32). Some women wore it daily, others only for ceremonials; Inf. 7 said that men sometimes wore it. This belt was also used as a support for women during childbirth; it was tied to a branch of a tree or post of the hogan. Forty-two Ramah informants, one from Pinedale, and two from Chaco Canyon confirmed this use for Bailey (1950:57). One of the most acculturated of the Ramah women, Inf. 82, had also used the belt for this purpose (Inf. 73).

According to Inf. 192, these belts became popular after the captivity at Fort Sumner. Although they are no longer part of the everyday attire, they are still made and worn on occasion. Various women now make belts; Inf. 85 made one for one of her daughters, and others for trade. Although belts may now be made of cotton, as in other areas, other details of manufacture have remained unchanged.

Hill (Central)

Only partial descriptions were obtained of woven belts, but these agreed in general with accounts from Ramah (MM and LW, Lukachukai; C, Chinle). C stated that the woven belt supplanted the one of buckskin. LW said that the woven belt was derived from Pueblo sources.

Comparative

Simpson (1850:101) apparently was the first to record the woven sash, the "girdle to confine their blankets." The next reference was from the post–Fort Sumner period. Palmer (1869:78, 80) noted a woven belt made from a red worsted bought from the traders, unraveled, then retwisted and woven. Both ends were fringed.

Many descriptions were given subsequently. Navaho men met by Dellenbaugh (1926:146) on the Colorado River in 1872 wore woven sashes. Shufeldt (1892:391–393) described belt weaving at Fort Wingate in the 1870's, Matthews (1884:389–390) at Fort Defiance in the late 1870's and 1880's, and Stephen, presumably at Keams Canyon about the 1890's (Stephen, ms. quoted in James, 1914:132–133). And finally, Reichard described the process as it was taught to her in the 1930's (Reichard, 1936:133–140; see also Amsden, 1949:106, pl. 21).

Matthews (1884:390) stated that belt designs were restricted, and he had seen about two dozen which he believed represented the range. According to the Franciscan Fathers (1910:248–249), the sash was originally black with a blue band in the center. After the introduction of bayeta, sashes were exclusively woven of red yarn with a small white design, and came to be known by the name "red girdle." A much wider range of colors was noted. Shufeldt (1892:393) stated that the leading colors were red, brilliant orange-yellow, blue, green, black, white, and gray. According to Stephen, a frequent combination of colors was dark blue, green, scarlet, and black (Stephen, ms. quoted in James, 1914:133). Reichard (1936:133) said that sashes were most commonly made of red and green Germantown wool. F. H. Douglas listed red, green, and white for the usual colors; he added that the basic source of these materials was undoubtedly the Pueblo (who used red, green, and black). Apparently the Navaho made these belts for Pueblo trade in Pueblo style and vice versa. Apparently such trading had been practiced for forty years (F. H. Douglas, personal communication).

Gifford's Western informant said that Navaho women wore a belt woven of red wool, but not of cotton. The Eastern informant said that the belt was a modern trait (Gifford, 1940:38, 130).

The woven belt is still worn in some parts of the Navaho area. It was worn in 1910 (Franciscan Fathers, 1910:249), observed in the 1930's (Kluckhohn, and by implication, Reichard, 1936:140), and in the 1940's (F. H. Douglas, personal communication).

Documentation of the employment of the woven belt in childbirth dates from the mid-nineteenth century. Letherman (1856:290) noted that Navaho women supported themselves with a rope during delivery. The Franciscan Fathers (1910:450, 453) said that a "stout cord" or belt was used, and Gifford's Navaho informants said that a parturient woman grasped a cord or stick (Gifford, 1940:40). Whether these comments refer to the woven sash is not clear.

Archaeological data support the possibilty that the woven belt was in use among the Navaho at an early date. Keur found a "flattened wooden slab, presumably of oak," (25 in. by $3\frac{1}{2}$ in. by $\frac{3}{8}$ in.) at a Gobernador site that dated between 1656 and 1771. The edge showed rubbing from use, and there was a series of parallel lines or grooves running diagonally across one face. The slab was asymetrical in form, rounded at one end, broadening out and tapering to a point at the other. It was identified by Wyman's informant DS (from the Pinedale-Coolidge-Smith Lake area) as a one-handed batten used on a narrow loom, thrust in from the side at a slant or angle. "This interpretation accounts for the asymetry of form, and for the diagonal slant of the lines worn by the warp" (Keur, 1944:81). The batten was found at a site where there was no evidence for the existence of sheep or goats. Malcolm (1939:9) also reported a find of four battens of this type, identified by Navaho of the Chaco Canyon region where the find was made. The material was not dated, but it was possibly from the early nineteenth century.

166. Cotton Skirt   ƛa·kaɬ (Lamphere, Haile)   "skirt" (CC)

Ramah
The long, fluted, calico skirt (see 166.a, 169.a), made either by hand or on a sewing machine, has become the "customary garb of the women and girls" (Roberts, 1951:17, 47). According to Griffith (1954), the Navaho women learned to make these skirts while at Fort Sumner.

Inf. 36 said the Ramah women differed from those of other areas in wearing skirts of two colors instead of one, and in facing the skirts on the outside. Inf. 82 said that the women wore "shortish" skirts until she taught them to make longer ones. New skirts were worn over a succession of older ones, which then served as petticoats. Clothing from the trading post is now commonly available.

Hill (Central and West)
Informants agreed that the present-day type of cotton skirt was of relatively recent introduction. C (Chinle) stated that the first ones were made from calico issued at Fort Sumner. According to SC (Crystal), they appeared on

the reservation about 1880. This date was confirmed by MB (Divide), who said they came in with the trading post and calico issues at Fort Defiance, and by SG (Keams Canyon), who said that Americans brought them in.

According to C, the first types were constructed by folding the material in a series of pleats and securing them at the waist with a cord. Somewhat later, cotton belts were sewn to the top to keep the pleats in place. Both C and MB agreed that ruffles were a recent addition.

Lamphere (East)

PM said that the skirt could just be called "clothing" but that the more specific name (above) meant "goes around the hips." She distinguished skirts of cotton, silk, and cloth with flowers "spotted." PM said that the word for a matching skirt and blouse also meant a man's suit if both the top and pants were of the same cloth.

Comparative

As noted above, the Navaho were apparently "going calico" (Amsden, 1949:97) at the turn of the century. Hollister (1903:61–62) noted that "gaudy calicos and bright red woolen cloths" were used for skirts, and by 1910 the long calico skirt plus shirt or tunic was the ordinary costume (Franciscan Fathers, 1910:245–246). Both of Gifford's informants denied a one-piece skirt made of cotton cloth (Gifford, 1940:39, 131).

166.a. Woman wearing cotton skirt and a velveteen blouse (Tr. 167)

167. Cotton Blouse   ʾeʾ deǯi (Lamphere)   "clothing top" (CC)

Ramah

Bright calico or velveteen long-sleeved blouses (see 166.a, 169.a) were worn with the long fluted skirt. Like the skirts, these were made either by hand or on sewing machines, usually by the mothers of the households; older girls also knew how to sew, and steel needles were purchased from the traders. Buttons of different sizes made of pounded and shaped silver were sewn across the shoulders and used to fasten the blouse at the wrist and down the front. Since no one had enough buttons for all her blouses, it was common to see a woman removing buttons from one blouse and sewing them on another (Roberts, 1951:17, 47; Griffith, 1954).

Hill (Central and West)

Cotton blouses patterned after men's shirts began to be worn by women after the return from Fort Sumner (C, Chinle; SC, Crystal; MB, Divide). According to MB, ruffles on the sleeves were a more recent innovation. Velveteen blouses were definitely assigned to the period following the establishment of reservation trading posts (C, SC, MB; SG, Keams Canyon).

Comparative

Descriptions of blouses were few, although many observers agreed that they were made of cotton, in "modern" style. The calico obtained in the late nineteenth century was undoubtedly made into blouses as well as skirts and dresses. By 1910, the women were usually dressed in calico shirts like those worn by men, but usually of brighter colors (Franciscan Fathers, 1910:465).

Many Navaho women have recently worn and still wear a distinctive and characteristic style of velveteen blouse. Underhill's informants stated that garments of this type appeared shortly before 1900 in the settlements near the railroad. At that time, preferred colors were orange and purple. Shirt styles were simple, with a V neck and hem hanging out over the skirt. Gradually they grew fancier, "with collars, tucks and lining, and with rows of silver buttons or silver coins on yoke, front and sleeves" (Underhill, 1953:224–225). Underhill's statement that these blouses were common until World War II stopped the supply of velveteen was not in accord with observations of many anthropologists who have been in the Navaho country since the war. All agreed that the bright colored, silver-decorated velveteen blouses were very much in style among Navaho women, both for everyday wear and for "dress up" occasions. All fifteen of the women and children in photographs published in *Arizona Highways* in August 1954 wore velveteen blouses (Tanner, 1954:18–26). That all were heirlooms is improbable.

168. Cotton Dress

ha·di·· ·e· (Lamphere) "clothing that goes all the way down"; "one-piece cloth" (CC)

Ramah

In the inventory of each of the three households studied by Roberts were several girl's dresses. These were apparently less common than the blouse and skirt. Although women's clothing was available at the trading stores, it was usually altered to fit at home (Roberts, 1951:17, 47). Other data were not obtained, presumably because the trait is of modern introduction.

Hill (Central and West)

C (Chinle) described a cotton dress of a pattern similar to the first type of buckskin dress (see Trait 161) except that it had a V neck. He said that this type of dress was worn by the women while they were at Fort Sumner. SG (Keams Canyon) also stated that cotton dresses were made.

Lamphere (East)

PM said that the word for cotton dress meant "clothing that goes all the way down."

Comparative

About 1877, one woman in the vicinity of Fort Wingate was wearing calico, or some approximation to the dress of white women, according to Shufeldt (1893:280). In 1903, Hollister (1903:61–62) stated that "the working dress of a squaw is usually a loose ill-fitting garment of calico reaching to the knees."

169. Shawl

bah do·Xizízí (Ramah, Franciscan Fathers) "about turquoise" (CC); "blue borders"

bi·l łagai (Ramah) "white shawl"

Ramah

A shawl about the size and shape of the modern shawl was woven on the loom. It was black with a blue border in which there were either white stripes

169.a. Woman wearing Pendleton blanket as a shawl; note also her cotton skirt and blouse (Tr. 166, 167) and her shell and turquoise necklace (Tr. 197)

or diamonds. A "white shawl" similar to that described by the Franciscan Fathers (see below) was also made.

The shawl was worn with the *bil* (Trait 164). According to Inf. 7, one would last about four years. Shawls were not inherited; the maker either wore them out or they were buried with the dead or burned at the death of the owner.

Shawls had been seen by Inf. 7, who implied that they ceased to be used about 1900, when commercially made Pendleton blankets became available (Roberts, 1951:47). Inf. 48, who gave most of the data, had only heard of the shawl. If shawls are now woven, they are made for trade; the women wear Pendleton blankets.

Comparative

Since shawls and blankets were apparently synonymous, it is probable that shawls or similar forms date from the middle of the eighteenth century (Hill, 1940a:398).

According to Amsden (1949:98–99, pl. 57), the shawl or "shoulder blanket" was worn by both men and women; that of the woman was always smaller than that of the man. Both were ancient styles, following the Pueblo tradition and certain general rules of proportion, color, and pattern. A woman in one of Möllhausen's drawings dating about 1858 was probably wearing the "white shawl."

The Franciscan Fathers (1910:246) described both types mentioned by Inf. 48 of Ramah. "The shawls were made in a single pattern and used after the manner of a shawl or wrap, much as the men use the blanket." The white shawl "was so called from the alternating white and red color which was woven horizontally in narrow strips throughout." Its border and tassels were blue. The Franciscan Fathers noted that it was "the only woman's garment in which white was used, and was therefore appropriately designated." As of 1910 the shawl and woman's dress were no longer used, although some were made for the market.

Both of Gifford's Navaho informants confirmed the use of a "woman's shawl of woolen material"; the Eastern informant said that "in the olden days" it was woven of mountain sheep wool (Gifford, 1940:37, 129).

For other data on weaving, consult Amsden (1934, or 1949), Reichard (1934), or their bibliographies.

Men's Garments

170. Skin Shirt   ꞌabaníꞌéꞏꞏ (Ramah, Lamphere, Haile)   "deerskin cloth" (CC)

Ramah

Most skin shirts were made of buckskin. Two buckskins were chosen, one for the front end and one for the back; large skins were not used, since the excess material would be wasted. Inf. 7 denied poncho-style shirts made from a single skin; however, he made one for an observer. Shirts could also be made from antelope skins; two were ordinarily enough, but three skins were used to make the best shirts, the third skin for sleeves. No shirts were made

Buckskin shirt, after Tschopik

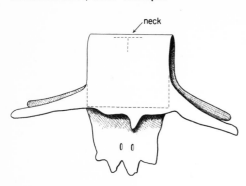

170.1. Buckskin folded for cutting (along dotted lines); sleeve is cut from remaining piece of buckskin

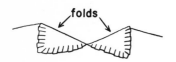

170.2. Folds at neck for lapels

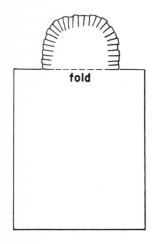

170.3. Back of shirt with fringed flap (skin side out)

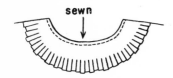

170.4. Back of shirt with collar sewn on (hair side out)

of mountain sheep skin, because of "danger from lightning." Elk skins were regarded as too thick for use.

The buckskins were usually dyed red, yellow, or black (see Traits 141–143). Occasionally skins were left the natural color, but "these get dirty awful quick and you can't clean them off again." After dyeing, skins were buried, dug up and hung to dry, then brushed to remove dirt and excess dye. Before cutting, the worker examined the skins to determine the best place "to fit all around." One man held the skins around his shoulders to measure while another cut down each side, forming two rectangular pieces (see 170.1). The buckskin for the front of the shirt was folded in half, and a mark was made at the center. The worker then cut down the fold for about three and a half inches, making V-shaped lapels from the resulting flaps (see 170.2). Sometimes a sleeveless shirt, but never one with sleeves, was cut open down the front, and tied together over the chest with a pair or series of tie strings. The back piece was sometimes cut to leave a triangular, square, or rounded U-shaped fringed flap at the neck (see 170.3) The flap hung down the back, skin side out. Sometimes a separate piece was used, in which case it was sewn with the hair side out (see 170.4). The front and back pieces were sewn together at the shoulders and beneath the sleeve opening to within four inches of the bottom on each side; buckskin thongs were used in a whip stitch and the seam was turned inside.

Sleeves were made from separate rectangular pieces (with one edge of the long axis untrimmed) cut and folded hair side in. The folded sleeve was measured against the arm opening in the shirt. It was unfolded, and sewn to the shirt; sewing began at the lower back edge. Six holes were made with an awl through the shirt back and sleeve, in that order, and through both pieces at once. The sewing thong was knotted, twisted to a firm point, and inserted through the awl hole. Stitches were not whipped, but paralleled the edges. The material was reversed for each punch, and the thong always followed the direction of the awl. When the sleeve was attached to the shirt, the seam from shoulder to wrist was sewn, also with a running stitch.

Shirts were decorated only with dye and fringe; no fur pendants, beadwork or quillwork were used. A fringe about two inches long was attached to the shoulder seams and down the sides, including the back flap and lapels. It was secured with a running stitch. The bottom was not fringed, except for the lowest four inches of the open sides.

The finished shirt was supposed to be three spans in length and reach to the pubic region. "Longer shirts don't look very good." The back flap extended from one third to halfway down the back.

Men usually made shirts, although Inf. 7 said that his mother had made such shirts for her small sons; Inf. 8 heard that only men made them. They were made in the fall, usually in November, after men went hunting and obtained buckskin (Inf. 8). They could be sewn in the house (Inf. 8).

In the old days, a man had two such shirts. One, described above, he kept for dress occasions. Another, without back flap or fringe, was used for daily wear. Shirts lasted four to five years "if not used too hard" (Inf. 7). According to Inf. 8, however, a good thick buckskin shirt would last about a year (worn daily?). They were stored in a sack hung on the wall in a dry place.

If a man died, soiled or worn shirts were buried with him. A shirt or hat that had never been worn might be given to someone (Inf. 8).

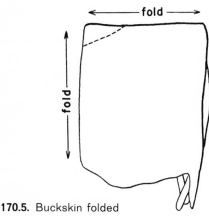

Buckskin shirts (Hill)

170.5. Buckskin folded
for cutting, after SG

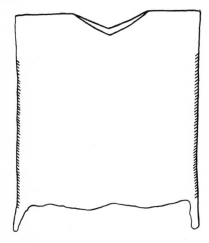

170.6. Sewing side seams, after SG

170.a. Buckskin shirt made by Inf. 7 in 1938

The shirt described above was made by Inf. 7 for Tschopik (see 170.a; it is in the Harvard Peabody Museum). Whether he or anyone else in his generation had made one before 1938 is not known. Inf. 7 said that he could remember seeing his mother and father making such clothing, and he and his younger brothers had worn shirts of this type. Inf. 32 had seen them in use; he said they were worn contemporaneously with woven shirts. According to Inf. 7, buckskin shirts began to disappear "about the time the railroad went through Gallup and stores opened up," in the early 1880's. None are worn today, although older members of the group know how to make them. Cotton, woolen, and silk shirts, and woolen or leather jackets are now purchased.

Hill (East, Central, and West)

According to C (Chinle), women made most of the buckskin garments. Two general types of buckskin shirts were produced. A poncho type, the oldest according to SG (Keams Canyon), was made from a single buckskin. The sides of the skin were squared, the head and sometimes the legs removed. If the legs remained, they were later fringed. The skin was folded head to tail, then side to side, to produce four thicknesses. It was placed on a log and a triangular section was cut out (see 170.5) to form an aperture for the head. Next the sides were sewn; room was left for the insertion of sleeves (see 170.6). The sleeves were cut from another buckskin, fitted, and sewn into the armholes (SG).

The second type of shirt was made from two buckskins, or from three antelope skins or goatskins when buckskin was unavailable. GH (White Cone) described a shirt made from three wildcat skins, one each for the front, back, and sleeves. Surplus from the sleeves was used for gussets under the arms and to enlarge the shirt. Less economically fortunate individuals had to be satisfied with shirts which were pieced together from scraps. One buckskin was placed upon another, the sides trimmed, and the back and front of the shirt cut simultaneously. The head of the animal was always at the top of the shirt (PP, Fort Defiance; MC, Sawmill). A shallow lunar section extending from below the armhole almost to the tail was often removed from each side

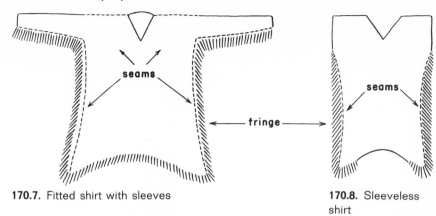

170.7. Fitted shirt with sleeves

170.8. Sleeveless shirt

to give the finished shirt a fitted appearance. If these sections were not removed, the stitching at the sides formed comparable arcs. In this case the selvage was later fringed (WH, Wheatfields; TLLSS, Crownpoint; see 170.7, 170.8).

There were two types of neck opening. Lapels were formed as at Ramah, but a six- or eight-inch cut was made. For a second type, a triangular section was detached from the shirt except at the apex. It formed a tippet and was allowed to hang from this point; its edges were usually fringed.

A lunate section was fully or partially detached from the back half of the garment. When not completely removed, this back tippet was fringed (WH, TLLSS).

According to LM (Canyon del Muerto) and TLLSS, buckskin shirts during the later period were completely open down the front "like coats." They were secured by thongs, later by buttons. "This was in imitation of Spanish and American styles." Hill saw such a coat worn by a Navaho in the 1930's.

The two halves of the shirt were sewn together at the shoulders and along the sides with sinew or with goatskin or buckskin thongs. A simple running stitch was used. Occasionally thongs spaced at intervals replaced the stitching. Seams could be either inside or outside (always on the outside, PP), although outside ones were the most common (SG, TLLSS, C; SC, Crystal).

Sleeves were usually added to the shirt. These were cut from a folded buckskin and tapered toward the wrist (SG, TLLSS, C). If the sleeve was not tapered in cutting, the seam tapered and the selvage was fringed (PP; see 170.8).

Most shirts carried ornamentation other than tippets. Customarily the tails were fringed, and fringed sections of buckskin were inserted in the side seams, around the armholes, and in the underseams of the sleeves. These fringes were said "to stiffen the garment." According to PP, strips of bayeta, sometimes studded with buttons, might be substituted for the fringes at the armholes. Fringed tippets (or tippets with holes punched in them, PP) were often appended in front and back at the neck of shirts which lacked them. More rarely, buckskin collars or yokes were sewn on the shirt (SG, TLLSS, C, PP, SC). On the wildcat skin shirt described by GH, the head skin at the rear of the shirt was removed, that in front allowed to hang for ornament.

Such garments were designed for winter use and were worn with the hair inside. Shirts with plain collars and cuffs were reported by PP. Shirts were often dyed yellow; less frequently they were dyed red (PP, C) or black (PP), or left natural (C).

According to WH, TLLSS, LM, and SC, buckskin shirts were common at the time of Fort Sumner although the last two informants said that the majority were made from sheepskins and goatskins. SG reported that some Navaho wore them after the return from Fort Sumner and MM (Lukachukai) remembered them as a child.

Lamphere (East)
EP and her mother confirmed the term for buckskin shirt.

Comparative
Buckskin shirts were common among the Navaho in the middle of the nineteenth century, and were noted by a number of observers, the earliest of whom seems to have been Pattie in 1827. He said that the Navaho wore buckskin shirts, belts, and moccasins, clothing similar to that of the Mescalero Apache save that the Navaho skins were better dressed (Pattie, 1905:164, 165). Bartlett (1854:329) also commented upon the similarity of Navaho and Apache dress, and Palmer (1869:67) noted that ordinary men's dress consisted of a deerskin hunting shirt or doublet or a blanket confined at the waist by a belt.

The only archaeological evidence for the buckskin shirt came from a single burial in Chaco Canyon presumably dating from the early nineteenth century. What may have been a shirt consisted of a large piece of buffalo hide placed next to the body. On one side were traces of cutting, possibly for a sleeve, and a U-shaped piece had been removed for the neck. Two rectangular pieces of buffalo hide (2 ft. by 1 ft.) were also found associated with the burial (Malcolm, 1939:16–17). Woodward (1938:9) believed that the Navaho adopted the short cloth or leather jackets from the Spaniards, copying Spanish costume of the eighteenth and early nineteenth centuries.

The types described in the literature are not unlike those mentioned by Ramah informants. The Franciscan Fathers (1910:457–458) illustrated a type of shirt which they believed was derived from the Pueblos; it was fringed along the front, shoulders, sleeves, sides, and lower edge. Thongs, later brass buttons obtained from the Utes, fastened the front. Shirts were dyed red, yellow, or left natural. Another open-front shirt was noted by Cremony (1868:305). Informants of Sapir and Hoijer described sleeved garments made of dressed skins which were stitched on both sides. Men also wore a poncho made by cutting a hole in the center of a deerskin, the sides of which were tied at several places (1942:413, 79).

Shirts in museum collections illustrate Hill's second type. A shirt in the American Museum of Natural History is fringed on the bottom, under the sleeves, and around the armholes. It has a Y-shaped tippet outlining the neck in front and a roughly triangular one in back; a deer tail is appended by a thong to each. A pocket is sewn on the lower left front of the shirt. Tippets and fringes are also illustrated in a photograph in the United States National Museum of a Navaho sub-chief (see Plate XI), allegedly taken prior to 1877.

Clothing   **XI.** Cabra Negra, a captain and sub-chief (prior to 1877). He is wearing a cloth headband (Tr. 183) and a fringed buckskin shirt with tippet (Tr. 170), which is decorated with appliqué ornaments of either bead or cloth. Note also the cotton trousers, slashed on the sides (Tr. 175), "middle part" type leggings (Tr. 177), and moccasins (Tr. 189). A quiver (Tr. 23) is by his feet.

170.b. Squirrel skin shirt

His shirt is decorated with beadwork and may be of Plains origin. In the United States National Museum is a squirrel skin shirt (see 170.b) collected by Dr. E. Palmer in New Mexico. It was presumably made for a child. Fourteen squirrel skins (*Sciurus Aberti*) were used in the body of the shirt; six in front, six in back, and one inserted under each arm.

Gifford's Navaho informants stated that men wore fringed, long-sleeved, buckskin shirts. The Western informant said that these were tied together at the neck opening and were sometimes open down the front; a design was sometimes painted on the shirt. The Eastern informant denied the open front and neck tie and said that shirts were sometimes decorated with porcupine quills. Gifford questioned his statements about the painting of shirts (Gifford, 1940:37).

The time of the disappearance of the buckskin shirt is obscure. Mid-nineteenth-century travelers such as Letherman and Davis did not mention it in their descriptions of Navaho clothing (Letherman, 1856:290; Davis, 1857:411–412), but other observers (for example, Pattie, Bartlett, and Palmer) did. If this was a period of transition, the change was probably complete within a few years; for among the eight Navaho met by the Powell expedition in the early 1870's, not one wore a buckskin shirt or jacket (Dellenbaugh, n.d.:170). The pre-1877 photograph in the National Museum is obviously posed and cannot be accepted as conclusive evidence for the ordinary use of buckskin shirts at that time. In 1881, when Bourke described the costume of the Navaho around Fort Defiance, he mentioned only cloth shirts and jackets (Bourke, 1936:223–224). By 1910 the Franciscan Fathers did not include it as part of the daily costume (Franciscan Fathers, 1910:465).

Mrs. Wetherill described a Navaho shirt of buckskin or mountain sheep, fringed around the armholes and painted in front and in back. The shirt was decorated with two squares of antelope skin or buckskin. She also mentioned a shirt made from prairie dog skins (Wetherill, n.d.:2 pp.).

171. Woven Shirt

ʼéˑˑ (Ramah, Haile) shirt; "cloth on" (CC)

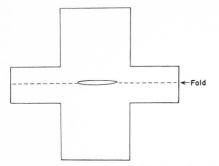

171.1. Woven shirt (Tschopik), after Inf. 16

Ramah

According to Inf. 32, a rectangular piece of material was woven, with a V-shaped slit left for the neck. The piece was usually blue, with red stripes across the bottom; however, some material was figured all over with small yellow geometric designs. It was folded and stitched down the sides under each arm; wrist-length sleeves of red cloth were attached to the body of the shirt. This garment was ordinarily waist length.

A similar shirt, also made in poncho style, was woven with sleeves attached (Inf. 16; see 171.1). It was black with no contrasting stripes or figures and it was sewn down the sides, but the sleeves were left open. It was tied at the waist. Both shirts lacked tassels and were apparently undecorated.

Women made these shirts but did not wear them. Men and boys wore them with short buckskin pants, in place of the buckskin shirt. The shirts were not well known. Inf. 7 had heard of the shirt described by Inf. 32 but he had never seen one, and he denied the black shirt described by Inf. 16. The latter denied the blue and red striped one.

Infs. 32 and 16 agreed that the shirts had been in use before the Navaho were taken to Fort Sumner. As far as is known, no one in the Ramah community today has made such articles, nor are any preserved as heirlooms. Only the very old have seen or heard of them.

Hill (Central)

The back and front of the shirt were woven separately and sewn together. Allowance was made for a round or V-neck during the weaving. When the material was removed from the loom, the warp threads in the neck area were cut and tied. These shirts were sleeveless and hip length (LW, MM, Lukachukai; WH, Wheatfields).

According to PP (Fort Defiance), shirts of this type were knitted, not woven; they were knitted in one piece and openings were left for the neck and sleeves. The sleeves were knitted separately and sewn into place. Occasionally ribbons were suspended from the shoulders.

Shirts were usually woven of wool dyed indigo, although sometimes alternating two-inch stripes of blue, black, and red were woven into the garment (LW). WH denied that such clothing was dyed.

Shirts of this type were never too prevalent. According to WH and PP, a few were being worn by the men about the time of Fort Sumner. LW remembered seeing one worn when she was a girl.

Comparative

The woven shirt is probably a development of the late eighteenth or early nineteenth century. There is no mention of it in the Rabal documents, which cover the first part of the eighteenth century. Most witnesses stated that the Navaho were dressed in buckskin (Hill, 1940a:412, 398).

A burial dated by Amsden at about 1800 provided the first evidence for the woven shirt; the mummified body of a man clothed in a woven shirt was found in a cave cist (Amsden, 1949:pl. 63). Later, observers said that Navaho men wore woven shirts. Letherman (1856:290) described a poncho or small blanket or piece of red baize that extended below the small of the back. The sides were partially sewn together, and the sleeves were formed of strips of red cloth attached at the shoulders. Davis (1857:411–412) described a similar garment, which he said was woven in light colors, open at the sides, and fastened at the waist with a belt. These observations confirmed statements that woven shirts came into use before the Fort Sumner period. By that time, however, the wealthy might wear ready-made coats and trousers, and the "middle class" frequently wore shirts and knee-length breeches of unbleached cotton. Simpson (1850:101) described Mariano, the chief, as dressed in "a sky-blue blanket great coat—apparently of American manufacture."

The Franciscan Fathers (1910:458, 248) described two types of woven shirts worn by men, both of which confirmed the types described at Ramah. A tassel at each corner decorated the black, poncho-like shirt. This garment was generally worn as an overcoat over the ordinary wool or calico shirt. The Franciscan Fathers believed that both types were originally borrowed from the Pueblo Indians. Amsden's description (1949:98) was substantially the same as that of the Franciscan Fathers. Gifford's Navaho informants were not asked about the woven shirt. The Western informant confirmed a poncho worn as an outer garment; the Eastern informant, however, denied it (Gifford, 1940:37).

It is doubtful that the blanket shirt survived long after the return from Fort Sumner. Neither Dellenbaugh (n.d.:170) nor Bourke (1936:223–224) mentioned it in his descriptions of Navaho clothing. But some old men were still wearing this type of shirt after the captivity: Louis Watchman remembered that Chief Barboncito and Cayetano, when they came in to Fort Defiance for supplies, wore such shirts, and his own grandfather was buried in one (Coolidge, 1930:99). The Franciscan Fathers stated that the blue shirt was no longer woven in 1910. The black poncho-like shirt had disappeared recently, but entirely by 1910 (Franciscan Fathers, 1910:247, 458; see also James, 1914:119, for a photograph of one from the Hubbell collection, pl. 140).

172. Cotton Shirt ʼeʼ deʒi (Lamphere) "cloth top" (CC)

Hill (Central)
Cotton shirts (see 156.a) patterned after buckskin ones were reported by C (Chinle) and PP (Fort Defiance). According to PP, these were made and worn for the first time while the Navaho were at Fort Sumner. They were worn only by men.

Lamphere (East)
PM said that the same word was used for the man's cotton shirt and the woman's blouse. It meant "shirt (or clothing) top."

Comparative
Neither of Gifford's Navaho informants was questioned about the cotton shirt (Gifford, 1940:38). The Franciscan Fathers (1910:464) stated only that the Navaho wore "a short shirt of bright-colored calico" in 1910. It was the typical costume.

173. Breechclout   ƛ̓eˑscoˑz (Ramah, Haile)

Ramah

The breechclout was made from a strip of buckskin or cloth about one foot wide and three feet long. It was not ornamented nor were the ends fringed. Each man made his own (Inf. 8) whenever one wore out; it could be made at any place.

The material was passed between the legs and over a belt so that the ends draped down in front and in back. The breechclout was worn with short trousers (Inf. 16) or with long leggings (Inf. 7). Infs. 7 and 8 said only men wore this garment, but Inf. 3 said that women and children also did. One woman (Inf. 32) has worn a buckskin undergarment in recent years, but it is not known whether this was a breechclout. Children began wearing one any time after the age of four years. Inf. 12 said that immature boys would wear the breechclout at ceremonials. According to Inf. 8, "in the old days" it was worn night and day and washed when it became dirty. He said breechclouts lasted a long time.

The breechclout is still worn by male patients in the ceremonials of the Shooting Way, and it is usually worn by the older men during sweat baths. That worn by Inf. 12 at his chant in 1940 was of white cloth held by a string belt. Inf. 7 said that only the cloth variety is used now, and it "for singing only." According to Inf. 45, Mr. Loincloth (Inf. 33's father-in-law) was the last to utilize the breechclout for daily wear and was thereby conspicuous in his dress. His was quite long, the front flap falling half way to the knees, the rear flap slightly shorter. Undergarments are now normally purchased at the stores (Roberts, 1951:17, other observers).

Hill (Central and West)

Breechclouts were made of carefully dressed buckskin (SC, Crystal; C, Chinle; WH, Wheatfields; SG, Keams Canyon), later of goatskin (PP, Fort Defiance). WH had seen one or two woven breechclouts, but they were uncommon. Breechclouts were not ornamented and, as at Ramah, were held in place by a belt, the ends hanging free. The front flap was the larger (C). According to SG, when men wore a breechclout they did not wear trousers.

Comparative

Earliest accounts of the breechclout date from the 1850's, but they did not designate the materials used. Enroute to Canyon de Chelly, Simpson saw a Navaho clothed only in a breechclout (Simpson, 1850:88; Letherman, 1856:290). Bourke reported that by the 1880's the breechclout was of "white calico, reaching to the mid thigh in front and about the same distance in back." For dances, this breechclout was replaced by a waist and hip band of black velvet or corduroy (Bourke, 1936:223).

By 1910, the breechclout was of goat hide or ordinary cloth, materials which replaced the earlier buckskin. At this time it was said to be "worn continuously by men" (Franciscan Fathers, 1910:460). In a photograph taken about 1914, S. J. Guernsey was shown with a Navaho wearing a breechclout and cotton trousers.

Both of Gifford's Navaho informants said that buckskin breechclouts were worn. The Western informant said that the ends formed two aprons, which the Eastern informant denied. The Eastern informant said that breechclouts were formerly made of woven juniper bark or grass (denied by the Western informant), or of shredded bark, or of woven rabbit skin. He said also that women sometimes wore a breechclout if they wore no skirt. In modern times, cloth has replaced the buckskin for breechclouts (Eastern informant; Gifford, 1940:39, 130).

At present, patients and other participants of Male Shooting Ways wear the breechclouts (Wyman, 1936a:642; later observations). It is often, but not always, worn by men taking sweat baths (Page, 1937b:19; Leighton, 1941c:20–21). Adair noted in 1938 that in the Pine Springs area breechclouts were made from sugar and flour sacks (Adair, personal communication).

Mrs. Wetherill described breechclouts of rabbit and rat skins, and of gopher skins. She said the costume worn by warriors consisted of a loincloth, sandals or moccasins, and a cap of deerskin. Other loincloths were made of wildcat skin, or of yucca cloth or buckskin (Wetherill, n.d.:2 pp).

174. Buckskin Short Trousers

λa·ǯi·é·· (Ramah, Lamphere, Haile) "bottom cloth" (CC)

Ramah

Short trousers were cut from two pieces of buckskin, which was usually dyed red, black, or yellow. The only seam was down the outside of the leg; it terminated in a short fringe. The trousers were secured at the waist by a drawstring which tied in front. These trousers extended to the knees (see 174.1).

Short trousers were worn by men with a breechclout, leggings (see Traits 176–178), and a buckskin shirt. The color of the trousers did not necessarily correspond to that of the shirt.

These were described by Inf. 16, but it is not known whether he ever wore or saw them. Inf. 8 was told about the short trousers by an old man. Inf. 7 denied that these were worn; he confirmed only the long leggings (see Trait 177).

Hill (East, Central, and West)

According to informants (C, Chinle; PP, Fort Defiance; MH, Head Springs), short, knee-length buckskin trousers were worn until about the time of Fort Sumner. These were made in the same manner as cotton trousers (see Trait 175). Full-length buckskin trousers of this type were reported by TLLSS (Crownpoint) and MH.

Lamphere (East)

EP and her mother confirmed the term for buckskin short trousers.

Comparative

References in the literature may have confused short and long trousers, and leggings. It is possible that the Navaho were wearing buckskin trousers in the early eighteenth century, for deponents of the Rabal documents mentioned buckskin clothing (Hill, 1940a:398). Woodward (1938:9) noted that Navaho trousers resembled types worn by the Spaniards of the eighteenth and early nineteenth centuries, a statement which strengthens this possibility.

174.1. Buckskin short trousers (Tschopik), after Inf. 16

Many of the nineteenth-century observers indicated that short trousers were common. An article appearing in 1824 noted that Navaho men dressed "in small clothes, sometimes of deer skin, tanned and handsomely colored" (*Missouri Intelligencer,* April 3, 1824, p. 3, quoted in Woodward, 1938). Letherman (1856:289–290) said that the men wore short breeches of brownish-colored buckskin or cloth. They buttoned at the knee and were worn with leggings. Skin breeches which extended to the knee were also mentioned by Davis (1857:411–412).

During the Fort Sumner period, short trousers were still worn, "sometimes ornamented up to the seams with pieces of silver or porcupine quills" (Palmer, 1869:46, 47). They were still seen in 1880, although Bourke reported that they were not decorated with porcupine quills, elk teeth, or much beadwork (Bourke, 1936:233).

By 1910, buckskin pants were rare. The Franciscan Fathers (1910:459) illustrated a pair which differed in several respects from those described at Ramah. These trousers were seamed on the inner leg and buttoned down the front, along the outer seam of the leg, and at the hip. There were no fringes. Informants said that seven days were required to finish a pair, for which reason they were rarely made. The Franciscan Fathers stated that long buckskin pants, decorated with fringes, were occasionally worn. The Navaho terms used for these garments confirmed those used at Ramah. That they disappeared at about this time was also indicated by the statement of one of Sapir's informants in 1929. He said that he could barely remember seeing men dressed in trousers of goatskin or very thin deer hide (Sapir and Hoijer, 1942:331).

Sapir and Hoijer (1942:79) recorded a mythological account of this article. The hero was dressed in a loincloth, and was thinking about making trousers. "So then, having sewn the deer skin up on both sides, he put one leg in one side, (the other) in the other side, and, with a string, he tied (the hide) around his waist."

175. Cloth Trousers

X̱aˑ ǯiˑé nakaˑigí (Ramah, Lamphere, Haile)   "bottom cloth pants, cotton" (CC)

Ramah

Cloth trousers extended either to the knee, in which case they were seamed all the way down the outside of the leg, or below the knee, in which case the last few inches were left open. They buttoned down the front and were tied at the waist with strings. Such trousers had no pockets and were undecorated; even silver buttons were absent.

Men made these if they knew how (Inf. 8); otherwise women might do so. They were worn by men. According to Inf. 7, boys began wearing them as soon as they started walking, but Inf. 8 said that boys were eight years old or so when they began to wear them.

If they were made of good material, these trousers would last about a year. Storage was no problem, for they were worn every day except when being washed or mended.

These trousers replaced the buckskin ones. According to Inf. 7, they were originally from the Spanish-Americans and were already in use before the

Fort Sumner period. Kluckhohn saw only three Ramah men (Infs. 2, 3, 265) wearing these trousers. It is possible that they are still worn by some as undergarments, but it is probable that they have generally been displaced by other garments adopted from the Americans or Spanish-Americans.

Hill (Central)

The trouser legs were cut separately. A rectangular section of material of proper length was folded, and a triangular piece was cut from one end of the folded edge of each leg (see 175.1). These two triangular sections were sewn together along their bases; the resulting diamond formed the crotch area of the trousers (see 175.2). A medial cut was made in the front of the diamond, slightly more than half the length. This cut facilitated getting in and out of the garment and was a convenience in urinating.

Trouser seams ran down the outside of the legs to within eight to twelve inches of the bottom. A piece of material was folded and sewn over the upper edge of the trousers to form a belt; the ends were tied in front to secure the garment. A breechclout was always worn with this garment.

Trousers were occasionally of double thickness. Materials with contrasting prints were utilized. This practice enabled the wearer to vary the outward design by reversing the garment (C, Chinle).

According to C, LM (Canyon del Muerto), and PP (Fort Defiance), the Navaho began wearing this type of trousers while at Fort Sumner; SC (Crystal) mentioned 1880 as the date of their introduction. A photograph in the United States Museum (see Plate XI), taken prior to 1877, illustrates this garment. LM was still wearing this type in 1933 and Hill noted several other cases of percale trousers worn as underclothing by older men.

Lamphere (East)

PM said that the first part of the term given above (*tlazhi ee*) is the general term for pants.

Comparative

Cotton trousers were known to be used among the Navaho before Fort Sumner. A Möllhausen print from 1853–1854 depicted a mounted Navaho warrior in what appeared to be cloth trousers bound just below the knee (Whipple *et al.,* 1855:pl. 22). A later work (1858) by the same artist showed two Navaho men, one with short trousers, the other with trousers which extended half way between the knee and ankle (Ives, 1861:pl. 7). Letherman (1856:290–291) also described trousers of "red flannel, buttoned at the knee."

By the early 1870's cloth trousers were common, and all of the eight Navaho men observed by the Powell party wore knee-length "wide flaring breeches" of muslin (Dellenbaugh, n.d.:170). A picture taken in 1869 of Navaho men from Fort Sumner showed all of them in cloth trousers, most of which were long and full (Bell, 1869:147). In 1881, the Navaho around Fort Defiance wore trousers "of colored calico made loose and split open from knee downward (*on outside*)" (Bourke, 1936:223; see also Bourke, 1884:pl. 8, a Navaho boy wearing cotton trousers). Welsh (1885:13) mentioned calico trousers, and a photograph taken by Shufeldt (1889:pl. 23) showed long trousers split on the bottom of the outside seam.

The Franciscan Fathers (1910:465) implied that these were the common

175.a. Man wearing cotton trousers; note also his cotton (velveteen) shirt (Tr. 172), headband (Tr. 183), necklace (Tr. 197), concho belt (Tr. 180), and pouch for personal equipment (Tr. 195)

Cloth trousers, after Hill

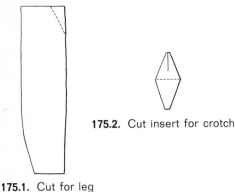

175.2. Cut insert for crotch

175.1. Cut for leg

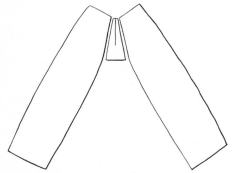

175.3. Pieces in position for sewing

garment or "undergarment" in 1910, and Woodward (1938:9) also confirmed the latter use. In 1914, Kidder and Guernsey observed a group of Navaho men, some wearing trousers with very wide stripes, probably of awning cloth. The sides of these garments were slit to the knees (Guernsey, 1914:n.p.).

176. Bark Leggings

ƛoh yisłé (Ramah, Haile)   "grass socks" (CC)

Ramah

Infs. 7 and 16 both denied the existence of leggings made from yucca (or bark). They had never heard of them.

Hill (West)

Woven leggings were made of juniper bark, according to GH (White Cone). The warp elements consisted of bundles of bark placed side by side; the weft was yucca fiber. Twined technique was employed. The fabricator measured for width and length as the work progressed. When the leggings were worn, the lower portions overlapped the sandals. These leggings were often lined with cliff rose bark to insure additional warmth.

Comparative

The Franciscan Fathers noted that by 1910 the "frail yucca leggings" had been displaced by those of buckskin, later of wool. The leggings were not described (Franciscan Fathers, 1910:460). Sapir and Hoijer (1942:79) confirmed the tradition that early leggings were of woven fiber, later of buckskin.

177. Buckskin Leggings

yisłé· bita xóló· (Ramah)   buckskin leggings, with wings; "socks, its wing is there" (CC)

yisłé· ·ałni·xa·nil (Ramah, Haile)   buckskin leggings, middle part; "socks, middle waist" (CC)

xadi·lži·í (Ramah, Haile)   long pants; "whole thing, all together garment" (CC)

Ramah

To make "leggings with wings," two rectangles were cut from buckskin, each notched in one corner. Each piece was folded across the base of the notch, forming a flap which was fringed for ornament. Sometimes a long flap was cut, or a triangular rather than a rectangular one. Leggings were sometimes dyed red according to Inf. 7.

Leggings of the second type, "middle part," were rectangular without flaps, and were so called only if the skin from which they were cut was from the central or most valued section of the buckskin (see 177.1). They were about eighteen inches long and about as wide. These were not fringed, but were often ornamented with a row of silver buttons (see Plate X). A pair made by Inf. 7 for Tschopik in 1938 were of red-dyed buckskin (see 177.a and 177.b). This type was worn with the breechclout and, according to Infs. 7 and 45, extended from the knee to the ankle. Storage was no problem, for these were worn every day (Inf. 7).

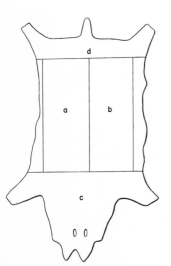

177.1. Cutting up a buckskin for leggings and moccasins, after Tschopik; *a* and *b*, leggings; *c*, moccasins; *d*, scrap

Hip-length leggings were also made, of natural, red, or according to Inf. 32, yellow buckskin. These extended from the hip to the ankle and were secured by a thong to a belt. A thong under the instep prevented creeping up. The only seam was on the outside of the leg; it was fringed, but other ornamentation, including silver buttons, was lacking. These leggings were worn for festive occasions and were called "dress clothes." They were worn with other leggings (Inf. 32).

Buckskin leggings were made by men. "Women don't know how to make them. They could make them if you teach them how" (Inf. 7). Inf. 7 made a pair of "middle part" leggings for Tschopik, and in 1947 was thinking of making another pair for himself.

Leggings were said to last four or five years (Inf. 7). They were worn as needed, or saved for ceremonial occasions.

According to Inf. 7, buckskin leggings existed at a time when the people were still "below the earth . . . The buckskin leggings were worn by the people who made turquoise basket—before there were any Navaho people. There is a song for the leggings." He denied the existence of leggings of fur or vegetable fiber, and ornamentation of beads, quills, hair, or scalps. According to Inf. 16, hip-length leggings were obtained from the Utes; Inf. 2 said that they were made by the Navaho.

The buckskin legging, mentioned in Navaho mythology, still survives, albeit rarely, among some of the older Ramah people. Inf. 7 said that hip-length leggings were worn only rarely after the Fort Sumner period, but in 1947 he believed that the short ones were still worn by some of the older men.

Hill (East, Central, and West)

Descriptions of knee-length "leggings with wings" coincided with those from Ramah except that no mention was made of the triangular flap. A flap extending the full length of the legging was sometimes cut if there was sufficient buckskin. If the available buckskin was limited in size, however, the flap might consist of a separate section sewn to the legging proper. The flap was wrapped about the upper part of the leg. Leggings were formerly secured at the top by a buckskin thong, later by a woven garter (C, Chinle).

177.a. Inf. 7 using an awl to make leggings

177.b. Buckskin leggings made by Inf. 7

Buckskin leggings, after Hill

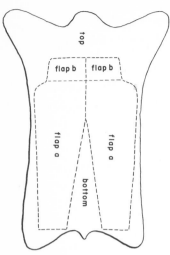

177.2. Pattern for cutting buckskin

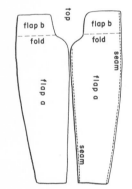

177.3. Seaming buckskin

Leggings of the type called "middle part" consisted of a rectangular section of buckskin wide enough to overlap the leg about three inches. The overlap might be worn either on the outside or inside of the leg. A thong under the instep prevented creeping up. Thongs, and later silver buttons, secured the legging along the outside of the leg. The top was held in place with a woven garter (C; PP, Fort Defiance). These leggings extended from just below the knee to the top of the moccasins (C).

Thigh-length leggings were also made. These tapered toward the bottom and were sewn or secured with buckskin thongs along the outside of the leg. They were fastened to a belt by a thong at the hip (PP). According to PP, earliest forms were without fringes. Later, fringes were added along the outside seams, to be replaced at a still later date by silver ornaments. TLLSS, (Crownpoint) described leggings of this type made from sheepskin. These were worn over trousers for additional warmth.

C described a variant of those above. According to him, one buckskin was laid upon another and four leg pieces cut (see 177.2). After cutting, the sections were reversed, left to right (see 177.3), and sewn. The reversal left room for the passage of the breechclout between the legs. This type was always fringed, and like that above, secured to the belt at the hip.

Short knee-length leggings were made by "poor men" who lacked sufficient buckskin for longer types and were forced to make this type. These were described by C and PP.

According to SC (Crystal) and SG (Keams Canyon), leggings disappeared from general use shortly after the return from Fort Sumner.

Comparative

There were many references to buckskin leggings in the literature, but the data did not always differentiate among the types described by modern informants.

The earliest reference appears to be that of Robinson; in 1846 he saw Navaho wearing deerskin leggings. Women apparently wore wrapped or "bandaged" leggings (Robinson, 1932:51). In 1849 Simpson noted that both men and women wore buckskin leggings in the Canyon de Chelly area (Simpson, 1850:88, 101). Palmer (1869:46) also noted that women wore wrapped leggings, which were wound around the legs several times, giving the leg a large and cumbersome appearance. These were fastened to the moccasins. Undoubtedly Robinson, Simpson, and Palmer were referring to the Pueblo type of woman's moccasin described on pages 284, 286, and 288. Letherman (1856:290–291) noted that men wore leggings of brownish-colored buckskin, and Cremony (1868:305) described a Navaho "dandy" who wore "highly ornamented" leggings. In the literature of the next thirty years there were repeated references to dyed buckskin leggings supported by woven woolen garters (Dellenbaugh, n.d.:170; Bourke, 1936:82; Stephen, 1893:355; Dyk, 1938:250; Bourke, 1884:pls. 7–8).

The Franciscan Fathers (1910:460) noted that buckskin leggings were wrapped about the leg and secured with a buckskin legging cord. This cord was eventually replaced by the wool garter, and the fringes along the edge of the legging disappeared. A legging wrap to supplement the moccasin on journeys or festive occasions was also described. It consisted of a buckskin "wound in regular folds around the lower leg, from ankle to knee," where it was secured by pieces of buckskin (Franciscan Fathers, 1910:465–466).

Gifford's Navaho informants agreed that buckskin leggings were worn by men only. The Western informant said that they were knee length, the Eastern that they were hip length, fringed, and sometimes "winged." They tied at the bottom with a cord passing under the foot. Both groups confirmed the calf wrapping, but said that it was a modern trait (Gifford, 1940:39, 131).

Woodward (1938:9) believed that the Navaho adopted knee-length wraparound leather leggings from the Spaniards, copying Spanish costume of the eighteenth and early nineteenth centuries. If this is true, it would be the earliest date for that type among the Navaho.

That the legging, whatever its origin, was in use by the early part of the nineteenth century is attested by a Navaho burial of this period. The body was dressed in deerskin leggings fastened with woven garters (Amsden, 1949:pl. 63).

178. Knitted Leggings

yisⱡé· do·ⱡiž (Ramah, Haile)   "socks, blue" (CC)

Ramah

Wool leggings were knitted without a seam, but two raised lines were knitted along the outside of the leg, to indicate the right from left. Four ridges were knitted about the top, two at the bottom. These leggings had no feet; a band under the instep kept them in place. According to Inf. 32, they were sometimes knitted with feet; she spoke of them as socks.

Leggings were usually dark blue (Infs. 7, 32) without designs, or black (Inf. 7). Inf. 32 said they were sometimes white; but Inf. 7 said that they were never white, although they might be knitted of white wool and then dyed.

Either men or women might make leggings (Inf. 7); Inf. 32 had done so. They were made throughout the year.

Knitted leggings were worn daily rather than reserved for dress occasions. They were worn inside moccasins and were tied at the top with a woven garter; if too long, they were folded over. They might be worn with or without buckskin leggings. According to Inf. 7, both men and women wore leggings, but Inf. 192 said that only men wore them. Blue leggings were worn by individuals of both sexes (Inf. 7). Women sometimes wore black ones but men never did (Inf. 7).

Inf. 32 said that she stopped making leggings soon after the return from Fort Sumner. There is no information as to whether any other woman now in the Ramah territory made leggings after this period; no leggings are now reported in the Ramah area.

Hill (Central)

Descriptions of manufacture coincided with those from Ramah except that informants (PP, Fort Defiance; C, Chinle) denied that ridges were produced in knitting. According to C, leggings occasionally had feet or, according to PP, the feet were knitted as far as the toes.

C said that the Navaho learned how to make knitted leggings from the Pueblos subsequent to the introduction of sheep. According to PP, however, they were introduced during the sojourn at Fort Sumner.

178.a. Knitted leggings and cap

Comparative

The earliest information on knitted leggings dates from 1857. At this time, Navaho men were wearing "blue stockings that cover the lower half of the leg" (Davis, 1857:411–412). Twelve years later, Palmer (1869:47) noted that men knitted leggings, although the young men considered it to be women's work. Thompson (1871:32) also said that men knitted leggings (see 156.a), adding that a knitted or plaited wool cord was attached under the instep. An example of these was collected by Governor Arny of New Mexico in 1875. Although they were called "riding leggings," they were knitted to cover the feet. They are forty-two inches long, decorated with red and white zigzag designs on a blue background (see 178.a). Bourke in 1881 referred to blue leggings knitted by men (Bourke, 1936:81, 223), and Matthews (1897:21) noted stockings "devoid of heels and toes." Only Hollister (1903:48) stated that these garments were commonly knitted by women.

The Franciscan Fathers (1910:255–256) stated that because leggings were considered part of the male attire, men did most of the knitting. In 1910, "women have begun to wear them only in recent years." Their description confirmed that from Ramah. The ridges at the top and bottom and down the outside of the leg were knitted with left (purl) stitches at the appropriate points. The top rim was said to prevent wear and tear in pulling on the legging, and it provided a hand grip.

Pepper observed a form of stocking made with feet. He stated that according to the trader Lorenzo Hubbell stockings with feet were made by the Isleta Indians and traded to the Navaho, but whether the Navaho also made them is not clear. The colors were white, blue, or black. White ones were commonly worn by old women; men wore the others (Pepper, quoted in Amsden, 1949:108).

Gifford's Western informant said that only men wore the footless stockings; his Eastern Navaho informant said that these were modern and that only men had worn them. Gifford believed that this trait was of Spanish derivation (Gifford, 1940:39).

179. Woven Garters

ʒá·néʒí· (Ramah, Haile)   "leg . . . (length wound around)" (CC)

yisλé λó·ł (Ramah, Haile)   string socks; "socks, string" (CC)

Ramah

Garters were made by weaving narrow red bands on narrow belt looms. No other color was used. These were made by "certain women" (Inf. 7); no more specific data could be obtained. Garters were used by both men and women to secure knitted leggings (Infs. 7, 32). Women probably did not use them (or wear leggings) before the Fort Sumner period (Inf. 192).

These were worn whenever leggings were worn (Inf. 7). Inf. 8 has seen them, and he said that some non-Navaho Indians still wear them. According to Inf. 256, there is an old blind man on the reservation who still wears them. Although they are no longer extant, the technique of their manufacture still exists, insofar as it is similar to that used in weaving belts (see Trait 165 and Plate X).

Hill (Central)

Descriptions of woven garters obtained from informants (IS, MM, LW, Lukachukai; C, Chinle; PP, Fort Defiance) coincided with those from Ramah. According to MM, they were woven on a belt loom or "ring" loom in only two colors blue and black. LW believed the use of this accessory was derived from the Pueblos.

Comparative

There is archaeological evidence for the existence of woven garters at an early date. Skin leggings tied with "woven garters" were found on the body of a Navaho man. Amsden believed that the burial dated from about 1800 (Amsden, 1949:pl. 63).

Nineteenth-century travelers also described woolen garters. Dellenbaugh (n.d.:170) spoke of the group of eight men encountered by the Powell expedition; they wore buckskin leggings "bound at the knee by bright woolen garters." Bourke reported that the men at Fort Defiance in 1881 wore woven red worsted garters with their blue leggings; he also reported that women wore garters to secure their leggings (Bourke, 1936:82, 223, 224). In describing the "modern" costume of the 1890's, Stephen (1893:355) said that the men wore "leggings of dyed deerskin, which are secured with garters woven of thread in fanciful designs." These were two inches wide and four feet long and were worn only by men (Stephen, quoted in James, 1914:133).

According to the Franciscan Fathers, garters were bands about two inches wide and two feet long, in red, black, and blue, although red was the preferred color. They were made either on the regular loom or with the aid of a forked pole. Garters were still in use in 1910, and a small loom was becoming popular for their manufacture (Franciscan Fathers, 1910:249–250, 465).

Gifford's informants did not mention garters (Gifford, 1940:39).

180. Buckskin Belt   sis (Haile)   "belt" (CC)

Ramah

A plain belt was made from dehaired hide; it was undecorated. It knotted in front. Only men made or used this type. Inf. 7 implied that its purpose was to support trousers, but he said that ordinarily men did not wear belts because their trousers tied in front. The belt was worn every day, if at all.

Only Inf. 7 had made a buckskin belt, although Inf. 16 had heard of this type. Both men denied any knowledge of the type described by the Franciscan Fathers (below).

Men now wear, and presumably have worn for decades, either the leather strap type of belt or one ornamented with silver conchos. The concho belt may also be worn by women (see Plates VII, VIII). Both also wear beaded belts, some of which are made by a few Ramah men and women including Inf. 45's daughters, Infs. 4121 and 4117, and their sister. Beading was learned by the school children.

Hill (Central and West)

The most desirable buckskin belt consisted of a strip taken from the center of the hide. Its length varied with the length of the hide. The woman's belt was three finger widths wide and was fringed at the end; the man's belt was narrower and unfringed. Both sexes tied the belt in front and allowed the ends to hang (C, Chinle).

Buckskin belts were used by the men to support trousers, breechclouts, and thigh-length leggings (C; SG, Keams Canyon; GH, White Cone; PP, Fort Defiance). Women wore the belts to gather in and secure the dress at the waist (C).

Comparative

Both of Gifford's Navaho informants mentioned a buckskin belt, which the Western informant said was a girdle worn only by men to hold the breechclout (Gifford, 1940:38, 130).

The Franciscan Fathers (1910:459–460) described a type of belt denied by Ramah informants. It consisted of two pieces of buckskin sewn together "so as to leave an opening in which to carry flint, medicine, tobacco, and such trifles." Both seams were fringed. It was fastened with thongs at the ends and was worn with the short trousers (see 180.1).

The buckskin belt had disappeared from general use by 1910, and was replaced by the cartridge belt or the concho belt (Franciscan Fathers, 1910: 459–460). The latter, according to Navaho quoted by Woodward, were first acquired through trade with the Utes. The first concho belt manufactured by a Navaho was made in 1868 or 1869 in the Fort Defiance area. It was produced by a man who learned silversmithing from the Spanish-Americans near Santa Fe (Woodward, 1938:61, 63, 66, 67).

Earliest accounts by observers date from 1855; except possibly for Palmer, they described the concho belt. In the Fort Defiance area Letherman (1856: 290) described such a belt, and Davis (1857:411) agreed that this was part of the costume "when the wearer can afford it." Palmer (1869:67, 86) said that the ordinary dress of the men was a hunting shirt confined at the waist by a belt which he did not describe. He specified that women's belts were of buckskin, "frequently richly ornamented with silver." Other reports (Dellenbaugh, n.d.:170; Robinson, 1932:43–51) contained no data on belts. In 1881, Bourke reported only the concho belts; they were so common that "the grand prize of the dandy Navajo buck is his belt." This leather belt was completely covered by silver conchos (each 4 in. by 3 in.), each of which contained "from $5 to $6 silver dollars and the workmanship is very striking" (Bourke, 1936:225, 226). Stephen (1893:355) described Navaho belts in terms of large silver conchos "strung upon a strip of leather"; these were worn by both men and women.

Since the mid-nineteenth century, though these belts have continued to be worn by Navaho, they have become increasingly articles made for the trader and subsequent developments have been largely influenced by the tastes of white customers (Adair, 1949:29–33). No description of silverwork will be attempted because of the extensive literature on the subject.

180.1. Buckskin belt, after the Franciscan Fathers

Headwear

181. Hair Tie   ċi·λół (Ramah, Haile)   "hair string" (CC)

ci·γé·ł (Haile)   "hair bundle" (CC)

Ramah

An inch-wide band about eighteen inches long was woven on the narrow loom. Inf. 32 said it was red; Inf. 7 specified red with white designs and green borders, each end having red tassels. Such bands were the only hair ties used in the old days. Buckskin thongs were never used for this purpose.

Cord obtained from the traders was also used. At Inf. 50's home someone was observed wearing a narrow cord made of strings tied tightly near each end and once loosely near the middle. The cord was about two feet long and half an inch thick at the knots. It was red, and shell beads were attached to the ends. Inf. 7 said that white cord was also used for a hair tie.

Women ordinarily made the hair tie at any time or any place where weaving might be done. It was used for tying the hair into a double loop at the back of the head.

The hair was first brushed tightly back with a grass brush (see Trait 90). The brush was grasped stubby end down in the fist, with the little finger down and thumb up. Strokes were made from the forehead back (Bailey, 1942:212). After brushing, the hair was held. The middle of the tie was placed across the hair close to the head, and the ends wound twice about the hair, then held. A person whose hair was being done held the ends of the tie in his hands while the helper brushed his hair, folded it over in a six-inch fold, and then passed the tie around the middle of the fold until only enough remained to tie. Folds above and below were arranged in small fans, and the hair dress was completed.

A person who was doing his own hair first tied the hair near the base of the head. Then, holding the tie in his teeth, he folded his hair back on itself, and finally secured it with the cord.

Both men and women used the same type of hair tie; they began to wear one as soon as their hair was long enough. Designs did not differ according to sex. Women usually had several hair ties, one or two for daily wear, others for special occasions. A well-made hair tie was said to last a year (Inf. 8). When not being worn, hair ties were kept in a bag in the hogan. When a woman died, her hair ties were buried with her.

Both Infs. 7 and 8 have seen woven hair ties in use, but Inf. 8 said that they are not worn by women at the present time. He added that women began to wear plain cord hair ties about 1907. Inf. 7 said that the Navaho began to cut their hair when the Spanish-Americans and Anglos arrived, but that some of the Pueblos still use the woven tie.

Inf. 129 was observed in 1937 wearing a small piece of turquoise in the end of his hair queue. This presumably was a token (*siitlool,* Kluckhohn and Wyman, 1940:38), presented by a singer to a patient on the final day of a chant.

At present, the hair tie is largely restricted to women, for most of the Ramah men have short hair. Women, however, generally continue to do their hair

Clothing   **XII.** Navaho woman brushing the hair of a young girl. The woman on the left wears the hair tie (Tr. 181). She is holding a grass brush (Tr. 90) and dressing the hair of the girl in front of her. Both are wearing cotton skirts (Tr. 166), as is the girl in the background. The two women in the foreground are wearing cotton blouses (Tr. 167). The girl in the background is wearing a velveteen blouse (Tr. 167) and a shell and turquoise necklace (Tr. 197). All three are wearing bracelets (Tr. 200). Note the wagon (Tr. 72) in the background and the hogan (Tr. 107), which is polygonal, probably hexagonal, with an earth-covered, cribwork roof.

in the double loop (see Plate XII); Inf. 50 and the women in Inf. 45's family were observed as they arranged their hair in this fashion. Roberts (1951:48) noted three grass hairbrushes in one of his households and one in another. The women used these as well as plastic combs to dress their hair, "a frequent activity in each household."

Hill (Central and West)

According to IS (Lukachukai), the Navaho formerly used lengths of mountain lion and otter skin for hair cords. C (Chinle) stated that buckskin was used. Later, hair cords were made in the same manner as garters, but were narrower in width; they were woven in alternating blue or black stripes (IS). Recently, according to the same informant, hair cords have been produced from several strands of Germantown yarn knotted together at each end.

Several informants (MH, Head Springs; C; IS, MM, Lukachukai) gave similar accounts of hair dressing, the fullest of which was by IS. The following account is his, unless otherwise designated. Formerly, cutting the hair was forbidden. "The hair was a dark cloud from which the rain came. If they cut off their hair they would cut off the rain. They were told to wear their hair that way and never cut it. The black hair stands for the black sky, the front of the body for the rising sun. When the hair is untied it stands for the falling darkness. The back of the body also stands for the falling darkness. On the right side you hold corn, on the left arrows. That is why we have the wind. These rules were made by the Holy People" (MH).

Women usually dressed the hair for both sexes. If a man was married his wife performed this duty; if not, his mother or sister. "If a girl friend did it, it would be embarrassing for both."

The hair was brushed and the ends folded back on themselves (see 181.1). The distance included in the first fold depended upon the length of the hair. "If you are to come out even you must know the right size of the fold from experience." Folding continued until the club fitted snugly against the back of the head at the desired height.

Next the hair cord was applied. A complete turn was taken around the center of the hair, but one end of the cord was left longer than the other (see 181.2). The short end was held while the hair dresser twisted the long end around the club until only enough remained to tie. The tie was either a square or a double bow knot. Finally the upper and lower portions of the club were spread to achieve the characteristic hour-glass shape (see 181.3).

The size and position of the club on the head varied somewhat with the taste of the wearer. A few Navaho wore their hair in two braids after the manner of the Ute. Otherwise all Navaho effected the style described above, and all informants insisted that this had always been the case. There were no style distinctions on the basis of sex, age, or marital status.

This form of hair dress was known as "hair bundle" (Haile, 1951:145). This was the name given to the mark placed on the "rattle stick" used in the Enemy Way and was the symbol of Changing Woman (IS). According to AS (Lukachukai) the symbol should be drawn as in the figure (see 181.4).

Feathers were never worn in the hair except by patients during a curing ceremony. Men over whom the Navaho or Chiricahua Wind Ways had been performed wore a turquoise bead in their hair as a talisman. Women who had been treated by the same chant wore an abalone shell bead. A combina-

Hair tie (Hill)

181.1. Folding the hair: first step (left) and second step (right)

181.2. Applying the cord, leaving long end for wrapping and short end for tying

181.3. Finished hair tie

181.4. Enemy Way symbol, after AS

tion of turquoise and olivella shell indicated the wearer had undergone the Blessing Way. "These charms were recognized by the Thunder, Wind, Snake Bear, and other Holy People connected with those chants and these protected the wearers" (IS).

Comparative

The earliest reference to the hair tie appears to be that of Letherman (1856:290), who noted that both men and women among the Navaho wore long hair tied up in back. Sick persons and children usually had short hair. Drawings by Möllhausen indicated at least two kinds of clubs in Navaho men's hair dressing in the 1850's (sketches reproduced in Whipple, *et al.,* 1855:pl. 22; Ives, 1861:pl. 7; Amsden, 1949:pl. 57).

The Franciscan Fathers (1910:249, 464) stated that the hair cord was of the same pattern as garters. By 1910, however, it had almost disappeared and had been superseded by "several strands of common twine." A "white woolen cord," to which a bead or two of turquoise or shell was attached, was sometimes worn at that time, but many men wore their hair short. Amsden agreed with the observation concerning the woven pattern and said that sashes, garters, and hair cords differed "mainly in size as determined by their function" (Amsden, 1949:106, pl. 21).

In 1914, while among a group of Navaho near Kayenta, Guernsey observed that "the hair of both men and women is tied with inch wide skeins of woolen string into a kind of a psyche" (Guernsey, 1914:31).

Gifford's Navaho informants agreed that both men and women wore their hair in a club tied with yarn or buckskin. Both informants used a grass brush for hair dressing; the Eastern informant said that a porcupine tail was also used as a hairbrush. The Western informant denied the woven hair tie, and the Eastern informant regarded it as modern (Gifford, 1940:36, 127).

182. Basketry Hat

ḳaiꞏ čah (Ramah, Haile)   "willow hat" (CC)

beꞏčaꞏhaꞏŏi (Ramah)   "shadow of the hat" (CC)

ciꞏzis (Ramah, Haile)   "hair bag" (CC)

Ramah

Willow, young oak, rabbit brush, sumac, and a possible species "which looks more like corn than a tree" (Inf. 267) were used to make basketry hats. A ring of twigs was made, and other flexible twigs were arched over one side to form the crown (Inf. 8). Leaves were left on the twigs, and those forming the crown were woven in checkerboard fashion. Other informants implied that these hats were made of the coiled (rod and bundle) basketry technique and were the shape of gathering baskets.

These were made by women and girls and used to protect their heads from the sun while they herded sheep in hot weather. According to Inf. 8, they were made mostly when goats were being herded, because sheep stay in the shade, but goats do not. These hats might also be used as containers for gathering the fruit of the *Yucca baccata* (Inf. 21). Or women and girls would wear them while traveling from home on foot or horseback. Only Inf. 7 stated

182.a. Wrapped-weave basketry hat

that men might wear them; Inf. 8 said specifically that men and boys did not wear them. They were worn until the twigs dried out and the leaves wilted; they were then replaced by new ones.

A hat of this type was found on the road near Ramah in 1937 (see 182.a). It was so identified by several informants (Infs. 3, 7, 21, 32), all of whom contributed to the data above; Inf. 32 said that she could remember girls wearing these hats when they herded sheep. Other informants in the same area (Infs. 12, 15, 36, 41, 42, 43) denied all knowledge of such hats. Some also denied all knowledge of the technique by which they were made and suggested that they were Chiricahua Apache work; it is possible that the trait was derived from the Chiricahua women who married into the group, and that use and knowledge of its construction was limited to their families. This type of hat was known by certain older informants, but others of almost equal age denied ever having seen it. It cannot have had a community-wide distribution at any period.

Hill (Central)
Basketry hats with hemispherical crowns and brims were woven from sumac; coil technique was employed. A rosette of turkey feathers and two eagle feathers was attached to the crown at the back.

According to the informant (PP, Fort Defiance), the idea of basketry hats was borrowed from the Paiute, and the Navaho secured many through trade with this group. He denied the use of the brimless basketry hat.

Comparative
The only reference to a basketry hat of the type known at Ramah apparently confirms its importation. In the autobiography of the Son of Old Man Hat, the narrator said, "I put on my straw hat . . . We used to get these hats from the Apache [about 1890]" (Dyk, 1938:322).

183. Headband
tˣábạstˣí·n (Ramah, Haile)   "forehead (top of the head) around it is there" (CC)

Ramah
A strip of beaver skin was used as a headband; according to Inf. 7, no other type of fur, buckskin, horsehair, or any form of woven material was used. It was worn at ceremonies as a "dress hat." Inf. 7 had heard of skin headbands but had never seen them. As far as is known, none exists in Ramah today.

Headbands of buckskin or cloth, however, are occasionally used. Inf. 7 was photographed wearing one of cloth, and Infs. 12 and 39 were seen with buckskin thongs tied about their heads; all three men were dressing or working skins (see 177.a). Neither Inf. 12 nor Inf. 39 explained this practice, but Inf. 39 said he always did this when dressing skins. Other men have been seen with a handkerchief bound about the head. A headband is required for male patients at chants; it, however, is called a "kerchief" (*atsii nazti*).

Hill (Central)
Headbands were made from strips of beaver or otter skin, carefully fitted to the wearer's head during the process of manufacture (PP, Fort Defiance;

C, Chinle). According to N (Coalmine), headbands were also made from squirrel and skunk hide. The heads were removed from two cased squirrel skins and the hides were sewn together at the shoulders. The rear sections of the skins were joined so that the tails crossed; the tails were looked upon as ornaments and were allowed to hang down the neck of the wearer. Similar fillets were made from skunk skin. Two hides were necessary; a strip down the back, including the tail, was used from each hide. "There is a treatment to take away the odor that I do not know" (N).

Comparative

According to the Franciscan Fathers (1910:462–464), headbands of beaver, muskrat, and otter skin were highly valued, and often decorated with precious stones. "These were a mark of wealth, while the poorer class were satisfied with buckskin headbands." These were worn only by men. By 1910, kerchiefs or "red silk sashes," often decorated with turquoise and silver, were common; these in turn were being displaced by the "western hat."

Gifford's Navaho informants confirmed the use of headbands by men (see Plate XIV). The Western informant said that these were of buckskin, wildcat, and "tiger"; the Eastern informant that they were of bear or wildcat skin (Gifford, 1940:36, 127).

Cloth headbands (see Plate XI) are known to date from 1849, since they appear in drawings reproduced by Simpson, and he noted that Navaho near Canyon de Chelly ordinarily wore red turbans (Simpson, 1850:88; pls. 44, 49, 50, 52; Whipple, *et al.*, 1855:pl. 22; Ives, 1861:pl. 7). Drawings and photographs of the 1870's and later frequently showed Navaho men wearing cloth headbands (see collection in Harvard Peabody Museum; Underhill, 1953:pls. 82, 86, 102, 106). In the early 1870's, Dellenbaugh met a group of eight Navaho men who were wearing "a piece of red cloth à la turban" (Dellenbaugh, n.d.:170; Dellenbaugh, 1906:318). Thompson observed a Navaho with a "handkerchief wound turban-like around head" (Thompson, 1871:30). In 1914, Guernsey noted that among a group of Navaho near Kayenta, most of the men wore red cloth headbands, but some wore broad-brimmed Stetson hats decorated with feathers (Guernsey, 1914, ms.), decoration which Dellenbaugh noted several decades earlier.

Mrs. Wetherill noted that a headband was made from a small beaver skin with the head still on (Wetherill, n.d.:2 pp.).

184. Buckskin Cap

čah xodolkǫh (Ramah, Haile)   rounded, smooth cap; "cap smooth" (CC)

čah da had cosi· (Ramah)   little pointed cap; "hat pointed little" (CC)

Ramah

Buckskin was the material most often used to make hats; sometimes other materials were utilized to make hats of the same construction as those made from buckskin. See Traits 186 and 187 for detailed data on mountain lion and wildcat skin caps.

To make a "smooth cap," a circular piece with an indentation in one side was cut from buckskin (see 184.1), either natural color or red or yellow, but not black. According to Inf. 7, antelope hide might also be used, but not

Buckskin cap (Tschopik)

184.1. Pattern

184.2. Pattern, showing serrated edge, after Inf. 7

184.3. Securing the feathers

184.4. Tying the rosette

184.5. Finished cap, made in four pieces

184.a. Buckskin cap made by Inf. 7

mountain lion, mountain sheep, or beaver. This piece (the crown) was fitted by measuring the skin against the wearer's head. When the desired size was achieved, the edge was folded, and small triangles were removed with a knife to produce a serrated edge (see 184.2). Decorative holes were cut with the aid of a wooden awl (see Trait 185).

Meanwhile, owl and eagle feathers were prepared; crow, hawk, quail, or other feathers were not used. The quills of the primary wing feathers of the big owl (great horned owl) were split, and the feathers were removed from the shaft with the right hand; the mid-ribs were discarded. The feathers were carefully straightened between the fingers, then buried in damp earth for about two hours. When removed, they were arranged in small bunches (about six half-feathers each), the ends of which were bent around a buckskin thong and lashed with a string (see 184.3). Six such bunches were prepared and then placed together to form a tuft, or, when the ends of the buckskin were tied together, a rosette.

The quills of two eagle feathers were perforated about an inch from their base and strung on two buckskin strips. These were loosely tied to the owl feather rosette to allow the eagle feathers to hang from the center of the tuft. A two-inch square of red-dyed buckskin was perforated at the center, and the thongs holding the tuft were pulled through the hole. Then small perforations were made with an awl along the edges of the square. A buckskin thong laced through these holes tied the rosette (see 184.4).

Although the finished cap was meant to sit on the head, the buckskin crown was fitted to determine the placing of chin straps. Two buckskin thongs, one on each side, were inserted and fastened in slits cut in the crown. Two holes were cut with the knife and awl (as above) in the center of the crown for the attachment of the feathers. The red buckskin at the base of the tuft was fringed with a knife, and the ends of the thongs tied to the feathers were pulled through the holes in the crown and knotted. "The feathers are the main hat. The buckskin just holds the feathers to your head" (Inf. 7; see 184.5).

No hats were made with horns or rawhide visors. Hats, however, might be decorated across the front with silver buttons, abalone shell, or a band of bayeta cloth.

Another cap was also made. For this, four pieces of natural, red, or yellow buckskin were cut and sewn together to form a cap with a slightly pointed top. A tuft of turkey feathers with two eagle feathers suspended from the center (presumably constructed as above) was secured to the top of the cap. A string was attached as a chin strap. None of these hats was decorated with painted designs; Inf. 7 did not know whether or not this type was decorated with bayeta and abalone shell.

Inf. 32 may have been describing a variation of this hat. According to her, buckskin skull caps sewn at the top and back were decorated with a tuft of short feathers on top and bunches hanging down behind the ear on each side and the center of the back. A few additional tufts were sewn on in front.

Although other types of skin caps were mentioned by Ramah informants, none specified the types described by the Franciscan Fathers, and Infs. 7 and 16 denied ever having seen or heard of hats of this description.

Only men made hats. "Women didn't wear them, and they didn't go to war, so they didn't have anything to do with them" (Inf. 7). Whether specialists among the men made hats, however, was not known.

These were worn for war and for dress occasions; Inf. 32 said that the type she described was worn at any time. Dancers in the Night Way formerly wore caps of this type, without the eagle feathers; these were called "enemy feathers" (*naaghee e atsos*) and were required for war. According to Inf. 16, caps without feathers might be worn on ordinary occasions, but Inf. 7 implied that this was not done.

Caps were worn only by adult men. Infs. 7 and 16 denied that clans were distinguished by caps. During a war raid, both the leader and other members of the war party might wear caps, and caps were not differentiated according to the rank of the wearer.

Caps were kept from one occasion to the next and "lasted a long time." When undyed buckskin caps became dirty, they were whitened with applications of white clay.

Information was obtained largely from Tschopik, who witnessed Inf. 7 making a rounded cap in 1938. Inf. 7 described the pointed cap, but he did not say that he had seen one. Infs. 2 and 16 had heard of the buckskin cap; Inf. 12's knowledge was derived from Inf. 7's father.

It is not known that Inf. 7—or any other Ramah person—ever made a cap before he made one for Tschopik. Inf. 7 stated that when he was a boy men wore caps of this type. None is now worn in the Ramah area. Men now wear felt hats, sometimes ornamented with beaded hatbands made in the Ramah area.

Buckskin caps (Hill)

184.6. Pattern for buckskin cap (Hill), after TLLSS

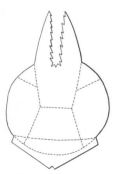

184.7. Pieced cap (Hill), after PP

Hill (East and Central)

Hats were made from buckskin, mountain lion, wildcat, badger, skunk, beaver, and weasel skin, ornamented with owl, eagle, and turkey feathers, abalone shell, bayeta, and silver buttons. All hats but those of buckskin were worn with the fur on them (C, Chinle). Methods of manufacture and styles of skin hats varied extensively; diversification existed even in those made from the same material.

A cap called by the same term as that for the Ramah smooth cap was constructed in a manner slightly different from that at Ramah; PP (Fort Defiance) translated the term as "tight fitting cap." Wet sand equal to the volume of the wearer's head was placed in a piece of buckskin. The edges of the buckskin were lifted from all sides, stretched around the sand forming a rounded bundle, and tied. When dry, the skin remained in the desired shape. The edges were trimmed and it was ready to wear.

A fitted cap was also made. Three triangular darts were cut from a roughly circular piece of buckskin (see 184.6). The edges left by the removal of the darts were drawn together and sewn; the resulting hemisphere was fitted to the wearer. Trial fittings were made and if the hat was too large, more material was cut from the sides before the final seams were sewn. Occasionally these hats were of double thickness. They were held in place by a chin strap (TLLSS, Crownpoint).

Ornamentation consisted of a row of abalone shell discs or rectangles placed on the hat above the forehead (TLLSS). These were usually four in number (SC, Crystal), but the number depended upon their size. Two tail feathers of an eagle were placed in a rosette of owl feathers (as at Ramah) and appended to the center of the crown by a thong (TLLSS, SC). According to SC, two owl feathers were also suspended from the back of the hat.

Another type of buckskin hat consisted of three pieces; a circular crown; a strip sewn to the crown at right angles, forming the sides, front, and back; and a buckskin chin strap to hold the hat in place (C). According to RH (Crystal), the sides of buckskin hats had flaps coming down over the ears to which the chin strap was attached. A large blackbird was sewn to the top. This hat was worn only by the leader in the Corral Way, together with an impromptu buckskin cloak (Hill, 1938:153). Badger, beaver, and weasel skins were also used to make this type of hat. Six weasel skins were required for one hat (C).

Hats were sometimes pieced together from buckskin or other kinds of skin. According to PP (Fort Defiance), as many pieces were used as necessary; he used ten (see 184.7). When assembled, the hat was either worked over the knee to shape it or darts were taken in the side to make it fit. According to C, sewing on all hats was done with sinew and with the aid of a bone awl.

The wearing of hats was a male prerogative, as at Ramah (MB, Divide; MM, Lukachukai; C, SC). A wide divergence of opinion existed, however, on whether or not the various kinds of hats were signs of economic status, badges of clan affiliation, or adjuncts to war and hunting. RH stated that the leader of the antelope hunt always wore a buckskin hat. C said that only the wealthy could afford hats of animals not frequently encountered: "Poorer men made theirs from scraps of buckskin."

C also stated that "in the beginning it was commanded that certain clans should wear a certain hat which had been set aside to distinguish them." An otter skin hat was to be worn by the *bitani* clan. The practice was not kept up, however, and "other hats which came into use later on were not set aside for any clan." He denied that hats were a necessary part of the equipment for war.

PP agreed that the privilege of wearing particular types of hats was accorded to specific clans, but he denied knowledge of the association cited by the Franciscan Fathers (see below). According to him, the sanction was derived from a raid on the Pueblos. Two men past fighting age (Bear and Big Snake) caught up with the war party at the first night's camp. "Bear wore a hat of mountain lion skin, Big Snake of buckskin." The two old men secured the scalp that the war party had sought, and after the fight the two clans most powerful in war ("Formed of her Back" and "Near the Water") and the three other linked clans of that group were given the right to wear buckskin and mountain lion skin caps. "If any other clans were to wear these hats it would bring them bad luck."

According to SC, "way back" one clan made a beaver skin hat with owl feathers as ornament. These hats distinguished them from other clans with other types of hats. He stated that copies were soon made by everyone and their significance was lost. TOMC (Red Rock), DM (Ganado), and IS denied the use of hats as clan insignia, saying that they were worn only for protection.

Comparative

Helmet-shaped caps of buckskin and other skins were noted by many of the nineteenth-century travelers among the Navaho. Simpson (1850:108) men-

Patterns for caps

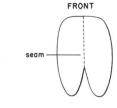

184.8. Collected by Matthews

184.9. Collected by Cushing

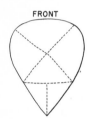

184.10. Collected by Fewkes

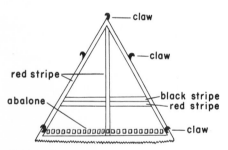

184.11. Decoration for Fewkes cap

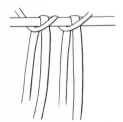

184.12. Method of securing dyed horsehair on Fewkes cap

tioned the use of such a cap decorated with bunches of eagle feathers. Later, Bartlett met a group of Navaho who wore helmet-shaped headdress similar to that used by the Apaches with whom he was then negotiating (Bartlett, 1854:I, 329). This may have been a war party, for Letherman (1856:290) said that regardless of the weather as a general rule neither men nor women wore any headdress, although "an old cap or hat, or dirty rag," was sometimes worn. The caps were probably worn until the time of the Fort Sumner captivity, for Palmer (1869:67) described one "surmounted with a plume of eagle or wild turkey feathers and fastened with a chin strap."

Four examples of Navaho hats are in the United States National Museum. The one collected by Washington Matthews (see 184.b) was cut from a single piece of buckskin, seamed down the center front; two flaps which hung down the wearer's neck in back were perforated along the outside edge (see 184.8). A tuft of owl feathers was secured at the crown with a thong, and two tightly rolled cylinders of buckskin were attached on either side of this tuft. Over the forehead were placed two strips of buckskin, one upon the other; the upper edge of the top strip was scalloped. A row of abalone shell discs and rectangles was sewn on this strip.

Another hat, collected by F. H. Cushing (see 184.c), was made from two pieces of buckskin, sewn medially over the crown (see 184.9). A tuft of turkey feathers decorated the top. A strip of cloth carrying a row of metal buttons was sewn over the forehead. Thongs were attached on each side to secure the hat to the head.

A third hat, collected by the War Department (see 184.d), was of blue-dyed buckskin, decorated over the forehead and sides with a red strip on which was sewn and laced a serrated and punched yellow strip. The bottom edges of the hat were punched. Two eagle feathers were attached to the top of the crown and on either side raised "ears" were fashioned. Thongs secured the hat on the head.

Another hat, collected by J. W. Fewkes at Keams Canyon (see 184.e), resembled the pointed type described at Ramah and by Hill. Six triangular pieces of buckskin were sewn together to make the cap (see 184.10). A buckskin strip with a serrated bottom edge was sewn over the forehead, over it a row of abalone discs and rectangles with a mountain lion claw at each end. Two additional claws, one on each side, were affixed along the seams of the crown, and one was placed at the peak of the hat. Red stripes were painted over the seams and down the middle in front; a red and a black stripe were painted transversely in front (see 184.11). At the back of the hat, a few inches below the peak, was appended a tuft of eagle and owl feathers, fashioned as described above. Red-dyed horsehair was attached at the bottom of the hat in back. The hair was looped over a cord and secured by another cord which was woven in and out (see 184.12).

An interesting variant of Navaho headwear in the 1870's is the knitted woolen cap collected by Governor Arny (see 178.a). In form, it is a faithful reproduction of the close-fitting skin caps, complete with tassel as a substitute for feathers and pattern squares (knit in) as a substitute for abalone shells or buttons. It is the only known occurrence of this type.

Both of Gifford's Navaho informants confirmed the use of buckskin caps with owl feathers. The Eastern informant said that any warrior could wear this type of cap; the Western informant said that without eagle feathers it was not necessarily a war cap (Gifford, 1940:32, 37, 71, 123, 129, 171).

Buckskin caps

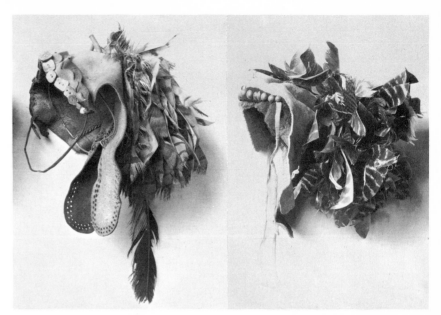

184.b. Collected by Matthews

184.c. Collected by Cushing

184.d. Collected by the War
Department

184.e. Collected by Fewkes

184.13. Buckskin caps, after the Franciscan Fathers

Clothing The Franciscan Fathers (1910:461) illustrated seven types of buckskin caps (see 184.13); all were made from two or more pieces of skin and were apparently more elaborate than those known at Ramah. "The smooth cap," called by the same term used at Ramah, had a flap in the rear, and "a single peak of hardened buckskin adorned the top." According to Matthews' informants, this same hat was "adorned with artificial ears . . . they wore such in the old days, and there are men still living who have seen them worn" (Matthews, 1897:184). The Franciscan Fathers also described "ears" decorating their hats, and a tuft of two eagle feathers "nestling in a cluster of turkey and crow feathers." The shapes varied as did the materials, and some caps had straight or curved peaks, and neck flaps. These were clan caps, worn by warriors on raids and journeys, and "hung up outside upon their return, as good custom forbade the use of the hat inside the hogan" (Franciscan Fathers, 1910:460–462).

Mrs. Wetherill, in her description of the ancient Navaho war costume, included a tight-fitting deerskin cap with a tuft of eagle or owl feathers on top (Wetherill, n.d.:2 pp.).

Bourke, in 1881, stated that by the time of his visit to Fort Defiance, "war bonnets" were no longer in use. These, he said, were once made of lion, wildcat, buckskin, goatskin, or lamb, decorated with eagle and wild turkey feathers. In rare cases, the Navaho used "the skin of the head itself, as the head of the lion." From their descriptions, he believed the caps to have been similar to those used by the Apache (Bourke, 1936:223, 231). Some of these caps were probably retained as heirlooms. A photograph taken in 1893 (see Plate XVI) shows a man decked out for war, wearing such a cap; it lacked the feather decoration.

Father Berard Haile stated that "native caps of buckskin, wild cat and mountain lion skins have disappeared, because they were worn only in war and raids" (Haile, 1951:42).

Hats of European style were observed among the Navaho as early as 1824; a Navaho killed on a war raid wore "a scarlet cloth cap, the folds of which were also secured by silver buttons" (Woodward, 1938:51, quoting an article in the *Missouri Intelligencer,* 1824). In 1849, Simpson noted that Chief Mariano was wearing a "tarpaulin hat," with a narrow brim and a semicircular crown (Simpson, 1850:101, 98). By 1900 the broad-brimmed felt hats purchased at the trading post were common (Franciscan Fathers, 1910:464). In many cases, particularly in the western and northern part of the Navaho area, they have been further ornamented with hatbands of silver stamped with simple designs (Adair, 1944:52–53). Thus, as an article of display, the felt hat performs part of the function formerly associated with the skin cap.

185. Wooden Awl

cin xá·xaščí·ʼ (Ramah, Haile) "pointed stick" (CC)

dóɣʷóži (Ramah, Haile) "greasewood" (CC)

Ramah
A length of pinyon (*Pinus edulis*) or greasewood (*Sarcobatus vermiculatus*) about a foot long and an inch in diameter was sharpened to a point at one end; the point was then carefully rounded. Infs. 7, 32, and 192 denied that awls of cactus spines or other woods were used.

The pinyon awl was used for working skin, and specifically for decorative perforations. Holes were not punched, but cut with a knife. The skin was placed hair side down over the point of the awl, and a knife cut was made around the point with a lateral sawing motion. The hide was reversed, and the edges of the holes were trimmed with the knife.

The pinyon awl was used by Inf. 7 in making a buckskin cap at Tschopik's request. There is no information on its use in other contexts.

According to Inf. 15, the greasewood awl was formerly used for making lightning mats (see Trait 215), and she was one of few who knew how to make them. Other Ramah informants denied the use of a wooden awl.

Comparative

There are few references to the wooden awl in the literature. Shufeldt observed such a tool in 1887, used in dressing a deerskin. A piece of soft pine was whittled to shape; to judge by the illustration, it was about four inches long. The edge of the skin was stretched over the handle of the awl, and twelve or thirteen holes were cut with a knife. The worker then put the awl in every hole, and holding the opposite edge with his left hand, "he was enabled to powerfully stretch the skin of the neck transversely" (Shufeldt, 1889:65, 66).

Although the Franciscan Fathers included perforations in the types of decorations for buckskin caps, they did not say how they were made. The wooden awl was mentioned, however, as "the only instrument used in platting" a quirt or rope (Franciscan Fathers, 1910:309–314, 460–462).

Gifford's Western informant confirmed the use of a greasewood awl for ear piercing; the Eastern informant denied this. Bone awls were used for working skin (Gifford, 1940:27, 115).

186. Mountain Lion Skin Cap

našdói coh čah (Haile) "mountain lion big cap" (CC)

Ramah

Hats made from mountain lion skin were denied by Infs. 7 and 16.

Hill (Central and West)

Mountain lion skin caps (see Plate X) were of two types. In one, the head skin of the lion was removed just below the eyes; about six inches of the neck were left attached. The skin was placed over the rounded end of a log to prevent shrinking while it dried. It was occasionally removed, worked, and stretched over the knee to produce the desired shape. Then it was dressed. First it was buried in damp earth; then brains were rubbed on it; and finally it was pounded with a stone or stick.

When the cap was complete, ornament was added. A strip of bayeta often decorated with abalone shell discs was placed on the rim above the forehead; it often extended to the ears of the wearer. The neck skin of the animal made a flap in back (PP, Fort Defiance; SG, Keams Canyon).

Hats of this type were also made of skunk skin. "If you wash the hide long enough in yucca root you get rid of the smell" (GH, White Cone).

According to C (Chinle), mountain lion skin hats like the three-piece buckskin cap he described were also made; a crown, side strip, and a buckskin chin strap were used, even with the mountain lion skin cap.

Mountain lion skin caps were also made by stretching the wet hide and fitting it over the head, then stuffing it with bark or wool to maintain the desired shape while it dried. Then a skin strap was attached, the tuft of eagle and owl feathers placed at the top, and abalone shell across the front. This type of cap (similar to the rounded cap, above) was also made from badger, wildcat, and skunk skin (Hill, 1936b:9).

Comparative
Data pertaining to the buckskin cap are equally appropriate to the mountain lion skin cap. Of the nineteenth-century travelers, Bourke specifically mentioned the use of mountain lion skin (Bourke, 1936:223, 231). According to the Franciscan Fathers (1910:460), this type of cap was used to distinguish the Tall House clan.

187. Wildcat Skin Cap

našdói čah (Ramah, Haile) "mountain lion (wildcat) cap" (CC)

Ramah
A tight-fitting cap was made with just enough skin to cover the head (Inf. 7; see 187.1). Beaver or coyote skins were not used for this type of cap. A chin strap was attached, and Inf. 7 said that sometimes a drawstring was placed around the edge to secure the cap.

Any man could make his own, and only men wore these caps. They were for everyday wear and "lasted a long time" (Inf. 7). They were stored in the hogan.

This type was seen by Inf. 7, but he had never made one. Inf. 16 knew about this type of hat, but did not specify whether he had ever made one, or seen one. It is possible that this type was derived from the Apache, for Inf. 16 is part Apache. No caps of this type are now extant.

187.1. Wildcat skin cap, after Tschopik

Hill (East and West)
Several kinds of wildcat skin hats were made. One type was made from the head of the wildcat (like the mountain lion skin cap). According to GH (White Cone), a rosette of owl feathers was placed on the crown between the ears.

TLLSS (Crownpoint) and GH described a second method of making hats from this skin. The whole skin of the animal was folded front to back and the edges were trimmed. The sides were sewn so as to leave the bottom opening the correct size for the head. "This makes a bigger hat. The head end of the skin was always worn in front" (GH). According to TLLSS, the fur was always worn on the outside and the hat was secured with a chin strap. TOMC (Red Rock) described a hat of the same type made from two pieces of hide; he said that badger skin might also be used.

Comparative
Data pertaining to the buckskin cap are also appropriate to the wildcat skin cap. According to one of the members of the Doniphan expedition, Navaho men were observed wearing "panther caps with eagle plumes" (Robinson, 1932:43). Whether these were part of the warriors regalia was not made clear. Bourke specifically mentioned wildcat skin caps (Bourke, 1936:223, 231). Again, the Franciscan Fathers (1910:460) stated that these were used to distinguish the Tall House clan.

Footwear

188. Sandals

ké biní·, xasti·i· (Haile) "foot (shoe) cinch, it goes around" (CC)

Sandals, after Hill

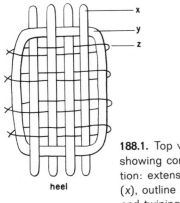

heel

188.1. Top view, showing construction: extension at toe (*x*), outline of foot (*y*), and twining (*z*)

heel

188.2. Side view, showing ties

Ramah

Infs. 7, 16, and 192 denied that yucca sandals—or any type of woven foot covering—were worn.

Hill (East, Central, and West)

Sandals belonged to the traditional period of Navaho history. None of the informants had actually made them, and descriptions were based on hearsay. According to RH (Crystal), his granduncle, who described the techniques, had made and used this type of footwear.

Twined sandals were made from three or four bundles of juniper bark about one inch in diameter, wrapped with yucca fiber and placed side by side (see 188.1). Bundles were long enough to extend several inches beyond the heel and toe (see *x* on 188.1). Another bundle of juniper bark was wrapped with yucca, then placed to outline the foot (see *y* on 188.1); at the heel and toe it was integrated in checker weave, and along the sides it paralleled the other bundles. These were secured by twining (see *z* on 188.1). Four sections of yucca fiber were introduced at spaced intervals. The ends of these twined elements were tied at the outside edge. LW (Ganado) said that sandals of this weave were made entirely of yucca, and the foot of the sandal was padded with cliff rose bark.

When the sandals were worn, the elements extending beyond the heel and toe were turned up and secured by ties around the ankle, instep, and toe (GH, White Cone; see 188.2).

Sandals in checker weave were made entirely of yucca (RH; PP, Fort Defiance; IS, Lukachukai), or of juniper bark (PP). Others had a juniper bark warp and a yucca weft (PP), or grass warp and yucca weft (RH). Elements were about half a finger width across. The weft element was a continuous strand, turned back over or under the last warp. Sandals of this type were secured by ties as above. According to C (Chinle), woven yucca sandals in which a diagonal pattern was produced by the weave were also made. Possibly this was twilled work, but the informant was unable to demonstrate this process. K (Mariano Lake) denied knowledge of woven types.

Wooden sandals were made from pinyon bark. A piece of bark was cut to fit the sole of the foot, with a section of wood extending upward in front to protect the toes. Wooden sandals were secured by yucca ties as above (SC, Crystal; TW, Keams Canyon).

According to GH, leather sandals were not used by the Navaho.

Comparative

Whether nineteenth-century observers of the Navaho saw yucca sandals is not known; they were, however, told about them. Stephen (1889:134) described shoes worn by men in the "snake or wind dance." These were of yucca, "the stems bound together at the sharp lips and braided in the center with cross strands."

The Franciscan Fathers (1910:308–309) cited Stephen's material, adding that a spur of twisted yucca secured at the heel was "for the purpose of effacing one's tracks in war," and that the shoe was made "for no other purpose than to elude an enemy." Yucca was used for the sole and the upper, unless badger or other hides were available for the latter. The sandal was decorated with porcupine quills. By 1910, these sandals were no longer used, but some specimens were still "kept as family relics." Both Stephen and the Franciscan Fathers believed these sandals to be the prototype of a peculiar form of moccasin collected by Stephen in the 1880's (see 189.a).

In his survey of North American footwear, Hatt (1916:159) suggested that this type of shoe was a "reminiscence" of a mid-eighteenth-century type worn by the Apache, as recorded by Venegas (1757:II, 554). The latter's description apparently confirmed the Franciscan Fathers' contention that this type was worn in warfare. The one-piece skin shoes of the Apache, however, made distinctive tracks instead of effacing the wearer's trail.

Gifford's Eastern informant said that sandals were made of badger hide or plaited yucca leaves, or cattail leaves. These were worn before moccasins were adopted. The Western informant had heard of a yucca "shoe," but he was unable to describe it (Gifford, 1940:40, 132).

References to bast footwear were found in Navaho mythology. Matthews noted that shoes were made with soles of hay and uppers of yucca fiber (Matthews, 1897:161, 184, 190). Stephen (1889:135–136) also recorded a myth which described footwear made from three kinds of grass, three kinds of yucca, and some of juniper bark.

Mrs. Wetherill, in her description of traditional and mythological Navaho dress, mentioned crude yucca sandals and sandals made from the neck skin of the antelope (Wetherill, n.d.:2 pp.).

189. Moccasins ké (Ramah, Haile) "shoe" (CC)

Ramah

The description of procedure was derived primarily from Tschopik's observation of Inf. 7 making a pair of moccasins. Moccasin soles were ordinarily made of rawhide, usually in recent years of cowhide. According to Inf. 16, however, before the Fort Sumner period deerskin was the favorite material. Inf. 7 said that several thicknesses of rawhide were used, taken from the neck of the deer where the toughest skin was found. Two or three layers were glued together with pinyon pitch to form a heavier sole. Inf. 7 said that badger, elk, and antelope skins were also used for this purpose.

Rawhide for the soles was buried in wet ground for about two days, then removed and stretched by the worker, who held one end of the skin on the ground with his foot (see 189.1). Then the worker cut the sole, flesh side inside, using his foot as a pattern and leaving a half-inch margin. The heel was cut square. Next the sole (*kekal*) was placed on a board and the edges were trimmed with a knife. The first sole was reversed, flesh side outside, and used as a pattern for cutting the second. Inf. 7 worked the soles with his hands, sometimes chewing them to shape them properly. The soles were buried for another two days before sewing began.

Moccasin uppers were formerly made only of buckskin; later goatskin was

Moccasins, after Tschopik

189.1. Pattern for sole; cutting starts at x, follows dotted line

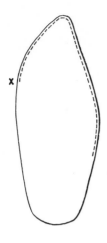

189.2. Pattern for upper, basted at points marked x

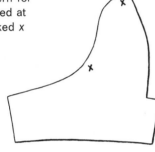

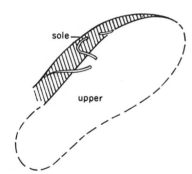

189.3. Stitching sole to upper

189.4. Stitching at heel

used. Inf. 7 denied that moccasins were made from skins dressed with the fur on. Buckskin was cut from the neck and shoulder area of the hide and buried for about an hour before sewing.

Each upper (*kelchi*) was made from a single piece, unless buckskin was scarce. If so, scraps were patched together to obtain a large enough piece. Both uppers were measured and cut at once, by doubling the buckskin along the spinal axis. The folded piece was then placed against the foot; holding the front (neck) of the skin on the outside of the ankle, the worker traced the inner outline of the foot (heel to toe) and trimmed the excess hide. Next the hide was divided along the fold, and the shaping of each piece continued. The worker outlined the outside of the foot, then trimmed and measured, repeating this procedure until the fit was satisfactory. He trimmed the hide by placing it on a board and cutting it with a knife. The area of the heel was cut large to compensate for the contraction in sewing, especially across the toe.

Next the sewing began. The worker sat cross-legged and held the moccasin on his left knee. The upper was first basted to the sole at two points (see 189.2); stitches between these two points were made close together to compensate for strain during wear. Next the worker bent the pliable rawhide sole and made two holes with one thrust of the awl; these were about one eighth of an inch apart. Sinew pointing to the left of the worker was inserted and pulled tight with the right hand. In like manner, holes were perforated and the sinew passed through the upper (see 189.3). When the stitch was completed, the moccasin was turned with the toe pointing away from the worker, who held the edge with his left hand and pulled the thread tight with his right. The stitch was called "sewn next to the rim" (*bitatai ichin*, see 189.20). Sewing continued around the sole until the heel was reached. The worker periodically molded the sole upward with the fingers of both hands, sometimes thrusting his right hand inside the toe and shaping with the left. When the heel was reached, the moccasin was fitted and the excess at the back was trimmed. Then the sewing of the heel was completed (see 189.4).

At this point the moccasin was placed on the end of a loom batten, which was held vertically with one end resting in the ground. The moccasin was pulled downward with both hands to stretch it and to mold the sole upward on the sides. Then four holes were punched close together through the upper and sole where the sewing terminated. A thin buckskin thong was laced through these and the ends drawn down and cut a quarter of an inch from the sole.

Next the flaps were cut to the proper shape, the moccasins tried on, and the location for the buttons marked. Two buttons were placed on the outside of each moccasin and two pairs of holes were punched in the inner flap. Buckskin thongs were cut; the buttons were threaded on them, the thongs passed through the holes, and the ends were tied inside in a hard knot. The moccasin was fitted once more to ascertain the location of the button holes on the upper flap. These were marked with the awl, then cut; during the cutting the upper flap was rested against an edge of the batten. Some moccasins were fastened with thongs only (Inf. 7). The thongs passed through slits in both the flap and upper and were tied on the outside.

Completed moccasins varied in height: some were ankle high, others extended four inches on the leg. None was calf high. According to Inf. 7, there was no difference in height between men's and women's moccasins of Navaho type.

According to Inf. 48, Navaho women were wearing the Pueblo woman's type of moccasin prior to Fort Sumner. Attached to the back of these moccasins was a large buckskin that wrapped around the calf. Inf. 7 said that these were worn for ceremonies. He said that they were wrapped about the calf of the leg and secured with a thong or woven garter. The wrap extended from just below the knee to the ankle, the bottom part extending over the ankle.

Ornamentation was a matter of individual preference and was apparently restricted to dyeing the buckskin and using buttons. Most moccasins were red, some (said to be worn with black leggings) were black; Inf. 7 said that moccasins were never yellow. Infs. 180 and 90 agreed that moccasins had to have some red on them or the wearer would become blind.

The greatest variation was perhaps in the stitches used. Inf. 7 recognized four in addition to the one he used, and said that any one was appropriate. The "pulled down" stitch (*bilya adlo,* see 189.21) was sometimes used to fasten the heel. The sinew passed through the outside edge of the sole and then the outside edge of the upper, alternating in that order, instead of through both at the same time. This stitch pulled the upper down and produced a puckered edge.

The "wound around" stitch (*biki deesdiz,* see 189.22) was a whipped running stitch, in which the edges of the upper and sole met and were flush. It was faster than any other stitch and was therefore used on "every-day moccasins" (Inf. 7). It did not wear as long as the "pulled down" stitch.

The "through the middle" stitch (*bikaii yii itsi,* see 189.23) was similar to that used by Inf. 7, except that the stitches passed diagonally through the outside of the sole and were hidden. Only one hole was punched at a time. This stitch was said to be less permanent than the "pulled down" stitch, but more permanent than the "wound around."

In the "two threads going at the same time" stitch (*naaki beenal kad,* or *ke alna ha ootsih,* see 189.24), two sinews were used. This was more permanent than any other stitch, but it required much more time. It is no longer used.

Moccasins were usually made by men, although women might make them. "Sometimes a man doesn't know how to sew them and a woman has to do it" (Inf. 7). Two women (Infs. 46, 76) were known to have made moccasins; in other cases they were made by men (Infs. 7, 180, 300). They could be made at any time and at any location that comfort and convenience dictated.

Men, women and children wore moccasins. Ordinarily, even in wet weather, all went barefoot around the dwelling to save their footwear. Men wore moccasins when hoeing or hunting, and women sometimes wore them about the house; both wore moccasins on ceremonial occasions. In winter, moccasins were lined with shredded juniper bark. No other linings were used "in the old days." More recently, old men and women have wrapped their feet in cloths or worn stockings with their moccasins.

Moccasins lasted a long time if properly cared for. If allowed to become wet, they deteriorated rapidly. If the stitching began to wear through, it was repaired. Before mending, damp earth was sometimes placed in the moccasins to soften the buckskin and rawhide (Infs. 15, 178). Moccasins made with soles of several layers of rawhide were repaired by adding another sole when the outer one deteriorated. The process was repeated until the upper was worn out. If the original material was of good quality and well dressed, and if they were not worn in the mud or rain, Inf. 46 estimated that a pair of moccasins would last about three years.

Moccasins were stored any place in the hogan (Inf. 7). Inf. 8 tied them together with the lacing thongs and hung them over a nail on the wall.

According to Inf. 8, when a man died, his best moccasins were part of his burial costume. Others that he had worn were also buried with him. Any that had not been worn were given to someone "who lives far away and is not a relation." Inf. 7 agreed that moccasins were probably not inherited.

Moccasins are still made and worn in the Ramah community, although shoes have somewhat replaced them. One woman (Inf. 46) said that she had never worn anything but moccasins, and in 1940 she owned no other footwear. Others probably have never owned moccasins, and in 1947 Inf. 8 said that they were worn only for ceremonials. Although moccasins are favored for the main participants in most chants and for all participants in certain chants, observers since 1947 have seen them worn at other times.

The technique of manufacture still exists, although goatskin is used when buckskin is scarce; and, if Inf. 16 is correct, rawhide replaced layers of deerskin for the sole. The wooden awl and chert chip knife have been replaced by metal implements.

The strength of the moccasin-making tradition remains, nonetheless, and is shown by various makeshift shoes worn presumably because of economic pressure. Inf. 138 was seen wearing an old pair of high leather shoes to which rawhide soles had been added. The stitching was of the "pulled down" type. Thick cowhide soles sewn with the concealed moccasin stitch to black shoe uppers were worn by Inf. 9. Inf. 196 once appeared in shoes with rubber soles sewn with thongs to a soft leather upper. Inf. 134 attached shoe uppers to a sole cut from an automobile tire by nailing a strip of leather around the edge of the uppers, through the rubber and cord.

Hill (East, Central, and West)

Moccasin soles were made of rawhide from various sources. Thick neck skin was taken from deer, badger, mountain lion, and buffalo (C, Chinle). Cowhide and horsehide have been used more recently (TLLSS, Crownpoint; C). Hide from the area of the hip was considered best. Moccasin uppers were made of buckskin.

Most informants contended that moccasin styles differed for men and women, although this was denied by PP (Fort Defiance). He and AM (Lukachukai) also denied that there were special types of moccasins used for dancing and warfare. Neither recognized the long moccasin illustrated and described by Stephen (see 189.a). Informants said that the current type of moccasin differs from those which were formerly worn, although the sole has remained essentially the same.

Soles always approximated the shape of the foot (see 189.5), but they were cut slightly larger to allow for the characteristic upturn of the edge. Both soles were cut back to back at the same time so they would be the same size (TOMC, Red Rock; C, PP).

In the old-style men's moccasin, several variations of the basic upper pattern occurred. In the most common form (see 189.6), the upper was split

Old-style men's moccasins, after Hill

189.5. Sole

189.6. Common form of upper

189.7. Alternative upper, worn by LH

189.8. Heel fastening

189.9. Instep strap

insert

189.10. Upper with tongue

189.11. Three-piece moccasin with sole (*a*), upper (*b*), and heel strip (*c*)

New-style men's moccasins, after Hill

189.12. Upper

189.13. Alternative pattern for upper   **189.14.** Sole

Old-style women's moccasins, after Hill

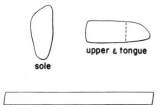

189.15. Pieces

189.16. Moccasin wrapped and tied   **189.17.** Wrapping with short heel piece

Pueblo-style women's moccasins, after Hill

189.18. Cutting a medium-sized buckskin; the neck (x) was sewn to the heel

in back into two strips which met at the back of the heel, where they were secured by a thong (C) or seamed (TLLSS; WH, Wheatfields; GH, White Cone). Sometimes one strip was cut longer than the other (see 189.7). If so, the thong or seam was at the side of the foot (TOMC). LH (Aneth) was wearing this type of moccasin. Occasionally the shorter strap was long enough to meet the other at the heel, at the bottom of which they were lightly fastened (TLFOS, Shiprock and Fort Defiance; TLLSS). The extra flap was brought around and fastened on the outside (see 189.8). According to informants, this type required less buckskin than modern types. The upper was sewn to the sole at all places except where the strips met at the heel (TLFOS, TLLSS, C).

Occasionally an instep strap (see 189.9) was sewn to the inside or outside of the moccasin near the sole. It was secured by a thong to the inside or outside of the upper near the sole (GH, C, TLFOS). Sometimes, instead, a wedge-shaped tongue was sewn in the open section over the instep (TLFOS, TLLSS; see 189.10).

An old type of three-piece moccasin consisted of a sole, an upper, and a heel strip (see 189.11). The upper was sewn to the front half of the sole and covered slightly more than the toes; the heel strip was sewn to the back of the sole and the ends lapped at the instep. The moccasin was secured by a tie on the outside of the foot. The upper was occasionally cut with a tongue.

The new-style moccasin was adopted "within the last thirty or forty years" (since 1890 or 1900; C), or after Fort Sumner (WH). The upper was cut in one piece (see 189.12, 189.13), and the sole (see 189.14) was cut with a square heel which was puckered to fit the foot (WH, C). This type was described at Ramah.

A three-piece moccasin was also worn by women just before the Navaho were taken to Fort Sumner (see 189.15). The upper, cut to include a tongue, was sewn to the sole as far back as the instep. The long heel piece was sewn from the back forward to meet the tongue and was wrapped twice around the ankle before being tied in front in a square knot (see 189.16). If a short heel piece was used, it went over the foot only once; the end hung as a flap on the outside (see 189.17). Women's moccasins were higher at the ankle than the men's (TLLSS, C, WH).

The popular style of women's moccasin was the Pueblo type, which, according to MM (Lukachukai), the Navaho began to use after their release from Fort Sumner. It was called "big shoe," and consisted of a sole, an upper, and a wrap. There were two methods of making it, the difference depending on the way the wrap was cut. In the first, a medium-sized buckskin, headless, not too thick, was placed in damp earth, then stretched and cut down the middle (see 189.18). The left half was used for the right moccasin, the right for the left moccasin. The neck of the skin was sewn to the heel part of the sole and the skin was wrapped around the leg from the inside out. The moccasin upper was cut from another piece and sewn to the forepart of the sole (MM, PP).

In the second method, the head and legs were left on the skin. It was folded along the back, marked by biting along the fold, then halved. A triangular section was removed from the back, to make a straight line from the neck back (see 189.19). The first piece cut was used as a pattern for the second. The front part of the moccasin was a combination upper and tongue, sewn to the sole as far back as the instep. The wrap was sewn from the heel forward

Pueblo-style women's moccasins, after Hill, con't.

189.19. Cutting buckskin: after the buckskin was halved (dotted line at *x*), a charcoal line (*y*) was drawn on each piece; next a triangular section (*z*) was removed and used as a pattern for the removal of its opposite (*w*). These pieces were later used as ties at the upper part of the wrap.

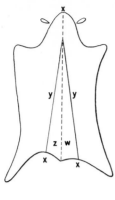

Moccasin stitches (Hill)

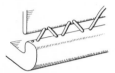

189.20. "Along the edge," or "sewn next to the rim"

189.21. "Pulled down"

189.22. "Wound around"

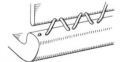
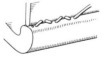

189.23. "Through the middle"

189.24. "Two threads going at the same time"

189.25. After C

to meet the tongue at the instep. The untrimmed halves of the buckskin were used to wrap around the legs; and the triangular sections from the back, sewn to the upper edge of the wraps, were used as ties. After the fitting, a thong was attached to secure the ties (C).

As at Ramah, several stitches were distinguished. Actually, only two basic varieties were used: one was some form of a simple running stitch (see 189.20–189.24); in the other (see 189.25), two threads were used at the same time, passing through the same hole in opposite directions. The Navaho, however, made distinctions in sewing on the basis of what position of the edge, side, or center of the material the sinew passed through. The stitch used by Inf. 7 at Ramah, "along the edge" (see 189.20) was known. The sinew passed through the inside edge of the sole and a little above the edge of the upper. The entire edge of the sole was visible. According to C, the seam did not show when this stitch was used. This stitch was used only to secure the upper to the front section of the moccasin sole (PP, C, GH; see 189.1). Other stitches confirmed Ramah types, and Hill's informants gave additional comments.

In the "pulled down" stitch (see 189.21), each stitch was pulled tight separately, and the edge of the sole did not show. The ends of the sinew were knotted and the knot pounded into the leather of the sole to hide it. This was the most common type of stitch; "it was used for rough work" (PP, C, GH).

The "wound around" stitches (see 189.22) were so close together that the edge of the sole did not show. For this type of stitch, a lighter sinew was used than for the other types (PP, C).

In the "through the middle" stitch (see 189.23) the sinew passed through the center of the edge of the sole and through the outside edge of the upper. When the stitch was pulled tight, only a small portion of the outside edge of the sole showed. The heel was usually sewn with this stitch (PP, C, GH).

The "two threads going at the same time" stitch (see 189.24) was the second general type of stitch. Both pieces were held with the edges together (not facing, as above). The two sinews passed through the holes in opposite directions (GH). In the finished moccasin the upper was pulled to a fold at this seam.

C mentioned another stitch (see 189.25). Again the edges of the sole and upper were placed together so that holes might be put through both at the same time. The sinew was passed over and through the edges.

Any stitch might be used in making repairs. Moccasins were formerly repaired and patched more often than at present, since buckskin was formerly more difficult to obtain (C).

Moccasins have been used by the Navaho throughout the historic period, but their use appears to have been somewhat sporadic. Both sexes customarily went barefoot. As at Ramah, the men went shod when hunting, and both went shod when traveling, doing field work, or at any important social or religious gatherings. Indications are that women wore moccasins less often than did men (MM, PP).

Sanction for the use of moccasins can be found in Navaho mythology. According to legend, the first true moccasins were worn by the gods living in the interior of the mountains. The heroes of the chant legends went to these holy places, and when they returned described these moccasins to the

Navaho, whereupon the people made them (SC). C attributed the introduction of moccasins to the Ute.

Fishler (West)

Moccasin soles were made either from cowhide or badger skin (GB, Tuba City), cowhide (TN, Kaibito), preferably badger skin but occasionally buffalo hide (TT, Coalmine). Uppers were made from buckskin (GB, TN). The foot was placed on the hide and the outline traced with a knife or pencil, with at least half an inch left for margin. The hide was soaked and molded to fit the foot.

TN said that men made moccasins but women helped. IJun (Kaibito) said that moccasins were traded from the Ute.

Comparative

The first reference to the use of the moccasin by the Navaho was by Pattie, and it dates from about the year 1827. The moccasin, he noted, was an article "of value to them" (Pattie, 1905:165, 166). In 1855, Letherman noted that moccasins for men and women were fashioned alike, with rawhide soles and buckskin tops coming well up the leg; the Pueblo style of wrapping was not mentioned (Letherman, 1856:290). Earlier, Simpson (1850:88) stated that the women of the Canyon de Chelly region ordinarily wore moccasins; he did not refer to the leg wrapping. Palmer, observing during the Fort Sumner period, spoke of different styles of moccasins. Men wore long ones, and women wore moccasins with wrapping attached, "wound round the leg several times and fastened, giving the leg a large, cumbersome appearance" (Palmer, 1869:67, 46). Robinson (1932:51) also noted these leg wrappings (see 164.b).

Palmer observed other types of moccasins, and deposited in the United States National Museum at least two pairs similar to those described above from Ramah. Mason remarked upon these in 1869, noting that they were made of three parts, a rawhide sole, buckskin vamp, and heel. The heel, he said, was "commonly called the quarters and legging" and consisted of a broad strip of buckskin attached at the heel and wrapped around the leg. The other pair was similar, but the wrap was "fastened with a thong rather than with buttons. Length ten inches" (Mason, 1896:354–355, figs. 63, 64).

Bourke described moccasins worn by both sexes. Those worn by men were of black, white, or red buckskin fastened on the outside of the instep by from one to six silver buttons. Leggings, also fastened by a row of silver buttons, and supported by garters, were worn with these moccasins. The leggings and moccasins worn by women, however, were usually of one piece, fastened at the knees by garters; "a narrow strip of buckskin also winds about the legs to keep the legging tight" (Bourke, 1936:224, 86; Dellenbaugh, n.d.:170).

According to Stephen, the three-piece Pueblo-style moccasin was typical of Navaho women in the Keams Canyon area in the 1890's. Here, of course, there was much contact with the Hopi (Stephen, 1893:356; 1889:133). Hatt illustrated and described a Hopi woman's moccasin, and said that it was worn not only by Hopi and Zuni, but by Navaho and Walapai women (Hatt, 1916:196, fig. 47).

Stephen collected an unusual pair of moccasins (see 189.a) worn in the Snake or Wind Dance. These were called "shoe sewed with single straight

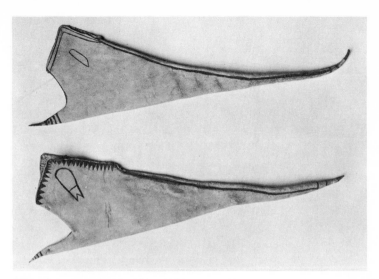

189.a. An unusual pair of buckskin moccasins

seam that makes a peculiar mark." They were stuffed with grass and tied on the feet for the dance. Each was marked with a footprint to designate right and left; as the dancers swung their legs, they made "marks on the sand like the trail of a snake" (Stephen, 1889:133–134; see also Trait 188, Comparative section.)

There are several long descriptions of moccasin making in the literature (Stephen, 1889:131–133; Franciscan Fathers, 1910:305–311; Sapir and Hoijer, 1942:419–421). According to the Franciscan Fathers (1910:305–306), the sole was formerly made from the thick neck skin of deer and badger, but by 1910 rawhide was used exclusively; the uppers were made from buckskin. Sinew from the loins of sheep, goat or deer was used for sewing according to Stephen. The upper (usually a single piece of buckskin) and sole were measured from the foot, basted together at certain points, and sewn with sinew. Several stitches were known, each of which confirmed those known at Ramah. The type demonstrated by Inf. 7, "shoe seamed in the groove," was described as an invisible and fancy stitch. The "pulled down" stitch made a "seam which draws it together." The "wound around" stitch, according to the Franciscan Fathers, was the most common. It was used for the heel and for repair work. The stitch "through the middle" was described as similar to that demonstrated by Inf. 7. The stitch using two threads was also used, and was known as "stitched through the center, or cross-stitched."

The Franciscan Fathers (1910:305, 465) indicated that Navaho women wore either the regular moccasin described for the men, or the Pueblo style, with wrapping. Moccasins were generally fastened by silver buttons, although thongs were also used. Moccasins were usually made by men, and most men were able to repair them. Newcomb (1940a:39) stated that moccasin making and any other work in leather was forbidden to women and could only be performed by men.

Gifford's Navaho informants spoke of rawhide, cowhide, and horsehide soles for moccasins, and the Eastern informant also mentioned skin from a badger's neck. They denied knee-length moccasins, and both informants said that three-piece moccasins were a modern trait (Gifford, 1940:39, 40, 131, 132; see also Sapir and Hoijer, 1942:77).

According to the Franciscan Fathers (1910:309), the two-piece buckskin moccasins were derived from the Ute, "who were better skilled in tanning and buckskin work, and at one time were not hostile to the Navaho." These moccasins were often "decorated with beads and porcupine quills, which later, however, disappeared entirely." According to Woodward (1938:9), the Navaho derived moccasins from the Mexicans of the eighteenth and early nineteenth centuries.

Moccasins survived as general foot covering into the early years of the twentieth century. Both cowhide and buckskin moccasins were common during the 1940's.

There are two instances of moccasins found archaeologically, and both pairs come from burials dated tentatively at the beginning of the nineteenth century. Wyman found a pair "of reddish color, badly decayed but recognizable as the Navaho type, of ankle height" (Wyman and Amsden, 1934:133). Malcolm (1939:19) found a pair in the Chaco Canyon region; these were one-piece moccasins. Neither report further described the moccasins. Moccasins were not mentioned in other reports.

Sanction for moccasin making was recorded by Stephen from Navaho mythology. The sole was to be made from the neck skin of the badger, the upper from deerskin; sinew for sewing was to come from the back of the mountain sheep. The foot was to be marked by "beginning at the toe and drawing the left side, then from the toe drawing the right side." The badger skin sole edge was to be concealed with red, yellow, blue or black paint. There was no mention of painting the uppers (Stephen, 1889:135–136).

190. Overshoes

ké· ·ečogi (Ramah, Haile) "shoe, (sound of pulling foot out of the mud), also rubber boots" (CC)

Ramah

Hides of sheep, goats, horses, or cows were used; Inf. 7 did not know what wild animal skins were used before these became available. The hide was cut into roughly triangular shape, with a rounded base and blunt apex. A string was laced through the apex, which was puckered and seamed with the whipped stitch ("wound around") to form the toe. Toes did not bend upward, nor were any such shoes laced over the instep. The heel was not seamed, but folded around the ankle and was tied with buckskin, rawhide, or yucca cord. Overshoes came up above the ankles.

Both men and women made them; Inf. 8 began to make his own at the age of fifteen. They were usually made in the winter, inside the dwelling.

Overshoes were worn over moccasins when there was snow on the ground. Men, women and children wore them. The children's were of sheepskin (Inf. 8). Overshoes would not last a month if worn every day (Inf. 8). They were apparently owned by those who wore them, including children. If a person died and left some, they were burned or thrown away.

Infs. 7 and 8 had made them and Inf. 2 had heard of them. They are

Overshoes (Hill)

190.1. After C

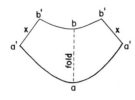

Top View

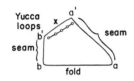

Side View

190.2. After TLLSS

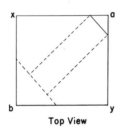

Top View

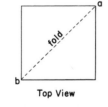

Side View

190.3. After SG and GH

Top View

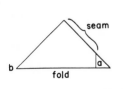 

Side Views

no longer made, having been replaced by commercially made overshoes available at the stores.

Hill (East, Central, and West)

Overshoes were made from the skins of mountain lions (C, Chinle), deer (C; T, Chaco Canyon), antelope (T), buffalo (TLLSS, Crownpoint), badgers (C, TLLSS), horses (T), goats, and sheep (SG, Keams Canyon; GH, White Cone; TLLSS). They were made with the hair inside and were quite often lined with juniper or cliff rose bark to give additional warmth (T, TLLSS, C, GH).

Several variations in style were produced. One type was somewhat tailored. The hide was folded, marked, and cut, the resulting pattern resembling a rim segment from a wheel (see 190.1). Both pieces were cut at the same time to assure uniformity. To make the overshoe, the skin was folded to a slanted U-shape, and two seams were sewn. Loops of yucca fiber were inserted around the top. A yucca drawstring through these loops secured the overshoe to the foot (C).

A second type was made from a square of hide (see 190.2). One corner was puckered for the toe and the seams sewn with yucca fiber. The two sides were drawn up along the foot and sewn down over the instep to the toe. The foot was then inserted and the rest of the square pulled up around the ankle. A thong tied about the leg secured the points of the shoe (corners of the square) above the ankle (TLLSS). Except for the shape of the original hide, this overshoe resembled the Ramah type.

In the third type, a square was folded diagonally (see 190.3). One corner and a side of the resulting triangle were seamed. The foot was inserted and the other corner drawn up about the back of the leg. This type was also secured by a thong or piece of yucca tied in front (SG, GH).

Fishler (West)

The fur was left on the hide, but the hide was not carefully dressed. Overshoes were cut much like moccasins, but the toes were pointed, and they were seamed to the toe. The top of the shoe extended halfway up the calf of the leg.

Both men and women made overshoes, during the winter. These were used only in snow, for they wore out rapidly.

Comparative

The earliest description of Navaho overshoes was apparently that by Stephen (1889:133). These, he stated, were of goatskin sewn with yucca. They were cut so that one straight seam from toe to ankle completed them. In 1910 they were still a part of the winter costume of the Navaho. The Franciscan Fathers (1910:308, 465) stated that these were wraps made of gunnysacks, or skins of kids, lambs, sheep, or goats, worn with the wool side in.

Gifford's Western Navaho informant confirmed the use of a "fur moccasin for winter," which he said was a sheepskin worn wool side in. The Eastern Navaho informant denied this trait, as well as hide overshoes (about which the Western informant was not questioned). The Eastern informant said that in winter, the Navaho wore juniper bark insoles or rabbit fur socks for warmth (Gifford, 1940:40, 131, 132).

191. Snowshoes

191.1. Snowshoe, after Tschopik

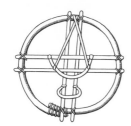

Snowshoes (Hill)

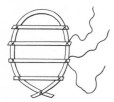

191.2. Juniper bark snowshoe, with bundles around foot (*x*), instep (*y*) and ankle (*z*); after TW, N

Side View

Side View Showing Ties

Top View

Side View Showing Ties

191.3. Oval frame snowshoe, after SC

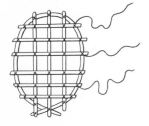

Top View

Side View Showing Ties

191.4. Oak snow shoe, after SC

Ramah

A circular wooden hoop was made from pine splints. Two pairs of cross sticks were tied to this with yucca cord (Inf. 3), and two buckskin straps were attached to the cross sticks (Inf. 16; see 191.1). One went over the toes, the other over the instep. These held the shoe in place. Snowshoes were sometimes colored with red ocher, according to Inf. 2.

These were made only at the time of a heavy snow (Inf. 2). Inf. 2 said that only those who knew the songs could make them. "If you don't know the songs, you can't stay on top of the snow." He said that the person who used snowshoes also had to know the songs. According to Inf. 3, they were used by the Chuska and Lukachukai mountain people; he implied that other groups of Navaho did not use them.

Data on snowshoes were obtained from three old men. None said that he had seen or used them, and Inf. 2 said that he had only heard of them. Whether this trait exists today or whether it has been replaced by a new one is not known. Members of Roberts' three households denied the use of snowshoes (Roberts, 1951:55).

Hill (East, Central, and West)

Snowshoes appear to have been extensively used by the Navaho, although because of ritual restrictions, they seldom, if ever, appear in collections. They were temporary devices produced to meet a particular situation.

SC (Crystal) stated that according to the legend of the Mountain Chant, the Bear People made the first snowshoes from an oak hoop and four crosspieces. Because of this association with the bear, the Navaho were instructed to dismantle the snowshoes and dispose of all parts when they were no longer needed. OTKM (Manuelito) said that the pieces were to be hidden under a tree. The snowshoe track was said to resemble that of the bear, and it would bring bad luck if the user brought snowshoes to his home (SC, OTKM; PP, Fort Defiance). PP said that they were normally used only once.

The most prevalent types of snowshoes were made from oak and secured with yucca ties. Juniper bark snowshoes were sometimes used, but according to C (Chinle), the type of snowshoe with rawhide web was never used by the Navaho.

For juniper bark snowshoes, three bundles of shredded bark (see *x*, *y*, and *z* on 191.2) were obtained. One bundle extended from the top of the foot, over the toes, beneath the foot, and back up the heel. The second encircled the instep, the third the ankle. These bundles were secured by yucca ties around the toes, instep, and ankle (TW, Keams Canyon; N, Coalmine).

Of other types, there was a considerable variety, presumably because of their temporary character. For one type, described by SC, a section of oak was heated over the fire, bent to form an oval, and tied where the ends crossed at the back (see 191.3). Four crosspieces were notched where they intersected with the frame and secured; they did not project any more than necessary. The shoe was fastened to the foot by yucca ties. One went over the toes. Two others were anchored to the second crosspiece from the back of the

Rectangular oak snowshoes (Hill)

Top View | Side View
Showing Ties

191.5. After RH

Top View | Side View
Showing Ties

191.6. After GH

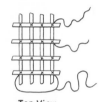

Top View | Side View
Showing Ties

191.7. After TLFOS

toe

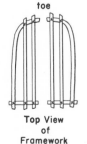

Top View
of
Framework | Top View
Showing Ties

Side View
Showing Ties

191.8. Pattern for framework of snowshoe (Hill), after TLLSS

191.9. Ties for 191.8

snowshoe. One of these went over the instep; the other was wrapped once around the ankle and tied to the opposite side of the same crosspiece. The informant said that he sometimes used wire for ties because it did not break easily.

SC also described another type similar to that above (see 191.4). An oak limb was whittled to about an inch diameter, then heated and bent. Three pieces were placed on the frame, from toe to heel, and secured. Six crosspieces were then added. All intersections were tied with yucca. The shoes were secured to the foot by three yucca ties, attached to the second, fourth, and toe crosspieces. Ties thus went over the toe, instep, and ankle, as above. "The shoes projected about four inches beyond the moccasin. You had to swing your feet in a half-circle to walk." These were used by hunters in the mountains, by others only in extreme cases.

Several types were made without a circular or oval frame. RH (Crystal) described the simplest (see 191.5), made from two pieces of oak slightly longer than the moccasin, to which were attached two crosspieces which went under the heel and the toe. These projected about two finger widths on either side of the foot. Intersections were notched and tied with yucca. The shoe was tied to the foot with yucca, one tie over the toe, and two attached to the back intersection; one to go over the instep, one around the heel in back. "It is necessary to swing the feet wide when wearing this shoe."

A similar type (see 191.6) was made with four pieces of oak two fingers wide, scraped flat on two sides; two similar crosspieces were attached and secured with split oak withes. The shoe was tied to the foot with two badger hide thongs, one over the toes, the other over the instep (GH, White Cone).

On a snowshoe described by TLFOS (Shiprock and Fort Defiance) (see 191.7), eight oak pieces, scraped flat, were used. Sticks were notched at the intersections and secured with yucca. Yucca ties crossed the instep and toe. A yucca loop was secured to each end of the heel crosspiece; it fit the heel and was tied by a string over the instep. These snowshoes projected about two inches in front, slightly less in back and at the sides. They were roughly rectangular in shape, tapering slightly toward the back.

When three long pieces and one short piece of oak were used, a different shape resulted (see 191.8). The sections were left round and were about the size of a finger in diameter. The short piece formed the heel, and the outside long piece was bent to form the toe. Sticks were notched and secured with yucca, the joints made as even as possible. Green yucca leaves were knotted together to form a continuous strand, which was woven at half-inch intervals across the frame. A second strand, woven lengthwise, produced a checkerboard pattern. Strands attached at the crosspiece of the heel were tied over the instep, as were those attached at the instep and the toe. An additional loop at the toe was tied to the toe and instep strings by a strand over the top of the foot (see 191.9). These snowshoes were about two inches longer than the foot. For warmth, juniper bark was placed around the foot before the strings were tied. An extra supply of yucca was always carried in case any strands should break (TLLSS, Crownpoint).

The last type of snowshoe (see 191.10) was used only in the deep snow (PP). It was constructed of five oak limbs, scraped flat on two sides, and varying in width. The center piece, about two inches wide, was placed over a diagonal cross (two pieces about an inch and a half wide). Two pieces,

Top View

191.10. Pattern for shoe used in deep snow (Hill), after PP

one that was narrow in front and a slightly wider one in back, were placed over the ends of the center piece and under the ends of the diagonal cross. The foot was placed over the intersection and secured with ties of pounded yucca fiber. These went over the instep and toe.

Comparative

There are references to the use of snowshoes in parts of the Navaho area other than Ramah, but none antedates the beginning of the twentieth century. The Franciscan Fathers (1910:47–48) stated that formerly a wooden snowshoe was used, made from pine, cottonwood, or even dried bark. The material was slightly pointed at both ends and secured to the foot by cords. Because the wearer often had difficulty regaining his balance in case of a fall, it was considered essential for him to carry a knife with which to cut the cords and extricate himself. By 1910, "overshoes, or covers made of burlap and sheepskin, as also foreign overshoes" were also designated as snowshoes. Navaho terms confirmed those known at Ramah.

Although the narrator of *Son of Old Man Hat* described trips through heavy snows, neither he nor any of his family or relatives used snowshoes. On one occasion, however, they wrapped their moccasins with cloths, and on another used a walking stick with three prongs to prevent breaking through the snow (Dyk, 1938:169).

Gifford did not ask his Navaho informants about wooden snowshoes with crosspieces, a trait which only one Southwestern group (San Ildefonso Pueblo) acknowledged. The Western Navaho said that bark snowshoes pointed at both ends were used. The Eastern informant denied this, and said that old grass-wrapped moccasins were worn (Gifford, 1940:40, 132).

Snowshoes were probably very uncommon. It is not known whether they are now used.

Miscellaneous

192. Fur Scarf
zé·dełco·z (Ramah, Haile)   "scarf, put over the head" (CC)

Ramah

A wildcat skin was dressed with the fur on. The legs were tied together, and the skin was tied about the shoulders with a buckskin thong. Men wore these scarves over buckskin shirts in cold weather. No other furs were worn.

Only Inf. 7 can remember seeing older people wearing this type of scarf. Whether any member of the Ramah community has ever made or used one is not known. Fur scarves are required for certain chants, but whether they are similar to the wildcat skin scarf is not known.

Hill (East and Central)

Wildcat skins were placed around the neck and secured in front by a thong. Worn for warmth, they were called "worn around the neck" (TLLSS, Crownpoint).

Fur collars or neckpieces somewhat resembling stoles were worn by chanters during the ceremonies (see Plate XIV). These were of beaver or otter skin. Sections of hide were sewn together to form a long strip. The width varied from two to six inches, depending upon the amount of available skin. The fur was worn on the outside, and the inside was often lined with cloth. They might be decorated with bayeta and feathers. According to PP (Fort Defiance), they were worn only during ceremonies, and represent a recent (as of the 1930's) addition to Navaho culture.

Comparative

According to the Franciscan Fathers, a fur collar made of wildcat skin was worn with a woven shirt to prevent scratchiness from the rough weave. It was tied with buckskin thongs. Collars made from beaver, otter, yellow fox, kit-fox skins, and spruce were worn for ceremonials (Franciscan Fathers, 1910:390, 413, 458; Matthews, 1902:10–27). Reichard (1950:711) also noted the ritual use of fur scarfs.

Neither of Gifford's informants confirmed the use of a fur scarf as such. The Western informant, however, said that a sheepskin or goatskin dressed with the hair on was worn. The Eastern informant denied this (Gifford, 1940:37, 129).

193. Skin Mittens

našdói· láȝiš (Ramah, Haile) "mountain lion glove (hand bag)" (CC)

Ramah

Mittens were made from two pieces of wildcat skin, dressed with the fur on. Holes were punched, and the two sections were sewn together with sinew. A separate section was made for the thumb. Inf. 7 first said that this section was not attached directly to the mitten, but was tied to the wrist with buckskin thongs; he later (1947) contradicted himself on this statement. Mittens were not fitted to the individual, but were made in general sizes.

Either men or women made them, at any time or place (Inf. 7). They were worn fur side in to keep the hands warm.

Inf. 7 has seen skin mittens, but has never made any. Inf. 8 heard about them and guessed that they were made "just before the winter time." They are no longer made. Mittens and gloves are now purchased. Roberts found one, two, and one pairs of gloves, respectively, in his three Ramah households; and in 1940, Inf. 12's son was seen wearing pigskin gloves (Roberts, 1951:17).

Hill (East, Central, and West)

Skin mittens were made from the hides of the wildcat (WH, Wheatfields; TLLSS, Crownpoint; C, Chinle), squirrel (GH, White Cone), and mountain lion (C; SG, Keams Canyon). The use of squirrel skin was denied by PP (Fort Defiance). The skins were dressed, and if large enough, were folded and marked for cutting, the hand being used for a pattern. When squirrel skins were used, two hides were necessary for each mitten. Occasionally mittens were made with thumbs, which were either cut in the pattern (WH, SG, GH), or cut separately and attached later (C). The mittens were then sewn with sinew along the top and inside. According to TLLSS and SG, they extended about five inches up the arm and were secured by a buckskin drawstring. According to WH and TLLSS, to prevent loss, the mittens were secured to each other by a long thong which passed around the neck of the wearer.

Comparative

The Franciscan Fathers (1910:460) stated that mittens were made of wildcat skin. They were not described, but the term used confirmed that used at Ramah. Gifford's Western Navaho informant said that wildcat skin mittens were made with separate thumbs and worn fur side in with a cord to hang them around the neck. The Eastern informant denied fur mittens (Gifford, 1940:39, 131).

194. Knitted Mittens

láǯiš (Ramah, Haile) "glove (hand bag)" (CC); "finger bag"

Ramah

Wool of any color was used, but black and white were most common; mittens were knitted in solid colors, with no patterned ridges. According to Inf. 32, knitting began at the wrist end, and the hand portion was knitted in one piece, like a sock. A hole was left at one side for the thumb, which was then knitted separately and sewn to the mitten. Inf. 7 said mittens were made in one piece. The finished product came up above the wrist. According to Inf. 7, one type of mitten required more wool and lasted from one season to the next.

Either men or women knitted mittens, but only during the winter, although "socks" were made all year round (Inf. 7). They were stored in the homes, but in no particular manner (Inf. 7).

Inf. 32 has made mittens, but she stopped soon after the return from Fort Sumner. Inf. 7 has not made them, and he said that he had no heirloom specimens. Apparently no one in the Ramah area now makes them.

Hill (Central)

Both informants (WH, Wheatfields; PP, Fort Defiance) had used knitted mittens. According to them, mittens were made both with and without thumbs.

Comparative

The use of knitted mittens has passed practically unnoticed among the Navaho. The only information on them comes from the Franciscan Fathers (1910:255), who reported that they were knitted of blue, white, and black yarns. Mittens were usually made with a separate thumb, but by 1910, some were made in glove form. Knitted mittens were not noted by Gifford (1940:39).

195. Pouch for Personal Equipment

da·na·γízi (Ramah) pouch

Ramah

Buckskin pouches were made in two pieces; they were either rectangular or rounded in shape. The pieces were sewn together with buckskin or sinew,

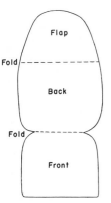

195.1. Pouch pattern, after Hill

195.a. Hashke Yazhe (1923) has a pouch for personal equipment over his shoulder. Note also his skin cap (Tr. 184), necklace (Tr. 197), concho belt (Tr. 180), and cotton (velveteen) shirt (Tr. 172).

hair side inside; a flap was left which was either fastened with silver buttons or tied with a thong which passed through two holes in the flap. A buckskin strap, dressed with the hair on, was then attached to the pouch. Completed pouches were about six inches long (see 175.a).

At first, pouches were not fringed, painted, beaded, or decorated with quills. Rawhide pouches began to be made about the time of white contact, and at this time beads and fringes were added. For protection from bears, snakes, or lightning, an arrow point or the cap of a horned toad, or both, were sewn on the pouch strap. An unperforated elk tooth might also be secured with a piece of buckskin, also to "scare the lightning."

Pouches were made by both men and women, but primarily used by men (Inf. 7) for carrying fire-making equipment. The strap was worn over either shoulder, and the pouch was carried at all times.

It is not known when these pouches ceased to be used by the Ramah people, or whether any Ramah informants have made or used them. They are no longer used. When fire-making equipment is still used, as in ceremonials, it is stored in the regular medicine bag. Other personal items are stored in pockets or in modern containers. Roberts noted a total of sixteen large imitation leather handbags or purses for the women of his three households, "while the men carried regular pocketbooks (a total of six)" (Roberts, 1951:17, 48).

Hill (Central and West)

Pouches were most frequently made of dressed mountain lion skin, sometimes of buckskin, and more recently of leather. When lion skin was used the fur was left on the hide. Buckskin, however, was dehaired, and the flesh side formed the inside. Pouches were cut in a single piece; the back and front were folded on each other and the sides were sewn with sinew (see 195.1). The flap was folded over the face and fastened there by a thong or button. Pouches varied from eight to twelve inches in width (PP, Fort Defiance; C, Chinle).

Shoulder straps were cut from the same material as the pouch. These were sewn along the side seams near the top (PP, C). There is some indication that shoulder straps were not always present. PP said that only some pouches had them, and SG (Keams Canyon) said that they were introduced after contact with the Americans.

C stated that pouches were undecorated until the advent of silverworking among the Navaho. According to PP, however, pouches were earlier ornamented with shells, which were later replaced by silver and turquoise.

Pouches were used as receptacles for a variety of articles, "everything necessary in everyday life" (C). Informants listed the following items: pollen (*ntliz*), ceremonial stuffs, flint and steel, tobacco, any valuables (PP); tobacco, pipes, cornhusks for cigarettes, flint and steel, a bag of pollen (C). "A man never went anywhere without a bag of pollen" (C).

Comparative

When the Navaho began to make and use these pouches is uncertain. One was found in a Navaho burial in Chaco Canyon, probably dating from the early part of the nineteenth century—"a plain, empty leather pouch tied at the top with a leather thong" (Malcolm, 1939:19). Simpson (1850:101), in describing the appearance of Mariano, stated that he wore a pouch at his side. Other nineteenth-century observers did not mention this trait, although many of the men photographed during this period carried pouches (Peabody Museum collection).

It is probable that Inf. 7 was unwarrantably restricting the use of the pouch he described when he said that it was used for fire-making equipment, although the narrator of the *Son of Old Man Hat,* speaking of his first encounter with matches, stated: "She handed me a little pouch, decorated with white beads around the edges and the middle, and said, 'Your brother gave it to you. There are some matches in it'" (Dyk, 1938:36).

The Franciscan Fathers (1910:311, 465) described a pouch formerly used for carrying "steel and flint, corn leaves and tobacco, pollen, and the dice used in gambling." It was carried on the left hip, with the strap over the right shoulder. Both the pouch and strap were often decorated with small silver buttons. By 1910, the pouch, when used, contained "tobacco, matches, pocket-knife, money, and other small articles." Only the older members of the tribe carried pouches, since the younger people wore modern clothes well supplied with pockets. In 1937, however, Adair saw a Navaho near Kayenta wearing a pouch decorated with fifty-two quarters on the shoulder strap, and "thirty rounded buttons made of quarters on the pouch itself, with a single fifty-cent piece in the center" (Adair, 1944:46).

196. Canes giš (Haile)   cane (CC)

Ramah
Members of the households studied by Roberts (1951:55) knew of canes (and crutches). Other data were not obtained.

Hill (East and Central)
Canes were made and used by the old and feeble to assist them in moving about (PP, Fort Defiance; TOMC, Red Rock). They might be fashioned from any kind of wood but were usually of oak or juniper (TOMC).

Comparative
The Franciscan Fathers (1910:390–391) mentioned the cane only in connection with the mask and actions of the personator in the Night Chant, the Hunchback.

Ornamentation

197. Necklace   yo·'diʒo·lí (Ramah)   "round bead"

báš̌žini· (Ramah)   "black shell"

do·X̌iži· (Ramah)   "blue shell"

yo·łgai (Ramah, Lamphere)   "white shell"

di·čiłí (Ramah)   "abalone"; "which always glitters"

Ramah

Variously shaped pieces of turquoise or shell were strung on a fine buckskin thong or thread. Turquoise pendants were worn separately or with other beads. Inf. 7 said that shell necklaces were made from black shell, blue shell, and white shell, and that an abalone shell pendant was sometimes worn with these (see Plate XIV, 107.e, 164.a, 164.b). Inf. 7 said that necklaces were not made of sweet grass, buckskin straps, snail shells, bone tubes, seeds, or claws from bears, wolves, wildcats, or eagles.

Necklaces were worn at any time, but especially at ceremonials and gatherings; both men and women wore them. They were stored in a safe place, such as a locker or suitcase. Inf. 7 still has some necklaces that belonged to his father. When the string became worn, the beads were restrung.

It is not known when necklaces were first worn. According to Inf. 7, the type he described was borrowed from the Pueblos, especially Zuni. Inf. 82 has a necklace of old coral beads bought at Zuni years ago. These old types were not made in the Ramah area. Necklaces of turquoise and shell are still worn in the Ramah community (see 82.a), although new types have been introduced which vie in popularity with the older forms. Many of these are at least partly of silver set with turquoise. Some are of cheap commercial glass beads.

Roberts was told in 1946 that no one worked bone or horn, but "everyone" made shell beads (his informant named three people). Beads were cut to size with a hacksaw and perforated with a knife. Roberts was extremely doubtful of this statement.

Inf. 55 described mountain lion claw ornaments. He told McAllester that they were used in ceremonial capacity. "And they put strings of mountain lion claws on you too. There are two that cross each other. They go over your shoulder and across your chest." He said that about fifteen claws were on each string. "And they put a small one around each wrist—about four claws on each one."

Hill (East and Central)

Both informants (PP, Fort Defiance; TLLSS, Crownpoint) agreed that the most common materials used for beads were abalone and clam shell, turquoise and red stone (coral?) (see Plate VIII). Most of these were finished products imported from the Pueblos. According to PP, the use of silver beads was comparatively recent (see Plate XIII). He placed the beginning of the manufacture of soldered silver beads about 1900, cast beads between 1915 and 1920.

Lamphere (East)
PM and EP said that there are several kinds of necklaces; the name depends upon the type of beads. The general term for necklace is "beads" (*yoo*). A coral necklace is called "red beads."

Fishler (West)
Wildcat claws were made into necklaces (FG, TT, Coalmine). TT had seen such necklaces.

Comparative
Necklaces of bear claws may have been one of the earliest forms of ornament. About 1827, members of Pattie's company "killed several bears, the talons of which the Indians took for necklaces" (Pattie, 1905:166). The next reference, in 1850, is a sketch of a Navaho wearing a necklace the details of which are not clear (Simpson, 1850:pl. 50). By 1855, the Navaho around Fort Defiance were noticed wearing "numerous strings of fine coral" (Davis, 1857:411). Letherman (1856:290), however, failed to mention such ornaments. Dyk (1938:3) told of a woman having a string of beads in 1868. Dellenbaugh (1906:103) published a photograph, apparently taken in the early 1870's showing a Navaho "chief" wearing a necklace similar to modern shell and turquoise ones. Neither he nor Thompson mentioned these in their manuscripts on this expedition (Dellenbaugh, n.d.:Thompson, 1871). At about this time, Powell (n.d.:50) mentioned amulets of scented grass which were worn "suspended from the ears or around the neck."

Adair was told by Chee Dodge that during the earlier part of the nineteenth century, before the exile at Fort Sumner, bits of scrap tin and other metal were strung on leather and worn about the neck or wrist. A photograph taken in the 1860's shows a man wearing one of these ornaments; another shows a women. In another photograph from this period, a woman is wearing what appears to be a necklace of hemispherical beads (Adair, 1944:43). (All three photographs are in the Laboratory of Anthropology in Santa Fe). These beads were certainly made by the Navaho in the early 1880's (Matthews, 1883:171–172), but it was some time later that the so-called squash blossom necklaces began to be popular (Adair, 1944:43).

Old photographs in the Harvard Peabody Museum collection confirm the use of turquoise and shell beads, although the year or period when they came into use is difficult to ascertain. By 1881, however, they were common, and worthy of note by Bourke. Heirlooms of coral (obtained in former years from the Spanish) and turquoise beads were prized, but those who had none wore "strands of silver hemispheres and balls of copper." Only pure silver and copper were used; the Navaho rejected plated ware at once. "Their chalchiutl beads are made by slicing the turquoise into narrow plates and boring these with *flint*." These beads were made by the Zuni, Santo Domingo, and other neighbors, and purchased by the Navaho. Necklaces were also made of sea shells, purchased from the Zuni who obtained them on frequent pilgrimages to the coast in the vicinity of Los Angeles, California, and from malachite. Some used the large varied blue and white trade beads. The silver necklace, however, was typical (Bourke, 1936:84, 86, 223, 224).

XIII. Navaho jewelry. In the center is a squash blossom necklace (Tr. 197). On the left, from top to bottom, are three bracelets (Tr. 200), a ring (Tr. 201), and brooch (cf. Tr. 202). Two bracelets, the ring, and the brooch are set with turquoise. On the right are two pairs of conchos, for buttons, cufflinks (modern), or earrings, a necklace ornament (*najahe;* Tr. 197), and a button (Tr. 202).

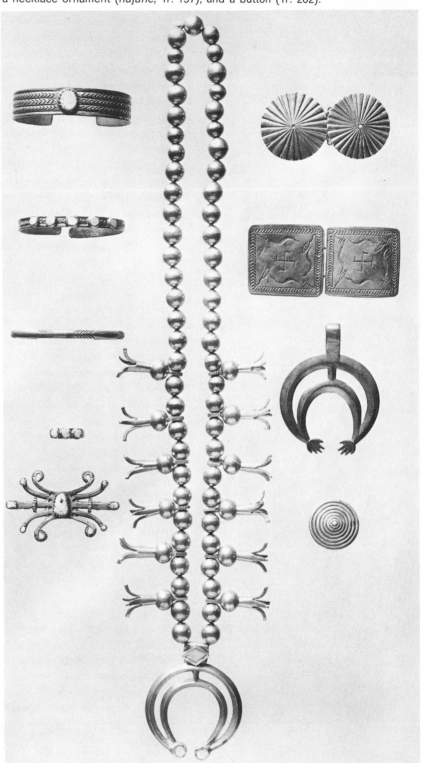

Clothing   Necklaces of "coral, thin discs of white shell and turquoise, and strings of globular silver beads and other ornaments of their own manufacture" were typical, according to Stephen (1893:355). In addition to these, the Franciscan Fathers listed beads of red stone, olivella shell, black stone, conch and tortoise shell obtained from the traders. Necklaces were made according to personal taste. If necessary, beads were perforated with the drill (see Trait 199), but more often they were obtained from traders or Pueblo Indians, especially the Zuni (Franciscan Fathers, 1910:300–301, 465).

Necklaces, according to Gifford's Navaho informants, were made from shell, turquoise, and cannel coal (jet), but not from bone or wood. Both informants agreed that olivella shell disc and whole shell beads were not made by the Navaho but were found in ruins or imported from the Pueblos or Spanish-Americans. Necklaces were not made from eagle talons or animal dewclaws, nor was haliotis shell used in inlay. The Western informant said that red shell beads and bear claws were used for necklaces or pendants, and that turquoise disc beads were found ready made. These were denied by the Eastern informant. The Eastern informant said that clamshell disc beads (about which the Western informant was doubtful), cylindrical shell beads sometimes found in ruins, and haliotis pendants (both denied by the Western informant) were known. In addition the Eastern informant confirmed the use of a turkey beard pendant "by shaman" and seed beads. He said that juniper seed beads were the only kind used in early times. These were ground down at one end until an opening appeared; the other end had a natural opening. They were threaded on sinew. The Eastern informant used turquoise in pendants, but not in disc beads; turquoise was imported, not found. He denied all necklaces of animal or bird claws (Gifford, 1940:33, 34, 123–125; see also Coolidge, 1930:109–112).

Beads have been found in Navaho sites dating from the seventeenth century. In the Gobernador area, Keur (1944:81) found perforated olivella shells, pendants of clay and chalcedony, a large fragment of a blue glass trade bead of a type "usually associated with late seventeenth and early eighteenth century historic sites." At Big Bead Mesa, which dates from the beginning of the eighteenth century, four small beads were found: a saucer-shaped one made from a univalve shell, and three bone beads with tiny perforations. A flat disc of turquoise was found on the surface; it probably represented an unfinished bead. Another uncut fragment was also found (Keur, 1941: 62–63).

In Canyon de Chelly, in the refuse area of some hogans regarded by Hurt as eighteenth-century, glass trade beads were discovered. These were identified by Woodward as a type in use between 1758 and 1860 (Hurt, 1942:96). Apparently investigators have found no beads at other sites.

198. Earrings

ʒaˑƛóˑł (Ramah, Haile)   ear pendant; "ear string" (CC)

ʒa ˑaɣánáˑáhí (Ramah, Haile)   "ear, going through pierced ear" (CC)

Ramah

According to Inf. 7, small pieces of turquoise were the earliest type of earrings. Later, long strings of glass beads were worn, then copper and silver. None

198.a. A prominent leader, near Dinnahotso, Arizona, wearing turquoise earrings; note the plaited buckskin lasso over his shoulder

was made of white shell, abalone, stone, or buckskin loops (Infs. 7, 16). Turquoise pieces were strung on thongs or thread (see Plate IV). Silver earrings were made by silversmiths at Ramah and elsewhere (see Plate XIII).

Both men and women wore earrings of the same type; Inf. 7 said that men wore turquoise, women wore turquoise and glass, and children wore glass. Other informants said that children also wore turquoise eardrops. Ages at which ears were pierced varied; Inf. 12's granddaughter's were pierced when she was a few hours old. Other informants said that piercing was done immediately after birth (Inf. 54), at the age of one day (Inf. 16), three or four days (Inf. 14), or between ten days and a month (Inf. 7). The operation was performed by the child's mother, who used a needle. A twisted string rubbed with sheep tallow was placed in the hole to keep it open until it healed. According to Inf. 7, not all men had their ears pierced.

Earrings are still worn by people of various ages. Men ordinarily wear the turquoise eardrops (Infs. 1, 63, 130; see 198.a). Inf. 9 said he had worn heavy silver rings, but stopped because they were so heavy they hurt his ears when he rode. Women commonly wear glass beads or silver earrings. Inf. 7 said that these are recent introductions. Others were observed wearing earrings, including Inf. 96's two daughters and Inf. 259's small son. Inf. 82 has two turquoise eardrops bought at Zuni "a long time ago," Inf. 97 wears blue bead earrings, and Inf. 41 has some of imitation turquoise.

Hill (East and Central)

Turquoise was ground to the desired shape and earrings were made (IS, Lukachukai). According to PP (Fort Defiance) and TLLSS (Crownpoint), these were the earliest type; metal ones came later. IS and PP stated that the first metal earrings consisted of a circle of copper wire inserted through two or three copper beads. Later they were made of silver.

Comparative

There is no archaeological evidence of earrings.

There is no information on earrings from the early historic periods. Observers such as Pattie, Letherman, Davis, and Thompson did not mention them nor were they evident in Simpson's pictures (Simpson, 1850:pls. 44, 49, 50, 52) or in those from the Powell expedition, 1871–1872 (Dellenbaugh, 1906:103, 318). Although some are shown in Dellenbaugh's photographs, it is likely that they were taken some time after the Powell expedition (Dellenbaugh, 1901:148, 152; Dellenbaugh, 1906:65). Dellenbaugh (1901:296) stated that he could not recall that any Navaho met on the Powell expedition wore silver ornaments of any kind.

By 1881, however, Navaho in the Fort Defiance area were wearing earrings of coral, turquoise, silver, sea shells, and malachite, "in the form of a simple solid ring . . . fastened by a sliding button at bottom." Bourke stated that Navaho earrings were similar to those of the Zuni, but the Navaho did not make imitations. His informant said that the Zuni took a small piece of hardwood and cut, polished, and stained it to look like stone (Bourke, 1936:86, 225).

By 1890, the men were wearing large silver earrings, and Stephen noted no other type for that period. He said that women no longer wore earrings, although their ears were pierced. The men explained this, attributing it to the "notorious" infidelity of their women. Formerly "when married women wore ornaments in their ears, an injured husband punished an unfaithful wife by tearing them through the lobes." When a girl married, she removed her earrings and wore them hanging from her necklace (Stephen, 1893:356; see also Newcomb, 1940a:35, who said that only unmarried girls wore turquoise pendants).

The Franciscan Fathers agreed that only the men wore earrings, although the women had pierced ears. Earrings for men were made of a small string of thin turquoise discs, or a flat piece of polished turquoise, or "of good sized silver rings, some of which have one or more loosely sliding beads strung upon them." Silver earrings were sometimes large and heavy, and to prevent discomfort when the wearer rode, they were often turned up over the ear (Franciscan Fathers, 1910:464–465, 284).

Gifford's Eastern Navaho informant said that women wore turquoise ear pendants and sometimes beads or a stick of wood, but not a haliotis pendant or a whole olivella shell. The Western informant said that both olivella and turquoise pendants were worn, but he did not indicate the sex of the wearer. Informants agreed that babies' ears were pierced with a bone awl. The Western informant said that a hardwood needle was also used; this was denied by the Western informant (Gifford, 1940:36, 37, 129).

Adair implied that either silver earrings were worn first or that early they displaced the turquoise ones, which later came into vogue again. At the end of the nineteenth century, Navaho men were wearing silver earrings which were either "a large, hoop-shaped ring with a small hollow silver ball at the bottom (sometimes a squash blossom bead instead of the ball)," or a pendant consisting of "one long, cone-shaped piece, which hung with the large end down, with a small squash blossom having short 'petals' hanging from it." These types were not stamped; sometimes a hoop, "flattened and stamped with dies," was worn. These types were abandoned when turquoise became available at the turn of the century. Men adopted the pendant earring, made from nuggets of turquoise perforated and fastened to the pierced ear by a piece of string. In the early 1940's, many of these earrings were worn, especially by "the older men of the tribe and those Navaho who live in the least accessible parts of the northern reservation" (Adair, 1944:48–49).

Earrings for women, according to Adair (1944:48–49), were quite different. Loops of small turquoise beads with several bits of red shell at the bottom were formerly worn. By the 1940's these were worn on necklaces, interspersed with larger pieces of turquoise. Silver earrings "often elaborate in design, set with many stones, and surrounded by bits of bent wire" were common. These reflected a Zuni influence.

Woodward (1938:28, 68) stated that nearly all the original forms of silver earrings were paralleled by earlier styles worn by Indians east of the Mississippi, and suggested the eastern area as the source for the Navaho. Some of the early earrings, according to him, were made of iron, like those in the Mindeleff collection at the United States National Museum.

Earrings are still worn by the Navaho, both men and women, apparently throughout the area. Adair noted no regional difference in styles in modern times. A great proportion of the earrings now made, however, are produced for the commercial market.

199. Drill be· bᵃγáda·ańiłí (Haile) "with it drilling" (CC)

Ramah

For perforating beads, either an unhafted arrowhead or an arrow was used, or in recent times, the pump drill. It was not extensively used, however, for whenever possible beads for necklaces and earrings were obtained through trade from the Pueblo Indians.

When the pump drill was introduced is not known (Inf. 16). Kluckhohn observed the use of a steel needle for perforating a shell used as a chant token.

Hill (Central)

Before the introduction of the pump drill, according to PP (Fort Defiance), the Navaho used a stone-pointed hand drill on those rare occasions when they wished to bore holes in turquoise. The bit of the drill was fashioned from a long flake of white chert or chalcedony; it was set in a hole in one end of the handle, or the handle was split and the stone inserted and bound in place.

A section the size and shape of the turquoise to be perforated was removed from a flat piece of wood. The turquoise was set in the hole, the wood acting as a vise and preventing the turquoise from slipping during the drilling.

The drill was operated with downward pressure in the same manner as the firedrill (see Trait 111), except that more pressure was necessary. Consequently the handle of this drill was larger than that of the firedrill to prevent blistering of the operator's hands. Turquoise beads were drilled from both sides to prevent splitting as the perforations were completed.

The use of the pump drill was confirmed by IS (Lukachukai) and PP. Both informants agreed that it was of recent introduction and of Pueblo provenience. It was used only for drilling beads.

Comparative

There is some evidence that at an earlier period the Navaho perforated objects by drilling. Gifford (1940:27, 115) recorded for both Navaho groups a tiny, unhafted chert drill held in the fingers. Both groups placed the object to be drilled in a wooden "vise" or in a hole in the ground. The Eastern informant confirmed but the Western denied a composite drill with a wooden shaft that varied in length. Both groups regarded the pump drill as modern, and the Western informant agreed that it was used for shell beads.

Other evidence indicated that the pump drill was being used in the later nineteenth century. Mooney photographed a Navaho using one in Keams Canyon around 1893 (Matthews, 1897:13). Bourke said that the Navaho in the Fort Defiance area in 1881 did not use the "bow drill" (Bourke, 1936:236).

According to the Franciscan Fathers (1910:301), the "bow drill"—which, from their description and illustration (see 199.1) is a pump drill, not a bow drill—was still being used for perforating beads of conch, tortoise, or olivella shells, turquoise, red stone, and other materials in 1910. Beads were polished and smoothed on sandstone before being perforated. The drill point, which usually consisted of a strong wire nail, was secured with sinew to a hardwood shaft. A crosspiece of soft wood was placed over the shaft to allow freedom of movement. A string was passed through each end of the crosspiece and

199.1. Pump drill, after the Franciscan Fathers

a hole in the upper end of the shaft. A stone disc was fitted to the shaft to steady it. For drilling, the operator twisted the crosspiece, wrapping the string around the shaft; then, by pumping up and down, he made the drill spin (see Plate V). This process continued until the perforation was made.

There is scant archaeological evidence for the drill. Keur apparently found none on Big Bead Mesa and only three in the Gobernador area (Keur, 1941; 1944:80), and Farmer (1942:73) found only one in his Upper Blanco and Largo sites. Even among the Zuni, who were recently notable in their employment of this implement, the only possible evidence for considerable age of the pump drill is a perforated tortoise shell disc from Hawikuh, which Hodge believed to be a whorl for a spindle or pump drill (Hodge, 1920:144, pl. 51b).

200. Bracelet

lácíní (Haile, Lamphere) "hand bracelet" (CC)

bé·š łičí·· (Ramah) copper bracelet; "red metal"

bé·š łagai (Ramah) silver bracelet; "white metal"

Ramah
Bracelets were made of copper and silver, in various sizes. They were set with turquoise or a flat, brown-black stone cut in circular form (Inf. 8). Other designs were stamped in the metal with steel tools (see Plates IV, XII, XIII). Bracelets were apparently made only by men but anyone could and did wear them.

According to Inf. 7, copper and silver bracelets were called by the term for the respective metals. He said that the first bracelets were of copper, and he thought that these were replaced by silver ones before Fort Sumner. Inf. 8 said that he saw copper bracelets being made for the first time about 1911 near El Morro, where he used to live. He said that silver ones "really came into use" about 1913, although some had been made earlier. His wife had a copper bracelet, but had lost it. He stated that Inf. 64 had recently made one. Only once was brass mentioned; Inf. 256 had seen brass bracelets worn by a woman.

In general, the Ramah Navaho now wear silver bracelets. These are obtained from Navaho in adjoining areas through trade and gift, purchased from the Zuni or in Gallup, inherited, or in some instances manufactured in the Ramah area. The majority are imported. Recently only five silversmiths have worked in the area, probably not more than three of them simultaneously (Infs. 128, 148, 12, 82, 81). Of these Infs. 82 and 148 have made bracelets.

Hill (East and Central)
Early bracelets were produced by hammering. Rude designs were punched on the surfaces with chisels. According to both informants (PP, Fort Defiance; TLLSS, Crownpoint), the manufacture of these by the Navaho postdates Fort Sumner. Both agreed that copper and brass were the first metals (after iron) to be introduced and that silver came later. According to PP, silver did not become plentiful until around 1890. "The railroad paid off in silver." He

said that leather punches used for stamping designs in silver jewelry were introduced through the trading posts about 1890 and that turquoise settings date from the same period.

Lamphere (East)
Lamphere's informants confirmed the term for hand bracelet.

Comparative
According to Woodward (1938:67), an old Navaho born about 1850 stated that before metal was used bracelets were made of deer horn. It was boiled, and when pliable bent in the desired shape. It was then drilled with a bone awl and set with turquoise in pinyon gum. Other references to nonmetal bracelets were lacking, except for Bourke's statement that as late as 1881 the Navaho were wearing "bracelets and garlands of braided sweet grass" as ceremonial costume (Bourke, 1936:223), and Inf. 55's statement at Ramah about mountain lion claw wristlets (see Trait 197, Comparative section).

Robinson, in 1846, saw Navaho men wearing brass arm rings, and was probably the earliest to record the use of bracelets (Robinson, 1932:51). References during the middle of the nineteenth century are lacking, except for Palmer's (1869:51) noting that both brass and silver were worn. He explained that formerly silver bracelets were made by the Navaho out of Mexican coin, "but of late the tribe has had many wars and ornamentations have been impossible for want of means." Dellenbaugh did not mention bracelets in his report from the expedition of the 1870's, but stated that later, after the Navaho obtained silver, they were able to plate copper bracelets with the more precious metal and sell them to the traders as silverwork (Dellenbaugh, n.d.; 1901:295).

By 1881, bracelets were made of "silver, copper, or brass, worn in any number on both wrists" (Bourke, 1936:224). Only silver bracelets were mentioned as part of the costume of the 1890's, and Stephen (1893:62) spoke of them only in connection with the woman's costume.

The Franciscan Fathers agreed that the Navaho made bracelets from Mexican silver coinage purchased from the traders, brass obtained from the Ute, and copper from the Mexicans and traders. Bracelets were made in various shapes with ridges and ornamental cuts, and were of varying widths (Franciscan Fathers, 1910:64, 276–283, 465).

Gifford's Western informants were apparently not questioned about metal bracelets. They denied those of shell, dewclaws, or wildcat claws. The Eastern informant said that turquoise disc beads were used in bracelets (Gifford, 1940:33–34, 125).

Woodward (1938:24–26) believed that the Navaho derived bracelets from neighboring tribes to the north and east, and that the types were similar to those found among the Iroquois, Cherokee, Yuchi, Delaware, and upper Plains people. The similarity was not only in form but in the engraved designs. The ridged or fluted type, for instance, was popular "in the Iroquois country one hundred years before the Navajo began making them. Originally they were made in brass and copper." During the 1830's and 1840's, these were common among the Plains and Rocky Mountain tribes, and the Navaho began to obtain them "in a secondary fashion through trade of spoils of war."

Adair (1944:36) stated that the first bracelets the Navaho made were of copper and brass. Lengths of round heavy wire were obtained and bent to fit the wrist. These bracelets were worn until well after 1900. J. W. Bennett, a trader, said that he "used to buy long bolts of heavy copper wire in hundred-pound lots. The Navajo men and women came into my post and bought lengths of it right off the spool." Mexican silver began to come into the country after 1885, but not until later was it plentiful.

Thereafter the silver bracelet was developed and rapidly became both an ornament and a trade article. (For the technique and development of silver-working, see, for example, Matthews, 1883; Franciscan Fathers, 1910:281–283; Woodward, 1938; Sapir and Hoijer, 1942:425–427; Adair, 1944.)

201. Rings

yoscah (Haile, Lamphere) "bead, ring" (CC)

Ramah
Copper finger rings came into use about the same time as copper bracelets (Infs. 7, 8). Inf. 8 said that he used to wear these copper ornaments and added that they were made near his former residence, El Morro. Whether they were made in Ramah is not known.

Silver rings (see Plates XIII and XIV), usually set with turquoise, are now frequently worn by people of all ages. A few are made by Ramah silversmiths; others are obtained from silversmiths from other areas or bought in Gallup or from the Zuni.

Hill (East and Central)
According to informants (TLLSS, Crownpoint; PP, Fort Defiance), rings were not made by the Navaho until after the return from Fort Sumner. The earliest ones were produced by hammering, either in copper or brass, and later silver.

Lamphere (East)
Lamphere's informants confirmed the term for rings.

Comparative
Rings have not been found in any Navaho sites, nor were they mentioned in any of the early accounts. They were apparently first noticed by Bourke, who found that silver rings were "very much in esteem" around Fort Defiance in 1881 (Bourke, 1936:224–225).

By 1910, according to the Franciscan Fathers (1910:283), the variety of rings was amazing. Women often wore half a dozen on each hand, although men were likely to wear only one or two.

Woodward (1938:28) derived rings, as well as bracelets and necklaces, from contact with northern and eastern Indian groups. Rings made from brass or German silver were patterned after those of the eastern tribes. Patterns and materials, he said, reached the Navaho "via the familiar Plains route which led through the Ute country." The basic forms—the long, oval bezel of plain or etched silver, or the square bezel—"laid the foundations for the turquoise settings which are so popular at the present time."

According to Adair (1944:49), the first rings were bands of plain metal without designs. Later these were marked with an awl, still later by dies, and about 1880 turquoise sets began to be used. These proved popular, and in succeeding years when turquoise was relatively scarce, other stones, such as malachite, cannel coal, garnets, and even bits of glass were also used. Later settings were almost exclusively of turquoise.

Since the 1900's rings have been made not only for sale among the Navaho but also for outside trade.

202. Silver Buttons

yo·· ǹłčíń (Haile)   "bead buttons" (CC)

Ramah
Silver buttons (see Plates VII and VIII) were used to embellish blouses and other garments and to secure moccasins (see Plates X and XIV). The three households studied by Roberts had, respectively, 135, 184, and 55 buttons (Roberts, 1951:22, 47). Other data were not collected, but buttons were a common adornment.

Hill (East and Central)
PP (Fort Defiance) and TLLSS (Crownpoint) stated that silver buttons of Navaho manufacture postdated Fort Sumner. According to them, the earliest forms were produced by hammering and had no stamped designs.

Comparative
According to the Franciscan Fathers, buttons were "the simplest kind of silver ornament." Shapes varied from simple hemispheres to those decorated with ridges, dies, or rectangles. An eyelet of copper wire was soldered to the back for fastening. These were worn on moccasins, leggings, and belts; they were also used on pouches (see 195.a), bridles, cradles, and other items that were "ornamented and set off with them" (Franciscan Fathers, 1910:279–281, 313, 470).

203. Face and Body Paint

λe·š (Ramah, Haile)   white clay

hanaíγa·štiš (Ramah)   charcoal

nakai· bičí·h (Ramah)   red paint; "Mexican red paint" (CC)

łico (Ramah, Haile)   yellow

Ramah
Red and white paint were mixed with grease, tallow, or pitch and rubbed on the face with the hands, or grease was rubbed on and dry pigment or charcoal applied. No brushes or sticks were used in the application. Deer, horse, or sheep bone marrow might also be used as an adhesive, but not water.

Red and white paint on the face or grease rubbed on the body were used to prevent sunburn or chapping, especially by men working in the hot sun. Red ocher mixed with mutton tallow and pitch was rubbed on the face for warmth and to prevent windburn. Men and women used either black or red paint under the eyes to prevent snow blindness; women ordinarily used the red.

According to Inf. 8, some kind of "white dirt" was used to protect the face from gnat and mosquito bites. Inf. 56 had used it for this purpose, and Inf. 1 for protection from the sun; Inf. 82 said that "the old people" used such things but she did not.

Painting was also used extensively in rituals. White paint was smeared on a girl at her *kinaalda* (puberty ceremony), early in the morning when she cut the corn cake (see Kluckhohn and Wyman, 1940:43, 150–152, for an account of painting for Chiracahua Wind Way). Relatives, after four days of mourning following death, painted their faces with *chee,* a line across the cheekbones over the nose. The body was also painted for hunting eagles (see Trait 4).

According to Infs. 7 and 16, paint was used to "frighten the enemy" in war. Faces might be painted in combinations of white, black, red, and yellow; the body was not painted. There were no clan colors, and all men did not paint alike. Inf. 7 said that some men covered their faces with black, yellow, or white paint and described a specific pattern: one side of the face was painted white, the other black; four parallel horizontal red lines were drawn across each cheek. Only warriors could make war paint, and only enough was made just before a foray for the particular occasion. There was no special place for making war paint.

As late as 1940 a number of Ramah people were observed using paint for various purposes. Three women (Infs. 41, 178, 203) wore red clay on their faces to prevent sunburn (Inf. 12). Inf. 12 said that formerly many people did this.

War paint has disappeared, but paint is still used. About the time that Inf. 7 was six (about 1875), "loose" women began to paint two red spots surrounded with a green ring on their cheeks. Both red and green paint for this purpose were obtained from the Spanish-Americans. He said that "in the old days" women did not paint their faces to make themselves more attractive. Today, an occasional Navaho woman is seen with her face rouged, particularly acculturated women, such as Inf. 73.

Hill (Central and West)

Informants agreed that red ocher mixed with tallow was rubbed on the face to prevent sunburn and chapping by wind and cold. "It is not done for beauty as the white women do" (C, Chinle). C said that white clay was sometimes substituted for ocher and that it was also used to protect field workers from gnats. He said that red ocher was occasionally substituted for charcoal in ceremonies.

According to PP (Fort Defiance), one clan ("Formed of her Back") was privileged to wear black face paint while hunting and during the Enemy Way. His explanation was based on mythology (see Trait 184, Hill section).

Body painting was also a feature of ceremonial eagle catching. The naked hunters were painted with white clay and spotted with corn smut (Hill, 1938:163).

For war, red ocher, white clay, blue paint, or charcoal were used to paint symbolic designs. Snakes were painted to give a man power and to make him feared, bear tracks "to make him fierce and brave like the bear." Human hands were thought to symbolize a man, a five-fingered being (Hill, 1936b:15).

Comparative

Accounts of face and body painting appear frequently in the literature of the Navaho. The earliest reference appears to be that of Simpson (1850:88), who noted in 1849, in the Canyon de Chelly region, a mounted Navaho man clad only in a breechclout, his entire body covered by "a kind of whitewash." Because of the military circumstances of the meeting it is possible that this was war paint. Palmer (1869:2) stated that before going to war Navaho men painted "their bodies according to their fancy."

Face painting alone seems first to have been noticed by Thompson (1871:32) in the early 1870's. He said that both Navaho men and women painted their faces. Bourke found that the Navaho at Fort Defiance "freely apply vermillion or red ochre to the cheek-bones and fore-head," according to individual fancy; they used red and white clay and vermilion. Bourke "noticed one with a pair of vermillion spectacles cleverly painted around his eyes" (Bourke, 1936:86, 225).

Later, Stephen (1889:133) noted that instead of carrying snakes in the Snake Dance, the Navaho painted a snake on his arms, "the tail on his shoulder, the body twining down the arm over the back of the hand and between the fingers, the head depicted on the palm." According to Voth (1905:261), in their last fight with the Hopi, the bodies of the Navaho were "decorated with red paint over which they had drawn their fingers when it was still wet, making their bodies full of lines."

The Franciscan Fathers stated that a mixture of red clay and tallow was rubbed on the face and forehead in summer to prevent sunburn and in winter to prevent chapping. The bodies of fire dancers were painted with white clay, as were those of girls in the puberty ceremony. Black was the only paint mentioned for war; it was put on the face for the Enemy Way. It was also used by gamblers when the moccasin game (see Trait 252) was played after sunrise (Franciscan Fathers, 1910:65, 70, 377, 446).

Gifford's Navaho informants agreed that face and body paint were used to prevent sunburn and chapping. The paint was applied with the fingers; red clay, white clay, and charcoal were used. The Eastern informant said that white paint (without fat) was applied for flies or mosquitoes, or in hot weather. Red, black, and white paints were used for war, according to the Eastern informant. He said that the face and trunk were painted, and that the hair was tied in a wild tuft on top of the head to "look like the devil" as battle was entered (Gifford, 1940:34–35, 126, 170).

Mrs. Wetherill recorded both traditional and mythological sanctions for body painting for war. She also said that the body was plastered with mud for warmth (Wetherill, n.d.:2 pp.).

The Navaho stopped using war paint when warfare disappeared as a tribal activity. Paints are still used, however, in ceremonies such as the Holy Way, Evil Way, and Life Way. Colors vary with the Way, but white, black, red, blue, and yellow are used. Reichard has summarized the roles of body painting in Navaho religious practices (Reichard, 1950:especially 628–629; see also Kluckhohn and Wyman, 1940:96–97, 125, 150–152).

204. Tattooing   ꞏakeꞏełčí (Haile, Lamphere)   "writing" (CC)

Ramah

At least one member in each of Roberts' households had letters tattooed on his wrists. Tattooing was reportedly done with cactus spines and was apparently a common practice at Indian schools (Roberts, 1951:48).

Hill (Central and West)

Informants agreed that tattooing among the Navaho was of recent introduction. GH (White Cone) attributed it to the Americans. PP (Fort Defiance) said that it was introduced by children who had become familiar with the trait during sojourns in the boarding schools.

Lamphere (East)

Lamphere's informants confirmed the term for tattooing. PM said that the word meant "written on" or "marked on."

Comparative

The Franciscan Fathers (1910:74, 505) stated that neither tattooing nor scarification was practiced. Gifford's Navaho informants also denied the practice (Gifford, 1940:37).

205. Tweezers   dáɣaꞏꞏ beꞏ ꞏiꞏniží (Ramah, Haile)   "with which the beard is plucked out"; "mustache with it to pull" (CC)

Ramah

Tweezers about one and one-quarter inches square were made from reasonably soft metal. A pair of homemade tweezers was seen at Inf. 53's place in 1940. A year or so later Inf. 7 was seen plucking his facial hair with tweezers, and a pair used for this purpose was owned by Inf. 259.

In 1948, Rapoport was told by Inf. 104 of a preparation he used to remove his beard. It was made for Inf. 104 by Inf. 17's father. He took bark from tree limbs at a point where they had rubbed together in the wind. The bark was worked into a paste and spread on the face. When it caked it was removed and the hair came with it. Inf. 104 thought that this method achieved permanent results in some instances, but not for him. It is possible that the method is similar to that recorded by Gifford.

Hill (Central and West)

Tweezers were made by bending double a piece of metal. According to AS (Lukachukai), they were made from brass or aluminum. IS (Lukachukai) said that they were obtained by trade from the Ute. C (Chinle) used a tin pair, and they were in general use by the older men in 1933–1934. Only hair from the face was removed (IS; MH, Head Springs); no body hair was removed. "It hurts too much" (MH).

Lamphere (East)

Lamphere's informants confirmed the term for tweezers.

Comparative

According to the Franciscan Fathers (1910:83, 284), "the hair[s] of the chin are scrupulously removed by means of a pair of tin tweezers." Silver tweezers were also made. They were called, as at Ramah, "with which the beard is plucked out."

Gifford's Navaho informants said that the beard was plucked with the fingernails. The Western informant said that beards were sometimes allowed to grow, and that inch-wide metal tweezers are now used. The Eastern informant denied these and said that pitch was put on a boy's face to remove the hair so that he would have little when grown (Gifford, 1940:35, 127).

According to Adair (1944:53), "all Navajo men pluck their facial hair." Tweezers, an inch or more wide, were made of a single piece of silver or brass bent double like a hairpin. Most of the men preferred brass ones, which retained a temper better than those of silver. Designs were stamped on the tweezers, which were often worn on a chain around the neck.

Hygiene

206. Menstrual Pad

x̣e·sco·z (Lamphere)   "breechclout" (CC)

Ramah

Informants used various materials, depending on the degree of acculturation. Bailey's oldest informants said they "used sheepskin pads tied to a rag on a buckskin belt." Others used flour sacks or soft cloths. The most acculturated informant had never heard of using sheepskins; she and several other women used sanitary napkins.

The belief in the dangerous character of the menstrual discharge necessitated careful disposal of the pads, although methods varied. Burning, burying, throwing away, and hiding were all mentioned to Bailey (1950:12).

Hill (West)

The menstrual pad was made of shredded bark, placed in a breechclout (MH, Head Springs).

Lamphere (East)

PM said that the word for menstrual pad was the same as that for breechclout; it means "the cloth [or flexible material] for the crotch." Modern sanitary napkins are called by the same term.

When her mother was a little girl, PM said, the women "just used sand"; during menstruation they sat on an area covered with clean sand, which was periodically removed and replaced with clean sand. Lamphere said that PM seemed to think that men had the breechclout first and the women saw it and decided to use it too. PM said that when the men were away, the women of the household or camp would prepare the sheep pelts for use. Unsheared pelts were cut into strips, about the size of a sanitary napkin; these were wrapped in cloth and secured to the waist with a piece of "sewn together cloth." PM said that the sheep pelt pad needed to be changed only once a day, unlike sanitary napkins which require changing several times.

Comparative

Reichard (Newcomb and Reichard, 1937:34) has noted a mythological sanction for the use of menstrual napkins in "The Story of the Navajo Shooting Chant," from the account of Blue Eyes. Haile (1938:53) noted that menstruation did not interfere in any of the features of Enemy Way. The pelt used by a menstruant was "employed as a robe by the medicine carrier of the Black Dancers. Even a small piece of this pelt . . . spotted with blood, is made to serve the purpose."

Dyk, in the life story of Left Handed, treated the fear which was associated with menstruation (Dyk, 1938:33ff). According to the Franciscan Fathers (1910:109), "the touch of a menstruous woman is said to cause stiffness and the hunchback." They did not mention the materials for the menstrual pad.

207. Abdominal Binding

ʾahidilkaˑdi (Lamphere)   "sewn together"

sis łičíˑ (Lamphere)   "red belt"

Ramah

According to Bailey's informants, after birth, a bundle of wool or a pillow was bound firmly across a woman's abdomen with her red belt. It was tied tightly "to make the hanging flesh go back in place" (Bailey, 1950:87–88).

Lamphere (East)

PM said that when a baby was born at home, cloth was sewn together and put around the mother's stomach. Any kind of cloth was used and it was called "sewn together." Later, the woman wore a red woven belt to keep her stomach flat. EP and her mother (MS) confirmed the latter.

208. Yucca Soap

cáˑásziˑ bitˣáláɣʷoš (Ramah, Haile)   "yucca with it suds" (CC)

Ramah

Yucca plants (*Yucca baccata Torr.* or *Yucca glauca Nutt.*) were not owned. They were dug as needed, and Inf. 7 said that excess roots were stored until they dried, then thrown away. All those gathered for ceremonials, however, had to be utilized in the course of the ritual (Inf. 267).

To make soap, a root was beaten between two sticks or rocks to remove the bark and soften it. The pulp was then stirred vigorously in warm water to produce suds. Formerly this was done in a woven basket; now it is done in a basin, except on ceremonial occasions when a basket is still required (see Kluckhohn and Wyman, 1940:90–92, 128–129, 149, 165–166, 173; Leighton, 1941b:19–20, and photographs).

Women made this soap, but it was used by men, women, and children. The soapy lather was rubbed in the hair, which was then rinsed with clear

208.a. Pounded yucca root to be used for hair-washing suds

water. Men washed their own hair, but a woman could help wash a child's hair. Previously yucca suds were also used to wash blankets (Inf. 15).

Formerly this was the only soap used. It is still used, especially as a shampoo and for ritual occasions. It has been seen by Kluckhohn, the Leightons, and Flora Bailey in several households (those of Infs. 12, 96, 50). Its function as a cleansing agent has, however, been largely displaced by commercial brands of soap (Vestal, 1952:21, has summarized all the uses of yucca known by the Ramah Navaho).

Hill (Central and West)
Informants (SG, Keams Canyon; GH, White Cone; LM, Canyon del Muerto; IS, Lukachukai) confirmed Ramah reports on the use of yucca root for soap in both religious and secular capacities.

Comparative
The use of the yucca root for soap has been confirmed by many observers, although early reports are apparently lacking. Matthews stated that all species of yucca have saponine in their roots, and all were used for cleansing purposes. In ceremonials such as the Mountain Chant, the suds were used for baths and shampoos (Matthews, 1887:251; 1897:229; see also Elmore, 1944:34–35; Wyman, 1936a:642ff).

The Franciscan Fathers (1910:340) stated that the Navaho used yucca suds, prepared as at Ramah, to wash their heads and hair once or twice a week. Gifford's Navaho informants agreed that the hair was washed with yucca suds, which also served to kill head lice. The Eastern informant added that after washing, the hair was rubbed in grease or marrow and the lice shaken out on hot stones in the sweathouse (Gifford, 1940:36, 128).

Wyman and Harris (1941:53) also cited the yucca shampoo, adding that "*Artemisia spp.* (*A. campestris*) may be added for its fragrance or to make the hair 'long and soft' and prevent its falling." Other plants were also used "to prevent falling hair and dandruff, or as hair restorers."

Chapter 4 Ritual

Navaho ritual has captured the imagination of almost every observer. Although many of the rites were and are not public, most of them have been witnessed, and a wealth of material describing chant procedures has been published. In addition, there are a number of comprehensive papers covering specialized areas of Navaho religion that deal with the problems of chant complexes (Kluckhohn and Wyman, 1940), the Navaho classification of chants (Wyman and Kluckhohn, 1938), and the utilization of botanical and other environmental resources in chant practice (Wyman and Harris, 1941). Most of these works contain information on the traits in this chapter. Because of the amount of published material available elsewhere, we have made no attempt to be all-inclusive. Our primary purpose is to make previously unpublished material available for the use of scholars. Those interested in the complete details on rites should consult works by Haile, Matthews, Reichard, Wyman, and others.

Traits discussed initially were selected to facilitate the transition from one chapter to another. In Chapter 3, the shading from clothing and ornamentation to ornamentation and hygiene is close; it is hygiene that bridges the gap between Chapters 3 and 4. Yucca soap is often used for ritual hair washings, just as the sweathouse, the first trait of ritual described, is often used for hygiene. Most of the other ritual items pertain to the chanter and the material equipment necessary for the chants he conducts. For the most part the principle utilized in the discussion of shelter, "the hogan, its insides," is applicable to ritual traits, and "the medicine bag, its insides" has been used as a guiding principle of organization. Unless otherwise specified, most ritual traits are still extant.

Some traits appearing elsewhere in the book, such as bows and arrows, and skin caps, are used in ceremonies as well as for secular purposes. These traits were only secondarily used for ritual, and thus have been described in the category of their primary usage. Traits pertaining to warfare are in most cases obsolete except in ritual context and have therefore been placed in this chapter. Acculturation has taken its toll over the years, and other traits, such as the firedrill, are also being retained in their original form for ritual use only or are being replaced by those more easily available. Tschopik's papers (1938, 1940) on the obsolescence of Navaho pottery and basketry indicate the manner in which such changes have occurred and the role of religious belief in accelerating or inhibiting change.

Ceremonies and Curing

209. Sweathouse

tˣáčéh (Ramah, Haile)

Ramah

The site selected was usually at some distance from the hogan "or the women might see [the men] without their clothes on" (Inf. 12). Sweathouses built near the dwelling in connection with certain ceremonials (for warfare or epidemics) had to be built on the north side and at a distance of about two

209.a. Sweathouse

hundred yards. According to Inf. 12, the sweathouse could be located in any direction from the hogan, at a place determined by the availability of suitable rocks. It was usually within a half mile of the hogan, since blankets and water had to be carried to it. Inf. 132 had two sweathouses in 1938, each located about two hundred yards east of a hogan group. Inf. 45 said that a man's sweathouse might be located in any direction but that a woman's had to be to the south of the hogan.

A pit was dug small enough to be effective: "A big sweathouse would not make you hot enough" (Inf. 8). Over the pit a framework of three interlocked forked poles (*sahdii*) was constructed. The poles were placed with the growing ends pointing up. "You don't have to do this if you are just going to use the sweathouse for taking your bath, but if you use it for medicines the growing ends of the sticks must point up." Two straight poles (*chee etii silaii* were placed against the framework, and another piece of timber was placed across their tops to form the doorway. It was covered with a blanket and always faced the east.

When the framework was in position, poles were added around the circumference. Next the structure was covered with pine needles and rabbit brush, then earth. The floor was lined with shredded juniper bark, grass, or rabbit brush. A pit for the heated rocks (*tse nanil*) was dug on the north side of the lodge (see Leighton, 1941c:20–21, for excellent photographs, taken at Ramah).

Men built the sweathouses, even if women used them. Sometimes a man built his own, or several men cooperated. Sweathouses were built in connection with ceremonials, or merely because a man or woman wanted a sweat bath. In the former case, the sweathouse could be utilized after the ceremony for nonritual purposes. For some Hunting Ways, a new sweathouse was required before the hunters departed. In that event, all the men in the hunting party helped in the construction. A sweathouse was sometimes built near the camping place of a hunting or war party, but this was merely a blanket-covered framework. Certain ceremonials connected with warfare or with the prevention or curing of epidemics also required special sweathouses.

In any event, a sweathouse had to be completed in a single day. If it were not finished when the sun began to set, it was covered with a blanket and used, and later furnished with a more permanent covering.

For a sweat bath, rocks were heated in a fire near the sweathouse, brought in on forked poles or sticks (see below), and placed in the firepit. According to Infs. 12 and 7, who provided most of the data about sweathouses, no water was used—the dry heat from the stones was enough to produce sweating. In winter, snow was placed on the stones when they began to cool. After sweating, the men rolled in the snow; in summer, they rubbed themselves with earth. Usually they returned to the sweathouse several times, until the stones were cool and no longer produced perspiration. According to Inf. 7, bathers sat where they liked, or lay down. They must not sleep, however; "it will kill you."

Men usually used sweathouses, and a few women also took sweat baths; the two sexes did not bathe together according to Infs. 7, 12, and 82, nor did they use each other's sweathouses. One or several men bathed at a time. Small boys sometimes accompanied the men, but they were not allowed to bathe alone. Informants gave various ages when boys were first allowed to take a sweat bath: Inf. 3 said at six years, Inf. 7 at eight or nine years; and when they were allowed to go in alone: Inf. 3 at ten years, Inf. 7 at ten or twelve years, Inf. 12 at twelve years. One elderly woman (Inf. 280) said that only old women might take sweat baths and that she had never heard of a young woman taking one. At least one woman (Inf. 36), however, said she had used the sweathouse when she was a young girl; and others have been known to do so. Men wore loincloths in the sweathouse (Infs. 7, 32, 258, 55); women wore skirts (Inf. 55).

Inf. 132 said that he bathed at intervals of two weeks to a month. Infs. 2 and 7 said that sweat baths were taken in the daytime. One taken during a war expedition might be taken at night, but a hole had to be left in the roof "or the Holy People wouldn't like it" (Inf. 2). According to Inf. 7, however, even this precaution did not justify taking a sweat bath at night. Sweat baths were mandatory for warriors returning from the raid (Inf. 2) and for undertakers four days after a burial (Inf. 7). A Holy Way singer had to take one the day he finished a chant, the patient on the fourth day following the ceremony (Inf. 45). Patients for other chants did not have to take sweat baths. Inf. 7 said that the sweathouse was used equally in summer and winter, but Inf. 8 did not like taking sweat baths in summer, "when snakes and mice were loose." The sweathouse was used "mostly when you're tired" (Inf. 7), but a sweat bath was never taken merely for cleanliness or because of fatigue. "You always pray and sing for good things."

Men usually sang sweathouse songs while bathing, and often used the sweathouse as a ritual center or men's club room where general plans were discussed and news imparted. Women did not sing songs, nor were they likely to gather there in numbers.

Either men or women could own sweathouses, but men usually did. Each man in the family might have his own (Inf. 8's family). Although the sexes were usually separated, Inf. 48 said that since she did not own a sweathouse, she used that belonging to the men of her family. According to Inf. 7, anyone might use the house without the owner's permission. "It was built for the people."

A sweathouse might last several years. An old one was torn down and the poles were moved to another site and reused. This was done at Inf. 12's place in 1940. A sweathouse was also dismantled and moved when the site became "dirty," or if the owner died. "This renews it" (Inf. 7). If wood was plentiful, however, new poles were used.

The Ramah Navaho regarded the sweathouse as part of the old Navaho culture, with origins firmly incorporated in legend and myth; yet the sweathouse remains a vital part of the present culture. The structure of the sweathouse has apparently undergone little change with regard to materials, technique of manufacture, or function.

Between 1936 and 1944, the construction of sweathouses was noted at several places (Infs. 2, 8, 9, 12). Twenty-one families reported that they had and used sweathouses; only four claimed to have none. Fifty-six men in the community took or were known to have taken sweat baths; only one was said never to have taken one. This trait is less strongly entrenched among the Ramah women, and data indicate that they seldom own sweathouses, and rarely take sweat baths. In three families women owned a sweathouse; nine women said they used the sweathouse, thirteen that they did not. A few of the latter had used it in the past; others claimed never to have used it.

According to Inf. 215, Navaho railroad workers spent their free time on Saturdays and Sundays taking sweat baths. He said that they always built a sweathouse whenever they moved on the railroad; there was then (1952) a string of Navaho sweathouses along all the major railroad lines from Chicago to California. Where juniper was not available (as in the Plains states), sweathouses were built of cottonwood; songs and other ritual requirements were maintained. If a train went by, the men ducked inside the sweathouse.

It is of interest that in some cases Spanish-Americans closely associated with the Navaho have adapted the sweathouse for their own use.

Hill (East, Central, and West)

The decision to make a sweathouse was normally settled at least one day in advance of actual construction "because, according to the rules laid down by the Holy People, the sweathouse had to be completed and used in one day" (PP, Fort Defiance; SC, Crystal; OTKM, Manuelito). Houses might rest directly on the ground or over a shallow pit. Any species of wood might be used for the framework, but juniper was preferred because it did not smell of pitch when heated (PP). Descriptions of the framework coincided with Ramah accounts (SC, PP, OTKM; C, Chinle; MH, Head Springs). The entrance did not have to face the east (OTKM, SC), but it usually did. A pit was dug inside and to the right (usually north) of the entrance; in this the heated rocks were placed. "The hot rocks were a protection against the evil [ghosts and the dead] located in the north" (PP, SC). The framework was covered with juniper bark and finally with wet earth. The floor was covered with one of several materials; juniper bark was the most frequently utilized (SC, OTKM), but sagebrush leaves and sweet clover were also used. Only cliff rose bark was barred from use: "That was only for babies" (SC). The bark absorbed the perspiration and prevented the floor from becoming muddy.

According to PP, a traveler, if pressed for time, might erect the frame of the house and use blankets for covering. MH stated that blankets were used when wet earth was not available.

Rocks were heated in front of the house. When hot they were placed in the pit and the entrance was covered with some heavy material. According to informants (PP, C), water was occasionally poured on the rocks to generate steam.

Several observances were mandatory prior to entering the sweathouse and during the sweat bath. Before entering, men pulled the prepuce over the glans of the penis and tied it; according to the myth explaining the origin of the sweathouse, blindness resulted from a failure to observe this custom. Before he entered the sweat bath for the first time, the bather shouted an invitation to the Holy People and people in general to come and join in the bath; this also had mythological sanction (SC, OTKM). While inside the bathers sang sweathouse songs, referring to the building of the first sweathouse and customs connected with its use. Other songs were those of the Monster Way; Thunder songs (SC); and songs which dealt with hard and soft goods, horses and sheep, and protection (OTKM).

Individuals stayed in the sweathouse as long as they could endure the heat. Navaho at Lukachukai attributed Hill's inability to withstand the high temperature of the sweathouse for an extended period to the fact that he did not know the songs. Those who succumbed were carried out and cold water was thrown in their faces. On the first exit, the bather rolled in the sand, or rubbed sand on his body, while delivering a prayer:

> May it be pleasant Mother Earth
> That I may live happily and pleasantly
> That I may have a long life.

This prayer could be extended at the option of the individual. As many re-entries could be made as desired. Prayers were said only after the first exit; if water was present the bathers plunged into it on subsequent occasions instead of applying sand (SC).

Women also took sweat baths, but not in company with men. "If they did they would go blind and get rheumatism" (SC, OTKM). "What man without clothes wants to stand before a crowd of women?" (SC). Pregnant women might take sweat baths, but were careful not to allow the heat to strike their backs, for fear the placenta would stick to the back during delivery. Menstruating women were prohibited the use of the sweathouse; "that would make it unfit for use" (SC).

There were other observances. Subsequent use of the sweathouse was always accompanied by an addition of earth to the roof. "This was commanded by the Sweathouse. 'Unless you throw something on me you will be a poor fellow; you will never get anything on yourself'" (SC). Sleeping in a sweathouse was prohibited. If an emergency arose, such as a sudden snowstorm, and a sweathouse was the only available shelter, a smokehole was pushed through the roof and the sweathouse was occupied. The smokehole in essence converted it to a hogan. If a smokehole was not made, it was believed that blindness and deafness would result (SC, PP). The same afflictions were thought to visit those who used wood from the sweathouse or its wood pile in preparing meals (PP, SC, OTKM). Flatulation in the sweathouses was believed to cause headaches (PP).

The sweathouse had a variety of uses. The baths cleansed and refreshed (SC, PP), and were thought to have therapeutic value and were often taken to cure colds. Occasionally emetics and purgatives were employed, "to cure illness" (PP) or "to get ugly things out of your body" (SC). Those engaged in ritual activities purified themselves before and after the performance in order to fit themselves for their normal roles in the community. On occasion, the sweathouse assumed the status of a club house, social center, and school. Visitors were entertained there, projects planned, business performed, and novices given instruction in ceremonies. These institutional aspects were summed up by PP and OTKM.

> The purpose of the bath was to make a man feel good. If he was tired and took a sweat bath he would feel fresh again. Also if a friend arrived you immediately started a sweat bath. Then you got in and he told you of his trip and the news of his community. Also if you were considering a ceremony you called in your relatives and discussed it with them. The men used it for purifying themselves after trading trips, hunting, war raids and ceremonies. Ceremonies were taught there. Leaders of war, hunting, and trading parties held sweat baths for their personnel before leaving. It is good for sweating out colds and sickness. It was also used for cleanliness.
>
> (PP, Fort Defiance)

> In a way a sweathouse was a kind of men's club. If a friend visited you it was good manners to build a sweathouse and take a bath with him. If some man went away and returned he usually built a sweathouse and all the neighbors came to hear the news. Plans for a trip were usually discussed in the sweathouse. Boys learning a ceremony usually built a sweathouse for the old men and received their instructions in it.
>
> (OTKM, Manuelito)

Ceremonial sweathouses differed in some respects from those used for ordinary purposes. One type was used in the Night Way and, according to SC, in the Big God Way (obsolescent as of 1933), but in no other ceremonials. For the Night Way, pinyon and juniper were used for the framework: the forked stick for the south was of pinyon, those for the north and west were of juniper. The southeast door pole was of pinyon, the northeast of juniper. The lintel and the lean-to poles might be of any wood. Spruce boughs were placed over the framework, then earth. Juniper bark was never used. Dodge weed, grama grass, rock sage, and "water carrier" (*toikaal*) were used on the floor, but not juniper bark. The tips of these plants were oriented toward the west. Spruce boughs, laid on top of these, completed the floor.

Over the exterior of the sweathouse a cross of sand, four fingers wide, was poured on the earth from east to west and from south to north, extending down the four sides. "These represent the framework poles." A dry painting of the Rainbow was drawn on the sand. The east and south figures were male; the west and north female. A circle of corn meal was drawn around the sweathouse. Twelve "wands" were placed upright on this line; six black, running sunwise (clockwise) from east to west; six blue, sunwise from west to east.

A blanket, quilt, or some heavy material covered the doorway, but a buckskin or piece of calico kept by the chanter was always included. Any convenient rocks were used for heating the sweathouse, and any convenient wood was used for fuel, although willow was preferred.

During the course of the Night Way, four sweathouses were built, in the east, south, west, and north, in that order, and with entrances facing in those directions. New materials were procured for each, the former sweathouse having been obliterated and its various parts "put away." The patient did not shout before entering the sweathouse, nor did he sing while in the bath. The chanter sang Night Way songs and Talking God performed in front of the sweathouse (SC).

Pit sweathouses were used in various ceremonials, such as the Bead Way (PP, SC), Water Way, Navaho Wind Way, and occasionally the Mountain and Night Ways (PP). Pits were dug, oriented to the four cardinal directions. Juniper and pinyon wood was placed in the pits with the growing tips pointing away from the ceremonial hogan. The wood was ignited, always with a firedrill (see Trait 111), and allowed to burn down. (According to SC, hot rocks might be placed in the pits.) The coals or rocks were covered with pinyon and juniper boughs and various grasses, including grama grass (PP). Patients were placed in the pits and covered with blankets (PP, SC). This arrangement was never used for ordinary sweat baths (SC).

Lamphere (East)

Lamphere participated in a sweat bath at Sheep Springs in 1966. She stated that most of the Sheep Springs people have their sweathouses in the mountains and that summer seems to be "sweathouse season," although she has seen one sweathouse at a winter home.

Preparation of the sweathouse was done by the men of the family with whom Lamphere was staying. Wood was gathered by the son the night before the sweat bath; in the morning, the men went out to prepare the sweathouse and to use it themselves.

Rocks heated outside the sweathouse were brought in on a pitchfork and placed on the north side of the sweathouse; on the south side, leaves from a fern-like plant (*deelda*, "sandhill crane food") were placed to form a mat for bathers to sit on. Several blankets were placed across the opening to keep the heat in; these were kept from slipping by stones or long sticks placed at the sides.

When the men finished their sweat bath, they replaced the *deeldaa* mat, then returned to the house to allow the women to bathe. Care was taken on exit to leave the blankets to retain as much heat as possible. PM said that this sweathouse would accommodate six people, although only three of the four bathers were in it at one time. One woman, menstruating, did not take a sweat bath. PM said that if a menstruating woman used the sweathouse the leaves on nearby trees would wither and die.

The women took all the bobby pins out of their hair and removed all clothes and jewelry before entering. For modesty's sake, a skirt or sheet was used to cover the lower part of the body until the individual had her feet and lower part of the body inside the sweathouse. Once inside, the woman placed her skirt at the side of the sweathouse to be put on when she came out. On this occasion, the sweat bath took about ten minutes, by which time the sweat was freely pouring, and it was rubbed around on the body to remove all dirt. Bathers then went outside, and returned for a second time a few minutes later. Finally they all went to bathe (with soap) in a nearby spring. Lamphere stated that sometimes bathers bring their clean clothes to put on after bathing; but in this instance the women returned home to change clothes.

Fishler (West)

An excavation was dug, approximately six feet in diameter and one and a half to two feet deep. Logs, much smaller than those used in a hogan, were secured and the framework erected. Two were placed for the entrance, which faced toward the west. Others were leaned around the circumference, caulked with brush and other material, and then covered with earth. The sweathouse was approximately three feet above the surface of the ground, and the inside height in many cases was less than four feet. Blankets or cardboard were used to cover the floor, and two blankets were usually placed over the entrance.

Men who were related, biologically or by marriage, usually made these structures. Sweathouses were owned by families, but not communally (FG, Coalmine; others). TN (Kaibito) said that a sweathouse was made only for the family and that everyone in the family helped to construct it. FG said that sweathouses might also be used by friends of the family and that they were large enough to accommodate from two to twenty people. (This many seems excessive.) Two sweathouses seen by Fishler were located near the hogans, one within fifty yards, the other a quarter of a mile away.

For a sweat bath, rocks were heated in a fire close to the sweathouse, brought in on a pitchfork, and placed in the northeastern corner. The door was covered with a blanket, and cardboard placed on the floor. Men removed their clothes. Strips of cloth or string—and on one occasion, yucca—were used to tie the foreskin of the penis, for fear the heat "would kill it. It would make you impotent. The heat would certainly kill it." The men (in one case, seven) entered the sweathouse and sat cross-legged or with their knees up under the chin and their arms around them.

The rocks produced enough heat for four baths. At each one four different songs were sung, by all the men in the sweathouse. Some series of songs dealt with the creation of the earth, the Twins, or other religious subjects. Men were obliged to take at least two baths, and the more stalwart completed four. After each bath, the men leaped out of the sweathouse, cupped their hands over their genitals, and lay on the sand. Sand was thrown on the body and rubbed to remove the sweat. While one group rested, a second might take a bath.

Informants agreed that the sweathouse was used for religious and therapeutic reasons (TN, FG) and as a meeting place (FG). GB (Tuba City) said that it was used for a thorough cleansing. "The person taking a water bath would only get the dirt from the outside off, while sweating opens the pores and all was cleaned out. When a person was tired he might take a sweat bath and then go to bed. When he got up he would be rested. Second, the sweat bath will cure disease." FG said that one type of sweathouse was used for a meeting place and another was used by the women.

Comparative

The extensive treatment of the origin and use of the sweathouse in Navaho mythology suggests that it is a very ancient trait (Mindeleff, 1898:500–502; Matthews, 1897:112; 1902:50). There are many references to the sweathouse in the literature on the Navaho. Letherman (1856:289) noted that "a small hut, about three feet in height, is erected for taking hot-air baths after any fatiguing exertion." It was heated and used as described above. Later, Bourke found that the Navaho around Fort Defiance "make great use of 'sweat lodges'" (Bourke, 1936:231).

Published descriptions of the sweathouse are remarkably similar. Stephen (1893:361) called it a miniature hogan, "just large enough to cover a man when squatted on his heels." Water was not thrown on the stones, but "the patient is filled with all he can drink" and "scoured dry with sand" on emerging. Mindeleff (1898:499–500) said the sweathouse was as high as "a man's hip," and designed to hold only one person at a time. His description was very similar to that given by Ramah informants. The doorway "invariably" faced the east. The patient was given "copious drafts sometimes of warm or hot water." After bathing, the subject rubbed himself with sand, or if ill and weak, he was rubbed dry by his friends. Mindeleff stated that men and women used the sweathouse at the same time only "under a certain condition medical in character." Presumably he was referring to the treatment of venereal disease (Dyk, 1938:92–95). The same sweathouse, however, might be used by a party of men on one day and by the women of the neighborhood on another day (Mindeleff, 1898:502).

Matthews (1897:16–17) said that the sweathouse had neither smokehole nor doorway structure. The materials of which it was constructed varied for different ceremonies, and for some the sweathouse was decorated with dry paintings. His description of the sweathouses made for the Night Chant is the most elaborate one available. A pit was dug, three feet or more in diameter, and nearly a foot deep. Over this a frame made of four forked sticks (two of pinyon, placed east and south; two of juniper, placed west and north) was constructed. His mention of this type of frame was apparently unique. The doorway faced the east. Other sticks were added, then a vegetal covering, preferably of spruce twigs; artemisia or any other plant was substituted or added if spruce was scarce. Earth or sand from the ground immediately around the house was placed next, and "lightly beaten down and smoothed with oaken battens used by the weavers." A part was smoothed with extra care and sometimes built up at the edges for a dry painting. The hut took an hour or more to build, and when finished measured "externally from five to six feet in diameter and about three feet high above the general surface of the ground." The doorway was about two feet high and tapered toward the top. Inside spruce twigs were strewn on the floor, to sit on. Meanwhile a fire was lighted to the east of the structure. Pinyon and juniper sticks were used, placed with their butts toward the sweathouse. Heated stones were transferred to the sweathouse by means of tongs. No water was thrown on the stones. "The Navaho sweat-bath is a hot-air bath, not a steam bath" (Matthews, 1902:50–52).

The Franciscan Fathers (1910:341–343) contradicted earlier writers, saying that water was sometimes sprinkled on the stones after the entrance was closed with a blanket. They described the structure as "the conical hogan in miniature, with the doorway structure omitted." The entrance usually faced west. Although the sweathouse was "frequently from four to five feet in diameter, and less in height," it was not uncommonly used by sixteen men simultaneously; this was "conducive to rapid perspiration." Bathers stayed inside as long as twenty minutes, came out to roll in the sand, and usually returned several times. In their locality, it was also common for bathers to plunge into streams after the bath. The Franciscan Fathers stated that the sweathouse was used in both summer and winter; ordinarily it was used only in the daytime, but in time of war or in exceptional cases, it was used also at night. Both men and women used it, but women always bathed alone and less frequently than men.

More recently, Page (1937b) described the building of a sweathouse and the taking of a sweat bath at Marsh Pass, Arizona. In this instance no excavation was made for the floor, which was covered with juniper bark. After ten or twelve minutes, participants emerged and sprinted up and down, rubbed themselves dry with sand, and drank warm water to induce perspiration. Heat in the rocks was sufficient for three ten-minute periods. Members of a household took sweat baths once or twice a month, men and women alternating.

Bailey collected data from the Smith Lake–Pinedale region, specifically about the use of the sweathouse by women; she was unable to obtain any definite information from the Chaco area. There were only vague reports that women there took sweat baths. In the Smith Lake area, women used a different sweathouse from that of the men. In Pinedale, she saw three women (aged 49, 26, 12) take a sweat bath. They used a house which had been used earlier in the day by the men of the family (Bailey, 1941:484–485).

Both of Gifford's Navaho informants regarded the conical sweathouse as a permanent structure. The Western informant said that it was covered with earth and that the entrance faced the sunrise. The Eastern informant, however, said that it was covered with juniper bark and earth and that the entrance faced north. Both agreed that the hot stones were placed to the right of the door. Both informants said sweathouses were used only in the daytime and that they were used by men. The Western informant estimated that between six and ten men took a sweat bath at one time. The Eastern informant said that women could also use the sweathouse; the Western informant said that they sometimes did. Both groups used the sweathouse for curing "all sickness." The Eastern informant specified rheumatism, fatigue, and venereal disease; the badly injured or very sick, however, were not allowed. He said that several treatments were necessary for a cure; the Western informant specified four. He also said that a chanter used the sweathouse before treating a patient; this was denied by the Eastern informant. Both groups agreed that the sweathouse was used before a ceremonial and before a war raid. The sweathouse in the Eastern area, but not the Western, was taboo to a man whose wife had recently born a child, to one associated with a menstruating woman, or after intercourse (Gifford, 1940:23–24, 110–111). According to Babington (1950:180), the Western Navaho sometimes poured water mixed with herbs over the hot stones to produce a fragrant steam.

Sweathouses from Navaho archaeological sites have been described by Keur and Hurt. Keur found them at Big Bead Mesa and in the Gobernador area, where presumably they date from the seventeenth and eighteenth centuries. Hurt's materials are from the Canyon de Chelly area and are regarded as dating from the eighteenth century.

At Big Bead Mesa, there was abundant evidence, usually "piles and disordered heaps of fire reddened stones, presumably those discarded and thrown out of the house after use." Many of the stones showed crumbling and splitting from excessive heat. In some cases, "the fireplace, where presumably the stones had been heated," was also found. The sweathouse associated with the E complex was excavated. Its circular floor, six and a half feet in diameter, showed excessive blackening from burning. "To the north and east, remnants of many badly charred beam ends were found. The entrance could not be determined." In the Big Bead sites, all sweathouses save one were located apart from the hogan groups (Keur, 1941:37, 38). The twenty sweathouses found at the Gobernador sites were also placed apart from the hogan groups, "according to good Navaho practice." These were distinguished by the tell-tale heap of fire-reddened stones, "so located as to suggest that they were thrown out of the doorway after use. In three cases, partially collapsed timbers were still present" (Keur, 1944:77). In the Canyon de Chelly area, Hurt found a small sweathouse (three feet high, six to seven feet in diameter, twenty-one feet in circumference). Large piles of burned sandstone were found on the north and east sides of the structure. "The inside had been filled with charcoal to a depth that made entrance impossible. Wyman suggests that the ash may have been deposited in the sweathouse as a part of a ceremony" (Hurt, 1942:91). Malcolm (1939) did not mention sweathouses in the Chaco Canyon area, nor did Farmer (1942) in his investigation of the Blanco–Largo Canyon area.

210. Sweathouse Rocks

cé ʾanaˑnitíˑ tˣáčéh góneˑ (Lamphere)   rocks that are put in the sweathouse; "rock, only one, sweathouse, in there" (CC)

cé łižin (Lamphere)   black rocks

cé cénX̣izizíˑ (Ramah)   hard rocks

Ramah

Stones, ranging from the size of a fist to the size of a human head, were used for heating the sweathouse. Those most easily available were chosen, but certain types were preferred. The best stones, according to Inf. 12, were white and very hard, and were called "hard rocks." These could not be identified, but may be malpais lava. Later Inf. 12 said that malpais was best since it held the heat. It was found on the Zuni reservation and probably in the Ramah area.

Rocks were heated in a fire built on the north or east side of the sweathouse, and when the fire burned down, they were rolled into a pit in the sweathouse. Infs. 7 and 12 repeated that neither water nor snow was put on them to make steam; the dry heat from the rocks was enough to produce perspiration.

The same rocks were used again and again. They were always removed from the sweathouse prior to the next bath and were usually piled in a heap nearby.

Hill (Central)

Any convenient rocks might be used to heat a sweathouse, according to SC (Crystal). PP (Fort Defiance) stated that once the rocks had been employed in this capacity they could not be used for any other purpose.

Lamphere (East)

PM said that these rocks would be called "rocks that are put in the sweathouse," the first term above. They were also called "black rocks" the second term above. The latter are basaltic rocks which are found in the Chuska Mountain region; they are said to hold the heat better than sandstone, and they do not burst.

Fishler (West)

About forty to fifty rocks, varying in size and shape, were kept in a neat pile on the northeastern side of the sweathouse. For a sweat bath, these were heated in a fire and brought into the sweathouse on a pitchfork. They were reused several times.

Comparative

According to Mindeleff (1898:499), stones for a sweat bath were heated until they were "nearly red-hot," then rolled into the sweathouse. According to Matthews (1902:52), four large stones, "of a kind that will not easily disintegrate when heated," were used. Rocks about one foot in diameter, preferably round, were specified in the Marsh Pass area (Page, 1937b:21). (See Comparative section of Trait 209 for further references.)

Some Navaho were said to plant sweathouse stones in the fields or at the base of fruit trees to prevent early frosts (Kluckhohn and Leighton, 1946:143).

211. Tongs (Forks)

bilaʼ naˑki (Lamphere)   forked stick "two fingers"; "two hands" (CC)

Ramah

Tongs seen at Inf. 28's place were made from two forked poles, one about six feet long, the other about two and a half feet long. At Inf. 7's place only one forked stick, about four feet long, was used. All had been whittled and slightly shaped. These were used for moving hot rocks into the sweathouse.

Wooden tongs have recently been observed and have been in use for a long time. By 1940, at least one family had substituted a long-handled shovel; others used steel pitchforks.

211.a. Forked-stick rock carrier

Hill (Central)

Forked sticks served as stone lifters in both domestic and semiritual capacity. In homes these implements were used to remove the pot and griddle support stones from the hot ashes. If none was available, the stone might be pushed aside with the poker (IS, Lukachukai). During a sweat bath the heated stones were lifted with two short-handled forked sticks (IS; PP, Fort Defiance). According to OTKM (Manuelito), rocks used in the sweathouse were rolled into place with a pole.

Lamphere (East)

PM said that juniper was used; it was called by the term for forked stick, "two fingers." A pitchfork bought from a store is now used; at a sweat bath in 1966, Lamphere noticed that wire was placed across the prongs to prevent the rocks from slipping through.

Fishler (West)

Informants said that a pitchfork was used for moving the hot stones for a sweat bath (FG, Coalmine; TN, Kaibito).

Comparative

In the myth which describes the origin of the Mountain Chant, two forked sticks were prescribed: one the length of the forearm for lifting in the hot stones and one longer stick for removing the stones from the fire. Sticks were chosen from trees against which a deer had rubbed its antlers (Matthews, 1887:389). In the description of the Night Chant, Matthews specified that the hot stones were transferred to the sweathouse "to the north of where the patient sits, with two sticks which are used as tongs" (Matthews, 1902:52).

212. Stone Boiling

·aze·· ha·nigaš (Lamphere)   "medicine boiling" (CC)

Hill (Central and West)

Stone boiling was practiced only in connection with curing. According to GH (White Cone), various herbs were placed in a pot of water and the solution brought to a boil by dropping heated stones into the container. The patient was placed under a blanket and inhaled the fumes from the pot. The treatment was used to cure body aches. "The sickness is sweated out of him. The sweat is what makes the person's body ache. When that is out the patient recovers." When the blanket was removed the patient was washed with a solution of cold water and herbs. IS (Lukachukai) stated that this treatment was given only when the individual was too ill to leave the hogan.

Both PP (Fort Defiance) and GH reported that stone boiling was never practiced in connection with the preparation of food.

Lamphere (East)

PM said this process would be called "medicine boiling."

Fishler (West)

Water and six or seven kinds of herbs were placed in a basket tray that had been waterproofed with pinyon gum. Rocks or small pebbles were heated in a fire, picked up with two small sticks, and placed in the water until it boiled. The sticks were used to hold the stones to avoid charring the basket. The patient leaned over the basket and inhaled the vapor.

Women made the baskets, but men conducted the ceremonies. Chanters owned these baskets. Stone boiling occurred in a ceremonial context, and there was some question as to whether it was ever used in a secular situation.

Comparative

There is nothing in the literature dealing with stone boiling among the Navaho. Gifford's Navaho informants denied boiling anything in baskets (Gifford, 1940:15). The question was asked, however, in connection with the preparation of food.

213. Splints

cin honesλǫ́ (Lamphere)   "stick tied up around"; "wood tied against" (CC)

Hill (East and West)

Splints were fashioned from any type of available wood. Chanters set the bone fractures and applied the splints (SG, Keams Canyon; TLLSS, Crown-point). TLLSS said that the chanter manipulated the broken limb until it was in the correct position. A heated rock was placed in a pit and the injured member placed on the rock; the heat was applied to reduce the swelling. Then the arm or leg was wrapped in soft cloth and the splint applied and secured in place with a "jointed" plant. One of the internodes of the plant was filled with eagle down and a medicine called *klitci*, and a second internode section was slipped over the first. "This is just like the bone and will make the break heal quickly." Finally a chant was held over the injured person.

Lamphere (East)

PM said that a splint would be called "stick, tied up around for healing."

214. Bugaboo Owl

ná·ášǯa·· (Ramah, Lamphere, Haile)   owl; "eared eyes"

Ramah

Bugaboo owls, for "good luck" and for frightening disobedient children, were made of sumac (*Rhus trilobata;* identification by Vestal, 1952:35). Several sticks were taken from the east side of the plant; branches were trimmed, and the bark removed with a knife. The sticks (about a third of an inch in diameter) were halved and thinned until pliable. Next, two halves were crossed at right angles about two inches from the butt ends. The long end of each piece was folded over about two inches from the intersection to make four thicknesses in the center of the cross (see 214.1). The next folds, making five, then six thicknesses, hid the butt ends in the middle of each arm of the cross. The maker continued to fold, alternating pieces over and over, until each strip was expended. The resulting cross-shaped bundle was tied at the center to prevent unwinding. It represented the body of the bird; one arm was the head of the owl, the others the tail and wings. Making the body took about fifteen minutes.

214.1. Bugaboo owl, after Tschopik

A piece of sumac, smaller in diameter than those above was trimmed and split, and the core removed. The stick was held in the teeth and four strips of bark were removed and cut into one-foot lengths. One of these lengths replaced the temporary string tied around the body of the owl. It was placed across the intersection and pulled tight beneath the body. A second strip was looped around the body at right angles to the first; a third went over the first, and the fourth over the second. The free ends of all strips were held

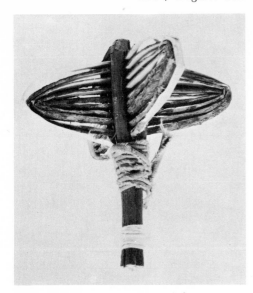

214.a. Bugaboo owl made by Inf. 15

in the left hand and tied with a piece of string in a bunch just below the body. The ends were trimmed to the same length. These were the "feet."

Such an owl (see 214.a) was made from Tschopik by Inf. 15, a woman, but whether men also made them is not known. Apparently children were not allowed to make them, for Inf. 15 told them not to watch her as she worked.

The owl was hung with the feet down. It was suspended by a string over one of the logs above the smokehole. Pulling on the string made it move up and down. According to Infs. 15 and 9, four owls were hung in the hogan, at the four cardinal points; Inf. 192 said that there were never more than three and that one was usual, hung on the west side. According to Infs. 15 and 192 these were for "good luck" and for frightening the children. Children were told that if they were disobedient, "the owl would get them." Owls were hung where "they could always watch the children." Inf. 9 had heard of owls and said that they were used to keep ghosts away; he had never heard of using them to frighten children.

Inf. 192 said that she had seen the type made by Inf. 15, but was not familiar with the one illustrated and described by the Franciscan Fathers. Inf. 54 said her parents had never used the owl, and neither had she.

Apparently there is none in Ramah at the present time, and with the exception of the one for Tschopik, none has been manufactured in recent years.

Hill (Central)
The description of the manufacture and use of the owl given by PP (Fort Defiance) was a condensed version of the Ramah account.

Lamphere (East)
PM said that she used to use a gourd dipper as an owl, to put the children to sleep. She would make eyes on the back of the gourd with charcoal, then hold it over the child who was in bed, saying, "you go to sleep."

Comparative
The Franciscan Fathers (1910:495) illustrated two different owls, one of which was faintly similar to that made by Inf. 15, except that it had no feet (see 214.2). The other type (see 214.3) resembled two diamonds on a wrapped stick. (The so-called God's Eye that occurs throughout the Southwest is similar in construction to this type of owl and has many of the same beliefs connected with it.) These owls were used to frighten insubordinate children, and four were hung from a beam of the hogan, usually "in the evening when, favored by the scant illumination of the hogan, the fancy of a child might easily be led to believe that the owl sitting there should carry it off." By 1910 the bugaboo was rarely seen.

Gifford's Navaho informants agreed that they used a "wound cross" as an "owl bugaboo" and were apparently the only ones among the groups he investigated to do so. (Others confirmed the use of an owl as "bugaboo," but it was not described.) The Eastern informant specified sumac for the material (Gifford, 1940:64, 160). Parsons (1916:338) mentioned a Navaho mother frightening her disobedient child by hooting like an owl.

Bugaboo owls, after the Franciscan Fathers

214.2   **214.3**

215. Lightning Mats

tˣeˑł náˑz bạsi (Ramah) round mat; "cattail mat"; "cattail round" (CC)

tˣéˑłcaˑˑ (Ramah) round mat

ƛohyaˑtˣeˑł (Ramah) mat; "grass under wide"

tˣeˑł daḱa nígí (Ramah) rectangular mat; "cattail rectangle" (CC)

Ramah

According to Inf. 15, both rectangular and round coiled mats were made. The round ones were "about the size of a large sheep pelt"; the rectangular ones were about five feet by three feet.

Four leaves were stripped from the cattail plant (*Typha latifolia, teel*; identifications from Wyman and Harris, 1941; see also Vestal, 1952:14). A coil was made with the butt ends in the center; it was tied with a strip of yucca (*Yucca glauca*). This formed the center of the mat. It was further secured before coiling began. The coil was held in the left hand, with the long ends of the leaves pointing to the left. A fifth leaf was threaded through the coil, away from the worker, pulled over and threaded through again to secure the loose end. With the bundle of cattail still free, wrapping started clockwise ("sunwise"). When a circuit was completed, direction was reversed, and the same coil was wrapped again. For a third circuit (clockwise as the first) an additional leaf was needed. At this point, with the ring thoroughly secured, coiling began, and the bundle of cattail leaves was incorporated into the sewing.

The initial coil was perforated with a pocket knife (formerly a greasewood awl was used). The cattail leaf was brought over the coil and bundle from the back and threaded through this perforation. Coiling was done counterclockwise (as was the second circuit). Additional coils were secured by wrapping the sewing element around the previous coil, rather than through a perforation. The rim was finished "any way"; no false braid was used. The cattail rushes were cut off with a knife and inserted one after another into holes in the rim. A pocket knife or awl was occasionally used.

No consistent system was followed in adding new sewing materials or bundle elements. There was no attempt, for example, to have all butt ends point toward the middle. New bundle elements were incorporated with previous ones and secured.

These mats were hung in the hogan "to scare the lightning so it will not hit your hogan or your sheep or your people." The round one (female) was hung in the west; the rectangular one (male) was hung in the east. The two mats were said to "give plenty of rain." They were not used for bedding (Inf. 15).

Several mats now in the Harvard Peabody Museum were made by Inf. 15 for Tschopik and Kluckhohn (see 215.a). She said that formerly men, not women, made these mats. She was unable to make the rectangular mat and may have forgotten how. When she tried to produce one, she made a kind of basket (see 215.b). Another woman, Inf. 32, denied knowledge of these mats. It is doubtful that any are made or used in the Ramah community today.

Comparative

There is apparently no information in the literature regarding the "lightning

Lightning mats made by Inf. 15

215.a. Coiled round mat

215.b. Rectangular woven rush mat

mat." The Franciscan Fathers (1910:467) illustrated a mat made from yucca woven sunwise, but it was used for bedding. Gifford stated that the Eastern Navaho did not make mats of tule or cattail because it was taboo to use materials taken from water. The Western informant was not questioned (Gifford, 1940:45, 137).

216. Wooden Box

ciča·ʼ (Haile) "box (wooden)" (CC)

Ramah
There is no information on the type of wooden box described by Hill's informants. According to Kluckhohn and Wyman's informants, pieces of bark from the Ponderosa pine were used as receptacles to hold the pigments for sandpaintings (Kluckhohn and Wyman, 1940:45).

Hill (Central)
A cottonwood log, eight to ten inches in diameter and of the desired length, was selected and squared on three sides. The fourth side and the interior of the log were removed by burning. The ends of greasewood limbs were put in the coals. When they ignited, the worker placed the end on the cottonwood and blew on it. The soft cottonwood was easily consumed, and this operation was repeated until the box interior was fashioned. A second piece of cottonwood was split and a cover carved to fit the box. In recent years boxes have been made with a knife.

These boxes were used as containers for the feathers employed in ceremonies. More recently, such ceremonial equipment has been wrapped in buckskin (PP, Fort Defiance).

217. Medicine Bag

ǯiš (Ramah, Haile) bag (generic term)

áλ̓čá·ʼazisí (Ramah, Hill) "two sacks together"

Ramah
Medicine bags were made from a variety of materials and varied greatly in size and form. Unwounded buckskin was the preferred material; it was obtained from a deer which had been killed by means other than shooting (Inf. 8). If buckskin was not available, cloth could be used. According to Inf. 1, for a big ceremony the bag should be of mountain sheep skin. He had a squirrel skin, however, and planned to make it into a medicine pouch.

The hide was dehaired, dressed, and trimmed to secure the largest possible rectangular piece. This was folded and sewn on two sides; a neck was left at one narrow end, which was tied with a small buckskin strip. Such bags were not fringed nor was there any other form of ornamentation. These were used for storing ceremonial paraphernalia, except for "jewels" (beads) and corn pollen. Each object inside was kept in a separate buckskin bundle or bag.

A second type of bag was also made of buckskin, though not necessarily unwounded. Dimensions varied; some were two and a half feet by one foot, others were only a few inches long. These bags were sewn as above or with a flap (see Trait 86, Storage Bag), and the stitching was placed some distance in from the edge to allow for a fringe. Beads, corn pollen, and other ritual equipment were stored in these.

A bag owned by Inf. 40 was fringed at the bottom; that owned by Inf. 7 was fringed on all sides, including the top. Some were decorated with beads around the edge. Inf. 9 had a small beaded buckskin bag; one shown Bailey by Inf. 82 was decorated with beads, shells, and silver buttons.

Infs. 7 and 40 said they had stored corn pollen in these containers, and others were observed doing so (Infs. 12, 56, 82, 97). In 1940, two buckskin bags seven to eight inches long were made at Inf. 12's place to hold prayersticks, which previously had been kept in a small canvas bag. The Leightons also observed two bags filled with pollen used at a chantway at Inf. 12's place. One was beaded; the other was of leather with the hair intact. These were also seen by Kluckhohn in 1937 (Kluckhohn, 1938:366; "Most of the men of middle age and older possess bags of pollen").

Bags were made during a ceremony in the hogan, but not necessarily while singing was actually in progress. A chanter might make his own, or it could be made by another chanter (Inf. 8). The Leightons were told by Inf. 269 of a ceremony in the Two Wells area where the singer told those attending, "If you have a buckskin of your own, you can sew up a sack. If you need a sack for yourself, make it up today. It is the right time to sew a sack." Pregnant women were excluded from making storage containers for fear of prolonging labor (Inf. 26; Bailey, 1950:41–42).

Bags of pollen were kept in the hogan, suspended from poles placed for this purpose. Other medicine bags were not usually kept inside but hung on a tree, although Inf. 8 had a cloth medicine bag hanging on the wall of his dwelling that appeared to be a double bag with a connecting piece used for hanging. Inf. 7 had always seen medicine bags hung east of the dwelling, but he did not know whether it was forbidden to hang them in the other three directions. Inf. 1 stored his ceremonial equipment in five flour sacks of various sizes.

Inf. 7 has seen medicine bags in use, but mentioned them in connection with earlier periods. These pouches are, however, used today, although in some cases they are not of buckskin but of cloth, and are different in pattern from those described above.

According to Inf. 270, a chanter's bundle was inherited by a son, brother, or mother's brother. It could not be used again for a year, and not before it had been sung over. First the Ghost Way (*hochooji*) was sung; then the Blessing Way (*hozhooji*). Inf. 1 received his Shooting Way bundle from his instructor, who in turn had been given it. He (Inf. 1) said that this particular bundle was made before the Fort Sumner period.

Kluckhohn and Wyman noted several requirements for the chanter's pouches [medicine bags]. They must be made from unwounded buckskin, sewn with sinew of wolf, deer, or mountain lion. Wolf sinew was preferred for pouches for Evil Way chants.

Kluckhohn and Wyman also mentioned "little medicine bags," made of buckskin or cloth and tied with buckskin thongs or wool yarn. These were used for carrying the various paraphernalia (Kluckhohn and Wyman, 1940:47; see also pp. 143, 159–160, for description).

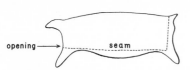

217.1. Unfringed medicine bag (Hill), after SC

Rectilinear medicine bag (Hill)

217.2. Cutting buckskin, after SC, PP

217.3. Folded and seamed bag

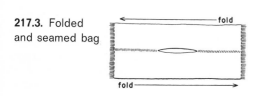

217.4. Stitch used for seam

217.a. Buckskin medicine bag

Hill (Central)

Several varieties of containers for ceremonial paraphernalia were distinguished by the Navaho. One type was made from the dressed skin of a young deer, not a "sacred" buckskin but one given to the chanter as partial payment for a ceremony he was about to perform. More recently, ceremonial containers have sometimes been made from heavy muslin acquired in the same manner. The buckskin was folded longitudinally and sewn across the rear portion and along the belly (see 217.1). The hide was never trimmed, and the opening was always at the head end of the skin. These bags were never decorated (SC, Crystal).

A second and more prevalent type of container was rectilinear. A buckskin was folded longitudinally and the largest possible rectangle cut out (see 217.2). The resulting rectangle was refolded longitudinally so that the long sides met in the center on top (see 217.3). Seams were sewn across the ends with a double stitch (see 217.4), about three inches in from the edge to allow for a fringe. The seam on top was sewn inward from either end in a simple running stitch; an opening was left in the center (SC; PP, Fort Defiance). One such bag collected at Coalmine (see 217.a) was about twenty-five inches long.

This type of container was used for storing and transporting all types of ceremonial materials, which were placed at each end of the sack. The container was grasped in the middle for carrying; this grip effectively closed the opening and separated the load in equal parts. For this reason it was called "two sacks together" (SC, PP), a term known at Ramah for the second type of bag.

Only those containers manufactured under ceremonial conditions could be used in ritual capacity (PP, SC). PP stipulated that the work should be done during the course of a Blessing Way.

The content of these large containers was made up of a variety of articles to which supernatural properties were attributed. These were kept in small receptacles of various types. Containers for "mountain dirt," for example, had to be made from "sacred" buckskin during the course of a ceremony. Buckskin strips about six inches long and an inch and a half wide were cut, always the length of the skin, and always from head to tail. The strips were buried in damp earth until they were thoroughly moist. An indentation was produced in the center of the strip with the butt of a stick, about the size of a pencil in diameter. The depression had to be made from the outside of the hide; "the head and tail must be up" (SC). "Mountain dirt" was placed in the indentation, and the ends of the strip were brought together and wrapped with a thong of "sacred" buckskin. Wrapping progressed from bottom to top until the length of the thong had been spent. The ends were secured by tucking them under the wraps (SC). Separate containers were used for earth from Blanco Peak, Mount Taylor, San Franciscan Peak, La Plata, Huerfano, and Gobernador. C (Chinle) stated that earth from buffalo tracks was treated in like manner.

Small sacks of "sacred" buckskin were made to store the herbs and clays used in ceremonies. There were several variants (see 217.5–217.8). A strip of hide was folded and sewn up the sides (217.5), or a rectangle was folded longitudinally and sewn across the bottom and up the open side (217.6). The opening was sometimes the width of the bag's diameter, or cut in the form

Small medicine containers (Hill)

217.5. Seamed on both sides, after SC

217.6. Seamed on end and one side, after SC

217.7. With constricted neck, after SC

217.8. Fringed and scalloped, after PP

of a constricted bottle neck (217.7). In some containers, two holes were punched near the upper edge; a thong was run through these and tied around the neck to close the sack. The container was fringed or not, depending on the whim of the maker (SC).

A sack (217.8) similar to that above was described by PP. It had a scalloped mouth and a fringe at the bottom. Containers of this type were used for pollen. They formed part of the ceremonial equipment or were carried with the individual. According to PP, beadwork has recently been applied to this type of container.

Two methods were in vogue for storing feathers used for ritual purposes. Either they were rolled up in a piece of buckskin or a buckskin sheath was made to fit the feathers (SC). "Jewels" used for offerings were carried and stored in squares of buckskin; the edges were gathered and tied (SC).

Fishler (West)

GB's niece (Tuba City) made him a buckskin bag decorated with beads. In it he kept many of his sacred objects, such as pollen and stone horses.

Comparative

Washington Matthews (1902:43) provided the earliest information on containers for ceremonial equipment, although he did not describe them. He noted that "ordinarily [pollen was] kept in small buckskin bags, which [were] carried on the person, not only by priests but by many of the laymen."

The chanter's pouch was described by the Franciscan Fathers (1910: 382–383). With the exception of the Blessing Way, each chant required a specific bag "containing the necessary paraphernalia for conducting the chant according to traditional ritual." They described it as "an oblong sack" made of sacred buckskin, secured by thongs of the same material. It contained "feathers, rattles, stones, pollens, animal tissues, native herbs, ochres and clays, and additional paraphernalia for specific chants, some of which are difficult to acquire." The chanter disposed of the pouch before death; its contents were sold by the heirs, "either in part or whole, as the profit may warrant."

The Franciscan Fathers (1910:410–411) also described the small buckskin sacks used for pollen and other specific chant materials. These consisted of "five wraps or bags of sacred buckskin into which precious stones and rock crystal" were inserted or sewn "together with dust gathered from the various sacred mountains." The five bags were wrapped with sacred buckskin. "The vigils can not be conducted properly without this pouch." This bag was called *azee*. Similar containers are in the Peabody Museum collection at Harvard; they are about an inch wide, two inches long, simple in shape, sewn on three sides, and fringed at the bottom.

218. Cased Bag   bi·hyá·aẓiš (Ramah)   "deer bag" (CC)

Ramah

The skin of a young fawn, killed by means other than shooting, was obtained. The hind legs and tail were skinned out and the hide cased. The hide was dressed with the hair on, and the hooves and head were removed (at Zuni the head was left on the skin). A circular piece of red-dyed buckskin was sewn over the neck opening to form the bottom of the bag. The upper end of the bag was tied about the hind legs with a length of cloth. The legs were left attached and hung down.

Both men and women made these bags (Inf. 7) and used them for storing sacred materials. Inf. 7 said that a person should own two, but he had only one. Formerly such bags were used to hold the seed corn which was planted first in the center of the field.

Bags of this type were hung from a pole on the west wall of the hogan. "All things like this have to go here—medicine bundles, seed corn, etc.," according to Inf. 7. At present, when the bag is not in use, it is stored in a trunk.

Bags of this type are still being made and used in the Ramah area; Inf. 7 made one within recent years and has used it. Whether it is or was a common type, however, is not known.

These are no longer being used for seed corn, however, since the ritual planting of the fields is now practiced by only a few people. The bag has now become a general container for sacred objects, but whether it is comparable to the chanter's bundle is not known.

Hill (Central)

When fawns were shot or caught the hide was cased. The hind legs and tail were skinned out and the hide pulled off the animal toward the head. The whole skin was used in the bag, dressed with the hair on. No ceremony was observed during the preparation. N (Coalmine) stated that cased squirrel skins were sometimes used as containers for ceremonial materials.

These bags were formerly used by the women for storing corn meal and tallow. They were also carried by the Talking God impersonator in the Night Way chant (C, Chinle).

Comparative

According to Matthews (1887:421), two fawn skin bags were used to carry the meal of the courier in the Mountain Chant. Pollen was also kept in fawn skin bags for occasions when it was needed in large quantities (Matthews, 1902:43).

Kluckhohn and Wyman (1940:23) noted that fawn skin was the preferred material for pouches for Blessing Way. The Navaho identified "the white stripe down the middle of the back with the Milky Way and various groups of spots with various constellations." Gifford's Eastern informant said that tobacco was kept in bags made from the cased skin of the ground squirrel (Gifford, 1940:58, 151).

219. Baskets   ċa·· (Haile)

Ramah

Ceremonial baskets were woven of sumac, as described in Trait 98, Basket Dish (see 98.a and 98.b). These were made by women. Special care was taken to observe ritual precautions, or a chanter could not use the baskets.

The basket was used to hold the contents of the ceremonial pouch prior to making a sandpainting. The ritual elements were transferred from the pouch to the basket "after the ceremony the previous night or before dawn in the morning" (Kluckhohn and Wyman, 1940:59–60).

In 1949 Edmonson noted that Inf. 7 used a flat basket caulked with pinyon to hold water for yucca soap during a chant; "it didn't leak a drop."

Hill (Central)

As at Ramah, there were no special weaves or restrictions in making a ceremonial basket, although special care was taken (LW, Lukachukai). Ceremonial baskets were used for holding prayersticks in rites for treating mild cases of delirium or insanity (PP, Fort Defiance). The basket was placed with the break in the design facing east. It was turned several times during the ceremony, and at the close faced west. The ceremony was called "turning the basket" (Hill, 1936a:71–72).

Comparative

The Franciscan Fathers (1910:397) stated that the baskets were used to hold prayersticks during the course of a ceremony.

There are several "Navaho-made" baskets in the collection of the Harvard Peabody Museum. One basket on display was a "wedding" basket, collected by Mrs. Henry Sturgis Grew in 1920. The design was a sort of chevron with an opening on one side, the ritually prescribed "trail," that was used to orient the basket during the ceremony. Another basket was collected by Grace Nicholson in 1908. According to the catalogue notation, a "fetich was buried in sacred meal in bottom of basket. These deep baskets took place of old 'Olla-shaped Basket.'"

The works of Mason (1904), with many excellent drawings of basketry techniques, are recommended to the interested reader, as are those of James (1902), who treated Indian basketry in general. James's work is amply illustrated with photographs showing different types of finished baskets.

220. Gourd Containers

ˈadeˑˑ ˈazeˑˑ beˑnaˑkahiˑ (Lamphere)   gourd cup; "cup, medicine, to hold it there" (CC)

Hill (Central)

In addition to their use for drinking and ladling liquids (see Trait 101, Gourd Ladle or Spoon), gourds were used as medicine containers in various ceremonies (PP, Fort Defiance; SC, Crystal; C, Chinle).

A special ceremonial utilization of a gourd receptacle was reported by PP. A large-necked gourd was procured, the end of the stem removed, and the interior cleaned. A plume from a live eagle was inserted in the neck. In the fall the gourd was taken to one of the sacred areas in the Chuska Mountains and tied with buckskin to the top of a high tree. The opening in the gourd was oriented to the southwest, or "windward side." "A ceremony was performed at this time."

The following fall the gourd was retrieved and the wind-carried "fog" and particles of earth which adhered to the plume were placed on a buckskin in the hogan. Next a Blessing Way was held over the accumulation and it was distributed among various chanters. These "particles carried by the wind" (*nestin*) were thought to possess the same qualities as pollen.

Lamphere (East)

EP said that the word for cup was a sufficient term for gourd containers. PM said that to be really specific, one should use the term above, meaning "gourd, medicine, with it, is repeatedly held."

Comparative

Gourds were used as medicine containers, according to the Franciscan Fathers (1910:407). They illustrated such a vessel (see 220.1), in which medicine was prepared, "stirred with the fingers or a feather, and administered directly from the cup or bowl." The chanter usually sipped it before offering it to the patient. Sometimes the medicine was "sputtered over the patient in the usual ritual manner."

There is a gourd cup similar to that illustrated by the Franciscan Fathers in the collections of the Harvard Peabody Museum. According to the catalogue, it was "found in a winter hogan, sometimes used as a medicine cup." The gourd was "used in preparing and serving liquid herb medicine to patient during a healing chant." It was found by Kidder and Guernsey in 1914 at Say-odd-ne-chee, Arizona.

220.1. Gourd medicine cup, after the Franciscan Fathers

221. Horn Containers

ꞌadeˑˑꞌakah bizis (Lamphere)   horn cup; "cup, fat, its container" (CC)

Ramah

Chanters carried deer, mountain lion, or bear grease in a mountain sheep horn. These horns had no handles. They were carried in the medicine bag. They are still part of the ceremonial equipment of a chanter.

Hill (East and Central)

Mountain sheep horns could be used only in ceremonial capacity. The container consisted of about six inches of the distal end of the horn, and in this was stored the tallow and fat from mountain sheep, buffalo, mountain lions, wolves, deer, or antelope. These substances were part of the equipment of various chantways (C, Chinle; PP, Fort Defiance; TLFOS, Shiprock; Hill, 1938:168). According to PP, buffalo horn could be utilized for the same purpose.

Lamphere (East)

EP said that deer fat was put in horn containers.

Comparative

Information on this use of horn containers by the Navaho is scanty. Gifford recorded that the Eastern Navaho chanters had a ladle for grease. It was made of mountain sheep horn with a wooden bottom (Gifford, 1940:26, 113).

222. Shell Containers

diˑčiłí łeˑčaˑˑ (Lamphere, Haile, Wyman)   "abalone shell dishes" (CC)

čéꞌh daɣáhi bičaˑ (Lamphere, Haile, Wyman) "turtle shell back" (CC)

Ramah

Small cups made from a sea shell were used in a curing ceremony. Powder,

Ritual water, and other forms of medicine were placed in them. Inf. 7 used shells for this purpose.

Roberts noted abalone shells in two of his Ramah households; these were obtained through gift or trade (Roberts, 1951:16, 38). There was no shell carving.

According to Inf. 6, a turtle shell was used as a medicine cup. The informant related the story of its origin: Monster Slayer's boy was stolen and cared for by the "turtle people," who taught him songs of the Female Shooting Way. He was given a turtle shell as a medicine container (Kluckhohn and Wyman, 1940:45–46, 51, 115, 143).

Hill (Central)
Abalone shells were employed as containers and formed a part of the ceremonial equipment (C, Chinle; PP, Fort Defiance). According to PP, their use as containers in this capacity began about 1905.

Lamphere (East)
PM and EP agreed that two kinds of shells were used for medicine, abalone and turtle. They said that in addition to the specific terms given above, a medicine container could be called simply "pot."

222.1. Tortoise shell medicine cup, after the Franciscan Fathers

Comparative
According to the Franciscan Fathers (1910:407), a special vessel was used for the preparation of medicine. It was sometimes made of a tortoise shell or a gourd, or "an ordinary earthen bowl" was used. Both of Gifford's Navaho informants said that a turtle shell was used as a medicine container, and both agreed that a mollusk shell ("shell [natural]") was not (Gifford, 1940:26, 113).

Wyman (1936a:640) also noted the use of abalone shell ("abalone bowl") or turtle shell ("turtle box") as a medicine cup. That his was apparently the earliest reference may confirm PP's claim that the trait is relatively recent among the Navaho.

223. Animal Fetishes

dibéči·n (Ramah, Haile) sheep fetish; "sheep" (CC)

łį·sčí·n (Ramah, Haile) horse fetish; "horses" (CC); "produced like a horse"

Ramah
Likenesses of sheep or horses were carved from stone. These charms were carried in the pollen sacks. They were meant to insure the well-being of the animals.

Whether the charms were widely used, or whether they were produced by the Ramah Navaho, is not known. Inf. 77 had such a fetish, which she bought from a Zuni.

Fishler (West)
Miniature horses and sheep were roughly shaped from "mirage quartz rock." Only the legs, head, body, and tail were differentiated. The animals were about two to two and a half inches long and about an inch high.

GB (Tuba City) owned an oblong stone a few inches long with a natural groove on one side. He had another stone, made of brown glass-like material, with diagonal lines running through it. It had rounded ends and was two to two and a half inches long and three quarters of an inch high. He believed these stones had the same powers as the animal fetishes.

Most informants did not know who made the fetishes. Some claimed they were made by Navaho, others that they belonged to the Anasazi or the gods.

Several explanations of their origin were given by informants. GB's grandfather, when a young man at Fort Sumner, was in the habit of running early each morning for exercise. One morning he saw a horse on the horizon and ran toward it. As he neared the area, the horse disappeared and he could find no tracks. He looked down and on a piece of earth, surrounded by tall grass, lay a small figure of a horse, about one and a half inches long and half an inch high, made of gray and black shiny material. The figure of the horse was perfect in all ways. He said a prayer to the sun and picked up the figure. It was passed down within the family. GB said that that grass was made by the Sun for the horse to use, and that was why the horse was found there. TH (Moenave) agreed, stating that both of the objects could be derived from Lightning or from the Cliff Dwellings.

According to TN (Kaibito), the long rounded chert (like GB's brown stone) was what Lightning actually shot at the earth. He agreed that the small stone horse and grooved stone were passed down from one generation to the next.

Both GB and TN said that the fetishes were used in curing ceremonies. They were used ceremonially to increase the number of horses and sheep, and as good luck charms to keep harm or evil from the animals. For this purpose the stones were kept inside a bag filled with pollen. The mere possession of a fetish, either in the hogan or on the person, gave a certain amount of power.

Comparative

The Franciscan Fathers (1910:399) stated that "sacred stones, such as rock crystal, turquoise, and the like, and sometimes animal fetiches" were carried in the pollen sacks. Wyman's informant X carried a horse image of white shell, and a sheep image of a translucent, yellow stone in his pollen bag (Kluckhohn and Wyman, 1940:48). Haile (1947b) gives an extensive description of the utilization of animal figurines.

Bird fetishes were also found. Hester (1962:118–119) described several which were "found with a cache of Puebloan pottery, prayer sticks, a buckskin mask" in the Gobernador locality, New Mexico. Fetishes resembling a macaw, magpie, woodpecker, and dove were carved from wood, possibly cottonwood. There were two raven fetishes, one "the pelt of a raven stuffed slightly with juniper bark and wrapped around the neck with a piece of broadleaf yucca." Braided grass cord and a piece of buckskin were wrapped around the body. The other was made from two raven skins "stuffed with grass and tied together with a flat braid of grass."

224. Cranebill   déłda·· (Haile)   cranebill; "beak" (CC)

Hill (Central and West)

The preparation of cranebills for use in the Flint Way was described by PP (Fort Defiance) and GH (White Cone). Their accounts were substantially the same as that of Father Berard Haile (1943) given below. C (Chinle) and SC (Crystal) were informants for Father Berard Haile.

Comparative

Cranebills were required for both Flint Way and Shooting Way. In both chants, "more commonly the cranebill [was] simply the pouch" (see Trait 217). The cranebill replaced "the living agate pouch of Gila Monster."

SC (Crystal) described the manufacture of the cranebill. Sandhill cranes were preferred, but in their absence the bill of a diving heron might be substituted, or (C, Chinle) that of a woodpecker. The birds were shot at their feeding places. The bills were cleaned of flesh, then dried thoroughly in the sun. Particles of the crane's heart, lungs, and stomach were dried, chips of jewels were inserted in them, and they were then replaced in the bill in the same order as they occurred in the body. Reeds obtained from Oraibi and Taos, "perhaps a good span in length," were added as containers for the medicines of Flint Way. The skin of the crane's breast and back, which was left on the bill, was next slipped over the reed joints. Pueblo foods were added to the medicines, and the whole was "stopped with red ocher and with pitch taken from a lightningstruck tree." The reed was then wrapped with un-wounded buckskin thongs. The male pouch was decorated with chert arrowheads, the female with olivella, abalone, white bead, and other available shells. "The pouches must be decorated in presence of Flintway and Shootingway singers at the five night ceremonial of [*azee niilghe alneehgi*] *making of the medicine preparation*" (Haile, 1943:22–23). It was usual for the male cranebill to be prominent for a male patient, and the female cranebill for a female patient; both, however, were necessary. Cranebills were "placed under the patients cover, while the corresponding song" was sung. Cranebills were also used as medicine spoons (Haile, 1943:23).

In the *Ethnologic Dictionary*, the Franciscan Fathers (1910:407–408) added that a twigbill crane might be substituted if sandhill cranes were scarce. They stated that the male cranebill was supposed to be slightly curved, the beak of the female straight; the curved cranebill illustrated, however, represented "a blue heron in female attire" (see 224.1).

224.1. "Blue heron bill in female attire," after the Franciscan Fathers

225. Medicine Stopper

ʼazeˑˑ bidádítˣįˑh (Ramah, Haile)   "medicine lid" (CC)

Ramah

"This was used to protect, stir, taste and sprinkle medicines" (Kluckhohn and Wyman, 1940:31).

Hill (Central)

The following description refers to medicine stoppers used in the Male and Female Flint Way. Both were made from wood reduced at one end to spatula form. Those for the Male Flint Way were made of lightning-struck oak; feathers were attached to the uncarved end. Those for the Female Flint Way were without feathers and were of lightning-struck mountain mahogany (SC, Crystal).

Comparative

Medicine stoppers were called "medicine spoons" by the Franciscan Fathers (1910:407), and two types were described (see 225.1). Both were about a foot long, made of mountain mahogany wound with yarn, calico, or wool. The "smooth stick" was decorated with olivella shell and the "fledged stick" with chert points; both were decorated with gray eagle feathers. The point of the "smooth" stopper was blunt, that of the other was slightly hollowed or flattened. Both were used in administering medicine to the patient and were held parallel over the medicine cup.

These were actually neither spoons nor stoppers but, according to Haile, served these purposes symbolically as part of the paraphernalia of Flint Way and Shooting Way. They were made from a feather of a "live (American) eagle and one of a live red shouldered hawk," found floating upon water, for the male and female stoppers, respectively. "The root of any live medicine" served as a support for the feathers, which were tied to it with unwounded buckskin thongs. The male stopper was decorated with chert, the female with beads or shell. The male stopper took precedence for a male patient, the female for a female, whenever both were "lined up with other parts of the pouch for the stepping ceremony." Medicine stoppers were made and used in accordance with the instructions of Gila Monster (Haile, 1943:32–33). Haile (1943:23) also stated that cranebills could be used as substitutes for medicine stoppers.

225.1. Medicine stoppers, after the Franciscan Fathers

226. Masks   ǯiš (Haile)   "pouch" (CC)

Ramah

Information on masks among the Ramah Navaho is scanty. Notes on the description of a Night Way in 1944 indicated several variations, including the wearing of headbands instead of masks by dancers (Inf. 12). "Singers own the masks, bring them along" (Inf. 12). Vogt observed a Night Way in 1949 at which some wore masks with ordinary clothing and others wore traditional garments. The masks were not described.

Hill (Central)

Masks were made from buckskin. The informant (SC, Crystal) stated that he had used twelve skins to construct the set he owned. Only "sacred" buckskin was formerly used, but because of the recent scarcity of the material, the principal of homeopathic medicine has been invoked and parts of one "sacred" buckskin have been used to impart sanctity to masks made from ordinary hides.

The buckskins were buried in damp earth and when thoroughly moistened were stretched. Next the hide was folded longitudinally and marked for cutting. The worker designated the point for the mouth, usually in the hip section of the skin. He placed his thumb on this point and described a circle using the thumb and middle finger as a radius. The hand was always twisted sunwise (clockwise). This circle corresponded to the general area used for the face of the mask and was used as a base for the more precise measurements which followed.

Next the position of the eyes was marked on the face. The worker placed his thumb in his mouth, his index finger in one eye, and his middle finger in the other eye. He then transferred this measurement to the buckskin, placing his thumb on the point designated for the mouth, and locating the points for the eyes at the point of contact of the middle and index fingers.

The top of the mask was determined by measuring five finger widths above the eyes; the sides were four finger widths from the eyes. A line was drawn five finger widths below the mouth. The mask below this area was later painted to symbolize evening twilight.

Finally the worker cut the mask from the skin following the outline formed by the measurements. The front and back were cut at the same time. These original halves were employed as patterns for subsequent masks.

SC said masks should be made in the following order: Talking God, House God (there are six of this type), Black God, Fringed Mouth, Water Sprinkler, and finally the six female masks. Whenever possible the male and the leader of the females should be made entirely of "sacred" buckskin.

Masks (Hill), after SC

226.1. Talking God mask

226.2. Mask worn by female impersonators

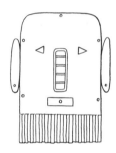

Sewing was accomplished with the aid of two awls from the right and left cannon bones of a "sacred" deer. Sinew was similarly selected, half from the right side of the animal's back, half from the left. Using the right awl and sinew, the worker sewed the halves together along the right side (the wearer's right) of the masks, starting from holes punched in the top of the two pieces of buckskin. The seam progressed from this point to the line designating the area of evening twilight and rain. A down feather of a bluebird was pressed on the moist sinew and included in each stitch. The worker repeated this operation on the left side of the mask using the left awl and sinew, but substituting the down feathers of a warbler. "The feathers are included because the gods inhabit the mountains. The birds live on the outside of the mountains, therefore you decorate the outside of the gods' heads with feathers."

When the sewing was completed, the mask was fitted. If the marks for the eye and mouth holes were properly located, circular sections were removed from these areas. These pieces were strung on a buckskin thong and tied inside near the respective apertures. "You must not lose these since they represent the eyes and mouth. If lost the worker would lose his eyesight and his mouth would become crooked."

Next the masks were painted and various appurtenances were attached. The lower portions of all were painted yellow for the evening twilight and striped with black to symbolize rain. The mask of the Talking God (see 226.1) was colored white. A black cornstalk was drawn on the forehead between the eyes. To the top of the mask was tied the tail of a deer and a white shell bead. The faces of the masks representing the House Gods were painted blue, and the eyes and mouths were outlined in black. The tail of a gourd was sewn in the mouths. An abalone and a turquoise bead were tied at the top of these masks. The remainder of the male masks bore abalone shell beads, with the exception of the Water Sprinkler, which had turquoise.

The six masks worn by the female impersonators were made from whatever sections of buckskin remained after the others had been completed. These merely covered the face; they were not equipped with backs. Two flaps representing ears were sewn to either side. Holes were punched in the bottom of each in which earrings were tied. Buckskin thongs through five holes, one

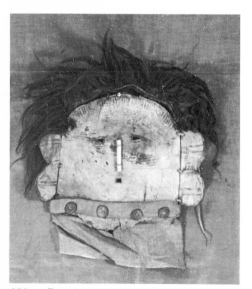

226.a. Female Impersonator mask

above and below each ear and one on top of the head, secured the mask to the performer.

Female masks were painted blue. A "feathered" ear of corn was drawn on the face; it was black outlined in white and divided into four sections by transverse white bars (see 226.2). It extended from between the eyes almost to the mouth. A turquoise bead and an eagle and a turkey feather were attached to the top of the leader's mask; the rest bore only eagle plumes.

SC was uneasy and disturbed throughout the description of the manufacture of masks, presumably because information of this type is not supposed to be divulged. This constraint may account for the fact that his description of the noses of the female masks does not agree with his drawing, the description stipulating four black sections while the drawing has five white ones. There are, however, variations in mask decoration among chanters, as Haile (1947a:37) has pointed out. In the case of the female mask, Haile's illustration (1947a:opposite p. 58) shows three sections in the ear of corn; Stevenson (1891:opposite p. 246) shows seven.

Comparative

In Matthews' monograph on the Night Chant, Navaho masks and other paraphernalia were well described. Details amplified and confirmed those obtained by Hill in most respects. Marking of facial features on unwounded buckskin was done with pollen "vitalized by a bird called *nikeni*" (probably an owl). There were occasional differences in ornamentation. Talking God and House God were described first, as by Hill's informant, but at that point the orders differed. Matthews stated that twenty masks completed a set, and agreed with Hill's informant that the six for female impersonators were only face masks. Masks were owned by a chanter, presumably the one who made them, and were stored in a bag when not in use. "One set of them may last a priest through his professional career" (Matthews, 1902:55–57).

According to the Franciscan Fathers (1910:384–388), the Night Chant properly required twenty-four masked impersonators, but by 1910 the number had been limited to fourteen: "the *yeibichai,* six male and six female masks, with . . . [*tonenili*], or water sprinkler." The masks were designated by the term for pouch [*jish*], but "strictly speaking they are . . . [*nikee*], or faceprints of the Holy Ones." (Note the similarity to the term for the bird, above.) The masks were "colored and decorated anew for each occasion." The Franciscan Fathers also presented an account similar to that of Hill's informant. In all descriptions, Talking God was white, with a corn plant drawn in the middle of the face; House God was blue; the female masks were merely face masks.

Worthy of particular note to one interested in Navaho masks is the monograph by Father Berard Haile, *Head and Face Masks in Navaho Ceremonialism* (1947a). It is illustrated with photographs of masks and color plates showing the manner in which they are painted. In another work he dealt with a set of masks bought in 1910. These had been made six years after the return from Fort Sumner by Largo, a signer of the treaty in 1868. On Largo's death, the masks were inherited by his sister's son, who bequeathed them to his brother (?), whose son, being untrained in ceremonialism, sold them. These transactions were common, and indicated that a son who was "able and willing to follow his father's profession" could inherit the paraphernalia. "Otherwise the ordinary rule of inheritance (uncle to nephew, sister's child)

Mask of yucca leaves used in the Night Way

226.b. Before trimming

226.c. After trimming with spruce

Ritual was followed and the masks were treated as merchantable property" (Haile, 1954:32–33).

227. Prayersticks

ke·tá·ń (Ramah, Haile)   "yucca stems" (CC)

Ramah
Prayersticks (see Plate XV) were made from cane reeds, mountain mahogany, wild cherry, juniper, or willow, "often lightning-struck, and sometimes from special directions" (Kluckhohn and Wyman, 1940:26). Eagle plumes taken from live birds were attached to the top of most by loops of buckskin or cotton string. Feathers from bluebirds, yellow birds, and others were also attached.

The size varied considerably. McAllester noted "a bundle of peeled sticks" like the one in Inf. 12's hogan at another hogan. "In both cases they were hanging on the wall up near the eaves." The sticks were "about the diameter of a pencil and from two feet to a yard long." Vogt believed this to be unusually long for a prayerstick.

Comparative
The Franciscan Fathers (1910:396–398) stated that "small sticks, varying in size and color, [were] offered with the sacrifice and dedicated by prayer."

"Talking prayersticks"

227.a. Used in Blessing Way rite

227.b. From Coolidge, N.M.

346

In some ceremonies these were very numerous and were made anew for each occasion; in a few ceremonies, they were not required. "The material to be used in their preparation is minutely described by ritual and tradition." Materials used corresponded with those at Ramah. During a ceremony, prayersticks were usually grouped in a ceremonial basket.

The Franciscan Fathers suggested "internode of reed" as a possible translation of the term for prayerstick. According to Father Berard, the term was "employed to designate a joint of reed or willow used for sacrificial purposes." One of L. Kluckhohn's informants called it "yucca stems."

Materials and sizes differed with ritual prescriptions, but a hollow reed was usually employed whenever the ritual required the insertion of tobacco; it was stoppered with pollen (Haile, 1943:38–39). Details of the preparation of prayersticks in a five-night ceremonial of the Male Branch of the Navaho Shooting Way were also described by Father Berard (Haile, 1947c; well illustrated with colored figs.).

Musical Instruments

228. Gourd Rattle

ʼade·· ʼaɣá·ł (Ramah, Haile) "gourd cup rattle" (CC)

Ramah

According to Inf. 12 in 1950, the rattle used in chantways was made from a gourd. A hole was drilled in the gourd, a piece of turquoise was put inside, and a handle was inserted in the hole. Other "jewels," pollen, and grains of corn were also placed inside the rattles. The surface of the rattles was "decorated with a perforated design representing constellations" (Kluckhohn and Wyman, 1940:41). Inf. 55 informed McAllester in 1950 that the rattle was made in the morning, after making the drum, but the type was not indicated.

Rattles have been used recently in the Ramah area; Roberts, in 1946, observed that Inf. 34 used the rattle but that Infs. 51 and 96 did not. Edmonson reported chanting to the accompaniment of a rattle at a Night Way in 1949, but he did not ascertain the kind of rattle used.

Hill (Central and West)

A mature, thoroughly dry, straight-necked gourd was selected. The end of the neck was cut off and a hole about half an inch in diameter was bored in the center of the ball of the gourd, directly opposite the neck opening. Gravel was shaken about in the gourd to loosen the seeds and pith, which were removed through the openings.

Prior to fixing the handle an indeterminate number of pieces of turquoise and white shell were placed in the rattle. According to PP (Fort Defiance), if the maker wished to insure a "loud rattle" he inserted a few commercial beads as well and punched holes in the sides of the rattle: "This makes it sound louder; otherwise it has a dull sound." GH (White Cone) stated that the inclusion of turquoise and white shell made the rattle "holy."

The handle was a tapered shaft, usually of juniper, which was inserted in the neck and passed through the rattle; it projected from half to three quarters of an inch beyond the hole in the ball. It was carefully made and fitted snugly at the points of contact. The handle was secured in one of two ways. Either the projecting end was notched and a cord or buckskin thong was wrapped and tied at this point (PP, GH), or a hole was bored through the end and a wooden key inserted (SC, Crystal). A buckskin wrapping was usually applied at the juncture of the handle and neck. According to informants (PP, SC), if the rattle was intended for use in the Night Way or Blessing Way, the handle must always be of juniper.

Finally the rattle was painted white, "because the dancers were painted white" (GH, SC). All rattles destined for commercial use had to be constructed under ritual conditions (SC).

One small rattle and six large ones of this type were used in the Night Way. When walking in for the dance, the dancers shook the rattles rapidly from side to side. They then presented their rattles to the west, "saluted," then, turning clockwise, presented them to the east. When the dance began the rattles were shaken with an up and down motion. GH and SC stated that the rattle used by the chanter in the Night Way was of the same type but smaller and had a punched design of a mountain sheep on the sides. PP said that large rattles were used in the Blessing Way.

Comparative

The Franciscan Fathers (1910:401–402) illustrated the gourd rattle, stating that it was used for the Night Way, various branches of the Wind Way, the Water, Big God, and Feather Ways. They stated that the decoration was "figures of the sun, moon, or some constellation."

Both of Gifford's Navaho informants confirmed the use of gourd rattles for accompanying dances and by chanters in curing. The Western informant said that pebbles or seeds were placed inside, but the Eastern informant questioned this information (Gifford, 1940:58, 151).

A rattle in the Peabody Museum (see 228.1), collected by Grace Nicholson and C. Hartman in 1908, is ten and one-half inches long; the diameter of the gourd is four inches.

228.1. Gourd rattle

229. Rawhide Rattle

ʼaka·ł ʼaɣá·ł (Ramah, Haile)

Ramah

These rattles "should be of bison rawhide, but today they are most often made of the hide of a cow or horse which has been given to the singer." The handle was made of lightning-struck wood to which a bison tail was attached. Inside were "jewels," as in the gourd rattles. Hide rattles were used in Shooting Way, Red Ant Way, Moving Up Way, and Beauty Way; those used for Beauty Way were shaped slightly differently (Kluckhohn and Wyman, 1940:42–43).

Hill (Central and West)

Rawhide rattles were formerly made from the tails of buffalo hides which the Navaho obtained from the Ute. In recent times, cowhide has been substituted. The hide from the upper end of the tail was utilized. It was fleshed

229 / *Rawhide Rattle*

XIV. Hastin Acani-Padanie, Navaho medicine man, administering Female Shooting Chant to mother and baby for better health, St. Michaels, Arizona. They are seated on a woolen blanket (Tr. 127) and sheepskin (Tr. 126). The woman wears the traditional hair tie (Tr. 181), a velveteen blouse (Tr. 167), a shell and turquoise necklace (Tr. 197), silver bracelet (Tr. 200), silver rings (Tr. 201), and a commercially made shawl (Tr. 169). The baby is in a cradleboard (Tr. 128) with an arched canopy (Tr. 131). Hastin Acani-Padanie is wearing a skin headband (Tr. 183), a velveteen shirt (Tr. 172), cloth trousers (Tr. 175), buckskin leggings (Tr. 177) decorated with silver buttons (Tr. 202) and secured by woven garters (Tr. 179), and moccasins (Tr. 189). He has a fur scarf (Tr. 192) and a shell and turquoise necklace (Tr. 197) around his neck, and is wearing several rings (Tr. 201), a bracelet (Tr. 200), and an ornamented wrist guard (Tr. 24). He holds a rawhide rattle (Tr. 229). She is holding two prayersticks (Tr. 227); another rests on the sheepskin blanket. On the blanket is a buckskin medicine bag (Tr. 217), a drum and drumstick, neither of which is Navaho in type, and a Plains saddlebag.

Rawhide rattles (Hill)

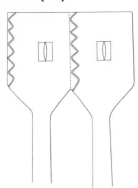

229.1. Pattern

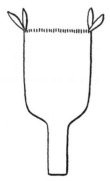

229.2. Applying quill wrapping, after IS

and dehaired, then soaked in water. When the hide was thoroughly pliable, the rattle was cut according to the established pattern (see 229.1). If the material was adequate it was cut in a single piece; if not, each side was cut separately. While the hide was still wet, two zigzag lines were cut in each of what would become the outside edges. The side or sides of the rattle were sewn, and the hide was reversed to conceal the stitching. The head of the rattle was filled with dry sand, compressed, and allowed to dry. Then the sand was removed and the rawhide retained the desired shape.

Next, pieces of white shell, turquoise, abalone shell, and jet were placed in the head; the sides of the handle area were sewn; and a wooden handle gauged to fit the opening was inserted. The handle was preferably made from pinyon; but mountain mahogany or oak might be substituted.

After the handle was placed, the rattle was painted black and set aside to dry. "This represented the dark sky." Then a representation of the "stubby" rainbow was painted on each face (see 229.1). These rainbows were rectangles bordered in white; the central sections were narrow white ovals. The left portions of the rectangles were colored blue, the right red (SC, Crystal).

The juncture of the handle with the rattle was wrapped with a finger-width three-ply braid of porcupine quills. SC said that the quills were strung longitudinally on a sinew string, the tip of one in the butt of the next. These were pressed flat with the fingernail. Three lengths were prepared in this manner and braided together.

IS (Lukachukai) gave an alternative for preparing the quill covering. He agreed that the quills were strung longitudinally, but said that they were left in the round. The chain was passed over and under two sinew strings, spaced a finger width apart, to produce a ribbon (see 229.2). The ends of the quill chain were tied in the square knots with the ends of the sinews. The ribbon was wrapped several times around the juncture. The overlap held one end in place, the other was fixed by passing the ends of the sinew around the shaft in opposite directions and tying them at the back. A slender otter skin thong was placed over the sinew and tied to cover it and the knot.

According to SC, the remainder of the handle was wrapped with buckskin, preferably "sacred" buckskin; at least one small piece had to be included to fulfill ritual prescriptions. Hair from the tail of a buffalo—more recently horsehair—was suspended from the base of the handle. It was held in place by the last few wraps around the base of the handle.

When the handle was completed, the zigzag cuts on the sides of the rattle were painted, each pair consisting of one red and one blue line. Finally, holes were punched in the upper corners, plumes were tied at these points, and the instrument was complete.

The account of the manufacture of this type of rattle by GH (White Cone) differed in some detail from the preceding one given by SC. Discrepancies in the second account appear to be compromises resulting from the difficulty of acquiring ritually prescribed materials. According to GH, the rattle was made from the upper portion of the tail of a cow that had been received in payment for the performance of a chantway. The tail skin was fleshed, dehaired, and shaped with dry sand. Beads were placed in the head; preferably these were of turquoise and white shell but commercial beads were substituted if necessary. The opening at the upper end was sewn. A cane

229.3. Rattle, after GH

handle was fitted in the base, and a buffalo tail attached to it. Feathers (type not specified) were tied to the upper corners (see 229.3). Finally, the rattle was painted black. No mention was made of painted designs.

PP (Fort Defiance) refused to describe the manufacture of a rawhide rattle. According to him, a description could be given only if a patient was present and undergoing a cure. In such a situation, the various parts of the rattle and their uses were explained by the patient.

Rawhide rattles were employed in a variety of chantways: the Shooting, Ghost, Ant, Big Star, and Mountain Ways (SC); the Shooting and Ghost Ways (IS); Shooting, Mountain, Blessing, and Mountain Top Ways (PP). According to GH, the rattle described by him might be used to accompany any song. The only restrictions he mentioned was that it must be shaken from side to side, never up and down. If this was not observed, it was believed that lightning would strike the operator. Use of the following types of rattles was denied by various informants: split stick (GH, PP); cocoon and tortoise shell (PP).

Comparative

The Franciscan Fathers (1910:401–402) illustrated a hide rattle (see 229.4) manufactured as described above, and stated that it was used in the Mountain and Witch chants and the Big Star Way, but not in the Blessing, Bead, and Feather Shaft chants. A badger hide rattle was used for the Beauty Way.

Gifford stated that the Western Navaho used a "buffalo-hide rattle formerly, from Ft. Sumner, New Mexico; nowadays cattle hide." It was used for curing. The Eastern informant was doubtful (Gifford, 1940:58, 151).

229.4. Rawhide rattle, after the Franciscan Fathers

230. Hoof Rattle

ʾakéšgaˑn ʾaɣáˑł (Ramah, Lamphere, Haile) "buffalo or deer hoof rattle" (CC)

Ramah

Hoofs from game animals (usually deer and bison), preferably from unwounded animals (Inf. 45), were strung on unwounded buckskin strips and tied to a stick. According to Infs. 2 and 7, antelope hoofs were never used. These rattles were used only in Flint Way. There were four in a set (Kluckhohn and Wyman, 1940:43–44).

Hill (Central and West)

Two variants of hoof rattle construction were recorded, the first by SC (Crystal). Deer hoofs or dew claws, buffalo hoofs, and elk horn were used. "A piece of elk horn may be added since elk are mentioned in some of the songs." Deer hoofs and dewclaws were boiled until soft, and the tips to be used for the rattle were cut off and perforated with a sharp stick. Buffalo hoofs, which were larger, were cut in several pieces before boiling. When perforated, all were strung on a string to dry.

A rectangular piece of "sacred" buckskin was fringed at one end. A section of hoof was threaded on each element of the fringe and a knot was tied in the end to secure the hoof. Hoofs were also attached in the same manner to several "sacred" buckskin thongs.

The rectangle was laid flat, and pollen and a "live medicine plant" were placed in the center. To obtain "live medicine plant" the man exposed part of the root system of a plant and pinched off one of the auxiliary roots. The scar left by the removal was treated with pollen, the roots were re-covered, and the plant continued to grow; hence, "live medicine plant."

Cane for the handle had to be obtained from the Hopi of Oraibi. "Oraibi stands for the west, Taos for the east." A section of cane was placed along one edge of the rectangle, extending above the center and below the lower edge. The top and bottom edges were then folded inward about half an inch. Next, one of the buckskin thongs was doubled and put beside the cane handle. It was so placed that the hoofs were aligned with those on the fringe.

Finally the buckskin rectangle was wrapped about the cane; the hide was wide enough to encircle the cylinder several times. After each complete coverage another doubled buckskin thong with rattles was inserted. The completed rattle was secured with a buckskin thong.

Other descriptions of the construction of hoof rattles (PP, Fort Defiance; GH, White Cone) agreed with that above with certain omissions. No mention was made of "live medicine plant" or the insertion of extra hoofs on thongs. PP stated that at least one piece of "sacred" buckskin must be included in the rattle, implying that most of the material could be ordinary buckskin. The principal difference in construction, however, was the lack of a cane handle. Both informants agreed that the hide was merely rolled on itself and that the lower portion was wrapped in buckskin to form the handle and give it rigidity.

These rattles were intended for ritual purposes and therefore could be constructed only during a special chantway held for the purpose of making ceremonial equipment (SC, Crystal; PP). PP stated that rattles of this type were used only in the Flint Way ("Hoof Way"); GH that they were part of the equipment of the Life Way. According to SC, an ordinary chanter was supposed to possess only three of these rattles; an authority of the Way, four.

GH stated that these rattles must be shaken only with an up and down movement, for fear of lightning. The same rule obtained for rawhide rattles and apparently for gourd ones.

Lamphere (East)

EP confirmed the term for hoof rattle.

Comparative

The Franciscan Fathers (1910:401–402) stated that the Knife Chant required a hoof rattle, made from the hoofs of the deer, antelope, bighorn sheep, and others. They illustrated one (see 230.1). Gifford's Western Navaho informant said that a rattle made of deer hoofs (in a bunch) was used. The Eastern informant gave no satisfactory answer (Gifford, 1940:58).

According to Haile (1943:39–40), the "buffalo people employed buffalo hoof rattles, therefore the hoof rattle was taken over by Flintway." Deer or fawn hoofs with buffalo or elk horn attached were used, since buffalo hoofs were not always available. The hoof rattle was meant to represent "the original flint rattle of Gila Monster."

230.1. Hoof rattle, after the Franciscan Fathers

231. Basket Drum ča·· ya·sit^xạ (Lamphere, Haile) "basket turned down" (CC)

Ramah
A ceremonial basket was used; it was turned over and beaten with a drumstick (see 98.b, 98.1–5; see also Tschopik, 1938; Kluckhohn and Wyman, 1940).

Hill (East, Central, and West)
"Wedding baskets" were inverted and used as drums in various chantways. Such baskets should not have been previously employed for utilitarian purposes. Once they had served ritually, however, they might be used in any capacity (SC, Crystal). The nonritual use of basket drums was reported by TLLSS (Crownpoint) in connection with corn grinding.

Certain types of sounding devices were denied. Three informants (TLLSS; PP, Fort Defiance; GH, White Cone) stated that drumming on the hogan walls was not permitted during a ceremony. The use of the plank foot drum and the double-headed Pueblo type of drum was denied by PP. MH (Head Springs) denied the use of the tambourine.

Lamphere (East)
PM confirmed the term for basket drum.

Comparative
Matthews observed that only two forms of baskets were made by Navaho women and that these were used for ceremonial purposes. The basket drum he called the most important variety; it was so called because of its use, "(inverted) chiefly as a drum." A regular drum or tom-tom was not used in any of the ancient Navaho rites. The sole decoration for the basket was "a colored band, red in the middle, with black serrated edges." The band was "intersected at one point by a narrow line of uncolored wood," a guide for orientation during the ceremony. After the ceremony, the basket was given to the chanter, who was "not to keep it but must give it away and he must be careful never to eat out of it" (Matthews, 1902:59). On some occasions, however, ceremonial baskets were sometimes used for food. Such a basket is in the Harvard Peabody Museum collection.

According to the Franciscan Fathers, the drum accompanied the rattle "at the close of some ceremonies," such as the Bead, Witch, and Star chants, and at all one-night ceremonies that ended in public exhibitions. The drum was furnished by the patient (Franciscan Fathers, 1910:402; the type of basket used is illustrated on p. 291).

Both of Gifford's Navaho informants said that a basket was used as a drum. The Eastern informant said that only the yucca drumstick was used; the Western informant said that the drum was beaten with a rattle. Both denied the use of a tambourine-type drum (Gifford, 1940:58, 151).

According to Father Berard Haile (1947c:21–22), the basket to be used as a drum was previously soaked with water. The basket was placed on a blanket, inverted over a corn meal cross; then the ends of the blanket were lapped over the basket. The chanter tapped the basket at the four cardinal points as he sang some twelve darkness songs. "After their completion he turns the basket up to indicate that the ceremonies for the night are completed."

232. Rawhide Drum

Hill (East, Central, and West)

TLLSS (Crownpoint) reported that he had once seen a rolled sheep pelt used as a drum during informal singing at Shiprock; it was beaten with moccasins. MH (Head Springs) stated that children in play occasionally rolled up a sheepskin in lieu of a drum and beat it with sticks. PP (Fort Defiance) said that men sang while the women were grinding corn in preparation for the girl's adolescent rite, and kept time on a rolled up sheepskin.

The idea of a rawhide drum was amusing to GH (White Cone). According to him, it was used by the White Mountain Apache, not the Navaho.

233. Pottery Drum

ʼása·· dáde·sʌ̨́ǫ́ (Lamphere, Haile) "pottery tied around" (CC)

Ramah

According to Inf. 55, a buckskin that had been soaked in water was stretched tightly over the neck of a pot. "It takes two or three guys to pull it down good and tight over the pot and then a guy wraps the string around. It's all done this way [clockwise] and four times."

A variation was reported by Roberts in 1946. Inf. 90 described to him a drum made by stretching a piece of rubber from an inner tube over a tin can. Inf. 90 implied that it was made by his wife. It is doubtful that such a drum would ever be used for ceremonial purposes.

Apparently anyone could make a pottery drum, but Inf. 55 told McAllester in 1950 that it had to be made after dark. Anyone could use it. "It doesn't make any difference; you just sort of pass it around. I've played it myself. Somebody else takes it when the man who has it gets tired" (Inf. 55). After the ceremony was over, the drum and the stick were taken back to the "Far Camp" (Inf. 55).

The pottery drum is still used in Ramah, and was observed in 1946, 1949, and 1950. In 1951 Mills was told that Inf. 264 had a "water drum" for use at chantways. This was probably the one seen by Roberts in 1946 at an Enemy Way; to make it several men tied "deer hide real tight over a pottery olla and put water in the jar."

Tschopik's informants (Infs. 7, 12, 15, 32) stated that no one in the Ramah area made pottery drums and that all were considered heirlooms. They were required for every Enemy Way ceremonial. Inf. 7 kept a drum in a sack hanging in a pinyon tree about twenty-five feet southeast of the hogan. He stated that the drum should not be kept in the house. According to Inf. 36, every two years or so the drum should be coated with more pinyon pitch to increase the noise (Tschopik, 1941:14).

Hill (Central and West)

An ordinary cooking pot was used for a drum. The only prescriptions were that it must not have been employed for utilitarian purposes prior to the ceremony (SC, Crystal), and that it have a decorative fillet around the neck (GH, White Cone). Before the ceremony the pot was carefully examined to make sure it contained no cracks. Next, about two cups of water were poured into the pot and the head was placed over the aperture. The head was formerly of buckskin (not "sacred"); more recently goatskin has been substituted. A buckskin thong or bowstring was used to secure the head. A loop was tied in one end and a short length of buckskin tied to this. The end of the initial cord was passed through the loop and the resulting larger loop placed over the drumhead and around the neck of the pot and drawn tight. The loose end was wrapped about the neck several times; finally this end and the end of the short length of buckskin were tied in a square knot (SC). The pot symbolized the earth, the drumhead the blue sky, the water the black sky (GH).

If the drum broke during the first night of the ceremony the ritual was terminated. The person responsible for the breakage had to have the Enemy Way performed at some later date. If breakage occurred after the first night, the chanter in charge prepared a new drum and the ceremony proceeded. Drums were never substituted during the ritual unless they were broken. If at the close of the ritual a crack was discovered in the drum, the ceremony was deemed ineffective and had to be repeated not only over the patient but also over the pole receiver (GH).

At the end of the ritual a song, "the mother song," purported to belong to Changing Woman, was sung. The drum was then brought to the pole receiver who untied the head and kept the tie-strings (GH).

Lamphere (East)
PM confirmed the term for pottery drum, and EP said that the Enemy Way drum was called "little pot."

Comparative
The Franciscan Fathers (1910:289) did not stipulate that the vessel must be unused or uncracked. In other respects, their description was essentially the same as that of Hill's informants. Gifford's Navaho informants agreed that a pottery drum with a skin head was used; it was beaten with a "ring drumstick" (Gifford, 1940:58).

Haile (1938:43) described the manufacture of the pottery drum, stating that it was to represent "beating the enemy ghosts into the ground." Water, not necessarily sacred water, was poured into the pot from the cardinal points and from above. Openings for eyes and mouth were punched into the cover. Songs were sung to accompany the preparation of this drum.

In the collections of the Harvard Peabody Museum is a pottery drum collected by Dr. A. M. Tozzer in 1908 (see 233.a). It is unusual in that the pot is equipped with a handle.

233.a. Pottery drum with loop drumstick (Tr. 234)

234. Loop Drumstick

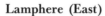

ˀasaˑˑ beˑiltˣaží (Ramah, Lamphere, Haile)   "pottery with it drumming" (CC)

Ramah
Roberts noted at an Enemy Way in 1949 a drummer "beating a tom-tom of some sort with an unusual curved implement." Mills in 1951 accompanied a group of Navaho who were preparing for a ceremonial: "Our next step was in order to obtain a twig from which to make the rounded drumstick. This has to be made of a special kind of material; Inf. 4 was the one who knew where this was growing."

Loop drumstick (Hill)

234.1. Bending the drumstick

234.2. Wrapping the drumstick, after SC

234.3. Securing the ends, after GH

Hill (Central and West)

Circular drumsticks must be made from juniper, oak, or wild cherry (SC, Crystal; GH, White Cone). "You have to obtain one of these woods even if it is necessary to travel two hundred miles" (GH). A section of wood slightly larger than a pencil in diameter was chosen for the drumstick, and the bark was removed. Next, the growing end of the stick was scraped or whittled to reduce its diameter to half-round; a small protuberance was left at the extreme tip. The half-round section occupied about a third of the over-all length. This operation was performed to make the area flexible, and flexibility was further increased by manipulating it with the hands. When sufficiently pliable, it was bent round side out to form a circle about three inches in diameter (see 234.1). Bending was accomplished without heat since the instrument was intended for ceremonial use and it was believed that fire would desecrate it. The distal three quarters of an inch of the end overlapped the handle of the drumstick, which was of any convenient length (SC, GH), and was held in place at that point by a buckskin wrap. The protuberance at the tip prevented the wrap from slipping (see 234.2).

The wrap that maintained the circle was formerly of "sacred" buckskin; recently this prescription has been lifted. It was put on clockwise and the wrapping proceeded from butt toward tip. The informants (GH, SC) disagreed on the correct methods of securing the ends (see 234.2, 234.3).

This type of drumstick was used on pottery drums and confined to the Enemy Way. The outside ("bottom") of the loop was used to produce the slow beats; the side of the loop in the same plane as the handle ("top") was used when rapid beats were desired. Prior to the ritual, the drum was kept in the hogan. When the time for singing approached, the drummer struck the drum once in each of the four cardinal points and once in the center. He then reversed the drumstick and sounded four rapid beats. The drum was removed from the hogan and the singing began after beats had again been sounded from the four cardinal directions and center (GH).

At the close of the ceremony, the drumstick was untied, soaked in water, and straightened. The pole or "baton" receiver did this, and kept the thongs. The drumstick was then placed under the bark of a growing juniper (SC) or under a rock where no rain could reach it (GH). When the stick was deposited a prayer was said. This was not a standardized prayer, the content being optional (SC).

Lamphere (East)

EP confirmed the term for loop drumstick.

Comparative

The Franciscan Fathers (1910:289) illustrated a loop drumstick in connection with the pottery drum, but did not describe it. Gifford's Navaho informants also confirmed the use of a "ring" drumstick on a pottery drum (Gifford, 1940:58; see also Haile, 1938, for an account of the Navaho Enemy Way).

The loop drumstick with the drum in the Peabody Museum, Harvard University (see 233.a), is eight and one-half inches long. The loop has a diameter of two and one-half inches.

235. Yucca Drumstick

Yucca drumstick, after Hill; *a* and *b* indicate ends of leaves, *x* location of corn kernels, *y* the wrappings, and *p* the strips that cross them

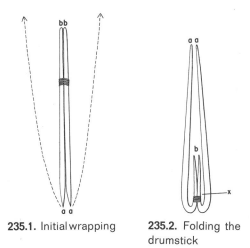

235.1. Initial wrapping

235.2. Folding the drumstick

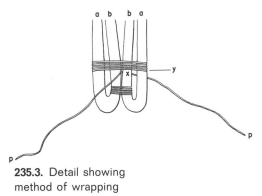

235.3. Detail showing method of wrapping

235.4. Side view, showing wrapping

ċa·· be·ikad (Lamphere, Haile)   "yucca with it to pound" (CC)

Ramah
There is no specific information on this trait. (See Kluckhohn and Wyman, 1940:44. They refer the reader to Matthews' description.)

Hill (Central)
Drumsticks were made from the leaves of a wide-leafed yucca. A leaf was chosen from each of the cardinal directions. Those from the east and west were placed back to back (see 235.1); the north and south leaves were divided into strips for wrapping and tying. One such strip was twisted around, slightly to one side of the center of the east and west leaves, and tied securely in a square knot. The bases of the two leaves were then folded back over the distal ends (see 235.2). Five kernels of corn (white, yellow, blue, black, and a duplicate of one color) were tied in a bundle and put between the two leaves, just above the initial wrapping (see 235.2, point *x*). Next, the proximal ends of yucca strips were tied in a square knot, and the knot placed on the corn kernels (see 235.3, point *x*). The loose ends (*p*) projected on either side. Then the worker took another strip and applied a wrapping (*y*) around the outside of the leaves above the cord. Four turns were taken, the wrapping progressing away from the worker. The ends of the strips (*p*) were then crossed over the wrapping; they passed between the leaves from opposite directions (see 235.4). Another wrapping was applied, and the strips were again crossed over this, and so on, until there were four wrappings. Finally the strips (*p*) were tied in a square knot and the ends allowed to hang between the leaves (see 235.4). The loops and wrappings were symbolic of the "four word songs" used in the chantways. The remainder of the drumstick below the head was wrapped solidly with yucca strips and finally covered with a cloth wrapping.

Yucca drumsticks were used with the basket drum in the Mountain, Night, Shooting (male and female), Wind, Bead, Beauty, Hail, and Water Ways. At the termination of the ceremony the stick was unwrapped, straightened, and deposited in the fork of a tree with a prayer. The content of the prayer was optional. If a man was present who was learning the chantway, he requested the kernels of corn, chewed them, and swallowed them. "This would make him learn faster and prevent him from forgetting." If no one requested the kernels, the chanter kept them and ground them up when he had occasion to make medicine (SC, Crystal).

Lamphere (East)
EP confirmed the term for yucca drumstick.

Comparative
Matthews published a complete description of the manufacture of the yucca drumstick. The chosen yucca leaves were to be "of proper length and absolutely free from wound, stain, withered point or blemish of any kind." They were gathered according to ritual directions, and the leaves pulled from the east and west were marked for later identification; those from the north and south, to be used for ties, were not. In the drumstick illustrated by Matthews, there were five wrappings, "one for each night" it was used. A grain or more of corn was usually placed in each section.

235.a. Yucca drumstick used in the Night Way

Matthews also stated that since the drumstick dried quickly and became brittle, it was buried in moist earth during the daytime. At dawn, on the last morning of the ceremony, it was dismantled by reversing the sequence of steps in its construction. The remnants, and the debris carefully saved from its original construction, were placed in the fork of a juniper tree or some large plant where they would not be trampled by cattle. There they remained until destroyed by the elements. The corn kernels were divided among the visiting chanters. They were later ground and put in their medicine bags (Matthews, 1902:61–63).

In the description published by the Franciscan Fathers (1910:297), corn pollen rather than corn kernels was inserted in the drumstick. Gifford's Eastern Navaho informant said that the basket drum was beaten only with a "plaited yucca-leaf drumstick." The Western informant denied this and said that a rattle was used (Gifford, 1940:151).

236. Drumming Stick

ʼasaˑˑ beˑiltˣažĭ (Lamphere)   drumstick; "pottery with it drumming" (CC)

Ramah
Edmonson noted at a Night Way in 1949 that the assistant pounded on the earth with a small club to produce a drumming effect.

Hill (East and West)
Any convenient piece of wood of proper size might be used as a drumming stick on informal and nonritual occasions. TLLSS (Crownpoint) said that young men sometimes sang to women who were preparing corn meal; songs were accompanied by drumming on an inverted basket (see Trait 231). MH(Head Springs) stated that children amused themselves by beating rolled sheep pelts with such sticks.

Lamphere (East)

PM said that the term for this stick was the same as that for the loop drumstick (see Trait 234).

Comparative

The Franciscan Fathers (1910:63) noted that in some legends Navaho ground corn side by side, Pueblo fashion, with a drummer or flute player timing them in accompaniment. In 1910 grinding was not done communally, nor is it now.

237. Stomping Pole

giš (Lamphere)   "cane" (CC)

Hill (East and West)

Wooden staffs about four feet long were used to beat time. Any available kind of wood was employed. According to the informant (TLLSS, Crownpoint), at large ceremonial gatherings young men and boys would assemble near the women who were grinding and preparing food, and sing. This was an informal social situation and the songs were purely for amusement. The chorus kept time by pounding the poles on the ground, clapping hands, or beating on an inverted basket with the drumstick. GH (White Cone) denied that poles were used in this capacity.

Lamphere (East)

PM said that there was a stomping pole for each of the sacred mountains.

Comparative

Material in Trait 236 from the Franciscan Fathers (1910:63) is appropriate here as well.

238. Flute

ṅdilnih (Lamphere, Haile)   "stick carved in the side"

Ramah

Roberts stated that Inf. 34 used to make flutes before he was in school in Albuquerque. He did not describe them.

Hill (East, Central, and West)

The flute was called "horn that makes a noise." Informants agreed that a mature stalk from a sunflower was always used to make a flute. The stalk was cut to size: ten inches (GH, White Cone), fourteen to sixteen inches (PP, Fort Defiance), fourteen to twenty-four inches (T, Chaco Canyon). The diameter was approximately the width of a finger (GH). The pith was removed from the interior and the holes were bored with a hot iron (PP). Four (T, GH) or four to six (PP) holes were bored. T stated that one end was plugged, but this was denied by PP and GH. The end forming the mouthpiece was tapered (PP). When the flute was played, the middle and ring fingers were used as stops.

A variant was reported by TLLSS (Crownpoint). He said that flutes were six inches long and equipped with ten holes. The holes were graduated in size, the largest toward the distal end; they were bored in pairs on opposite sides of the flute. When played, this instrument was held in the same position as a fife and moved back and forth across the mouth.

The instrument was utilized in several ways. T stated that flutes were toys. TLLSS reported that they were part of the orchestration accompanying songs sung by young men to girls who were grinding corn. PP said the flute was part of the equipment in one of the branches of the Bead Way. According to GH, flutes were used to compel girls to make assignations.

> Boys have love songs which they sing at home. Even though they were sung at home the power of the song would reach the girl and make her like the boy. A boy would also make a flute from a sunflower stalk. When he had finished his song he would take his flute and go to the girl's home. When he got there he would blow the flute once. Then he would say "Let me see you" and leave. Then he blew his flute again and the girl would follow him. He would walk until he came to a rock or reached the forest. Then he sat down and waited for the girl. When the girl arrived he had intercourse with her. The note from the flute would make her want to. You should not let the girl hold the flute because if she should blow on it, it would make her kind of crazy; she would get dizzy. This is because you sing over the flute when you make it.   (GH)

The flute appears to have been a recent acquisition of the Navaho. K (Mariano Lake) stated that it was derived from the Ute. T said that the Navaho obtained it from the Comanche while at Fort Sumner, and TLLSS that it was introduced just prior to the Fort Sumner period.

Lamphere (East)
PM said that the term for flute means "stick carved in the side."

Comparative
According to the Franciscan Fathers (1910:511), "the ancient custom of timing the grinding of corn at the war dance by means of a flute made of the stalk of the sunflower, and provided with four keys, is mentioned as a tradition only."

Both of Gifford's Navaho informants agreed that a flute was used. It was made of cane; the Eastern informant specified a sunflower stalk. Four stops were made, spaced according to convenience. According to the Western informant, the flute was used only for amusement, and only by children. The Eastern informant said that only chanters used flutes, and denied their use for amusement or at dances (Gifford, 1940:59, 152).

According to Haile (1951:126), the flute was mentioned in the songs of the Navaho Enemy Way "as an instrument for rejoicing played by returning warriors." It is now no longer in vogue.

239. Whistle
cisǫ́·s (Ramah, Lamphere, Haile) "whistle (sound)" (CC)

Ramah
Pine pitch from a lightning-struck tree (pinyon or Ponderosa) was used to stop the opening of whistles. According to Inf. 2, it should be gathered "by

men or women who have been captured in youth by enemies and who have returned to the Navaho after many years." "Blow sickness off, blow sickness off on all four sides of the sick man, that's what it's for," stated Inf. 1 (Kluckhohn and Wyman, 1940:33).

Whistles, after Hill

239.1. Type I; *x* indicates mouthpiece, *y* is filled with pitch

239.2. Type II; *z* indicates mouthpiece, secured with pitch

Hill (Central and West)

Whistles for ceremonial purposes were made from cane or the femur of an eagle. Two types were described. In one type, (see 239.1), a notched section of bone or cane was removed from the upper side, about an inch from the mouthpiece. A loosely rolled section of cornhusk was fitted into and filled the area of the mouthpiece behind the notch (*x*). It was fixed in place with pitch; pitch was also used to seal the distal end of the whistle (*y*). According to PP (Fort Defiance), pitch used in whistles had to be obtained from outside sources, preferably from the Ute or Paiute.

The second type (see 239.2) of whistle had an over-all length of about seven inches and was notched in the same manner as the first. Instead of a cornhusk "reed," however, a layer of pitch was placed back of the notch opening and anchored to the side walls (*z*). A cornhusk was wrapped loosely around the outside of the tube. The husk was moved back and forth to vary the tone (GH, White Cone). C (Chinle) made no mention of a cornhusk.

According to PP, whistles were part of the equipment of the Lightning and Mountain Ways; according to GH, of the Night Way.

Two whistle-like noise-making implements were reported by GH. The first was constructed by splitting a bone, placing a piece of tissue from the ear of a rabbit between the halves, and binding the two together. When blown, the dry membrane vibrated and gave forth a sound. For the second, green leaves were placed between the thumbs and blown upon to create a similar sound. These were used by small boys for amusement.

Lamphere (East)

PM said that whistles were made from reeds.

Fishler (West)

A whistle made from a cane was blown by a singer as he probed for a lump on the body of a sick person (GB, Tuba City).

Comparative

The leg bone of a jack rabbit killed by an eagle was the material specified for making a whistle, according to the Franciscan Fathers. The bone was split and the marrow removed. A piece of the inner ear was placed between the two pieces of bone and wound with sinew. The whistle, when dry, produced "a shrill, piercing sound." As part of the Bead chant equipment, this whistle was meant to imitate the cry of the eagle and hawk (Franciscan Fathers, 1910:141, 403, 511).

Gifford's Eastern Navaho informant said that a cane whistle was used for turkey hunting. The Western informant denied this trait, and both informants denied the use of bone whistles (Gifford, 1940:59, 152).

240. Bullroarer

cin diṅi· (Ramah, Haile)   "wood sound" (CC)

Ramah

Oak or Ponderosa pine from a lightning-struck tree was required. There was apparently no correlation between the kind of wood and the ceremonial (Inf. 1; Kluckhohn and Wyman, 1940:34).

240.a. Bullroarer bearing three turquoise sets made from Gamble's oak

240.1. Bullroarer, after the Franciscan Fathers

Hill (Central and West)

Informants agreed that only wood from a lightning-struck tree could be used to construct a bullroarer. PP (Fort Defiance) mentioned pine and further specified the section of wood detached and hurled farthest toward the east by the bolt of lightning. The bullroarer was spatulate in form. The growing tip of the wood formed the point of the instrument, and unless the growing end could be determined the wood could not be used. Either the base was notched or a hole was bored in it, in which case the base was wrapped with buckskin to prevent splitting (PP). A thong of mountain sheep hide was attached. A loop was tied in the end of this thong to prevent it from slipping off the finger of the operator (GH, White Cone), but no handle was attached. Three small pieces of turquoise were set with pitch in one side of the wood; these represented the eyes and mouth. Finally the whole instrument was painted with hot pitch (PP).

The bullroarer was used in the Shooting, Blessing and Wind Ways (see Plate XV). It was never used except in ceremonies (GH). The interpreter (AS, Lukachukai) said that as a boy he had made one and used it as a toy.

Comparative

The Franciscan Fathers (1910:414) stated that the bullroarer ("groaning stick") was constructed according to minute prescriptions. It was made of lightning-struck pine, inset with turquoise ("eyes" and "mouth") on one side and an abalone shell ("pillow") on the other. The whole was covered with yucca pitch, lightning-struck pitch, and charcoal gathered from a lightning-struck tree. A thong made from bighorn or "sacred" buckskin was attached to the butt end, and wound about this end when not in use. For use, the bullroarer was placed in the medicine bowl, and the thong was soaked with medicine by one of the assistants. "He then encircles the hogan once or twice and violently whirls the roarer, during which time all remain in silence within." After his return to the hogan, the thong was wrapped about the bullroarer, which was used for pressing the limbs; the front (with eyes and mouth) was always pressed toward the limb.

Both of Gifford's Navaho informants confirmed the use of bullroarers. Both agreed that they were about eight inches long, made of lightning-struck wood. The Eastern informant said that they were about one and one-quarter inches wide, with a four-foot cord; the Western informant said that they were about one and one-half inches wide, with a two-foot cord, looped at one end. Both denied the use of a wooden grip. The Western informant said that the edges of the bullroarer were notched. According to the Eastern informant, the operation of this instrument might be witnessed by the public. The Western informant, however, said that if used in public it would make no sound. Both agreed that it was not seen during a curing rite. This somewhat ambiguous statement and the differentiation between seeing and hearing is clarified by the Franciscan Fathers above in their description of the ceremonial use of the bullroarer. Both informants stated that it was never used at dances. The Eastern informant stated that if the bullroarer came off the cord, or if it did not sound, the sick person was doomed (Gifford, 1940:58–59, 151–152)

XV. Ritual equipment of the Navaho Wind Way. The object in the foreground is a bullroarer (Tr. 240); immediately behind it on the ground are talking prayersticks (Tr. 227). Standing in the background are bundle prayersticks including (left to right) two slender sticks, a straight snake stick, two crooked snake sticks, another straight snake stick, and two slender sticks.

According to Haile (1947c:24), the bullroarer was meant to reproduce the voice of the Flint People; it was Flint Man who conducted the Holy Way ceremonials. "The stick itself represents him and the sound, his voice."

241. Musical Bow

Hill (East, Central, and West)

The musical bow had cultural significance among the Navaho only as a toy. Children, especially small boys, occasionally amused themselves with this instrument. One end of the bow was placed in the mouth and the bowstring was picked to produce the sound (GH, White Cone; WH, Wheatfields; K, Mariano Lake). The bow was held away from the body, the string near the operator (WH). According to K, the bowstring might be rubbed with a stick rather than picked. PP (Fort Defiance) denied that this instrument was used, even as a toy.

Comparative

Gifford's Western Navaho informant denied the use of the musical bow; his Eastern informant confirmed it. He said that the hunting bow was used, against the teeth (Gifford, 1940:59).

242. Musical Rasp

deł dá· (Lamphere)   musical rasp; CC said this term was the name of a plant but could not identify it.

Hill (Central and West)

This instrument consisted of two pieces of wood: the rasp and the scraper. Both pieces were about fourteen inches in length and an inch in diameter, constructed from any kind of wood conveniently available. The scraper was left in the round; either four, seven, or nine notches were cut in the rasp. These instruments were made in sets of four. One set was painted black, a second blue, a third yellow, and the last white (GH, White Cone).

The musical rasp was used in the Night Way (GH), the Mountain Way, and the Corral Dance (WH, Wheatfields). The resonance chamber was an inverted "wedding basket" (PP, Fort Defiance; GH). The butt of the rasp was placed about three inches above the edge of the inverted basket and was scraped with the scraping stick. According to GH, rasps were played simultaneously by four men. The butt of the black one was placed on the east side of the basket, the blue on the south, the yellow on the west, the white on the north. Players scraped either up or down in unison, taking their time cue from the chanter in charge of the ceremony. GH mentioned that occasionally baskets were held in a vertical position and their edges scraped only with a rasp to produce a sound.

Lamphere (East)

PM said that the musical rasp was just a stick rubbed across a basket.

Comparative

According to the Franciscan Fathers (1910:402), tradition mentioned the use of a "notched stick which was drawn over the basket instead of the present drumstick" in some ceremonies. Both of Gifford's Navaho informants confirmed the ceremonial use of the notched rasp. According to the Western informant, it was used in the "feather dance." Both also said that a coiled basket was scraped with a stick (Gifford, 1940:24, 151).

Warfare

243. Lance

ci·dítˣá (Ramah, Haile)

Ramah

Cottonwood, juniper, and sometimes oak was used for the shaft. According to Inf. 7, the shaft was short, about the length of the butt of a .22 caliber rifle and one and a half inches in diameter; Inf. 16 said the shaft was about six feet long. A hole was drilled in one end.

Before iron was introduced the spear had only a hardwood point (Inf. 16). No stone points were used. Iron points varied from six to twelve inches in length, and were diamond-shaped in cross section and triangular in profile, sloping sharply on each side. The base was a roughly rounded peg. Points were obtained from siversmiths, and the peg was then beaten and filed to fit the hole in the shaft. The point was bound to the shaft with sinew, and further secured with a sleeve of wet rawhide, which was allowed to dry in place.

There were no composite handles. According to Inf. 16, the shaft was not decorated, but the point was poisoned in the same manner as arrow points. Inf. 16 said two eagle feathers were tied near the tip, "to look pretty," but Inf. 7 said no paint or feathers were used.

Men made lances. They were used in warfare for thrusting, but not for throwing. Inf. 7 said that they were sometimes used to kill horses when nothing else was available.

No spears are extant in the Ramah area, and there is no reason to believe that either Inf. 7 or Inf. 16 ever made them or saw them made.

Hill (Central and West)

Shafts varied from three to six feet in length. They were made of oak, willow (C, Chinle), or alder (PP, Fort Defiance) that had been hardened by pounding with a stone. According to PP, an alder limb about three inches in diameter was reduced to about an inch and a half. "This made the wood both straight and strong." Shafts were left unsmoothed, to prevent them from slipping.

According to C, one end of the shaft was split, and the base of the point was inserted and secured with buckskin wrapping. A piece of wet buckskin was sewn around this juncture and allowed to dry in place. PP said that an iron cylinder was forced over one end of the shaft, a hole was burned in the same end with a hot iron, and the point driven into this hole. If the iron cylinder was lacking, a piece of wet rawhide was sewn around the juncture.

According to C, the lance head was of hardwood worked down to a fine point and polished on a stone. It was from eight to ten inches long and three fingers wide at the widest part. "The diameter must not be too great or it will be hard to pull out." Lance points were painted black and "poisoned" as were arrows. PP denied that wood or stone points were used on lances and said that points were not painted. Pieces of iron were filled to the desired shape (SG, Keams Canyon; PP), or iron was heated and pounded to shape the head (PP). According to SG, iron points formed an obtuse-angled triangle in cross section.

Two eagle tail feathers were appended at the juncture of shaft and point. According to C, an arrow point was tied at the butt of the shaft. "This was believed to give the spear added power." A thong was attached near the butt of the shaft. It was worn over the wrist to allow a man to use his bow and arrow, yet keep the lance at hand.

According to PP, lances should be made only during the performance of an Enemy Way, and preferably by an individual who knew this ceremonial.

Lances were primarily weapons of war, generally employed by mounted warriors, but they could also be used by men on foot. Secondarily, they were used in hunting deer (SG) and buffalo (PP). There was no agreement as to when lances came into use. According to C, they were quite ancient; according to PP, they represented an idea borrowed from the Ute, Apache, and Comanche, and did not become prevalent until iron was introduced from

Spanish sources. SG stated that lances were introduced by the Spanish (see also Hill, 1936b:10).

Blows were usually struck with an overhand motion, but occasionally an underhand blow with a short shoveling swing was practiced.

Fishler (West)

A large section of oak was chosen, the bark stripped off, and the wood allowed to season. It was shaped and cut to the desired length. TT (Coalmine) said that shafts were straightened with a mountain sheep horn.

Points were of stone, chert, (TN, Kaibito), or wood. Stone points were prepared as were arrow points; when they were not available, the end of the shaft was merely sharpened. TT said that wooden points were fire-hardened or hardened by an application of cactus juice.

Lances were made by men, owned by hunters and warriors. TN said that they were used on horseback in warfare. They were also used for buffalo hunting (GB, Tuba City); TT stated that two men rode up on either side of the buffalo and speared it in the sides.

Comparative

There is some question as to whether the lance was an early Navaho weapon, although it seems to have been used throughout the area. Pike (1811:377) stated that the Navaho used spears, as did Simpson (1850:108, pl. 52). In 1854, Letherman saw Navaho in the Fort Defiance area with spears eight to ten feet long, including eighteen-inch iron points (Letherman, 1856:293). Möllhausen portrayed Navaho warriors armed with long spears during the following four years (reproduced in Whipple, *et al.,* 1855:pl. 22, and Ives, 1861:pl. 7). The weapons attributed to the Navaho in their last fight with the Hopi, which occurred before 1863, did not include lances (Voth, 1905:262), nor are lances mentioned in the text on old weapons published by Sapir and Hoijer (1942:427–429). There were no references in Navaho mythology (Reichard, 1950; Spencer, 1947).

The spear lingered in some areas after warfare had disappeared. Bourke mentioned that it was still commonly seen in the Fort Defiance area in 1881 (Bourke, 1936:88). A photograph of an old Navaho warrior taken in the Keams Canyon region showed the subject holding what appeared to be an iron-pointed, buckskin-sleeved spear (see Plate XVI).

By 1910, however, the lance was obsolete. The Franciscan Fathers described the one formerly used as a "stout shaft, about seven to eight feet in length, to which a point of flint, and later of iron, was fastened and decorated with a tuft of eagle feathers" (Franciscan Fathers, 1910:465, 316).

Both of Gifford's Navaho informants said that the spear was used in warfare, and only as a thrusting lance. The Eastern informant confirmed the wooden spear with a flat, two-edged hardwood blade. The Western informant denied the wooden spear and was doubtful of a stone point, which was denied by the Eastern informant. The Eastern informant said that the spear was sometimes used to kill deer caught in pitfalls. Both groups regarded the iron-pointed spear as modern; both denied feather decorations (Gifford, 1940:32, 122).

Farmer's informants in the Blanco–Largo Canyon area told of spears made of oak or cherry wood used in warfare. Sometimes these had stone points (Farmer, 1938:5).

XVI. An old warrior with lance (Tr. 243) and shield (Tr. 245), near Keams Canyon, Arizona. He is also carrying a quiver (Tr. 23). He is wearing a skin cap (Tr. 184), buckskin shirt (Tr. 170), necklace of round silver beads (Tr. 197), cloth trousers (Tr. 175), knitted leggings (Tr. 178), and moccasins (Tr. 189).

244. War Club

Ramah

Inf. 7 said that he had heard of rawhide-covered stone war clubs among the Zuni, but the Navaho did not use them. He denied that the axe was used as a war club. Inf. 16 had never heard of a rawhide-covered stone club. Both said that sticks and stones were thrown during warfare when arrows had been expended.

Hill (East and Central)

No wooden clubs were used in warfare. According to informants (RH, Crystal; PP, Fort Defiance), stone-headed clubs manufactured in the same manner as axes were used long ago in war.

More recently, a club similar to that used by the Apache came into use (RH; C, Chinle; TLLSS, Crownpoint). It was constructed in the following manner. The bone from the upper end of a cow's tail was removed and a round stone inserted in its place. The opening was then sewn up and the hide allowed to dry over the stone. The lower section of the tail was cut to the desired length and the club was ready for use. PP had never heard of this type of club.

Comparative

Bourke's evidence from the Fort Defiance area is contradictory. On his first visit, he stated that "the only stone implement to be found among them now is the war-club." On his second visit, apparently about a month later, he stated, "They have not been at war since 1864. Have no war-clubs or anything of that kind." He was told that "the 'old men say' that in former days they used to make hatchets for war and other purposes of a hard, black stone like flint (evidently obsidian)." Bourke found none of these (Bourke, 1936:88, 231).

A Hopi tradition describing their last fight with the Navaho, recorded by Voth (1905:262), stated that the Navaho were armed with war clubs, as well as bows and arrows, shields, and a few guns obtained from the Spanish. There was no further description of the weapons.

The Franciscan Fathers (1910:322) reported that "the stone axe was used at close range," but Gifford's Navaho informants denied this use of the grooved axe or hammer. His Western informant said that a stone and stick encased in rawhide was used; it was an ancient form of club. This club was denied by the Eastern informant, who mentioned a ball-ended club made from a root knob, a weapon denied by the Western informant (Gifford, 1940:33, 123; see also Hill, 1936b:10–11).

In Navaho mythology, there was an apparent merging of the magic axe, which destroyed anyone who took hold of it (other than its owner), and the club. Both were used as weapons, and the chert club was both swung and thrown (see Reichard, 1950, for discussion and references; also Kluckhohn and Wyman, 1940:35).

245. Shield

na·gʸé (Ramah, Haile)

Ramah

Shields were made away from the dwelling, since women and children were not allowed to watch the process (Infs. 7, 16). According to Inf. 7, the shield maker went to an uninhabited location alone or accompanied by other men who knew how to make shields. There they erected a brush circle where the work was done; this structure opened toward the east.

A piece two to three feet in diameter (Infs. 7, 16) was selected and cut from the hip or neck area of a cleaned but not dressed cowhide or horsehide; buffalo hide was not used (Infs. 7, 16). A heap of earth was prepared and a fire built on it (Inf. 7). When it was hot, the coals were removed and the dirt smoothed. The rawhide was placed over the mound. Heat shrank and shaped the rawhide. According to Inf. 16, however, wet rawhide was placed directly on a heap of hot coals and staked down; no heap of earth was used. Both informants denied molding shields over anthills.

When removed from the shaping mound, the hide was cut in a circle. Inf. 7 said it was kneaded from both sides with the knee to give it flexibility. Two holes were cut near the center (Inf. 16), or four were burned (Inf. 7). Two strings were passed through these to serve as a handle for carrying the shield.

Shields were ornamented with eagle tail feathers. These were suspended from short, inch-long buckskin thongs passed through holes burned in the edge of the shield. Infs. 16 and 2 said that in addition there were two eagle feathers suspended from buckskin thongs about three feet long in the center of the shield. According to Inf. 16, these served "to make you invisible" to the enemy.

Inf. 7 stated that shields were not further ornamented, but Infs. 16 and 2 agreed that occasionally wet rawhide was incised with a stick. Designs included bear paws, snakes, lightning, rainbow, sun, half-sun, and others. Inf. 16 said that shields were not painted. Infs. 7 and 16 denied the existence of oval or square shields or shields with wooden rims.

Only men who knew one of the war chants such as Enemy Way, Enemy Monster Way, Bear Way, or Big Snake Way could make shields. According to Inf. 16, each chantway had a different motif; Bear Way had the bear paw, Big Snake Way, the snakes, Enemy Monster Way, lightning. Those who did not know a way would be afraid to make shields (Inf. 7). Shields were sometimes obtained from other tribes; Inf. 7's father was given a shield by Chiricahua Apache friends in the period before Fort Sumner.

Warriors used shields to parry bullets and arrows. Inf. 7, who is left-handed, said that the shield was held in the right hand, and a warrior could handle the shield and shoot at the same time. Inf. 16 said that the shield was fastened over the left upper arm.

A shield was supposed to last a lifetime (Inf. 7). When not in use, it was kept in a buckskin bag. It was not folded, but kicked in the center and the concavity reversed (Infs. 7, 16). The feathers were placed in the concavity for protection, and the shield slipped into the bag. A shield was never stored in the hogan, but somewhere in the vicinity.

Whether any of the informants ever made a shield is not known. Inf. 16 saw shields made by Navaho south of Quemado; Inf. 7 saw and handled his father's shield and said that he returned it to the Chiricahua Apache years ago. This may have been the shield Kluckhohn saw in his possession in 1923, or Inf. 7 may have owned one at that time. Inf. 8 knew that shields had been used in war, but knew nothing more about them.

Hill (Central and West)

Shields were made under strict ritual conditions. When the appropriate materials had been gathered, the warriors—and only warriors—gathered at an appointed place. "The leader directed the work, and with the men, sang songs which were believed to impart invulnerability." Women and children especially were excluded, "as it was thought that the songs which were sung would cause them harm" (Hill, 1936b:9–11).

Shields were made of deerskin, later of cowhide (rawhide) and horsehide. Skin from the hip of the animal was always used, since it was thickest in that area. To allow for shrinkage during drying, the hide was cut slightly larger than the diameter for the finished product, which was from eighteen to twenty-four inches. According to three informants (SG, Keams Canyon; OTKM, Manuelito; C, Chinle), sand was arranged in a heap about the size of an anthill. The hide was soaked until it was soft, placed over the knoll, and pegged down or covered with dirt (C). SG said the sand was moistened before the hide was placed on it; OTKM said the sand was heated to dry the hide quickly and to harden it. The drying and hardening process normally took about two days.

PP (Fort Defiance) described a variant of the process. According to him, a shallow bowl-like depression was dug in hard ground. The hide was placed in this and pounded with a water-worn boulder until it was dry and had assumed the convex shape. "You can tell when you have pounded the hide enough because it gives out a wooden sound."

Shields made from two thicknesses of hide were not uncommon. In such cases, one section was made slightly smaller than the other and when dry fitted into the first. The two were secured by buckskin lashing around the circumferences.

A shield might be finished in several ways. According to SG and PP, holes were bored on either side of the center, midway from the edge, and thongs were tied at these points for handles. Eagle feathers (SG) or eagle feathers and a strip of bayeta eight inches wide (PP) were sewn around the edge of the shield with sinew. "These will protect you from the enemy and help you kill other Indians." According to OTKM, the circumference of the shield was laced with buckskin to strengthen it, and eagle feathers were added to the lacing. C said that a small branch was cut the size of the circumference and laced to the shield; crosspieces were added and a buckskin loop fixed to them for holding the shield on the arm. PP had never heard of this type. A pinch of Rio Grande ground squirrel pollen was tied to each shield. This was thought to make the warrior invisible to the enemy (C).

Next the shield was painted black (unpainted, according to PP), and designs were applied. These consisted of the Big Snake, bears' paws (C, PP, SG), the sun and moon (C, PP), hands and stars (C), lions (SG), and zigzag lightning (OTKM). According to SG and C, these represented the chantway in which a man went to war. OTKM and PP said that they were put on the shield because "they were powerful and feared and because they strengthened the warrior." While painting was in progress, a war leader held a special Blessing Way over the shields (C). According to PP, shields should be made during an Enemy Way.

When the shield was not in use, the owner pressed his knee against the center, reversing the concavity. The bayeta and eagle feathers were folded toward the center. The shield was covered with a buckskin bag equipped with a drawstring at the back which was pulled tight to make the cover fit snugly over the face of the shield. The upper halves of shield covers were usually decorated with a strip of bayeta about eight inches wide. Three pairs of eagle tail feathers and plumes (PP) were attached to the bayeta at evenly spaced intervals. The covered shield was hung in the hogan.

PP denied that the Navaho had ever used the folded type of shield described by the Franciscan Fathers (see below). He had never heard of a curtain shield.

Fishler (West)
A length of wood was heated and bent to produce a circular form. It was reinforced with wooden crosspieces. Deerskin, horsehide, or cowhide was then stretched over the frame and secured, and the shield was complete.

Shields were made by men and used primarily for protection against arrows, although some used them against lances. According to FG (Coalmine), the Navaho formerly trained for war by standing on one leg, holding their shield on their arm and parrying arrows and other weapons. "This they learned from the War Twins."

Comparative
It is not known when the Navaho first used the shield, but their Pueblo neighbors were using it in 1540 (Winship, 1892–1893:548). Simpson, in 1849, was apparently the first to note the shield among the Navaho; he observed that Navaho warriors were generally armed with the shield, bow, and lance. In one of the drawings he published was what appeared to be an ovoid hide shield, about three feet in diameter, with a tuft of hair affixed to its center. No other decoration was evident (Simpson, 1850:108, pl. 52).

The first description of a Navaho shield (Whipple *et al.,* 1855:30, 52, pl. 21) dates from the next few years. The shield was circular, made of rawhide, and painted in colors, including an "alleged head of Montezuma." Around the circumference was a strip of red cloth trimmed with feathers. This type of shield was said to be common among the Apache, Pueblo, and Navaho Indians. The shields were "impervious to arrows, and frequently hard enough to turn aside a ball." The gay colors and feathered cloths were meant to dazzle the eyes of their adversaries; while the shield diverted arrows, the warrior was able to use his bow.

The vivid account recorded by Voth (1905:261) of the last fight between the Hopi and the Navaho related how the more numerous Navaho surrounded groups of their opponents, using their shields to "cover themselves completely when encircling the Hopi"; but the Hopi said that they managed to threaten the Navaho, then turn quickly and "shoot at somebody else from the side and past their shields." By 1881, shields were uncommon, and Bourke at Fort Defiance stated that "shields have been discarded," although "they were in use up to the year 1868" (Bourke, 1936:88, 231). Probably the last and one of the few photographs of a Navaho warrior with a shield was taken at Keams Canyon in 1893 (see Plate XVI).

By 1910, the Franciscan Fathers reported that the shield had disappeared save for a few family heirlooms. They stated that some shields had been elliptical, others round. They were made of horsehide or rawhide, burnt

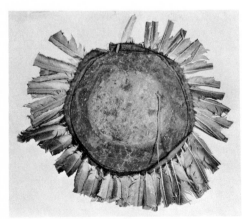

245.a. Navaho shield

slightly, shaped over an anthill, and weighted down with earth. The rim was decorated with eagle feathers, and the face of the shield was further ornamented by figures of sun, rainbow, crescent, and bear paw. A buckskin sling worn on the left arm served as a handle; there was also a buckskin band which passed over the right shoulder. To preserve the feather decorations, some shields were "provided with a crease in the center, so that they might quickly be opened and closed by stepping on them" (Franciscan Fathers, 1910:317).

Gifford's Navaho informants confirmed the use of circular rawhide shields with feather decorations and painted designs. The Western informant noted horsehide or cowhide, with crow or other large feathers for decoration. The Eastern informant said that elk neck skin was used, staked out and dried. A permanent buckskin cover was put on the front, painted red and black, but with no realistic design. Eagle feathers were preferred, but "yellow-tailed" hawk feathers were also used for ornamentation. They helped to conceal the shield bearer. Both informants denied shields made of buffalo hide, or curtain shields (Gifford, 1940:32, 122–123).

An informant from the Upper Blanco–Largo Canyon district told Farmer that the Navaho formerly used round leather shields made from buffalo or other skins. These were decorated with feathers around the edge and two eagle plumes hanging from the middle (Farmer, 1938:5).

246. "Armor" ʾabaníʾéʾʾ (Ramah) "deer shirt" (CC)

Ramah
Buckskins were glued (Inf. 7) or sewn (Inf. 2) together to make a four-ply material which was then made into a shirt. These articles, according to Inf. 2, were made as were other shirts (see Traits 170–172). Inf. 3 stated that two "unshot" buckskins were used; one hung over the chest, the other over the back. A plant was chewed and this material spat on the side of the buckskin next to the body. These shirts were used for warfare.

With the possible exception of Inf. 3, none of the informants had seen buckskin armor. Several (Infs. 2, 7, 8, 12) had heard of it. According to Inf. 3, none was preserved in the Ramah area; Inf. 16 denied all knowledge of armor. Horse armor was mentioned by Infs. 7 and 16; both had heard that there was such an article, but neither could describe it.

Hill (East and Central)
Descriptions in Hill (1936) were given by RH (Crystal) and TLLSS (Crownpoint). A warrior chose the thickest buckskin possible for making a war shirt; some wealthy men used four thicknesses of buckskin. The shirt had sleeves reaching nearly to the elbow. It fitted tightly around the neck and was laced with thongs across the chest. In making one, the buckskin was first laid flat and cut to pattern. Leaves of the "wide cactus" were rubbed over it to create a sticky surface to which the cuttings and trimmings of the buckskin would adhere. This process was repeated until the four layers were in place; the shirt was then quilted to maintain its shape. This armor was quite heavy and was used only during an attack.

Another kind of buckskin shirt was made using eight buckskins. It reached the knees, and because of its weight could be worn only on horseback. It was slit in back and front for this purpose. According to PP (Fort Defiance), sleeveless shirts made of double thicknesses of hide from the neck of a deer were also used as armor.

In addition to body armor, several kinds of caps were worn, made of skin of the heads of badgers, wildcats, skunks, and lions. They differed from the caps used on everyday occasions in that a plume was attached just before the attack. Another type was made of two thicknesses of buckskin secured by a chin strap. See also Skin Caps, Traits 184–187.

Fishler (West)

TN (Kaibito) claimed armor was not used by the Navaho.

Comparative

Accounts of the buckskin four-ply shirt among the Navaho indicated that it had long been abandoned, even by 1887. Neither Letherman (1856) nor other early reporters on the Navaho mentioned buckskin armor, nor did Bourke refer to it in his description of weapons and costume for war (Bourke, 1936:88, 231). In a myth text recorded by Matthews (1887:416), suits of armor were said to be made of several layers of buckskin. "The warriors in those days wore such armor, but they wear it no longer."

The Franciscan Fathers (1910:458–459) said that the so-called "big shirt" was made of four-ply buckskin glued with pitch; it was impenetrable to the thrust of a spear or arrow.

Gifford's Navaho informants denied the trait for their groups (Gifford, 1940:32), thus confirming the Hopi account of their last fight with the Navaho, during which the Hopi wore rawhide armor, but the Navaho did not (Voth, 1905:261).

A number of armor types were mentioned in the myths, among them the rawhide armor worn by Cicada as protection against Turtle's lightning and arrows. Most frequently cited was chert armor of several colors. Cattail fiber armor was also noted, and may be associated with Spanish quilted armor. Turtle shells, scales, and feathers were also said to protect the individual (Reichard, 1950:511, 553).

Secoy (1953:17) noted that the Navaho armor, with glued multiple thicknesses, was similar to that of the Northern and Plains tribes. Quilting, however, was probably derived indirectly through the Pueblos from some Middle American source. The unusual coincidence of techniques, according to Secoy, probably indicated an area of transition or overlap.

Chapter 5   Recreation

Recreational activities include games, toys, and smoking. Games, the first and largest category of traits in this chapter, form an appropriate transition between the related topics of ritual and recreation. Just as ritual has social recreational aspects, so many Navaho games contain religious elements. Many are sanctioned by mythology and because of this association can be played only during certain seasons of the year. Games are frequently played during intervals in ceremonials. Smoking also has religious connotations.

Most Navaho games involve gambling, except when played "for practice" by children, or "just for fun." The Navaho love to gamble and gambling can be a part of any game. Navaho names in this category refer not only to the game equipment, but also to the playing of the games themselves. Slight differentiations in the methods of play and scoring occurred, depending on the players involved. Rules for play and stakes were agreed upon before any game began. Although children learned the adult games by watching and by playing modified versions, their activities were usually considered in terms of "practice" and no stakes were involved. Except in these respects, their participation did not differ from that of adults.

Toys, as opposed to games, were used principally by children, only rarely by adults. Traits in the toy category are further differentiated by the number of persons involved. Toys seem to have been used by one or two individuals; games usually occupied the attention of a larger group.

Games

247. Hoop and Pole   ná·ážǫ·š (Ramah, Haile)   hoop and pole game; "bridge" (CC)

bą·s (Ramah)   hoop; "gambling"

bé··éna·ažǫ·ší (Ramah)   pole

na·ažǫ·š ·axą̨desX̧óní (Haile)   pole, "bound together"

na·ažǫ·š dilkǫ·h (Haile)   pole, "slick or polished"

na·ažǫ·š diX̧oi (Haile)   pole, "strung profusely"

na·ažǫ·š dilkǫ·h (Haile)   pole, "polished"

Ramah
There are two pieces of equipment: the hoop (*baas*) and the pole (*bee enaazhooshi*). Various materials were used to make the hoop. Inf. 61 thought it was made of twigs; Inf. 16 said that it was of twigs and rags wrapped with buckskin and measured about six inches in diameter. Inf. 1 said that it was made of rags wrapped with buckskin; and Inf. 7 said that the hoop was of buckskin stuffed with rolled buckskin, and measured about eight inches

in diameter. Formerly, Inf. 7 said, the hoop was made of mountain lion skin and other materials which he could not remember; it was not covered with buckskin.

The pole was made of two pieces of wood bound together with buckskin. According to Inf. 7, the bark was removed. Inf. 16 said that it was about four and a half feet long; Inf. 7 said that each piece was about three and a half feet long. One end was pointed; the other (the butt end) was cut square. Ten strings (called "turkey feet") were tied to the pole, five to each section. According to Inf. 180, the pole was wrapped with buckskin. According to Inf. 7, the buckskin thongs, or rawhide wrapped with buckskin to keep it rigid, hung from the foreshaft only. Inf. 16 said that a red or black band was painted on the poles at the point where the shafts were bound together. This band enabled each team to distinguish its pole. Inf. 7, however, said that the poles were not decorated with paint or feathers.

Each man apparently made his own equipment. "Every man sings to his ring and stick when he makes it. He talks to them and prays to them. They do this at home when no one is around. The man who has the strong prayer will win all the time" (Inf. 7).

The game was played only by men (Infs. 8, 16, 77, 111, 192), two at a time (Inf. 16); Inf. 7 said that it might never be played by women or children. Inf. 7 implied that only specialists who knew the songs were likely to play. "A boy twenty-five if a man taught him how to play would have to have a song to play. If you don't know, the people who play can cheat you pretty bad."

The game might be played anywhere, at any time of the year (Infs. 7, 8, 16), but it was commonly played during ceremonials. Infs. 7, 8, and 77 specified that it should be played during the day; otherwise players could not see to play (Infs. 7, 8). Inf. 77 expressed the fear that those who played it at night would go blind.

For playing, a course about ten feet wide was cleared; it was approximately twelve to fifteen yards long, oriented east and west. Neither end was marked, nor was the course measured by shooting an arrow in either direction (Inf. 16). According to Inf. 7, the course measured about fifty feet, and "as far as the level goes, that's the mark."

Only one hoop was used for the game, although each man had his own; Inf. 7 did not know how the choice was made. To begin the game, the owner of the hoop rolled it toward the east. He next rolled it toward the west, and so on. Both men ran after the rolling hoop and threw their poles at it simultaneously. The players jostled each other, each trying to push his opponent out of position and thus gain clear access to the ring.

Inf. 16 described the scoring; Infs. 7 and 180 did not know the count. If the pole fell on the hoop, but not through it, there was no count. If the hoop fell on the pole, or if one string could be seen through the hoop, the count was one. Two strings were scored two, three strings, three, and so on. If the middle strings of the two poles touched under the hoop, the man whose stick was under the hoop was given four points. Each play was named according to the number of strings visible through the hoop. If the middle string passed through the hoop, the play was called *azanzi;* if none passed through, the play was called *hokah.*

The loser paid after each roll of the hoop. Before beginning play, each man assembled various items which he evaluated according to points. When his opponent scored, he took the point equivalent in goods. Play continued until one man exhausted his pile of goods.

Only three informants (two of whom are brothers) said that they had played the hoop and pole game (Infs. 7, 1, 16). Inf. 1 said that he had played only on a few occasions as a young man, and his brother (Inf. 7) said that he had played only as a boy. Inf. 7 had made the equipment "just any way," implying that he did not know the proper songs or ritual and was not really a qualified player. Inf. 16 said that their (Inf. 1 and Inf. 7's) father used to play and knew a song. According to Inf. 61, Inf. 16 had formerly played a great deal and had been considered an expert. Inf. 16 said he had learned from other boys and had played when he lived in Thoreau. He added that the hoop and pole game was played after the return from Fort Sumner but had lapsed shortly thereafter.

Both of the men known to have participated in the game at Ramah are elderly, and neither knew the scoring. No others claimed to have seen the game (except Infs. 45 and 180 at Two Wells long ago), but various individuals had heard of it and knew something of the rules (Infs. 8, 12, 20, 61, 77, 99, 111, 115, 175, 259). Inf. 8 said that the last time it was played was seventy years ago; Inf. 20, fifty years ago. Infs. 20 and 111 specified that it has not been played recently. Inf. 248 had never heard of the game. No equipment is known to exist in the Ramah community.

Hill (Central and West)

According to SG (Keams Canyon), the foundation of the hoop was twigs bent and overlapped to form a circle. A buckskin wrapping formerly held the twigs in place, but more recently twine and rags have been used. PP (Fort Defiance) said that the hoop consisted of the lips of a mountain lion wrapped in "sacred" buckskin. The inside diameter of the hoop was about seven inches; the hoop was two inches thick (SG).

The pole was approximately six feet long with a diameter of an inch to an inch and a half. It was made from two pieces of wood joined together at the center in a diagonal splice. The joint was wrapped with buckskin (SG) or rawhide (PP), which covered about a foot and a half of the center of the pole. One end of the pole was pointed; the other was left blunt. Grooves were cut near the ends and at either end of the center wrapping. Goatskin (SG) or rawhide (PP) thongs were tied to these points. The ends of the thongs were eight to ten inches long and were allowed to hang. Only one end was allowed to hang from the center grooves, to which two cross thongs were

Hoop and pole game, after Hill

 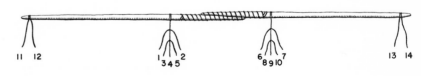

247.1. Detail of hoop   **247.2.** Pole; strands numbered to show scoring

tied at intervals, to produce in all five loose ends (SG). These were called "turkey tracks" (PP).

The game was played with two contestants. PP said that a single hoop was used, rolled by the winner of the previous cast. SG agreed, but said that each man might roll a hoop. After the hoop (or hoops) was rolled, the contestants waited until it began to waver in its course before casting their poles; jostling the thrower was considered legal. The objective was to have the pole come to rest with the hoop on one or more of the ends of the suspended thongs.

Informants differed in their system of scoring. According to SG, points were counted as follows: seven points if the hoop rested on the ends of the thongs at either end of the pole or on both the center thongs; two or three points if the hoop rested on one center thong or if the hoop fell on the pole and the pole was visible in the circle. The contestant scored a miss if the pole fell on the hoop.

PP practiced a more complicated system of scoring. Values were assigned to certain thongs and combinations of them; certain combinations were named. PP said that one point was scored each time the following thongs were visible through the hoop (thongs are numbered for descriptive purposes; see 247.2): the ends of four or nine (long thongs at the center), called *axiditi*; the ends of both four and nine, called *akenezi*, "something between others"; two and six or five and eight, or any three or all; eleven or thirteen, called *alaltlol*. There was no score if the hoop rested on numbers one, two, three, five, six, seven, or eight alone. When the hoop fell on the pole, it was called *datsaani*. If the pole was thrown through the hoop it scored a miss.

Scoring values and the extent of the game were decided prior to play. According to SG, sticks were used as counters, and the game ended when one contestant had won them all. Both informants agreed that betting was usual and indulged in by both spectators and contestants. The hoop and pole game might be played at any time.

According to SG, some individuals knew songs to insure victory. "You always sang these when no one could see or hear you." There was a general feeling that behavior of this type verged on dishonesty. Two methods of cheating were described; these were employed when close or questionable decisions were involved. A contestant, on pretense of making a close examination, either pushed the hoop over the thong ends with his nose, or blew them into the desired position.

Comparative

There is no archaeological evidence for the hoop and pole game, but ethnographic accounts indicate that it has long been played. Robinson in 1846 was apparently the first to record it. He saw men playing the game with a lance and puck, a solid ring of buckskin from six to eight inches in diameter (Robinson, 1932:47). In 1854, Backus wrote that this was the Navaho's favorite game, and one "in which they are said to exhibit much skill." He had not seen it, and was unable to describe its details (Backus, 1854:214). During the Fort Sumner period, Palmer (1869:42) collected a set of poles and a hoop of "buckskin wound on the ring." He said that the number of counts for a game was determined, and as the hoop was rolled, the poles were pushed after it. The number of strips of buckskin which touched the pole were "so many counts for the owner. They will gamble everything they possess at this game." Bourke in the 1880's gave the game only passing mention, saying the Navaho "have the 'Apache billiards' with hoops and staves or lances" (Bourke, 1936:226).

Matthews (1897:226) stated that the poles were usually of two pieces of alder, bound at the joint by a long, branching strap called "turkey-claw." One pole was marked with red, the other with black. In playing, a hoop was rolled along the ground and the poles thrown at it. According to Navaho legend, the hoop and pole game was among those brought from the lower world.

The hoop and pole game equipment illustrated (see 247.a) was collected by Washington Matthews at Fort Wingate in 1885, except for one of the hoops, which was collected by Edward Palmer. One pole is six feet long; the other is five feet six inches long. There is a black gum stripe at one end of the shorter pole. The "turkey tracks" are made of leather and are wrapped in buckskin at the juncture. One hoop, wrapped in buckskin, is nine inches in diameter. The other hoop, covered with ticking wrapped in buckskin that has been wet, is eight inches in diameter.

Culin illustrated equipment obtained at Keams Canyon about the beginning of the twentieth century. It consisted of a hoop about six and a half inches in diameter, wrapped with sheep hide, and two poles, each about nine feet long; these overlapped about a foot at the joint and were lashed with hide, the ends of which had crosspieces of hide fastened to them with bands of sheepskin. Culin quoted a personal communication from Haile. According to Haile, the pole was decorated with buckskin "turkey feet," and sometimes with claws of wildcats or of mountain lion, bear, or eagle, attached to the strings. As the claws caught the hoop a point was scored (Haile, in Culin, 1907:457).

Haile discovered that there were four types of poles. The first, "bound together," was made of two pieces lashed together with buckskin, the ends of the string allowed to hang down; the second, "slick or polished," was of one piece, with two strings at the butt and one at the point; the third, "strung profusely," was decorated with many strings; in the fourth, "polished," the hoop or wheel was only about an inch in diameter and was thrown toward a mark or point. Each player had a stick, about the length of an arm, which

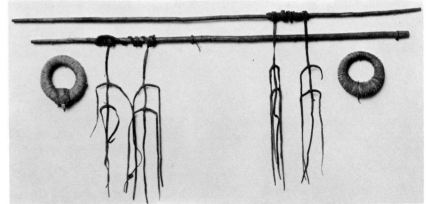

247.a. Two poles and two hoops

in a stooped position he tried to throw through the ring. Points were determined in advance, and the number necessary for a game varied "according to the value of the article put at stake." To distinguish the first and fourth games, the Navaho "also called the latter *laaze* . . . varnished (with juice of yucca and paint)" (Haile, in Culin, 1907:457–460). Haile also stated that another game, played with forked sticks and a ring, may be a form of the hoop and pole game.

Haile (1933:39–40) later published another account, based on information obtained from a Red Rock man. "To avoid the labor of preparing a course for the game, certain localities where level ground free of weeds could be found were selected," one of which was in the lower Lukachukai Mountains. Poles of cottonwood or quaking aspen were selected and lashed together with buckskin thongs, "to the ends of which five so-called turkey feet were wound. The center toe was longer than the rest," thus the designation. Thongs were also tied at the tip and butt of the pole, known as the "first cord" and the bottom cord"; and the space on the pole below the first cord was called the "twig," because the cord suggested a twig tied to the tip of the pole.

There were a number of possibilities for scoring, depending on the manner in which the hoop "bridged" the pole; the term *na azhoosh* meant "the bridging." The point count and stakes were determined before the game began, and the winner was paid accordingly. "Both players had their own poles and the winner of a thrust always had the privilege of rolling the hoop" (Haile, 1933:39–40).

The account presented by the Franciscan Fathers (1910:482–482) confirmed other accounts. Several types of pole were known, decorated with thongs; and "counts were taken as these strings, called turkey feet, lay across the hoop," an apparent reversal of scoring.

Both of Gifford's Navaho informants confirmed the hoop and pole game. Both agreed that the pole was decorated with buckskin and that the game was played by men only, two contestants at a time. Poles were cast simultaneously, and scores were given to the pole(s) under the hoop. At this point, accounts differed. The Eastern informant said that the hoop was made of Spanish bayonet yucca leaves; there was "supposed to be a bull snake inside wrapping of hoop." There was a lump on the hoop for counting. He said that the pole was made of two pieces. In play, a contestant might try to knock his opponent's pole aside. Contestants agreed on the number of points required to win; for five points a buckskin was wagered. Pebbles were used as counters, and at the start were placed in two piles. A contestant scored a game if the hoop lay on all six center buckskin cords, two points if over the terminal pairs of thongs, five points if over the joint of the pole, and one point if over one thong. According to the Western informant, the hoop was buckskin-wrapped. The pole, he said, was made of juniper. A fixed number of points—eight—was required to win. Each successful throw was scored two points; four in succession won the game. Points were subtracted, with one side always zero (Gifford, 1940:53, 144–145).

The hoop and pole game seems to have lapsed throughout the Navaho area. Reagan declared in 1932 that it had long since disappeared (1932:68), but Haile wrote a year later that the discontinuance of the game "need not be placed too far back in the past." About 1916, Haile asked a Mexican clan man, a headman from Red Rock, Arizona, to reproduce the hoop and pole. He made a hoop about six to seven inches in diameter and a pole of two pieces, about eight feet long. He made another pole of a single piece, called "a complete hoop pole in one" (*naazhoosh la azee*). He noted the obvious inconvenience of carrying a long pole in the saddle and of finding a course "over which the hoop could be conveniently trundled." These inconveniences, he believed, gradually led to the abandonment of the game (Haile, 1933:37).

Hoop and pole equipment in the Harvard Peabody Museum was acquired in 1905. The poles are nine feet four inches long; each joint is wrapped with rawhide. On one side of the joint the pole is painted red, on the other, black. The three buckskin-wrapped hoops are seven, seven and a half, and eight inches in outside diameter.

248. Shinny

ńdilka·l (Ramah, Haile) "bat and ball" (CC); "wild gourd"

ʒo·ł (Ramah) puck; "ball" (CC)

be·ekalí (Ramah) shinny stick; "bat" (CC)

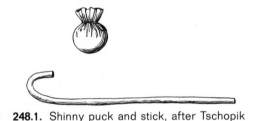

248.1. Shinny puck and stick, after Tschopik

Ramah

This game was played with a puck or ball and a stick. The puck was round, about three inches in diameter. Inf. 16 said that it was made from two pieces of buckskin stuffed with deer hair and sewn together around the edges; others (Infs. 7, 77) said that wool was wrapped in buckskin, then sewn and pulled tight and the loose edges of buckskin cut off (see 248.1).

The ball used by Inf. 8 was of buckskin packed with wool or rags; Inf. 259 said he used one made of blue denim stuffed with wool. The shinny stick was about three feet long, with a crook at one end (Inf. 7). It was made from green juniper or oak.

According to Inf. 16, the game was played only by adults, and men did not play against women. Inf. 7 said that children could play and that women might play with the men. "Might be one woman on each side—maybe only one woman on one side." Other informants said that shinny was exclusively a man's game (Infs. 61, 63, 77, 101, 106, 157, 259), and Inf. 106 said that old women taught their daughters not to handle the ball "or they would get big breasts." Several informants (Infs. 1, 61, 101, 106, 259) said they had played as children; Inf. 63 said that shinny was played by young boys.

Infs. 7 and 16 agreed that each team had the same number of players, although the number was variable. They said that the game began with two men on each team, and others joined later. According to Inf. 63, any number could play; but Inf. 8 specified three or four to a team, Inf. 106 five to a team, Inf. 192 said there were four to six to a team.

Shinny was played wherever there was level ground. Most informants agreed that it was played in the early spring, before the crops were planted (Infs. 16, 20, 63, 77, 81, 101, 259); others said that it was played in the winter (Infs. 1, 7, 61, 63, 192) if there was no snow on the ground (Inf. 7). It could not be played during planting time, and no one stated that it might be played in summer. For obvious reasons it was not played after dark.

The boundaries of the playing field were not marked, but goals at either end were designated by trees. According to Infs. 7 and 16, the ball was buried in the center of the field prior to the game. Inf. 106 and his mother, Inf. 192, denied burying; Inf. 63 said that a mound of earth six inches high was erected and the ball put in it. Two men, one from each team, stood on either side of the ball and struck it with the stick, knocking it from the hole. Each team then tried to drive the ball past the goal (Inf. 16). One goal counted as a win (Infs. 7, 16). The ball must always be hit with the stick; it could not be carried or kicked. Players were not allowed to grapple. There was no referee.

Information was obtained principally from Infs. 16 and 7. Although there was only one report of the game in recent years in the Ramah area, many Ramah men both old and young have played shinny in the past (Infs. 1, 8, 16, 20, 61, 90 at school, 101, 106, 259). Inf. 63 had watched shinny but had never participated. A number of women had also watched the game; but only Inf. 192 said that she had played, and only at Fort Sumner. Infs. 115 and 248 had never heard of the game, and others (Infs. 1, 61, 81, 259) said that it had not been played recently. The last time it was played was about 1924 or 1925 (Infs. 61, 90, 259), or about 1890 (Infs. 8, 101). As far as is known, no shinny equipment exists in the Ramah area today except that manufactured by school boys. Inf. 16 denied that he had any and said he knew of none.

The disappearance of the game was attributed by some to the opposition of the older members of the community, who warned young men against games that might involve gambling. Infs. 16 and 61 were specifically advised not to play, and Inf. 192 said that her brothers were given this advice. Others (Infs. 1, 63, 101, 259) said that they had not been told that the game "was bad," and that they thought it "a good game because it trained men to run fast." Whatever the cause, the game seems to have lapsed until the last few years.

Inf. 256 claimed to have played shinny recently. He learned at school; he had never heard of it from his parents. Later he played at home with his younger brother (Inf. 84) and others (Infs. 260, 261, 264). They used oak sticks with a natural L-shape and a tin can for a puck. Goals were marked by juniper trees. At another time they used a ball made of sheepskin and wool, constructed by Inf. 267, who had learned the game from Inf. 256.

Hill (Central and West)

The game was played with a ball and clubs. The ball was covered with buckskin. A circular piece was cut, and a drawstring introduced along the edge. The skin was soaked in water and drawn tightly around a filler of grass or, more recently, of wool. The drawstring was tightened and tied. Contraction of the skin in drying produced a ball "as hard as a baseball" (PP, Fort Defiance; SG, Keams Canyon).

Shinny sticks were preferably made from oak although juniper and pinyon were also used. A limb of the desired size was selected, the bark removed, and when necessary the club was roughly shaped. A curve was produced in the head by heating and bending, either manually (SG) or in the crotch of a tree where it was secured and allowed to set (PP).

According to PP, both men and women played; according to SG, only men participated. There was no interclan or interphratric significance. Any number of individuals might participate. Opposing teams of equal numbers were chosen by men selected as leaders.

Shinny was played only during the winter. "If it were played in the summer it would bring wind and rodents" (PP). It was commonly an adjunct of one-night ceremonies (SG).

The size of the playing field was, in part, determined by the terrain. PP said that goals might be located from a quarter to a half a mile apart. The objective of the game was to drive the ball across the opponent's goal line. The ball was buried midway between the two goals, three inches (PP) or five inches (SG) in the earth. The two leaders faced each other on either side of the ball and at the signal from their teammates, began to dig out the ball and start play. Throwing the ball was prohibited. SG said that tripping or striking an opponent with a club was legitimate; PP said that it was not.

Wagers were commonly placed on the outcome of the game. SG related an incident in which a leader, having chosen an excellent team, bet heavily and lost because his teammates, without telling him, placed their wagers on their opponents and allowed them to win.

Neither informant had heard of ritual being associated with this game, although PP stated that a nighthawk that had been soaked in water was occasionally batted about with shinny sticks in the belief that it would bring rain.

Comparative

Bourke, in the Fort Defiance area in 1881, was apparently the first observer to refer to the game. He said that both boys and girls played the game, with a ball "of buckskin, stuffed with wool" (Bourke, 1936:225). Matthews (1897:84) stated that in "the game *tsol*, or ball, the object was to hit the ball so that it would fall beyond a certain line," and noted that it was mentioned in the Origin Legend.

The first extensive description was by Haile, quoted by Culin. According to him, shinny was played with the same ball and according to the same rules regulating the game of tossed and batted ball. The shinny ball was a small filled leather pouch, sewn at the end and not in the center. The stick was the reversed ball stick. The game was played over a long course. Whoever first brought the shinny ball over the opponent's line was the winner. Culin illustrated a shinny ball, one and a half inches in diameter, and a stick, a sapling thirty-two inches long and curved at the end, both of which were collected at Chinle in 1903 (Haile, in Culin, 1907:623–624).

The Franciscan Fathers (1910:487–488) stated that a "bag-shaped ball, sometimes enclosing a smaller one of buckskin, was used, and the ball struck with the curved end of a stick or bat" (see 248.2). "The game of shinny is mentioned in some legends as played by the divinities, but is not often witnessed at present," although "it is still played by school children."

Gifford recorded the game for both Eastern and Western Navaho. Only men played, in evenly matched teams; and according to the Eastern informant, any number constituted a team. A curved stick was used. The Eastern informant said that another curved stick was carried to prevent the opponent

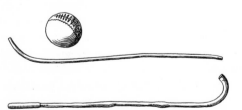

248.2. Shinny ball and sticks, after the Franciscan Fathers

from hitting the ball while it was being driven. The Western informant said that a stuffed buckskin ball was used, the Eastern informant said that this was modern, and that a "wild gourd" was formerly used as a puck. Both informants agreed that the ball was completely buried at the start of the game and that grappling was permitted. The Eastern informant said that the ball could also be driven with the feet. Lines on the ground marked the goals, although the Eastern informant said that bushes were sometimes covered with deerskins for this purpose. The Western informant denied betting, the Eastern informant confirmed it (Gifford, 1940:52, 144).

249. Archery   yiskah (Lamphere)   "shooting with an arrow"

Ramah

An arrow was used as a target in the archery game. Several informants had played (Infs. 1, 20, 81, 106), but not in recent years. Inf. 1 said in 1940 that he had not played in fifty years, and that no one did at Ramah, but Navaho did on the reservation.

A ball of yucca leaves was obtained and used for target practice. One man threw it up, and others shot at it with bows and arrows. Such practice was not considered a game at Ramah, and there was no betting.

Although Inf. 16 described the target, it was not clear whether he had seen or used one; nor was it clear that this was a Ramah trait, since Inf. 16 is part Apache and spent his early life in an atypical Navaho group at Puertocito.

Hill (Central and West)

The Navaho engaged in several types of archery contests. One was called "shooting for distance"; no target was used. Each contestant endeavored to shoot as far as possible, and the winner was the participant whose arrow covered the greatest distance. Both men and boys played this game, but in separate groups. Bets were placed on the outcome; boys wagered arrows, men blankets, horses, money, or personal equipment (SG, Keams Canyon).

Targets for boys were usually set at twenty-five yards; those for men at fifty to a hundred and fifty yards (PP, Fort Defiance; SG). According to PP, a broad leaf of yucca was placed upright in the ground and served as a target; he said the game was called "shooting at the back," referring to the back of a man. Exceptional marksmanship was required and the contest often continued for a period of four or five hours without a hit being scored.

Arrows were also used as targets in tests of skill. An individual selected as "leader" shot an arrow, and it represented the target. The line of play was thirty or forty yards back. The next three or four contestants attempted to hit or place their arrows as close as possible to the first; those following were privileged to select any of the previous arrows as their targets. The final arrow was discharged by the "leader."

Wins were scored on the basis of proximity to the first or subsequent three or four arrows. The "bull's-eye" was decided upon prior to play and was either the length of the little finger or the width of three fingers. A new game began as soon as a contestant scored, even though only a few of the participants had shot; the winner collected an arrow from each participant. Two unpointed arrows were considered equal in value to a pointed one (PP). This game was played in the intermissions during a ceremony; it had no ritual association (PP).

Hill witnessed archery contests at Lukachukai in 1933. On that occasion, a small paper carton set up at a distance of fifty yards was used as a target.

Lamphere (East)

PM said that "back in the old days" two of the women around Sheep Springs used to shoot with bows and arrows as a game. They would prop up boxes of Crackerjacks, then see who could shoot them through with an arrow. This was called "shooting with an arrow." One could also say, "both are going to shoot with arrows."

Comparative

Target practice was fairly common to judge from the literature. Bourke, in 1881, said that the Navaho boys and men around Fort Defiance, "make bets to determine who can shoot farthest or straightest and are very fond of shooting at the tall slim stalk of the soap-weed or amole (a species of Yucca common in their country)" (Bourke, 1936:225).

The first description of a target ball was based on data supplied by Haile. Bayonet-shaped yucca leaves were heated in hot ashes; when flexible and moist, fibers were detached and wound around bark or other soft material. A buckskin string was included in the wrapping when the ball was nearly finished. A small piece of oak was fastened to the end of the string. The stick and ball were then thrown into the air. The stick, being heavier, had a tendency to steady the ball as it fell to the ground. Players shot at the falling ball, and scored if they were successful (Haile, in Culin, 1907:385–386).

A similar target was described by the Franciscan Fathers (1910:488); according to them, the stick was attached "to give momentum to the light ball." By 1910, however, the game was obsolete, although "the game of shooting at an arrow [was] still in vogue in some districts."

Both of Gifford's Navaho informants agreed that archery games were played. The Eastern informant said that arrows were shot for distance; the Western Navaho informant was not questioned on this point. Both groups shot at a stationary target, which the Western informant said was an arrow. The closest shot won the original arrow. For a moving target, he said that something soft which an arrow might penetrate was used. Shooting arrows at a rolling hoop he considered a boys' game. Shooting at a moving target was denied by the Eastern informant. He said that boys played warfare games, shooting at a mark (Gifford, 1940:53, 57, 145, 149).

250. Stick Race

na·lžagí (Ramah)   stick race

na·lžagí (Ramah)   puck

be·na·alžagí (Ramah)   stick

Ramah

This game was played with a puck and a stick. The puck consisted of two grooved sticks about two inches (Inf. 7) or four inches (Inf. 1) long, connected with a string (Infs. 1, 7). The completed puck was H-shaped (Infs. 63, 101). The puck was propelled by a straight stick about a foot and a half (Inf. 7) or two feet long (Inf. 1). It was unpointed and had a diameter a little larger than the index finger (Inf. 7).

The game was played only by boys and men (Infs. 7, 101); Inf. 81 said that "women can't run." According to Inf. 7, it was meant to train boys for distance running. Races were held in the daytime, at any time of the year (Inf. 101).

According to Inf. 7, any number of players participated, each man for himself. According to Inf. 2, however, players were divided into two teams of six to ten players each. They ran barefoot unless the ground was covered with rocks and cactus; clothing or lack of it was optional. At the start, runners lined up and someone threw in the puck. It was tossed ahead with the stick, and the object was for all the players to keep abreast of it. The group ran toward a designated mark, such as a tree or a rock, circled it, and returned. Sometimes a distance of four to five miles (Inf. 1), or six to seven miles was covered. The winner was the man who drove the puck across the starting line.

According to Inf. 7, there was neither betting nor a referee; and this race was therefore not considered a game. Others (Infs. 1, 2), however, said that betting was involved. According to Inf. 7, there was no kick-stick race.

Most of the information was obtained from Inf. 7, some from his brothers (Infs. 1, 101), and some from Inf. 2. Only Inf. 1 said he had played, and he had done so infrequently; Inf. 7 had played alone, but not in a game. Both he and Inf. 101 had watched the game, but not for many years. Inf. 7 thought that this was "fifty years ago" (in 1890). He thought that Inf. 16 (d. 1942) had played and still knew the rules and procedure. Infs. 20 and 63 had heard of the game but had not seen it; Inf. 20 believed that it had not been played for thirty-five years (since 1905). Infs. 8, 77, and 256 claimed no knowledge of the game.

A stick race has been held in neighboring areas in recent times. Happy of Two Wells said that it was played during a fiesta in his community, but whether any Ramah people were present or participated is not known. Its existence at Ramah may have been due to Zuni influence, since it is played every year at that Pueblo. No stick race equipment is extant in the Ramah area.

Hill (Central)

This game was played with a puck and a stick. Formerly, according to PP (Fort Defiance), the puck was made from two three-inch pieces of wood. These were crossed and tied at the intersection. The puck described at Ramah was familiar to both informants. The stick used for propelling was pointed (AS, Lukachukai).

Two teams composed of four members played the game. Some object such as a tree, rock, or horse was designated. It was at a distance of a quarter of a mile or more. The team which first succeeded in propelling the puck around this objective and back to the starting point was victorious (PP, AS).

PP was familiar with the Hopi and Zuni kick-stick and kick-ball games of this type, but denied that the Navaho played them. AS had seen the stick race during his lifetime.

Comparative

The stick race appears to be a variant of Culin's "Double Ball," a game common throughout North America. He stated that in general this was a woman's game. Although it appeared among the surrounding tribes, Culin did not indicate that it was played by the Navaho (Culin, 1907:561–562, 647–664).

The Franciscan Fathers (1910:484) stated that a "ball race" was held in the cooler seasons of spring and fall; it "consisted in kicking a small round stick over a course previously agreed upon," usually a distance of some miles. No propelling sticks were used. Runners wore only a breechclout.

Gifford's Navaho informants also confirmed the kick race, but did not mention the stick race. Men and boys raced along a straight course about three miles long. The Western informant ran the course and returned; the Eastern informant ran it one way. The Western informant said a stuffed buckskin was used for a puck. The Eastern informant said that one team kicked a stick painted red on one side, black on the other; the other team, a yellow and white stick. Sides represented places, not clans. Groups ran to a stick (Western informant) or a line (Eastern informant) on the ground (Gifford, 1940:51, 143).

251. Horse Race

łį·· biǯá·dtˣah (Haile)   "horse racing together" (CC); "legs among"

Ramah

Horse racing was a favorite recreation, enjoyed on an impromptu basis.

Hill (Central and West)

Horses were trained for racing both long and short distances. They were also taught to jump ditches. The first step in training a race horse was to tie the reins to a cinch and let the horse loose so he could run. When the horse turned, the reins pulled; consequently he learned to turn quickly. When horses were about two years old, they were tied to a post all night; in the morning when they were hungry, they were raced about a quarter of a mile. "They run faster when they are hungry" (SG, Keams Canyon). He said that geldings made the best racers. When horses were castrated, medicine believed to make them fast racers was applied.

SG said that in the old days only two horses were chosen to race. Two communities brought together their best horses and put them in separate groups. Each side chose its best horse. AS (Lukachukai) said that one side chose two horses which they knew or thought to be equal in speed. These two horses were then walked out before the opposing side, and the opponents were given the choice of the horse they wished to bet on (AS). Before the horses left for the start, members of each group placed wagers. Items wagered included buckskins, saddlebags, blankets, bridles, and other equipment (SG). Each side then put up a jockey and the race was run. "In the old days they would race to a stake, turn, and then come back to the starting point." It was considered a great joke if one side entered an inferior horse which looked fast, but which was hopelessly slow, and persuaded the opponents to select that horse and place bets on it.

There were several methods of fixing a race: the best horse was "pulled" at the owner's order and the slow horse allowed to win. The owner bet on the other horse. When a fixed race went wrong because the rider was unable to hold back the horse, it was considered a great joke. Boys, not the owners, usually rode the horses.

The night before a race, one side would sometimes steal the sure winner and run him all night, then slip him back into the corral. The next day he would be exhausted and barely able to run. A side might run its own horse at night, and bet on the opponent's horse. This was also considered hilariously funny.

Some of the men knew songs to insure success in horse racing. They would sing over their horses before they were led onto the track. To fix a race ritually, a man would rub some medicine on his hands; then, pretending to feel the horse's legs, he would say, "This horse will win all right," and rub on the medicine that was believed to make the horse lose.

Another form of gambling was to draw a line and then put a blindfolded man on a horse. The horse was started toward the line and bets were placed on whether the left or right foot of the horse crossed the line first (AS).

Evenly matched boys were also raced. "They got to be crooked so we had to stop this" (AS).

Comparative

According to the Franciscan Fathers, horse racing with light betting was frequent. Betting on festive occasions was heavy, "losses being sustained with as much indifference as gains are accepted with joy and laughter." The Navaho was considered a cheerful loser as well as winner and often staked "his most treasured possessions on a single issue." Good horses were well cared for and were "often practiced and trained long before a race." By 1910, horse and foot racing had "long since displaced the ball race" or kick race (Franciscan Fathers, 1910:154, 484).

In the term for horse race recorded by Father Berard Haile (1950:119), the suffix specifically implied the racing of two animals: *lii nihil alghadiitaash,* "we two are having a horserace."

252. Moccasin Game

kéšžé·' (Ramah, Haile) "shoe game" (CC)

t^xólaštóši· (Ramah) round ball; "stone" (CC)

kétą·z (Ramah) yucca leaf counters; "moccasin cut"

be·'edecili (Ramah) stick; "with it to search" (CC)

Ramah

Equipment for this game included a round ball cut from the root of a yucca plant (Infs. 12, 16, 175, 180); 102 yucca leaf counters; a cornhusk disc the size of a quarter, blackened on one side with charcoal; eight moccasins; and a blanket. Pits were dug on the north and south sides of the playing area, each about six inches deep and large enough to contain four moccasins. A stick about a foot long, which Inf. 12 said had to be of pinyon, was cut and placed on the west side between the two pits.

Both men and women might play, according to several informants (Infs. 1, 12, 16, 41, 61, 115, 180); Inf. 7 said that women might play, but not often, and were not really supposed to. In a game observed at Inf. 12's place, women did participate. Infs. 63 and 77 said that women were not supposed to play. According to Inf. 16, the game was forbidden to children; they sometimes substituted a rock for the yucca ball, omitted the yucca leaf counters and pinyon stick, and played in pairs, "just for fun." "It is the children's way of practicing for the moccasin game" (Inf. 16). Inf. 8 said that he learned to play from his parents. Any number of people could play, although how sides were chosen was not clear.

According to several informants (Infs. 1, 16, 63, 175), the game was played only in the hogan. Others (Infs. 12, 41, 81, 115, 180) said that it might be played either outside or in. It was apparently played at ceremonials, for Inf. 12 told of two occasions when it was added to the ritual of a chantway. It is not known that this was done at Ramah.

The moccasin game was played only in the winter (Infs. 1, 7, 16, 61, 63, 99, 106, 115, 175, 180, 192), or through spring until the first thunder was heard (Inf. 12). Some said it was played only at night (Infs. 16, 63, 99, 180). Others said that it might be played during the daytime, or into the morning if players blackened their eyes to prevent blindness (Infs. 1, 7, 12, 81, 106, 180), or if the door and smokehole of the hogan were covered (Infs. 1, 12, 99, 101, 180, 192), or if the ball were put in the fire for a moment to blacken it (Inf. 115). Inf. 115 denied the first two practices; others (Infs. 77, 106, 192) had never heard of blackening the eyes or the ball.

The blackened cornhusk was used to decide the order of the play. "The man who blackens the cornhusk, his side is black. The other side is white." Four moccasins were buried in each pit. The "blackener" stood on the west side of the hogan between the two opposing groups and dropped the cornhusk. If the black side was up, the black team began play; if the white, then white began.

To start the game, two men stood and held the blanket to conceal the player hiding the ball. Meanwhile, the men of this group sang moccasin game songs. Then the moccasins were filled with earth.

The other team took the bundle of yucca leaves and the pinyon stick. A man chosen as "pointer" stood before the buried moccasins, and pointed to the one which he believed contained the hidden ball. If he was correct, his side paid nothing. If he missed, his side paid according to the value placed on the moccasins—four points for the outside moccasins, ten points for the inside moccasins. The ball was rehidden after each guess. If the pointer was relatively sure, however, that a moccasin did not contain the ball, he beat it several times with the pinyon stick. If he was correct, the moccasin was considered "killed," and the pointer attempted to find the ball among the other three. For a wrong guess his team lost ten counters, and the ball was rehidden. The game ended when all counters were won by one of the teams.

Various methods of cheating were practiced. The most common one was to hold the ball instead of hiding it (Infs. 1, 63, 192). Several people (Infs. 1, 12, 180) said that some men prepared for the game by rubbing corn pollen (Infs. 12, 180) or a preparation made from the acqueous humor from the eye of a bird like a chicken (*naa atso tlozi*) mixed with red ocher, beneath their eyes. This procedure enabled the pointer to see, even underneath the ground.

After the game, the equipment was "put away," outside and away from the hogan. It was hidden in any kind of bush (Inf. 12).

The description of the game was obtained primarily from Inf. 16, with some corroboration from Inf. 180 and others; and a game was observed at Inf. 12's place in Two Wells in 1940. Several people said that they knew how to play and had done so occasionally (Infs. 1, 7, 8, 20, 63, 101), but estimated that it was between nine and fifty years before 1940. Some (Infs. 77, 106, 192) reported that others had played in recent years (Infs. 19, 22, 24, 57, 101, 112, 120, 121, 125, 138, 186, 219, 261). These are among the younger and middle-aged men in the community. According to Inf. 256, Infs. 258, 261, and 4903 knew songs associated with the game. Inf. 256 had played at school but had never been in a real game. Several (Infs. 99, 115, 180, 256) had watched adults play games, although they had not played; Inf. 175 watched a game at Fort Wingate in 1926, Inf. 256 saw games played about 1937 at Inf. 57's place, and Inf. 1 watched a game about 1938 at Inf. 22's place. Infs. 61, 248, and 259 said they had never seen the game. According to Inf. 256, Ramah people participated in real games and "games for fun" at pinyon-gathering camps. Others agreed and explained that at the camps there was a concentration of people, whereas at Ramah the population was scattered and it was difficult to obtain players. All informants were aware that the game was still played in other parts of the Navaho country. In 1950 Inf. 283 deplored the fact that local people did not play the "shoe game" although it was played at Kayenta and Shiprock.

The decrease in popularity of the game in the Ramah area was generally attributed to the antagonism expressed by the older generation. They maintained that those who played wasted their time and money and tried to prohibit the younger generation from playing.

Hill (Central and West)

Data were obtained at Sawmill and Keams Canyon. Descriptions and names given the counters, ball, and pointer used in the moccasin game coincided, except in small details, with the Ramah material. One variation included juniper pointers, about ten inches long, "to dig something out with." Moccasins were hidden on the north and south sides of the hogan in separate holes rather than in a trench. Those on the outside were called "on each side"; those in the center, "something between others." According to SG (Keams Canyon), the ball was formerly hidden in one of four piles of sand instead of in moccasins. He also reported that a special name (*bichoi*) was applied to the last two counters; these were valued at five points instead of one.

Some innovations in play were also reported. SG said that the moccasin game was played in the hogan and was a regular adjunct of four-night ceremonies. Bets were made and play began after it was determined which side should hide the ball. This was accomplished by throwing some object, black on one side, white on the other, into the air. The group which called the toss won. Colors on the object thrown had no directional association with the moccasin pits.

A blanket was held up, the ball was hidden, and play began. All play was accompanied by song. There were one hundred and two songs associated with the game.

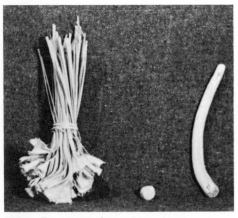

252.a. Equipment for moccasin game: counters, ball, pointer

Several options were open to the individual selected to guess the location of the ball. He might say "it is gone," one, two or three times, or he could elect to locate the ball on the first, second, or third guess. Scoring was as follows. If a man attempted to locate the ball on the first try and was unsuccessful, his group lost ten points; if on the second, six points; if on the third, four points. When the contestant guessed correctly his group won the privilege of hiding the ball and won either ten, six, or four counters, depending upon which guess located the ball.

The moccasin game seems to have had a certain amount of ritual significance. An offering of turquoise was given to the yucca plant that furnished the ball and counters; it was deposited by the chanter in charge of the ceremony. When the game ended, the same individual hid the counters and ball and made another turquoise offering. At this time a prayer was said asking for the quick recovery of the patient. It was also customary for a contestant who had scored ten points to pray for the patient or blow smoke through the smokehole in order to insure fast recovery.

Several methods of cheating were in vogue. The side which hid the ball sometimes hid two in order to lessen the odds of negative guesses. Occasionally one group located a confederate among their opponents. This man signaled the location of the ball by rubbing the inside or outside of his right or left leg. A ritualistic method of taking advantage of opponents involved the use of "eye water" from the roadrunner and magpie and parings from the claws of the roadrunner. The player combined these with red ocher and surreptitiously rubbed the mixture on his hands and cheeks. This mixture was believed to give the individual power to locate the correct moccasin. When cheating was discovered, play was terminated (SG).

Lamphere (East)

Lamphere took part in a moccasin game played at Sheep Springs in 1966. Players sat on the north and south sides of the hogan, each side behind a row of four shoes. In each row the shoes nearest the door were called "outside side," next were "next to outside," "next to inside," and "inside." A piece of paper blackened on one side was dropped from the ceiling to decide which side first hid the rock; the side correctly calling the fall started the game; the side winning one game started the next one. Before each game, bets from both teams, consisting of quarters, dimes, and nickels, were placed in a kerchief and this "pot" was hung on the west side of the hogan.

In play, one person keeps track of the 102 counters for each game, and all are tied in a bundle at the beginning. As points are awarded in play, the correct number is taken from the bundle and given to the winning side. When all counters in the bundle have been distributed, the winning side takes counters from the loser. The game ends when one side wins all the counters; the winning side gets the "pot."

As elsewhere, one team hides the rock in a shoe while singing Moccasin Game songs (many of which are about animals); one member of the other team tries to find the rock. This person, "the guesser," may try to eliminate the shoe or shoes he believes to be empty, or he may try to locate the ball immediately. Scoring depends not only on his success but on the actual location of the ball and on the number of questions required to locate it. For each incorrect guess, the side hiding the ball is awarded counters.

For the strategy of elimination, the guesser may use a juniper stick to clear away excess sand, and "kill" a shoe, or he may dig in one or two shoes with his bare hands. He indicates his choice or choices by saying *adin hei,* "nothing's in here." If he means to kill the shoe and finds the rock, he loses ten counters when the rock is in the right-hand shoe (inside) and six counters if it is in the left-hand shoe (outside). He gets another guess each time he correctly "kills" a shoe. When two shoes remain, he chooses the location of the rock; if he misses, he loses six points if the rock is in the right shoe, four if it is in the left one. If he locates the rock, his side wins the chance to hide the rock.

For the strategy of location, the guesser will dig in one shoe, saying "it's in here." If he chooses the correct shoe, his side wins the chance to hide the rock. He loses ten points for digging two shoes away from the rock; he loses six points if he digs next to an inside rock, four points if he digs next to an outside rock. The side which hid the rock continues singing while guessing is in progress.

Fishler (West)

Both informants (FG, Coalmine, and TN, Kaibito) have played the game. They said a yucca ball was carved about three quarters of an inch in diameter (FG). According to TN, a stone ball was used. Both informants agreed that yucca leaf counters, a juniper pointer, and a small stick colored on one side were used, as described above.

The game was played in the winter at night. If it was played in the summer, the smokehole and door had to be covered.

Players were divided into two groups and wagers were made. One side took the ball and hid it in the toe of one of the moccasins or in the hand. The moccasins were then filled with earth, which was tramped down tightly so the ball would not roll around. When hit with the juniper club, the moccasin containing the ball was said to make a sharp sound different from that made by the empty moccasins.

Counters were placed between the opponents and the appropriate number deducted after an incorrect guess. When the center pile was exhausted, counters were taken from piles accumulated by the two teams. The game ended when one group won all the counters.

Points were counted as follows. (For descriptive purposes, the moccasins, four in a row on each side, have been numbered from left to right.) If the ball was in the first moccasin, four, ten, and four points were deducted for selecting the second, third, and fourth moccasin; if the ball was in the second moccasin, four, six, and ten points were deducted for guessing the first, third, and fourth moccasin; if the ball was in the third moccasin, ten, six, and four points were deducted for selecting the first, second, and fourth moccasin; if the ball was in the fourth moccasin, four, ten, and four points were deducted for wrong guesses. Ten points were deducted for an initial wrong guess. If a player guessed that a moccasin was empty, and it was, he got no points. If a player located the ball, his side got the ball, but was given no points.

Comparative

Bourke in 1881 reported that the Navaho were playing the "odd and even" game of the Shoshones, Bannocks, and Zunis, played for one hundred points.

"One side with much ceremony and a great deal of singing and gesticulation will bury four moccasins in the ground, concealing themselves meantime behind a blanket." A small white stone was hidden (Bourke, 1936:225).

Eight years later, Matthews (1889:2–6) published an extensive description of the game. The game was played in winter, "the only time when their myths may be told and their most important ceremonies conducted," and during the darkness. According to Matthews, they played at night because the stone could not successfully be hidden by daylight; but informants were inclined to give a mythical explanation, saying that one who played in daylight would be struck blind. His description of the equipment coincided with the accounts above, except a "roundish stone or pebble about an inch and a half in diameter" was the object hidden, and two of the yucca counters were notched on the margin.

Moccasins were placed "side by side a few inches apart in two rows, one on each side of the fire." The pointer "strikes with a stick the moccasin in which he supposes the ball to lie." For a correct guess he was rewarded with the stone, and the opportunity to hide it. For an incorrect guess, the hiders won four, six, or ten of the counters according to the position of the moccasin struck and that of the moccasin containing the stone. Matthews' account here paralleled that of Fishler. Matthews stated that the pile of counters was held by "some uninterested spectator and handed to either side according as it wins"; the two notched counters, called "grandmothers," were given out last. These were placed in the rafters of the hogan and were told to "go seek your grandchildren," or bring back the other counters. The possession of the "grandmothers" was supposed to bring good luck. Songs were thought to assist the gamblers, "probably under the impression that the spirits of the primeval animal gods were there to help such as sing of them" (Matthews, 1897:141, 240; see also Eaton, 1854:218–220; Newcomb and Reichard, 1937:31; Spencer, 1947:94).

Culin (1907:346) amplified this material and published pictures and descriptions of the equipment collected by Matthews. These included a sandstone ball, an inch and a quarter in diameter, "marked on one side with a cross, with one line painted red and the other black"; also one hundred yucca counters, eight inches long, "and a club of cottonwood, slightly curved, thirteen inches in length." In the collection was a set of 102 yucca leaf counters, eight and three-quarters inches long. Two of these were notched on the margins, "to represent a snake, called the grandmother snake."

Culin also quoted from an unpublished manuscript of A. M. Stephen, who witnessed a game on January 23, 1887. Details of equipment and procedure largely paralleled those described above; yucca leaf counters, a small sandstone nodule, and a pinyon club six inches long were used. "The game was played in a hogan erected for a ceremony." Pits were dug and moccasins placed "very leisurely, with no ceremony apparent." The stakes, "consisting of saddle, bridle, leggings, buttons, manta, prints, blankets," were discussed and, after some difficulty in appraisement, placed beside the buried shoes. "After an hour one side held a blanket between them and the fire and sang, then dropped the blanket," and an opponent struck the shoe to find the hidden stone. "One of the players spat on the stick to hoodoo it for the strikers." As the game proceeded, there was "much droll by-play." "One player, whose side appeared victorious, tried to copulate with the fire. Another, winning, covered his head with his blanket and imitated the cry of the owl(?)." Much jesting prevailed. Amid great uproar, one "player went around the fire as an old man, followed by another as a Ye, imitating masks." Stephen said that to win the maximum number of counters—ten—the pointer should designate two empty shoes, and locate the sandstone nodule on the third try (Stephen, in Culin, 1907:349).

The Franciscan Fathers described the moccasin or "hidden ball" game, stating that it furnished "an innocent pastime for the long winter months," and it was played only then and at night. Equipment was similar to that described above: a small pebble was hidden and a "bicolored stick, or a playing card, or a coin," was tossed to determine the first team to hide the ball. To preclude fraud, moccasins were "exchanged, and placed alternately in a line running east and west, so that no two moccasins belonging to one set of players [were] set side by side." Each pointer had three chances to locate the ball, and struck the moccasin with a small stick to indicate the choice. If a player staked all chances on one guess, and lost, he lost ten points. He lost six points after the second guess, and four after the third. "As the counts of four, six and ten will even up at a hundred, the remaining two strips [the grandmothers] equal either four, six or ten counts, as the player stakes his fortune on one, two or three chances." Stakes ranged from twenty-five cents upward, and it was not considered unusual to spend a whole night on a single game. According to legend, the moccasin game "was first played by the people (or animals) of the day and night for the purpose of deciding whether a difference between day and night should exist." Dawn and the sunrise interrupted the game, so the question was never settled, "in consequence of which the night always succeeds the day." If, at dawn, players decided to continue the game, they painted a charcoal line just below the eyes, as prescribed by the legend (Franciscan Fathers, 1910:485–487).

Both of Gifford's Navaho informants indicated that this game was played in the winter; the Eastern informant specified winter for fear of snakes and bears in summer. The Western informant said that a piece of wood, called "man," was hidden. Ten points were scored for the last two counters, one point each for the other hundred. A stick was set up in the ground for each game won. The Eastern informant said that the game could be played with heaps of sand as well as moccasins; a pebble, stick, or yucca root ball was hidden. A die, black on one side and white on the other, used to determine the start, represented the sun; according to the Eastern informant, the game was taught by the giant son of Sun. The yucca leaf counters represented the sky roads which the sun traveled. Information on scoring was given by the Eastern informant, although both agreed that a count of ten, six, and four points was used. A stick pointer was used to locate the ball hidden in the moccasin; the hand sufficed when the ball was hidden in sand. Sometimes only a single guess was allowed. Both positive and negative scoring were allowed, but negative scoring was apparently usual; the pointer sought to eliminate empty piles before locating the ball. His side lost ten, six, or four points if he inadvertently found the ball on his first, second, or third guess. If he eliminated all three empty piles or moccasins successfully, his side took the ball. For positive scoring, if the ball were hidden in one of the inside moccasins, six points were lost for a guess on either side, ten for a guess at the opposite end. If the ball were hidden at one end, and a player guessed the other, he lost four points. If the hiders forgot the location of the ball, the opponents gained possession of it. A variant game was played, using three moccasins; the count was six or four, not ten (Gifford, 1940:54–55, 146).

There was some difference of opinion concerning the present distribution of the game. According to Reagan (1932:68), the game was tabooed and was no longer played. More recently, Dyk (1947:205) stated that it has been "largely supplanted by cards." Haile, however, stated that it was not unusual to find the young men playing at some hogan during a winter's evening, wagering "a few matches, a silver button, or a quarter of a dollar—in a word, negligible." But the counters passed back and forth, the traditional gambling songs were sung, becoming more lively as the game progressed. "The appearance of full dawn alone puts a stop to the sport, but there is no reason why a fresh start cannot be made on the following night" (Haile, 1933:36–37).

253. Seven Cards

dá·ka cosčed (Ramah, Haile) "card seven" (CC)

Ramah

A basket and seven dice were used for this game. The dice were round and flat, about the size of half dollars (Infs. 2, 16). On one side they were white or "natural"; on the other they were painted red.

Inf. 15 denied that baskets were used with dice. Inf. 16 denied the dice games described by the Franciscan Fathers, although Inf. 2 had heard of them.

According to Infs. 16, 63, and 106, seven cards was a man's game, although Inf. 63 claimed that his mother had played. Infs. 1 and 259 said that either men or women had played. It could be played either outside or in the hogan (Infs. 1, 106, 259), during the day or at night (Infs. 1, 259), at any time of the year (Infs. 1, 16), or only in winter (Inf. 259).

The dice were tossed up and caught in the basket. If seven red sides or seven white sides showed it was a winning throw. No other combination counted.

None of the informants stated that they had ever played the game, but Infs. 3, 16, and 138 were said to have been familiar with it and to have played. Several (Infs. 16, 63, 81, 106) said that they had seen games, although on another occasion Inf. 63 said that he had only heard about it from his grandfather. Several others (Infs. 1, 7, 20, 180, 259) had only heard of it; Inf. 180 claimed to have heard only the name, and he knew nothing about the game. Infs. 56 and 175 denied having heard of the game.

According to Infs. 1 and 7, the game had not been played in the Ramah area for many years. Inf. 81 said that he had seen it played in Arizona in 1920 and 1928. Some (Infs. 7, 192, 259) said that they had been warned against playing the game; Inf. 63 said he was not warned.

None of the equipment has been preserved.

Hill (Central and West)

The dice, according to SG (Keams Canyon), could be any of three types, all made from cottonwood. One form (253.1) was about an inch long, half an inch wide, and half round in cross section; a second (253.2) was an inch long, three quarters of an inch wide, with one side slightly rounded; a third (253.3) was of the same dimensions as the second but flat on both sides. Types

Dice for seven cards, after Hill; top row showing shapes, bottom row showing cross sections

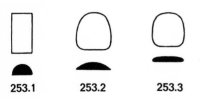

253.1   253.2   253.3

one and three were confirmed by PP (Fort Defiance), who described the third as being as large as a fifty-cent piece.

On all dice the flat sides (or one flat side) were blackened with a charcoal-base paint. On six of the dice the other surfaces (rounded) were colored white or left the natural color of the wood. The remaining surface on the seventh die was painted with red ocher; this die was called *bichi* (PP, SG).

Formerly only two persons at a time played this game; they sat facing each other. Each player held an equal number of twigs used as counters. Onlookers placed wagers on one side or the other to win. The dice were cast by each man in turn, the owner of the dice first. They were thrown from a basket and caught as they fell. When the player failed to catch all the falling dice, his opponent was given one point, although the scoring value of the cast was not impaired.

Methods of scoring differed in accordance with prearranged rules, but in general there were six possible combinations on which points were counted. Seven points were scored for "white" (*xooga*), six white surfaces and a red; six black and a red, or six white and a black (*bichi*); and for "darkness" (*xootcil*), all black. One point was scored for "something round is set on top" (*dasaan*), five white, one black, one red, and for *bichi,* six black and one white. All other combinations were regarded as misses (SG). The game ended when one man gained possession of all the counters.

It was difficult to cheat in this game since play was watched by many bystanders. One possibilty was to turn a die that missed the basket without being seen. Songs believed to bring success were sung in secret before play began. "If a man began to sing during the game he would be thrown out as if he had been cheating" (SG).

Fishler (West)

FG (Coalmine) described a game played with seven colored flat sticks, which were thrown from a basket. The game was popular among women, and scoring was similar to that of the women's dice (see Trait 254). TN (Kaibito) said that women sometimes gambled, but not as much as the men.

Comparative

There is no record of the seven dice equipment in Navaho archaeology. The first reference to the game is apparently that of Bourke, who said that the Fort Defiance Navaho had "dice made of round or square blocks of wood, seven in number, six black and one red: these are shuffled in a basket and thrown out on the ground" (Bourke, 1936:226; see also Goddard, 1933:141; Spencer, 1947:95). Whether this game was the one described at Ramah is not known.

Matthews (1897:83–84) mentioned a similar game, played with thirteen chips, red on one side and white or uncolored on the other. "Success depends on the number of chips which, being thrown upwards, fall with their white sides up." This game was mentioned in the Origin Legend.

Apparently there was considerable variation in the dice. Culin (1907:95–97) published some detail on four sets of seven dice, the last three made by Little Singer, who gave their name as "seven cards" (as above). The first set was of juniper ($\frac{3}{4}$ in. by $\frac{7}{16}$ in. by $\frac{1}{4}$ in.) with unpainted hemispherical backs; six had flat sides blackened, the seventh was painted red. This set was collected by Matthews. The second set was also of wood ($\frac{3}{4}$ in. long), flat on one side and rounded on the other, with the ends cut square. The third set was circular, an inch in diameter; the fourth was oval, one and one-quarter inches in diameter. The dice were all black on the flat side. Six of the rounded sides were unpainted, the seventh was red.

A set of seven dice in the Harvard Peabody Museum (see 253.a) was collected in 1914 at Marsh Pass from a *chiindi* hogan (one in which death has taken place). These were five and a half inches long, one and a quarter inches wide; the flat sides were black, the rounded sides red. The seventh die was smaller than the others.

A description of the game by Haile was quoted by Culin (1907:96–97). He said that players usually carried with them a small pouch with four sets of chips of seven each, and a basket. "These chips were made of oak or of a certain species of wood easily polished after removing the bark, perhaps mahogany." One set was flat on both sides and square; another flat and half rounded; another had rounded corners; and the other set tapered "to a point on both sides, with rounded back and a ridge in the center." Each set had six chips black on one side and white or natural on the other; the seventh (*bichi*) was red and white and of greater value than all the rest. Only one set of chips was used at a time, and points were scored according to the fall of the chips. "Six white and the seventh red won the game, while all blacks did not score as much." Haile's interpreter, Frank Walker, recognized the name given by Matthews for thirteen cards "as that of a similar game which is so called in legends," but he said that the seven cards game was more generally known.

Culin also quoted a description by A. M. Stephen. The game was played with seven small chips about an inch in diameter, all blackened on one side. One was red on the other face and marked with a cross, the others were uncolored. Dice were thrown with the hands, not from a basket. Scoring was not given by Stephen. He added that an even number of players was sought, and that it was a man's game, although women might sometimes play, but under protest from the men. According to Matthews, however, the game was played by women (Culin, 1907:95–96).

According to the Franciscan Fathers (1910:479), dice were cut from mountain mahogany or black greasewood twigs; they were usually disc-shaped, or half round, or with rounded corners. They were colored as described above and were carried "in the leather shoulder pouch, which today is used for tobacco and other trifles, and the basket used in shaking the dice was carried below the arm." The number of points "was decided before the game unless one wished to stake his fortune on a single throw." By 1910, the game was "not in vogue at present, but is mentioned frequently in the legends as the pastime of the Holy People."

Gifford did not include this game in his trait list for the Southwestern groups (Gifford, 1940:51–56).

253.a. Seven cards dice

254. Women's Stick Dice

cidił (Ramah, Lamphere, Haile)   "wood game" (CC); "bouncing sticks"

Ramah

The game required three cottonwood (Inf. 56) dice, each about five inches long (Inf. 16); Inf. 1 said that those he had seen were from six to eight inches long. They were plano-convex—one side rounded and unpainted, the other flat and painted black. Small, apparently unshaped, sticks were used for counters.

A circle about three feet in diameter was drawn on the ground, and a mark was made in the east; this was the only break according to Inf. 16. A flat stone was placed in the center, and forty stones were placed around the circle; Inf. 16 denied that the stones were divided into quadrants of ten. According to Inf. 1, however, there were fifteen stones in each quadrant; the resulting total of sixty stones was not confirmed by other sources. Gambling occurred in this game but, according to Inf. 16, bets were not placed under the rock in the center. According to some (Infs. 7, 20, 81, 101, 157, 175, 180), a blanket was suspended over the center rock; Inf. 41 said that there was no blanket in the game she saw.

Most informants said that players might be of either sex (Infs. 1, 7, 16, 20, 41, 81, 99, 192); two (Infs. 1, 7) said that women played more often than men; and Inf. 175 said that it was a game for women only. Inf. 157 said that men never played and added that only women who knew the songs and rules played. Inf. 16 said that children did not play this game.

Most informants agreed that the game was played either inside or outside the hogan (Infs. 20, 41, 63, 99, 115, 157, 192), but Infs. 7 and 81 said it was only played outside. It could be played at any time of the year according to Infs. 7, 16, 20, 41, 99, and 175, but some (Infs. 81, 82, 115, 180, 192) maintained that it could be played only in winter. Like the hoop and pole game, it was often played at large ceremonies and the time of an Enemy Way; Inf. 45 had seen it played during a ceremonial.

According to some (Infs. 20, 99, 115), the game could be played at any time, either day or night. Others (Infs. 7, 41, 81, 157) said that it was played only while there was light enough to see. Inf. 192 said that those who played at night would become blind.

Two of three players (Inf. 1) sat in a circle. Inf. 1 said that each person sat on the side of the quadrant where his counters were located; Inf. 16 said that players progressed about the circle in either direction. All players used the same dice. Stick dice were held in the hand—grasped in the middle of the dice (Inf. 1)—and dropped on the flat center stone.

Methods of scoring differed. According to Inf. 16, black sides were counted: three, two, or one scored five, three, or two points, respectively. Ten points and an additional cast were given for three whites. If the dice of one player landed on another's counter, "this sent him home." Songs accompanied the play. According to Inf. 1, white sides were counted: three whites, ten points; two whites, one point; one white, three points. According to Inf. 115, three blacks won the game, two blacks scored two points, one black scored one.

Although it is not played at the present time in the Ramah area (Infs. 7, 8, 16, 20, 61, 99, 101, 106, 157, 180, 259), considerable knowledge of the game exists. Inf. 1 stated that it was a good game, but he had never learned to play because he "never had anything to bet." Some (Infs. 8, 16, 78) have played it, although Inf. 78 claimed to have played only when visiting in Gallup. Some were known to have played. Inf. 157 said that Inf. 16's wife and her sister were good players, and that her own mother (Inf. 32) knew the game and was a good player. According to one informant (Inf. 81, 82, or 115), Inf. 32 still played around 1940. Several informants watched games in progress (Infs. 7, 20, 41, 45, 63, 77, 81, 82, 106, 157, 180): Inf. 81 said he was in a game about 1925 in the Bluewater area; Inf. 45 said that during the 1940 pinyon-gathering season she witnessed a game between some Navaho from other regions; Inf. 180 said he had only seen it played below Two Wells, never in Ramah. Others questioned (Infs. 61, 99, 115, 175) had heard of the game but had never seen it. Inf. 256 had seen neither the game nor the dice. Inf. 259, born in 1915, said he knew nothing of it. Some (Infs. 20, 101, 106, 157) estimated that the game had not been played in the Ramah area for thirty or forty years (before 1940).

Several informants felt that this game had disappeared "when those who are not old were young" as the result of a ban against gambling by some of the influential Navaho men of the area, especially Inf. 7's father, "Many Beads." They (Infs. 77, 81, 99, 101, 180, 192, 259) added that they had been warned against playing. Others (Infs. 8, 20, 41, 157) were unaware of this warning. Inf. 16 thought the game's disappearance was due to the influence of the government. Others (Infs. 77, 180) were "afraid of sticks." As far as is known, no dice are preserved in the Ramah area.

Hill (West)

The three wooden dice used in this game were made from well seasoned cottonwood, which SG (Keams Canyon) said was less apt to split than other varieties. Dice (see 254.a) were about seven inches long and slightly over an inch wide. One side was flat and blackened with charcoal, the other rounded and left natural.

Forty small stones were used for scoring. These were divided into units of ten, arranged in a roughly circular form (see 254.1) called "rock circle," with a major opening toward the east called "a river." A flat rock, "way down in the bottom," was placed in the center of the circle. A blanket was suspended on four poles four feet above the circle.

The game was played by either men or women; five or six individuals usually participated. Wagers were placed before the game began, and were put beneath the stone in the center of the circle. Players arranged themselves in rows behind the quadrants on either side of the major opening (*A* and *D* on 254.1), each holding a stick to mark his progress around the circle. The third person from the opening on either side (*A3* or *D3*) made the first cast. Once play began and the sequence of casts had been established, the participants could take any position that they desired.

Each contestant cast the dice in turn. They were grasped in one hand and thrown so that the ends struck the stone in the center of the circle. Unless the dice bounced high enough to touch the blanket the player scored a miss. Points were counted as follows: two white and one black, one; two black and one white, three; all black, five; all white, ten. When a player scored ten he was entitled to another cast; it was possible for a player to score forty points and win the game without ever losing control of the dice. "The man who will win the game is a person who likes everyone."

Players attempted to cheat by counting more spaces than they had scored. "If you get caught you put the counter back where it belongs."

Lamphere (East)

PM gave Lamphere a long account of the women's stick dice game, and

254.a. Women's stick dice of cottonwood root, black on one side, white on the other

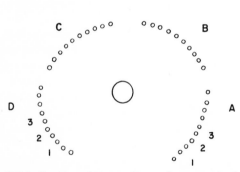

254.1. Position of stones (in quadrants marked by letters) and players (marked by numbers) for women's stick dice game, after Hill

confirmed the term for it. She said that players sit around the hogan in a circle; each person has a partner directly opposite her. Small rocks are placed around the hogan in front of the players, to be used in the counting. Three sticks are used, black on one side, white on the other. Money for bets is placed under a rock in the center; Lamphere thought each player would bet against her partner.

In play, sticks are bounced off the center rock. Ten points are awarded the thrower when the sticks land with all three white sides up. If all three are black, five points are awarded. Three points are awarded for one white and two black, or two white and one black sticks. To keep score, small sticks are placed next to the stones (between them). To win, a player must consistently get more points than the opponent.

Fishler (West)

Three wooden dice were used, one side convex, the other flat. These were about two to two and a half inches wide, four inches long, and about three quarters of an inch thick. Forty rocks were arranged in a circle; every tenth rock was a large one. A large rock was placed in the center. Counters were used to mark the scores.

Dice were usually made by men; they could be made at any time, but usually in the summer or early fall. Both men and women played the game, although women played more frequently than men.

There were two, three, or four players. Each cast in turn until one achieved the required number of points. The dice were thrown into the air, with a basket or by hand. Some players held the dice in the right hand and brought them down forcefully upon the rock in the center, releasing them just before they touched the rock so that they rebounded. The fall of the dice determined the number of points.

Comparative

Stick dice are the only game equipment used by the Navaho for which there is archaeological evidence. In the Gobernador region, Keur found two small cottonwood slabs ($4\frac{7}{8}$ in. long), "flattened on one surface, and with rounded ends." The flat surfaces showed "remnants of black paint. They were evidently used in a variety of stick-dice game" (Keur, 1944:81). These apparently dated between 1660 and 1770. Malcolm also found wooden dice associated with a burial believed to date early in the nineteenth century. Two sets were found, one flat and rectangular, six in number, and the other, flat and boat-shaped, seven in number. Older Navaho, both in the Chaco Canyon region and at Ramah, identified the dice, stating that the rectangular ones were said to be male, the boat-shaped ones female. "But several informants affirmed that the female type was very unusual." According to informants, the "dice were used in almost the same way as the familiar 'bouncing sticks' . . . [*tsidil*], which are similar in appearance though longer" (Malcolm, 1939:19).

Reference to the stick game in literature dates from the early part of the nineteenth century. Robinson, in 1846, saw women playing with three "bones" that were tossed on a flat rock. One hundred pebbles placed in a ring were part of the equipment (Robinson, 1932:47).

Palmer, about 1869, procured some stick dice and described them. "A square marked off and surrounded by small stones" was divided into four parts, each with ten stones. "A stake four or five feet long" was set at each corner of the space, and a blanket stretched over it. A player sat at each of the four divisions, "while young and old stand or sit around to enjoy the sport." Three dice were thrown, to rebound against the blanket and fall onto the square. Three blacks scored five; three whites, ten; one white and a black scored two; two whites and a black, three. Score was kept "by scratching a notch on a stick with a stone." The Navaho women, fond of gambling, "manifest great spirit in playing, and will frequently stake all they have upon" this game (Palmer, 1869:41).

The account by Bourke, who called it an "Apache game," was similar. Three dice, five to eight inches long, were bounced on a flat stone surrounded by a ring of forty pebbles. The pebbles served as counters, and the "count" depended on whether black or white sides of the dice turned up (Bourke, 1936:227).

According to Matthews (1897:77), the stick game was given mythological origin by the Navaho; in the Origin Legend, it was one of the four games brought by the Navaho from the lower world (see also Aberle, 1942:144–154). Matthews noted, as did Palmer, that the pebble counters were placed in a square rather than a circle. "These are not moved, but sticks, whose position are changed according to the fortunes of the game, are placed between them" (Matthews, 1897:219).

Culin (1907:94–95) published descriptions of the dice. One set was made of cottonwood root, eight inches long, about one and three-quarters inches wide, and half an inch thick, "one side flat and blackened, the other rounded and unpainted . . . one stick tied near the end to prevent splitting." Not all dice were black and white; another set consisted of "three flat blocks, 6 inches in length, one face painted with equal bands of green, blue, and red, and the other face half blue and half red." If all three dice fell with three bands up, five points were scored; all three with two bands up scored ten; two with three bands and one with two scored three; one with three bands and two with two scored two.

Both types of dice were mentioned by the Franciscan Fathers (1910: 480–482). The banded dice were slightly rounded on both sides, with two black bands in watercolor on one side and three on the other. Other details confirm those described above, although the Franciscan Fathers specified that this was a woman's game, not played after sunset. Points were lost by dropping the stick outside the stone circle. This game was still popular about 1910.

Aberle (1942:144) published a complete description of the game based on information from fifteen informants from the Chaco Canyon area. According to his account, the circle of stones was about two feet across, and four "rivers" separated the quadrants. As few as two people could play, or as many as could crowd around the circle, sitting or standing. "The throws are counted off with twig markers on the circle of stones. The first person to complete the circuit of forty stones wins." Bets ranged "from a button to a saddle horse or more." "It should be noted that although stick-dice is played by people of both sexes, it is considered a woman's game."

Gifford's Navaho informants confirmed the data above. The Western informant said that four persons played, the Eastern that there were two sides. Both groups denied the use of a square of stones for counting as described by Matthews (Gifford, 1940:55, 147).

Haile (1933:37) noted the decline of the game after 1910; "the sheep industry, weaving and increased domestic duties are not favorable to the pastime." Reagan (1932:68) mentioned its decline and said that for some reason it had become "tabooed." It is possible that at Navaho Mountain, however, the game is still played; according to Eubank (1945:138–140), "the same ritual remains intact."

255. Button Game

Fishler (West)

Two holes were made in a small piece of bone or stone about one inch in diameter. A long string was inserted in the perforations and the ends tied in a loop. The length of the string depended on the number of people who were to play the game.

Men gathered in a circle facing the center and the button was passed from man to man. One man stood in the center of the circle and guessed who had the button. If he guessed correctly, the loser went to the center and the winner took his place. All the men waved their arms and pretended to pass the button in order to confuse the guesser. The string prevented the button from being palmed or hidden in the clothing (TN, Kaibito).

Toys

256. Figurines

xašʎiš da·né·é (Ramah, Haile)   "mud . . ." (CC)

Ramah

Clay figurines were described by Tschopik (1941:13), who was told by several individuals (Infs. 15, 36, 192) that the Navaho made toy figures of animals (horses, sheep, and goats), and of men and women. Facial features were indicated by a few incised lines. Miniature dishes were also made. According to Infs. 15 and 36, figurines were fired; Inf. 192 said that they were not.

These were made for children by their mothers. They were often made by children as well (Inf. 15). Inf. 97 stated that everyone in her family made clay animals. She and Inf. 96 had made them as children, and their children currently made horses, cows, sheep, dogs, men, women, and babies.

At the present time Ramah children make model toys; Inf. 261 made small clay figures of goats and sheep, which were seen by Dorothea Leighton in 1942. From time to time, observers have given Ramah children modeling clay, and they have proceeded to model figures and to play with them.

Many of the small girls have been seen playing with dolls, which were probably gifts from observers. Lacking them, children were not above improvising. Inf. 96's daughters had dolls they had fashioned from dry pine branches and cloth. Another child made herself a doll from rags. A rag was rolled into a small ball and covered with another to make the head. A scrap of black material was tied over the head to simulate hair. A skirt was attached at the neck. In 1944, children at the Ramah day school were taught to make dolls in their sewing class.

256.a. Child's corral containing clay figurines

Hill (East and West)

Dolls were modeled from clay (SG, Keams Canyon; TLLSS, Crownpoint) or made from hide (SG). Figures representing horses and sheep were also produced in clay. These were dried in the sun (Hill, 1937:10). Both children and women of the household made clay toys; hide dolls were manufactured by adult females (SG). "The children played with these. They would make hogans and Enemy Way poles. They would talk to their toys as if they were real" (TLLSS).

Comparative

Bourke, in 1881, reported that "little girls are fond of making their own dolls of adobe mud baked in the sun and provided with dresses and bark cradles" (Bourke, 1936:225). Later, dolls were reported from various parts of the reservation. Fewkes (1923:559–563; see 256.c) illustrated a collection of figurines representing animals and humans. They were said to have been made by a four-year-old child.

According to the Franciscan Fathers (1910:495–496), wooden figures representing Navaho deities were not made "for the amusement of their children, or similar purposes. Dolls and images of some animals, however," were sometimes "carved in cottonwood for ceremonial purposes." One such was illustrated (see 256.1). Clay figurines were not mentioned.

Gifford's Western informant said that small bird figures were modeled from clay; these were denied by the Eastern informant. The Eastern informant denied all toy dolls—"lest the child sicken." The Western informant was not questioned on this point (Gifford, 1940:51, 57, 142, 150).

Figurines have not often been reported from archaeological sites, but Keur found an unfired miniature clay bowl at Big Bead mesa (Keur, 1941:62). Kidder (1932:128–133) found clay figurines at Pecos but was at a loss to explain their cultural significance.

Adelaide Bullen (1947) studied clay figurines "made as toys by contemporary Navaho children living in the region between the Chaco and Blanco

256.b. Wooden dolls

256.1. Wooden doll, after the Franciscan Fathers

256.c. Clay figurines

Canyons, New Mexico." They created animals, such as dogs, horses, goats, and a sheep, ram, mare, donkey, buck, and chicken. Small cooking vessels were made, as were figurines of two Navaho women with the characteristic skirt and headdress. (For an enlightening discussion of clay figurines in the Southwest in general, see also Morss, 1954.)

Two wooden figurines are in the collections of the Harvard Peabody Museum (see 256.d). One was collected by Dr. A. V. Kidder and S. J. Guernsey in 1914 in the Chinle Valley; its over-all length is ten inches. The other was collected by H. O. Ladd in 1887; its over-all length is eight and one-half inches.

256.d. Two wooden dolls

257. Tops

ńdóstˣázi· (Ramah, Haile) "spinning" (CC)

Ramah

Tops were made from wood; they were about two inches in diameter and three inches high. They were spun with a buckskin string on an undressed sheepskin. One end of the string was looped for the fingers.

Men and boys played with tops "in the old days." Tops were spun only in winter and spring. If used in summer, they were said to "bring lots of wind." Three or four boys played together, one spinning the top and the others attempting to split it. There was no betting.

Information was given by Inf. 16 and confirmed by Inf. 2, the two oldest members of the Ramah community. Whether they played with tops is not known. No tops have been noted by observers in the area and it is not known that commercial tops are used.

Comparative

No tops have been found at any archaeological site regarded as Navaho. Apparently the first to report them was Bourke, who said that the Navaho around Fort Defiance "provide their children with tops, (made much as our own)" (Bourke, 1936:225).

According to Culin (1907:733), the top was "one of the most widely diffused of Indian children's playthings." Although its recent introduction has been asserted, "its general use, taken in connection with its existence in prehistoric times in Peru, would seem to point to its having been known before the period of contact with the whites."

The Franciscan Fathers (1910:488) reported the existence of tops but implied that they were borrowed from the whites; children played "such modern games as marbles, top spinning, and the like." Gifford's Navaho informants denied the trait (Gifford, 1940:56).

258. Willow Horses

łį· cinbe··a·lyá na·ni· (Lamphere) "horse, stick with it you play"; "horse, wood with it pulling" (CC)

ńdí·ɣíli· łį· (Lamphere) "horse; sunflower horse"; "black horse" (CC)

·áłčíní biłį· (Lamphere) "horse; children's horse"

Ramah

Children cut willow switches, which they rode like horses. They cut only the larger end, leaving the small branches. According to tradition, before the Navaho had horses the rattle stick of Enemy Way was moved on one of these willow horses.

This trait was described only by Inf. 2. He said that willow horses were used "in the old days," implying that they are no longer made.

Lamphere (East)

Lamphere said that the best way to describe willow horses was by the first term. PM said that horses were also made out of large sunflower branches;

these were called "sunflower horses." They could also be called "children's horses."

Comparative
Apparently the only reference in the literature is by Dyk (1938:13), whose informant said that as a boy in the Black Mountain area he had broken off a willow limb and used it as a horse.

259. String Figures

na·ałoˀ (Haile) "motion of the strings" (CC)

Ramah
Pieces of string were used to create cat's cradles. They could be made any time except in the summer—between May and September. Everyone, according to one of Roberts' informants, knew how to make them; Inf. 1 did not, but said that his wife did. Little girls did not always know how, but tried. Roberts' informant stated that everyone in the household was familiar with all designs; he proceeded to demonstrate one that was unfamiliar to his wife.

Hill (Central)
Both informants (PP, Fort Defiance; LW, Lukachukai) indicated that cat's cradle was a popular form of amusement. It was indulged in by both children and adults. Children were taught to make the figures by members of their family and there were stories, often allegorical in nature, associated with each figure. Some of the more common ones included Breastbone, Two Cloud Peaks (259.a), Attached Stars, Star with Horns, Many Stars (259.b), the Pleiades, Butterfly, Arrow (259.c), Birds' Nests, (259.d), Two Coyotes Running Apart (259.e), Three Cloud Peaks, the Owl (259.f), First Hogan (259.g), and Lightning (259.h).

String figures

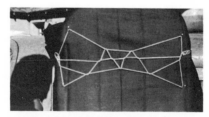

259.a. Two Cloud Peaks

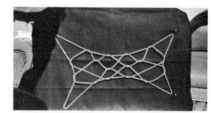

259.b. Many Stars

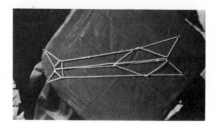

259.c. Arrow

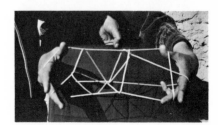

259.d. Birds' Nests

259.e. Two Coyotes Running Apart

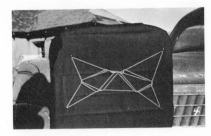

259.f. The Owl

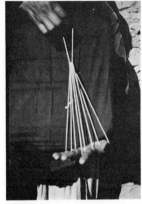

259.g. First Hogan

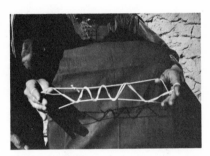

259.h. Lightning

Fishler (West)
TN (Kaibito) denied the cat's cradle.

Comparative
According to the Franciscan Fathers (1910:488–489), the cat's cradle was played by children in the winter, "when the Spider People, to whom it is attributed, are at rest." Its object was "ostensibly to educate the children by riveting their attention, and to supply them with an innocent occupation." Figures included those of stars (the Pleiades, Many Stars, the Horned Star), of animals (Snake, Coyote, Coyotes Running in Opposite Directions, Horned Toad, Owl), and others (Bow, Arrow, Cloud Effect, Nest, Single Hogan, Double Hogan, Man, Wood Carrier, a Standing Tooth, a Bent Tooth).

Both of Gifford's Navaho informants agreed that cat's cradle was played by men, women, and children. It was played only in the winter when spiders were not about, lest they bite (Gifford, 1940:56, 149).

Culin (1907:763–767) collected a number of cat's cradles from St. Michaels, Arizona. Figures he illustrated included the Lightning, Many Stars, Horned Stars, Twin Stars, the Pleiades, Hogan, Coyotes Running Apart, the Owl, Snake, Horned Toad, Poncho, and Carrying Wood. The illustrations of the first eight figures corresponded to photographs taken by Hill. The Owl was apparently constructed in a similar fashion but was pulled to set differently: the extremities were extended, the inner strings were close together. A figure of Carrying Wood collected from Chaco Canyon was also illustrated; Culin reported that other figures had been collected among the Navaho.

260. Swings

ndiba·ł (Lamphere)

ni·ž daba·ł (Lamphere)

Hill (Central and West)

Swings for children were made by tying the two ends of a rope to the limb of a tree. A board seat was fitted in the bottom of the loop formed by the rope. SC (Crystal) stated that this trait had been taken over recently from the whites.

According to GH (White Cone), one end of a rope was tied to the limb of a tree. The child grasped the rope in his hands and swung back and forth.

Lamphere (East)

EP gave the first word for swing; PM called it by the second.

Comparative

The only swing mentioned by the Franciscan Fathers (1910:472) was used for the baby's cradle (see Trait 132, Cradle Swing). The trait was not mentioned by Gifford's Navaho informants (Gifford, 1940).

261. Buzzer

Hill (Central and West)

Buzzers consisted of flat, circular discs of wood, squash rind (PP, Fort Defiance), pumpkin rind, or rawhide (GH, White Cone). The edges were sometimes notched to increase the noise-making potential. Two holes were bored in each disc, one on either side of the center. A cord ran through both holes and extended about a foot on either side of the buzzer.

The operator placed a finger in each of the loops formed by the cord and twisted the disc, thus twining the cord on either side of the buzzer. When pulled taut, the cord unwound and propelled the buzzer. When the tension was lessened at the proper time, the momentum of the disc would cause the cord to rewind in the opposite direction. The buzzer could be spun continuously if these movements were repeated, and it gave a humming or buzzing sound. It was used as a toy and confined to children.

Comparative

Gifford's Navaho informants denied the buzzer (Gifford, 1940:57).

Smoking

262. Pipes

nátosce· (Ramah, Haile)   "tobacco rock, paper" (CC)

Ramah

Tschopik has devoted considerable attention to the manufacture of Navaho pipes (1940:55–65, Part III, Pipes). He describes in detail the technology and ritual prescriptions involved in their construction (see also 262.a).

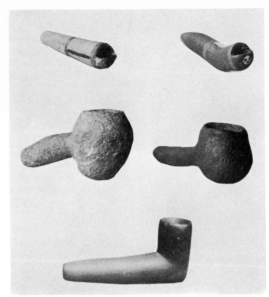

262.a. Clay pipes

Little additional information is available on the use of pipes in the Ramah area. One informant (JP), describing a Blessing Way, mentioned using "an old rock pipe" which was passed around. Possibly this was a stone pipe recovered from a ruin and used in the ceremony.

Hill (Central)

Short lengths of seasoned cane were occasionally used as pipes. Tobacco was placed in one end; the other formed the mouthpiece. These were not used extensively since they soon became overheated (PP, Fort Defiance).

Comparative

Pipes have been reported from the Gobernador region in an area and period of close Navaho-Pueblo contact, between 1660 and 1770. Two clay pipes were found. One "of tubular form, grayish black in color, of smooth finish but undecorated, occurred in the fill of a Pueblito Canyon hogan." This pipe tapered for half its length toward the stem. The second pipe was a "fragment of a cylinder made of very fine, hard paste." It was "grayish in color and unbelievably smooth in surface finish," decorated with three slightly raised bands, "separated from each other and from the body of the cylinder by deeply cut grooves." Keur found the workmanship "so excellent that it almost suggests lathe turning rather than hand manufacture." Wyman's informant DS identified this fragment as part of a pipe used in a ceremonial hunt. He named Antelope Corral Way as the specific ceremony involved (Keur, 1944: 81–82).

Stemless, conical clay pipes were made, when necessary, of clay mixed with broken pottery; pipes found in old ruins were often used. For ceremonial use, the pipes were filled with the appropriate mixture of medicines ignited with a punk of corncob pith or symbolically lighted with a rock crystal. The pipe was smoked first by the chanter, then by the patient and all present. Smoking in general was "enjoyed by both men and women, and boys early acquire the habit." Ordinarily, "they smoke cigarettes made of foreign tobacco, wrapped in paper or cornhusks," usually inhaling the smoke. Chewing was a recent introduction in 1910 (Franciscan Fathers, 1910:287, 395, 506).

Gifford's Navaho informants said that pipes found in ruins were smoked, as were cigarettes made with cornhusk wrappers, according to the Western informant, or oak leaf wrappers, according to the Eastern informant. The Eastern informant said that an elbow pipe was used, with a stone or shell bowl and a cane or alder stem. He described a turquoise and white shell elbow pipe with a cane stem. A tubular cane or alder pipe was denied by both informants. The Eastern informant said that women made a tubular clay pipe, which was "not very satisfactory" (Gifford, 1940:57, 150).

263. Tobacco Pouch

nátoszis (Ramah, Haile)   "tobacco bag" (CC)

Ramah

Smoking tobacco was kept in a pear-shaped buckskin or rawhide pouch. According to Inf. 8, it was made from two pieces, probably sewn together. For shaping, the bag was filled with wet earth, then left to dry. A wooden plug sealed the opening. According to Inf. 7, the tobacco pouch was similar to the pollen pouch (see Trait 217). He said that tobacco might also be kept in "powder horns."

According to Inf. 8, any man could make the type he described. These pouches lasted a long time because they were carried in the pocket. After some time they became smooth and polished. Tobacco pouches were buried with a man when he died.

No Ramah Navaho is known to have made or used tobacco pouches like those described above. Inf. 7 still has a silver tobacco canteen made for his father; it was the only one known in the community. No silver canteens are made by the Ramah Navaho at present.

Hill (Central)

There were two types of tobacco pouches, according to PP (Fort Defiance). One consisted of a small buckskin sack that was closed with a drawstring. The other was made from a rectilinear strip of cloth, folded back on itself for a third of its length and sewn along the sides. The loose end formed a flap. Tobacco was placed in the lower part of the pouch; cornhusks or cigarette papers in the upper. These containers were rolled up and carried in the shoulder pouches.

Comparative

Bourke observed tobacco pouches "of buckskin and muslin, made plain; I have also seen a number of very gorgeous affairs of silver, one of which I tried in vain to purchase" (Bourke, 1936:232). The use of tobacco pouches was also mentioned in a myth recorded by Washington Matthews (1897:176). According to the myth, the pouch was "adorned with pictures of the sun and moon." Earlier, Matthews (1883:pl. 16) illustrated a metal tobacco canteen. Leather pouches made with a flap were similar to those used for carrying matches and other small objects, according to the Franciscan Fathers (1910:311).

Gifford's Navaho informants said that wild tobacco was gathered, and the Eastern informant said that its seed was cultivated where it was found. The Western informant said that tobacco was kept in a buckskin bag, the Eastern informant that it was kept in a bag made from the cased skin of a ground or tree squirrel, along with the pipe. According to the Eastern informant, only women smoked; the Western informant said that only married men smoked, saying that "first a young man must have captured a coyote," that is, married (Gifford, 1940:57–58, 150–151).

According to Adair (1944:51–52), small silver tobacco cases shaped like canteens were derived from the Mexicans, who made them of rawhide and copper, and later of silver. They were purchased until the Navaho learned to make them. Silver ones "were very expensive, and there were only a few Navajo who had enough money to buy them," stated an old informant. Only tobacco was carried in these canteens; other containers were used for corn pollen and medicine. Tobacco cases were carried in the leather pouches which medicine men then wore on the right side and which other men wore on the left. Silver tobacco cases were rare, and only older men knew what they were. Adair stated that these were difficult to make and required "more technical ability than any other silver object," which was one of the reasons for their rarity. In recent years, traders have encouraged a few men to make imitations of the old cases, but these are for sale to whites rather than for Navaho use.

Chapter 6 Summary and Analysis

The purpose of this chapter is to explore some problems relating to cultural ecology, manufacture, and use, and to determine the distribution of Navaho material culture in various areas and through time. We are fully aware that any conclusions drawn from the data presented in Chapters 1–5 are at best tentative or represent approximations. Frequently the data are not comparable because of the many differences in the mode of data collection within and between studies (see fieldwork acknowledgments in the Introduction). For example, the number of investigators in any area and their individual interests varied, as did the duration of their research. In like manner there was considerable disparity in the numbers, interests, ages, and degree of acculturation of informants who were questioned. All of these and other factors make statistical treatment of the data difficult if not impossible. Negative data are particularly difficult to evaluate. Where information on a trait is lacking, it is not always known whether this lack indicates that the trait was absent, denied, or merely unreported. In spite of these reservations, however, generalizations of limited scope are possible and are attempted in order to provide a better understanding of the total picture of Navaho material culture.

Materials

Data on materials used in the manufacture of traits were abstracted from the manuscript during the writing of the third draft. These data and Colson's original manuscript on materials form the basis of this section.

Animal Products

Animal products were the most extensively used raw materials. Hides were used whole, or cut into strips to make thongs and sewing materials. Sinews were also used as sewing materials. Horn and bone were less extensively used but were required for certain implements.

Deer were the most important source of animal products. Buckskin was used for bedding and for clothing; for armor, shields, quivers, and wrist guards; for bridles, saddles, cruppers, saddlebags, pouches; for hafting tools; and for glue. Clothing, feathers, and food were wrapped in buckskin for storage and transport. Strips were used for thongs, tumplines, handles, and wrapping for hoops and the joints of drills and lances; for reinforcing bows and tying. Sinews were used for bowstrings and sewing and for the sinew-backed bow. "Sacred" buckskin, obtained from deer killed by means other than shooting, was required or preferred for certain ritual items such as medicine bags, masks, and the wrapping on hoof rattles. Cased skins were also used as containers.

Specific bones were used. Scapula hoes were made. Ribs were utilized for beaming tools; leg bones were made into arrow wrenches or straighteners and awls. Antlers were used for hafting and awls. Hoofs were tied to rabbit skin blankets, made into glue (as were horns), and used for rattles.

Other wild animals frequently used by the Navaho included antelope, buffalo, elk, mountain sheep, mountain lion, and bear. Antelope were used for most of the same purposes as deer, but were specifically mentioned for men's shirts, rope, and buckskin caps. Buffalo hides were preferred by the wealthy for robes and bedding, occasionally for shirts and moccasin soles or overshoes, and for hoof and rawhide rattles. Buffalo fat was used in ceremonies. Although TT (Coalmine) said buffalo were hunted, they did not occur in Navaho territory and hides were usually obtained in trade from the Ute. Elk were hunted until about 1850, when they gradually disappeared from the Navaho area; hides were usually secured from the Ute. Elk hide was prized for its durability and was used for saddlebags, for making rawhide and buckskin, for moccasins, and for shields. Horns were used for bows, ladles, and rattles; scapulae, for hoes; and teeth were affixed to a man's pouch "to scare lightning."

The mountain sheep, mountain lion, and bear were considered ritual animals and their use was restricted. Mountain sheep horns were used for arrow wrenches and lance straighteners, and as containers for ritual substances. The use of mountain sheep hide was taboo, and it was believed that violators of this proscription would become crippled or be struck by lightning. Mountain lion hides were preferred for quivers, and the sinew was used for backing ceremonial bows and for sewing ritual pouches. According to C (Chinle), mountain lion skin was used in caps, moccasins, overshoes, mittens, and pouches. These uses were confirmed by the Franciscan Fathers (1910: 461), but other informants denied or did not mention them. Claws were sometimes used in necklaces and for wristlets, or in other decoration. Bear was seldom used, but the skin was specified for use in a headband by Gifford's Eastern Navaho informant. The claws were used for necklaces and wristlets, and for the turkey feet in the hoop and pole game. Bear fat was used in rituals.

Wildcat skin was used for caps and mittens and was preferred for scarves. Claws were utilized for decorative purposes, and were also suspended from the turkey feet of the pole in the hoop and pole game. Wildcat skin was used for arrow cases, but not for the bow cases.

A variety of small wild animals was used. Badger hide was pieced together to produce quivers; it was specified for moccasin soles, made into caps, and used for wrist guards, overshoes, and thongs. Live rabbits were used as decoys in trapping eagles. Rabbits were also used for food, and their skins were made into blankets, used for swaddling, and for breechclouts. Whistles were made from their ear tissue and leg bones. Squirrel skins were often cased and used to store sewing equipment, medicine, or tobacco. Mittens and headbands were sometimes made from squirrel hide; and a bit of the hide, or a squirrel tail, was occasionally attached to the cradle to "protect" the baby or to attract his attention. Otter and beaver skins were used for headbands, hair ties, caps, and scarves, and otter occasionally for quivers and robes. Not all informants, however, agreed on these usages. Fox and prairie dog skins sometimes were used to make shirts. The blood of the prairie dog was specified for smearing on arrow shafts. This animal was also used for food, as was the porcupine, whose quills decorated shirts, trousers, sandals, and rattles. Pack rat skins were used by those who could not obtain or afford larger skins to finish blankets and for swaddling; formerly they were used for thread.

Skunk skin was mentioned for use in headbands and caps. Wolf sinew was the preferred sewing material for sewing Evil Way pouches.

Domestic animals included sheep, goats, horses, and cattle. Goatskin and cowhide have replaced hides of deer and antelope in the manufacture and uses of buckskin and rawhide; dressed goatskin, as the most readily available material, was preferred for making rope. Cased hides were used for water bags. Goatskins and sheepskins were used for bedding, and scapulae from both animals for hoes. Sheep pelts were also used for overshoes. Sheep tallow and marrow were required for seasoning wood and as adhesives for paint. Rawhide derived from cattle and horses was used for moccasin soles, wrist guards, saddles, ropes, overshoes, rattles, and shields. Their ribs were used for beaming tools, their scapulae made into hoes, and their sinew used for sewing. Horsehair was used in bird snares and was braided or twisted into ropes, quirts, and rattle handles.

Wool was spun for the warp in fur blankets and sleeping mats; it was woven into blankets, saddle blankets, saddlebags, and articles of clothing and belts for men and women. Wool ropes, tumplines, and cord were manufactured; and wool was used to stuff pucks for shinny and other games. Bayeta cloth, obtained from the soldiers at Fort Sumner and later from trading posts, was valued for its color and used for decoration. Strips were often placed on quivers and buckskin caps. It was frequently unraveled and the strands introduced in blanket weaving for ornamental effect.

Birds

Birds were used chiefly for their feathers. Eagles were ritually hunted, and one was sometimes tethered as a decoy. Eagle feathers were preferred for fletching arrows and were used to decorate basketry and buckskin hats, masks, prayersticks, lances, shields, and armor. Eagle claws were used on necklaces and tied to the ends of the turkey feet of the pole in the hoop and pole game. Down was placed in the internodes of splints, and femurs were made into whistles. Turkey feathers were sometimes substituted for eagle feathers in fletching arrows; they were used with eagle feathers in decorating basketry and buckskin hats, masks, and sometimes quivers. Hawk, crow, and owl feathers were used for fletching and for decorating shields. Feathers from bluebirds, warblers, and other small birds were also used for decorating masks and ceremonial equipment. Feathers were fastened to hair ties worn by patients in curing ceremonies.

Wood and Plants

Wood was used in connection with or as part of approximately half of the traits. It was usually employed in the form of sticks, logs, twigs, or brush. The Navaho lacked complex woodworking tools, and until the late nineteenth century stone axes were used to fell trees. Consequently there was little woodworking. Jointing techniques were simple; and often pieces of wood were merely lashed together, or forked sticks were interlocked and secured by lashings. Wooden artifacts were chopped, whittled, or hollowed by burning; wedges were unknown.

A particular species of wood or plant was seldom stipulated for a specific artifact. Convenience and availability were the main criteria for the choice, unless the finished product were associated with ritual. Exceptions included *tselkani,* which was preferred in all areas for making bows and was acquired from the Apache a hundred miles south of Ramah as well as from other sources; indigo, which was obtained from Mexico; alder, from the Zuni mountains, which was utilized in red and black dyes, and occasionally for the pole in the hoop and pole game, and for lances and pipe stems; and cane from Oraibi, which was required for hoof rattle handles.

Juniper was most frequently used, but for many traits pinyon was equally acceptable. Oak, pinyon, pine (Ponderosa?), and cottonwood were also used. Both pinyon and juniper were used for corrals, shades, hogans, sweathouses, bows and arrows, hoes, snow drags, pokers, firewood, brooms, cradles, beaming posts, and shinny sticks. Juniper was also utilized for making throwing clubs, cactus pickers, digging sticks, flails, carrying poles and litters, wringing sticks, prayersticks, rattle handles, lances, poles for the hoop and pole game, and pointers for the moccasin game. Juniper bark was used for tinder, torches, as a pad for cradles, for kennels, sleeping mats, and formerly for clothing. In solution, juniper (or juniper ashes) was used in arrow poison and dyes, to harden gourd ladles and to remove the taste from gourds used as canteens. Pinyon was stipulated for beaming posts (but not always used); wild animals were placed on pinyon boughs when they were dressed and skinned. Pinyon was the preferred material for the handles of rawhide rattles and was used for saddletrees. Pinyon and juniper bark were used for padding and lining, and formerly for clothing, particularly sandals. Pinyon nuts were eaten.

Pinyon provided pitch to caulk water baskets, to glue layers of hide for moccasin soles, and to remove facial hair in place of tweezers. Pinyon pitch was the mordant in black and red dyes. Pitch from lightning-struck trees (Pinyon or Ponderosa) was used to stop the holes of whistles. It was also used to set stones in the bullroarer.

Oak was the principal hardwood, and was used for bows and arrows, throwing clubs, sometimes for lances, for cactus pickers, pinyon beaters, gathering baskets, digging sticks, hoes, flails, stirrups, snowshoes, canes, and for hafting implements. It was preferred for cradle canopies and shinny sticks. Galls were used for tinder. Lightning-struck oak was used for drill tips, medicine stoppers, and for the bullroarer.

Cottonwood was specified for the earliest type of wrist guard; the roots were used for firedrills and shovels. It was used in the manufacture of saddletrees and hearths. Torches were made from the bark. Burls were hollowed to make ladles, and sections of trunk to produce wooden boxes. Dice and pointers for games were often made from cottonwood, as were figurines.

Pine was preferred for hogan building and for the solid-back cradle. The burls were used to make ladles, the needles to cover the sweathouse. Bark was used in making red dye, and as a receptacle for pigments for sandpainting. Lightning-struck pine was utilized for making a bullroarer. Pine branches were used to make dolls. Aspen was used only for burl drinking cups and ladders.

Greasewood was sometimes substituted for oak in making bows and arrows, digging sticks, and hoes. It was preferred for stirring sticks at Ramah, and

Materials was used for knitting needles, awls in making lightning mats, and for burning out cottonwood in making wooden boxes. Greasewood was an ingredient in red, yellow, and blue dyes. It was used for the shaft in the firedrill, for pokers, and for firewood.

Other woods and plants were also used. Fendlerbush was utilized in all areas for arrows; it was used for quiver supports and knitting needles. Mountain mahogany was used for arrows, in making red dye, prayersticks, rattle handles, and dice. Lightning-struck wood was used for medicine stoppers. Cliff rose was used principally for its bark, for making woven doorway mats, sleeping mats, cradle pads, and in connection with rabbit skin blankets, and, formerly, for bast clothing. In this respect, it was specifically mentioned for winter clothing: bast leggings, sandals, and the lining of overshoes. Its use for lining the sweathouse floor, however, was denied by one informant, who said it was used "only for babies."

Several woods were mentioned for making arrows, among them Apache Plume, which Gifford's Eastern Navaho informant said was also used for the sleeping mat; currant also used for quiver supports; and ash, preferred, according to Newcomb, for pokers and cradle canopies. Cane was used, occasionally, for the composite arrow; it was also used for ritual purposes for prayersticks, rattle handles, flutes and whistles, and pipes. Cherry was used occasionally for bows; it was also used for digging sticks, prayersticks, and loop drumsticks.

Spruce was a wood with ceremonial associations; for this reason it was used for sweathouses but not for hogans. Wild animals were placed on spruce boughs when dressed and skinned, and the bark was boiled for red dye.

Sumac and willow were the principal basketry materials and were used almost interchangeably. They were also used for rod cradles. Sumac leaves or bark were essential for black dye and were used in other dyes as well. Willow was the preferred fuel for the sweathouse fire and was used for the firedrill hearth and for prayersticks. Children rode willow horses.

Yucca was the most frequently used plant. It was employed extensively for lashings and ties and for weaving. Yucca juice was an element in arrow poison and in black dye; yucca ashes, in red dye. The root produced soap. Balls formed from leaves were used as archery targets and as the hidden object in the moccasin game. Leaves were used as counters and for drumsticks.

Gourds, wild and domesticated, were used for canteens and cups, for parts of masks, rattles, and formerly for shinny pucks.

Grasses were utilized for brushes, tinder, bast for clothing, and caulking for buildings. Sagebrush was used for bottle stoppers, firedrills (and tinder), brooms, antelope corral wings, and in sweathouses. Rabbit brush was used for composite arrows, hats, and for covering sweathouses. Bird snares and flutes were made from sunflower stalks. The last two plants, and many others, were utilized in the preparation of dyes. These have been treated in Traits 141 to 147.

Corn and corn products were used in the manufacture of several traits. The cob was used as a blunt arrow point, and to apply dyes. Kernels were employed as rodent bait, and were placed in yucca drumsticks and in rattles. Husks provided materials for spoons or swabs, for plugging whistle holes, for the discs in the moccasin game, and for cigarette wrappings. Pollen was used for the consecration of cradles and hogans; pollen and meal were and still are used for other ritual purposes as well. Corn was, of course, a staple food.

The use of cotton was learned from the Pueblos, but not until yard goods were available from the trading posts was this material extensively used. Other textiles derived from the trading posts included canvas, velveteen, and calico. Canvas was preferred for the ram apron and tumplines, and was split to form cordage. Velveteen was a favorite for women's clothing; and cotton cloth was used not only for clothing, but for swaddling, for covering the cradle, and as a substitute for buckskin and wool.

Stone and Minerals

The Navaho did little stonework, and whenever possible they used implements obtained from nearby ruins. Chert, chalcedony, sandstone, and lava were the dominant materials. Stones were chosen for their hardness or softness and for their similarity in shape to the finished product. Chips of chert or chalcedony were used as knives for shaping wood, scraping hides, and cutting buckskin; they were used for drill points, strike-a-lights, hammers, and formerly, arrow points. Whether these tools were fabricated or appropriated by the Navaho is not always known. Sand from "lightning-struck" chert or chalcedony was required for use with the firedrill. Obsidian chips were also used for arrow points and knives. Arrow points frequently found in the area were used as knives, scrapers, drills, and for tipping arrows. Sandstone was used for shaping and smoothing wooden and bone tools and for rubbing rawhide and buckskin. It was occasionally a building material, used in dams, ditches, wells, water troughs, animal enclosures, and houses. Rocks for the sweathouse were of sandstone, as were griddles and pot supports, hammers, and axes. Lava was also used for heating the sweathouse, for metates and manos, or as a rubbing stone in the preparation of rawhide and buckskin. Stone of unspecified type was used for sealing storage caves, for mortars and other stone utensils associated with the preparation of food, for axe heads, and hammers. Pebbles were utilized as sling stones, with pitch for repairing leaks in basket bottles, for rattles, for hiding in the moccasin games, and in the button game. Mica or selenite was used for reflectors.

Some semiprecious stones were used for ornamentation and in connection with ritual. Turquoise was preferred for this purpose, but coral or other red stone, a black stone (cannel coal, jet, or obsidian), malachite, and garnets were also used. Chalchuitl was imported from Mexico. Glass was occasionally included in necklaces and earrings.

Some use was made of other minerals. A rock-alum mordant was used in most dyes, as occasionally was gypsum. Clay was utilized infrequently, but was an important material for face and body paints, dyes, sandpaintings, and pottery. Except for pottery clays, white clay was required more often than other colors; it was used for dyeing yarn and in paints and sandpaintings. Red ocher was used in these capacities and also for coloring cradles and occasionally snowshoes. Yellow ocher was also used for dye and paints. "Blue clay" was apparently the only imported clay. It was obtained from the Mexicans, via the Ute, and utilized in blue and green dyes. Trips were made to deposits thought to have particularly good clay. One such was a deposit of white clay near Ramah.

Earth was used in the construction of dams, ditches, wells, and ovens, and generally for covering hogans, sweathouses, eagle pits and other such structures. Hides were buried in earth during part of the skin-dressing process, and a mound of earth was erected to shape the shield. Earth gathered from the four sacred mountains was kept in the medicine bag. Mud was sometimes used to cover the body for warmth.

Salt was also gathered on trips. Used for seasoning food and in rituals, it was also used in yellow dye, and has recently been utilized in dressing mountain lion hides.

Shells

Shells obtained in trade from nearby peoples (Pueblo and Ute) were used for ornamentation and ritual containers. A variety of shells was specified for use in necklaces, such as abalone and olivella. Black, white, and blue shells of unnamed varieties were used for necklaces as well. Abalone and haliotis shells were used for containers. They were also used on ritual items such as cranebills, masks, bullroarers, and armor, as well as in other religious capacities.

Metals

Various metals were used. Tin, iron, silver, copper, and brass were all known. Tin cans, used as containers for products obtained at the trading posts, provided an easy source for this metal. From it the Navaho fashioned reflectors, sheep shears, knives, sizers, scrapers, and drums. Wire or nails were frequently used, for engravers, drill points, small arrow points, bullets, and branding irons; for boring holes in wooden saddletrees or cradles; for knitting needles; and for tying. Arrow points were made from barrel hoops. Copper, brass, and especially silver were used for ornamentation. These materials were made into conchos and buttons and used to decorate clothing, horse equipment, and cradles. Metal artifacts were obtained from the traders as well. These included wire screening for pinyon gathering, hoes, rakes, pitchforks, barbed wire, bits, horseshoes, wagon wheels, axes, hammers, knives, hangers, pots and pans, and umbrellas, the ribs of which were used for knitting needles.

Areal Variation

The area occupied by the Navaho comprises much of Arizona, parts of New Mexico, southwestern Colorado and southeastern Utah. Geologically part of the Colorado Plateau, it varies in altitude from five to over ten thousand feet. It is dotted by mesas, ridges, and mountains, and frequently cut by valleys and arroyos. Vegetation varies with elevation and with seasonal rainfall. Sagebrush and grasses cover the lowest elevations; pinyon and juniper trees grow between five and eight thousand feet over most of the

Navaho area; and in the mountains, these give way to forests of pine, fir, spruce, and scrub oak. Rainfall is slight, averaging about fifteen inches annually, and most of it occurs during the summer months in showers which are often violent and sometimes accompanied by hail. Resulting washouts can ruin crops and disrupt communications. Temperature variations are great: summer days are hot, but nights are refreshingly cool; winters can be bitterly cold.

Natural resources and geographical features are duplicated in each of the areas arbitrarily designated (Introduction, p. 3) Ramah, East, Central, and West. In order to discover whether there were instances of individual and areal preference and selectivity of one material over another from this common environment, lists of material were totaled for each area and the number of traits for which a particular material was specified was tabulated. This revealed that in the use of resources throughout the Navaho area some individual and areal selectivity did occur.

In those rare instances where the use of a material was reported for one area only, this could often be attributed to the specialized knowledge, or lack of it, on the part of investigators or informants, the limited range of a particular resource, or factors of differential acculturation. For example, the otter was mentioned only by informants from the Central area. The animal is known to inhabit Colorado, and although it may be indigenous to the Navaho area, it is not common. Only Ramah informants reported the use of coyotes or wolves and chipmunks. Their use of coyote or wolf was unique, for these animals are generally taboo. Perhaps it is the result of the comparatively acculturated character of this area. A plant used for a hearth material (*niihikahi*) was mentioned at Ramah but not elsewhere; a plant (*hactan*) used in blue dye only for the Central area; sorrel only at Mariano Lake. These, like snakeweed and redscale at Ramah, were probably known throughout Navaho territory, although their use in only one area was specified. The uses of plant coffee and rabbit brush were reported only for the Ramah area, but their uses elsewhere were confirmed by Elmore (1944:89, 83). Elmore, Wyman and Harris, and others reported many plants not mentioned by informants. These instances of single usages are, however, probably not examples of areal variation but reflect the knowledge by the investigator or the informant of the identity of the material—its colloquial or scientific name—rather than the uniqueness of the material. Fendlerbush was considered a hardwood and used for arrows, according to informants in all areas. An informant from Black Mountain, however, said it was used for tobacco, boiled "with juniper berries, pinon buds, and corn meal for mush-eating ceremony of Plumeway, Nightway, Male Shootingway, and Windway" (Wyman and Harris, 1951:25). By the same token, only Keur identified basalt or quartzite as materials used for the hammers she found; others merely identified these minerals as stone.

Insights into the process of individual and areal selectivity were more abundant when other materials were examined. For example, wildcat, although used in all areas in two traits (arrow case, skin mittens), was used for five in the Eastern area, and for six in each of the other areas. It is one of few materials that were reported by informants from the Eastern area with a frequency comparable to that from other areas. For many traits, data from the Eastern area were scarce or absent. Alder was an exception. Identified by Elmore, it was apparently used more in the Eastern area than in any other, and there is scant information on its use in the Western area. The use of cattails was reported only for Ramah and in the East.

The use of mountain sheep horns for arrow wrenches was reported for all areas, but more often by informants from the Western area. Protected by taboo, the animal was less frequently used at Ramah, except in ceremonial capacity. Robes of buffalo hide were used throughout the region but were noted specifically only for the Ramah, Western, and Central areas.

In the Central area, badger, fox, beaver, porcupine, and skunk were noted with greater frequency than elsewhere. Badger skins were used in all areas for moccasin soles before the Fort Sumner captivity. There was no mention by Western informants of the use of the other four animals, all of which were utilized in at least one trait at Ramah. The others were known in the Eastern area, but used infrequently. Elk was used more often in the Central area than elsewhere; the use of elk horn was recorded only in the Central area. The mountain lion was used more often in the Central area than at Ramah, and in these areas much more frequently than in the Eastern and Western areas. In all areas it was used for making quivers.

Although Hill stated (1938:145) that there were more antelope in the Western part of the Navaho territory, according to informants from Ramah and the Central areas, greater use was made of them in those regions than in the East or the West. Bear were universally used, but more specific references were recorded at Ramah than elsewhere; the bear was a ritual animal, and only those chanters who knew the Mountain Way could kill it. Small animals, such as rabbits, squirrels, and rats, were also reported as used more often by Ramah informants than others.

Domestic animals were universally used, but the preferences for these between and among the different areas were interesting. Sheepskin bedding and overshoes were common to all areas; for other purposes, sheep provided raw materials for Ramah Navaho far more often than did horses, goats, or cattle. The Navaho in the Central area preferred goats to horses, sheep, or cattle. Navaho in the Western area apparently had a slight preference for horses over both goats and sheep. Those in the East used goats, sheep, and horses with about the same frequency, but used cattle less often than the others.

The uses of wood and plants also varied among localities. There were more references to goldenrod, cliff rose, grasses for bast, gourds, and yucca by informants from the Central area than by those from other areas. Yucca, for example, was used in twenty-three traits in the Central area, in fourteen, fifteen, and nineteen traits in the Ramah, Eastern, and Western areas, respectively. Although most areas overlapped, on only seven of these traits were informants from all areas in agreement. Again, this difference may be interpreted on the basis of degree of acculturation. Yucca fibers were used largely for ties and twining, materials which have been replaced. On the use of juniper, informants from the Central area specified it for thirty-three traits, as opposed to twenty-five traits for Ramah and the Western area, and fifteen traits for the Eastern area. Only four of these traits showed universal agreement.

Willow, sumac, aspen, oak, pinyon, cottonwood, greasewood, and mountain mahogany were reported more often by Ramah and Central area informants than by those from the East or the West.

There were few areal differences in the use of stone among the Navaho. Here particularly, convenience was a major criterion. Any convenient cobble became a smoother, and any nearby ruin a source of arrow points or metates. Lava was abundant in the Ramah area and was used more often by the Ramah Navaho than by those from other areas. Red ocher was mentioned more often by informants from the Eastern area and Ramah than by others.

Eagle feathers were used in all of the areas for fletching arrows and decorating shields and (except for Gifford's Navaho informants) lances. Rosettes of owl and eagle feathers adorned caps in all areas; turkey was substituted for the owl more often in the Central area than elsewhere. Crow feathers were also used for this purpose by informants from the Central area, but not by those from Ramah. Other birds, such as bluebirds, warblers, blackbirds, hawks, doves, and flickers were variously specified by informants from all areas. Data on these usages are far from complete, as the feathers adorned ceremonial equipment, which has been treated here superficially.

Informants from the Ramah area reported the use of metal in the form of wire or nails more often than did informants from other areas. Tin cans were used in all areas. Informants from the Central area more frequently mentioned brass; and all used silver and copper. Data from the Western area are lacking on these metals: Fishler included little information on clothing or ornamentation; and Gifford's Western informant provided data where possible on traits current before the introduction of metals—metals were designated as "modern." Informants from all areas used earth for building and other purposes (described above).

Informants from the Central area more often reported the use of shell for decoration than did informants from other areas. Shells were, as stated, obtained in trade from nearby Pueblo or Ute Indians.

Data revealed overwhelming conformity in the use of a specific material in producing a given trait both within a given area and throughout the reservation. Individual and areal variation was most apparent in the choice of alternatives when the preferred material was not used. Here, however, no consistent pattern emerged. Alternatives could not be ranked in order of preference; selection was random. The determining factors appear to have been appropriateness, availability, and personal preferences or specialized knowledge. The consensus of fieldworkers, reinforced by data, was that differences in material use were no greater between the four areas than those based on individual preference in a single area.

Manufacture and Use

This analysis of the manufacture and use of each trait takes into account not only the time and place of construction or use, but also the person or persons who performed actions necessary for the completion or utilization of the product. Such analysis reveals insights concerning the division of labor on the basis of sex and age, and information on specialization and cooperation.

Time

"Any time" was appropriate for the manufacture of most traits of Navaho material culture; materials were rarely worked except to satisfy an immediate need. Restrictions imposed were largely functional, with only an occasional cultural addition. Seasonal factors of need and availability were determinants for the most part. Overshoes were made when an old pair wore out in the winter and were stored during the warmer months. Snowshoes were made when necessary; after use they were dismantled, according to ritual prescription. Dyes were said to lose their color if stored for long periods; they were made as required. Some materials were available only at certain times of the year. Goldenrod, for yellow dye, was gathered when in bloom. Buckskin and rawhide were prepared when the animals were available and stored, as was wool. Other raw materials not readily available or easily acquired were gathered and stored. Expeditions or hunts were organized to procure raw materials such as animals for hides and food, eagles for feathers, clays, sandpainting pigments, and salt.

There appeared to be an unstated rhythm in the handicraft work, actually an accommodation to periods of comparative leisure as opposed to intensive preoccupation with economic pursuits. In spring and late summer the Navaho were occupied with livestock and agriculture and had little time for making articles. Visits to Pueblo festivals during the summer interfered with the production of material objects. Handicrafts and recreation were left to the winter.

As expected, agricultural tools were used during the planting season; storage pits during the winter; seed beaters and pinyon beaters during the fall, when the seeds and nuts ripened. Otherwise, articles were in daily use, except for many objects of recreation for which there was a summer ritual prescription. Seasonal taboos on ritual pursuits were observed; taboos were also observed on the telling of myths, many of which embodied discussions of the origins of material objects and directions for their construction.

A few articles could be manufactured only in connection with ritual occasions. Certain chantways were held for the express purpose of making ceremonial equipment, such as rattles, medicine bags, and other items. Frequently the manufacture of these ritual items was limited to chanters or men over whom chants had been performed. Although no rituals were required for the production of quivers, the best were said to be made during a performance of an Enemy Way. When a cradle was to be made, work was not begun until several days or a week or more after the baby was born, for fear the child would die. Although infant mortality among the Navaho was (and is) high, this fear was expressed in terms of cause and effect.

Time of manufacture might also be affected by other types of negative sanctions. Although there seems to have been little dread of the contaminating influence of women as such, prohibitions were frequently imposed on pregnant and menstruating women and their husbands. Taboos associated with pregnancy were dictated by concern for the welfare of the mother and unborn child; those with menstruation with possible loss of efficacy of the item or person with which the menstruant came in contact. Restrictions were enforced only so long as the condition existed.

Most traits were made during the day, for obvious reasons. Exceptions were the items of a religious nature, which were made during the chantways.

Place

"Any place" that was convenient was the location for manufacture of most traits of Navaho material culture. Only for silverworking or weaving was the worker dependent upon tools that were cumbersome and likely to tie him or her to one location. In or near the hogan—in winter—with company and tools nearby, was usually the most convenient. In summer, life centered around the shade or remada, and much of the work was done there or nearby. Animals killed on a hunt were skinned and dressed in the field, domestic animals near the hogan or corrals. Ditches and dams were naturally built where there was water, and snares and traps where they were appropriate. Sweathouses were built at a distance from the hogan to insure privacy.

Ritual requirements dealt largely with the presence of onlookers and were proscriptive. The fletching of arrows and the making of shields, pipes, and pottery were supposed to be done without witnesses, which usually meant at a distance from the hogan. There was no prescribed location. Children were not supposed to watch the preparation of bugaboo owls, but there was no prescribed or proscribed location for making them. Dehairing hides of wild animals had to be done at a distance from the hogan because the hair was considered dangerous. Snowshoes were made, used, and dismantled away from habitations because the track was said to resemble that of the bear, and bad luck was believed to follow if the user brought the shoes home.

The sweathouse was not used for handicraft, although it served in part as a men's club. There men discussed general events, planned work, and learned ritual songs and myths. Actually, the sweathouse was an unsuitable structure for craft work.

Workmanship

The transformation of raw materials into usable form was characterized by great simplicity. In most instances processing was carried only to the point of minimum efficiency. Where it was more complicated, the tool or finished product was often imported. The Navaho used the drill to perforate beads, for example, but when possible imported beads already drilled.

The lack of interest in objects, as such, was reflected in the deficiency in refinement and paucity of ornamentation that characterized most finished products. Many observers have commented on the crudeness of the Navaho material culture and the lack of Navaho interest in virtuosity. Weaving and silverworking were notable exceptions. When it became available, silver was freely applied to leather, bridles and other objects, and used to decorate clothing. Otherwise, traits of ritual significance used in ceremonies, in war, or in hunting were the usual sources of aesthetic expression; and these in most cases were rigidly prescribed. Dyeing and painting were the principal methods of ornamentation. Red, yellow, black, blue, and white were the colors most frequently used. Occasionally skin objects were fringed. Feathers, shells, turquoise, and porcupine quills were occasionally attached to the garments, especially hats or pouches. Recently beadwork has been used to decorate hat bands and other objects. Sculpture and carving and the use of decorative lashings were virtually absent. In general, Navaho material culture was characteristically functional rather than aesthetic.

Specialization was not highly developed. It was principally associated with the manufacture of items used in chantways, warfare, and ritual hunting. Weapons were usually made carefully and under conditions of taboo. Though all men were capable of making bows, arrows, and quivers, superior craftsmen who were frequently ritualists were often engaged to perform these tasks. The technical aspects of manufacture of shields, eagle pits, pitfalls, and antelope corrals could be accomplished by anyone, but their construction was restricted or at least supervised by those who knew the associated rites. It was the extensive ritualization of life rather than technological complexity that led to a modified apprentice system and specialization in some areas of Navaho material culture.

Though most specialization was connected with religion, superior competency, if not virtuosity, was recognized in the production of some secular items. For example, outstanding craftsmen might be hired to make a saddle, buckskin rope, or a hogan, and the belt or blanket produced by a master weaver was highly prized.

Mutual assistance in the production and use of items of material culture was also rare. Articles tended to be made and utilized by individuals. Cooperative efforts usually occurred only when the mechanics of the task precluded the accomplishments of the desired result by a single individual. Thus, help was solicited in the construction of twisted hair ropes, rabbit skin blankets, pottery drums, sweathouses, hogans, storage pits, wells, dams, antelope corrals, stalking costumes, and pitfalls. In general such assistance, when possible, was recruited from within the family or from the local segment of the clan.

Division of Labor by Sex and Age

Informants often specified that men, women, or children could, could not, did, or did not manufacture or use specific traits; or this information was implied either by the nature of the article or other criteria. A résumé of these data is presented here in order to determine whether any significant division of labor existed on the basis of sex and age in the utilization of raw materials and the manufacture and use of traits.

Men utilized raw materials to a much greater extent than women. Their use of raw materials derived from animal sources far exceeded that by women. Nearly all products of horn, hooves, and bone were made by men. Hides were employed twice as often by men as by women and twice as often by boys as by girls. This ratio also applied in the use of sinew by men and women. Only in the use of wool did women exceed men by the same degree. Wood was utilized primarily by men. Both sexes used plants. However, because of their association with religious aspects of the culture plants were used in greater number and variety by men. Only plants employed in basketry, carrying baskets excepted, fell principally in the woman's domain, since men were forbidden to make these products. Males were predominantly concerned with those areas of the culture that utilized stone, earth, minerals, including semiprecious stones, and metal. Only in the use of clay did women exceed men.

Both men and women participated in the manufacture and use of traits; some groups of traits were the prerogative of men, some of women.

Ritual hunting was entirely an adult male pursuit except for the instruction received by boys. Men made and used the equipment associated with it. Bows and arrows and blinds utilized in hunting large animals were made by males. Women were forbidden to manufacture them or the tools employed in their fabrication, although occasionally a woman might make a quiver. Ritual sanctions were strictly enforced. When boys made bows and arrows they were presumably subject to fewer restrictions than men, since these weapons were used for secular purposes, the nonritual hunting of small game and archery contests. Items associated with firearms and other modern weapons such as powder horns and ammunition were usually made by men, but prohibitions against their use by women were less stringent. Negative sanctions, however, applied to the use or manufacture of weapons by girls.

Nonritual hunting was dominated by males, though there were few restrictions against participation by women and children. Anyone could set deadfall traps and use rodent sticks; women did not make, but sometimes used, throwing clubs. Children, usually boys, made and used bird snares and boys made bird blinds.

Anyone could manufacture most of the traits related to gathering and almost everyone used them. Gathering bags and burden baskets were made by both men and women, although men used the former less and manufactured the latter less frequently than women. The only pursuit in this category prohibited to women and children was the highly ritualized one of salt gathering. Salt, however, was used by everyone.

Traits associated with agriculture were largely manufactured by men, although used about equally by men and women. Women could make flails, digging sticks, and hoes. Children did not use flails because of the arduous character of the work. Men and boys constructed dams, ditches, and wells, although everyone benefited from their use. The manufacture and use of agricultural traits by children was extremely limited.

Traits associated with animal husbandry were manufactured almost entirely by men. None was said to have been made by women. Use, however, was not strictly dominated by men. Care of the sheep and goats traditionally was in the hands of the women and children; traits associated with sheep such as corrals and shears, ram aprons, and water troughs were made by men, or derived from traders or other sources.

Both men and women owned and used horses, and both made and used the associated equipment, although men perhaps more frequently than women, and boys more often than girls. Men, for instance, usually made bridles, although women could do so; both made saddles. However, neither a pregnant woman nor her husband could work on a saddle.

The makers of most traits associated with transportation and burdens were not stated. Most traits were made as required, probably by the persons who needed them. It was stated that men made carrying poles, and implied that they made sleds, rafts, and bridges. Both men and women used the carrying poles and tumplines. Children were not specified either for the manufacture or for the use of traits in this category.

In general, women manufactured almost twice as many traits associated with food as did men, and they used more than three times as many of the traits. Traits associated with the storage of food were largely manufactured by women; they made water bags and basket bottles. Both sexes made storage bags and both shared the work on storage caves and pits, although Ramah informants indicated that women performed most of the labor on pits. It was implied that anyone could use these traits. Traits associated with the preparation of food were manufactured by both men and women; both made mortars, metates, manos, brushes, and stirring sticks, but only women were specified for the manufacture of stirring paddles. Metates and manos were, however, frequently obtained from prehistoric sites or inherited. Women made the griddles. Both men and women dug roasting pits. Cooking was done mostly by women. Utensils such as dishes, bowls, ladles, and spoons were more often made by women, except that men made wooden utensils. Both sexes made gourd ladles and spoons. These utensils were much more often used by women than by men.

Heavy construction on hogans and other house types was done by men and older boys, some finishing by the women and girls. Men and boys probably made the shades and ladders, but informants did not so state. The whole family used these.

Men manufactured firedrills and pokers; women also made pokers. Formerly these traits were used by anyone. The firedrill reserved for ceremonies is now used only by ritualists. All members of the family gathered firewood.

Multipurpose tools, such as the axe, hammer, knife, and knife sheath, were most frequently made by men, although anyone could and did use them. These implements were often recovered from prehistoric sites and used without further refashioning. Women made most of the bedding, although men made sleeping mats and rabbit skin blankets. Woolen blankets were woven only by women. Bedding was used by everyone.

Both men and women made cradles. Men ordinarily fashioned the wooden parts, and the women helped to assemble the lashings, bedding or swaddling, and the cradle canopy.

Both sexes contributed to the preparation of materials for clothing, but a division of labor was apparent. Men prepared most of the rawhide and buckskin; they made and used the tools connected with their manufacture: beamer, beaming pole, and wringing stick. Women used buckskin and rawhide as often as did the men. They dyed most of the buckskin, wool, and cotton cloth, although men were not prohibited from so doing, and occasionally did. Dyes used for basketry were prepared only by women.

Both men and women made and used sewing equipment such as metal awls, sinew thread, buckskin thongs and cord, and knitting needles. Women were specified as the makers of the sewing bags in which this equipment was kept. Both sexes used the equipment, although in practice it is probable that women did so more often than men.

Women made most of their own clothing and that of their daughters. Men made many articles of their clothing, especially buckskin shirts, breechclouts, trousers, and leggings, though they occasionally wore some items made by women, for example, rope or woolen belts. Informants denied the manufacture of buckskin leggings and the buckskin belt by women. Women rarely wore articles of men's clothing, and informants denied their use of the woven shirt and buckskin belt.

Both men and women made headgear. Women made and wore the hair tie and the basketry hat; men also made hair ties and headbands. Caps of buckskin, mountain lion, or wildcat were made by men but were neither made nor worn by women. These were utilized for warmth and worn on military expeditions.

Sandals, moccasins, overshoes, and snowshoes were all made by men, although women could also make moccasins and overshoes. Everyone wore moccasins—or more recently shoes obtained at the trading post or some combinations of types—as well as overshoes, but snowshoes were apparently used only by men. A ritual prescription required the dismantling of snowshoes when the wearer was through with them. Both men and women made mittens. Pouches for personal equipment were made by both sexes; everyone used them, but particularly men. Canes were used by the aged or infirm.

Though informants did not specify sex and age with respect to the manufacture of necklaces and earrings, presumably men made them as they were the specialists in metalwork and semiprecious stones. They made such articles as bracelets, rings, and buttons and these were often embellished with semiprecious stones, turquoise, cannel coal, and coral. Both sexes wore articles of adornment. Jewelry, however, was more indicative of wealth or inclination than of sex or age. Men were possibly more apt to use paint for decorative purposes than were women. Tweezers were used by men.

Yucca soap was used by everyone; the other articles in the category of hygiene were functionally required only by women.

Most items of ritual nature were manufactured and used by the men. In many instances women were forbidden to make or use these articles. Traits associated with warfare were made and used only by men. Men built sweathouses, which were used by members of both sexes, but not simultaneously. Women made the bugaboo owls used to frighten children. Ritual containers were supposed to be made by chanters. Women made the cased bags and woven baskets. Chanters used these articles in the ceremonies.

Musical instruments, except for basketry and pottery drums, were made by men, who used them particularly in ritual context. Informants stated that children made and used rawhide drums; they also used the stomping pole, whistle, and musical bow. These were playthings, however. Anyone could use the pottery drum or the stomping pole.

Men made most of the game equipment. Both parents and children made toys utilized by anyone. Men played all games; the women played some, but were said not to participate in the stick race or hoop and pole. Children did not play the women's stick dice game, but boys participated in the races, and both boys and girls played shinny.

Smoking was primarily a male prerogative, although both men and women smoked. Men made the tobacco pouches.

The roles of men, women, and children are defined in Navaho mythology. The functions of each sex and age are detailed in the Emergence Myth, recorded by Curtis (1907:84–86), Fishler (1953:24–26), the Franciscan Fathers

(1910:349–350), Goddard (1933:128–129, 138), Matthews (1897:70–72, 93), Newcomb and Reichard (1937:25), Oakes (1943:6), and Wheelwright (1942:45–48). Except in a few instances, however, the mythological ideal is seldom achieved and the division of labor on the basis of sex and age tends to be loosely structured. It was most pronounced in those areas of Navaho material culture associated with warfare, ritual hunting, and religion. These activities were overwhelmingly adult male prerogatives, and traits associated with them were both made and used by men.

In the secular area there appears to have been only one clear division affecting both manufacture and use—clothing. Adults, with few exceptions, made and wore costumes appropriate to their sex. Aside from this, use was not generally restricted though manufacture might be. Men produced most of the traits associated with agriculture and animal husbandry, and did the bulk of the work in stone, metal, and wood. Women made most of the articles associated with the processing and preparation of food including pottery and most basketry. They did most of the weaving. Though one sex or the other dominated, use roles tended to be mixed. For example, women made and used pottery and most baskets; on occasion, however, these were used by male chanters. Men dressed buckskin, but women made and used many of the articles manufactured from it, including ropes, saddles, moccasins, and skin bags. Men did not grind corn, but used the metate and mano to grind pigments for a sandpainting or bark for dyeing buckskin. The batten used by a women in weaving might be borrowed by a man to smooth a sand-painting. In addition, there was evidence that not only was the same type of tool used by men and women, but the same tool was transferred from one to another as needed.

The distinctions based on age were largely functional. Ability and experience dictated usage.

Distribution of Traits by Area

The areal distribution of the traits was examined in an attempt to discover whether local or regional variations occurred and to determine the degree of homogeneity that existed in Navaho culture as a whole. In terms of analysis an equivalent sample of data from each area (Ramah, East, Central, and West) would have been desirable, but this was not possible. Data from different areas were collected at different times and under a variety of circumstances. Most were collected incidentally. In order that the reader will be in a position to evaluate the results, a résumé is given of the conditions of fieldwork and of the source materials.

Clyde Kluckhohn described the Ramah study as being both extensive and intensive. Work was done over an extended time by many people, and included research not only in ethnology but in other behavioral sciences, as well as in botany and geography. More observers worked at Ramah than anywhere else, and in general those at Ramah used a greater number of informants than others. Ramah investigators whose works or notes have been used included Aberle, Adair, Bailey, Griffith, C. Kluckhohn, Landgraf, the Leightons, McAllester, McCombe, Mills, Murray, Roberts, Spencer, Spuhler, Tschopik, Vestal, and Vogt.

Some of these investigators emphasized material culture, notably Tschopik, but even he was primarily interested in data on Navaho basketry and pottery. Roberts compiled minute inventories of the three households he studied in 1946. The field check by Mills in 1947 was specifically oriented to material culture traits, based on a list compiled after Hill wrote the first draft of his material.

Hill's fieldwork was done in approximately fifteen months during 1933 and 1934. He worked throughout the reservation, but primarily in the Eastern and Central areas. The major focus of his research was on subsistence practices and this factor determined the selection of informants. Since hunting in particular, and agriculture to a considerable extent, were highly ritualized, whenever possible information was derived from individuals who were familiar with the chantways and minor rituals associated with these pursuits. In a sense many informants—namely the intellectual elite—were nonrepresentative of the total population. Emphasis on material culture was subordinate to the subsistence inquiries; gaps in the Eastern or Western data can be explained by the fact that the attempt was made there only to isolate regional variations in hunting and agriculture. However, since production and consumption entailed the utilization of many items of material culture, information on these was correspondingly rich. The list compiled by the Franciscan Fathers (1910) was used as a point of departure and elaborated. No attempt was made to stress modern innovations.

The period of time spent by Hill with each informant varied considerably. In part it depended upon the depth of knowledge possessed by the individual and his other commitments. In some instances services were engaged for only a day and the informant reported on a single specialty; others were employed for several weeks. Occasionally fortuitous circumstances were the determining factors. For example, the relatively extensive use of PP (Fort Defiance) resulted not only from his qualifications but also from a heavy snowstorm which interrupted transportation for a considerable period.

Lamphere's fieldwork was done in the Eastern area at Sheep Springs over a fifteen-month period in 1965–66. Work specifically directed at Navaho material culture was done in several interviews between April and September 1966. Lamphere was specifically asked to verify the Navaho names of the traits, and where possible to provide translations for these terms. She was also asked to question her informants about additional Navaho terms for traits. The resulting data were sufficiently plentiful to warrant a separate heading in the descriptive chapters and in Appendix 1, where the data on distribution of traits by area are presented in tabular form.

Fishler's fieldwork was done in the Western part of the Navaho reservation during the first months of 1950. Obtaining data on material culture was not his primary purpose; hence information is lacking on many traits and there is frequently insufficient information on those that are described.

In the Comparative sections, data from the Franciscan Fathers (1910) and Gifford (1940) were utilized insofar as possible for each trait. The Franciscan Fathers' *Ethnologic Dictionary of the Navaho Language* was largely the work of Father Berard Haile, with the collaboration of Anselm Weber, Leopold

Ostermann, and Marcellus Troester. During his ten years in the Central area at St. Michaels, Father Berard spent much time in the study of the Navaho language and culture. The *Dictionary* was planned and edited during 1907–1909 and printed the following year (Wilken, 1955:118). As at Ramah, data were gathered from a relatively limited area, over a long period of time.

Gifford did fieldwork among twenty Southwestern Indian groups from July to November 1935. Two of his informants were Navaho. He questioned the Western Navaho informant first; later, after investigating several other tribes, he worked with the Eastern Navaho informant. During the interval Gifford had added to his trait list many new elements, about which he was unable to question the Western informant. Consequently his data for the Eastern area are more comprehensive than for the West.

In addition to the work mentioned above, other sources were frequently utilized for plotting traits according to area and for comparative purposes. Spanish sources were in general disappointing for the purposes of this book, with the exception of Benavides (1630; cf. Ayer, 1916) and the deponents of the Rabal manuscript (1744; cf. Hill, 1940a), who gave pertinent information on the Eastern region. Other than these and a few fragmentary and other hearsay accounts, the bulk of the data on the East was collected in the twentieth century.

A number of investigators worked at Chaco Canyon, New Mexico, during the twentieth century. Among these were Aberle, Bailey, Elmore, M. James, Malcolm, Toulouse, Whittemore, and Woodbury. Goddard recorded texts from an informant at Shiprock, and Oakes from one at Crownpoint. Wyman did research in the areas of Mariano Lake, Pinedale, and Smith Lake, and Bailey at Pinedale and Mariano Lake. Both Wheelwright and Newcomb worked at or from Newcomb (Nava), midway between Gallup and Shiprock, New Mexico; and Tremblay and others were at Farmington. Most of the early archaeology on the Navaho was done in the Eastern area. Malcolm, Toulouse, Whittemore, and Woodbury all worked at Chaco Canyon with C. Kluckhohn and Reiter. Dittert's archaeological study was in the area between Shiprock, Farmington, and Newcomb, New Mexico. Other investigations were made by Keur at Big Bead Mesa and Gobernador Canyon in the Gobernador region, and by Farmer in Blanco and Largo Canyons.

Fort Defiance was the point of departure or destination for nineteenth-century travelers to the Central Navaho country. Backus, Davis, and Eaton were there in the 1850's, as was Letherman, who spent three years at the Fort. Dellenbaugh visited Fort Defiance in his travels, which took him among other places to Kanab, Utah; Pueblo, Colorado; Flagstaff and Keams Canyon, Arizona; and Manuelito and Fort Wingate, New Mexico. Palmer's notes did not indicate the extent of his visit, but several references to the Navaho Agency imply that he was also at Fort Defiance. He also visited Keams Canyon in the West.

Between April 1881 and June 1882, Bourke was released from his position as aide-de-camp to General Crook "to the special duty of investigating the manners and customs of the Pueblo, Apache, and Navaho Indians" (Hodge, 1897:247). His descriptions of the Navaho were largely obtained at Fort Defiance during one or the other of his trips from Fort Wingate to the Navaho country in April and May 1881; he also visited Canyon de Chelly and Keams Canyon.

Fort Wingate was also a point of departure for investigations among the Central Navaho. Washington Matthews was the post surgeon there from October 1880 until April 1884, and again from 1890 to 1894. Between these two western tours of duty, he made two trips to the Navaho country, one of which was with the Hemenway Expedition in 1887. Shufeldt was also at Fort Wingate, where he apparently collected a number of artifacts for the U.S. National Museum. Many of these were later reported by Mason. Canyon de Chelly was visited in the nineteenth century by both Simpson and Mindeleff. It is probable that Simpson went through Washington Pass (east of Crystal, New Mexico) to explore the country east of the Chuska Mountains.

Many twentieth-century workers have also done research in the Central Navaho area. Newcomb and Reichard obtained data from informants at Lukachukai; Sapir and Hoijer at Crystal; Adair and Reichard at Ganado; Underhill and Young at the Navaho Agency at Window Rock; Bryan and Young did research on native dyes at Fort Wingate. Most of the investigations by the Coolidges were in the Central area, although they traveled widely throughout the reservation. Archaeological investigations in the Canyon de Chelly were pursued by Hurt and De Harport, among others.

The Western part of the Navaho area was included in the itineraries of a number of nineteenth-century travelers. Bourke visited Keams Canyon as did Dellenbaugh, Mooney, and Voth. Stephen lived there, with the trader Thomas Keam, from 1880 until his death in 1894 (McNitt, 1962:170). Culin visited Keams Canyon at the turn of the century. At Kayenta and in the surrounding area were Babington, Guernsey and Kidder, the Wetherills, and nearby at Marsh Pass, Page. Observations of Navaho houses by Page, however, encompassed a number of different areas. Dyk's informants in the *Son of Old Man Hat* (1938) were familiar with the Navaho country between Black Mountain and Keams Canyon; his later informant, Old Mexican, came from an area a few miles south of Aneth, Utah.

Appendix 1 (see p. 453) details the distribution of traits by source according to area. Symbols used in Appendix 1 indicate whether the trait was confirmed; denied; confirmed more often than denied; denied more often than confirmed; present but considered to be modern; whether a variation of the trait accomplished the same purpose; whether the trait was probably present but the data were not clear; and when the trait was unreported or data were lacking. Traits are grouped in categories and are discussed here in those groupings.

The category of ritual hunting includes four traits. The antelope corral, pitfall, and eagle pit occurred in all areas. The antelope or deer disguise was reported everywhere except at Ramah. Nonritual hunting includes eight traits. Seven of these (bird snare, blind, rodent snare, deadfall, reflector, rodent stick, and throwing club) were confirmed in all areas, although the throwing club was little used in the East. The rabbit net was reported by only one informant for the West; others denied its occurrence. It was unreported at Ramah, denied and unreported for the East and Central areas. The evidence for its presence is suspect.

Weapons include sixteen traits. In all areas the bow (either sinew-backed or self) was known, as were the associated traits—glue, bowstrings, and arrows.

The trussed bow was confirmed except at Ramah, and the elkhorn bow was confirmed only by Hill's Central and Western informants. Horn bows were denied by Hill's other informants, and at Ramah. This areal difference is possibly explained by Ute-Navaho contacts or a greater number of elk in the more remote parts of the reservation. Arrow tools were used in all areas, although the engraver was unreported for the East. The quiver, wrist guard, and sling were known in all areas. Firearms, powder horns, and ammunition were present in all areas although, except for the powder horn, unreported by informants in the East.

Gathering includes eight traits. The cactus picker, pinyon beater, carrying basket, and gathering of salt were reported by informants from all areas. There was no Ramah information on the cactus brush, but it was reported in the other three areas. The pinyon screen was reported at Ramah, but confirmed only by Lamphere's informants in the East and by informants of Sapir and Hoijer in the Central area. Both of Gifford's Navaho informants denied the occurrence of the seed beater (as did Hill's Eastern and Central informants) and the gathering bag. There was no evidence from the Western area, but both were confirmed by informants at Ramah and in the Central area.

Agriculture includes nine traits, of which six (digging stick, hoe, rake, flail, some device for drying corn, and dam) were universal. The digging stick and hoe were well known in all areas. The rake, present in all areas, was regarded by most as modern. The shovel was reported by Lamphere's informants, by Hill's Central and Eastern informants, and by the Franciscan Fathers; Ramah informants did not differentiate terminologically between shovel and hoe and used the same implement for both purposes. The drying of corn above the ground was reported in all areas, but there was considerable variation in the methods used to accomplish this task. Hill believed that dams were constructed in all areas, but Gifford's Western informant denied this trait. Ditches were reported except in the Ramah area; wells were reported except in the Western area.

Animal husbandry includes eight traits. Reported in all areas were corrals, sheep shears, and eagle cages. Kennels and ram aprons were reported except at Ramah. Water troughs were known only in Ramah and the Central area. The snow drag was reported in the East and by one informant from Ramah, who apparently used it only once. Chicken and turkey pens were known only at Ramah and in the East.

The category of horse equipment includes eighteen traits. There is a noticeable lack of information from the Eastern area. Gifford's informants were apparently questioned on only six of the traits, and Hill's data are derived mostly from informants in the Central and Western areas. The quirt, skin saddlebag, the yucca, rawhide, buckskin, and horsehair ropes, rope twister, and the branding iron were the only traits reported in all areas. The Ramah informant regarded the branding iron as modern, as did Gifford's Eastern informant the horsehair rope and rope twister. Traits for which there were no data from Hill's or Gifford's Eastern informants, but which otherwise were well reported, included the saddle, bridle, quirt, woven saddlebag, and hobble. There were no data from the Western area on chaps or on wool rope; none from Ramah or the Eastern area on the crupper. The pack saddle and rope wrench were reported only in the Central area, and the hitching post was reported only by Fishler's informant (FG) from Coalmine. The last is a trait largely of ritual significance.

Eight traits are included in the category of transportation and burdens, of which only the tumpline and some form of raft were reported in all areas. The wagon and sled were reported in Ramah and the Central area; litters and buckskin "trunks" were known in all areas but Ramah. The carrying pole was reported only at Ramah, and bridges were reported only by informants in the Central area.

The food category has been subdivided into traits dealing with storage, preparation, cooking, and utensils. Of the seven traits pertaining to storage, five (the water bag, pitched basket bottle, storage cave, storage pit, and storage bag) were known in all areas. The gourd canteen was reported everywhere except at Ramah; the sizer was reported only in the Eastern and Central areas. Given the sizer's function, however, and the prevalence of the pitched basket bottle, its distribution is probably universal. Of the six traits associated with the preparation of food, only two—the mortar and the stirring paddle—were not known in all areas. The mortar was denied in the Central area by Hill's informants, but confirmed by both of Gifford's informants, at Ramah, and by Fishler's informants. The stirring paddle was denied at Ramah, but confirmed for all other areas. Five traits pertained to the cooking of food; griddles, skewers, roasting pits, and the earth oven were universally acknowledged. Gifford's Western Navaho informant denied using rocks to support cooking pots. This trait was unreported by other Western sources but informants from all other areas confirmed the practice. Utensils were grouped into nine varieties, of which wooden utensils, gourd or pottery spoons, and liquid swabs were confirmed in all areas. Horn spoons were denied at Ramah and by Hill's and Lamphere's Eastern informants; Gifford's Eastern informant maintained that their use was restricted to chanters. Basket dishes were not reported by informants from the Western part of the Navaho area, but were undoubtedly used. Stone bowls were denied by Gifford's Eastern informant and by one of Hill's Western informants, but other informants in the Central and Western areas confirmed them. The use of a cornhusk for a spoon was reported only by one of Hill's Eastern informants; toothpicks only at Ramah.

The housing category includes four traits, the various house types being considered as a unit. These were known in all areas, as were shades. Woven doorway mats were reported in all areas but Ramah. Ladders were reported only in the Eastern and Central areas; they were denied by both of Gifford's Navaho informants.

The five fire-making traits, firedrill, strike-a-light, slow match and torch, wooden poker, and firewood, were reported in all areas, although both of Gifford's Navaho informants regarded the strike-a-light as modern.

Of the four traits in the category of multipurpose tools, the axe, hammer, and knife were known in all areas, but data on the knife sheath were rare and the trait was not reported in the Western area. The category of miscellaneous equipment includes three traits. The grass brush was confirmed as a broom at Ramah and in the Central area; it was known by Gifford's informants, but its use as a broom was not specified. Clothes hangers were reported in all areas. The fly swatter was reported only by Hill's White Cone informant (GH); Lamphere's informant knew only of the modern fly swatters.

All varieties of bedding (sleeping mat, rabbit skin blanket, dressed skin blankets and robes, sheepskin bedding, and woolen blankets) were reported by at least one informant from each area. No data for the five traits in the category of cradles were provided by Hill or Fishler for the West. Both the split- and the solid-back cradle were probably known in all areas, but from Gifford's description it is impossible to tell which is indicated. The laced rod cradle was reported in the Central area by Hill's informants, the Franciscan Fathers, and the Coolidges, but not elsewhere. At Ramah a flimsy temporary cradle was used until the child was old enough for the more permanent type. Canopies and some version of the cradle swing were reported in all areas, although data were scanty.

Six of the eight traits in the skin-dressing category were reported in all areas, rawhide, buckskin, beaming post, bone beaming tool, rubbing stone, and wringing stick. The other two, the metal beaming tool and the stone scraper, were recorded everywhere but in the Eastern area, where the former was not recorded and the latter was denied.

The category of dyes and paints consists of six dyes and stirring sticks. There is little information for the Western area. Red, black, and probably white were known in all areas. The Franciscan Fathers confirmed the use of white clay, but did not specify its use for making dye. Yellow and blue dyes and stirring sticks were confirmed at Ramah, and in the Eastern and Central areas, but not in the West. Green dye was not known at Ramah, but was confirmed by several informants in the Central and Eastern areas; Gifford's Western informant denied it.

Sewing equipment includes nine traits, seven of which (bone awl, metal awl, yucca thread, sinew thread, thongs, knots, and knitting needles) were confirmed in all areas. Data on sewing bags were recorded only at Ramah, and buckskin cord only at Ramah and by Gifford's Eastern informant.

The category of apparel was subdivided according to type. Women's garments includes thirteen traits, of which six were known in all areas. Bast and skin clothing were confirmed except by informants at Ramah, where there was no information. Note that Ramah was settled after the return from Fort Sumner and that informants stated that bast and skin clothing were used until the captivity. The first type of women's woolen dress (Type A), described at Ramah, was confirmed in the Central area but not elsewhere, as was the accompanying belt. Clothing confirmed by informants from all areas included the *bil* (woolen dress, Type B) and belt (which Gifford's Eastern informant regarded as modern), the cotton dress, shawl, and the cotton blouse and skirt. Men's garments included eleven traits, of which seven (skin shirt, breechclout, buckskin short trousers, cloth trousers, buckskin and knitted leggings, and buckskin belt) were confirmed by informants from all areas. Woven garters were confirmed everywhere except in the East, where they were unreported. The woven shirt was reported in the Ramah and Central areas. The men's cotton shirt was reported only in the Eastern and Central areas, although this garment has been universal in the Navaho area in recent years. Bark leggings were denied by informants from Ramah and unreported in the East, but confirmed by informants from the Central and Western areas.

Headwear includes seven traits, of which five (hair tie, headband, buckskin and wildcat skin caps, and wooden awl) were known in all areas. There was no information from the Eastern area on the basketry hat, and data on its occurrence in other areas were scanty. Caps of mountain lion skin were reported only in the Central area and by Hill's Western informants; they were denied at Ramah, but confirmed by informants from other areas. Of the four footwear traits, moccasins, overshoes, and snowshoes were confirmed by informants from all areas, although Gifford's Eastern informant disagreed with others concerning the use of overshoes and snowshoes. Sandals were denied at Ramah, but confirmed by informants from other areas. Of the miscellaneous traits, the fur scarf and skin mittens were confirmed in all areas, as was the pouch for personal equipment. Knitted mittens were acknowledged by informants from Ramah and the Central area, and canes by informants in all areas but the West, where there was no information.

Ornamentation includes nine traits. The common forms of ornament—the necklace, earrings, and bracelet—were reported in all areas, as were face and body paint. Drills and tweezers were also noted in all areas. Rings and silver buttons were reported except in the Western area. Tattooing was denied by Gifford's informants, and regarded as modern by Hill's Central and Western informants.

Of the three traits in the category of hygiene, yucca soap and the menstrual pad were reported in all areas. Only Bailey and Lamphere supplied data on abdominal binding.

In the ritual chapter, nineteen traits are included in the category of ceremonies and curing. Of these, seven (sweathouse, sweathouse rocks, tongs, bugaboo owl, medicine bag, shell containers, and animal fetishes) were reported in all areas, and an additional six were reported in three areas. The latter included cased bags, horn containers, and masks, all unreported in the West; also stone boiling and gourd containers, unreported at Ramah, and baskets, unreported in the East. Medicine stoppers and prayersticks were confirmed at Ramah and in the Central area; it is probable that both were used throughout the Navaho area. Informants from the Eastern and Western areas confirmed the use of splints. Ramah informants alone reported lightning mats. Informants in the Central area alone confirmed the use of wooden boxes. The cranebill was reported from the Central and Western areas, but since it was used in the Flint Way, it can be assumed to be reservation-wide.

Fifteen traits make up the category of musical instruments. Ten of these (gourd, rawhide, and hoof rattles, basket and pottery drums, loop drumstick and drumming stick, flute, whistle, and bullroarer) were reported in all areas. Four more (rawhide drum, stomping pole, musical bow, and musical rasp) were reported in all areas except Ramah, and one (the yucca drumstick) by informants from the Eastern and Central areas. The last was denied by Gifford's Western informant; since it was used in several chantways, however, there is no question of its universality. In view of the high degree of homogeneity of these traits throughout the Navaho area, it is probable that any gaps in these data, as well as in the category of ceremonies and curing, are the result of deficient fieldwork, or, as noted above, of a superficial coverage for comparative purposes of the published sources on religion.

Warfare includes four traits, plus the bow and arrow and the buckskin cap discussed above. Of the four, the lance, some form of war club, and the shield were confirmed by informants from all areas. Gifford's informants disagreed with others about the form of the war club. "Armor" was reported from the Eastern and Central areas and at Ramah; both Gifford's and Fishler's informants denied this trait.

In the chapter on recreation, the category of games includes nine traits, of which seven (hoop and pole, shinny, archery, stick race, moccasin game, seven cards, and women's stick dice) occurred in all areas. The horse race was not described by informants from the Eastern area, and the button game, an easily improvised pastime, was recorded only by Fishler.

Six traits are included in the category on toys. There is variation among the areas. Figurines and string figures (cat's cradles) were reported in all areas. Tops were reported in all but the Eastern area; willow horses were recorded at Ramah, Sheep Springs, and Black Mountain, and swings were reported except at Ramah. Buzzers were reported in the Central and Western areas, but were denied by both of Gifford's Navaho informants.

In the category on smoking, both pipes and the accompanying tobacco pouches were reported in all areas.

In order to arrive at some approximation of the degree of homogeneity between areas and throughout the reservation, a summary tally was made of the data in Appendix 1 (see p. 460). For purposes of tabulation a trait was considered present if it was confirmed by at least one source (whether completely confirmed, more confirmed than denied, or more denied than confirmed), if it was probable but the data were not clear, if the trait was reported to be modern, and if a variation of the trait was used. Percentages were then computed on the basis of a total of 263 traits.

Of the 263 traits, 215 or almost 82 per cent were confirmed at Ramah. Six were denied and there were no data on 42 traits. If the unreported traits are examined it is evident that the percentage figure can be increased. Some form of the fly swatter was probable; the hitching post, musical rasp, yucca drumstick, and stone boiling all have ritual associations and were presumably present. The cotton shirt was also certainly present. In addition, there were no data on the bast apron, skin apron, skin skirt, skin dress, bark leggings, sandals, and the woven doorway mat. Lack of information on these traits is understandable since they were all obsolescent by Fort Sumner times, and Ramah was founded in the post–Fort Sumner period.

The data on the Eastern area show 218 traits, or 83 per cent confirmed, 11 denied, and 34 unreported. As is the case with Ramah, when unreported items are examined, a re-evaluation is possible. For example, Hill was aware of the existence of the following traits in the Eastern area, but failed to record or question informants concerning them because of the pressure of time and focus on other interests: firearms, ammunition, water trough, bridle and bit, saddle, hobble, and wagon. Other traits were undoubtedly used in the area, such as toothpicks, the hitching post, and such traits in the ritual category as baskets, cranebills, medicine stoppers, prayersticks, and possibly lightning mats.

Two hundred and forty-eight of the 263 traits, or 94 per cent, were confirmed for the Central area. This is not surprising, since it was the most thoroughly worked area of the reservation. Only two items were denied and 13 unreported. Abdominal binding and buckskin cord were probably known, as were several of the traits that have been assumed present in other areas, such as toothpicks, the fly swatter, lightning mats, and possibly splints. If these are considered present, then all but seven of the traits were present in the Central area.

An analysis of the Western data shows 212 traits confirmed, 13 denied, and 38 unreported, almost an 81 per cent confirmation. When the previous procedures are followed and items unreported but observed by Hill (wagon, water trough, chaps, baskets, rings, buttons, cotton shirts) are included and the probable ones (well, blue and yellow dye, dye stirring sticks, horn containers, medicine stopper, mask, prayerstick, and yucca drumstick) are added, as well as those considered in the other areas (snow drag, toothpick, and lightning mat), the West has a confirmation percentage second to the Central area.

Even though the Navaho are scattered over an area of some twenty-five thousand square miles, this homogeneity of culture is predictable. It stems from several causes. First, the natural resources are similar throughout the area. Second, because the majority of the tribe was held captive at Fort Sumner from 1864 to 1868 and was thus restricted in area and activity, the Navaho had ample opportunity for the exchange of knowledge and ideas. The cultural homogeneity encouraged by the captivity was abetted, on their return to the reservation, by the issuance of government supplies and equipment, which included such items as livestock, clothing, and wagons, and by the subsequent arrival of traders and missionaries who made new but similar products and ideas available even to the remote areas of the territory. In recent years this cultural homogeneity has become even more marked.

Distribution of Traits through Time

In this section an attempt is made to show the distribution of Navaho traits through time and to indicate changes that have taken place during various periods. Among the Navaho, change has been a constant feature for many centuries, as Aberle (1963) has stressed; therefore, any attempt to define a static "aboriginal" or "native" culture is not only doomed to failure, but also presents a distorted picture of Navaho life.

A variety of sources has been utilized for our data on change. These include archaeological reports, historical accounts, Navaho mythology, the results of past and contemporary research by ethnologists, as well as the information derived from our own informants.

Prior to the last decade there were few reports on Navaho archaeology. In the last ten years, however, much has been done, particularly in connection with Navajo Land Claims cases and the Salvage Archaeology program of the Museum of New Mexico in cooperation with the National Park Service. Works by David M. Brugge (1963) and Edith L. Watson (1964) are among those published based on Land Claims archaeology. Other monographs by Alfred E. Dittert (1958) and James J. Hester (1963), together with others (Dittert, Hester, and Eddy, 1961; and Hester and Shiner, 1963) are among the Navajo Project Studies in salvage archaeology. The trait descriptions and tabulations were completed before most of these works were available and therefore much of the data contained in them has not been utilized in this book.

Mythology has been sparingly used to assess time because it is frequently misleading. It is known, for example, that the Spanish introduced horses into the Southwest in the sixteenth century. Lacking historical documentation, one might infer a greater antiquity since legends dealing with the origin of horses among the Navaho have become thoroughly integrated in the body of Navaho mythology; horses were created for Turquoise Boy, the son of Changing-Woman (Sapir and Hoijer, 1942:109–127; also Hill field notes).

Historical sources cover a span of over three hundred years. Those prior to 1800 provide meager information, although such early visitors as Benavides and the deponents of the Rabal manuscript are exceptions. After 1800 there were substantial increases in the number of reports dealing with the Navaho. These observations by early travelers have also been utilized with caution because they were often fragmentary and incomplete. Pattie, Pike, and Jacob Robinson traveled through the area at this time. Their failure to mention a trait need not mean that the trait was absent, a point which is often overlooked by anthropologists. Conversely, obsolescent traits kept as heirlooms must be treated in proper perspective.

Sources available for the period between 1850 and 1864 include Backus, Bartlett, Davis, Eaton, Letherman, Simpson (1849), and Whipple and Ives. Between the 1870's and 1890's men who were to lay the ground work for ethnology arrived in the area. Among others, these included Culin, Dellenbaugh, Mindeleff, Palmer, Powell, Putnam, Thompson, Bourke, Matthews, Shufeldt, Stephen, Voth, and Welsh. The next decade saw works by Curtis, the Franciscan Fathers, Hollister, Hough, James, and Pepper, as well as those mentioned above.

Our own material was collected over a long period of time. In terms of informants' experience it covers more than a century of first-hand and second-hand knowledge. The age span of informants is greatest at Ramah (the oldest informant was born in 1845, the youngest in 1940), and observations there covered the longest time period of any area. The dividing line between generations is often marked. Thus, an informant's familiarity with various traits might give clues to the date of obsolescence, although not necessarily to the antiquity of the items. Several of Hill's informants were fourteen years old when they were taken to Fort Sumner; the oldest for whom a birth date is available was born in 1843, the youngest in 1900. Lamphere's oldest informant was born in 1891, the youngest in 1926. Fishler's best (and oldest) informant was born in 1868, others between 1878 and 1910.

A list of the date and place of birth of each informant is given in Appendix 2. Although it was anticipated that age differentials might be useful for placing traits in time, analysis demonstrated no consistent relationship between age and knowledge of culture content. Younger individuals were frequently as well informed as those years their senior.

The data from our own informants were variable. Hearsay evidence only was available for some traits; informants recounted what parents had told them about the way of life "a long time ago." In other instances, those questioned had seen items but had not used them. In still other cases, informants had both manufactured and utilized the objects.

The information from our informants plus that from all sources mentioned above was examined for data on the time and place or agent of introduction of each trait and its obsolescence or extent of obsolescence. The data were ordered on a chart in accordance with the date of introduction or obsolescence; gaps, however, were sufficiently numerous to render the tabulation relatively useless. In an attempt to determine whether broader patterns could be discerned, we then tabulated the data by decade (using the same criteria of date of introduction or obsolescence), but for several reasons this too proved to have little utility. In the first place materials from earlier and contemporary writers as well as much of our own were collected without the idea of time and change in mind. In many instances descriptions were not comparable and the dates of introduction and obsolescence were educated guesses.

Granting the variability of the data and the way in which they were collected, it is still possible to propose some generalizations concerning change through time, and these are presented in the following pages.

Most traits in the ritual hunting grouping (the antelope and deer disguise, the pitfall, and the eagle pit) were obsolete shortly after the turn of the twentieth century; the antelope corral was probably used in some areas until the mid 1920's. Wild game became increasingly rare and was replaced to a large extent by domesticated animals. Eagles are still taken for their feathers, but the current practice is to rob the nests of the young rather than to utilize the eagle pit.

Several traits of nonritual hunting were extant in the 1930's and are probably still used to a limited extent; these include the bird snare, the reflector, and the rodent stick. Only one informant knew of the rabbit net; other informants denied its occurrence. It is probable that it was never a part of the Navaho culture. The blind was not commonly used after 1900, but may have remained in use in the mountain areas (Lamphere's informant PM knew of its construction). The throwing club was apparently little used after 1920, and the rodent snare was obsolete by 1930. The deadfall probably became obsolete between 1910 and 1920.

Among weapons, the bow and arrow (Traits 13–19) became obsolete except for ceremonial or recreational use about 1900. The sling also declined in use except as a toy. Arrow tools (arrow wrench, sandstone smoother, and engraver) probably were retained since arrows continued to be made for recreational and ceremonial purposes. There was, however, no evidence that they were manufactured much after 1900 and those that exist can be classed as heirlooms, as can the quiver. The wrist guard is now ornamental rather than functional. Modern firearms, introduced in the nineteenth century, gradually replaced the earlier weapons.

Some of the traits associated with gathering, such as the cactus picker, gathering bag, and carrying basket, appear to have become obsolete. Others are apparently still used, including the cactus brush, seed beater, pinyon screen, and possibly the pinyon beater. Salt from the saline deposits is still preferred to that purchased in the trading posts.

Agricultural traits appear to be retained to a large extent. Flails and drying platforms or frames are still used. The digging stick, hoe, and wooden rake and shovel have been replaced by modern implements. Irrigation (dam, ditch, well) was introduced after the return from Fort Sumner, and its use continues. Although animal husbandry has existed among the Navaho since at least

1700, early sources fail to mention traits associated with this occupation. Data from informants indicate that except for the corral and eagle cage, most traits pertaining to animal husbandry were of reasonably recent introduction. Sheep shears and the ram apron assuredly are. All these traits, plus the snow drag, kennels, chicken and turkey pens, and the water trough, are still used. Water for livestock is now often obtained from wells drilled by the tribe. Windmills are used to operate the pumps.

Traits pertaining to horse equipment give evidence of greater antiquity than those pertaining to other branches of animal husbandry. The hitching post was said to have been used by the "early Navaho" and was not generally known. The rope and buckskin bridles are no longer used; the silver-mounted bridle, introduced in the early nineteenth century, was rare by 1940. Modern equipment, homemade or purchased (or a combination) has replaced the more traditional tack. The same applies to saddles. The western stock saddle was introduced about the turn of the century, and it gradually replaced the wooden forked-stick saddle, although this was still used until the 1940's. The crupper and skin saddlebag were rarely used by 1920; at the same time, chaps were beginning to be worn. Whether or not the pack saddle is still used is unknown. The quirt, woven saddlebag, and hobble are still used. Ropes are required for working livestock and setting up the loom. Earlier these were made of buckskin, rawhide, horsehair, wool, and yucca. Some ropes made of these materials may still be used, but by 1940 they had been almost entirely replaced by commercial products obtained at the trading posts. For obvious reasons the use of the rope twister and rope wrench has lapsed. The branding iron is used today.

Of the traits associated with transportation and burdens, the litter and carrying pole are probably obsolete, as is the buckskin "trunk," which has been replaced by blankets, boxes, or suitcases. The tumpline is obsolete except for its possible use with the cradle. When bridges were introduced is unknown, and the sled is probably a modern device; both are still used when and where required. Individuals may also use some form of raft if no other means is available to cross a body of water. The wagon is still seen on the reservation, but as more roads are built or improved it is being rapidly or entirely replaced by the pickup truck.

The traits pertaining to the storage of food, except those still used for ritual purposes, are now obsolete, and have been for several decades. These include the means of carrying water (water bag, gourd canteen, and pitched basket bottle), which have been supplanted by modern containers. The sizer continues in use in the preparation of materials for such basketry as is made—usually for ceremonial purposes. The storage cave was rarely used after the turn of the century, but apparently the storage pit was used until the 1930's, as was the storage bag. As a container for ritual items, the storage bag retains its original purpose.

The old methods of preparing and cooking food are still used, but less than formerly. The mortar and stirring paddle are obsolete. The metate and mano and the grass brush and stirring sticks are usually reserved for ceremonial requirements. Stirring sticks, however, are as effective as they ever were and are occasionally used in nonritual cooking. Most traits used in cooking (griddle, skewer, or spit, pot supports, roasting pit, and earth oven) are extant, and are used especially for ceremonials—the roasting pit, for example. The stone griddle was replaced by the metal griddle in the 1930's, and since that time the Pueblo-style earth oven has increased in use.

Most older utensils (including stone bowls, most wooden utensils, gourd, horn, and pottery ladles) have become obsolete and have been replaced by commercial wares. Where older forms remain extant they are reserved primarily for ceremonial use. Cornhusk spoons, liquid swabs, and toothpicks are undoubtedly still extant.

Hogans and shades are still popular. Few now use the conical, forked-pole type, but polygonal hogans with cribwork roofs are plentiful, and both types are more plentiful in the more remote areas of the Western reservation than in the East. Innovations such as windows and plank and tarpaper roofs are in evidence, and doorway mats have been replaced by blankets or framed doors. Houses of the Spanish-American type have been adopted by a number of the Navaho. Cinderblock houses are also becoming prevalent, especially in the more populated areas near the trading posts or towns. Ladders, except for purchased ones, are obsolete.

Most of the traits pertaining to fire making are obsolete. The firedrill, slow match and torch, and wooden poker are still used for ritual purposes, but the strike-a-light was replaced by matches before the turn of the century, and any convenient stick or piece of metal is used as a poker. Firewood is still gathered, and often used in oil drum stoves as well as open fires.

Stone axes, hammers, and knives have been replaced by their metal counterparts, although the stone knife is still used in a ceremonial capacity. The knife sheath may be of recent introduction, and is reserved for use with metal knives; it is probably extant. Brooms, fly swatters, and clothes hangers are still used.

Sheepskins and goatskins and modern woolen blankets are the common forms of bedding; sleeping mats, rabbit skin blankets, and dressed skin blankets and robes are now obsolete. The various types of cradles, with the possible exception of the rod type, are still used, and some sort of cradle swing is probable.

Skin dressing methods are still employed, although buckskin and rawhide are less used than at the end of the nineteenth century. The bone beaming tool has become obsolete and has been replaced by one of metal. The stone scraper has apparently become obsolete except for ceremonial use. The rubbing stone and wringing stick may still be used.

Native dyes and paints are less used than formerly. All were apparently known in the 1930's. Dye stirring sticks and white dye are still used; blue dye was common until the 1890's. The others, though still known, have often been replaced by commercial forms. Their continued use is frequently at the instigation of traders.

The buckskin sewing bag has probably been replaced by a cloth one or another container, although some of its contents have been retained; sinew thread is still used in making moccasins, yucca thread may be used as a temporary measure and is still used for ritual purposes. The bone awl or needle may be used occasionally in making baskets, but its general use ended by 1910. The metal awl, introduced after the Fort Sumner period, was widespread in the early part of the twentieth century and is still used. Wooden knitting needles were rare by 1890; wire needles were introduced about then and had become common by 1910. Men continued knitting long after women stopped, but by the 1930's knitting was rare. Thongs used to sew buckskin clothing were no longer used after Fort Sumner, but thongs and buckskin cord were probably used as needed in the absence of other threads long after that time. Thongs are still used as saddle ties.

A great number of changes have taken place in Navaho clothing. Bast clothing, including aprons, bark leggings, and sandals, was obsolete or rare before most of the informants were born. Skin clothing for women (the skin apron, skirt, shirt, and dress) was worn until the Fort Sumner captivity. The less common form of women's woolen dress became obsolete shortly thereafter, and the rope belt worn with it was replaced by the woven sash or belt. The more common woolen dress (the *bil*) was largely replaced by cotton in the 1870's and 1880's, though some were seen in the early twentieth century. The belt worn with this dress is still used, especially on dress occasions or for ritual. The introduction by the traders in the 1870's and 1880's of calico cloth created a stylistic revolution among the Navaho women, who quickly adapted the style of the pioneer women's long calico dresses to their own use (Gilpin, 1968:72). Navaho women generally preferred the long skirt and a blouse (which most frequently was of velveteen), but many wore a simple cotton dress. The woven women's shawl has largely been replaced by the Pendleton blanket, introduced by C. N. Cotton in the 1890's (Gilpin, 1968:72). These blankets are worn today.

Men's clothing was slower to change than women's. Buckskin shirts, short trousers, and leggings were still worn to a limited extent in the 1870's and 1880's; but by 1900 buckskin clothing was obsolete. Contrary to our initial opinion, the plain woven shirt apparently went out of vogue by the 1880's. It was never very common. The cotton shirt and cloth trousers introduced by the traders in the 1870's and 1880's quickly became the usual apparel for men, as were calico dresses for women. The breechclout was little seen after 1920, but it was worn ceremonially in 1945 and is presumably so worn today. Evidence on knitted leggings is contradictory. One informant thought that they were introduced during the Fort Sumner captivity; another observer saw them a decade earlier. Some thought they disappeared just after the Fort Sumner period, others that they continued to be worn into the twentieth century. Woven garters were worn with both knitted and buckskin leggings, and were apparently still worn at the beginning of the twentieth century. The buckskin belt has been replaced by the ornamental concho belt, which is still popular.

Hair ties were replaced by simple cord about the turn of the century, and skin headbands by those of cloth; both are still worn. The basketry hat may still be worn, but it is not, and never has been, a popular item. Skin caps (buckskin, mountain lion skin, and wildcat skin) were worn in warfare and for warmth until shortly after the Fort Sumner captivity; then those that were available were retained for ceremonial use. The wooden awl, originally used only in the decoration of hats, may still be used for other purposes.

Sandals made of woven fibers were part of the earliest Navaho costume, and were early replaced by moccasins. These are extant, although in many instances they have been replaced by shoes. Hand-made overshoes and snowshoes have been superseded by commercial products.

The fur scarf, worn to protect the neck from the scratchy woven shirt, ceased to be worn when the woven shirt did, in the late nineteenth century.

Skin scarves are occasionally worn as part of ceremonial attire. Both skin and knitted mittens have been replaced by commercial products. Pockets in modern garments have taken the place of the pouch for personal equipment, and women carry pocketbooks. Navaho at Kayenta still may carry their belongings in a pouch, for an elaborately decorated leather one was observed in 1937, and in 1968, L. Kluckhohn saw a man carrying a khaki pouch over his shoulder, a modern variant of the trait. Canes are still used as necessary to assist the infirm, and in the Night Chant.

Most ornaments are extant. Turquoise and shell beads were used in necklaces and earrings; they are worn today and old ones are prized heirlooms. Brass and copper were used to make bracelets and rings in the middle of the nineteenth century, but by 1890 silver was plentiful, and it came to be the more common medium. Rings apparently came into vogue in the middle of the nineteenth century, and by 1910, a great variety of the styles were being produced. Silver buttons postdated the Fort Sumner captivity, and areas may have adopted stylistic differences in decoration, as Gilpin noticed at Navaho Mountain in 1954 (Gilpin, 1968:72). Face and body paint is now reserved for ceremonial requirements, except for commercially produced cosmetics worn by acculturated Navaho women. Tattooing was said to be a common practice at boarding schools, and thus is of recent (early twentieth-century) introduction. Tweezers were made when metal became available, in the latter part of the nineteenth century.

Yucca soap and other traits associated with hygiene are extant. Since many births now take place in hospitals, the use of abdominal binding may be declining. Materials for menstrual pads have changed—modern types are now purchased.

Traits pertaining to ritual (Chapter 4) are, for the most part, still extant. Certainly the sweathouse and sweathouse rocks are still used, and in all areas. By the 1930's, however, pitchforks and shovels were being used in place of wooden tongs to move the hot rocks. Fishler's description of stone boiling from the Western area in the 1950's indicates that it is still practiced in connection with healing. Splints are probably still applied as necessary to set broken limbs. The bugaboo owl was rare by 1910, but was well enough known that informants could make specimens at Ramah in the 1930's.

Lightning mats were known only at Ramah, and by the 1940's informants had difficulty reproducing them. Wooden boxes are probably still used on occasion; both the medicine bag and the cased bag were commonly seen in the 1940's and are probably retained today, though cloth bags have sometimes been used when unwounded buckskin was not available. Baskets no longer are used in a non-ceremonial capacity, but are retained in ritual as are the gourd, horn, and shell containers, wherever they are available. Shell for containers was introduced shortly after the turn of the century. It is probable that animal fetishes are still carried in pollen sacks. The use of cranebills and medicine stoppers in Flint Way insures that these traits are still preserved. Masks were observed at Ramah in 1949, and are included in the paraphernalia of the Night Chant. Prayersticks are also presumably extant.

Among the musical instruments, the gourd rattle is extant, but the nineteenth-century form of the rawhide rattle—made of bison hide—has been replaced by one of cowhide; and hoof rattles, also made with the hooves of game animals, are rarely made, though some may be preserved as heirlooms. The basket drum is still used, and with it the yucca drumstick, as are the pottery drum and loop drumstick. Spontaneous timekeepers, such as the rawhide drum and the stomping pole, may still be used. The drumming stick has become an item of spontaneous usage also, like the stomping pole. The flute was introduced in the middle of the nineteenth century, and appears to have lost favor in the 1920's. Whistles have a wide distribution and some form is doubtless extant; the bullroarer is ritually important and thus extant. The musical bow appears to be a spontaneous toy, and the musical rasp, as such, is also in use at present.

Traits pertaining to warfare (the lance, war club, shield, and "armor") are obsolete and have been since the Fort Sumner period. Some Navaho, especially in the Western area, may have kept the lance and shield as heirlooms.

Most games were obsolescent at the end of the nineteenth century and have been played infrequently since then. Among these are the hoop and pole game, shinny, the stick race, and seven cards. Shinny was often played in the nineteenth century; by 1900 it was rarely played except by school children. Recently, however, the game has been revived and has been played at Ramah. Archery contests enjoyed decreasing popularity as the bow ceased to be used as a weapon, and they were probably obsolete by 1920. Individual contests, however, continued long after. The moccasin game is not often played at Ramah, but it is still enjoyed elsewhere on the reservation. The women's stick dice game is another pastime that seems to have gone out of vogue and then to have been revived. The button game is probably extant.

Toys are extant. Whether old forms or modern ones are used probably depends upon availability and individual preference. This is especially true of figurines and dolls. Navaho-made wooden tops seem to have been especially popular at the turn of the century, but whether or not they have been replaced by modern ones is not known. Although willow horses were said to be obsolete at Ramah in the 1940's, it is likely that such an impromptu pastime was known on the reservation much later and may be extant today. Swings were said to be of recent (1920's) introduction. String figures and the buzzer are probably extant.

Navaho smoke, but pipes and the tobacco pouch were little used after the end of the nineteenth century. Modern cigarettes are preferred.

Since the completion of this manuscript there have appeared several historically oriented publications dealing with change in Navaho culture through time. Among them are Underhill (1954), Wilken (1955), Hester (1962), Smith (1966), Gilpin (1968), and Young (1968). Young's carefully researched paper is of particular value because it covers the totality of Navaho history. In it he delineates a number of epochs and demonstrates how historical circumstances have fostered or inhibited cultural changes. Where his area of inquiry overlaps our own he confirms our findings.

It is generally accepted that the North American homeland of the Athabaskan-speaking peoples was and is the interior of Alaska and Canada, a region of limited natural resources. As segments of this old core of population moved into other territories, they brought with them a meager inventory of culture and tended to absorb the habits of surrounding groups. The Navaho are no exception. Adair and Vogt (1949:557) commented on this "astonishing capacity to borrow elements of Pueblo, Spanish, and white American culture and fit them into pre-existent patterns" in all categories except language.

Pueblo contact was the source of the first of several far-reaching changes in Navaho culture. This took place prior to the arrival of Europeans in the sixteenth century. Cultural innovations included the adoption of the Pueblo agricultural complex, which profoundly altered the Navaho economic base, and, at the same time, the adoption of a few elements of Pueblo social structure and religion. Once inaugurated, Navaho-Pueblo relationships continued to be a source of innovation, periodically intensified by later Spanish pressure when people from many Pueblo groups took refuge among the Navaho prior to the Pueblo Revolt of 1680 and during the Reconquest, 1693–1698.

Shortly after this first adjustment Europeans arrived in the Southwest and the scene was set for other important changes in Navaho culture. There is no evidence that the Coronado Expedition (1540) had any impact on Navaho culture. When the Spanish returned in 1580, however, their influence began to be felt. This next period of Spanish-Mexican domination over the Navaho (roughly three hundred years) was characterized by turmoil, strife, and fighting, the result of repressive measures by the Spanish and their descendants. Although this created a climate that was anything but conducive to the free exchange and dissemination of ideas, radical changes did occur in Navaho culture.

The most important of these resulted from the introduction of livestock—sheep, goats, some horses and cattle. Just when they became available is a matter of conjecture. It is known, however, that by the beginning of the eighteenth century the Navaho were engaged in pastoralism, thus adding another dimension to their economic base. As with agriculture the diffusion appears to be that of a whole complex of traits rather than individual items. Weaving, a trait previously borrowed from the Pueblo, increased markedly during this same period because of the ready availability of wool.

Although agriculture and pastoralism were the two major innovations, before 1800–1850 there is evidence that the Navaho became familiar with metals and possibly with metallurgy. Alterations also took place in the warfare complex, and in clothing and clothing styles.

The long span of Spanish-Mexican domination in the Southwest was terminated in 1846 when the United States assumed political authority in the area. The early years of the American period were characterized by the same instability, friction, raiding, and inept administration that had existed under earlier regimes. Finally in 1864 increased military pressure was brought to bear: Col. Kit Carson was sent to round up the Navaho. Eventually 8,354 were confined at Fort Sumner, where they remained until 1868, when by the Treaty of 1868 the Navaho Reservation was established. This was a traumatic experience to the Navaho, and Kit Carson and the "Long Walk" home are still remembered. It successfully terminated their ability to function effectively as a military force.

Although the sojourn at Fort Sumner was brief, it was to have consequences for both immediate and later change. For the first time many Navaho were able to observe and see in use traits of American material culture current in that period. The fact that many of these were in short supply and technical knowledge for their production was unavailable to the Navaho barred their diffusion at this time. This familiarity, however, created a climate favorable to a rapid takeover in later years when the individual traits became more readily available.

One noteworthy exception to this occurred in the area of clothing. When cotton cloth was introduced in quantity, it was rapidly accepted and substituted for older materials; styles of dress also shifted to conform to the American ones of that era. The obsolescence of older clothing materials and styles was very rapid and for all practical purposes was accomplished in two decades. A slightly slower transition took place in the war complex; as warfare became only a memory, its associated traits disappeared from use or were retained only for use in a ritual context.

There is also evidence for another type of change during the Fort Sumner period, and one that is unique in Navaho culture. Before 1864 the Navaho were located in widely scattered groups that functioned more or less independently of each other. Communication between these groups and with other peoples was sporadic. This fostered differentials in the degree of cultural change. At Fort Sumner the Navaho were forced to live in close proximity and for the first time had an opportunity to share each other's knowledge. Presumably this resulted in a consolidation of the total inventory of culture and led to a degree of cultural homogeneity that had previously been lacking. We believe that the high degree of similarity in the areal distribution of traits (see Appendix 1) was in part a carry-over from this experience.

On their return from Fort Sumner in 1868 the Navaho were faced with the formidable task of reestablishing their economy. There was a continual shortage of food. Government rations frequently failed to materialize or were in short supply. Droughts were common and crops were inadequate or failed to mature. In an effort to survive the Navaho began drifting away from government centers—Fort Wingate and later Fort Defiance. They occupied their former territories or settled in new areas, thus reestablishing the old pattern of semi-isolated autonomous groups. This in turn led to disputes over land rights and conflict between Navaho and American settlers, earlier European settlers, and other Indian tribes. But the Navaho survived and by 1890 they were faced not only with the problem of overpopulation but also with that of overgrazing.

In spite of these adverse conditions, however, the period between 1868 and 1900 was marked by developments that both helped alleviate some of the Navaho's problems and provided the foundations for the accelerated change that was to continue to the present. The first of these was the establishment of trading posts among the Navaho. Beginning in the 1870's, these continued to grow in numbers throughout the years. In part at least this growth was due to the advent of the railroad, another great event. By 1882–83 construction on the Atlantic and Pacific Railroad (later the Santa Fe) had reached within a few miles of the reservation and communication with the rest of the country was assured. A third development in this same period was the establishment of permanent missions among the Navaho. Often these combined schools and medical facilities with the teaching of Christianity. The advantages derived from the trading posts, the railroad, and the missions in terms of new ideas and products are obvious. They also meant a ready outlet for Navaho surpluses, especially wool and blankets, and to a lesser extent livestock.

Some gauge of the magnitude and rapidity of change following the return from Fort Sumner is apparent from the summary on pages 440–445. In terms of Navaho material culture, however, the emphasis shifted after 1880. Before that time the number of introductions and obsolescences remained about equal. After 1880, the number of obsolescent traits exceeded new ones by three or four to one until 1930, the last year for which we have adequate documentation. In some cases, such as ritual hunting, whole complexes and associated traits disappeared. In other instances single items disappeared from the cultural inventory. Partial obsolescence also occurred, either as a shift from one material to another, or as a change from practical to ceremonial use (for example, the firedrill). This is not to say that most of the "old" Navaho traits no longer exist; they still do, particularly in areas other than material culture.

The Navaho are notably acquisitive, and momentum for change has usually been derived from the outside. Sources have varied through time, as was indicated above. Not that the Navaho accepted blindly anything that was offered: There is ample evidence for selectivity and there is also evidence that the Navaho modified borrowed elements to conform them to prevailing Navaho patterns.

There are also several instances where the Navaho elaborated relatively simple traits; they sometimes achieved a complexity and perfection far beyond that practiced by the donor culture. One example of this is blanket weaving, derived from the Pueblo, in which the Navaho achieved technical perfection and virtuosity in design beyond that of the Pueblo. Another is the sand-painting altar, again derived from the Pueblo, which the Navaho developed into one of the finest expressions of nonliterate art.

There is no evidence that change in any culture has ever been uniform over time or area. Differential acculturation, with the possible exception of the Fort Sumner period, has always characterized the Navaho. The tribe has occupied a vast area and the settlement pattern has been one of small groups; communications and contacts have been extremely variable both within and outside the reservation. This has encouraged cultural diversity and the creation of cultural enclaves, some of which still exist. It has been facetiously stated that the number of miles from railroads can be used as an accurate gauge of the degree of the acculturation of any specific group. If interpreted in terms of equal accessibility to all forms of communication this is probably true. When data on the four areas Ramah, East, Central, and West are examined there is evidence that the Western area, the most isolated, exhibits the greatest degree of differential acculturation, suffers most from cultural lag, and retains a greater number of "old" Navaho traits than the other three.

The mid 1930's was a time of rapid change on the Navaho Reservation, as it was throughout America. Tremendous alterations have taken place in Navaho culture since the Great Depression and the Roosevelt era. Specific details on these can be consulted in the recent publications cited at the beginning of this section. An examination of these sources leads us to predict that differential acculturation is about at an end, and that in a relatively short time the material culture of the Navaho will become homogeneous. This prediction is based upon the tremendous recent developments in all media of communications. Improved and paved roads are common, the automobile and pickup truck have replaced older forms of land transportation, air fields are springing up on and near the reservation, telephones, radios and television sets are becoming more numerous, and literacy is increasing. All these factors have contributed to the eradication of regional differences and to the equal sharing of the total cultural heritage throughout the reservation.

Appendix 1. Distribution of Traits by Source According to Area

The following symbols are used in the table.

+	present	− +	trait more denied than confirmed
−	trait denied	+?	trait probable but data not clear
0	trait unreported or data lacking	m	trait reported to be modern
+ −	trait more confirmed than denied	v	variation of trait used

In the summary at the end of the table, a trait was considered present if it was designated + −, − +, m, v, or +? in the body of the table. Gifford's material and that of the Franciscan Fathers (FF) has been added to the appropriate areas. The "other" columns include data derived from all other published sources.

Distribution of Traits by Source According to Area

Trait	Ramah	East				Central			West			
		Hill	Lamphere	Gifford	Other	Hill	FF	Other	Hill	Fishler	Gifford	Other
					Subsistence							
Ritual Hunting												
1. Antelope corral	+	+	+	+	0	+	+	+	+	+	+	0
2. Disguise	0	0	0	+	0	+	+	0	+	+	+	0
3. Pitfall	+	0	0	+	0	+	+	+	+	+	+	0
4. Eagle pit	+	0	0	+	+	+	+	+	+	0	−	0
Nonritual Hunting												
5. Bird snare	+	+	0	v	0	+	+	0	+	+	+	0
6. Blind	+	+?	+	−	0	+	0	0	+	0	+	0
7. Rodent snare	+	+	0	0	0	+	0	0	+	0	0	0
8. Deadfall	+	+	0	+	0	+	+	+	+	+	+	0
9. Reflector	+	+	v	0	0	+	+	0	+	+	+	0
10. Throwing club	+	0	0	− +	−	+	+	0	0	+	− +	0
11. Rodent stick	+	0	0	+	0	+	0	+	0	+	+	0
12. Rabbit net	0	−	−	−	0	−	0	0	−	− +	−	0
Weapons												
13. Sinew-backed bow	+	0	0	+	+	+	0	+	+	+	+	+
14. Glue	+	+	0	+	0	+	0	0	+	+	+	0
15. Self bow	+	0	0	+	0	+	+	0	0	+	+	0
16. Trussed bow	0	+	0	0	0	+	0	0	+	0	0	0
17. Elkhorn bow	−	−	−	0	0	+ −	0	0	− +	0	0	0
18. Bowstring	+	0	+	+	0	+	+	0	+	+	+	0
19. Arrow	+	+	+	+	+	+	+	+	+	+	+	+
20. Arrow wrench	+	+	0	+	+	+	+	0	+	+	+	0
21. Sandstone smoother	+	0	0	+	+	+	0	0	+	+	+	+
22. Engraver	+	0	0	0	0	+	0	0	+	0	+	0
23. Quiver	+	0	0	+	+	+	+	+	+	+	+	+
24. Wrist guard	+	0	0	0	+	+	+	+	0	+	0	0
25. Sling	+	0	+	+	0	+	+	0	0	+	+	0
26. Firearms	+	0	0	0	0	+	+	0	+	0	0	0
27. Powder horn	+	0	+	0	0	+	+	0	+	0	0	0
28. Ammunition	+	0	0	0	0	0	+	0	+	0	0	0

Trait	Ramah	East				Central			West			
		Hill	Lamphere	Gifford	Other	Hill	FF	Other	Hill	Fishler	Gifford	Other
Gathering												
29. Cactus picker	+	0	0	+	+	+	+	0	+	0	+	0
30. Cactus brush	0	0	v	+	0	+	+	0	0	0	v	0
31. Seed beater	+	−	0	−	0	−	0	+	0	0	−	0
32. Pinyon beater	+	+	+	−	0	+	0	0	0	+	+	+
33. Pinyon screen	+	0	+	0	0	0	0	+	0	0	0	0
34. Gathering bag	+	+	0	−	0	+	+	0	0	0	−	0
35. Carrying basket	+	+	0	+	0	+	+	0	+	+	+	0
36. Salt	+	+	0	+	0	+	+	0	0	+	+	0
Agriculture												
37. Digging stick	+	+	0	+	+	+	+	0	+	+	+	0
38. Hoe	+	+	+	+	+	+	+	0	+	0	+	0
39. Shovel	+	+	+	0	0	+	m	0	0	0	0	0
40. Rake	m	+	0	0	0	0	m	0	+	0	0	0
41. Flail	+	+	+	+	0	+	0	0	+	0	+	+
42. Drying platform	+	+	v	v	0	v	0	0	v	+	v	0
43. Dam	+	+	0	+	0	+	+	+	+	0	−	0
44. Ditch	0	+	+	+	0	+	+	0	+	+	+	+
45. Well	+	0	+	0	0	+	−	0	0	0	0	0
Animal Husbandry												
46. Water trough	+	0	0	0	0	0	+	0	0	0	0	0
47. Corral	+	+	0	+	0	+	+	+	+	0	+	0
48. Snow drag	+	0	+	0	0	0	0	0	0	0	0	0
49. Ram apron	0	0	+	0	0	+	0	0	+	0	0	0
50. Sheep shears	+	+	0	0	0	+	+	+	+	0	0	0
51. Kennel	0	0	+	0	0	+	0	0	+	0	0	0
52. Chicken, turkey pens	+	0	+	+	+	0	−	0	0	0	0	0
53. Eagle cage	+	+	0	−	0	+	−	0	+	0	−	0
Horse Equipment												
54. Bridle and bit	+	0	0	0	0	+	+	+	+	+	0	0
55. Saddle	+	0	0	0	0	+	+	+	+	0	0	0
56. Crupper	0	0	0	0	0	+	+	0	+	0	0	0
57. Quirt	+	0	+	0	0	+	+	+	+	+	0	0
58. Chaps	+	0	+	0	0	+	0	+	0	0	0	0
59. Pack saddle	0	0	0	0	0	+	+	0	0	0	0	0
60. Skin saddlebag	+	+	0	+	0	0	+	+	+	0	0	0
61. Woven saddlebag	+	0	0	0	0	0	0	+	0	0	0	+
62. Hobble	+	0	0	0	0	+	+	+	+	0	0	+
63. Hitching post	0	0	0	0	0	0	0	0	0	+	0	0
64. Yucca rope	+	0	+ −	+ −	0	+	0	+	0	0	+ −	0
65. Rawhide rope	+	0	+	−	0	+	+	0	+	0	−	0
66. Buckskin rope	+	+	+	+	0	+	+	+	0	0	+	0
67. Wool rope	+	0	+	0	+	+	+	+	0	0	0	0
68. Horsehair rope	+	+	0	m	0	+	+	+	+	0	+	0

Distribution of Traits by Source According to Area (cont.)

Trait	Ramah	East				Central			West			
		Hill	Lamphere	Gifford	Other	Hill	FF	Other	Hill	Fishler	Gifford	Other
69. Rope twister	+	+	+	m	0	+	0	0	+	0	+	0
70. Rope wrench	0	0	0	0	0	+	0	0	0	0	0	0
71. Branding iron	m	+	+	0	0	+	+	0	+	0	0	0
Transportation and Burdens												
72. Wagon	+	0	0	0	0	+	+	0	0	0	0	0
73. Tumpline	+	+	+	+	0	+	+	0	0	0	+	0
74. Carrying pole	+	0	0	−	0	0	0	0	0	0	−	0
75. Litter	0	0	v	+	0	+	+	0	0	0	+	0
76. Buckskin "trunk"	0	0	+	+	0	+	0	0	0	0	+	0
77. Sled	+	0	0	0	0	0	m	+	0	0	0	0
78. Raft	+	+	0	v	+	+	+	0	0	0	v	0
79. Bridge	0	0	0	−	0	+	+	+	0	0	−	0
Food Storage												
80. Water bag	+	0	0	+	0	+	+	0	+	0	+	+
81. Gourd canteen	0	0	+	+	0	+	0	0	0	0	+	0
82. Pitched basket bottle	+	+	0	+	+	+	+	+	0	+	+	0
83. Sizer	0	+	v	0	0	+	0	0	0	0	0	0
84. Storage cave	+	0	0	+	+	+	0	0	0	0	+	0
85. Storage pit	+	+	0	+	0	+	+	+	+	+	+	+
86. Storage bag	+	+	0	+	+	+	0	0	+	+	+	+
Food Preparation												
87. Mortar	+	0	0	− +	0	0	0	0	0	+	− +	0
88. Metate	+	+	+	+	+	+	+	0	+	+	+	+
89. Mano	+	+	+	+	+	+	+	+	+	+	+	0
90. Grass brush	+	+	+	+	0	+	+	+	+	+	+	0
91. Stirring sticks	+	+	+	+	0	+	+	0	+	+	+	0
92. Stirring paddle	−	+	−	−	0	+	0	0	+	0	−	0
Cooking												
93. Griddle	+	0	0	+	0	+	+	+	+	+	+	0
94. Skewer	+	+	0	+	0	+	+	+	+	+	0	0
95. Pot supports	+	0	+	+	+	+	0	+	0	0	−	0
96. Roasting pit	+	+	+	+	+	+	+	+	+	0	+	+
97. Earth oven	+	0	+	−	0	+	m	0	0	+	−	0
Utensils												
98. Basket dish	+	0	0	+	0	+	+	0	0	0	0	0
99. Stone bowls	0	0	0	−	0	+	0	0	+ −	0	+	0
100. Wooden utensils	+	+	0	+	0	+	+	+	+	−	+	0
101. Gourd ladle, spoon	+	+	+	+	0	+	+	+	+	+	+	0
102. Horn spoons	−	−	−	+	0	+	0	+	+	0	0	0
103. Pottery	+	+	0	0	+	+	+	0	+	+	0	0
104. Cornhusk spoon	0	+	−	−	0	0	0	0	0	0	−	0
105. Liquid swab	+	+	v	+	0	+	0	0	0	0	+	0
106. Toothpicks	+	0	0	0	0	0	0	0	0	0	0	0

Distribution of Traits by Source According to Area (cont.)

		East				Central			West			
Trait	Ramah	Hill	Lamphere	Gifford	Other	Hill	FF	Other	Hill	Fishler	Gifford	Other

Shelter

Housing

Trait	Ramah	Hill	Lamphere	Gifford	Other	Hill	FF	Other	Hill	Fishler	Gifford	Other
107. House types	+	+	0	+	+	+	+	+	+	+	+	+
108. Woven doorway mats	0	+	+	0	0	+	+	+	+	0	0	0
109. Shade	+	+	0	+	+	+	+	+	+	+	+	+
110. Ladder	0	+	0	—	0	+	+	0	0	0	—	0

Fire Making

Trait	Ramah	Hill	Lamphere	Gifford	Other	Hill	FF	Other	Hill	Fishler	Gifford	Other
111. Firedrill	+	0	0	+	+	+	+	+	0	+	+	+
112. Strike-a-light	+	0	0	m	+	+	+	+	0	+	m	+
113. Slow match and torch	+	0	0	+	0	+	+	+	+	+	+	+
114. Wooden poker	+	0	0	0	+	+	+	+	+	+	0	+
115. Firewood	+	0	0	+	0	+	+	0	+	0	+	0

Multipurpose Tools

Trait	Ramah	Hill	Lamphere	Gifford	Other	Hill	FF	Other	Hill	Fishler	Gifford	Other
116. Axe	+	+	0	+	+	+	+	+	+	+	+	0
117. Hammer	+	+	0	—	+	+	+	0	0	0	+	0
118. Knife	+	0	0	+	+	+	+	0	+	+	+	+
119. Knife sheath	+	0	0	+	0	+	0	+	0	0	0	0

Miscellaneous Equipment

Trait	Ramah	Hill	Lamphere	Gifford	Other	Hill	FF	Other	Hill	Fishler	Gifford	Other
120. Broom	+	0	0	0	0	+	+	0	0	0	0	0
121. Fly swatter	0	0	m	0	0	0	0	0	+	0	0	0
122. Clothes hangers	+	0	+	0	0	+	0	0	+	0	0	0

Bedding

Trait	Ramah	Hill	Lamphere	Gifford	Other	Hill	FF	Other	Hill	Fishler	Gifford	Other
123. Sleeping mat	+	+	0	+	0	+	+	+	+	—	+	0
124. Rabbit skin blanket	+	+	0	+	0	+	+	0	+	+	—	+
125. Dressed skin blankets	+	+	—	+	+	+	+	+	+	+	0	0
126. Sheepskin bedding	+	+	+	0	0	+	+	0	+	+	+	0
127. Woolen blanket	+	0	0	+	0	0	+	0	0	0	+	0

Cradles

Trait	Ramah	Hill	Lamphere	Gifford	Other	Hill	FF	Other	Hill	Fishler	Gifford	Other
128. Split-back cradle	+	+	+	m	+	+	+	+	0	0	+	+
129. Solid-back cradle	+	0	0	m	0	+	+	+	0	0	+	0
130. Laced rod cradle	0	0	0	0	0	+	+	+	0	0	0	0
131. Cradle canopy	+	0	+	+	+	+	+	+	0	0	+	0
132. Cradle swing	+	0	0	+	0	0	+	0	0	0	+	0

Clothing

Skin Dressing

Trait	Ramah	Hill	Lamphere	Gifford	Other	Hill	FF	Other	Hill	Fishler	Gifford	Other
133. Rawhide	+	+	0	+	+	+	+	+	0	0	+	0
134. Buckskin	+	+	0	+	+	+	+	+	+	+	+	+
135. Beaming post	+	+	0	+	+	+	+	0	0	0	+	0
136. Bone beaming tool	+	+	0	+	+	+	+	0	0	0	+	0
137. Metal beaming tool	+	0	0	0	0	0	+	+	0	+	0	0
138. Stone scraper	+	0	0	—	0	+	+	0	+	+	+	0

Distribution of Traits by Source According to Area (cont.)

Trait	Ramah	East				Central			West			
		Hill	Lamphere	Gifford	Other	Hill	FF	Other	Hill	Fishler	Gifford	Other
139. Rubbing stone	+	+	0	−	+	+	0	0	+	+	+	0
140. Wringing stick	+	+	0	+	0	+	+	0	+	0	+	0
Dyes												
141. Red dye	+	+	0	+	+	+	+	+	0	0	+	+
142. Yellow dye	+	+	+	+	+	+	+	+	0	0	0	0
143. Black dye	+	+	0	+	+	+	+	+	+	0	0	0
144. Blue dye	+	0	+	+	+	+	+	+	0	0	−	0
145. White dye	+	0	+	0	+	0	+?	0	0	0	+?	0
146. Green dye	0	+	+	0	+	+	+	+	0	0	−	0
147. Dye stirring sticks	+	+	+	0	0	+	+	0	0	0	0	0
Sewing Equipment												
148. Sewing bag	+	0	0	0	0	0	0	0	0	0	0	0
149. Bone awl	+	+	0	+	+	+	+	+	+	+	+	0
150. Metal awl	+	+	0	0	0	+	+	0	0	0	0	+
151. Yucca thread	+	0	0	+	0	0	+	0	+	0	+	0
152. Sinew thread	+	+	0	+	+	+	+	0	+	+	+	0
153. Thongs	+	+	0	+	0	+	+	+	+	+	0	0
154. Buckskin cord	+	0	0	+	0	0	0	0	0	0	0	0
155. Knots	+	+	0	0	+	+	+?	+	+	0	0	0
156. Knitting needles	+	0	0	m	+	0	+	+	0	0	+	+
Women's Garments												
157. Bast apron	0	+	0	+	0	+	+	0	+	0	−	+
158. Skin apron	0	0	−	+	0	+	0	0	+	0	0	0
159. Skin skirt	0	0	−	+	0	0	+	+	+	0	0	+
160. Skin shirt	0	0	−	+	0	+	+	0	+	0	+	+
161. Skin dress	0	+	−	+	0	+	0	+	+	0	+	+
162. Woolen dress, Type A	+	0	0	−	?	0	0	+	0	0	−	0
163. Rope belt	+	0	0	0	0	0	+	0	0	0	0	0
164. Woolen dress, Type B	+	+	+	+?	+	+	+	+	+	0	+?	+
165. Woolen belt	+	0	0	m	+?	+	+	+	0	0	+	+
166. Cotton skirt	+	0	+	−	+	+	+	+	+	0	−	+
167. Cotton blouse	+	0	+	0	0	+	+	+	+	0	0	+
168. Cotton dress	+	0	+	0	+	+	0	0	+	0	0	+
169. Shawl	+	0	0	+	0	0	+	+	0	0	+	0
Men's Garments												
170. Skin shirt	+	+	+	+	+	+	+	+	+	0	+	+
171. Woven shirt	+	0	0	0	0	+	+	+	0	0	0	0
172. Cotton shirt	0	0	+	0	0	+	+	0	0	0	0	0
173. Breechclout	+	0	0	+	+	+	+	+	+	0	+	+
174. Buckskin short trousers	+	+	+	0	0	+	+?	+	+	0	0	0
175. Cloth trousers	+	0	+	0	+	+	+	+	0	0	0	+
176. Bark leggings	−	0	0	0	0	0	+	+	+	0	0	0
177. Buckskin leggings	+	+	0	+	0	+	+	+	+	0	+	+
178. Knitted leggings	+	0	0	m	+	+	+	+	0	0	+	+
179. Woven garters	+	0	0	0	0	+	+	+	0	0	0	+
180. Buckskin belt	+	0	0	+	0	+	+	+	+	0	+	+

Distribution of Traits by Source According to Area (cont.)

Trait	Ramah	East				Central			West			
		Hill	Lamphere	Gifford	Other	Hill	FF	Other	Hill	Fishler	Gifford	Other
Headwear												
181. Hair tie	+	0	0	+	0	+	+	+	+	0	+	+
182. Basketry hat	+	0	0	0	0	+	0	0	0	0	0	+
183. Headband	+	0	0	+	0	+	+	+	0	0	+	+
184. Buckskin cap	+	+	0	+	+	+	+	+	0	0	+	+
185. Wooden awl	+	0	0	−	+	0	v	0	0	0	v	0
186. Mountain lion skin cap	−	0	0	0	0	+	+	+	+	0	0	0
187. Wildcat skin cap	+	+	0	0	0	0	+	+	+	0	0	0
Footwear												
188. Sandals	−	+	0	+	+	+	+	+	+	0	+	+
189. Moccasins	+	+	0	+	+	+	+	+	+	+	+	+
190. Overshoes	+	+	0	−	0	+	+	0	+	+	+	+
191. Snowshoes	+	+	0	−	0	+	0	0	+	0	v	+
Miscellaneous												
192. Fur scarf	+	+	0	0	0	+	+	+	0	0	v	0
193. Skin mittens	+	+	0	−	0	+	+	0	+	0	+	0
194. Knitted mittens	+	0	0	0	0	+	+	0	0	0	0	0
195. Pouch	+	0	0	0	+	+	+	+	+	0	0	+
196. Canes	+	+	0	0	0	+	+	0	0	0	0	0
Ornamentation												
197. Necklace	+	+	+	+	+	+	+	+	0	+	+	+
198. Earrings	+	+	0	+	+	+	+	+	0	0	+	+
199. Drill	+	0	0	+	+	+	+	+	0	0	+	+
200. Bracelet	+	+	+	0	0	+	+	+	0	0	v	+
201. Rings	+	+	+	0	0	+	+	+	0	0	0	0
202. Silver buttons	+	+	0	0	0	+	+	0	0	0	0	0
203. Face and body paint	+	0	0	+	+	+	+	+	+	0	+	+
204. Tattooing	+	0	+	−	0	m	−	0	m	0	−	0
205. Tweezers	+	0	+	−	0	+	+	+	+	0	m	+
Hygiene												
206. Menstrual pad	+	0	+	0	0	0	0	+	+	0	0	+
207. Abdominal binding	+	0	+	0	0	0	0	0	0	0	0	0
208. Yucca soap	+	0	0	+	+	+	+	0	+	0	+	+?
Ritual												
Ceremonies and Curing												
209. Sweathouse	+	+	+	+	+	+	+	+	+	+	+	+
210. Sweathouse rocks	+	0	+	+	+	+	+	+	0	+	+	+
211. Tongs (forks)	+	0	+	0	+	+	0	0	0	+	0	0
212. Stone boiling	0	0	+	−	0	+	0	0	+	+	−	0
213. Splints	0	+	+	0	0	0	0	0	+	0	0	0
214. Bugaboo owl	+	0	v	+	0	+	+	0	0	0	+	0
215. Lightning mats	+	0	0	0	0	0	0	0	0	0	0	0

Distribution of Traits by Source According to Area (cont.)

Trait	Ramah	East				Central			West			
		Hill	Lamphere	Gifford	Other	Hill	FF	Other	Hill	Fishler	Gifford	Other
216. Wooden box	0	0	0	0	0	+	0	0	0	0	0	0
217. Medicine bag	+	0	0	0	+	+	+	0	0	+	0	0
218. Cased bag	+	0	0	+	+	+	0	0	0	0	0	0
219. Baskets	+	0	0	0	0	+	+	0	0	0	0	+
220. Gourd containers	0	0	+	0	0	+	+	0	0	0	0	+
221. Horn containers	+	+	+	+	0	+	0	0	0	0	0	0
222. Shell containers	+	0	+	+	+	+	+	0	0	0	+	0
223. Animal fetishes	+	0	0	0	+	0	+	+	0	+	0	0
224. Cranebill	0	0	0	0	0	+	+	+	+	0	0	0
225. Medicine stopper	+	0	0	0	0	+	+	+	0	0	0	0
226. Masks	+	0	0	0	+	+	+	+	0	0	0	0
227. Prayersticks	+	0	0	0	0	0	+	+	0	0	0	0

Musical Instruments

Trait	Ramah	Hill	Lamphere	Gifford	Other	Hill	FF	Other	Hill	Fishler	Gifford	Other
228. Gourd rattle	+	0	0	+	0	+	+	0	+	0	+	0
229. Rawhide rattle	+	0	0	+?	0	+	+	0	+	0	+	0
230. Hoof rattle	+	0	+	+?	0	+	+	+	+	0	+	0
231. Basket drum	+	+	+	+	0	+	+	+	+	0	+	0
232. Rawhide drum	0	+	0	0	0	+	0	0	+	0	0	0
233. Pottery drum	+	0	+	+	0	+	+	+	+	0	+	0
234. Loop drumstick	+	0	+	+	0	+	+	0	+	0	+	0
235. Yucca drumstick	0	0	+	+	+	+	+	0	0	0	−	0
236. Drumming stick	+	+	+	0	0	0	+	0	+	0	0	0
237. Stomping pole	0	+	+	0	0	0	+	0	+	0	0	0
238. Flute	+	+	+	+	0	+	+	+	+	0	+	0
239. Whistle	+	0	+	+ −	0	+	+	0	+	+	−	0
240. Bullroarer	+	0	0	+	0	+	+	+	+	0	+	0
241. Musical bow	0	+	0	+	0	+	0	0	+	0	−	0
242. Musical rasp	0	0	+	+	0	+	+	0	+	0	+	0

Warfare

Trait	Ramah	Hill	Lamphere	Gifford	Other	Hill	FF	Other	Hill	Fishler	Gifford	Other
243. Lance	+	0	0	+	+	+	+	+	+	+	+	+
244. War club	+	+	0	− +	0	+	+	+	0	0	+ −	+
245. Shield	+	0	0	+	+	+	+	+	+	+	+	+
246. "Armor"	+	+	0	−	+	+	+	0	0	−	−	0

Recreation

Games

Trait	Ramah	Hill	Lamphere	Gifford	Other	Hill	FF	Other	Hill	Fishler	Gifford	Other
247. Hoop and pole	+	0	0	+	+	+	+	+	+	0	+	+
248. Shinny	+	0	0	+	+	+	+	+	+	0	+	+
249. Archery	+	0	+	+	+	+	+	+	+	0	+	0
250. Stick race	+	0	0	v	0	+	+	0	0	0	v	0
251. Horse race	+	0	0	0	0	+	+	+	+	0	0	0
252. Moccasin game	+	0	+	+	+	+	+	+	+	+	+	+
253. Seven cards	+	0	0	0	+	+	+	+	+	+	0	+
254. Women's stick dice	+	0	+	+	+	0	+	+	+	+	+	+
255. Button game	0	0	0	0	0	0	0	0	0	+	0	0

Distribution of Traits by Source According to Area (cont.)

Trait	Ramah	East Hill	Lamphere	Gifford	Other	Central Hill	FF	Other	West Hill	Fishler	Gifford	Other
Toys												
256. Figurines	+	+	0	−	+	0	+	+	+	0	0	0
257. Tops	+	0	0	−	0	0	m	+	0	0	−	+
258. Willow horses	+	0	+	0	0	0	0	+	0	0	0	0
259. String figures	+	0	0	+	0	+	+	+	0	−	+	0
260. Swings	0	0	+	0	0	+	0	0	+	0	0	0
261. Buzzer	0	0	0	−	0	+	0	0	+	0	−	0
Smoking												
262. Pipes	+	0	0	+	+	+	+	0	0	0	+	0
263. Tobacco pouch	+	0	0	+	+	+	+	+	0	0	+	0

SUMMARY

Category	Number of Traits	Ramah +	−	0	East +	−	0	Central +	−	0	West +	−	0
Subsistence													
Ritual hunting	4	3	−	1	4	−	−	4	−	−	4	−	−
Nonritual hunting	8	7	−	1	6	2	−	7	1	−	7	1	−
Weapons	16	14	1	1	12	1	3	16	−	−	16	−	−
Gathering	8	7	−	1	7	1	−	8	−	−	5	2	1
Agriculture	9	8	−	1	9	−	−	9	−	−	7	0	2
Animal husbandry	8	6	−	2	7	−	1	6	1	1	5	−	3
Horse equipment	18	14	−	4	10	−	8	17	−	1	14	−	4
Transportation and burdens	8	5	−	3	4	2	2	7	−	1	4	2	2
Food storage	7	5	−	2	7	−	−	7	−	−	6	−	1
Food preparation	6	5	1	−	6	−	−	5	−	1	6	−	−
Cooking	5	5	−	−	5	−	−	5	−	−	4	1	−
Utensils	9	6	1	2	7	1	1	7	−	2	6	1	2
Shelter													
Housing	4	2	−	2	4	−	−	4	−	−	3	1	−
Fire making	5	5	−	−	5	−	−	5	−	−	5	−	−
Multipurpose tools	4	4	−	−	4	−	−	4	−	−	3	−	1
Miscellaneous equipment	3	2	−	1	2	−	1	2	−	1	2	−	1
Bedding	5	5	−	−	5	−	−	5	−	−	5	−	−
Cradles	5	4	−	1	4	−	1	5	−	−	4	−	1
Clothing													
Skin dressing	8	8	−	−	6	1	1	8	−	−	8	−	−
Dyes	7	6	−	1	7	−	−	7	−	−	3	2	2
Sewing equipment	9	9	−	−	8	−	1	7	−	2	7	−	2
Women's garments	13	8	−	5	11	1	1	13	−	−	11	1	1
Men's garments	11	9	1	1	8	−	3	11	−	−	9	−	2

Distribution of Traits by Source According to Area (cont.)

Trait	Ramah	East				Central			West					
		Hill	Lamphere	Gifford	Other	Hill	FF	Other	Hill	Fishler		Gifford		Other
Headwear		7	6	1	–	5	–	2	7	–	–	7	–	–
Footwear		4	3	1	–	4	–	–	4	–	–	4	–	–
Miscellaneous		5	5	–	–	4	–	1	5	–	–	3	–	2
Ornamentation		9	9	–	–	9	–	–	9	–	–	7	–	2
Hygiene		3	3	–	–	3	–	–	2	–	1	2	–	1
Ritual														
Ceremonies and curing		19	14	–	5	13	–	6	17	–	2	12	–	7
Musical instruments		15	10	–	5	15	–	–	15	–	–	14	1	–
Warfare		4	4	–	–	4	–	–	4	–	–	3	1	–
Recreation														
Games		9	8	–	1	7	–	2	8	–	1	9	–	–
Toys		6	4	–	2	4	2	–	6	–	–	5	–	1
Smoking		2	2	–	–	2	–	–	2	–	–	2	–	–
TOTALS		263	215	6	42	218	11	34	248	2	13	212	13	38

Appendix 2. Informants According to Area

Data, when available, are given in the following order: sex, date of birth, date of death, and additional information.

RAMAH

Inf. 1; m; b. 1878; d. 1950
Inf. 2; m; b. 1851; d. 1940; born near Mt. Taylor
Inf. 3; m; b. 1853? d. 1942
Inf. 4; m; b. 1882
Inf. 5; m; b. 1887; d. 1945
Inf. 6; m; b. 1890? d. 1959
Inf. 7; m; b. 1866; d. 1954; Hill's informant MM
Inf. 8; m; b. 1888?
Inf. 9; m; b. 1899
Inf. 11; f; b. 1885; d. 1938
Inf. 12; m; b. 1893
Inf. 13; m; b. 1885; d. 1939
Inf. 14; f; b. 1875; d. 1944
Inf. 15; f; b. 1876; d. 1945
Inf. 16; m; b. 1868; d. 1942; born at Fort Sumner
Inf. 17; m; b. 1898
Inf. 18; m; b. 1884; d. 1948; born in Arizona, south of railroad and Route 66
Inf. 19; m; b. 1890
Inf. 20; m; b. 1894
Inf. 21; m; b. 1894? d. 1951
Inf. 22; m; b. 1906? d. 1958; suicide
Inf. 24; m; b. 1897
Inf. 26; f; b. 1896
Inf. 27; m; b. 1906?
Inf. 28; f; b. 1892
Inf. 29; f; b. 1911
Inf. 30; f; b. 1903
Inf. 32; f; b. 1860? d. 1944; born 5 miles northwest of Gallup
Inf. 34; m; b. 1897
Inf. 35; m; b. 1907; d. 1946
Inf. 36; f; b. 1903
Inf. 39; m; b. 1901
Inf. 40; m; b. 1898
Inf. 41; f; b. 1892; d. 1950
Inf. 42; f; b. 1902
Inf. 43; f; b. 1902
Inf. 44; m; b. 1863? d. 1939
Inf. 45; m; b. 1886?
Inf. 46; f; b. 1890; d. 1954
Inf. 47; f; b. 1874; d. 1942; tuberculosis
Inf. 48; f; b. 1874? d. 1947
Inf. 50; f; b. 1860; d. 1945; cancer
Inf. 51; m; b. 1897
Inf. 53; m; b. 1886; d. 1941
Inf. 54; f; b. 1899
Inf. 55; m; b. 1918

Inf. 56; f; b. 1895
Inf. 57; m; b. 1918
Inf. 58; f; b. 1907? d. 1938
Inf. 60; f; b. 1902
Inf. 61; m; b. 1904
Inf. 63; m; b. 1874; d. 1949
Inf. 64; f; b. 1890
Inf. 73; f; b. 1916?
Inf. 76; f; b. 1872
Inf. 77; f; b. 1880? d. 1945
Inf. 78; f; b. 1898; d. 1939
Inf. 81; m; b. 1903
Inf. 82; f; b. 1914
Inf. 83; f; b. 1909
Inf. 84; m; b. 1896
Inf. 85; f; b. 1901
Inf. 86; m; b. 1904
Inf. 90; m; b. 1913
Inf. 95; m; b. 1914; d. 1948; tuberculosis
Inf. 96; m; b. 1916
Inf. 97; f; b. 1917
Inf. 99; m; b. 1915?
Inf. 101; m; b. 1893
Inf. 102; m; b. 1876? d. 1944
Inf. 104; m; b. 1890
Inf. 106; m; b. 1899; d. 1941
Inf. 107; m; b. 1884? d. 1938; after automobile accident
Inf. 109; m; b. 1903; d. 1943
Inf. 111; f; b. 1877; d. 1950
Inf. 112; m; b. 1892; d. 1942; of syphilitic heart disease
Inf. 115; f; b. 1912
Inf. 120; f; b. 1897?
Inf. 121; m; b. 1916
Inf. 125; m; b. 1899; d. 1957
Inf. 128; m; b. 1916
Inf. 129; m; b. 1868; d. 1956; born near Inscription Rock
Inf. 129's mother; b. 1850; d. 1899
Inf. 130; m; b. 1896
Inf. 132; m; b. 1906
Inf. 134; m; b. 1882; d. 1942
Inf. 138; m; b. 1880? d. 1950
Inf. 139; m; b. 1913; d. 1941
Inf. 147; m; b. 1880; d. 1942
Inf. 148; m; b. 1885
Inf. 153; m; b. 1909
Inf. 157; f; b. 1886? d. 1942
Inf. 166; f; b. 1912

Inf. 169; f; b. 1877
Inf. 172; f; b. 1894
Inf. 175; m; b. 1911
Inf. 177; f; b. 1888
Inf. 178; f; b. 1910
Inf. 180; m; b. 1878
Inf. 182; m; b. 1919; d. 1957
Inf. 186; f; b. 1908
Inf. 192; f; b. 1858; d. 1942
Inf. 196; m; b. 1908? d. 1950
Inf. 203; f; b. 1936
Inf. 210; m; b. 1922
Inf. 215; m; b. 1909; d. 1954
Inf. 216; m; b. 1916; d. 1957
Inf. 219; m; b. 1923?
Inf. 234; m; b. 1931
Inf. 242; m; b. 1940; d. 1948; of pneumonia at Black Rock
    Hospital
Inf. 248; f; b. 1921
Inf. 256; m; b. 1923
Inf. 257; m; b. 1847; d. 1929
Inf. 258; m; b. 1907
Inf. 259; m; b. 1915
Inf. 260; m; b. 1904? d. 1949

Inf. 261; m; b. 1921
Inf. 262; m; b. 1904
Inf. 263; m; b. 1921
Inf. 264; m; b. 1921
Inf. 265; m; b. 1845; d. 1923; born near Tohatchi
Inf. 267; m; b. 1928
Inf. 269; m; b. 1917
Inf. 270; Tschopik's interpreter; Inf. 12's brother-in-law from
    Two Wells
Inf. 273; m; b. 1917
Inf. 274; m; b. 1907? d. 1956
Inf. 276; f; b. 1932
Inf. 277; m; b. 1924; Zuni
Inf. 278; f; b. 1904? d. 1926
Inf. 279; f; b. 1916
Inf. 280; f; b. 1867?
Inf. 283; no data
Inf. 300; m; b. 1890's; brother of Inf. 12
Inf. 4027; m; b. 1918
Inf. 4117; m; b. 1919
Inf. 4121; m; b. 1924
Inf. 4415; m; b. 1929? d. 1955
Inf. 4903; m; b. 1911
JP; m; no data

EAST

Hill

Aneth, Utah
    LH; m; b. 1843? no ceremonial experience; born near the
    Four Corners
Cañoncito, New Mexico
    WP; m; b. 1890
Chaco Canyon, New Mexico
    T; m; b. 1865
Crownpoint, New Mexico
    D; f
    JJ; m; b. 1895
    MLH; m; b. 1850; born near Crownpoint; taken to Fort
    Sumner when about 14 years old
    TLLSS; m; b. 1875; born between Taylor and Newcomb
Mariano Lake, New Mexico
    K; f; b. 1850; berdache; went to Fort Sumner when about
    14 years old
Red Rock, Arizona
    TOMC; m; b. 1860; born at Red Rock
Shiprock, New Mexico
    TLFOS; m; b. 1871; born near Fort Defiance
    TLHO; possibly from Newcomb, but age and area unknown
    MM; m; b. 1866; d. 1954; Ramah Inf. 7

Gifford

Shiprock and Tohatchi, New Mexico
    EN (Eastern Navaho informant); m; b. 1869; born near
    Tohatchi, moved to Shiprock in 1891

L. Kluckhohn

Thoreau, New Mexico
    DS; f; b. 1920's
Sheep Springs, New Mexico
    CC; f; b. 1948

Lamphere

Sheep Springs, New Mexico
    PM; f; b. c. 1926
    EP; f; b. 1932
    MS; f; b. 1891

Hill

Black Mountain, Arizona
  K; m; b. 1883
  BV; m; b. 1890; also from Nazlini
Canyon del Muerto (Canyon de Chelly), Arizona
  LM; m; b. 1854; born at Canyon del Muerto, taken to Fort
    Sumner when about 10 years old
Chinle, Arizona
  C; m; b. 1871; chanter; born at Lukachukai; informant for
    Father Berard Haile
Coalmine, New Mexico
  N; f; b. 1857 at Black Mountain
  SS; m; b. 1867
Crystal, New Mexico
  RH; m; b. 1863; chanter; born at Crystal
  SC; m; b. 1871; chanter; born at Lukachukai; informant
    for Father Berard Haile
Divide, New Mexico
  MB; f; b. 1900
Fort Defiance, Arizona
  PP; m; b. 1866; chanter; born at Fort Defiance
  TLFOS; m; b. 1871; also from Shiprock
Ganado and Hunters Point, Arizona
  DM; m; b. 1853; taken to Fort Sumner when about 11
    years old
  LW; f; b. 1850; born at Black Mountain; taken to Fort
    Sumner when about 14 years old

Lukachukai, Arizona
  AM; m; b. 1868; knew hunting ways
  AS; m; b. 1895; informant for Father Berard Haile
  IS; m; b. 1876; born at Lukachukai
  LW; f; b. 1872
  MM; f; b. 1853
  RMW; f; b. 1886
Manuelito, New Mexico
  OTKM; m; b. 1869; born near Manuelito
Nazlini, Arizona
  SW; f; b. 1858
  BV; m; b. 1890; also from Black Mountain
Red Lake, Arizona-New Mexico
  YLH; m; b. 1870
Round Rock, Arizona
  MLH; m; b. 1865; born at Fort Sumner
  TM; m; b. 1853
Sawmill, Arizona
  MC; m; b. 1880; chanter
  MS; f; b. 1895
Wheatfields, Arizona
  WH; m; b. 1857; at Wheatfields; went to Fort Sumner

L. Kluckhohn

Morenci, Arizona
  AB; m; b. 1941?

Informants who contributed to the work of the Franciscan Fathers (1910, 1912) and who worked for Father Berard Haile have been considered as being from the Central area.

WEST

Hill

Head Springs, Arizona
  MH; m; b. 1880
Jeddito, Arizona
  MDW; m; b. 1865; chanter
Keams Canyon, Arizona
  BW; f; b. 1895; born at Keams Canyon
  SG; m; b. 1863
  TW; f; b. 1890
White Cone, Arizona
  GH; m; b. 1863; chanter; born in the Jeddito Valley

Fishler

Coalmine, Arizona
  FG; m; b. 1890
  TT; m; b. 1868

Kaibito, Arizona
  BN; m; b. 1910
  IJmo; f; b. 1902
  IJun; m; b. 1890; brother of IJmo
  TN; m; b. 1900
Moenave, Arizona
  TH; m; b. 1898
Tuba City, Arizona
  GB; m; b. 1878
  FrJfa; m; b. 1904

Gifford

Leupp, Arizona
  WN (Western Navaho informant); m; b. 1855; chanter;
    taken to Fort Sumner

Bibliography

Aberle, David F.

1942   "Mythology of the Navaho Game Stick-Dice," *Journal of American Folklore*, 55:144–154.

1963   "Some Sources of Flexibility in Navaho Social Organization," *Southwestern Journal of Anthropology*, 19:1–8.

Adair, John

1944   *The Navajo and Pueblo Silversmiths*. Norman: University of Oklahoma Press.

Adair, John, and Evon Z. Vogt

1949   "Navaho and Zuni Veterans: A Study of Contrasting Modes of Culture Change," *American Anthropologist*, 51:547–561.

Amsden, Charles Avery

1932   "Navaho Weaving," *The Masterkey* (Los Angeles), 6:5.

1934   *Navaho Weaving*. Santa Ana, Calif.: Fine Arts Press.

1949   *Navaho Weaving*, 2nd ed. Albuquerque: University of New Mexico Press.

Ashley, Clifford W.

1944   *The Ashley Book of Knots*. Garden City, N. Y.: Doubleday, Doran and Co.

Ayer, Mrs. Edward E., trans.

1916   *The Memorial of Fray Alonso de Benavides, 1630*. Chicago: privately printed.

Babington, S. H.

1950   *Navajos, Gods, and Tom-Toms*. New York: Greenberg.

Backus, Major E.

1853   "Navoho Wigwams," vol. 3, p. 70, in Schoolcraft, (see Schoolcraft, 1860).

1854   "An Account of the Navajoes of New Mexico," vol. 4, pp. 209–215, in Schoolcraft (see Schoolcraft, 1860).

Bailey, Flora

1940   "Navaho Foods and Cooking Methods," *American Anthropologist*, 42:270–290.

1941   "Navaho Women and the Sudatory," *American Anthropologist*, 43:484–485.

1942   "Navaho Motor Habits," *American Anthropologist*, 44:210–234.

1950   *Some Sex Beliefs and Practices in a Navaho Community: With Comparative Material from Other Areas*. Cambridge, Mass.: Papers of the Peabody Museum of American Archaeology and Ethnology, Harvard University, vol. 40, no. 2.

Bandelier, Adolf

1890–   *Final Report of Investigations among the Indians of the Southwestern United States.*
1892   *Carried on Mainly in the Years from 1880 to 1885*. Papers of the Archaeological Institute of America, American Series III. Part 1, 1890, part 2, 1892. Cambridge: At the University Press.

Bartlett, John R.

1854   *Personal Narrative of Explorations and Incidents in Texas, New Mexico, California, Sonora, and Chihuahua: Connected with the United States and Mexican Boundary Commission, During the Years 1850, '51, '52, '53*, vol. 1. New York: D. Appleton and Co.

Bibliography

Bell, William A.
1869   *New Tracks in North America: A Journal of Travel and Adventure; Whilst Engaged in the Survey for a Southern Railroad to the Pacific Ocean During 1867–8,* vol. 1. London: Chapman and Hall.

Bourke, John Gregory
1884   *The Snake Dance of the Moquis of Arizona.* London: Sampson Low, Marston, Searle, and Rivington.

1936   "Bourke on the Southwest," ed. Lansing S. Bloom, *New Mexico Historical Review,* 11:77–122, 217–244.

Brugge, David M.
1963   *Navajo Pottery and Ethnohistory.* Navajoland Publications, Series 2. Window Rock, Ariz.: Navajo Tribal Museum.

Bryan, Kirk
1929   "Flood Water Farming," *The Geographical Review,* 19:444–456.

Bryan, Nonabah G., and Stella Young
1940   "Navajo Native Dyes—Their Preparation and Use," *Indian Handcrafts,* 2:1–75. Chilocco, Okla.: Education Division, U.S. Office of Indian Affairs.

Buck, Peter H.
1950   *Material Culture of Kapingamarangi.* Honolulu: Bernice P. Bishop Museum, Bulletin 200.

Bullen, Adelaide Kendall
1947   "Archaeological Theory and Anthropological Fact," *American Antiquity,* 13:2:128–134.

Carroll, H. Bailey, and J. Villasana Haggard, trans. and eds.
1942   *Three New Mexico Chronicles.* Albuquerque: Quivira Society Publications, vol. 11.

Carroll, John B., and Joseph B. Casagrande
1958   "The Function of Language Classifications in Behavior," pp. 18–31 in *Readings in Social Psychology,* ed. Eleanor E. Maccoby, Theodore M. Newcomb, and Eugene L. Hartley, 3rd ed. (New York: Holt, Rinehart, and Winston).

Coolidge, Dane, and Mary Roberts Coolidge
1930   *The Navajo Indians.* Boston and New York: Houghton Mifflin Co.

Corbett, John Maxwell
1940   "Navajo House Types," *El Palacio,* 47:5:97–107.

Cremony, John C.
1868   *Life Among the Apaches.* San Francisco: A. Roman and Co.

Culin, Robert Stewart
1907   *Games of the North American Indians.* Washington, D.C.: Bureau of American Ethnology, Annual Report, no. 24.

Curtis, Edward S.
1907–1908   *The North American Indian.* Seattle, Wash.: E. S. Curtis.

Bibliography **Davis, William W. H.**

1857   *El Gringo: Or New Mexico and Her People*. New York: Harper and Bros.

De Harport, David Lee

n.d.   "Archaeological Research in Canyon de Chelly, 1948–1957." MS. in Peabody Museum, Harvard University, Cambridge, Mass.

1951   "An Archaeological Survey of Cañon de Chelly. Preliminary Report of the Field Sessions of 1948, 1949, and 1950," *El Palacio,* 58:2:35–48.

1959   "An Archaeological Survey of Cañon de Chelly, Northeastern Arizona: A Puebloan Community Through Time." Ph.D. diss., Harvard University.

Dellenbaugh, Frederick S.

n.d.   "Diary." MS. in New York Public Library, New York.

1901   *The North Americans of Yesterday*. New York: G. P. Putnam's Sons.

1906   *The Romance of the Colorado River*. New York: G. P. Putnam's Sons.

1926   *A Canyon Voyage: The Narrative of the Second Powell Expedition*. New Haven: Yale University Press.

Denver Art Museum

1937   "Seven Navaho Pots," *Material Culture Notes,* 3:9–14.

Dittert, Alfred E., Jr.

1958   *Preliminary Archaeological Investigations in the Navajo Project Area of Northwestern New Mexico*. Navajo Project Studies, I. Santa Fe: Museum of New Mexico, Papers in Anthropology, no. 1.

Dittert, Alfred E., Jr., Jim J. Hester, and Frank W. Eddy

1961   *An Archaeological Survey of the Navajo Reservoir District, Northwestern New Mexico*. Santa Fe: School of American Research and the Museum of New Mexico, Monograph no. 23.

Dixon, Roland B.

1928   *The Building of Cultures*. New York: Charles Scribner's Sons.

Dunn, Roy

1939   "Bow and Arrow of the Deneh," *Southwest Tourist News,* Sept.

Dyk, Walter

1938   *Son of Old Man Hat*. New York: Harcourt, Brace and Co.

1947   *A Navaho Autobiography*. New York: Viking Fund Publications in Anthropology, no. 8.

Eaton, J. H.

1854   "Description of the True State and Character of the New Mexican Tribes," vol. 4, pp. 216–221, in Schoolcraft (see Schoolcraft, 1860).

Elmore, Francis H.

1944   *Ethnobotany of the Navajo*. Albuquerque: University of New Mexico and the School of American Research, Monograph no. 7.

Eubank, Lisbeth

1945   "Legends of Three Navaho Games," *El Palacio,* 52:138–140.

Bibliography

Farmer, Malcolm F.

1938   "Field and Laboratory Reports: Archaeological Work Done in the Old Navaho Country, Summer of 1938." MS. in Clyde Kluckhohn's files, Peabody Museum, Harvard University, Cambridge, Mass.

1942   "Navaho Archaeology of Upper Blanco and Largo Canyons, Northern New Mexico," *American Antiquity,* 8:65–79.

1947   "Upper Largo Navaho, 1700–1775," *The Kiva,* 12:15–24.

Fewkes, J. W.

1923   "Clay Figurines made by Navaho Children," *American Anthropologist,* 25: 4:559–563.

Fishler, Stanley A.

1953   *In the Beginning: A Navaho Creation Myth.* Salt Lake City: Department of Anthropology, University of Utah, Anthropological Papers, no. 13.

Ford, Clellan S.

1937   "A Sample Comparative Analysis of Material Culture," pp. 225–246 in *Studies in the Science of Society,* ed. G. P. Murdock (New Haven: Yale University Press).

Franciscan Fathers

1910   *An Ethnologic Dictionary of the Navaho Language.* St. Michael's, Ariz.

1912   *A Vocabulary of the Navaho Language.* St. Michael's, Ariz.

1948   "Navaho Baby-Carrier," *The Masterkey* (Los Angeles), 22:3:99.

1952   "Home Heating Navaho Style," *The Padre's Trail* (St. Michael's, Ariz.), Jan.:11–12.

Frisbie, Charlotte Johnson

1967   *Kinaalda: A Study of the Navaho Girls' Puberty Ceremony.* Middletown, Conn.: Wesleyan University Press.

Gifford, E. W.

1928   "Pottery-Making in the Southwest," University of California Publications in American Archaeology and Ethnology, no. 23, pp. 353–373. Berkeley: University of California Press.

1940   *"Culture Element Distributions XII. Apache-Pueblo,"* University of California Anthropological Records, vol. 4, no. 1, pp. 1–207. Berkeley: University of California Press.

Gilpin, Laura

1968   *The Enduring Navaho.* Austin and London: University of Texas Press.

Goddard, Pliny Earle

1933   *Navajo Texts.* New York: American Museum of Natural History, Anthropological Papers, vol. 34, part 1, pp. 1–179.

Gregory, Herbert E.

1916   *The Navajo Country.* U.S. Geological Survey, Water Supply Paper 380. Washington, D.C.: Government Printing Office.

Griffith, Charles R.

1954   "Navaho Clothing." MS. based primarily on Ramah Navaho data.

Bibliography

Guernsey, Samuel J.
1914   "Diary of Arizona Exploration." Part of MS. with photographs in Clyde Kluckhohn's files.

Guernsey, Samuel J., and Alfred V. Kidder
1921   *Basket-Maker Caves of Northeastern Arizona.* Cambridge, Mass.: Papers of the Peabody Museum of American Archaeology and Ethnology, Harvard University, vol. 8, no. 2.

Haile, Berard
1917   "Some Mortuary Customs of the Navajo," *The Franciscan Missions of the Southwest,* 5:29–32.

1933   "Navaho Games of Chance and Taboo," *Primitive Man,* 6:35–40.

1937   "Some Cultural Aspects of the Navaho Hogan." MS. in Peabody Museum, Harvard University, Cambridge, Mass.

1938   *Origin Legend of the Navaho Enemy Way.* New Haven: Yale University Publications in Anthropology, no. 17.

1942   "Why the Navaho Hogan," *Primitive Man,* 15:39–56.

1943   *Origin Legend of the Navaho Flintway.* Chicago: University of Chicago Publications in Anthropology, Linguistic Series.

1946   *The Navaho Fire Dance or Corral Dance.* St. Michaels, Ariz.: St. Michaels Press.

1947a   *Head and Face Masks in Navaho Ceremonialism.* St. Michaels, Ariz.: St. Michaels Press.

1947b   *Navaho Sacrificial Figurines.* Chicago: University of Chicago Press.

1947c   *Prayer Stick Cutting in a Five Night Navaho Ceremonial of the Male Branch of Shootingway.* Chicago: University of Chicago Press.

1950   *A Stem Vocabulary of the Navaho Language: Navaho-English.* St. Michaels, Ariz.: St. Michaels Press.

1951   *A Stem Vocabulary of the Navaho Language: English-Navaho.* St. Michaels, Ariz.: St. Michaels Press.

1952   "*Blessingway,* Version One, Introduction." MS. in Special Collections Division, University of Arizona Library, Tuscon. Cf. Wyman, 1970:1–106.

1954   *Property Concepts of the Navaho Indians.* Washington, D.C.: Catholic University of America, Anthropological Series, no. 17.

Hatt, Gudmund
1916   *Moccasins and Their Relation to Arctic Footwear.* Memoirs of the American Anthropological Association, vol. 3, no. 3, pp. 147–250.

Hester, James J.
1962   *Early Navajo Migrations and Acculturation in the Southwest.* Santa Fe: Museum of New Mexico Papers in Anthropology, no. 6.

Hester, James J., and Joel L. Shiner
1963   *Studies at Navajo Period Sites in the Navajo Reservoir District.* Santa Fe: Museum of New Mexico Papers in Anthropology, no. 9.

Bibliography

Hill, W. W.

1936a   "Navaho Rites for Dispelling Insanity and Delirium," *El Palacio,* 41:71–74.

1936b   *Navaho Warfare.* New Haven: Yale University Publications in Anthropology, no. 5.

1937   "Navaho Pottery Manufacture," University of New Mexico Bulletin (Albuquerque), Anthropological Series, no. 2, pp. 5–23.

1938   *The Agricultural and Hunting Methods of the Navaho Indians.* New Haven: Yale University Publications in Anthropology, no. 18.

1940a   "Some Navaho Culture Changes During Two Centuries," *Smithsonian Miscellaneous Collections,* 100:395–415.

1940b   "Navajo Salt Gathering," University of New Mexico Bulletin (Albuquerque), Anthropological Series, no. 3, pp. 3–25.

1944   "The Navaho Indians and the Ghost Dance of 1890," *American Anthropologist,* 46:523–527.

Hill, W. W., and Dorothy Hill

1943   "The Legend of the Navajo Eagle-Catching Way," *New Mexico Anthropologist,* 6–7:31–36.

Hodge, Frederick Webb

1896   "John Gregory Bourke," *American Anthropologist* (O.S.), 9:245–248.

1920   "Hawikuh Bonework," *Indian Notes and Monographs,* 3:2:63–151. New York: Museum of the American Indian Heye Foundation.

Hoijer, Harry

1945   *Navaho Phonology.* Albuquerque: University of New Mexico Publications in Anthropology, no. 1.

1951   "Cultural Implications of Some Navaho Linguistic Categories," *Language,* 27:111–120.

Hollister, U. S.

1903   *The Navajo and His Blanket.* Denver: United States Colortype Co.

Hough, Walter

1901   "Apache and Navaho Fire-Making," *American Anthropologist,* 3:585–586.

1902   "A Collection of Hopi Ceremonial Pigments," United States National Museum Annual Report for 1900 (Washington, D.C.), pp. 463–471.

1928   "Fire-Making Apparatus in the United States National Museum," Proceedings of the United States National Museum (Washington, D.C.), vol. 73, part 14.

Hurt, Wesley R., Jr.

1942   "Eighteenth Century Navaho Hogans from Canyon de Chelly National Monument," *American Antiquity,* 8:89–104.

Ives, Joseph Chester

1861   *Report Upon the Colorado River of the West: Explored in 1857 and 1858 by Lt. Joseph C. Ives.* U.S. Congress, House Exec. Doc. 90, 36th Congress, 1st session.

Bibliography

James, George W.
1902   *Indian Basketry,* 2nd ed. New York: Henry Malkan.

1914   *Indian Blankets and Their Makers.* Chicago: A. C. McClurg and Co.

James, Marjorie
1937   "A Note on Navajo Pottery Making," *El Palacio,* 43:85–86.

Jeançon, Jean Allard, and F. H. Douglas
1930   *Navaho Spinning, Dyeing, and Weaving.* Denver: Denver Art Museum, Department of Indian Art, Leaflet no. 3.

Kearney, Thomas H., and Robert H. Peebles
1942   *Flowering Plants and Ferns of Arizona.* Washington, D.C.: U.S. Department of Agriculture, Miscellaneous Publication no. 423.

1951   *Arizona Flora* (2nd ed. of above). Berkeley and Los Angeles: University of California Press.

Keur, Dorothy
1941   *Big Bead Mesa: An Archaeological Study of Navaho Acculturation, 1745–1812.* Society for American Archaeology Memoirs, no. 1.

1944   "A Chapter in Navaho-Pueblo Relations," *American Antiquity,* 10:75–86.

Kidder, Alfred V.
1932   *The Artifacts of Pecos.* Phillips Academy, Andover, and the Carnegie Institution, Papers of the Southwestern Expedition, no. 6. New Haven: Yale University Press.

Kluckhohn, Clyde
1938   "Participation in Ceremonials in a Navaho Community," *American Anthropologist,* 40:359–369.

1942   "The Navahos in the Machine Age," *Technology Review,* 44:1–6.

1945   "A Navaho Personal Document with a Brief Paretian Analysis," *Southwestern Journal of Anthropology,* 1:260–283.

1956   "Aspects of the Demographic History of a Small Population," pp. 359–381 in *Estudios Antropológicos,* publicados en homenaje al doctor Manuel Gamio (Mexico City: Direccion General de Publicaciones).

1960   "Navaho Categories," pp. 65–98 in *Culture in History: Essays in Honor of Paul Radin,* ed. Stanley Diamond (New York: Columbia University Press).

Kluckhohn, Clyde, and Dorothea Leighton
1946   *The Navaho.* Cambridge, Mass.: Harvard University Press.

Kluckhohn, Clyde, and Paul Reiter
1939   *Preliminary Report on the 1937 Excavations, Bc 50–51, Chaco Canyon, New Mexico.* University of New Mexico Bulletin (Albuquerque), Anthropological Series, vol. 3, no. 2.

Kluckhohn, Clyde, and Leland C. Wyman
1940   *An Introduction to Navaho Chant Practice.* Memoirs of the American Anthropological Association, no. 53.

Bibliography

Kroeber, Alfred L.
1948   *Anthropology.* New York: Harcourt Brace, and Co.

Landgraf, John L.
1954   *Land-Use in the Ramah Area of New Mexico: An Anthropological Approach to Areal Study.* Cambridge, Mass.: Papers of the Peabody Museum of American Archaeology and Ethnology, Harvard University, vol. 42, no. 1.

Leighton, Alexander H., and Dorothea C.
1941a   "A Navaho Builds a House: A Story in Pictures," *Natural History,* 47:272–273.

1941b   "A Navaho Makes Soap," *Natural History,* 48:19–20.

1941c   "A Navaho Takes a 'Turkish Bath,'" *Natural History,* 48:20–21.

1949   *Gregorio, the Hand Trembler.* Cambridge, Mass.: Papers of the Peabody Museum of American Archaeology and Ethnology, Harvard University, vol. 40, no. 1.

Leighton, Dorothea C., and Clyde Kluckhohn
1947   *Children of the People.* Cambridge, Mass.: Harvard University Press.

Letherman, Jonathan
1856   "Sketch of the Navajo Tribe of Indians, Territory of New Mexico," Smithsonian Institution Annual Report for 1855 (Washington, D.C.), pp. 283–297.

Maclay, Howard
1958   "An Experimental Study of Language and Non-Linguistic Behavior," *Southwestern Journal of Anthropology,* 14:2:220–228.

Malcolm, Roy L.
1939   "Archaeological Remains Supposedly Navaho, from Chaco Canyon, New Mexico," *American Antiquity,* 5:4–20.

Mason, Otis T.
1889   "Cradles of the American Aborigines," United States National Museum Annual Report for 1887 (Washington, D.C.), part 2, pp. 161–212.

1894   "North American Bows, Arrows, and Quivers," Smithsonian Institution Annual Report for 1893 (Washington, D.C.), pp. 631–680.

1896   "Primitive Travel and Transportation," United States National Museum Annual Report for 1894 (Washington, D.C.), pp. 237–593.

1904   "Aboriginal American Basketry," United States National Museum Annual Report for 1902 (Washington, D.C.), pp. 171–548.

Matthews, Washington
1866   "Navajo Names for Plants," *American Naturalist,* 20:767–777.

1883   "Navajo Silversmiths," Bureau of American Ethnology Annual Report for 1880–81 (Washington, D.C.), part 2, pp. 167–178.

1884   "Navajo Weavers," Bureau of American Ethnology Annual Report for 1881–82 (Washington, D.C.), part 3, pp. 371–391.

1887   "The Mountain Chant: A Navajo Ceremony," Bureau of American Ethnology Annual Report for 1883–84 (Washington, D.C.), part 5, pp. 379–467.

Bibliography

1889   "Navajo Gambling Songs," *American Anthropologist* (O.S.), 2:1–19.

1893'   "Navajo Dye Stuffs," Smithsonian Institution Annual Report for 1891 (Washington, D.C.), pp. 613–616.

1897   *Navaho Legends.* New York: American Folklore Society Memoirs, no. 5.

1902   *The Night Chant: A Navajo Ceremony.* New York: American Museum of Natural History Memoirs, no. 6.

1904   "The Navaho Yellow Dye," *American Anthropologist,* 6:194.

McCombe, Leonard, Evon Z. Vogt, and Clyde Kluckhohn
1951   *Navaho Means People.* Cambridge, Mass.: Harvard University Press.

McNitt, Frank
1962   *The Indian Traders.* Norman: University of Oklahoma Press.

Mera, H. P.
1944a   *Navajo Woven Dresses.* Santa Fe: Laboratory of Anthropology, General Series, Bulletin no. 15.

1944b   *Indian Silverwork of the Southwest, Illustrated: Bridles.* Santa Fe: Laboratory of Anthropology, General Series, Bulletin no. 17.

Mindeleff, Cosmos
1898   "Navaho Houses," Bureau of American Ethnology, Annual Report for 1895–96 (Washington, D.C.), no. 17, part 2, pp. 475–517.

Morris, Earl H.
1939   *Archaeological Studies in the La Plata District.* Washington, D.C.: Carnegie Institute of Washington, Publication no. 519.

Morss, Noel
1954   *Clay Figurines of the American Southwest,* Cambridge, Mass.: Papers of the Peabody Museum of Archaeology and Ethnology, Harvard University, vol. 49, no. 1.

Murdock, George Peter
1938   *Outline of Cultural Materials.* New Haven: Institute of Human Relations.

1950   *Outline of Cultural Materials.* New Haven: Human Relations Area Files.

Newcomb, Franc Johnson
1940a   *Navajo Omens and Taboos.* Santa Fe: Rydal Press.

1940b   "Origin Legend of the Navajo Eagle Chant," *Journal of American Folklore,* 53:50–77.

Newcomb, Franc J., and Gladys A. Reichard
1937   *Sandpaintings of the Navajo Shooting Chant.* New York: J. J. Augustin.

Oakes, Maud
1943   *Where the Two Came to Their Father: A Navaho War Ceremonial.* Bollingen Series, 1. New York: Pantheon Books.

O'Connell, Daniel T.
1939   "The Black Dye of the Navajos," *Science* (N.S.), 90:272 (Sept. 22).

Bibliography

Osgood, Cornelius

1940   *Ingalik Material Culture.* New Haven: Yale University Publications in Anthropology, no. 22.

Osterman, Leopold

1917   "Navajo Houses," *The Franciscan Missions of the Southwest,* 4:20–28.

Page, Gordon B.

1937a   "Navaho House Types," *Museum Notes,* 9:47–49. Flagstaff: Museum of Northern Arizona.

1937b   "The Navajo Sweat House," *New Mexico Anthropologist,* 2:1:19–21.

Palmer, Edward

1869   "Notes on the Navajo Indians of New Mexico Made in 1869." MS. in Peabody Museum, Harvard University, Cambridge, Mass.

Parsons, Elsie C.

1916   "The Zuni A'Doshle and Suuke," *American Anthropologist,* 18:338–347.

1923   "Navaho Folk Tales," *Journal of American Folklore,* 36:368–375.

Pattie, James O.

1905   *The Personal Narrative of James O. Pattie of Kentucky.* Cleveland: Arthur H. Clark Co.

Pepper, George H.

1902   "The Navajo Indians," *The Papoose,* 1:1:3–9.

1903   "Native Navajo Dyes," *The Papoose,* 1:3:1–12.

1923   "Navaho Weaving." MS. in the Museum of the American Indian, Heye Foundation, New York. Quoted in Amsden, 1949.

Pike, Zebulon M.

1811   *Exploratory Travels Through the Western Territories of North America: Comprising a Voyage from St. Louis on the Mississippi, to the Source of that River, and a Journey Through the Interior of Louisiana, and the North-Eastern Provinces of New Spain.* London: Longman, Hurst, Rees, Orme, and Brown.

Pope, S. T.

1923   "A Study of Bows and Arrows," University of California Publications in American Archaeology and Ethnology, vol. 13, no. 9, pp. 329–414. Berkeley: University of California Press.

Powell, John W.

n.d.   "Legends, Customs, Superstitions, etc." MS. (Navaho 3247) in Bureau of American Ethnology, Washington, D.C.

Putnam, Frederick W.

1879   *Reports upon the Archaeological and Ethnological Collections from the Vicinity of Santa Barbara, California, and from Ruined Pueblos of Arizona and New Mexico, and Certain Interior Tribes.* U.S. Geographical Surveys West of the One Hundredth Meridian, vol. 7, Archaeology. Washington: Government Printing Office.

Bibliography

Reagan, Albert B.

1932   "Navajo Sports," *Primitive Man,* 5:68–71.

1934   "A Navaho Fire Dance," *American Anthropologist,* 36:434–437.

Reichard, Gladys A.

1934   *Spider Woman.* New York: Macmillan Co.

1936   *Navajo Shepherd and Weaver.* New York: J. J. Augustin.

1944   *The Story of the Navajo Hail Chant.* New York: Gladys A. Reichard.

1950   *Navaho Religion,* 2 vols. Bollingen Series, 18. New York: Pantheon Books.

Roberts, John M.

1951   *Three Navaho Households.* Cambridge, Mass.: Papers of the Peabody Museum of American Archaeology and Ethnology, Harvard University, vol. 40, no. 3.

Robinson, Jacob S.

1932   *A Journal of the Santa Fe Expedition under Colonel Doniphan.* Princeton: Princeton University Press.

Sapir, Edward

1936   "Internal Linguistic Evidence Suggestive of the Northern Origin of the Navaho," *American Anthropologist,* 38:224–235.

Sapir, Edward, and Harry Hoijer

1942   *Navaho Texts.* Iowa City: Linguistic Society of America.

Schoolcraft, Henry R.

1860   *Archives of Aboriginal Knowledge: Information Respecting the History, Condition, and Prospects of the Indian Tribes of the United States.* Philadelphia: J. P. Lippincott and Co. Part 3, 1853; part 4, 1854.

Secoy, Frank Raymond

1953   *Changing Military Patterns on the Great Plains, 17th–Early 19th Centuries.* American Ethnological Society, Monograph 21. New York: J. J. Augustin.

Shapiro, Harry L.

1956   *Man, Culture, and Society.* New York: Oxford University Press.

Shufeldt, Robert W.

1887   "Arrow Release among the Navajos," *American Naturalist,* 21:784–786.

1889   "The Navajo Tanner," Proceedings of the United States National Museum for 1888 (Washington, D.C.), vol. 11, pp. 59–66.

1892   "The Navajo Belt-Weaver," Proceedings of the United States National Museum for 1891 (Washington, D.C.), vol. 14, pp. 391–393.

1893   "The Evolution of House-Building among the Navajo Indians," Proceedings of the United States National Museum for 1892 (Washington, D.C.), vol. 15, pp. 279–282.

Simmons, Leo, ed.

1942   *Sun Chief: The Autobiography of a Hopi Indian.* New Haven: Yale University Press.

Bibliography　　Simpson, James H.

1850　*Journal of a Military Reconnaissance from Santa Fe, N.M., to the Navajo Country, 1849*. In Report of the Secretary of War, U.S. Congress, Senate Exec. Doc. 64, pp. 56–168. Also published separately, Philadelphia, 1852.

Smith, Anne M.

1966　*New Mexico Indians: Economic, Educational, and Social Problems*. Santa Fe: Museum of New Mexico Research Records, no. 1.

Spencer, Katherine

1947　*Reflection of Social Life in the Navaho Origin Myth*. Albuquerque: University of New Mexico Publications in Anthropology, no. 3.

Spuhler, James N., and Clyde Kluckhohn

1953　"Inbreeding Coefficients of the Ramah Navaho Population," *Human Biology*, 25:295–317.

Steggerda, Morris, and Ruth Eckhardt

1941　"Navajo Foods and Their Preparation," *Journal of the American Dietetic Association*, 17:217–225.

Stephen, Alexander M.

1889　"The Navajo Shoemaker," Proceedings of the United States National Museum for 1888 (Washington, D.C.), vol. 11, pp. 131–136.

1893　"The Navajo," *American Anthropologist* (O.S.), 6:345–362.

Stevenson, James

1891　*Ceremonial of Hasjelti Dailjis and Mythical Sandpainting of the Navajo Indians*. Bureau of American Ethnology Annual Report for 1886–87, vol. 8.

Tanner, Clara Lee

1950　"Navajo Silver Craft," *Arizona Highways*, 30:8:16–33 (August).

Thompson, Almon H.

1871　"Diary of the Colorado River Expedition." MS. in New York Public Library, New York.

Titiev, Mischa

1937　"A Hopi Salt Expedition," *American Anthropologist*, 39:2:244–258.

Toulouse, Joseph, Jr.

1939　"Arrow-Shaft Tools," pp. 80–89 in Kluckhohn and Reiter, 1939.

Tremblay, Marc A., John Collier, Jr., and Tom T. Sasaki

1954　"Navaho Housing in Transition," *América Indígena*, 14:3:187–219.

Tschopik, Harry S., Jr.

1938　"Taboo as a Possible Factor Involved in the Obsolescence of Navaho Pottery and Basketry," *American Anthropologist*, 40:257–262.

1940　"Navaho Basketry: A Study of Culture Change," *American Anthropologist*, 42:3:444–462.

1941　*Navaho Pottery Making: An Inquiry into the Affinities of Navaho Painted Pottery*. Cambridge, Mass.: Papers of the Peabody Museum of American Archaeology and Ethnology, Harvard University, vol. 17, no. 1.

Bibliography

Underhill, Ruth
1953   *Here Come the Navaho! Indian Life and Customs.* Lawrence, Kansas: United States Indian Service.

1956   *The Navajos.* Norman: University of Oklahoma Press.

Venegas, Miguel
1757   *Noticia de la California y de su conquista temporal, y espiritual, hasta el tiempo presente,* 3 vols. Madrid: en la Imprenta de la Viuda de Manuel Gernandez.

Vestal, Paul A.
1952   *Ethnobotany of the Ramah Navaho.* Cambridge, Mass.: Papers of the Peabody Museum of American Archaeology and Ethnology, Harvard University, vol. 40, no. 4.

Vogt, Evon Z.
1951   *Navaho Veterans: A Study of Changing Values.* Cambridge, Mass.: Papers of the Peabody Museum of American Archaeology and Ethnology, Harvard University, vol. 41, no. 1.

Voth, H. R.
1905   *The Traditions of the Hopi.* Chicago: Field Columbian Museum Publication 96, Anthropological Series, vol. 8.

Watson, Edith L.
1964   *Navajo Sacred Places.* Navajoland Publications, Series 5. Window Rock, Arizona: Navajo Tribal Museum.

Welsh, Herbert
1885   *Report of a Visit to the Navajo, Pueblo, and Hualapais Indians.* Philadelphia: Indian Rights Association.

Wetherill, Louisa Wade
n.d.   Miscellaneous brief MSS. on Navaho myths and traditions.

1946   "Some Navaho Recipes," *The Kiva,* 12:1:5–6.

1947   "Navaho Recipes," *The Kiva,* 12:3:39–40.

Wheelwright, Mary C.
1942   *Navajo Creation Myth.* Told by Hasteen Klah. Santa Fe: Museum of Navajo Ceremonial Art.

Whipple, A. W., Thomas Ewbank, and Wm. W. Turner
1855   "Report Upon the Indian Tribes," pp. 1–127 in *Reports of Explorations and Surveys to Ascertain the Most Practicable and Economical Route for a Railroad from the Mississippi River to the Pacific Ocean, 1853–1854,* vol. 3, part 3. U.S. Congress, Senate Exec. Doc. 78, 33rd Congress, 2nd session.

Whipple, A. W., and J. C. Ives
1854   "Report of Explorations for a Railway Route near the 35th Parallel," pp. 1–136 in *Reports of Explorations and Surveys to Ascertain the Most Practicable and Economical Route for a Railroad from the Mississippi River to the Pacific Ocean, 1853–1854,* vol. 3, part 1. U.S. Congress, Senate Exec. Doc. 78, 33rd Congress, 2nd session.

Whittemore, Mary
1939   "Artifacts of Bone, Antler, and Shell," pp. 131–146 in Kluckhohn and Reiter, 1939.

Wilken, Robert L.
1955   *Anselm Weber, O.F.M.: Missionary to the Navaho.* Milwaukee: Bruce Publishing Co.

Winship, George Parker, trans. and ed.
1904   *The Journey of Coronado, the First Explorer of the West.* New York: A. S. Barnes and Co.

Wissler, Clark
1915   *Riding Gear of the North American Indians.* New York: American Museum of Natural History, Anthropological Papers, no. 17, part 1, pp. 1–38.

1922   *The American Indian.* 2nd ed. New York: Oxford University Press.

1938   *The American Indian,* 3rd ed. New York: Oxford University Press.

Woodbury, Richard B.
1939   "Ground and Packed Stone Artifacts (Other Than Arrow Shaft Tools)," pp. 58–79 in Kluckhohn and Reiter, 1939.

1954   *Prehistoric Stone Implements of Northeastern Arizona.* Cambridge, Mass.: Papers of the Peabody Museum of American Archaeology and Ethnology, Harvard University, vol. 34, no. 1.

Woodward, Arthur
1938   *A Brief History of Navajo Silversmithing.* Museum of Northern Arizona Bulletin 14. Flagstaff: Northern Arizona Society of Science and Art.

Worcester, D. E.
1945   "The Use of Saddles by American Indians," *New Mexico Historical Review,* 20:139–143.

Wyman, Leland C.
1936a   "The Female Shooting Life Chant: A Minor Navaho Ceremony," *American Anthropologist,* 38:634–653.

1936b   "Origin Legends of Navaho Divinatory Rites," *Journal of American Folklore,* 49:134–142.

1957   *Beautyway: A Navaho Ceremonial.* Bollingen Series, 53. New York: Pantheon Books.

1970   *Blessingway with Three Versions of the Myth Recorded and Translated by Father Berard Haile, O.F.M.* Tucson: University of Arizona Press.

Wyman, Leland C., and Charles H. Amsden
1934   "A Patchwork Cloak," *The Masterkey* (Los Angeles), 8:133–137.

Wyman, Leland C., and Flora L. Bailey
1943   "Navaho Girl's Puberty Rite," *New Mexico Anthropologist,* 7:3–12.

Wyman, Leland C., and Stuart K. Harris
1941   *Navajo Indian Medical Ethnobotany.* Albuquerque: University of New Mexico Bulletin no. 366, Anthropological Series, vol. 3, no. 5.

Bibliography 1951 *The Ethnobotany of the Kayenta Navaho.* Albuquerque: University of New Mexico Press.

Wyman, Leland C., and Clyde Kluckhohn
1938 *Navaho Classification of Their Song Ceremonials.* Memoirs of the American Anthropological Association, no. 50.

Young, Robert W.
1958 *The Navajo Yearbook, VII.* Window Rock, Ariz.: Navajo Agency.

1961 *The Navajo Yearbook, VIII.* Window Rock, Ariz.: Navajo Agency.

1968 *The Role of the Navajo in the Southwestern Drama.* Gallup, N.M.: Gallup Independent.

Young, Robert W., and William Morgan
1949 *The Ramah Navahos.* Navaho Historical Series, no. 1. U.S. Indian Service, Phoenix Indian School.

Index of Traits

Abdominal Binding (Tr. 207) 314, 436–437, 444

Ammunition (Tr. 28) 55–56, 369, 371, 419, 426, 433, 437

Animal Fetishes (Tr. 223) 340–341, 436, 444

Antelope and Deer Disguise (Tr. 2) 10–11, 234, 425, 432, 440

Antelope Corral (Tr. 1) 8–10, 173, 234, 275, 416–417, 425, 432, 440. *See also* Corral (Tr. 47)

Apron: bast (Tr. 157); ram (Tr. 49); skin (Tr. 158)

Archery (Tr. 249) 24–26, 29, 35–36, 384–385, 417, 426, 437, 445

"Armor" (Tr. 246) 372–373, 413, 415, 419, 436, 445

Arrow (Tr. 19) 10, 13, 16, 19–20, 26–29, 33–43, 46–51, 55, 75, 109, 163, 207, 210, 297, 317, 365, 368–369, 371, 373, 384–385, 415–422, 425–426, 436, 440

Arrow Smoother: *See* Sandstone Shaft Smoother (Tr. 21)

Arrow Wrench (Tr. 20) 33, 36, 39, 43, 44, 413–414, 421, 433, 440

Awl: bone (Tr. 149); metal (Tr. 150); wooden (Tr. 185)

Axe (Tr. 116) 66, 78, 116, 136–137, 143–144, 146–147, 150, 152, 169, 171, 173–175, 193, 195, 211, 368, 415, 418–419, 427, 434, 442

Bag: buckskin "trunk" (Tr. 76); cased (Tr. 218); gathering (Tr. 34); medicine (Tr. 217); pouch (Tr. 195 and Tr. 261); saddle (Tr. 60 and Tr. 61); sewing (Tr. 148); storage (Tr. 86); water (Tr. 80)

Bark Leggings (Tr. 176) 260, 416–417, 435, 437, 443

Basket: baskets (Tr. 219); carrying (Tr. 35); dish (Tr. 98); drum (Tr. 231); hat (Tr. 182); pitched bottle (Tr. 82)

Basket Dish (Tr. 98) 3, 57–58, 61, 119–120, 134–137, 141, 217–229, 314–317, 329, 337–338, 395–397, 400, 417, 425, 427, 437–438, 441

Basket Drum (Tr. 231) 120, 353, 357–359, 364, 417, 428, 436, 438, 445

Basketry Hat (Tr. 182) 270–271, 417, 428, 436, 443

Baskets (Tr. 219) 134–136, 337–338, 347, 354, 415, 417, 425, 428–429, 436, 438, 444

Bast Apron (Tr. 157) 203, 236–237, 416–417, 435, 437, 443

Beaming Post (Tr. 135) 204–205, 208, 211–212, 416, 427, 435

Beaming Tool: bone (Tr. 136); metal (Tr. 137)

Beater: pinyon (Tr. 32); seed (Tr. 31)

Bedding: dressed skin blankets and robes (Tr. 125); rabbit skin blanket (Tr. 124); sheep skin (Tr. 126); sleeping mat (Tr.

Bedding: (*Cont.*)
123); woolen blanket (Tr. 127)

Belt: buckskin (Tr. 180); concho (Tr. 180); rope (Tr. 163); woolen (Tr. 165)

Bird Snare (Tr. 5) 14–15, 232, 415, 417, 432, 440

Black Dye (Tr. 143) 221–223, 240–243, 248, 254, 257, 263–265, 269, 284, 288, 296, 416–417, 424, 435, 442

Blankets: dressed skin blankets and robes (Tr. 125); rabbit skin (Tr. 124); saddle (Tr. 55); sheep skin (Tr. 126); sleeping mat (Tr. 123); woolen (Tr. 127)

Blind (Tr. 6) 16, 426, 432, 440

Blouse: cotton (Tr. 167)

Blue Dye (Tr. 144) 223–225, 240–243, 254, 263–265, 269, 276, 296, 416–418, 420, 424, 435, 438, 442

Bone Awl (Tr. 149) 87, 107, 138, 179, 227–229, 273, 275, 279, 283, 304, 307, 344, 413, 435, 442

Bone Beaming Tool (Tr. 136) 204–205, 212–213, 413, 415, 427, 435, 442

Bow: elkhorn (Tr. 17); musical (Tr. 241); self (Tr. 15); sinew-backed (Tr. 13); trussed (Tr. 16)

Bowls: pottery (Tr. 103); stone (Tr. 99); wooden (Tr. 100)

Bowstring (Tr. 18) 24–27, 32, 230–234, 354, 363, 413, 432

Box: wooden (Tr. 216)

Bracelet (Tr. 200) 118, 158, 203, 301, 306–308, 349, 428, 436, 444

Branding Iron (Tr. 71) 98, 419, 433, 441

Breechclout (Tr. 173) 256–257, 262, 266, 313, 427, 435, 438, 443

Bridge (Tr. 79) 105, 427, 434, 441

Bridle and Bit (Tr. 54) 81–84, 94, 96, 309, 387, 393, 413, 419, 424, 426, 433, 437, 441

Broom (Tr. 120) 123–124, 143, 179–180, 416–417, 434, 442. *See also* Brush (Tr. 90)

Brush: broom (Tr. 120); cactus (Tr. 30); grass (Tr. 90)

Buckskin (Tr. 134) 24, 26, 32, 46, 49, 51, 61, 67, 72, 84–94, 100–103, 106–110, 114–115, 121, 163, 167, 173–174, 176, 178, 182, 184, 186, 188, 192–198, 200, 206–211, 214–222, 226, 228, 231, 237–239, 273, 276, 279, 283–290, 296–297, 333, 346, 351, 354, 362, 365–366, 375–381, 384, 387, 410, 414–415, 418, 423–424, 427, 435, 442. *See also* Buckskin Cord (Tr. 154); Thongs (Tr. 153)

Buckskin Belt (Tr. 180) 146, 158, 161, 203, 238, 240, 242, 248, 256, 259, 265–266, 309, 313, 352, 419, 425, 428, 435, 443. *Includes also* concho belt

Buckskin Cap (Tr. 184) 225, 257, 264, 272–278, 317, 367, 373, 414–415, 422, 425, 428, 435–436, 443

Buckskin Cord (Tr. 154) 229, 231–232, 380, 427, 435, 437, 443